Tolley's Tax Co
2020/21

Disclaimer

In the preparation of this guide, every effort has been made to offer current, correct and clearly expressed information. However, the information in the text is intended to afford general guidelines only. This publication should not be regarded as offering a complete explanation of the tax matters referred to and is subject to changes in law and practice.

No responsibility for any loss occasioned to any person acting or refraining from action as a result of any material included in or omitted from this publication can be accepted by the authors or publishers. This work does not render legal, accounting or tax advice. Readers are encouraged to consult with professional advisers for advice concerning specific matters before making any decision.

Tolley's Tax Computations 2020/21

by

Tolley's Editorial Team

LexisNexis® UK & Worldwide

United Kingdom　　RELX (UK) Limited trading as LexisNexis®, 1–3 Strand, London WC2N 5JR and 9–10 St Andrew Square, Edinburgh EH2 2AF

LNUK Global Partners　LexisNexis® encompasses authoritative legal publishing brands dating back to the 19th century including: Butterworths® in the United Kingdom, Canada and the Asia-Pacific region; Les Editions du Juris Classeur in France; and Matthew Bender® worldwide. Details of LexisNexis® locations worldwide can be found at www.lexisnexis.com

First Published in 1987

© 2020 RELX (UK) Ltd.

Published by LexisNexis

All rights reserved. No part of this publication may be reproduced in any material form (including photocopying or storing it in any medium by electronic means and whether or not transiently or incidentally to some other use of this publication) without the written permission of the copyright owner except in accordance with the provisions of the Copyright, Designs and Patents Act 1988 or under the terms of a licence issued by the Copyright Licensing Agency Ltd, Saffron House, 6–10 Kirby Street, London EC1N 8TS. Applications for the copyright owner's written permission to reproduce any part of this publication should be addressed to the publisher.

Warning: The doing of an unauthorised act in relation to a copyright work may result in both a civil claim for damages and criminal prosecution.

Crown copyright material is reproduced with the permission of the Controller of HMSO and the Queen's Printer for Scotland. Any European material in this work which has been reproduced from EUR-lex, the official European Communities legislation website, is European Communities copyright.

A CIP Catalogue record for this book is available from the British Library.

ISBN for this volume: 9780754556824

Printed and bound by Hobbs the Printers Ltd, Totton, Hampshire

Visit LexisNexis at www.lexisnexis.co.uk

About This Book

Tolley's Tax Computations is an established annual publication, having been first published in the early 1980s in response to interest shown by Tolley tax subscribers in worked examples, both to assist in understanding UK tax legislation and to provide guidance as to layout. The book is divided into six parts covering income tax, corporation tax, capital gains tax, inheritance tax, value added tax and national insurance contributions. In each part, chapters are arranged in alphabetical order by subject to assist reference. Most of the computations have explanatory notes, and statutory references are given wherever appropriate. The book also includes a table of statutes and an index.

This 2020/21 edition has been fully updated to take account of the provisions of the Finance Act 2020 and other relevant information.

Comments on this annual publication and suggestions for improvements and additional computations are always welcome.

Contents

About This Book   v

Abbreviations and References   xi

Table of Statutes   xiii

Table of Statutory Instruments   xxv

INCOME TAX
1. Allowances and Tax Rates
2. Accrued Income Scheme
3. Capital Allowances
4. Capital Allowances on Plant and Machinery
5. Charities
6. Compensation for Loss of Employment
7. Deceased Estates
8. Double Tax Relief
9. Employment Income
10. Enterprise Investment Scheme
11. Herd Basis
12. Intellectual Property
13. Late Payment Interest and Penalties
14. Life Assurance Policies
15. Losses
16. Married Persons and Civil Partners
17. Non-Residents
18. Partnerships
19. Pension Provision
20. Personal Service Companies etc
21. Post-Cessation Receipts and Expenditure
22. Property Income
23. Remittance Basis
24. Savings and Investment Income
25. Seed Enterprise Investment Scheme
26. Self-Assessment
27. Settlements
28. Share-Related Employment Income and Exemptions
29. Social Security Income
30. Trading Income
31. Trading Income — Cash Basis for Smaller Businesses
32. Venture Capital Trusts

CORPORATION TAX
101. Accounting Periods
102. Capital Allowances
103. Capital Gains
104. Close Companies
105. Double Tax Relief
106. Group Relief
107. Income Tax in relation to a Company
108. Intangible Assets
109. Interest on Overpaid Tax
110. Interest on Unpaid Tax
111. Investment Companies and Investment Business
112. Liquidation

Contents

113 Loan Relationships
114 Losses
115 Payment of Tax
116 Profit Computations
117 Research and Development
118 Returns
119 Transfer Pricing

CAPITAL GAINS TAX
201 Annual Rates and Exemptions
202 Anti-Avoidance
203 Assets
204 Assets held on 6 April 1965
205 Assets held on 31 March 1982
206 Business Asset Disposal Relief (formerly Entrepreneurs' Relief)
207 Capital Sums Derived from Assets
208 Companies
209 Computation of Gains and Losses
210 Double Tax Relief
211 Enterprise Investment Scheme
212 Exemptions and Reliefs
213 Hold-Over Reliefs
214 Indexation
215 Investors' Relief
216 Land
217 Losses
218 Married Persons and Civil Partners
219 Offshore Settlements
220 Overseas Matters
221 Partnerships
222 Payment of Tax
223 Private Residences
224 Qualifying Corporate Bonds
225 Remittance Basis
226 Rollover Relief — Replacement of Business Assets
227 Seed Enterprise Investment Scheme
228 Settlements
229 Shares and Securities
230 Shares and Securities — Identification Rules
231 Social Investment Relief
232 Wasting Assets

INHERITANCE TAX
301 Accumulation and Maintenance Trusts
302 Agricultural Property
303 Anti-Avoidance
304 Business Property
305 Calculation of Tax
306 Charities
307 Close Companies
308 Deeds of Variation and Disclaimers
309 Double Taxation Relief
310 Exempt Transfers
311 Gifts with Reservation
312 Interest on Tax
313 Liability for Tax
314 Mutual Transfers
315 National Heritage
316 Payment of Tax
317 Protective Trusts
318 Quick Succession Relief

Contents

319 Settlements: Interests in Possession
320 Settlements: Relevant Property
321 Transfers on Death
322 Trusts for Bereaved Minors
323 Trusts for Disabled Persons
324 Trusts for Employees
325 Valuation
326 Woodlands

VALUE ADDED TAX
401 Bad Debt Relief
402 Capital Goods
403 Catering
404 Hotels and Holiday Accommodation
405 Input Tax
406 Motor Cars
407 Output Tax
408 Partial Exemption
409 Records
410 Reduced Rate Supplies
411 Retail Schemes
412 Second-Hand Goods

NATIONAL INSURANCE CONTRIBUTIONS
501 Age Exception
502 Aggregation of Earnings
503 Annual Maximum
504 Class 1 Contributions: Employed Earners
505 Class 1A Contributions: Benefits in Kind
506 Class 1B Contributions: PAYE Settlement Agreements
507 Class 4 Contributions: On Profits of a Trade etc.
508 Company Directors
509 Deferment of Payment
510 Earnings from Self-Employment
511 Earnings Periods
512 Intermediaries
513 Partners

Index

Abbreviations and References

Abbreviations

ACT	=	Advance Corporation Tax
Art	=	Article
BPR	=	Business Property Relief
b/f	=	brought forward
C & E	=	Customs and Excise
CA	=	Court of Appeal
CAA	=	Capital Allowances Act
CCAB	=	Consultative Committee of Accountancy Bodies
Ch D	=	Chancery Division
c/f	=	carried forward
CGT	=	Capital Gains Tax
CGTA	=	Capitals Gains Tax Act
CRCA	=	Commissioners for Revenue and Customs Act
CT	=	Corporation Tax
CTA	=	Corporation Tax Act
CTT	=	Capital Transfer Tax
CVS	=	Corporate Venturing Scheme
CY	=	Current Year
DTR	=	Double Tax Relief
EIS	=	Enterprise Investment Scheme
ESC	=	Extra-Statutory Concession
ESP	=	Expected Selling Price
FA	=	Finance Act
F(No 2)A	=	Finance (No 2) Act
FIFO	=	First In, First Out
FII	=	Franked Investment Income
FY	=	Financial Year
FYA	=	First-Year Allowance
HL	=	House of Lords
HMRC	=	Her Majesty's Revenue and Customs
IBA	=	Industrial Buildings Allowance
ICTA	=	Income and Corporation Taxes Act
IRPR	=	Inland Revenue Press Release
IHT	=	Inheritance Tax
IHTA	=	Inheritance Tax Act
IT	=	Income Tax
ITA	=	Income Tax Act
ITEPA	=	Income Tax (Earnings and Pensions) Act
ITTOIA	=	Income Tax (Trading and Other Income) Act
LEL	=	Lower Earnings Limit
LIFO	=	Last In, First Out
LLPA	=	Limited Liability Partnerships Act
NBV	=	Net Book Value
NIC	=	National Insurance Contributions
para	=	paragraph
PAYE	=	Pay As You Earn
P/e	=	Period ended
PET	=	Potentially Exempt Transfer
PR	=	Personal Representative

Abbreviations and References

PY	=	Previous Year
Reg	=	Regulation
RNRB	=	Residence nil rate band
s	=	section
SC/S	=	Scottish Court of Session
Sch	=	Schedule
SI	=	Statutory Instrument
SSAP	=	Statement of Standard Accounting Practice
TCGA	=	Taxation of Chargeable Gains Act
TIOPA	=	Taxation (International and Other Provisions) Act
TPA	=	Taxation of Pensions Act
TMA	=	Taxes Management Act
UEL	=	Upper Earnings Limit
VAT	=	Value Added Tax
VATA	=	Value Added Tax Act
VCT	=	Venture Capital Trust
WDA	=	Writing-down Allowance
WDV	=	Written-down Value
Y/e	=	Year ended

References

STC	=	Simon's Tax Cases (LexisNexis, 30 Farringdon Street, London EC4A 4HH)
TC	=	Official Tax Cases (H.M. Stationery Office, P.O. Box 276, SW8 5DT)

Table of Statutes

1970 Taxes Management Act
- s 42(10A) .... IT 1.6
- (11A) .... IT 26.2
- s 59A .... IT 26.1; 26.2(A)(B)(C)
- s 59B .... IT 13.1(A)
- (4) 15.1
- s 59D .... CT 101.3; 115.1
- s 59E .... CT 115.1
- s 59FA .... CGT 220.1
- s 86 .... IT 27.1
- (1)(2) .... IT 13.1(A)
- s 87A .... CT 110.1
- s 91 .... CT 110.2(B)
- s 94(3) .... CT 118.2
- ss 109B–109F .... CGT 220.1
- s 118(2) .... CT 118.2
- Sch 1B .... IT 26.2
- para 5 .... IT 21.1
- Sch 3ZB .... CGT 220.1

1980 Finance Act
- s 79 .... CGT 205.2; 213.1(C)

1984 Inheritance Tax Act
- s 3 .... IHT 305.1; 305.2
- (3) .... IHT 307.3
- s 3A .... IHT 305.1; 305.2
- s 5 .... IHT 305.2
- s 7 .... IHT 305.1; 305.2
- s 8A .... IHT 308.1; 310.3; 310.3(A)–(C)
- s 8B .... IHT 310.3; 310.3(A)(B)
- s 8C .... IHT 310.3; 310.3(B)(C)
- ss 8D–8M .... IHT 310.5(A)
- s 8D .... IHT 310.5(D)
- s 8FA .... IHT 310.5(B)
- s 8G .... IHT 310.5(C)
- s 8L .... IHT 310.5(C)
- s 16 .... IHT 302.1(B)
- s 17 .... IHT 308
- s 18 .... IHT 303.1(C); 310.4; 319.3
- s 19 .... IHT 310.1
- (1)(2) .... IHT 310.1(A)
- (3A) .... IHT 310.1(B)
- s 21 .... IHT 310.2;
- ss 30–32 .... IHT 315
- s 31 .... IHT 315.3(B)
- (1)(5) .... IHT 315.1
- ss 32, 32A .... IHT 310.3(C)
- s 33 .... IHT 315
- (2ZA) .... IHT 315.2(B)
- (5) .... IHT 315.2(C); 315.5(A)
- (7) .... IHT 315.4
- s 34 .... IHT 315; 315.5(A)
- s 34(1) .... IHT 315.2(C)
- s 35 .... IHT 315
- ss 36–39 .... IHT 305.3; 305.3(C)
- s 39A .... IHT 305.3; 305.3(B)(C)

1984 Inheritance Tax Act – *cont.*
- s 40 .... IHT 305.3; 305.3(C)
- ss 41, 42 .... IHT 305.3
- s 49 .... IHT 317.2; 319
- (1A) .... IHT 319.1; 319.2; 319.3
- s 49A ... CGT 228.5; IHT 317.2; 319; 319.1; 319.2; 319.3
- s 49B .... IHT 317.2; 319; 319.2; 319.3
- s 49C ... CGT 228.5; IHT 317.2; 319; 319.2; 319.3
- ss 49D, 49E ... IHT 317.2; 319; 319.2; 319.3
- s 51(1)–(1B) .... IHT 319
- s 52(1)(2A) .... IHT 319
- s 54A .... IHT 319
- s 54B .... IHT 319
- s 57 .... IHT 319
- s 57A .... IHT 315
- s 59(1)(2) .... IHT 319.1; 319.2; 319.3
- s 62B(1) .... IHT 320.2(A)
- s 62C .... IHT 320.2(A)
- s 64 .... IHT 320.1(A)(B)
- (1A) .... IHT 320
- s 65 .... IHT 320.2(A); 320.3
- s 66 .... IHT 320.1(A)(B)
- s 68 .... IHT 320.2(A)
- s 69 .... IHT 320.3
- s 70 .... IHT 306
- s 71 .... IHT 301
- (1)(1A) .... IHT 301.1
- (1B) .... IHT 322.1(A)
- s 71A ...... CGT 228.5; IHT 322; 322.1(A)
- ss 71B, 71C .... IHT 322; 322.1(A)
- s 71D ...... CGT 228.5; IHT 301.2(A); 322; 322.1(B)
- s 71E ...... IHT 301.2(A)(B); 322; 322.1(B)
- (2) .... IHT 301.2(A)(B)
- ss 71F, 71G . IHT 301.2(A)(B); 322; 322.1(B)
- s 71H .... IHT 322
- s 72 .... IHT 324
- s 73 .... IHT 317.1
- s 74 .... IHT 323
- s 77 .... IHT 315
- s 78 .... IHT 315
- (3) .... IHT 315.2(C); 315.5(A)
- s 78(4)(6) .... IHT 315.5(A)
- s 79 .... IHT 315; 315.5(B)
- s 88 .... IHT 317.2
- s 89 .... IHT 323
- s 89A .... IHT 323; 323.4
- s 89B(1) ..... CGT 228.5; IHT 317.2; 319.1; 319.2; 319.3
- s 94 .... IHT 307
- (1) .... IHT 307.2
- (2)(*b*) .... IHT 307.1
- ss 95–97 .... IHT 307
- s 98 .... IHT 307

xiii

Table of Statutes

1984 Inheritance Tax Act – *cont.*

s 98(3)	IHT 307.3
s 102	IHT 307
s 103	IHT 304
s 104	IHT 304
s 105	IHT 304
ss 106–110	IHT 304
s 111	IHT 304; 304.1(A)
ss 112, 113	IHT 304
s 113A(3)	IHT 304.1(D)
s 113B	IHT 304.1(D)
s 114	IHT 302.2; 304
(2)	IHT 326
s 115	IHT 302
s 116	IHT 302
(1)	IHT 302.1(A)(B)
(2)	IHT 302.1(A)(B)
(7)	IHT 302.1(A)(B)
ss 117–121	IHT 302
ss 122, 123	IHT 302; 302.2
s 124A	IHT 302
(1)(3)	IHT 302.1(A)
s 124B	IHT 302
s 125	IHT 326
s 126	IHT 310.3(C); 326
s 127	IHT 326
(2)	IHT 326.1(B)
ss 128–130	IHT 326
s 131	IHT 313.3
s 141	IHT 314.1; 318
s 142	IHT 308
(2)	IHT 308.1
(3A)(3B)	IHT 308.1
s 159	IHT 309
s 161	IHT 303.1(B); 325.2
ss 178–189	IHT 325.3
s 190	IHT 325.1
s 191	IHT 325.1; 325.1(A)
s 192	IHT 325.1
s 192(1)	IHT 325.1(B)
ss 193–197	IHT 325.1
s 197A	IHT 325.1; 325.1(A)
s 197A(3)	IHT 325.1(B)
s 198	IHT 325.1
s 199	IHT 305.1; 313.4
(1)	IHT 313.1
(2)	IHT 313.3
s 200(1)	IHT 313.2
(3)	IHT 313.2
s 201	IHT 313.4
(2)	IHT 313.3
s 204	IHT 305.1; 313.4
(1)	IHT 313.2
(2)(3)	IHT 313.1; 313.2
(5)	IHT 313.1; 313.2
(6)	IHT 313.1
s 207	IHT 315
(1)	IHT 315.2(C)
s 208	IHT 326
s 211	IHT 313.2
s 218A	IHT 308; 308.1

1984 Inheritance Tax Act – *cont.*

s 226(4)	IHT 326
ss 227, 228	IHT 316
s 233	IHT 312
s 234	IHT 316
s 267	IHT 310.4
ss 267ZA, 267ZB	IHT 310.4
s 268	IHT 303.1(C)
s 269	IHT 304
Sch 1A paras 1–3	IHT 321.2(A)
para 5	IHT 321.2(A)
para 7	IHT 321.2(B)
para 8	IHT 321.2(A)
para 9	IHT 321.2(A)(B)
Sch 2 para 3	IHT 319.3
4	IHT 326
5	IHT 315; 315.2(C)
6	IHT 315; 315.6
Sch 4	IHT 315
paras 8, 12–14	IHT 315.6
Sch 5	IHT 315
Sch 6 para 4	IHT 315.3(B)
Pt VI, Chapter IV	IHT 325.1(A)

1985 Companies Act

s 249AA(4)–(7)	CT 119.1(A)

1986 Finance Act

s 81	IHT 311
ss 102–102C	IHT 311
s 103	IHT 321.1
s 104	IHT 314; 321.1
Sch 20	IHT 311

1988 Income and Corporation Taxes Act

s 9(1)	CT 101.3
s 87	CGT 216.3(G)
s 247	CT 104.2(B); 118.2(A)
s 338(1)	CT 101.3
(4)	CT 101.3
s 825	CT 109
s 826	CT 109
(7A)	CT 109.2
Sch 4	CT 116.1

1988 Finance Act

s 34	CGT 218.3

1989 Finance Act

s 43	CT 116.1
s 178	CT 109; IHT 312

1991 Finance Act

22, 23	CT 109

1992 Taxation of Chargeable Gains Act

s 1(3)	CGT 217.1; 219.1(A)
s 1A(3)	CGT 216.4; 220.2
s 1B	CGT 220.2
s 1C	CGT 216.4
s 1E	CGT 217.1
(4)	CGT 217.2
s 1F	CGT 217.1
s 1G	CGT 216.4
s 1H	CGT 201.1
(7)(8)	CGT 228.1

Table of Statutes

1992 Taxation of Chargeable Gains Act – *cont.*

s 1I	CGT 201.1
s 1J	CGT 201.1
(6)	CGT 201.1(A)(C)
s 1K	CGT 201.2; 228.1
(4)	CGT 217.1(B)
(5)	CGT 206.1(B)(C); 215.1(C)
ss 1M, 1N	CGT 220.4
s 2A	CGT 208.1
s 2A(1)	CT 101.3; 103.1
ss 2B–2F	CGT 287.1,
s 2B(4)	CGT 216.4; CGT 220.1
s 2B(5)	CGT 216.4
s 3(2)	CT 103.3(E)
s 12	IT 23.1
ss 14B–14H	CGT 208.1
s 16ZA	CGT 225.1
s 16A	CGT 208.2
s 17	CT 103.2(A)
ss 19, 20	CGT 202.3
s 22	CGT 207.3
(1)	CGT 207.1
s 23	CGT 207.3; 207.3(B)(C)
(2)	CGT 207.3(D)
s 24	CGT 217.1(B)
(1)	CGT 209.1(C)
s 25	CGT 220.1; 220.3
(1)(3)(8)	CGT 220.3
s 25ZA	CGT 220.2
s 29	CGT 202.1
s 30	CGT 202.2
s 35	CGT 205.2; 216.3(E); 221.5; 232.3(B)
(1)	CGT 205.1; 205.2(A)
(2)	CGT 205.2(A); 204.3(B); 205.2(A); 216.3(E)
(3)	CGT 204.3(C); 205.2(A); 209.2(A)
(*a*)	CGT 204.3(A)(B)(C); 216.3(E)
(*b*)	CGT 204.1(B); 204.3(D)
(*c*)	CGT 204.1(B); 205.2(B)
(*d*)	CGT 205.3; 214.2(A)
(4)	CGT 204.3(B); 205.2(A)
(5)	CGT 204.1(A); 205.1(A)(B)
(9)	CGT 204
s 35A	CGT 214.2(A)
s 38	CGT 209.1(A)(C)
s 39	CGT 209.1(A); 216.3(G)
s 41	CGT 209.1(B); 220.2
s 42	CGT 204.3(E); 208.2; 216.3(B); 218.3; 229.3
(4)	CGT 209.2(A)
s 44	CGT 203.1; 232.1; 232.2
(1)(*d*)	CGT 232.3
s 45	CGT 232.1; 232.1(A)
s 46	CGT 203.1; 232.1; 232.2
s 47	CGT 232.1
s 52A	CGT 214.2(A)
s 53	CGT 211.1(B); 214.1

1992 Taxation of Chargeable Gains Act – *cont.*

s 53(1)(1B)	CT 103.2(A); 103.3(A)–(C)(E); CGT 204.1(A)(B); 204.2; 204.3(A)–(F); 205.2(A)(C)(D); 205.3; 207.3(C); 208.1; 214.1(B)–(D); 216.3(E)(F); 229.3(C); 230.2
(2A)	CGT 214.1(D)
(3)	CT 103.2(A)
s 54	CGT 214.1
(1A)	CGT 213.1(C)
(1B)	CT 103.2(A); 103.3(A)–(C)(E); CGT 204.1(A)(B); 204.2; 204.3(A)–(F); 205.2(A)(C)(D); 205.3; 207.3(C); 208.1; 2089.1(B); 214.1(B)–(D); 216.3(E)(F); 229.3(C); 230.2
(4)(*b*)	CGT 216.3(F)
s 55	CGT 214.1
(1)(2)	CGT 204.1(A); 204.3(A)(C); 205.2(A); 208.2(A); 214.1(D) 216.3(E); 230.2
(5)(6)	CGT 214.2(A)(C)
(7)–(9)	CGT 214.2(C)
s 56	CGT 214.1
(2)	CT 103.3(B); CGT 214.2(A)–(D)
(3)	CT 103.3(B); CGT 214.2(D)
(4)	CGT 214.2(D)
s 58	CGT 214.2(A); 218.1; 218.1(B); 218.2
s 59	CGT 221.1
s 62	CGT 214.1(C)
(2)(2A)	CGT 217.1(C)
s 67	CGT 213.1(B)
s 70	CGT 228.3
s 71	CGT 228.4
(1)	CGT 222.1(B)
(2)–(2D)	CGT 228.4(B)
s 72	CGT 228.5
(1)	CGT 222.1(B)
s 76	CGT 228.5(B)
s 77	CGT 217.2
s 86	CGT 217.2; 219.1(A)
s 87	CGT 217.1(C); 217.2; 219
s 87A	CGT 219.1(A)(B)
ss 87D–87J	CGT 219.1
ss 87K, 87L	CGT 201.2; 217.2; 219.1
s 87M	CGT 219.1
s 89(2)	CGT 201.2; 217.1(C); 217.2; 219.1(A)
s 91	CGT 219.1(B)
s 103KA(2)(3)	CGT 201.1(C)
s 104	CGT 230.1; 230.2
s 105	CGT 230.1; 230.2
s 106A	CGT 224.1; 230.1
s 107	CGT 230.2
s 108	CGT 230.2
(1)	CGT 224.1
s 109	CGT 230.2
(4)	CGT 204.1; 204.1(A)
(5)	CGT 204.1

xv

Table of Statutes

1992 Taxation of Chargeable Gains Act – *cont.*
- s 110 .... CGT 230.2
- s 115 .... IT 2.1; CGT 224
- s 116 .... CGT 224; 224.2
  - (10) .... CGT 206.5; 224.2
- s 117 .... CGT 217.3; 224; 224.1
  - (1) .... CGT 224.1; 229.6
  - (7)(*b*)(8) .... CGT 224.1
- s 119 .... IT 2.1; CGT 214.3
- s 119A .... IT 28.1; 27.5
- s 122 .... CGT 229.4(A); 229.8(A); 229.8(B)
  - (2) .... CGT 229.8(B)
- s 123 .... CGT 229.8(B)
  - (1) .... CGT 229.3
- s 125 .... CT 103.2
  - (1)(5) .... CT 103.2(A)
- s 125A .... CGT 217.3
- s 126 ...... CGT 206.4; 215.2; 229.1; 229.2
- s 127 ...... CGT 206.4; 215.2; 224.2; 229.1; 229.1(A); 229.2; 229.3(C); 229.4(A)
- s 128 ... CGT 224.2; 229.1; 229.2; 229.3(C); 229.7
  - (4) .... CGT 229.3
- s 129 .... CGT 224.2; 229.1; 229.1(A)
- s 130 .... CGT 224.2; 229.1; 229.1(B); 229.2
- s 131 .... CGT 229.1
- s 132 .... CGT 229.4(E); 229.6
- s 135 ... CGT 206.4; 215.2; 229.4; 229.4(A)
- s 136 .... CGT 206.4; 215.2; 229.5
- s 137 .... CGT 229.4
- s 138 .... CGT 229.4; 229.5
- s 138A .... CGT 229.4(C)
- s 140 .... CGT 220.4
- s 141 .... CGT 229.7
- s 142 .... CGT 229.7
- s 144 .... CGT 203.1
  - (3) .... IT 28.1
- ss 144ZA–144ZD .... CGT 203.1
- s 145 .... CGT 203.1
- s 146 .... CGT 232.2; 232.2(B)
- s 150A .... IT 10
  - (1) .... IT 10.2(B); CGT 211.2; 211.3; 211.3(B)
  - (2)(2A)(3) ... IT 10.2(C); CGT 211.1; 211.2
- s 150B .... IT 10; 9.2(C)
- s 150D .... CGT 211.3(B)
- s 150E ...... IT 25.2(B); CGT 227.1; 227.2
- s 150G .... CGT 227.3
- s 151A .... IT 32; 31.3
- s 151B .... IT 32
  - (1) .... IT 32.3
- s 152 .. CT 103.3(D); CGT 208.2; 226; 226.1
  - (7)(9) .... CGT 226.2(B)
- s 153 ...... CT 103.3(D); CGT 226; 226.2(A)
- s 154 .... CGT 226; 226.3
- s 155 .... CT 103.3(D); CGT 226
- ss 156–158 .... CGT 226
- s 161 .... CT 103.3(B)(C)
  - (2) .... CT 103.3(C)
  - (3) .... CT 103.3(B)

1992 Taxation of Chargeable Gains Act – *cont.*
- s 162 .... CGT 213.3
- s 164A .... CGT 213.3
- s 165 .... CGT 213.1(C); 213.2; 222.1(B)
  - (10) .... CGT 213.1(C)
- ss 169B–169G ..... CGT 213.1(A); 228.3(A)
- s 169C(7) .... CGT 222.1(B)
- s 169H .... CGT 206.1(A)
- s 169I .... IT 28.5; CGT 206.1(A)(C)
  - (8) .... CGT 206.2
- s 169J .... CGT 206.1(A)
- s 169K .... CGT 206.1(A); 206.3
- s 169L .... CGT 206.1
- s 169LA .... CGT 206.1
- s 169M .... CGT 206.1
  - (1)–(3) .... CGT 206.1(A)
- s 169N .... CGT 206.1(B)
- s 169P .... CGT 206.3
- s 169Q .... CGT 206.4
- s 169S(2)–(4) .... CGT 206.1(C)
  - (5) .... CGT 206.1(C); 206.3
- ss 169SB–169SH .... CGT 206.6
- ss 169T–169V . CGT 206.1(A); 206.5; 211.3; 231.3
- s 169VC .... CGT 215.1
- ss 169VD–169VG .... CGT 215.1(B)
- s 169VK .... CGT 215.1; 215.1(C)
- s 169VM .... CGT 215.1(A)
- s 169VT .... CGT 215.2
- s 171 ... CT 103.3(A)(E); CGT 214.2(C)(D)
  - (1) .... CT 103.3(B)(C)
- ss 171A–171C .... CT 103.3(A)
- s 173(1) .... CT 103.3(B)
  - (2) .... CT 103.3(C)
- s 175 .... CT 103.3(D)
- s 176 .... CGT 202.4
- s 177A .... CT 103.3(F)
- s 179 .... CT 103.3(E)
- s 179ZA .... CT 103.3(E)
- ss 185, 187 .... CGT 220.1
- s 187B .... CGT 220.2
- s 222 .... CGT 223.1; 223.1(B)
  - (5) .... CGT 223.2
- s 223 .... CGT 223.1
  - (1) .... CGT 223.1(A)(B)
  - (3)(*a*)(*b*) .... CGT 223.1(B)
  - (4)(7) .... CGT 223.1(A)(B)
- s 225 .... CGT 228.4(A)
- s 225E .... CGT 222.1(A)
- s 236B .... CGT 218.2
- ss 241, 241A .... IT 22.2; CGT 226.4
- s 242 .... CGT 209.2(D); 216.1
  - (2) .... CGT 216.1
- s 243 .... CGT 216.2; 216.2(B)
- ss 244–246 .... CGT 216.2
- s 247 .... CGT 216.2; 216.2(A)
- s 248 .... CGT 216.2
- s 255B .... CGT 231.1
  - (1) .... CGT 231.2(A)(B)
- ss 255C, 255D .... CGT 231.1
- s 258(8) .... IHT 315.3

Table of Statutes

1992 Taxation of Chargeable Gains Act – *cont.*
- s 260 .... CGT 213.1; 222.1(B); 228.3(A)(B)
  - (5) .... CGT 213.1(B)
  - (7) ...... CGT 213.1(C); IHT 302.1(C)
- s 261B .... IT 15.2
- s 261C .... IT 15.2
- ss 261D, 261E .... IT 21.2
- s 262 .... CGT 202.3
  - (2) .... CGT 212.1(A)
  - (3) .... CGT 212.1(B)
  - (4) .... CGT 212.1(C)
- ss 279A–279D .... CGT 217.4
- s 280 .... CGT 222; 222.1(A)
- s 281 .... CGT 222; 222.1(B)
- s 288(7B) .... CGT 220.4; 230.1
- Sch B1 .... CGT 228.1
- Sch 1 .... CGT 225.1
- Sch 1C .... CGT 228.1
- Sch 2 para 1 .... CGT 204.1
  - 2 .... CGT 204.1
    - (1) .... CGT 204.1(B)
  - 3 .... CGT 204.1
- Sch 2 para 4 .... CGT 204.1; 204.1(A)
  - 5 .... CGT 204.1
  - 6 .... CGT 204.1
  - paras 7, 8 .... CGT 204.1
  - 9–15 .... CGT 204.2
  - para 16 .... CGT 204.3; 204.3(D)
    - (3)–(5) .... CGT 204.3(E)
    - (8) .... CGT 204.3(E)
  - paras 17, 18 .... CGT 204.3
  - para 19 .... CGT 204.3
    - (1) .... CGT 204.3(C)
    - (2) .... CGT 204.3(D)
    - (3) .... CGT 204.3(C)(D)
- Sch 3 para 1 .. CT 103.3(D); CGT 213.2(A)
  - 4(1) .... CGT 204.3(E); 209.2(B); 229.4(A)
    - (2) .... CGT 207.3(D)
  - 6 .... CGT 204.3(B)
  - 7 .... CGT 205.2(A)
  - paras 8, 9 .... CGT 205.2(A)
- Sch 4 .... CGT 205.3; 213.3
  - para A1 .... CGT 205.3
  - 1 .... CGT 205.3
  - 9 .... CGT 205.3
  - .... CGT 216.4
- Sch 5B .... CGT 211.3
  - para 1(5A) .... CGT 206.1(A)
- Sch 5BB .... CGT 227.3
- Sch 5C .... IT 32
- Sch 7 .... CGT 213.2
- Sch 7ZB .... CGT 215.1(A)
- Sch 7A .... CT 103.3(F)
  - 10 .... CT 103.3(B)
- Sch 7AC .... CT 103.4
- Sch 7D para 5 .... IT 28.4
- Sch 8 para 1 ... CGT 216.3 (A)(D)(E)(F)(G)
  - (2) .... CGT 216.3(A)
  - (4)(*b*) .... CGT 216.3(F)
  - 2 .... CGT 216.3(B)(C)

1992 Taxation of Chargeable Gains Act – *cont.*
- Sch 8 para 4 .... CGT 216.3(H)(J)
  - 5 .... CGT 216.3(C)(H)(J)
  - (2) .... CGT 216.3(H)(J)
- Sch 8B .... CGT 231.3

1992 Social Security Administration Act
- s 13A .... IT 29.1

1992 Social Security Contributions and Benefits Act
- s 6(3) .... NIC 501.1; 501.1(A)
  - (4) .... NIC 502.3
- ss 8–9A .... NIC 504.1
- s 10 .... IT 9.3(A); NIC 505.1
- ss 10ZA, 10ZB .... NIC 505.1
- s 10A .... NIC 506.1
- s 15 .... NIC 502.7
- s 19(1)(2) .... NIC 509.1
- s 122(1) .... NIC 501.1(B)
- Sch 1 para 1 ...... NIC 502.1; 502.2; 502.3; 502.4;
- Sch 2 para 3 .... NIC 510.1
  - 4 .... NIC 513.1

1992 Finance (No 2) Act
- Sch 14 para 8 .... IHT 304
  - 9 .... IHT 304

1994 Finance Act
- s 93(1)(2) .... CGT 207.1(B); 207.2(D); 208.2(B); 212.1(D)
  - (3) .... CGT 211.1(B)
- Sch 12 .... CGT 217.4

1994 Value Added Tax Act
- s 24(5) .... VAT 405.2
- s 26A .... VAT 405.1
- s 29A .... VAT 410.1
- s 36 .... VAT 401
- ss 56, 57 .... VAT 406.1
- Sch 46 .... VAT 406.1
- Sch 6 .... VAT 406.1
  - para 9 .... VAT 404.1
- Sch 11 para 2(6) .... VAT 410

1995 Finance Act
- s 155 .... IHT 302.1(B)

1995 Pensions Act
- Sch 4 .... NIC 501.1(B)

1996 Finance Act
- s 185 .... IHT 302.1
- Sch 13 para 1 .... IT 22.1(A)

1997 Finance Act
- s 90 .... CGT 211.3

1998 Finance Act
- s 121(1) .... CGT 224.1(A)
  - (2) .... CGT 224.2
- s 122(1) .... CGT 221.1
  - (2) .... CGT 213.1(C)
  - (3) .... CGT 213.1(C)
  - (4) .... CGT 209.4(E); 221.1
- s 144 .... CGT 203.1
- Sch 18 paras 3–7 .... CT 118.1
  - 5(1) .... CT 118.1(A)(B)(C)

xvii

Table of Statutes

1998 Finance Act – *cont.*
Sch 18 para 5(2) .... CT 118.1(A)(B)
         (3) .... CT 118.1(C)
        14 .... CT 101.3
Sch 20 .... CGT 227.4
Sch 27 Part III(31) .... CGT 227

1998 Scotland Act
Part 4A .... IT 1.8
ss 80D–80F .... IT 1.8

2000 Finance Act
s 101 .... CT 103.3(A)

2000 Limited Liability Partnerships Act
s 10(1) .... IT 18.4

2001 Capital Allowances Act
s 6 .... IT 4.1
  (6) .... IT 4.1(B)
s 18 .... CT 111.1
s 33A .... IT 4.5
s 36(1) .... IT 9.2(A)
s 38ZA .... IT 31.1
s 38A .... IT 4.6
s 38B .... IT 4.2; 4.6
s 45A .... CT 102.1
s 45D .... IT 4.3
s 45H .... CT 102.1
s 46(2) .... IT 4.2
s 47 .... CT 102.1
s 51A .... IT 4.6; CT 101.3
  (6) .... IT 4.1(A)
s 51C .... CT 102.1
s 55 .... CT 102.1
s 56 .... CT 102.1
  (1) .... IT 4.1(B); 4.5
  (3) ...... IT 4.1(A)(B); CT 101.3; 102.1
s 56A .... IT 4.5
s 61(2) .... IT 4.3
  (4) .... IT 4.3
ss 83–89 .... IT 4.4
ss 90–104E .... IT 4.5
ss 104A, 104AA .... IT 4.3
s 206 .... IT 4.3
s 213 .... IT 4.3
s 214 .... IT 4.2; 4.3
s 217 .... IT 4.2; 4.3
s 218 .... IT 4.3
ss 217, 218 .... IT 4.3
ss 234–246 .... IT 4.7
s 253 .... CT 111.1
ss 265–268 .... IT 4.2
s 270AA .... IT 3.1
ss 270IH .... IT 3.1
ss 310–313 .... CT 102.1
s 396(2)(3) .... IT 3.3
s 404 .... IT 3.3
s 418(1) .... IT 3.3
s 424 .... IT 3.3
ss 437–451 .... IT 3.5
ss 464–483 .... IT 3.4
ss 484–487 .... IT 3.2
s 488(4)(5) .... IT 3.2

2001 Capital Allowances Act – *cont.*
s 489 .... IT 3.2
ss 546–548 .... IT 4.7
s 549 .... IT 4.7
ss 550–551 .... IT 4.7
s 559 .... IT 4.2
s 569 .... IT 4.2
s 575 .... IT 4.3

2001 Finance Act
s 77 .... CT 103.3(A)
s 78 .... CGT 232; 232.2(B)
Sch 15 para 10 .... CGT 211.3

2002 Finance Act
s 51 .... CGT 216.7
s 84 .... CGT 225.1(A)
s 120 .... IHT 308; 308.1
Sch 29 .... CGT 213.2(B)
    para 95 .... CGT 213.3
    paras 117, 118 .... CGT 213.3
    para 121 .... CGT 213.3
        132 .... CGT 213.1
Sch 30 para 1 .... CT 101.3

2003 Income Tax (Earnings and Pensions) Act
s 18 .... CT 116.1
s 22 .... IT 23.1
ss 48–55 .... IT 19
s 56 .... IT 20; 20.1
ss 57–61 .... IT 20
s 75 .... IT 9.6(A)
ss 87, 88 .... IT 9.6(A)
ss 97, 98 .... IT 9.4
s 99 .... IT 9.4
  (1)(2) .... IT 9.4(A)
s 100 .... IT 9.4; 9.4(A)
ss 101–104 .... IT 9.4
ss 105, 106 .... IT 9.4; 9.5
s 107 .... IT 9.4; 9.4(B)
ss 108–113 .... IT 9.4
ss 114–121 .... IT 9.3(A)
ss 122–124 .... IT 9.3(A); CT 104.3
ss 125–153 .... IT 9.3(A)
ss 154–164 .... IT 9.3(B)
s 170(1A)(2)(5) .... IT 9.3(B)
ss 173–180 .... IT 9.3(D)
s 181 .... IT 9.3(D); 9.5
ss 182–191 .... IT 9.3(D)
s 201 .... IT 9.6(A); NIC 505.1(A)
ss 202, 203 .... NIC 505.1(A)
s 204 .... IT 9.3(A)
ss 203–208 .... IT 9.3(C)
ss 216, 217 .... IT 9.6(A)
s 218 .... IT 9.6(A)(B)
ss 219, 220 .... IT 9.6(A)
ss 229–236 .... IT 9.2(A)
ss 240, 241 .... IT 9.6(A)
ss 271–289 .... IT 9.5
ss 289A–289E .... IT 9.3(A)
s 313 .... IT 9.4; 9.4(A)
s 314 .... IT 9.4; 9.4(A)

Table of Statutes

2003 Income Tax (Earnings and Pensions) Act – *cont.*

s 315	IT 9.4
(5)	IT 9.4(A)
s 325	IT 9.6(B)
s 336	IT 9.2(B)
ss 337–340	IT 9.2(B); 20.1
ss 346–350	IT 9.3(A)
ss 370, 371	IT 9.1
ss 402–402E	IT 6.1
s 403	IT 6.1
s 404	IT 6.1
ss 415, 416	IT 6.1
s 420(8)	IT 28.1
ss 422–432	IT 28.2
ss 435–444	IT 28.3
ss 471–474	IT 28.1
s 475	IT 28.1; 28.4
s 476	IT 28.1; 28.5
ss 477–484	IT 28.1
ss 488–515	IT 28.4
ss 527–541	IT 28.5
ss 681B–681H	IT 29.1
s 693	IT 9.6(A)
Sch 5	IT 28.5

2004 Finance Act

s 117	CGT 222.4
ss 188–195A	IT 19.1
ss 214–226	IT 19.2
ss 227–238A	IT 19.3
Sch 19 paras 4–7	CGT 229.5
Sch 36 paras 7–11D	IT 19.2
para 39	IT 19.1
40	IT 19.1

2005 Income Tax (Trading and Other Income) Act

ss 13, 14	IT 17.1
s 25A	IT 31.1
ss 31A–31F	IT 31.1
s 33A	IT 31.1
ss 36, 37	IT 30.4
ss 45–47	IT 30.4
s 51A	IT 31.1
s 55	IT 30.4
s 57	IT 30.4
s 57B	IT 31.1
s 58	IT 31.4
ss 60–63	IT 22.5(B); CGT 216.3(G)
s 64	IT 22.5(B)(C); CGT 216.3(G)
ss 65–67	IT 22.5(B); CGT 216.3(G)
ss 94B–94I	IT 31.1
ss 111–129	IT 11
ss 148A–148J	IT 29.7
ss 163, 164	IT 20; 20.1
ss 169–172	IT 30.9
s 172B	IT 30.4
s 198	NIC 507.1
s 200	NIC 507.1
ss 198 200	IT 30.1
s 201	NIC 507.1

2005 Income Tax (Trading and Other Income) Act – *cont.*

s 202	IT 30.3
s 203	IT 18.1(B)
s 204	IT 30.1
s 205	IT 30.3
s 214	IT 30.2
(1)	IT 30.2(C)
s 215	IT 30.2
s 216	IT 4.1(B); 30.2; 30.2(A)(B)
s 217	IT 4.1(B); 30.2; 30.2(A)(B)(C)
s 218	IT 30.2
s 219	IT 30.2; 30.2(C)
s 220	IT 30.2; 30.2(B)
ss 221–225	IT 30.6; 30.7
s 227A	IT 31.1
ss 240A–240D	IT 31.1
ss 241–247	IT 21
s 248	IT 21
(3)(4)	IT 21.2
s 249	IT 21
s 250	IT 21; 21.2
ss 251–254	IT 21.1
s 255	IT 21
(4)	IT 21.2
s 256	IT 21
s 257	IT 21; 21.2
ss 263–272ZA	IT 22.1
ss 272A, 272B	IT 22.4
ss 273, 274	IT 22.1
ss 274A, 274AA, 274B, 274C	IT 22.4
s 275	IT 22.1
s 276	IT 22.5
s 276A	IT 22.1
s 277	IT 22.5; 22.5(A); CGT 216.3(C)
ss 278–281	IT 22.5; CGT 216.3(C)
ss 282–286	IT 22.5
ss 287, 288	IT 22.5; 22.5(C)
ss 289–307	IT 22.5
ss 307B–307F	IT 22.1
ss 308A–308C	IT 22.1
s 311A	IT 22.1
ss 321–328B	IT 22.2
ss 334B–334E	IT 22.1
s 397A	IT 28.4
s 399	IT 17.1
ss 427–429	IT 24.1
ss 430–436	IT 24.1; 24.1(A)
ss 437–452	IT 24.1
s 453	IT 24.1; 24.1(A)(B)
s 454	IT 24.1; 24.1(B)
s 455	IT 24.1; 24.1(A)
ss 456–460	IT 14.1; 24.1
ss 461–490	IT 14.1
s 491	IT 14.2
ss 192–498	IT 14.1
s 499	IT 14.2
ss 500–506	IT 14.1
s 507	IT 14.2
ss 508–527	IT 14.1
s 528	IT 14.1; 14.3

Table of Statutes

2005 Income Tax (Trading and Other Income) Act – *cont.*

s 529	IT 14.1
s 530	IT 14.1(A)(B)
s 531	IT 14.1(A)
ss 532–535	IT 14.1
s 536	IT 14.1(A)(B)
s 537	IT 14.1(B)
ss 538–541	IT 14.1
s 542	IT 14.1(A)
ss 543–546	IT 14.1
s 629	IT 27.4
ss 631, 632	IT 27.4
ss 633–638	IT 27.5
ss 649–651	IT 7
s 652	IT 7.1
s 653	IT 7
s 654(3)	IT 7.2
s 655	IT 7
s 656	IT 7.1
ss 657–660	IT 7
s 661	IT 7.2
ss 662–664	IT 7
s 665	IT 7.1
ss 666–678	IT 7
s 679	IT 7.1; 7.2
ss 680–682	IT 7
ss 783A–783AR	IT 30.5
ss 784–802	IT 22.3
ss 803–828	IT 30.8
s 832	IT 23.1
ss 846–849	IT 18.1
s 850(1)	IT 18.1(A)
(2)–(5)	IT 18.2
s 851	IT 18.1(B)
ss 852, 853	IT 18.1(A)
ss 854–856	IT 18.1(B)
s 863	IT 18.1
(2)	IT 18.3
Sch 2 para 133	IT 27.4

2005 Finance Act

ss 23–45	CGT 228.2
Sch 1	CGT 228.2
Sch 1A	CGT 228.2

2005 Finance (No 2) Act

s 38	CT 114.3(A)

2006 Finance Act

s 32	CGT 220.4
s 69	CGT 208.2
s 70(3)	CT 103.3(F)
Sch 12 paras 34, 36	CGT 219.1(A)
41	CGT 219.1(A)
Sch 15 Pt 1	IT 27.9

2007 Income Tax Act

s 7(1)	IT 1.3
(2)	IT 1.2
s 8	IT 1.1
s 9	IT 27.2
s 11A	IT 1.8
s 12	IT 1.3

2007 Income Tax Act – *cont.*

s 12A	IT 1.2
s 12B	IT 1.2; 1.8
s 13	IT 1.1
s 13A	IT 1.1
s 16	IT 1.1; 1.2; 1.3
s 19	IT 1.1
s 25(2)	IT 1.1(B)(C); 1.3; 1.4
ss 26, 27, 29	IT 10.1(A)
s 35	IT 1.5; 5.1(C); 19.1(B); 32.2
s 42	IT 1.7
s 43	IT 1.7
s 44	IT 1.7; 16.1
s 45	IT 1.7
(4)	IT 1.3(C)
s 46	IT 1.7
s 47	IT 1.7
ss 48–50	IT 1.6; 16.1
s 51	IT 1.7
s 52	IT 1.7; 16.1
s 53	IT 1.7
(1)–(3)	IT 17.1
s 54	IT 1.7; 16.2
s 55	IT 1.7
s 55A	IT 1.6
s 55B	IT 1.6; 16.1
ss 55C–55E	IT 1.6
s 56	IT 17.1
s 58	IT 1.5; 1.7; 19.1
s 61(2)	IT 15.3(A)(B)
s 62	IT 18.2
s 63	IT 15.4
s 64	IT 15.1; 15.3(A)(B); 15.4; 18.3; 18.4; 29.5; 29.6; CGT 201.2; NIC 510.1
(2)	IT 1.4; 15.2
s 71	IT 15.2
s 72	IT 15.3; 15.3(A)(B); 18.4; NIC 510.1
ss 73, 73	IT 15.3
s 83	IT 15.3(A)(B); NIC 510.1
ss 89–91	IT 15.4
ss 96–101	IT 21.2
ss 103–106	IT 18.3
ss 107–109	IT 18.4
ss 113A, 114	IT 18.3; 18.4
s 118	IT 22.4
ss 125, 126	IT 21.2
s 127	IT 21.2
s 127ZA	IT 22.2
ss 131, 132	IT 10.2(B); 15.5; CGT 217.3
ss 133–151	IT 15.5; CGT 217.3
ss 156, 157	IT 10
s 158	IT 10; 10.1(A)
(2)(2ZA)(2ZB)	IT 10.1(B); CGT 211.1
(4)(5)	IT 10.1(B)
s 159	IT 10
(2)	IT 10; CGT 211.1; 211.2(B)
(4)	IT 10.2(B)
ss 160–162	IT 10
s 163	IT 10; CGT 211.3
ss 164, 165	IT 10
ss 166–168	IT 10; CGT 211.3

Table of Statutes

2007 Income Tax Act – *cont.*
ss 169, 170	IT 10; 10.1(A); CGT 211.3
s 171	IT 10; CGT 211.3
ss 172–200	IT 10
s 201	IT 9; 10.1(B)
(6)	IT 10.2(A)
ss 202–208	IT 10
s 209	IT 10; 10.2(A)(B); CGT 211.2(B)
s 210	IT 10; 10.2(A); CGT 211.2(B)
(2)	IT 10.1(B)
ss 211, 212	IT 10
ss 213–217	IT 10; 10.2(B)
ss 218, 219	IT 10
s 220	IT 9; 10.2(B)
ss 221–233	IT 10
s 234	IT 10
(1)	IT 10.2(B)
s 235	IT 10; 10.2(A)(B)
ss 236–245	IT 10
s 246	IT 10; 10.2(A)
ss 247–257	IT 10
ss 257A–257EG	IT 25.1
s 257AB(5)	CGT 227.3
s 257EA	CGT 227.3
ss 257FA, 257FB	CGT 227.2(B)
ss 257FC–257GI	IT 25.2(A)
ss 257R, 257RA	CGT 231.2(B)
s 257HA	IT 25.2(A)
ss 258–260	IT 32
ss 261–263	IT 32; 32.1(A)
ss 264, 265	IT 32
ss 266–270	IT 32; 32.1(B)
ss 271–332	IT 32
ss 414, 415	IT 5.1
s 423	IT 5.1; 5.1(C)
ss 424, 425	IT 5.1
ss 426, 427	IT 5.1(A)
ss 453–456	IT 16.2
s 460	IT 17.1
s 461	IT 12.1
ss 479–483	IT 27.2
ss 484–486	IT 27.2; 27.2(B)
s 487	IT 27.2
ss 491, 492	IT 27.2; 27.2(A)
ss 493–495	IT 27.2
ss 496–498	IT 27.2; 27.2(C)
s 503	IT 27.3(A)
ss 615–681	IT 2
s 643	IT 2.1
s 809B	IT 23.1; CGT 220.2; 225.1
s 809C	IT 23.1; CGT 225.1
s 809D	IT 23.1
s 809G	IT 23.1
s 809H	IT 23.1; CGT 225.1
s 809J	CGT 225.1
ss 809Q, 809R	IT 23.1
ss 809RA–809RD	IT 23.1
ss 810–828	IT 17.1
s 836	CGT 218.3
s 837	CGT 218.3
s 851	IT 1.2

2007 Income Tax Act – *cont.*
ss 874, 875	CT 107.1
s 876	IT 1.2; CT 107.1
ss 877–938	CT 107.1
s 1005	IT 24.1(A)(B)
Sch 2 paras 14–17	IT 17.1
para 101	IT 16.2

2007 Finance Act
s 27	CGT 208.2

2008 Finance Act
s 31	IT 10
s 77	IT 4.3
s 80(2)	IT 4.1(B)
s 83	IT 4.5
Sch 1 para 20	IT 25.2
Sch 2 para 37	IT 22.2
59	CGT 214.2(A)
60	CGT 214.2(A)
65	CGT 205.2; 214.2(A)
Sch 3 para 6	CGT 206.3
7	CGT 206.1(A)(B); 206.5
8	CGT 206.1(A)(B)
Sch 4 para 10	IHT 310.3(B)
Sch 7 paras 120–125	CGT 219.1(A)
Sch 19	IT 5.1(A)
Sch 24 para 3	CT 102.1

2009 Corporation Tax Act
s 2	CGT 207.1
s 8	CT 101.2
s 9	CT 101.1; 112.1
s 10(1)	CT 101.1; 101.3
s 12	CT 101.1; 112.1
s 18A	CT 105.2; 105.2(A)(B)
ss 18A–18E	CT 105.2
s 18F	CT 105.2; 105.2(A)
ss 18G–18I	CT 105.2
ss 18J–18N	CT 105.2; 105.2(B)
ss 18O–18Q	CT 105.2; 105.2(A)(B)
s 18R	CT 105.2; 105.2(A)
s 18S	CT 105.2
s 53	CT 101.3
s 56	CT 116.1
ss 62–67	CGT 216.3(G)
s 104A	CT 117.2
s 104B	CT 117.1; 117.2
ss 215, 216	CGT 216.3(C)
ss 217, 218	CT 116.1; CGT 216.3(C)
ss 219, 220	CT 116.1
ss 274–276	CT 116.1
ss 295–298	CT 113.1
s 299	CT 113.1; 113.2
ss 300, 301	CT 113.1
s 304	CT 113.1
ss 306A–310	CT 113.1
s 328	CT 113.1
ss 456–463	CT 113.3(A)
ss 463A–463I	CT 113.3(B)
ss 726–744	CT 108.1
ss 751–753	CT 108.2
ss 754–763	CT 108.3

Table of Statutes

2009 Corporation Tax Act – *cont.*

ss 849B–849D	CT 108.1(A)
ss 879A, 879B	CT 108.1(C)
s 879C	CT 108.1(A)(C)
ss 879D–879P	CT 108.1(C)
ss 882–884	CGT 213.3
s 1040A	CT 117.2
ss 1044–1062	CT 117.1
ss 1218–1222	CT 111.1
s 1223	CT 106.2; 111.1
ss 1224–1231	CT 111.1
ss 1248, 1255	CT 111.1
s 1307	CT 101.3
Sch 1 para 536	CT 117.1

2009 Finance Act

s 4	IT 5.1(C); 19.1(B); 28.2
s 27	CT 27
s 101	IT 13.1(A)(B); CT 110.1(A)
s 102	IT 26.2(A); CT 109.1
s 107	IT 13.1(A)
s 122	IHT 302
para 6	IT 5.1(C)
Sch 6 paras 1, 2	IT 14.1(B)
Sch 8 paras 1–5	IT 10
para 6	IT 10; 10.1(B)
7	IT 10
8	IT 32
paras 11, 12	IT 10
13	IT 1; 10.1(B)
Sch 27 para 5	CGT 225.1
Sch 35	IT 19.1
Sch 53	CT 110.1(A)
para 1	IT 13.1(B)
Sch 54	CT 110.1(A)
para 5	IT 26.2(A)
Sch 56	IT 13.1(A)

2010 Corporation Tax Act

s 24	CT 115.1
s 37	CT 106.5; 109.2
(3)	CT 103.1; 114.1; 114.3(A)(B); 117.1
(4)	CT 114.3(A)
s 38	CT 114.3; 114.3(B)
s 39	CT 109.2; 114.3; 114.3(A)
ss 40–44	CT 114.3
s 45	CT 106.2; 106.5; 114.2(A); 114.3(A)(B); 117.1
s 45A	CT 106.5; 114.2; 114.3(A)
s 45B	CT 114.2; 114.3(A)
ss 45C–45E	CT 114.2
s 45F	CT 114.3(A)
ss 62–67	CT 114.4
ss 68–81	CT 114.4
ss 82–86	CT 114.4; 116.1
ss 87–90	CT 114.4
ss 97, 98	CT 106.1
s 99	CT 106.1; 106.2; 106.5
ss 100–102	CT 106.1; 106.2
s 103	CT 106.1; 106.2; 111.1
s 104	CT 106.1; 106.2; 108.2
s 105	CT 106.1; 106.2; 106.5

2010 Corporation Tax Act – *cont.*

ss 106–129	CT 106.1
s 130	CT 106.1; 106.7
s 131	CT 106.1
s 132	CT 106.1; 106.7; 106.7(D)
s 133	CT 106.1; 106.7; 106.7(B)
ss 134–137	CT 106.1
s 138	CT 106.1; 106.3; 106.4
ss 139, 140	CT 106.1; 106.3; 106.4; 106.7(A)
ss 141, 142	CT 106.1; 106.3; 106.4
s 143	CT 106.1; 106.7(A)(C)
s 144	CT 106.1; 106.7(D)
s 145	CT 106.1
s 146	CT 106.1; 106.7(B)
s 147	CT 106.1
s 148	CT 106.1; 106.7(B)
ss 149, 150	CT 106.1
s 151	CT 106.1; 106.7(C)
s 152	CT 106.1
s 153	CT 106.1; 106.7(C)
ss 154–156	CT 106.1
s 188BB	CT 106.2
s 279F	CT 115.1
ss 188AA–188EK	CT 106.6
s 189	CT 114.1; 116.1
s 190	CT 116.1
ss 269ZA–269ZQ	CT 114.7; 114.7(A)
s 269ZBA	CGT 208.3
s 269ZR	CT 114.7; 114.7(A)(B)
ss 269ZS—269ZZA	CT 116.1; 114.7(A)
s 269ZZB	CT 116.1; 114.7(A)(B)
s 439	CT 104.1(A)(C)
ss 440–445	CT 104.1
s 446	CT 104.1; 104.1(A)
ss 447–449	CT 104.1
s 450	IT 17.2; CT 104.1; 104.1(B)(C)
s 451	IT 17.2; CT 104.1; 104.1(B)
s 452	CT 104.1; 104.1(B)
s 453	CT 104.1
s 455	CT 104.2; 104.2(B)
ss 456, 457	CT 104.2
s 458	CT 104.2; 104.2(B)
ss 459–464	CT 104.2
s 464A	CT 104.2; 104.2(A)
s 464B	CT 104.2
ss 464C, 464D	CT 104.2; 104.2(A)
s 535	CT 103.3(E)
ss 626–629	CT 112.1
ss 677–703	CT 111.1
ss 940A–944	CT 102.1; 114.5
ss 945–947	CT 102.1; 114.5; 114.5(A)
ss 948–951	CT 102.1; 114.5
s 952	CT 102.1; 114.5; 114.5(A)
s 953	CT 102.1; 114.5; 114.5(B)
ss 963–966	CT 110.1(D)
s 967	CT 107.1
s 1060	CT 117.1
ss 1064–1069	CT 104.3
s 1172	CT 101.3
Sch 1 para 117	CT 109.2

Table of Statutes

2010 Taxation (International and Other Provisions) Act
- ss 2–6 .... CT 105.1
- ss 18–20 .. IT 8.1(A); CT 105.1; CGT 210.1
- ss 21–30 .... IT 8.1(A); CGT 210.1
- ss 31–34 .. IT 8.1(A); CT 105.1; CGT 210.1
- s 35 .... IT 8.1(A); CGT 210.1
- s 36 .... IT 8.1(A)(B); CGT 210.1
- ss 37–41 .... IT 8.1(A); CGT 210.1
- ss 42–56 .... CT 105.1
- s 113 .... CT 105.1
- ss 146–173 .... CT 119.1
- ss 174–178 .... CT 119.1; 119.1(B)
- ss 179, 180 .... CT 119.1
- ss 181–184 .... CT 119.1; 119.1(B)
- s 185 .... CT 119.1; 119.1(A)
- ss 186–230 .... CT 119.1
- ss 372–498 .... CT 119.1(B)
- Sch 7A .... CT 119.1(B)

2010 Finance Act
- s 1 .... IT 1.5; 1.6

2011 Finance Act
- Sch 14 para 2 .... IT 22.1
- para 14 .... CGT 226.4
- Sch 17 paras 29–31 .... IT 19.3

2012 Finance Act
- s 4 .... IT 22.2
- s 6 .... CT 101.3
- s 9 .... IT 1.6
- s 10 .... IT 14.6
- s 20 .... CT 117.1
- Sch 3 .... CT 117.1
- Sch 7 paras 12, 23 .... IT 10.1(B)
- Sch 39 para 48 .... IT 24.1(A)

2013 Finance Act
- s 29 .... CT 106.2
- s 48 .... IT 19.2
- s 49 .... IT 19.3(A)
- s 56 .... IT 25.1
- s 229 .... CGT 220.1
- Sch 2 paras 2, 5 .... IT 4.6
- Sch 4 para 24 .... IT 28.4
- Sch 4 para 32 .... IT 30.6; 30.7
- Sch 4 para 39 .... IT 21.1
- Sch 4 para 40 .... IT 22.3
- Sch 4 para 56 . IT 11.1; 21.1; 22.3; 30.6; 30.7
- para 4 .... IT 23.1
- para 6 .... IT 23.1
- Sch 6 paras 5, 6, 8 .... IT 21.1
- Sch 22 .... IT 19.2
- Sch 23 para 17 .... CGT 218.2
- Sch 24 para 1 .... IT 28.5
- paras 5, 6 .... IT 28.5
- para 6 .... CT 104.2(A)
- Sch 38 .... VAT 406.1
- Sch 45 para 77 .... IT 21.1
- paras 109–115 .... CGT 219.1(A)
- para 119 .... CGT 219.1(A)
- para 153 .... 21.1; CGT 219.1(A)
- paras 25–27 .... IT 23.1

2013 Finance Act – *cont.*
- Sch 46 para 35 .... IT 2.1
- Sch 49 .... CGT 220.1

2014 Finance Act
- s 1 .... IT 1.5
- s 11 .... IT 16.1
- s 22 .... IT 9.3(D)
- s 54 .... IT 25.1
- Sch 6 para 10 .... IT 19.2(B)
- Sch 7 paras 13, 16 .... IT 19.1
- Sch 10 .... IT 32

2014 National Insurance Contributions Act
- ss 1–9 .... NIC 504.1

2014 Taxation of Pensions Act
- Sch 1 paras 26, 27 .... IT 19.2
- Sch 1 para 76 .... IT 19.2
- Sch 2 paras 19–24 .... IT 19.2

2015 Finance Act
- s 5 .... CT 101.1
- s 11 .... IT 1.6
- s 13(1)(4) .... IT 9.6(A)
- s 26 .... CT 108.1(A)
- Sch 4 paras 4–7 .... IT 19.2

2015 Finance (No 2) Act
- s 7 .... IT 9.4
- s 9 .... IHT 310.5(A)(C)(D)
- s 21(7)(10) .... IT 19.2

2016 Finance Act
- s 5 .... 1.6; 27.2
- s 7 .... IT 9.4
- s 19 .... IT 19.2
- s 24 .... IT 31.1
- s 25 .... IT 30.6; 30.7
- s 31 .... IT 32
- s 74 .... IT 22.1
- s 83 .... CGT 228.1
- s 84 .... CGT 206.3
- s 85 .... CGT 206.1(A)
- s 88 .... CGT 218.2
- Sch 1 para 63 .... IT 5.1; 27.2; 27.2(C)
- Sch 1 para 73 ..... IT 6.1; 7.1; 17.1; 27.2; 27.2(C)
- Sch 4 .... IT 19.2
- Sch 6 .... CT 107.1
- Sch 6 para 1 .... IT 1.2
- Sch 6 para 2 .... IT 1.2
- Sch 6 para 28 .... IT 1.2
- Sch 14 para 2 .... CGT 215.1; 215.2
- Sch 15 .... IHT 310.5(A)
- Sch 15 para 1 .... IHT 310.5(B)(C)(D)
- Sch 15 para 2 .... IHT 310.5(D)
- Sch 15 para 5 .... IHT 310.5(B)
- Sch 15 para 6 .... IHT 310.5(C)

2016 Scotland Act
- ss 13, 14 .... IT 1.8

2017 Finance Act
- s 8 .... IT 9.3(C)
- Sch 5 .... CT 107.1

Table of Statutes

2017 Finance (No 2) Act

s 5(3)–(5)(10)	IT 6.1
s 8	IT 1.1
s 16	IT 31.1
ss 27, 28	CT 103.4
Sch 2 paras 1, 4	IT 31.1
Sch 2 paras 13–15	CT 22.1
Sch 2 para 17	CT 22.1
Sch 2 paras 22, 23	CT 22.1
Sch 2 para 64	CT 22.1
Sch 3 para 1	IT 30.5
Sch 4 para 4	CT 113.3(B)
Sch 4 para 5	CT 108.2
Sch 4 para 6	CT 111.1
Sch 4 para 10	CT 114.2
Sch 4 para 11	CT 114.2; 114.2(B); 114.3(A)
Sch 4 paras 13, 14	CT 114.6
Sch 4 paras 16	CT 114.7; 114.7(A)(B)
Sch 4 para 23	CT 106.6
Sch 4 paras 62–68	CT 114.5
Sch 4 para 190	CT 106.6; 108.2; 111.1; 113.3(A)(B); 114.2; 114.2(B); 114.3(A); 114.6; 114.7; 114.7(A)
Sch 4 paras 191, 192	CT 106.6; 114.6
Sch 8 paras 11, 14	CGT 225.1

2018 Finance Act

s 14	IT 10; 25.1; 32
ss 15, 16	IT 10; 32
s 17	IT 32
s 26(2)(3)(6)	CT 103.2(A); 103.3(A)–(C)(E); CGT 204.1(A)(B); 204.2; 204.3(A)–(F); 205.2(A)(C)(D); 205.3; 207.3(C); 208.1; 214.1(B)–(D); 216.3(E)(F); 229.3(C); 230.2
s 27	CGT 220.3
s 28	CGT 202.4
s 36	IT 22.1
Sch 4	IT 10; 32
Sch 5	IT 32
Sch 4 paras 1, 10	IT 10.1(B); CGT 211.1
Sch 10 para 1	CGT 219.1
Sch 10para 2	CGT 219.1

2019 Finance Act

s 7	IT 9.3; 4.5
s 30	IT 3.1; 4.5
s 31	IT 4.1; 4.5
s 32	IT 4.1; 4.6; CT 101.3
ss 33, 34	IT 4.1
s 35	IT 4.5
s 39	CGT 206.1
s 66	IHT 310.5; 310.5(B)
s 88	CT 109
Sch 1 para 2	CT 101.3; 103.1; CGT 201.1; 201.1(A)(C); 201.2; 206.1(B)(C); 208.1; 215.1(C); 217.1; 217.2; 220.1; 220.2; 220.4; 228.1

2019 Finance Act – *cont.*

Sch 1 para 3	CGT 225.1
Sch 1 para 13	CGT 225.1
Sch 1 para 16	CGT 228.1
Sch 1 paras 25, 26	CGT 220.2
Sch 1 para 28	CGT 221.1
Sch 1 para 29	CGT 217.1(B)
Sch 1 para 33	CGT 217.2
Sch 1 para 35	CGT 219.1(A)
Sch 1 para 43	CGT 219.1(B)
Sch 1 para 54	CT 103.3(B)(C)
Sch 1 paras 62, 63	CT 103.3(A)
Sch 1 para 67	CGT 220.1
Sch 1 para 74	CGT 223.1
Sch 1 paras 97, 98	CGT 228.2
Sch 1 para 111	CT 105.2; 105.2(A)
Sch 1 para 120	CT 101.3; 103.1; 105.2; 105.2(A); CGT 201.1; 201.1(A)(C); 201.2; 217.1; 217.2; 220.1; 220.2; 220.4; 223.1; 228.1
Sch 2	105.2(A); CGT 201.1; 209.2; 213.1
Sch 5 para 12	CT 105.2; 105.2(A)
Sch 5 para 35	CT 105.2; 105.2(A)
Sch 8 paras 1–9	CGT 220.1
Sch 9 para 6	CT 108.1(A)(C)
Sch 9 para 7	CT 108.1(C)
Sch 10 para 12	CT 114.7
Sch 13	IT 4.6; CT 101.3
Sch 16 para 1	CGT 206.3
Sch 16 para 2	CGT 206.1; 206.1(A)(C); 206.3
Sch 16 para 3	CGT 206.6
Sch 16 para 4	CGT 206.1(A)(C); 206.3; 206.6

2020 Finance Act

s 1	IT 1.1
s 2	IT 1.1
s 3	IT 1.1; 1.2
s 4	IT 1.1; IT 1.3
s 6	IT 1.1; 1.2; 1.3
ss 8–10	IT 9.3
s 23	CGT 206.1
s 29	IT 3.1
s 26	CT 115.1
s 28	CT 117.2
s 30	IT 3.1
s 37	IT 14.1
s 38	IT 15.5
s 73(5)	IHT 320.1
s 73(6)	IHT 320.2; 320.3
s 107	IT 28.5
s 110	IT 25.1
Sch 3	CGT 206.1
Sch 3 para 4	CGT 206.4
Sch 4 para 2	CGT 208.3
Sch 4 paras 39, 42	CT 103.1
Sch 5	IT 3.1

Table of Statutory Instruments

1978/1689 Social Security (Categorisation of Earners) Regulations
Sch 3 para 2 .... NIC 502.4

1987/530 Income Tax (Entertainers and Sportsmen) Regulations .... IT 17.2

1987/1130 Inheritance Tax (Double Charges Relief) Regulations ... IHT 311; 311.1(B); 314; 321.1
Reg 4 .... IHT 314.1
Reg 5 .... IHT 311.1(B)
Reg 6 .... IHT 321.1
Reg 7 .... IHT 314.2

1988/1013 Personal Pension Schemes (Relief at Source) Regulations .... IT 21.1(A)

1989/1297 Taxes (Interest Rate) Regulations
.... CT 109; IHT 312

1992/3122 Value Added Tax (Cars) Order
Art 8(7) .... VAT 412.3

1993/2212 Taxes (Interest Rate) (Amendment No 3) Regulations .... CT 109

1995/1268 Value Added Tax (Special Provisions) Order
Art 12(7) .... VAT 412.3
Art 13 .... VAT 412.2

1995/2518 Value Added Tax Regulations
Regs 66–75 .... VAT 403.1; 411
Regs 99–109 .... VAT 408.1; 408.2
Regs 112–116 .... VAT 402.1
Regs 165–172E .... VAT 401.1
Regs 172F–172J .... VAT 405.1

1998/3175 Corporation Tax (Instalment Payments) Regulations . CT 109.1(A)(B); 110.1; 115.1

1998/3176 Taxes (Interest Rate) (Amendment No 2) Regulations . CT 109.1(A)(B); 110.1

1999/684 Income Tax (Cash Equivalent of Car Fuel Benefits) Order ..... IT 9.3(A)

1999/1928 Taxes (Interest Rate) (Amendment No 2) Regulations . CT 110.1(A)(B); 111.1

1999/3120 Value Added Tax (Special Provisions) (Amendment) (No 2) Order
.... VAT 412.2

2000/727 Social Security Contributions (Intermediaries) Regulations
.... NIC 512.1

2000/2315 Personal Pension Schemes (Relief at Source) (Amendment) Regulations
.... IT 19.1(A)

2001/1004 Social Security (Contributions) Regulations
Reg 2 .... NIC 511.1
Reg 3 .... NIC 511.1; 511.1(A)(B)

2001/1004 Social Security (Contributions) Regulations – *cont.*
Reg 4 .... NIC 511.1; 511.1(C)
Reg 5 .... NIC 511.1
Reg 6 .... NIC 511.1
Reg 7 .... NIC 501.1; 512.1
Reg 8 .... NIC 502.5; 508.2; 511.1; 511.3
Reg 9 .... NIC 511.1
Reg 12 .... NIC 504.2
Reg 14 .... NIC 502.1; 502.1(A)
Reg 15(1) .... NIC 502.2; 502.3; 502.4
Reg 18 .... NIC 511.2
Reg 19 .... NIC 511.3
Reg 21 .... NIC 503.1
Reg 22(2) .... NIC 508.1; 508.2
Regs 28, 29 .... NIC 501.1; 501.1(A)
Reg 36 .... NIC 505.2(A)(B)
Reg 68 .... NIC 509.1
Reg 84 .... NIC 509.1
Reg 94 .... NIC 507.1
Reg 100 .... NIC 503.2; 503.2(A)
Sch 3 Pt X para 2 .... NIC 508.1

2004/773 Retirement Benefits Schemes (Indexation of Earnings Cap) Order
.... IT 19.1(A)

2005/720 Retirement Benefits Schemes (Indexation of Earnings Cap) Order
.... IT 19.1(A)

2006/912 Energy-Saving Items Regulations
.... IT 22.1

2009/730 Enactment of Extra-Statutory Concessions Order
Art 4 .... CGT 218.1(B)

2011/701 Finance Act 2009, Sections 101 to 103 (Income Tax Self Assessment) (Appointed Days and Transitional and Consequential Provisions) Order
.... IT 13.1(A)(B)

2011/702 Finance Act 2009, Schedules 55 and 56 (Income Tax Self Assessment and Pension Schemes) (Appointed Days and Consequential and Savings Provisions) Order .... IT 13.1(A)

2012/1359 Income Tax (Entertainers and Sportsmen) (Amendment) Regulations
.... IT 17.2

2014/2409 Corporation Tax (Instalment Payments) (Amendment) Regulations
.... CT 115.1

2014/2896 Van Benefit and Car and Van Fuel Benefit Order .... IT 9.3(A)(B)

2015/1539 Income Tax (Limit for Rent-a-Room Relief) Order 2015 .... IT 22.3

xxv

Table of Statutory Instruments

2015/1979 Van Benefit and Car and Van Fuel Benefit Order .... IT 9.3(A)(B)

2016/352 Social Security (Contributions) (Amendment) (No 2) Regulations 2016 Reg 5 .... NIC 503.2

2017/293 Income Tax (Relevant Maximum for Calculating Trade Profits on the Cash Basis) Order 2017 .... IT 31.1

2017/1072 Corporation Tax (Instalment Payments) (Amendment) Regulations 2017 .... CT 109.1(B); 110; 115.1

2018/931 Finance Act 2018, Section 14 and Schedules 4 and 5 (Commencement) Regulations 2018 .... CGT 211.1

2019/201 Devolved Income Tax Rates (Consequential Amendments) Order 2019 .... IT 5.1(B)

2019/1087 The Capital Allowances (Structures and Buildings Allowances) Regulations 2019 .... IT 3.1

2020/333 The Capital Gains Tax (Annual Exempt Amount) Order 2020 .... CGT 201.2

Income Tax

1	Allowances and Tax Rates
2	Accrued Income Scheme
3	Capital Allowances
4	Capital Allowances on Plant and Machinery
5	Charities
6	Compensation for Loss of Employment
7	Deceased Estates
8	Double Tax Relief
9	Employment Income
10	Enterprise Investment Scheme
11	Herd Basis
12	Intellectual Property
13	Late Payment Interest and Penalties
14	Life Assurance Policies
15	Losses
16	Married Persons and Civil Partners
17	Non-Residents
18	Partnerships
19	Pension Provision
20	Personal Service Companies etc.
21	Post-Cessation Receipts and Expenditure
22	Property Income
23	Remittance Basis
24	Savings and Investment Income
25	Seed Enterprise Investment Scheme
26	Self-Assessment
27	Settlements
28	Share-Related Employment Income and Exemptions
29	Social Security Income
30	Trading Income
31	Trading Income — Cash Basis for Smaller Businesses
32	Venture Capital Trusts

1 Allowances and Tax Rates

Cross-reference. See also **16.1** MARRIED PERSONS AND CIVIL PARTNERS for transfer of married couple's allowance.

1.1 DIVIDEND ALLOWANCE

[ITA 2007, ss 8, 13, 13A, 16, 19; F(No 2)A 2017, s 8; FA 2020, ss 1–4]

(A)

Cicero has property income of £34,500, bank interest of £800 and UK dividends of £2,200 for 2020/21. Cicero is not a Scottish taxpayer.

His taxable income and tax liability are computed as follows

	Savings income	Dividend income	Non-savings income	Total income
	£	£	£	£
Property income			34,500	34,500
Savings income	800			800
Dividend income		2,200		2,200
Total income	800	2,200	34,500	37,500
Personal allowance	–	–	(12,500)	(12,500)
Taxable income	£800	£2,200	£22,000	£25,000
Tax payable:				
22,000 @ 20% (basic rate on property income)			4,400.00	4,400.00
800 @ 0% (personal savings allowance)	—			—
2,000 @ 0% (dividend allowance)		—		—
200 @ 7.5% (dividend ordinary rate)		15.00	–	15.00
£25,000				
Tax payable				£4,415.00

Notes

(a) The dividend allowance for individuals for 2020/21 is £2,000. It was £5,000 for tax years 2016/17 and 2017/18. The dividend allowance is not a deduction in arriving at total income or taxable income. Instead, the first £2,000 of dividend income attracts a zero rate of income tax (the 'dividend nil rate'). See SAIM1080 and *Simon's Taxes* E1.101.

1.1 IT   Allowances and Tax Rates

(b) Dividend income in excess of the dividend allowance is charged at special rates. Where taxable income does not exceed the basic rate limit the rate applied is the 'dividend ordinary rate', 7.5%. To the extent that dividend income exceeds the basic rate limit but not the higher rate limit of £150,000, the rate is the 'dividend upper rate', 32.5%.

To the extent that dividend income exceeds the higher rate limit, the rate is the 'dividend additional rate', 38.1%. In determining the extent to which dividend income does fall above the basic rate or higher rate limit, dividend income is treated as the top slice of income (with certain limited exceptions).

(c) See **1.2** below for the personal savings allowance.

(B)

Terentia has employment income of £10,500, savings income of £7,000 and dividends of £3,500 for 2020/21. She is not a Scottish taxpayer.

	Savings income	Dividend income	Non-savings income	Total income
	£	£	£	£
Total income	7,000	3,500	10,500	21,000
Deduct Personal allowance	(1,000)	(1,000)	(10,500)	(12,500)
Taxable income	£6,000	£2,500	—	£8,500
Tax payable:				
£5,000 @ 0% (starting rate for savings)	—			—
£1,000 @ 0% (personal savings allowance)	—			—
£2,000 @ 0% (dividend allowance)		—		—
£500 @ 7.5% (dividend ordinary rate)		37.50		37.50
Tax payable	—	£37.50		£37.50

Note

(a) The personal allowance is treated as reducing income of different descriptions in such manner as will result in the greatest reduction in tax liability. [*ITA 2007, s 25(2)*]. In this example, what remains of the personal allowance (£2,000) is set firstly against savings income but only to the extent necessary to produce a nil liability on that income. If the £2,000 were set wholly against savings income there would have been a total liability of £112 (£1,500 @ 7.5%) on the dividend income. If the £2,000 were set wholly against dividend income it would wipe out the liability on dividend income but produce a liability of £200 on savings income (£1,000 @ 20%).

(C)

Crassus has trading income of £47,300, bank interest of £700, UK dividends of £1,300 and overseas dividends £2,550 (net of 15% foreign withholding tax) for 2020/21. He is not a Scottish taxpayer.

His taxable income and tax liability are computed as follows

	Savings income £	Dividend income £	Non-savings income £	Total income £
Trading income			47,300	47,300
Bank interest	700			700
Dividend income:				
UK dividends		1,300		1,300
Overseas dividends £2,550 × 100/85		3,000		3,000
Total income	700	4,300	47,300	52,300
Personal allowance	(200)	(2,300)	(10,000)	(12,500)
Taxable income	500	2,000	£37,300	39,800

Tax payable:

37,300	@ 20% (basic rate on trading income (note (a))		7,460.00	7,460.00
500	@ 0% (personal savings allowance)	—		—
2,000	@ 0% (dividend allowance)	—		—
			7,460.00	7,460.00
Less: Foreign withholding tax £3,000 @ 15%		—	(450.00)	(450.00)
Tax payable		—	£7,010.00	£7,010.00

Tax on income excluding foreign dividends

	Savings income £	Dividend income £	Non-savings income £	Total income £
Trading income			47,300	47,300
Bank interest	700			700

1.1 IT Allowances and Tax Rates

Dividend income:				
Dividend income (UK dividends only)		1,300		1,300
Total income	700	1,300	47,300	49,300
Personal allowance	(200)		(12,300)	(12,500)
Taxable income	500	1,300	£35,000	36,800
Tax payable:				
35,000 @ 20% (basic rate on trading income (note (b))			7,000.00	7,000.00
500 @ 0% (personal savings allowance)		—		—
1,300 @ 0% (dividend allowance)		—		—
Tax payable		—	£7,000.00	£7,000.00

The difference between the two calculations of tax payable (before withholding tax) is £460 (£7,460 – 7,000). This is greater than the foreign withholding tax of £450, so the withholding tax is deductible in full.

Notes

(a) The personal allowance is treated as reducing income of different descriptions in such manner as will result in the greatest reduction in tax liability. [*ITA 2007, s 25(2)*]. In this example, £2,300 of the personal allowance has been set against dividend income, £200 has been set against savings income, leaving £10,000 to be set against trading income. The advantage of doing this is that it removes £2,300 of dividend income that would otherwise be taxed at the dividend upper rate of 32.5%. The cost is an additional £2,300 of non-dividend income chargeable at the basic rate of 20%. The tax saving is £287.50 (£2,300 @ (32.5% - 20%)). See SAIM1090 and *Simon's Taxes* E1.101B.

Allowances and Tax Rates   IT 1.2

(b) Overseas dividends are taxed at the same rates, and attract the dividend allowance in the same way, as UK dividends. Credit for the withholding tax on the overseas dividends is given against the UK tax due on them to the extent that it does not exceed that UK tax. See also 8.1 DOUBLE TAX RELIEF. In the calculation of tax on income excluding foreign dividends, the personal allowance is set entirely against trading income; there is no longer an advantage in setting it partly against dividend income as the latter is fully covered by the dividend allowance.

(c) The personal savings allowance is £500 as the taxpayer has income above the basic rate limit but not above the higher rate limit. See **1.2** below.

1.2 PERSONAL SAVINGS ALLOWANCE

[*ITA 2007, ss 7(2), 12A, 12B, 16; FA 2020, ss 3, 4*]

Servilia has pension income of £45,600, bank interest of £2,500 and dividends of £2,000 for 2020/21. She is not a Scottish taxpayer.

Her taxable income and tax liability are computed as follows

	Savings income	Dividend income	Non-savings income	Total income
	£	£	£	£
Pension income			45,600	45,600
Savings income	2,500			2,500
Dividend income		2,000		2,000
Total and net income	2,500	2,000	45,600	50,100
Personal allowance			(12,500)	(12,500)
Taxable income	£2,500	£2,000	£33,100	37,600

Tax payable:

33,100	@ 20% (basic rate on pension income)		6,620.00	6,620.00
500	@ 0% (personal savings allowance)		—	—
2,000	@ 20% (basic rate on savings income)	400.00		400.00
1,900	@ 0% (dividend allowance — part)	—		—
37,500	Basic rate limit			
100	@ 0% (dividend allowance — part)	—		—
£37,600				
Tax payable		—	— £7,020.00	£7,020.00

1.2 IT Allowances and Tax Rates

Notes

(a) The personal savings allowance is £1,000 for basic rate taxpayers, i.e. individuals who have no income chargeable at the higher or additional rates or the dividend upper and additional rates. For individuals with income chargeable at the higher rate or dividend upper rate but not at the additional rate or dividend additional rate, the allowance is £500. Individuals with income chargeable at the additional rate or dividend additional rate are not entitled to the allowance. If dividend income is, in fact, chargeable at the dividend nil rate because of the dividend allowance but would otherwise have been chargeable at the dividend upper or additional rate, it is treated as if it had been chargeable at the dividend upper or additional rate for the purpose of determining the amount (if any) of the personal savings allowance. See *Simon's Taxes* E1.101.

(b) The personal savings allowance is not a deduction in arriving at total income or taxable income. Instead, the savings income covered by the allowance (whether the allowance be £500 or £1,000) attracts a zero rate of income tax (the 'savings nil rate') instead of the basic or higher rate (whichever would otherwise apply).

(c) For the purpose of applying these rules, savings income is treated as the highest part of an individual's total income apart from dividend income and other limited exceptions.

(d) The personal savings allowance operates in conjunction with the starting rate for savings where the latter is available (see **1.3** below).

(e) Deduction of basic rate tax at source by banks and building societies was abolished for 2016/17 onwards, so interest is receivable gross. [*ITA 2007, ss 851, 876; FA 2016, Sch 6 paras 1, 2, 28*]. See *Simon's Taxes* A4.425.

(f) See **1.1** above for the dividend allowance.

1.3 STARTING RATE FOR SAVINGS

[ITA 2007, ss 7(1), 12, 16; FA 2020, s 4]

(A)

Catalina has earned income of £12,180, bank interest of £6,590 and UK dividends of £500 for 2020/21. Catalina is not a Scottish taxpayer.

His income tax position is as follows

	Savings income	Dividend income	Non-savings income	Total income
	£	£	£	£
Earnings			12,180	12,180
Savings income	6,590			6,590
Dividends		500		500
Total — income	6,590	500	12,180	19,270
Personal allowance	(320)		(12,180)	(12,500)
Taxable income	£6,270	£500	—	£6,770
Tax payable:				
5,000 @ 0% (starting rate for savings)	—			—
1,000 @ 0% (personal savings allowance)	—			—
270 @ 20% (basic rate on savings income)	54.00			54.00
500 @ 0% (dividend allowance)		—		—
£6,770				
Tax payable	£54.00	—	—	£54.00

Notes

(a) To the extent that an individual's savings income (excluding dividends) does not exceed the starting rate limit, it is taxed at the 0% starting rate for savings instead of the basic rate. The starting rate limit for 2020/21 is £5,000. For the purpose of determining whether savings income exceeds the starting rate limit, it is treated as the highest part of the individual's total income apart from dividend income and other limited exceptions. See SAIM1112 and *Simon's Taxes* E1.101.

(b) It follows that wherever the amount of an individual's taxable income, apart from savings income and dividend income, equals or exceeds the starting rate limit, the starting rate for savings cannot apply to any of the income.

(c) The personal allowance is treated as reducing income of different descriptions in such manner as will result in the greatest reduction of the tax liability. [*ITA 2007, s 25(2)*]. In this example, it is set firstly against earnings and then against savings income, which gives the best result (see also **1.1(B)(C)** above).

1.3 IT Allowances and Tax Rates

(d) The starting rate for savings operates in conjunction with the personal savings allowance (see **1.2** above) but takes priority.

(e) Savings income includes interest, income from purchased life annuities, profits on deeply discounted securities, accrued income profits and chargeable event gains on life policies etc. See *Simon's Taxes* E1.401

(B)

Clodia has a pension of £13,400, on which tax of £180 has been paid under PAYE, and building society interest of £5,350 for 2020/21. She is not a Scottish taxpayer.

Her income tax position is as follows

	Savings income	Non-savings income	Total income
	£	£	£
Pension income		13,400	13,400
Savings income	5,350		5,350
Total and net income	5,350	13,400	18,750
Personal allowance		(12,500)	(12,500)
Taxable income	£5,350	£900	£6,250
Tax payable:			
900 @ 20% (basic rate on pension income)		180.00	180.00
4,100 @ 0% (starting rate for savings)		—	—
1,000 @ 0% (personal savings allowance)		—	—
250 @ 20% (basic rate on savings income)	50.00		50.00
Tax liability	£230.00		£230.00
Less: PAYE			(180.00)
Tax Payable			£50

Notes

(a) The building society interest is the highest part of the individual's income, and £4,100 of this interest is within the 0% starting rate band of £5,000. The personal allowance has been set against the pension income as this gives the best result.

(b) See also the notes to (A) above.

1.4 USE OF LOSSES

[ITA 2007, s 25(2)]

Hortensius has traded for a number of years. He prepares accounts to 30 June, and his tax-adjusted profits for the year ended 30 April 2020 are £21,530. His other 2020/21 income consists of building society interest of £2,500, interest on UK company loan stock of £1,200 (net of basic rate tax deducted at source) and dividends of £4,500.

For the year to 30 April 2022 Hortensius sustains a tax-adjusted trading loss of £3,228 and makes a claim under *ITA 2007, s 64(2)(b)* to carry it back against general income of 2020/21. He is not a Scottish taxpayer.

Allowances and Tax Rates IT 1.4

His 2020/21 tax liability after loss relief is computed as follows

	Savings income	Dividend income	Non-savings income	Total income
	£	£	£	£
Trading income			21,530	21,530
Building society interest	2,500			2,500
Loan stock interest (£1,200 × 100/80)	1,500			1,500
Dividends	—	4,500	—	4,500
Total income	4,000	4,500	21,530	30,030
Loss relief under *ITA 2007, s 64(2)(b)*			(3,228)	(3,228)
Net income	4,000	4,500	18,302	26,802
Personal Allowance			(12,500)	(12,500)
Taxable income	4,000	4,500	5,802	14,302

Tax payable:

5,802	@ 20% (basic rate on net trading income)		1,160.40	1,160.40
1,000	@ 0% (personal savings allowance)	—		—
3,000	@ 20% (basic rate on savings income)	600.00		600.00
2,000	@ 0% (dividend allowance)		—	—
2,500	@ 7.5% (dividend ordinary rate)		187.50	187.50
14,302		£600.00	£187.50 £1,160.40	£1,947.90
Less: tax deducted at source				(£300)
Net tax payable				£1,647.90

Notes

(a) Although dividend income is generally regarded as the top slice of income and savings income as the next slice, this does not mean that a loss must be set against those types of income first. Deductions allowable in computing net income are treated as reducing income of different descriptions in such manner as will result in the greatest reduction of the tax liability. Here the loss has been set against trading income. Savings income and dividend income are left intact, and attract the personal savings allowance and dividend allowance respectively.

(b) In this example, the whole of the personal allowance is also set against trading income as doing otherwise would not give a better result, but see 1.1(B)(C) above as regards optimum use of the personal allowance in other cases in accordance with the principle stated in (a) above.

1.5 IT Allowances and Tax Rates

1.5 RESTRICTION OF PERSONAL ALLOWANCE

[ITA 2007, ss 35(2)–(4), 58]

Cato has employment income of £118,200 for 2020/21 (and no other income) and makes Gift Aid donations of £4,800. He is not a Scottish taxpayer.

His 2020/21 tax liability is computed as follows

	£	£
Employment income		118,200
Total and net income		118,200
Deduct Personal allowance	12,500	
Less reduction for excess adjusted net income over £100,000 (¹/₂ × 12,200) (note (b))	6,100	(6,400)
Taxable income		£111,800
Tax liability:		
£43,500 @ 20% (note (c))		8,700.00
£68,300 @ 40%		27,320.00
Tax payable		£36,020

Notes

(a) The personal allowance is reduced by one-half of the excess of adjusted net income over £100,000. See PAYE10010 and *Simon's Taxes* E1.910.

(b) Net income of £118,200 is reduced to adjusted net income of £112,200 by deducting the grossed up amount of the Gift Aid donations (£4,800 x 100/80 = £6,000).

(c) Whilst the Gift Aid donations are deductible in arriving at adjusted net income, they are not deductible in arriving at taxable income. Instead, the basic rate band is extended by the grossed up amount of the donations. So the expanded band is £37,500 + £6000. See **5.1(C)** CHARITIES.

1.6 TRANSFERABLE TAX ALLOWANCE

[ITA 2007, ss 55A–55E; TMA 1970, s 42(10A)]

Irina, a married woman receives income (net of allowable expenses) of £11,510 in 2020/21 from occasional freelance proofreading. She has no other taxable income. Irina elects under *ITA 2007, s 55C* to transfer part of her personal allowance to her husband. Her husband, Arkady, has employment income of £44,000 but no other taxable income. The couple are not eligible for married couple's allowance and neither is a Scottish taxpayer.

	£	£
Arkady		
Total income		44,000
Deduct Personal allowance		(12,500)
Taxable income		£31,500
Tax on £31,500 @ 20% (basic rate)		6,300.00
Deduct Transferable tax allowance £1,250 @ 20%		250.00
Tax liability		£6,050.00
Irina		
Total income		11,510
Deduct Personal allowance	12,500	
Less transferable tax allowance	(1,250)	
		(11,250)
Taxable income		£260
Tax liability: £260 @ 20% (basic rate)		£52.00

Notes

(a) An individual may elect to transfer part of his or her personal allowance to a spouse or civil partner. The amount transferable (known as the '*transferable tax allowance*' or '*marriage allowance*') is equivalent to 10% of the basic personal allowance for the year, e.g. it is £1,250 for 2020/21. Relief is given to the transferee by means of a tax reduction at step 6 of the calculation. See *Simon's Taxes* E1.910B.

(b) The election is valid only if neither the transferor nor the transferee are liable to income tax at the higher or additional rate or the dividend upper or additional rate. It cannot be made if either the transferor or transferee claims married couple's allowance for the year.

(c) This couple save tax of £198 by electing to use the transferable tax allowance. Arkady makes the maximum saving of £250.00 (£1,250 @ 20%) while Irina has to pay tax of £52.00 to which she would not otherwise have been liable. If Irina's income had been £11,250 (90% of the personal allowance) or less, the couple would have achieved the maximum saving of £250.00.

1.7 MARRIED COUPLE'S ALLOWANCE

[*ITA 2007, ss 42–55, 58*]

(A)

Vlad and Nadia are a married couple born in 1934 and 1942 respectively. Vlad's net income for 2020/21 amounts to £31,600 and Nadia's to £35,300. Neither spouse has any dividend income or savings income. The couple were married before 5 December 2005 but they made a joint election for the primary claimant to be Nadia (rather then her husband) as she has

1.7 IT Allowances and Tax Rates

the higher net income. The election is irrevocable (see *Simon's Taxes* E1.920). Neither is a Scottish taxpayer, although as far as tax devolution in Scotland and Wales is concerned, the married couple's allowance is a reserved matter, which means the level of the allowance is set by the UK Government.

Taxable income and tax payable are calculated as follows

	Vlad	Nadia (the primary claimant)
	£	£
Net income	31,600	35,300
Deduct Personal allowance	12,500	12,500
Taxable income	£19,100	£22,800
Tax payable:		
19,100/22,800 @ 20%	3,820.00	4,560.00
Reduction for married couple's allowance:		
£6,525(see below) @ 10%		(652.50)
Total liabilities	£3,820.00	£3,907.50
Calculation of married couple's allowance		
Unrestricted married couple's allowance		9,075
Deduct $1/2 \times £5,100$ (being the excess of the primary claimant's adjusted net income over £30,200 ie £35,300–30,200)		2,550
		6,525

Notes

(a) The restriction in the married couple's allowance is by reference to the primary claimant's income only. Relief is given at Step 6.

(b) Also see *Simon's Taxes* E1.926 for further examples of transfers of unused married couples allowance.

(B)

Before 6 April 2020, Mr and Mrs Scarlet made a joint election under *ITA 2007, s 48* to transfer from husband to wife the whole of the basic married couple's allowance with effect for 2020/21 and later years. Mr Scarlet was born on 29 May 1934 and his wife on 6 January 1953. The couple married before 5 December 2005 and have not made the joint election under *ITA 2007, s 44* to be treated in the same way as couples marrying on or after that date, so the allowance is available in the first instance to the husband. Neither is a Scottish taxpayer. For 2020/21, their incomes are as follows.

Allowances and Tax Rates IT 1.7

	Mr Scarlet	Mrs Scarlet
	£	£
Employment income	—	39,865
Pension income	12,180	—
Dividends	2,000	2,000
Building society interest	10,000	—

The couple's tax position for 2020/21 is as follows

	£	£
Employment income	—	39,865
Pension income	12,180	—
Dividends	2,000	2,000
Building society interest	10,000	—
Total and net income	24,180	41,865
Deduct Personal allowance	(12,500)	(12,500)
Taxable income	£11,680	£29,365

Tax payable:

			£	£
5,000	@ 0% (starting rate for savings)		—	
1,000	@ 0% (personal savings allowance)		—	
3,680	@ 20% (basic rate on savings income)		736.00	
2,000	@ 0% (dividend allowance)		—	
27,365	@ 20% (basic rate)			5,473.00
2,000	@ 0% (dividend allowance)		—	—
			736.00	5,473.00

		£	£
Deduct Married couple's allowance (£9,075):			
	£5,565 @ 10%	556.50	
	£3,510 @ 10%		351.00
Tax liabilities (subject to PAYE deductions)		£179.50	£5,122.00

Notes

(a) Married couple's allowance is available only where one of the spouses/civil partners was born before 6 April 1935.

(b) An individual can elect to receive half the basic married couple's allowance (i.e. the minimum amount below which the age-related allowance may not be reduced by reference to the income of the claimant) otherwise due to his or her spouse or civil partner or, as illustrated in this example, a couple can jointly elect for the whole of

1.7 IT   Allowances and Tax Rates

the basic amount to be transferred between them. An election is not dependent on levels of income but, except for the year of marriage or the year in which the civil partnership is entered into, must be made before the start of the first year for which it is to apply (e.g. before 6 April 2020 to have effect for 2020/21). [ITA 2007, ss 47–50]. See Simon's Taxes E1.923, E5.103.

(c) If the individual's income is too low to fully utilise the married couple's allowance so allocated, he or she may transfer the excess allowance back to the other spouse or civil partner. [ITA 2007, s 52].

(d) As the married couple's allowance attracts tax relief at a fixed rate of 10%, an election to transfer the basic allowance does not save any tax, although the election may have cash flow advantages where one spouse or partner pays tax under PAYE and the other does not.

(e) As they have claimed married couple's allowance, no part of the personal allowance can be transferred between spouses as in **1.6** above. [ITA 2007, s 55B(2)]. See Simon's Taxes E1.910B.

1.8   SCOTTISH RATES OF INCOME TAX

[ITA 2007, s 11A; Scotland Act 1998, Pt 4A; Scotland Act 2016, ss 13, 14(8)–(10)(15)]

Duncan is a Scottish taxpayer (within the definition at Scotland Act 1998, ss 80D–80F). For 2020/21 he has earnings of £44,300, bank interest of £1,400 and no other taxable income.

Duncan's taxable income and tax liability are computed as follows

		Savings income	Non-savings income	Total income
		£	£	£
Employment income			44,300	44,300
Savings income		1,400		1,400
Total and net income		1,400	44,300	45,700
Personal allowance			(12,500)	(12,500)
Taxable income		£1,400	£31,800	£33,200
Tax payable:				
2,085	@ 19% (Scottish starter rate on non-savings/ non-dividend income)		396.15	396.15
10,573	@ 20% (Scottish basic rate on non-savings/ non-dividend income)		2,114.60	2,114.60
18,272	@ 21% (Scottish intermediate rate on non-savings/ non-dividend income)		3,837.12	3,837.12
870	@ 41% (Scottish higher rate on non-savings/ non-dividend income)		356.70	356.70
1,000	@ 0% (personal savings allowance)	—		—
400	@ 20% (basic rate on savings income)	80.00		80.00
£33,200				
Tax payable		£80	£6,704.57	£6,784.57

Allowances and Tax Rates IT 1.8

Notes

(a) With effect for 2017/18 onwards, the Scottish Parliament is empowered to set its own income tax rates and thresholds for Scottish taxpayers independently of, and not linked to, UK rates. The Scottish rates and thresholds apply only for the purpose of calculating tax on income that is neither savings income nor dividend income; UK rates and thresholds still apply to those types of income. The Scottish rates for 2020/21, as set by the Scottish Parliament are divided into five different tax rates and bands as follows:

- Starter rate — £1 – £2,085 @ 19%
- Basic rate — £2,086 – £12,658 @ 20%
- Intermediate rate — £12,659 – £30,930 @ 21%
- Higher rate — £30,931 – £150,000 @ 41%
- Top rate — Over £150,000 @ 46%

(b) In this example, the personal allowance is set against employment income as this gives the best result. This leaves taxable non-savings/non-dividend income of £31,800 which is taxed at the rates in (a) above. However, the savings income falls entirely within the UK basic rate band and is thus chargeable at the basic rate (to the extent that it exceeds the personal savings allowance).

(c) In determining the amount of the personal savings allowance (PSA), a Scottish taxpayer is assumed to pay income tax by reference to UK rate thresholds. [*ITA 2007, s 12B*]. In this example, the PSA is £1,000 because taxable income does not exceed the UK basic rate limit of £37,500 and the taxpayer would not be liable above basic rate if he were not a Scottish taxpayer. See **1.2** above for the PSA generally.

2 Accrued Income Scheme

[*ITA 2007, ss 615–681*]

2.1 The following transactions take place between individuals during the year ended 5 April 2021.

Settlement day	Sale by	Purchase by	Securities
14.8.20	X (cum div)	Y	£4,000 6¼% Treasury Loan 2024
17.9.20	X (ex div)	P	£4,000 8% Treasury Loan 2022
4.4.21	S (cum div)	Y	£2,500 4% Treasury Loan 2023

Interest payment days are as follows

6¼% Treasury Loan 2024	25 May, 25 November
8% Treasury Loan 2022	27 March, 27 September
4% Treasury Loan 2023	7 March, 7 September

Both X and Y owned chargeable securities with a nominal value in excess of £5,000 at some time in either 2019/20 or 2020/21, and both are resident in the UK. P is non-resident in the UK throughout 2020/21. The maximum value of securities held by S at any time in 2020/21 and 2021/22 is £4,000.

14.8.20 transaction

The transaction occurs in the interest period from 26.5.20 to 25.11.20 (inclusive).

Number of days in interest period	184
Number of days in interest period to 14.8.20 (see note b)	81
Interest payable on 25.11.20	£125

The deemed payment is

$$£125 \times \frac{81}{184} = £\underline{55}$$

X is treated as receiving a payment of £55 on 25.11.20. Assuming no other transfers in this kind of security in the interest period, this will also be the figure of accrued income profit chargeable.

Y is treated as making a payment of £55. Assuming no other transfers in this kind of security in the interest period, this will also be the figure of accrued income loss to set against the interest of £125 he receives on 25.11.20. £70 remains taxable.

IT Accrued Income Scheme

17.9.20 transaction

The transaction occurs in the interest period from 28.3.20 to 27.9.20 (inclusive).

Number of days in interest period	184
Number of days in interest period from 17.9.20 (see note c)	10
Interest payable on 27.9.20	£160

The deemed payment is

$$£160 \times \frac{10}{184} = £\underline{9}$$

X is treated as making a payment of £9. Assuming no other transfers in this kind of security in the interest period, this will also be the figure of accrued income loss to set against the interest of £160 he receives on 27.9.20. £151 remains taxable. P is an excluded transferee (see note (a)).

4.4.21 transaction

The transaction occurs in the interest period from 8.3.21 to 7.9.21 (inclusive)

Number of days in interest period	184
Number of days in interest period to 4.4.21	28
Interest payable on 7.9.21	£50

The deemed payment is

$$£50 \times \frac{28}{184} = £\underline{7}$$

S is an excluded transferor as his holdings do not exceed £5,000 at any time in 2020/21 or 2021/22 (the year in which the interest period ends).

Y is treated as making a payment of £7. Assuming no other transfers in this kind of security in the interest period, this will also be the figure of accrued income loss to set against the interest of £50 he receives on 7.9.21. £43 remains taxable.

Notes

(a) P is an excluded transferee as he is non-resident in the UK throughout the tax year in which the transfer is made (2020/21). Different rules apply where a non-UK resident is trading in the UK through a branch or agency. [*ITA 2007, s 643*]. See SAIM4230 and *Simon's Taxes* D9.436.

(b) If the transfer is with accrued interest (i.e. with the right to receive the next interest due, or 'cum div') the transferor is treated as receiving a payment from the transferee. The accrued interest is given by the formula I x A/B, where I is the interest due on the first payment day following the settlement day, A is the number of days in the interest period up to and including the settlement day and B is the number of days in the whole period.

Accrued Income Scheme   IT 2.1

(c) If the transfer is without accrued interest (i.e. without the right to receive the next interest due 'ex div') the transferor is treated as making a payment to the transferee. The accrued interest is given by the formula I x A/B, where I is the interest due on the first payment day following the settlement day, A is the number of days from the day after the settlement day up to and including the payment day and B is the number of days in the whole period.

3 Capital Allowances

Cross-reference. See also **4** CAPITAL ALLOWANCES ON PLANT AND MACHINERY.

3.1 STRUCTURES AND BUILDINGS

[*CAA 2001, ss 270AA–270IH; FA 2019, s 30; FA 2020, ss 29, 30, Sch 5; SI 2019 No 1087*]

(A)

Mini draws up accounts to 5 April each year. In her accounting period ending 5 April 2021, Mini incurs the following expenses on the construction of a building on land in the UK held freehold which she intends to use for the purposes of her trade as a flat pack furniture manufacturer.

	£
Cost of land	300,000
Cost of obtaining planning permission	20,000
Foundation works	50,000
Construction costs	200,000
Installation of electrical and plumbing systems	40,000

She begins to use the building for the purposes of the trade on 1 October 2021. Mini can claim structures and buildings allowances as follows.

The amount of the expenditure on which the SBA can be claimed is:

	£
Foundation works	50,000
Construction costs	200,000
Total	250,000

Y/e 5 April 2021

No allowance is due as the building has not been brought into qualifying use before the end of the period.

Y/e 5 April 2022

The building is brought into qualifying use on 1 October 2021. The allowance is therefore due for the period 1 October 2021 to 5 April 2022 (187 days).

£250,000 x 3% x 187/365 = £3,842

Y/e 5 April 2023

£250,000 x 3% = £7,500

Assuming that Mini continues to own the freehold and to carry on a qualifying activity, and that the building is not demolished or brought into residential use, she will continue to be entitled to an allowance of £7,500 for each year up to and including the year ended 5 April 2054. For the year ended 5 April 2055, only the period up to 31 January 2055 falls within the period of $33^{1}/_{3}$ years from first use, so the allowance will be the remaining unrelieved qualifying expenditure £6,158.

3.1 IT Capital Allowances

Notes

(a) Mini incurs qualifying expenditure of £250,000, so the annual SBA will be 3% of this amount, i.e. £7,500. However, Mini can only claim the SBA from the date the factory starts to be used for trade purposes, which is 1 October 2021. The factory is therefore in use for 6 months in the year ended 5 April 2022, so the SBA is proportionately reduced to £3,842. The expenditure will be fully relieved over a writing-down period of $33^{1}/_{3}$ years.

(b) Before 6 April 2020 (1 April 2020 for corporation tax purposes), the rate of SBA was 2% and the writing-down period was 50 years. For the purpose only of computing the allowance for a period straddling 6/1 April 2020, that period is split into two separate notional chargeable periods, the second beginning on that date. A proportion (calculated on a time basis) of the 2% allowance is then given for the first period and a proportion of the 3% allowance for the second. [*CAA 2001, s 270AA; FA 2020, s 29*].

(c) The reduction from 50 to $33^{1}/_{3}$ in the number of years comprised in the writing-down period applies equally to qualifying expenditure which had already attracted an allowance at the old 2% rate before 6 April 2020 (1 April 2020 for CT purposes). This is achieved by enabling the shortfall in allowances to be claimed in the chargeable period in which the writing-down period of $33^{1}/_{3}$ years comes to an end. It applies only if the person entitled to the allowance on 5 April/31 March 2020 does not dispose of the relevant interest in the building before the time that the writing-down period ends and continues to be entitled to an allowance in respect of the expenditure at that time. [*CAA 2001, s 270GD; FA 2020, s 29*].

(d) The costs of the land and obtaining planning permission are not qualifying expenditure. The electrical and plumbing systems are integral features. The costs relating to these will qualify for plant and machinery capital allowances and so are excluded from SBA. [*CAA 2001, ss 270BG, 270BI*]. See CA94000; *Simon's Taxes* B3.271– B3.272.

(e) Further expenditure for which SBA cannot claimed includes expenditure on any residence or any structure located in the grounds of a residence; expenditure on financing, such as loans; expenditure on public enquiries or legal expenses; expenditure on landscaping or land reclamation and expenditure in respect of which a grant or contribution is received.

(f) An SBA cannot be claimed unless the person who incurred the qualifying expenditure makes an allowance statement. A claimant who is not that person must obtain the allowance statement (or a copy of it). The statement must identify the building to which it relates and must state the date of the earliest contract (written or oral) for the construction of the building, the amount of the qualifying expenditure and the date on which it was first brought into non-residential use. [*CAA 2001, s 270IA; FA 2020, Sch 5 paras 7, 10*].

(B)

Mini in (A) above in fact sells the freehold to Mickey, another furniture merchant, on 30 June 2023 for £600,000. Mickey draws up accounts to 5 April each year. Assuming that both of them claim the maximum structures and buildings allowance, their entitlement will be as follows.

Mini

For the year ending 5 April 2024, Mini will be entitled to an allowance for the period 6 April 2023 to 30 June 2023 of £250,000 × 3% × 86/366 = £1,762.

Mickey

For the year ending 5 April 2024, Mickey will be entitled to an allowance for the period 1 July 2023 to 5 April 2024 of £250,000 × 3% × 280/366 = £5,738.

Assuming that Mickey continues to own the freehold and to carry on a qualifying activity, and that the building is not demolished or brought into residential use, he will be entitled to an allowance of £7,500 for the year ended 5 April 2025 and will continue to be entitled to an allowance of £7,500 for each year up to and including the year ended 5 April 2054. For the year ended 5 April 2055, only the period up to 31 January 2055 falls within the period of $33^1/_3$ years from first use, so the allowance will be the remaining unrelieved qualifying expenditure £6,158.

Notes

(a) In the year of disposal, Mini only owns the factory for three months, so the SBA is proportionately reduced.

(b) Although Mickey actually paid £600,000 for the factory, the SBA continues to be calculated on the original qualifying expenditure. Mickey owns the factory for nine months in the year of acquisition, so the SBA is reduced accordingly.

(c) On the sale of the relevant interest in a building or structure, the seller (and not the purchaser) is treated as having the relevant interest on the day of the transfer. [*CAA 2001, s 270DA(4)*].

(d) Where a person disposes of an interest in land by reference to which he has obtained an SBA, the following applies. If the expenditure by reference to which the allowances has been made is allowable in computing the gain or loss on disposal, the consideration for the disposal is treated as increased by the amount of the allowances given to the seller. [*TCGA 1992, s 37B*].

3.2 DREDGING

[*CAA 2001, ss 484–489*]

D is the proprietor of an estuary maintenance business preparing accounts to 30 June. Expenditure qualifying for dredging allowances is incurred as follows

	£
Year ended 30.6.19	4,000
Year ended 30.6.20	5,000

On 2 January 2021, D sells the business to an unconnected third party.

3.2 IT Capital Allowances

The allowances available are

Date of expenditure	Cost	Residue brought forward	Allowances WDA 4%	Residue carried forward
	£	£	£	£
2019/20 (year ended 30.6.19)				
2019	4,000	—	160	3,840
2020/21				
Year ended 30.6.20				
2019	4,000	3,840	160	3,680
2020	5,000	—	200	4,800
			£360	£8,480
Six months ended 2.1.21				
Balancing allowance note (a)			£8,480	
Total allowances 2020/21 (£360 + £8,480)			£8,840	

Note

(a) On permanent cessation of the trade by the person carrying it on, including a sale other than one falling within *CAA 2001, s 488(4)(5)*, a balancing allowance is given and is equal to the excess of expenditure over writing-down allowances previously made. There are no provisions for a balancing charge or a transfer of allowances to a purchaser. See CA81600 and *Simon's Taxes* B3.803.

3.3 MINERAL EXTRACTION

[*CAA 2001, Pt 5*]

X has for some years operated a mining business with two mineral sources, G and S. Accounts are prepared to 30 September. On 31 December 2019 the mineral deposits and mineworks at G are sold at market value to Z for £80,000 and £175,000 respectively. A new source, P, is purchased on 30 April 2020 for £170,000 (including land with an undeveloped market value of £70,000) and the following expenditure incurred before the end of the period of account ended 30 September 2020.

	£
Plant and machinery	40,000
Construction of administration office	25,000
Construction of mining works which are likely to have little value when mining ceases	50,000
Staff hostel	35,000
Winning access to the deposits	150,000
	£300,000

Capital Allowances IT 3.3

During the year to 30 September 2020, X incurred expenditure of £20,000 in seeking planning permission to mine a further plot of land, Source Q. Permission was refused.

		£
Residue of expenditure brought forward		
(based on accounts to 30 September 2019)		
Mineral exploration and access	– Source G	170,000
	– Source S	200,000
Mineral assets	– Source G	95,250
	– Source S	72,000

The mineral extraction allowances due for the year ending 30.9.20 are as follows.

Source G	£	£
Mineral exploration and access		
WDV b/f	170,000	
Deduct: Proceeds	175,000	
Balancing charge	£5,000	(5,000)
Mineral assets		
WDV b/f	95,250	
Deduct: Proceeds	80,000	
Balancing allowance	£15,250	15,250
Total allowances		
Source S		
Mineral exploration and access		
WDV b/f	200,000	
WDA 25%	(50,000)	50,000
WDV c/f	£150,000	
Mineral assets		
WDV b/f	72,000	
WDA 10%	(7,200)	7,200
WDV c/f	£64,800	

3.3 IT Capital Allowances

Source P
Mineral exploration and access

Expenditure	150,000	
WDA 25%	(37,500)	37,500
WDA c/f	£112,500	
Mineral assets		
Expenditure	100,000	
WDV 10%	(10,000)	10,000
WDV c/f	£90,000	
Mining works		
Expenditure	50,000	
WDA 25%	(12,500)	12,500
WDV c/f	£37,500	

Source Q
Mineral exploration and access

Expenditure	20,000	
WDA 25%	(5,000)	5,000
WDV c/f	£15,000	
Total allowances (net of charges)		£132,450

Notes

(a) Expenditure on the acquisition of mineral assets, which includes expenditure on the acquisition of, or of rights in or over, both the site of a source and of mineral deposits, qualifies for a 10% writing-down allowance. Other types of expenditure qualify for a 25% writing-down allowance. [*CAA 2001, s 418(1)*]. See OT26315 and *Simon's Taxes* B3.420.

(b) Allowances are not due on either the office or staff hostel. The plant and machinery qualify for plant and machinery allowances under *CAA 2001, Pt 2* rather than for mineral extraction allowances.

(c) Abortive expenditure on seeking planning permission is qualifying expenditure by virtue of *CAA 2001, s 396(2)(3)* as if it were expenditure on mineral exploration and access. See CA50300, OT26355 and *Simon's Taxes* B3.406.

(d) The undeveloped market value of land is excluded from qualifying expenditure and from disposal receipts. [*CAA 2001, ss 404, 424*]. See CA50330, CA50440 and *Simon's Taxes* B3.410.

3.4 PATENT RIGHTS

[*CAA 2001, ss 464–483*]

P, who prepares accounts to 31 December, acquires two new patent rights for trading purposes

	Date	Term	Cost
Patent 1	19.4.19	15 years	£4,500
Patent 2	5.10.20	5 years	£8,000

On 1.12.20 P sold part of his rights under patent 1 for £2,000.

The allowances for each patent are

	Pool £	WDA £
Y/e 31.12.19		
Expenditure (patent 1)	4,500	
WDA 25%	(1,125)	£1,125
	3,375	
Y/e 31.12.20		
Expenditure (patent 2)	8,000	
Disposal proceeds (patent 1)	(2,000)	
	9,375	
WDA 25%	(2,344)	£2,344
WDV c/f	£7,031	

Note

(a)   See CA75020 and *Simon's Taxes* B3.602.

3.5 RESEARCH AND DEVELOPMENT

[*CAA 2001, ss 437–451*]

C is in business manufacturing and selling cosmetics, and he prepares accounts annually to 30 June. For the purposes of this trade, he built a new laboratory adjacent to his existing premises, incurring the following expenditure

		£
April 2018	Laboratory building	50,000
June 2018	Technical equipment	3,000
March 2019	Technical equipment	4,000
July 2019	Plant	2,500
August 2020	Extension to existing premises comprising 50% further laboratory area and 50% sales offices	30,000

3.5 IT Capital Allowances

In September 2019 a small fire destroyed an item of equipment originally costing £2,000 in June 2018; insurance recoveries totalled £3,000. In March 2020, the plant costing £2,500 in July 2019 was sold for £1,800.

The 100 per cent R&D allowances due are

	£
Y/e 30.6.18	
Laboratory building	50,000
Technical equipment	3,000
	£53,000
Y/e 30.6.19	
Technical equipment	4,000
	£4,000
Y/e 30.6.20	
Net allowance on plant sold (note (a))	£700
Balancing charge on equipment destroyed (note (b))	(£2,000)
Y/e 30.6.21	
Extension (note (d))	£15,000

Notes

(a) As the plant was sold in the period of account in which the expenditure was incurred, the disposal value of £1,800 is set against the expenditure of £2,500, resulting in a net allowance of £700.

(b) The destruction of the equipment in the year to 30 June 2020 results in a balancing charge limited to the allowance given. The charge accrues in the period of account in which the event occurs.

(c) A capital gain of £1,000 (£3,000 − £2,000) will also have arisen on the destruction of equipment and insurance recovery. However, the gain will be exempt from capital gains tax under the chattels exemption. [*TCGA 1992, s 262*]. See CG76573 and *Simon's Taxes* C3.1811.

(d) Capital expenditure which is only partly for research and development is apportioned on a just basis to arrive at the amount qualifying for allowances. [*CAA 2001, s 439(4)*]. See CA60400 and *Simon's Taxes* B3.703.

4 Capital Allowances on Plant and Machinery

Cross-reference. See also 31 TRADING INCOME — CASH BASIS FOR SMALLER BUSINESSES.

4.1 PERIODS OF ACCOUNT

[*CAA 2001, s 6, FA 2019, ss 31–34*]

(A) General

James commenced business on 1 October 2017 preparing accounts initially to 30 September. He changed his accounting date in 2019, preparing accounts for the 15 months to 31 December 2019. The following capital expenditure is incurred

	Plant	Car
	£	£
Year ended 30 September 2018	74,400	4,000 (no private use)
1 October 2018 to 31 December 2019	7,500	
Year ended 31 December 2020	4,000	

An item of plant was sold for £500 (original cost £1,000) on 25 September 2019. All of the expenditure on plant additions is AIA qualifying expenditure. (AIA = Annual Investment Allowance.) The expenditure on the car is not special rate expenditure. James chooses to claim a reduced AIA of £60,000 for the year ended 30 September 2018.

Profits *before* capital allowances but otherwise as adjusted for tax purposes are as follows

	£
Year ended 30 September 2018	96,000
Period ended 31 December 2019	81,000
Year ended 31 December 2020	100,000

4.1 IT Capital Allowances on Plant and Machinery

The capital allowances are

	AIA qualifying expenditure	Main pool	Allowances
	£	£	£
Year ended 30.9.18			
Qualifying expenditure	74,400	4,000	
AIA 100% (note (b))	(60,000)		60,000
Transfer to main pool	(14,400)	14,400	
		18,400	
WDA 18%		(3,312)	3,312
WDV at 30.9.18		15,088	
Total allowances			£63,312
15 months ended 31.12.19			
Additions	7,500	7,500	
AIA 100% (maximum £1,050,000 — note (c))		(7,500)	7,500
Disposals		(500)	
		14,588	
WDA 18% x 15/12 (note (d))		(3,281)	3,281
WDV at 31.12.19		11,307	
Total allowances			£10,781
Year ended 31.12.20			
Additions	4,000	4,000	
AIA 100% (maximum £1m (note (f))		(4,000)	4,000
		11,307	
WDA 18%		(2,035)	2,035
WDV at 31.12.20		£9,272	
Total allowances			£6,035

Taxable profits for the periods of account concerned are

	Before CAs	CAs	After CAs
	£	£	£
Year ended 30 September 2018	96,000	63,312	32,688
Period ended 31 December 2019	81,000	10,781	70,219
Year ended 31 December 2020	100,000	6,035	93,965

Capital Allowances on Plant and Machinery IT 4.1

Taxable profits for the first four tax years of the business are

	£	£
2017/18 (1.10.17–5.4.18) (£32,688 × 6/12)		16,344
2018/19 (y/e 30.9.18)		32,688
2019/20 (1.10.18–31.12.19)	70,219	
Deduct Overlap relief £16,344 × 3/6 note (e)	(8,172)	
		62,047
2020/21 (y/e 31.12.20)		93,965

Notes

(a) Capital allowances are calculated by reference to periods of account and are treated as expenses of the trade or other qualifying activity. [*CAA 2001, ss 2, 6, 247*]. For this purpose, a period of account may exceed 12 months (but cannot exceed 18 months — see (B) below). See CA11510, CA29320 and *Simon's Taxes* B3.102, B3.380.

(b) The maximum AIA for the twelve-month period of account to 30 September 2018 is £200,000. All of James's qualifying expenditure of £74,400 would attract AIAs but he has chosen to claim only £60,000.

(c) The maximum AIA for the 15-month period of account to 31 December 2019 is £1,050,000 (£200,000 × 3/12 + 1,000,000 × 12/12). However, for expenditure incurred before 1 January 2019 the maximum AIA is £250,000. The overriding rule for expenditure incurred in the part of the chargeable period falling before that date is that the maximum allowance is calculated for the 15-month chargeable period as if the annual limit had remained at £200,000.

(d) Where a period of account exceeds 12 months as is the case with the 15-month period to 31 December 2019 in this example, both the maximum AIA and the WDAs are proportionately increased. [*CAA 2001, ss 51A(6), 56(3)*]. See CA23085, EIM36605 and *Simon's Taxes* B3.329.

(e) The overlap profit is £16,344 being the profit taxed twice under the commencement rules. This represents 6 months' profit (1 October 2017 to 5 April 2018). As the basis period for 2019/20 is 3 months greater than one year, 3/6 of the overlap profit is relieved in that year, the balance being carried forward. For further examples on the basis of assessment for businesses see **30.1–30.3 TRADING INCOME**.

(f) The maximum AIA for the twelve-month period of account to 31 December 2020 is £1 million. For expenditure incurred on or after 1 January 2021 it is £200,000.

(B) **Period of account exceeding 18 months**

Anastasia commenced business on 1 October 2017 preparing accounts initially to 30 June. She changed her accounting date in 2019/20, preparing accounts for the 21 months to 31 March 2020. The following capital expenditure was incurred

4.1 IT Capital Allowances on Plant and Machinery

	Plant	Motor Car
	£	£
9 months to 30 June 2018	60,000	20,000 (no private use)
21 months to 31 March 2020	10,600	
Year ended 31 March 2021	8,000	

Of the £10,600 of expenditure incurred in the 21-month period of account to 31 March 2020, £3,600 was incurred in January 2019 and £7,000 in the nine months to 31 March 2020. Apart from the car, all expenditure is AIA qualifying expenditure. The expenditure on the car is special rate expenditure. Anastasia chooses to claim a reduced AIA of £48,000 for the nine-month period to 30 June 2018.

An item of plant was sold for £512 (original cost £1,100) on 3 November 2019.

Profits *before* capital allowances but otherwise as adjusted for tax purposes are as follows

	£
Period ended 30 June 2018	64,000
Period ended 31 March 2020	112,000
Year ended 31 March 2021	85,000

The capital allowances are

	AIA qualifying expenditure	Main pool	Car	Total allowances
	£	£	£	£
9 months ended 30.6.18				
Qualifying expenditure	60,000		20,000	
AIA (note (d))	(48,000)			48,000
	12,000			
Transfer to main pool	(12,000)	12,000		
WDA 18% × 9/12 (note (e))		(1,620)		1,620
WDA 8% × 9/12 (note (e))			(1,200)	1,200
WDV at 30.6.18		10,380	18,800	
Total allowances				£50,820
12 months ended 30.6.19				
Additions	3,600			
AIA 100% (note (d))	(3,600)			3,600
WDA 18%		(1,868)		1,868
WDA 7.5% (note (e))			(1,410)	1,410
WDV at 30.6.19		8,512	17,390	
Total allowances				£6,878
9 months ended 31.3.20				
Additions	7,000			

Capital Allowances on Plant and Machinery IT 4.1

	AIA qualifying expenditure	Main pool	Car	Total allowances
	£	£	£	£
AIA 100% (note (d))	(7,000)			7,000
Disposals		(512)		
		8,000		
WDA 18% × 9/12		(1,080)		1,080
WDA 6% × 9/12			(783)	783
WDV at 31.3.20		£6,920	£16,247	
Total allowances				£8,863
Year ended 31.3.21				
Additions	8,000			
AIA 100% (note (d))	(8,000)			8,000
WDA 18%		(1,246)		£1,246
WDA 6%			(975)	£975
WDV at 31.3.21		£5,674	15,283	
Total allowances				£10,221

Taxable profits for the periods of account concerned are

	Before CAs	CAs	After CAs
	£	£	£
Period ended 30 June 2018	64,000	50,820	13,180
Period ended 31 March 2020	112,000	(6,878 + 8,863)	96,259
Year ended 31 March 2021	85,000	10,221	74,779

Taxable profits for the first four tax years of the business are

	£	£
2017/18 (1.10.17 − 5.4.18) (£13,180 × 6/9)		8,786
2018/19 (1.10.17 − 30.9.18):		
1.10.17 − 30.6.18	13,180	
1.7.18 − 30.9.18 (£96,259 × 3/21)	13,751	
		26,931
2019/20 (1.10.18 − 31.3.20) (£96,259 × 18/21)	82,508	
Deduct Overlap relief (note (f))	(8,786)	
		73,722
2020/21 (1.04.20 − 31.03.21)		74,779

4.1 IT Capital Allowances on Plant and Machinery

Notes

(a) Where a period of account for capital allowances purposes would otherwise exceed 18 months, it is broken down into shorter periods, the first beginning on the first day of the actual period and each subsequent period beginning on an anniversary of the first day of the actual period. No period can therefore exceed 12 months. [*CAA 2001, s 6(6)*].

(b) The capital allowances computed for the notional periods of account referred to in (*a*) above are deductible in aggregate in arriving at the adjusted profit for the actual period of account.

(c) A period of account exceeding 18 months cannot normally result in an immediate change of basis period, because of *ITTOIA 2005, ss 216, 217(1)(3)*. However, the conditions of *ITTOIA 2005, s 217* do not have to be satisfied if the change of accounting period occurs in the second or third tax year of a new business, as in this example. See BIM81045 and *Simon's Taxes* B4.110.

(d) Where there is a change in the AIA limit, the appropriate proportion of the AIA limit corresponding to the period of account is taken to determine the overall AIA limit for the period. The maximum AIA for the nine-month period of account ended 30 June 2018 is £150,000 (200,000 x 9/12). All of Anastasia's qualifying expenditure of £60,000 would attract AIAs but she has chosen to claim only £48,000.

The maximum AIA for the notional twelve-month period of account ended 30 June 2019 is £600,000 ((£200,000 × 6/12) + (£1,000,000 × 6/12)). There is an overriding rule for expenditure incurred in the part of the period of account falling before 1 January 2019, that the maximum allowance is calculated for the twelve-month period as if the annual limit had remained at £200,000. Accordingly, for expenditure incurred in the period 1 July 2018 to 31 December 2018, only expenditure of up to £200,000 can qualify for AIA.

The maximum AIA for the notional nine-month period of account ended 31 March 2020 is £750,000 (£1,000,000 × 9/12)).

The maximum AIA for the notional twelve-month period of account ended 31 March 2021 is £800,000 ((£1,000,000 × 9/12) + (£200,000 × 3/12)). There is an overriding rule that, for expenditure incurred on or after 1 January 2021, the maximum allowance is what would be the maximum allowance for a notional period beginning on 1 January 2021 and ending at the end of the period of account. So in the twelve months period of account to 31 March 2021, the maximum of any expenditure incurred on plant on or after 1 January 2021 for which AIA can be claimed is £50,000 (£200,000 × 3/12).

(e) The hybrid special rate of writing-down allowance for the year to 30 June 2019 is 7.5%, computed as follows (where 279 is the number of days from 1 July 2018 to 5 April 2019, 86 is the number of days from 6 April 2019 to 30 June 2019 and 365 is the total number of days in the period of account).

$$R = \left(8 \times \frac{279}{365}\right) + \left(6 \times \frac{86}{365}\right) = 7.5\%$$

(f) Where the period of account is less than 12 months, WDAs are proportionately reduced. [*CAA 2001, s 56(3)*]. See CA23220 and *Simon's Taxes* B3.332.

(g) In this example, the overlap profit is £8,786 being the profit taxed twice under the commencement rules. This represents 6 months' profit (1 October 2017 to 5 April 2018). As the basis period for 2019/20 is 6 months greater than one year, the whole of the overlap profit is relieved in that year. For further examples on the basis of assessment for businesses, including commencement and cessation rules, overlap relief and changes of accounting date, see **30.1–30.3** TRADING INCOME.

4.2 SUCCESSIONS

[*CAA 2001, ss 265–267, 268, 559*]

Michael, who had been in business for a number of years, decided to retire, and he transferred the business, as a gift, to his son, Alec, on 1 May 2020. Accounts, prepared by both Michael and Alec to 30 April annually, reveal the following expenditure on, and proceeds of, plant and machinery.

	Expenditure £	(Disposal Proceeds) £
Michael		
Period 1.5.19 – 30.4.20	7,200	–
Alec		
Period 1.5.20 – 30.4.21	5,000	(600)

The plant and machinery disposed of by Alec was an item transferred to him by Michael. The market value of plant and machinery at 1.5.20 totalled £18,000. In no case did an item's market value exceed its cost. The written-down value brought forward at 1.5.19 was £10,000.

The capital allowances are as follows.

(i) **No election under CAA 2001, s 266**

	AIA qualifying expenditure £	Main pool £	Total allowances £
Michael			
Period of account y/e 30.4.20			
WDV b/f at 1.5.19		10,000	
Additions		7,200	
Disposals (at market value)		(18,000)	
		(800)	
Balancing charge		800	£(800)

4.2 IT   Capital Allowances on Plant and Machinery

Alec
Period of account y/e 30.4.21

Additions qualifying for AIA	5,000		
AIA 100%	(5,000)	—	5,000
Other additions		18,000	
Disposals		(600)	
		17,400	
WDA 18%		(3,132)	3,132
WDV at 30.4.21		£14,268	
Total allowances			£8,132

Note

(a) If no election is made under *CAA 2001, s 266* (see (ii) below), plant and machinery is treated as sold by the predecessor to the successor at market value, but no annual investment allowance is due to Alec on the assets transferred. [*CAA 2001, s 265*]. See CA29030, CA15100 and *Simon's Taxes* B3.109, B3.390. Similar rules apply for other assets. [*CAA 2001, s 559*]. No annual investment allowance is due for expenditure incurred in the period of account at the end of which Michael permanently ceases to carry on the trade. [*CAA 2001, ss 38B, 46(2)*]. See CA23084 and Simon's Taxes B3.329.

(ii) **Election under CAA 2001, s 266**

	AIA qualifying expenditure £	Main pool £	Total allowances £
Michael			
Period of account y/e 30.4.20			
WDV b/f at 1.5.19		10,000	
Additions		7,200	
Disposals (at written-down value)		(17,200)	
Balancing allowance/charge		Nil	Nil
Alec			
Period of account y/e 30.4.21			
Additions qualifying for AIA	5,000		
AIA 100%	(5,000)	—	5,000
Other additions		17,200	
Disposals		(600)	
		16,600	
WDA 18%		(2,988)	2,988

Capital Allowances on Plant and Machinery IT 4.3

WDV at 30.4.21	£13,612	
Total allowances		£7,988

Notes

(a) Under *CAA 2001, s 267*, plant and machinery passing to the successor is deemed to have been sold by the predecessor to the successor at such a price as to leave no balancing allowance or balancing charge. An election must be made (under *CAA 2001, s 266*) for these provisions to apply. See CA29040 and *Simon's Taxes* B3.390.

(b) An election under *CAA 2001, s 266* may be made only between connected persons, as defined by *section 266(5)*, must be made jointly by predecessor and successor and must be made within two years of the succession, i.e. by 1 May 2022 in this example.

(c) Annual investment allowances are not available to the successor on plant and machinery transferred under a *CAA 2001, s 266* election (by virtue of *CAA 2001, ss 214, 217*). See CA28300 and *Simon's Taxes* B3.365.

(d) For certain assets other than plant and machinery, a similar election is available under *CAA 2001, s 569* for certain transfers between connected persons. See CA13200 and *Simon's Taxes* B3.108.

4.3 POOLING, ANNUAL INVESTMENT ALLOWANCE, WRITING-DOWN ALLOWANCES, CARS, PARTIAL NON-BUSINESS USE, ACQUISITIONS FROM CONNECTED PERSONS AND BALANCING ADJUSTMENTS

A has for some years been in business as a builder and demolition contractor. He makes up his accounts to 5 April. The accounts for the year to 5 April 2021 reveal the following additions and disposals.

	£
Additions	
Plant	
Wagon	30,000
Concrete mixer	45,000
Excavator 1	32,000
Excavator 2	80,000
Dumper Truck	5,000
Bulldozer	20,000
Miscellaneous	570,000
Fittings	
Office furniture and equipment	52,000

4.3 IT Capital Allowances on Plant and Machinery

Motor Vehicles

Van	7,000
Car 2	21,000
Car 3	2,000
Car 4	15,000

Disposals	Cost	Proceeds
	£	£
Excavator 1	32,000	30,000
Digger loader	15,000	4,000
Car 1	14,200	3,600
Fittings	3,500	500

The dumper truck was bought second-hand from Q, brother of A, but had not been used in a trade or other qualifying activity. The truck had originally cost Q £6,000, but its market value at sale was only £2,000.

Excavator 1 was sold without having been brought into use.

The bulldozer and Car 3 were both purchased from P, father of A and had originally cost P £25,000 and £3,500 respectively. Both assets had been used for the purposes of a qualifying activity. In both cases the price paid by A was less than the market value.

Car 1 sold and the new Car 2 are both used for private motoring by A. Private use has always been 30%. Car 2 has CO_2 emissions of over 110g/km. Car 3 is occasionally borrowed by A's daughter, and the private use proportion is 20%. Car 3 has CO_2 emissions of less than 110g/km.

Car 4 was purchased new and unused on 1 July 2020 and is used for business purposes only. It is a car with low CO_2 emissions and qualifies for 100% first-year allowances under *CAA 2001, s 45D*.

All of the expenditure on plant and machinery was incurred before 1 January 2021.

The written-down values at 6 April 2020 of the main plant and machinery pool and Car 1 are £80,500 and £3,225 respectively.

Capital Allowances on Plant and Machinery IT 4.3

The capital allowances for 12-month period of account to 5.4.21 are as follows

	Expenditure qualifying for AIA	Main pool	Car 1 partial use pool	Car 2 partial use pool	Car 3 partial use pool	Total allowances
	£	£	£	£	£	£
WDV b/f		80,500	3,225			
Additions						
Miscellaneous	570,000	570,000				
Wagon	30,000	30,000				
Concrete mixers	45,000	45,000				
Excavator 1 (note (a))	32,000	32,000				
Excavator 2	80,000	80,000				
Dumper truck (notes (b)(c)(d))		2,000				
Bulldozer (notes (b)(d)(e))		20,000				
Furniture	52,000	52,000				
Van	7,000	7,000				
Cars				21,000	2,000	
	816,000					
Car 4	15,000					
FYA 100%	15,000					15,000
AIA (100% on 800,000)	(800,000)					800,000
Disposals						
Excavator		(30,000)				
Digger		(4,000)				
Fittings		(500)				
Car 1			(3,600)			
		84,000	(£375)	21,000	2,000	
WDA (18%)		(15,120)			(360)	15,480
WDA (6%)				(1,260)		1,260
Private use restriction:						
Car 2 — £1,260 @ 30%						(378)
Car 3 — £360 @ 20%						(72)
WDV c/f		£68,880		£19,740	£1,640	
Total allowances						£831,290
Balancing charge (Car 1) £375 less 30% private use						£263

4.3 IT   Capital Allowances on Plant and Machinery

Notes

(a) The annual investment allowance (AIA) and writing-down allowances are available even though an item of plant or machinery is disposed of without being brought into use, always provided that the expenditure is, respectively, AIA qualifying expenditure and general qualifying expenditure.

(b) If an AIA is made in respect of an amount of AIA qualifying expenditure, the expenditure is nevertheless added to the appropriate pool (or pools). Such allocation is necessary to enable a disposal value to be properly brought into account when a disposal event occurs in relation to the item in question. Following the allocation, the available qualifying expenditure in the pool (or in each pool) is reduced by the amount of the AIA on the expenditure allocated. [*CAA 2001, s 58(4A)*]. It follows that any excess of the AIA qualifying expenditure over the AIA made will qualify for WDAs beginning with the chargeable period in which the expenditure is incurred. See CA23080 and *Simon's Taxes* B3.329, B3.333, B3.336.

(c) No AIA is available in respect of an item of plant or machinery purchased from a connected person (within *CAA 2001, s 575*). [*CAA 2001, ss 213, 214, 217*]. See CA11630 and *Simon's Taxes* B3.108B.

(d) Qualifying expenditure (and AIA qualifying expenditure) on the dumper truck is restricted to the lowest of

  (i) market value

  (ii) capital expenditure incurred by the vendor (or, if lower, by a person connected with him)

  (iii) capital expenditure incurred by the purchaser

  [*CAA 2001, ss 213, 214, 218(3)*]. See CA28300 and *Simon's Taxes* B3.303.

(e) Qualifying expenditure on the bulldozer is the lesser of A's actual expenditure and the disposal value brought into account in the vendor's computations. [*CAA 2001, ss 213, 214, 218(2)*]. (The vendor's disposal value would have been market value but for the fact that the purchaser is himself entitled to claim capital allowances on the acquisition. [*CAA 2001, s 61(2)(4)*].) A's qualifying expenditure is thus equal to his actual expenditure. The same applies to the purchase of Car 3. See CA23250 and *Simon's Taxes* B3.334.

(f) Cars 2 and 3 are allocated to separate single asset pools by virtue of their being partly used for non-business purposes. [*CAA 2001, s 206*]. See CA27005 and *Simon's Taxes* B3.359. Car 2 qualifies for writing-down allowances at the special rate of 6% because of its CO_2 emissions level. [*CAA 2001, ss 104A, 104AA*]. See CA22320 and *Simon's Taxes* B3.342. See note (e) above as regards the amount of qualifying expenditure to be brought into account in respect of Car 3. Car 4 qualifies for 100% first-year allowances under *CAA 2001, s 45D*; if the full 100% had not been claimed, the balance of the expenditure would have entered the main pool. See CA23153 and *Simon's Taxes* B3.320, B3.324A.

4.4   SHORT-LIFE ASSETS

[*CAA 2001, ss 83–89*]

A prepares trading accounts to 30 September each year and buys and sells machines for use in the trade as follows

Capital Allowances on Plant and Machinery   IT 4.4

	Cost	Date of acquisition	Disposal proceeds	Date of disposal
Machine X	£40,000	30.4.11	£13,000	1.12.12
Machine Y	£20,000	1.9.12	£1,500	1.12.20

A elects under *CAA 2001, s 83* for these machines to be treated as short-life assets. It is assumed for the purposes of the example that no annual investment allowance is claimed for any of the expenditure. His pool of qualifying expenditure brought forward at the beginning of period of account 1.10.10–30.9.11 is £80,000.

A's capital allowances are as follows

	£ Main Pool	£ Short-life asset pools Machine X	£ Short-life asset pools Machine Y	£ Total Allowances
Period of account 1.10.10–30.9.11				
WDV b/f	80,000			
Additions		40,000		
WDA 20%	(16,000)	(8,000)		£24,000
	64,000	32,000		
Period of account 1.10.11–30.9.12				
Additions			20,000	
WDA 19.03% – note (d)	(12,179)	(6,090)	(3,806)	£22,075
	51,821	25,910	16,194	
Period of account 1.10.12–30.9.13				
Disposal		(13,000)		
Balancing allowance		£12,910		12,910
WDA 18%	(9,328)		(2,915)	12,243
				£25,153
	42,493		13,279	
Seven periods of account 1.10.13–30.9.20				
WDA for 7 years – note (e)	(31,900)		(9,969)	£41,869
	10,593		3,310	
Period of account 1.10.20–30.9.21				
Transfer to pool	3,310		(3,310)	
	13,903		—	
Disposal	(1,500)			
	12,403			
WDA 18%	(2,232)			£2,232
	£10,171			

4.4 IT Capital Allowances on Plant and Machinery

Notes

(a) Only plant and machinery which is not specified in *CAA 2001, s 84* is eligible to be treated as short-life assets. See CA23620 and *Simon's Taxes* B3.343.

(b) Where separate identification of short-life assets is impracticable, a form of pooling may be adopted (HMRC Statement of Practice SP 1/86).

(c) The eighth anniversary of the end of the chargeable period in which the expenditure on Machine Y is incurred is 30.9.20 (the cut-off date). The balance of expenditure on Machine Y is thus transferred to the main pool in the period of account 1.10.20–30.9.21, this being the first chargeable period ending after the cut-off date. See CA23640 and *Simon's Taxes* B3.343.

(d) The hybrid rate of writing-down allowance for the year to 30 September 2012 is 19.03%, computed as follows (where 188 is the number of days from 1 October 2011 to 5 April 2012, 178 is the number of days from 6 April 2012 to 30 September 2012 and 366 is the total number of days in the period of account).

$$R = \left(20 \times \frac{188}{366}\right) + \left(18 \times \frac{178}{366}\right) = 19.03\%$$

(e) For convenience the writing-down allowances for the seven periods of account from 1 October 2013 to 30 September 2020, calculated at 18% p.a. on the reducing balance, have been combined in this example.

4.5 SPECIAL RATE POOL

[*CAA 2001, ss 90–104, 104A–104E, FA 2019, ss 30, 31, 35*]

B begins trading on 1 January 2020 and makes up accounts to 31 December. In the year ending 31 December 2020, B incurs capital expenditure on plant and machinery of £2,000,000, of which £1,500,000 is special rate expenditure and the remainder falls to be allocated to the main pool. B carries on no other qualifying activity and is entitled to the maximum annual investment allowance of £1 million. None of the capital expenditure qualifies for first-year allowances.

B's plant and machinery allowances for the year ended 31 December 2020, assuming she claims all allowances to which she is entitled, will be calculated as follows.

	Main pool of expenditure £	Special rate pool £	Total allowances £
Additions	500,000	1,500,000	
AIA (note (a))		(1,000,000)	1,000,000
		500,000	
WDA (18% p.a.)	90,000		90,000
WDA (6% p.a.)		30,000	30,000
WDV c/fwd	£410,000	£470,000	
Total allowances claimed			£1,120,000

Notes

(a) Certain expenditure qualifies for writing-down allowances (WDAs) at a special rate of 6% of the amount (if any) by which available qualifying expenditure exceeds the total of any disposal values falling to be brought into account. This is known as '*special rate expenditure*'. The special rate was 8% before 6 April 2019 (and a hybrid rate for periods straddling 6 April 2019). Special rate expenditure comprises the following:

  (i) expenditure on thermal insulation;

  (ii) expenditure on integral features of buildings and structures;

  (iii) long-life asset expenditure;

  (iv) expenditure on cars other than electric cars, cars with low emissions and cars registered before 1 March 2001;

  (v) expenditure on the provision of cushion gas, i.e. gas that functions, or is intended to function, as plant in a particular gas storage facility; and

  (vi) expenditure on the provision of solar panels.

(b) If special rate expenditure is incurred wholly and exclusively for the purposes of the qualifying activity, and does not fall to be allocated to a single asset pool, it is allocated to a class pool known as the '*special rate pool*'. Even if allocated to a single asset pool, the special rate of WDAs still applies.

(c) B is free to choose how to allocate the annual investment allowance to expenditure. In this example the allowance has been allocated to special rate expenditure as this maximises the writing-down allowances available.

4.6 ANNUAL INVESTMENT ALLOWANCE — STRADDLING PERIODS

[*CAA 2001, ss 38A, 38B, 51A; FA 2019, s 32, Sch 13 paras 1, 2*]

(A) **Periods straddling 1 January 2019**

Paul is a trader making up accounts to 30 June each year. For the year ended 30 June 2019, he incurs expenditure of £550,000 on plant and machinery. Of this amount, £230,000 is incurred before 1 January 2019 and £320,000 on or after that date. All the expenditure is AIA qualifying expenditure.

Paul's maximum annual investment allowance for the year ended 30 June 2019 is computed as follows

Period 1.7.18 to 31.12.18 (184 days)

$$\text{Maximum} £200,000 \times \frac{184}{365} \qquad 100,822$$

Period 1.1.19 to 30.6.19 (181 days)

$$\text{Maximum} £1,000,000 \times \frac{181}{365} \qquad \underline{495,891}$$

4.6 IT Capital Allowances on Plant and Machinery

Maximum qualifying for AIAs for the year	£596,713

Further adjustment

On the face of it, all of Paul's expenditure of £550,000 would qualify for AIAs as it is below the maximum of £596,713 computed above. However, there is an overriding rule, as regards expenditure incurred in the part of the period of account falling before 1 January 2019, that no more than £200,000 can qualify for the AIA. Paul can claim AIAs of £520,000 (£200,000 + £320,000), which is within the overall limit of £596,713.

If the total expenditure of £550,000 had been split as to, say, £180,000 incurred before 1 January 2019 and £370,000 thereafter, the overriding rule would not have come into play and the whole of the expenditure would have qualified for AIAs.

Note

(a) See CA23080 and *Simon's Taxes* B3.329.

(B) **Periods straddling 1 January 2021**

Paula is a trader making up accounts to 30 April each year. For the year ended 30 April 2021, she incurs expenditure of £720,000 on plant and machinery. Of this amount, £480,000 is incurred before 1 January 2021 and £240,000 on or after that date. All the expenditure is AIA qualifying expenditure.

Paula's maximum annual investment allowance for the year ended 30 April 2021 is computed as follows

Period 1.5.20 to 31.12.20 (245 days)

$$\text{Maximum} £1,000,000 \times \frac{245}{365} \qquad 671,233$$

Period 1.1.21 to 30.4.21 (120 days)

$$\text{Maximum} £200,000 \times \frac{120}{365} \qquad 65,754$$

Maximum qualifying for AIAs for the year	£736,987

Further adjustment

On the face of it, all of Paula's expenditure of £720,000 would qualify for AIAs as it is below the maximum of £736,987 computed above. However, there is an overriding rule, as regards expenditure incurred in the part of the period of account falling after 31 December 2020, that no more than the appropriate proportion of £200,000 can qualify for the AIA. The appropriate proportion is the figure of £65,754 above.

Therefore, of the expenditure of £240,000 in the period 1.1.21 to 30.4.21, only £65,754 qualifies. The remaining expenditure of £480,000 qualifies in full, as the resulting maximum AIA for the year of £545,754 (480,000 + 65,754) is within the overall maximum of £736,987.

If the total expenditure of £720,000 had been split as to, say, £680,000 incurred before 1 January 2021 and £40,000 thereafter, the overriding rule would not have come into play and the whole of the expenditure would have qualified for AIAs.

Note

(a)   See CA23080 and *Simon's Taxes* B3.329.

4.7   **VAT CAPITAL GOODS SCHEME**

[*CAA 2001, ss 234–246, 546–551*]

T Ltd carries on a trade which is partially exempt for VAT purposes, and draws up accounts to 31 March each year. Its partial exemption year also runs to 31 March. On 1 May 2017, the company acquired computer equipment at a cost of £340,000 plus VAT of £68,000. The company had a written-down value of £143,000 on its plant and machinery main pool at 1 April 2017 and, for the purposes of this example, it is assumed that there are no other acquisitions and no disposals during the period covered.

T Ltd's claimable percentage of non-attributable input tax for the partial exemption years ended 31 March 2018, 2019, 2020 and 2021 is as follows

Year ended	
31.3.18	75%
31.3.19	80%
31.3.20	65%
31.3.21	65%

The input tax position is as follows

	Computer
Year ended 31.3.18	
Initial input tax claim:	
£68,000 × 75%	£51,000
Year ended 31.3.19	
Additional VAT rebate:	
$\dfrac{68,000}{5} \times (80 - 75)\%$	£680
Year ended 31.3.20	
Additional VAT liability:	
$\dfrac{68,000}{5} \times (75 - 65)\%$	£1,360

4.7 IT Capital Allowances on Plant and Machinery

Year ended 31.3.21
Additional VAT liability:

$$\frac{68,000}{5} \times (75-65)\% \qquad \qquad £1,360$$

T Ltd deals with the appropriate VAT capital goods scheme adjustments in its quarterly VAT return to 30 September following each partial exemption year.

The capital allowances computations are as follows

Plant and machinery

	Qualifying for AIAs	Main pool	Total allowances
	£	£	£
Year to 31.3.18			
WDV at 1.4.17		143,000	
Addition (£340,000 + £(68,000 – 51,000))	357,000		
AIA 100% (maximum £200,000)	(200,000)	157,000	200,000
		300,000	
WDA 18%		(54,000)	54,000
			£254,000
		246,000	
Year to 31.3.19			
WDA 18%		(44,280)	£44,280
		201,720	
Year to 31.3.20			
Disposal value		(680)	
		201,040	
WDA 18%		(36,187)	£36,187
		c/f 164,853	
		b/f 164,853	
Year to 31.3.21			
Addition	1,360		
AIA 100%	(1,360)	—	1,360
WDA 18%		(29,674)	29,674
		c/f 135,179	
			£31,034

Capital Allowances on Plant and Machinery   IT 4.7

Plant and machinery

		b/f	
		135,179	
Year to 31.3.22			
Addition	1,360		
AIA 100%	(1,360)	—	1,360
WDA 18%		(24,332)	24,332
WDV at 31.3.22		£110,847	
			£25,692

Notes

(a) For the purpose of determining the chargeable period in which capital allowances are to be adjusted by reference to any additional VAT rebate/liability, the rebate/liability is treated as accruing on the last day of the VAT return period in which the adjustment is made (i.e. the return for the quarter to 30 September in the chargeable period). [*CAA 2001, s 549*]. See CA11900 and *Simon's Taxes* B3.104.

(b) Where expenditure was AIA qualifying expenditure (i.e. it qualified for the annual investment allowance), any additional VAT liability incurred in respect of that expenditure at a time when the plant or machinery is provided for the purposes of the qualifying activity, is also AIA qualifying expenditure — for the chargeable period in which the liability accrues. [*CAA 2001, s 236(3A)–(3C)*]. See CA29230 and *Simon's Taxes* B3.393.

# 5 Charities

5.1 DONATIONS TO CHARITY

[*ITA 2007, ss 414, 415, 423–425; FA 2016, Sch 1 paras 63(4), 73*]

(A) **Higher rate taxpayer**

Ronan has total income of £51,425 for 2020/21, which consists entirely of employment income. During that year, he makes a number of payments to charity, all of them qualifying donations, amounting in total to £600. Ronan is not a Scottish taxpayer.

Ronan's income tax liability for 2020/21 is as follows

		£
Total income		51,425
Less Personal allowance		(12,500)
Taxable income		£38,925
Tax liability		
38,250	at 20%	7,650.00
675	at 40%	270.00
£38,925		£7,920.00

Notes

(a) The basic rate limit of £37,500 is increased by the grossed up amount of the qualifying donations (£600 × 100/80 = £750) and becomes £38,250. Ronan thereby saves tax of £150 (£750 × 20% (40% − 20%)). The charities will reclaim basic rate tax of £150 (£750 × 20%) and will thus receive £750 in all. The net cost to Ronan is £450 (£600 − £150), a saving of 40%. (The tax relief can, in fact, exceed 40% where the effect of extending the basic rate limit is that an additional amount of dividend income falls within the basic rate band and is taxed at 7.5% instead of at 32.5% (see (B) below). See *Simon's Taxes* E1.811.

(b) Gift aid donations may, by election, be treated as made in the preceding tax year. The election must be made on or before the date the donor submits his tax return for that preceding year and not later than 31 January following that year. An election cannot be made if insufficient income tax or capital gains tax was payable for the preceding year to cover the tax deducted from the payment. [*ITA 2007, ss 426, 427*].

5.1 IT Charities

(B) Higher rate taxpayer with dividend income

The facts are as in (A) above except that £7,000 of Ronan's income is dividend income.

Ronan's income tax liability for 2020/21 is as follows

		£
Employment income		44,425
Dividend income		7,000
Total income		51,425
Less Personal allowance		(12,500)
Taxable income		£38,925
Tax liability		
31,925	at 20%	6,385.00
2,000	at 0% (dividend nil rate)	—
4,325	at 7.5% (dividend ordinary rate)	324.37
675	at 32.5%	219.37
£38,925		£.6,928.74

Note

(a) As in (A) above, the basic rate limit (£37,500) is increased by the grossed up amount of the qualifying donations (£750) and thus becomes £38,250. But this time the tax saving is £187.50; this reflects the fact that the donation has the effect of pushing £750 of dividend income back into the basic rate band, a saving of 25% (32.5% − 7.5%) instead of the usual 20% (40% − 20%). Ronan's relief at source is still £150 (£750 − £600). His total relief is thus £337.50 which gives him total relief of 45% (not 40%) on the grossed up amount of the gift (£750).

(b) Where the Scottish basic rate or Welsh basic rate is higher than the main basic rate, the donor of a gift-aid donation is effectively taxed only at the main basic rate on so much of the grossed-up donation as would otherwise be more heavily taxed at the Scottish, or Welsh, basic rate. The legislation ensures that where the Scottish basic rate or Welsh basic rate is lower than the main basic rate, the donor of a gift-aid donation is effectively taxed at the main basic rate on so much of the grossed-up donation as would otherwise be more lightly taxed at the Scottish, or Welsh, basic rate. It does not make a donor worse off as a result of having made gift-aid donations. [SI 2019 No 201, Reg 12].

(C) Additional rate taxpayer

Rikki has total income of £175,000 for 2020/21, none of which is dividend income. During that year, he makes qualifying donations to charity of £2,400. Rikki is not a Scottish taxpayer.

Charities   IT 5.1

Rikki's income tax liability for 2020/21 is as follows

	£
Total and net income	175,000
Less Personal allowance (note (b))	Nil
Taxable income	£175,000

Tax liability		£
40,500	at 20%	8,100.00
112,500	at 40%	45,000.00
22,000	at 45%	9,900.00
£175,000		£63,000.00

Notes

(a) Both the basic rate limit of £37,500 and the higher rate limit of £150,000 are increased by the grossed up amount of the qualifying donations (£2,400 × 100/80 = £3,000) and become £40,500 and £153,000 respectively. Rikki thereby saves tax of £750 (£3,000 × 25% (45% − 20%)). [*ITA 2007, s 414(2)(b)*]. The charities will reclaim basic rate tax of £600 (£3,000 × 20%) and will thus receive £3,000 in all. The net cost to Rikki is £1,650 (£2,400 − £750), a saving of 45%.

(b) No personal allowance is available in this example as income is too far above the £100,000 income limit. [*ITA 2007, s 35*]. The grossed up amount of the gift is deductible in arriving at adjusted net income for the purpose of applying the restriction of the personal allowance where adjusted net income exceeds £100,000. See *Simon's Taxes* E1.910.

(D) **Low income taxpayer**

Rod, a single person, has a State pension of £10,850 and UK dividends of £2,000. He makes a qualifying donation of £400 to charity. Rod is not a Scottish taxpayer.

Rod's income tax liability for 2020/21 is as follows

		£
Pension income		10,850
Dividends		2,000
Total and net income		12,850
Less Personal allowance	12,500	
Restricted by (see note (a))	2,150	(10,350)
Taxable income		£2,500

Tax liability		
£500	at 20% (basic rate)	100.00

5.1 IT Charities

£2,000 at 0% (dividend nil rate) —

£100.00

Note

(a) The personal allowance is restricted by such amount as is necessary to leave tax of £100.00 in charge. The tax computation shows the impact on the personal allowance. However software packages will often simply present this as an addition of the tax due at basic rate on the gift aid donation, to the tax liability.

6 Compensation for Loss of Employment

6.1 TAXATION OF POST-EMPLOYMENT NOTICE PAY

[*ITEPA 2003, ss 402, 402A–402E, 403, 404, 415, 416; F(No 2)A 2017, s 5(3)–(5)(10)*]

Yujin is a monthly-paid employee on a salary of £66,000 per annum (£5,500 per month). On 10 April 2020 her employment is terminated. She is given three months notice as required by her employment contract, and it is agreed that she will receive a £35,000 termination payment. On 1 May 2020 the employer asks her to leave immediately and pays her a PILON (payment in lieu of notice) of £12,200, which was not required under the terms of her contract. It is assumed for the purposes of the example that Yujin is not entitled to a statutory redundancy payment.

'*Post-employment notice pay*' is given by the formula:

$$\left(\frac{BP \times D}{P}\right) - T$$

where:

- BP = the employee's basic pay (as defined) from the employment in respect of the last pay period to end before the trigger date (as defined);
- P = the number of days in that pay period;
- D = the number of days in the post-employment notice period (as defined); and
- T = the total amount of any payments or benefits received in connection with the termination which are already taxable as earnings apart from these provisions, but excluding bonuses and holiday entitlement pay for a period before the employment ends. The purpose of deducting T in the formula is to avoid any double charge.

Applying the formula to Yujin's circumstances:

- BP = £5,500 (Yujin's basic pay for the last monthly pay period ended before 10 April 2020 (the trigger date)
- P = 31 (the number of days in that pay period)
- D = 69 (the number of days in the post-employment notice period, which runs from 2 May to 9 July 2020 inclusive)
- T = Nil

		£
Post-employment notice pay	$\left(\dfrac{5,500 \times 69}{31}\right) - 0$	£12,241

The post-employment notice pay of £12,241 is less than the total termination awards of £47,200. Therefore, £12,241 is treated as taken out of the special provisions for termination payments (*ITEPA 2003, s 403*) into the charge on general earnings. The balance of the

6.1 IT Compensation for Loss of Employment

termination awards is £34,959, and this is taxable under the special provisions for termination payments and thus subject to an exemption for the first £30,000. Therefore, £12,241 is taxable as earnings and £4,959 under the special provisions. See EIM13020, EIM13110, EIM13880, EIM13876 and *Simon's Taxes* E4.802C, E4.812A, E8.232.

For NICs purposes, £12,241 is liable to employer and employee Class 1 NICs. £4,959 is liable to employer Class 1A NICs.

Notes

(a) The income tax treatment of termination payments is amended with effect for 2018/19 onwards. Whether or not they are entitled to a contractual payment in lieu of notice, employees pay tax on the amount of basic pay that they would have received had they worked their notice in full.

(b) If the post-employment notice pay had equalled or exceeded the total termination awards, the full amount of the termination awards would have been treated as taken out of the special provisions for termination payments and into the charge on general earnings. The exemption for the first £30,000 would not have been available at all. For these purposes, a termination award does not include a statutory redundancy payment.

(c) Before 6 April 2020, an amount of payments and benefits within the charge to income tax under the special provisions (disregarding the availability of the £30,000 threshold) was subject to neither employer nor employee national insurance contributions (NICs). For 2020/21 onwards, any excess over the £30,000 threshold is liable to employer Class 1A NICs, but the pre-existing exemptions for employer NICs on the first £30,000 and employee NICs on the full amount remain in place. The change in the rules does not apply to termination awards received on or after 6 April 2020 in respect of employment terminated before that date. In the case of awards received in instalments, the change does not apply to instalments received on or after 6 April 2020 if the first instalment was received before that date. [*Social Security Contributions and Benefits Act 1992, s 10(1A)–(1C)(3A)(4A); Social Security Contributions and Benefits (Northern Ireland) Act 1992, s 10(1A)–(1C)(3A)(4A); National Insurance Contributions (Termination Awards and Sporting Testimonials) Act 2019, ss 1, 2, 5; SI 2020 No 285, Reg 2*].

The above Class 1A charge on termination awards must be reported and paid to HMRC through PAYE in real time. There is an exception where the award consists of the benefit of the use of an asset without any transfer of ownership; in this case the Class 1A charge is payable after the year end in line with other types of Class 1A liability. [*SI 2001 No 1004, Reg 40C; SI 2020 No 300, Regs 1, 7*].

7 Deceased Estates

[*ITTOIA 2005, ss 649–680A, 681, 682*]

7.1 ESTATE INCOME: ABSOLUTE INTEREST

C died on 5 July 2018 leaving his estate of £400,000 divisible equally between his three children. The income arising and administration expenses paid in the administration period which ends on 25 January 2021 are as follows

	Period to 5.4.19		Year to 5.4.20		Period to 25.1.21	
	£	£	£	£	£	£
UK dividends		16,875		9,900		3,720
Dividend ordinary tax thereon payable by personal representatives		(1,266)		(743)		(279)
		15,609		9,157		3,441
Administration expenses						
chargeable to income		(1,500)		(750)		(366)
		14,109		8,407		3,075
Other income (gross)	10,000		3,200		975	
Basic rate tax thereon payable by personal representatives	(2,000)		(640)		(195)	
		8,000		2,560		780
Net residuary income		£22,109		£10,967		£3,855
Each child's share		£7,370		£3,656		£1,285

Dates and amounts of payments to each child are as follows

	Payment
	£
30.4.19	5,000
16.10.19	3,500
21.6.20	2,500
22.1.21	1,000
30.7.21	311

7.1 IT Deceased Estates

Each child's assumed income entitlement is as follows

	2018/19 £	2019/20 £	2020/21 £
Cumulative income entitlement (net)	7,370	11,026	12,311
Deduct net equivalents of amounts taxed in previous years	Nil	Nil	(8,500)
Assumed income entitlement	£7,370	£11,026	£3,811

For all years other than the final tax year (i.e. the year in which the administration period ends), compare the assumed income entitlement with the payments made.

	2018/19	2019/20
Assumed income entitlement	£7,370	£11,026
Payments made	Nil	£8,500
Lower amount is the taxable amount (subject to grossing up)	Nil	£8,500

For the final tax year (202021), the taxable amount (subject to grossing up) is the amount of the assumed income entitlement (£3,811).

The children's income from the estate for tax purposes is as follows

	2018/19	2019/20	2020/21
Each child's share of income (net)	Nil	£8,500	£3,811
Each child's share of basic rate income	Nil	3,520*	260
Basic rate tax	Nil	880	65
Grossed up basic rate income	Nil	£4,400	£325
* £(8,000 + 2,560) × 1/3 = £3,520.			
Each child's share of dividend income	Nil	4,980	3,551
Dividend ordinary rate tax (7.5/92.5)	Nil	404	288
Gross dividend income	Nil	£5,384	£3,839

Notes

(a) A beneficiary with an absolute interest is chargeable to income tax on income treated as arising in a tax year from the interest if he has an 'assumed income entitlement' (see *ITTOIA 2005, s 665)*, (see Simon's Taxes C4.120, C4.121) and TSEM7678 for the year and a payment is made in respect of the interest in the year and before the end of the administration period. For the year in which the administration period ends (the '*final tax year*'), income is treated as arising if the beneficiary has an assumed income entitlement for the year (whether or not any payments are made). [*ITTOIA 2005, s 652*]. See TSEM7604 and *Simon's Taxes* C4.121.

(b) Payments to a beneficiary of an estate are deemed to be made out of his share of income bearing tax at the basic rate in priority to his share of income bearing tax at the dividend ordinary rate. [*ITTOIA 2005, s 679*]. Therefore, administration expenses chargeable to income are effectively relieved primarily against dividend income. See *Simon's Taxes* C4.118.

(c) Each beneficiary would receive tax certificates (Forms R185 (Estate Income)) showing the gross amount of his entitlement and the tax paid by the personal representatives. Where the estate has dividend income bearing tax at the dividend ordinary rate, the tax certificate shows such income separately from income which has borne tax at the basic rate.

(d) Estate income which has borne tax at the dividend ordinary rate is treated as dividend income in the hands of a beneficiary. [*ITTOIA 2005, s 680A*]. For example, such income will attract the dividend allowance. See TSEM3017.

(e) The beneficiaries' shares of income are grossed up at the rate for the year in which the income is treated as arising to them, rather than, if different, the year in which the income is received, and tax accounted for, by the trustees. [*ITTOIA 2005, s 656*]. See *Simon's Taxes* C4.118, C4.121.

(f) Personal representatives are not entitled to the dividend allowance.

7.2 ESTATE INCOME: LIMITED INTEREST

Mrs D died on 5 January 2019 leaving her whole estate with a life interest to her husband and then the capital to her children on his death. The administration of the estate was completed on 7 February 2021. Mr D received payments on account of income of £1,200 on 30 September 2019, £2,500 on 31 December 2019, £1,050 on 7 February 2021 and £360 on 31 May 2021.

The actual income and deductible expenses of the estate were as follows

	2018/19 (from 6.1.19)	2019/20	2020/21 (to 7.2.21)
	£	£	£
Bank interest received	750	3,000	2,500
Basic rate tax thereon payable by personal representatives	(150)	(600)	(500)
	600	2,400	2,000
Other income (gross)	500	600	200
Basic rate tax thereon payable by personal representatives	(100)	(120)	(40)
Expenses	(80)	(450)	(400)
Net income available for distribution	£920	£2,430	£1,760

7.2 IT Deceased Estates

D's income from the estate for tax purposes is calculated as follows

	2018/19	2019/20	2020/21
	£	£	£
Net income	Nil	1,200.00	3,910.00
Basic rate tax	Nil	300.00	977.50
Gross income	Nil	£1,500.00	£4,887.50

Notes

(a) Subject to note (b) below, the beneficiary's net income is equal to distributions received in each tax year.

(b) The £360 paid to D in May 2021 remains payable on completion of administration and is thus treated as income of the beneficiary for the tax year in which the administration period ends, i.e. 2020/21. [*ITTOIA 2005, ss 654(3), 661*] See TSEM7650– TSEM7660 and *Simon's Taxes* C4.122.

(c) For 2020/21, D is also likely to have taxable income from his life interest in his wife's settlement. This will be income covering the period 8 February 2021 to 5 April 2021. It does not enter into the above calculations, but is dealt with as in **27.3(A)** SETTLEMENTS.

(d) Personal representatives are not entitled to the personal savings allowance.

(e) See generally notes (b) to (f) to **7.1** above.

8 Double Tax Relief

8.1 RELIEF BY CREDIT

[*TIOPA 2010, ss 18–41*]

(A)

A UK resident non-Scottish taxpayer has, for 2020/21, UK earnings of £23,955 and foreign income from property of £2,000 on which foreign tax of £300 has been paid.

(i) *Tax on total income*

	£
Employment income	23,955
Income from property (foreign tax £300)	2,000
	25,955
Deduct Personal allowance	(12,500)
Taxable income	£13,455
Tax on £13,455 @ 20%	£2,691.00

(ii) *Tax on total income less foreign income*

	£
Employment income	23,955
Deduct Personal allowance	(12,500)
Taxable income	£11,455
Tax on £11,455 @ 20%	£2,291.00

The difference in tax between (i) and (ii) is £400. The foreign tax is less than this and full credit of £300 is available against the UK tax payable. If the foreign tax were £600, the credit would be limited to £400 and the balance of £200 would be unrelieved.

Note

(a) For a further example, involving overseas dividends, see **1.1(C)** ALLOWANCES AND TAX RATES.

(b) See INTM151060 and *Simon's Taxes* E6.429A, E6.453.

(B)

A UK resident non-Scottish taxpayer has the following income, allowances and UK tax liability for the year 2020/21 before double tax relief.

8.1 IT Double Tax Relief

	£
Earned income	
UK directorship	38,215
USA directorship (foreign tax £1,200)	6,000
Dutch partnership (foreign tax £3,750)	7,500
	51,715
Unearned income	
UK dividends	1,600
Foreign bank interest (foreign tax £250)	2,500
Total income	55,815
Deduct Personal allowance	(12,500)
Taxable income	£43,315
Tax on £37,500 at basic rate (20%)	7,500.00
£1,715 at higher rate on earnings (40%)	686.00
£500 at savings nil rate (0%)	—
£2,000 at higher rate on savings (40%)	800.00
£1,600 at dividend nil rate (0%)	—
Tax borne before double tax relief	£8,986.00

The maximum double tax relief is obtained by progressively taking relief for each foreign source with the source with the highest rate of foreign tax being eliminated first. [*TIOPA 2010, s 36*]. See INTM161210 and *Simon's Taxes* E6.433A.

	£	£	£
Taxable income from all sources	43,315	43,315	43,315
Deduct foreign income			
Dutch partnership	(7,500)	(7,500)	(7,500)
USA directorship		(6,000)	(6,000)
Interest			(2,500)
	£35,815	£29,815	£27,315
Tax thereon (see note (a))	6,643.00	5,443.00	5,143.00
Tax on income before eliminating foreign source under review	8,986.00	6,643.00	5,443.00
Tax attributable to that source (A)	£2,343.00	£1,200.00	£300.00
Foreign tax suffered (B)	£3,750.00	£1,200.00	£250.00
Double tax relief i.e. lesser of (A) and (B)	£2,343.00	£1,200.00	£250.00
The UK income tax borne after credit for double tax relief is			
As computed before double tax relief		£8,986.00	
Deduct Double tax relief		(3,793.00)	
		£5,193.00	

Double Tax Relief IT 8.1

Note

(a) The recalculation of tax after each element of foreign income has been deducted is as follows

	£	£	£
Earned income	44,215	38,215	38,215
Deduct Personal allowance	(12,500)	(12,500)	(12,500)
	31,715	25,715	25,715
Savings income	2,500	2,500	
Dividend income	1,600	1,600	1,600
	£35,815	£29,815	£27,315
Basic rate tax (20%) on net earned income	6,343.00	5,143.00	5,143.00
Personal savings allowance £1,000 at 0%	—	—	
Basic rate tax (20%) on savings income	300.00	300.00	
Dividend allowance £1,600 at 0%	—	—	—
	£6,643.00	£5,443.00	£5,143.00

In the first two of these calculations, the personal savings allowance is £1,000 as there is now no income above the basic rate limit.

9 Employment Income

Cross-reference. See also **6** COMPENSATION FOR LOSS OF EMPLOYMENT.

9.1 DUTIES PERFORMED ABROAD — TRAVEL COSTS AND EXPENSES

[*ITEPA 2003, ss 370, 371*]

M, a married man resident in the UK, is employed by Bigbuild Ltd in Milnrow at a salary of £50,000 per annum and is involved in the management of the following construction projects.

29.8.20 – 30.11.20	Office block in Philippines
9.12.20 – 15.1.21	Factory in Germany
19.3.21 – 27.6.21	Housing development in Spain

Details of travel expenses incurred in 2020/21 are

		Paid by M	Reimbursed by Bigbuild	Paid by Bigbuild
		£	£	£
28.8.20	Milnrow – Heathrow Airport (M) (not an allowable deduction as not reimbursed, see note a)	40		
29.8.20	Heathrow – Philippines (M)			400
20.10.20	Milnrow – Philippines (wife and children)			1,000
30.10.20	Philippines – Milnrow (wife and children)			1,000
30.11.20	Philippines – Milnrow (M)	500	500	
9.12.20	Milnrow – Manchester Airport (M)	10	10	
9.12.20	Manchester – Germany (M)			100
10.12.20	Milnrow – Germany wife and children (not an allowable deduction, see note a)			300
3.1.21	Germany – Milnrow wife and children (not an allowable deduction, see note a)	350	350	
15.1.21	Germany – Milnrow (M)			100

9.1 IT Employment Income

19.3.21	Milnrow – Spain (M)	150	150	
31.3.21	Milnrow – Spain (wife - allowable as more than 60 days but only to the extent that it is reimbursed, see note a)	60	—	150
		£1,110	£1,010	£3,050

M's 2020/21 taxable income is as follows

	£	£
Salary		50,000
Cost of expenses incurred by Bigbuild		3,050
Reimbursed travel expenses		1,010
		54,060
Allowable part of expenses incurred by Bigbuild (£3,050 – £300 note (a))	2,750	
Allowable expenses incurred by M to the extent that they are reimbursed (£1,010 – £350 note (a))	660	
Personal allowance	12,500	(15,910)
		£38,150

Note

(a) A deduction is allowed for travelling expenses of the employee from any place in the UK to take up the overseas employment. In addition where the employee is out of the UK for 60 days or more continuously, an allowance is available for up to two outward and two return trips per fiscal year for the employee's wife and minor children provided the expense is borne or reimbursed by the employer. As M is away for less than 60 days in Germany, he cannot deduct the cost of his family's Christmas and New Year trip. The part of the cost of his wife's trip to Spain not reimbursed cannot be deducted.

(b) See EIM34050, EIM34060, EIM34070, and *Simon's Taxes* E4.703H.

9.2 ALLOWABLE DEDUCTIONS

(A) **Mileage allowances**

[*ITEPA 2003, ss 229–236*]

D is employed as a buyer by CB Ltd and uses his own car for business. CB Ltd pays its employees a standard mileage allowance of 62 pence per business mile for 2020/21. D's business mileage is 18,000 in 2020/21.

The amount to be included in D's taxable employment income for 2020/21 is as follows

	£	£
Mileage allowances received 18,000 × 62p		11,160
Tax free rates:		
First 10,000 business miles at 45p	4,500	
Balance of 8,000 miles at 25p	2,000	(6,500)
Taxable amount		£4,660

Notes

(a) Mileage allowance payments are taxable only to the extent that, in total for the year, they exceed the approved rates. The approved rates for cars and vans are 45 pence per mile for the first 10,000 miles and 25 pence per mile thereafter. The same rates apply to all cars and vans, regardless of cylinder capacity. [*ITEPA 2003, ss 229, 230; SI 2011 No 896*]. See EIM31415 and *Simon's Taxes* E4.704.

(b) Where no mileage allowance payments are made, or payments are made at a rate lower than the approved rates, the employee may claim a deduction ('mileage allowance relief') for business mileage of an amount equal to the approved rates or, as the case may be, equal to the excess of the approved rates over the payments. [*ITEPA 2003, ss 231, 232*]. See EIM31330 and *Simon's Taxes* E4.704.

(c) In addition to the mileage allowances, employers can make 'approved passenger payments', taxable only to the extent that they exceed 5 pence per mile. If no such payment is made, however, the employee may not claim a deduction as in (*b*) above. [*ITEPA 2003, ss 233, 234*]. See EIM31400, EIM31415 and *Simon's Taxes* E4.704.

(d) Relief as in (a) and (b) above is also available in respect of business use of a cycle or motorcycle. The approved rates are 20 pence per mile for cycles and 24 pence per mile for motorcycles.

(e) No other method can be used to calculate relief for business use of an employee's own vehicle, and capital allowances are not available. [*CAA 2001, s 36(1)(a)*]. See CA20015 and *Simon's Taxes* B3.311, E4.795.

(B) **Travelling expenses generally**

[*ITEPA 2003, ss 336–340*]

Three employees of Fixit Ltd, which has offices in Central London and a main depot in Chelmsford in Essex, incur travelling expenses as follows in 2020/21.

(1) A, who lives in Surrey, normally works in the London office, travelling in by train. She has to attend a monthly meeting of managers in Chelmsford, to which she travels direct by car. She is able to claim a deduction for the costs of travel to Chelmsford.

(2) B, who lives in North London and normally drives to work in the Chelmsford office, occasionally calls in at the London office to pick up urgent packages. He also frequently visits, on his way to the Chelmsford office, a customer whose offices are close to Fixit Ltd in Chelmsford, to check on work in progress. He is allowed the costs of travel on days when he visits the London office. It is unlikely that he will

9.2 IT   Employment Income

be allowed the costs of travel when he visits the customer in Chelmsford; an employee cannot turn what is really an ordinary commuting journey into a business journey simply by arranging a business appointment along the way (HMRC Employment Income Manual EIM32060).

(3) C is an operative living in a defined area of Kent, in which he has responsibility for serving all the company's customers. He occasionally calls at the Chelmsford office to discuss new contracts, but generally arranges call-outs by telephone. He is allowed in full the costs of travel within the defined area, the whole of which is defined as his 'permanent workplace'. He is also allowed the costs of travel to the Chelmsford office, as this is not a permanent workplace.

See *Simon's Taxes* E4.703C.

9.3   THE BENEFITS CODE

(A) **Cars and fuel**

[*ITEPA 2003, ss 114–153; FA 2019, s 7; FA 2020, ss 8–10*]

(i) *Example*

A, B and C are employees of D Ltd. Each is provided with a company car throughout 2020/21. The company also bears at least part of the cost of petrol for private motoring.

A is provided with a 1,800 cc car first registered in January 2017 with a list price (including VAT, car tax (but not road tax), delivery charges and standard accessories) of £19,000. The car was made available to A in April 2017. It has a diesel engine and a CO_2 emissions figure of 155 g/km. An immobilisor was fitted in September 2017 at a cost of £200. A is required to pay the company £250 per year as a condition of using the car for private motoring, and duly pays this amount in 2020/21.

B is provided with a 1,400 cc car first registered in March 2016 with a list price of £9,000. It has an emissions figure of 90g/km. B was required to make a capital contribution of £1,000 on provision of the car in January 2017. B leaves the company in March 2021 and returns the car to D Ltd on 16 March. B was required to pay the company £50 per year as a condition of using the car for private motoring, and duly paid this amount in 2020/21.

C is provided with a luxury car first registered in April 2020 with a list price of £88,000 (which includes the list price of non-standard accessories). He made a capital contribution of £3,000 in 2020/21. The car's CO_2 emissions figure is 280g/km.

Employment Income IT 9.3

Car and fuel benefits for in 2020/21 are as follows

	A £	B £	C £
List price	19,000	9,000	88,000
Later accessories	200	—	—
	19,200		
Capital contributions	—	(1,000)	(3,000)
Price of car	£19,200	£8,000	£85,000
Cash equivalent — Max 37% (36% + 4%) see note (d)			
(including diesel supplement — note (d))	7,104		
— 23%		1,840	
— 37%			31,450
Deduction for unavailability			
($£1,840 \times 20/365$)		(101)	
		1,739	
Contribution for private use	(250)	(50)	—
Car benefit	6,854	1,689	31,450
Fuel benefit ($£24,500$ @ 37%)	9,065		
($£24,500$ @ 23%)		5,635	
($£24,500$ @ 37%)			9,065
Deduction for unavailability			
($£5,635 \times 20/365$)		(309)	
Total car and fuel benefits	£15,919	£7,015	£40,515

Notes

(a) For cars which have an approved carbon dioxide emissions figure, the benefit is a percentage of the car's list price determined by reference to the level of those emissions. Different percentages may apply depending on whether the car was first registered before or on or after 6 April 2020 (but the 37% maximum still applies). [*ITEPA 2003, ss 133–142*]. See EIM24500 and *Simon's Taxes* E4.626A.

(b) The price of the car is ascertained under *ITEPA 2003, ss 122–132*. See EIM24100 and *Simon's Taxes* E4.627.

(c) The fuel benefit charge is computed by taking the car benefit percentage ascertained in (a) above and applying it to a set figure of £24,500 (£24,100 for 2019/20). [*ITEPA 2003, ss 149–153; SI 2015 No 1979; SI 2016 No 1174*]. See EIM25510 and *Simon's Taxes* E4.629.

(d) The diesel supplement for company cars is 4% from 2018/19 onwards, (3% for 2017/18). In the case of A the appropriate percentage excluding the diesel supplement is 36%. When the diesel supplement is added this becomes 40% but it is restricted to a maximum of 37% overall for 2020/21.

9.3 IT   Employment Income

(ii)

J is Managing Director of K Ltd and during the year ended 5 April 2021 the company provided two cars for his use. Car 1 was a two-year old car (2,200 cc with CO_2 emissions of 155g/km and a list price of £20,000) and it was used by J for both business and private purposes until 31 October 2020 when it was written off as a result of an accident. J was subsequently prosecuted for dangerous driving, banned for one year and incurred legal costs of £800 which were ultimately paid for by K Ltd. In the period 6 April 2020 to 31 October 2020 J had paid the company £30 per month as a contribution towards private fuel. J was then provided with the use of a new 2-litre car (Car 2) and, since at first he had injuries which prevented him from driving and later lost his licence, a chauffeur. This replacement car was to be used for business purposes only.

J's benefits for 2020/21 relating to the cars are

	£
Car 1	
Car benefit £20,000 @ 36%	7,200
Fuel benefit £24,500 @ 36%	8,820
	£16,020
Proportion for period 6.4.20–31.10.20	
($^{209}/_{365}$ × £16,020)	9,173
Legal costs	800
Car 2	
Annual scale charge	—
Provision of chauffeur	—
	£9,973

Notes

(a) For 2020/21 the percentage used to compute the car and fuel benefits is 16% for a car first registered before 6 April 2020 and 14% for a car first registered on or after 6 April 2020 at carbon dioxide emissions levels of 55g/km or more, plus 1% for each additional 5g/km up to a maximum of 37%. The maximum is reached at 160g/km and 170g/km respectively.

(b) The car benefit and car fuel scale charges for Car 1 are reduced because the car was not available for use for part of the year. [*ITEPA 2003, ss 143, 152*]. See EIM23010–EIM23885 and *Simon's Taxes* E4.626A

(c) Since J makes a contribution only towards private fuel as distinct from private use, a reduction in the car benefit under *ITEPA 2003, s 144* will not be available. See *Simon's Taxes* E4.626A. As J is not *required* to make good the *whole* of the expense incurred by K Ltd in providing fuel for private use, his contributions do not reduce the fuel benefit. [*ITEPA 2003, s 151*]. See *Simon's Taxes* E4.629.

(d) The legal costs will be taxable as a benefit following *Rendell v Went HL 1964, 41 TC 641*. No relief is available under *ITEPA 2003, ss 346–350* (employee liabilities) as the expenses are incurred in connection with a criminal conviction. [*ITEPA 2003, s 346(2)*]. See *Simon's Taxes* E4.787.

(e) Since Car 2 is not available for private use, no benefits will arise. [*ITEPA 2003, ss 114, 118*]. See EIM22745, EIM22740 and *Simon's Taxes* E4.625. No benefit arises in respect of the chauffeur's wages as they relate to business travel only and J would have been eligible for a deduction had he incurred and paid the equivalent expense himself. [*ITEPA 2003, ss 289A–289E; FA 2015, s 11*]. See EIM30210 and *Simon's Taxes* E4.729.

(f) K Ltd will be liable to employers' Class 1A NIC for 2020/21 in respect of Car 1, under *Social Security Contributions and Benefits Act 1992, s 10*. See NIM16381–16389 and *Simon's Taxes* E8.271.

(B) **Vans**

[*ITEPA 2003, ss 155–164, 170(1A)(2)(5)*]

W is an employee of C Ltd, earning £37,000 per annum. From 1 October 2020 to 5 April 2021, W is provided by his employer with exclusive use of a one-year old company van (Van A) on terms such that the restricted private use requirements are not met and which provide for a deduction of £4 per month to be made from his net salary at the end of each month in consideration for private use. Van A was off the road and incapable of use for a three-week period in January 2021; no replacement was provided.

X, Y and Z are also employees of C Ltd, each earning £32,500 per annum. Throughout 2020/21, a single two-year old company van (Van B) is made available to the three of them. The terms are such that the restricted private use requirements are met in relation to X but not in relation to Y and Z. No payment for private use was required from any of them. Van B was damaged and incapable of use for 40 consecutive days in February/ March 2021; no replacement was provided. The facts show that a just and reasonable allocation of the benefit for 2020/21 is 0% to X (whose private use was insignificant), 60% to Y and 40% to Z.

Both vans have a normal laden weight not exceeding 3,500 kilograms.

It is not the policy of C Ltd to provide fuel for private travel in its vans. All employees are required to make good the full cost of any fuel used for private purposes and have done so in 2020/21.

The taxable benefits to W, X, Y and Z for 2020/21 of company vans are calculated as follows.

	£
W	
Cash equivalent of benefit before adjustment	3,490
Exclude Period of unavailability (see note (b) below):	
$£3,490 \times \dfrac{178}{365}$ (6.4.20 – 30.9.20)	(1,702)
	1,788
Deduct Payment for private use (6 × £4 per month)	(24)
Cash equivalent of benefit	£1,764

9.3 IT   Employment Income

X

Cash equivalent of benefit	Nil

Y

Cash equivalent of benefit before adjustment	3,490
Exclude Period of unavailability:	
$£3,490 \times \dfrac{40}{365}$	(382)
	3,108
Exclude Reduction for sharing (40%)	(1,243)
Cash equivalent of benefit	£1,865

Z

Cash equivalent of benefit before adjustment	3,490
Exclude Period of unavailability (same as for Y):	(382)
	3,108
Exclude Reduction for sharing (60%)	(1,865)
Cash equivalent of benefit	£1,243

Notes

(a) The cash equivalent of the benefit is £3,490 (£3,430 for 2019/20). [*ITEPA 2003, s 155(1); SI 2015 No 1979; SI 2016 No 1174*]. See EIM22790 and *Simon's Taxes* E4.630B.

(b) In W's case, the period of unavailability in January 2021 does not count towards the reduction as it is a period of less than 30 consecutive days.

(c) No fuel benefit arises in this example due to C Ltd's policy on fuel for private travel and the fact that the employees have reimbursed the company for any private fuel used.

(C) **Assets given and leased**

[*ITEPA 2003, ss 203–208*]

During 2020/21 P Ltd transferred to R a television set which it had previously leased to him for a nominal rent of £4 per month. The company also leased a suit to R under similar arrangements but at a rent of £2 per month.

Television

First leased to R on 6 April 2019 (when its market value was £860); transferred to R on 1 March 2021 for £100, the market value at that time being £375.

R's benefits are	£	£
2019/20		
Cost of benefit 20% × £860		172
Deduct Rent paid by R		(48)
Cash equivalent of benefit		£124
2020/21		
Cost of benefit 20% × £860 × $^{330}/_{365}$ (note (a))		155
Deduct Rent paid by R (11 months)		(44)
Cash equivalent of benefit		111
Greater of		
(i) Market value at transfer	375	
Deduct Price paid by R	(100)	
	£275	
and		
(ii) Original market value	860	
Deduct Cost of benefits note (b)	(327)	
	533	
Deduct Price paid by R	(100)	
	£433	
		433
Total		£544

Suit

First leased to R on 31 July 2020 (when its market value was £580).

R's benefit for 2020/21 is		
Cost of benefit 20% × £580 × $^{249}/_{365}$ (note (a))		79
Deduct Rent paid by R (8 months)		(16)
Cash equivalent of benefit		£63

Notes

(a) Where the benefit consists in the use (without transfer) of an asset, the cost of the benefit is time-apportioned by reference to the number of days in the tax year on which the asset is available for private use. An asset is *unavailable* for private use on any day if, inter alia, that day falls before the day on which the asset is first available to the employee (without any transfer of property) or after the day on which it is last so available. [*ITEPA 2003, ss 205(1B)–(1D), 205A, 205B; FA 2017, s 8(1)–(3)(5)*]. See EIM21200, EIM21637.

9.3 IT   Employment Income

(b) On the transfer of the television set, the cost of the benefits to date (£172 + £155), not the cash equivalents, is deducted from the original market value. [*ITEPA 2003, s 206*]. See EIM21650 and *Simon's Taxes* E4.616.

(c) It is assumed that the television set and suit have been bought by P Ltd and are not goods provided from within its own business. If the latter was the case, R would be taxed on the marginal or additional cost to P Ltd in providing the benefit (*Pepper v Hart* HL 1992, 65 TC 421).

(D) **Cheap loan arrangements**

[*ITEPA 2003, ss 173–191*]

D, who is an employee of A Ltd earning £40,000 per annum, obtained a loan of £10,000 from the company on 10 October 2007 for the purpose of buying a car. Interest at a nominal rate is charged annually on the outstanding balance while the principal is repayable by instalments of £1,000 on 31 December and 30 June commencing 31 December 2007. The interest paid by D in 2007/08 amounted to £50 and in 2008/09 to £250. The official rate of interest is 6.25% p.a. until 28 February 2009 and 4.75% p.a. thereafter. The average rate for 2008/09 is 6.1%.

D will be chargeable for 2007/08 as follows

Normal method (averaging)   £

$$\text{Average balance for period } \frac{£10,000 + £9,000}{2} \qquad £9,500$$

£9,500 × $^5/_{12}$	£3,958
£3,958 × 6.25%	247
Deduct Interest paid in year	50
Cash equivalent of loan benefit	£197

Alternative method

Period	Balance of loan in period	Interest at official rate on balance	
	£		£
10.10.07 – 31.12.07	10,000	£10,000 × 6.25% × $^{83}/_{365}$	142
1.1.08 – 5.4.08	9,000	£9,000 × 6.25% × $^{95}/_{365}$	146
			288
Deduct Interest paid in year			50
Cash equivalent of loan benefit			£238
Amount chargeable to tax	note (b)		£238

Employment Income IT 9.3

D will be chargeable for 2008/09 as follows

Normal method (averaging) £

Average balance for year $\dfrac{£9,000 + £7,000}{2}$ £8,000

	£
£8,000 × 6.1%	488
Deduct Interest paid in year	250
Cash equivalent of loan benefit	£238

Alternative method

Period	Balance of loan in period £	Interest at official rate on balance	£
6.4.08 – 30.6.08	9,000	£9,000 × 6.25% × $^{86}/_{365}$	132
1.7.08 – 31.12.08	8,000	£8,000 × 6.25% × $^{184}/_{365}$	252
1.1.09 – 28.2.09	7,000	£7,000 × 6.25% × $^{59}/_{365}$	71
1.3.09 – 5.4.09	7,000	£7,000 × 4.75% × $^{95}/_{365}$	33
			488
Deduct Interest paid in year			250
Cash equivalent of loan benefit			£238
Amount chargeable to tax	note (b)		£238

Notes

(a) The period 10 October 2007 to 5 April 2008 is, for the purpose of calculating the average balance, five complete months (months begin on the sixth day of each calendar month). However, for the purpose of applying interest rates, the actual number of days (178) during which the loan was outstanding is taken into account.

(b) HMRC will probably require the alternative method to be applied for 2007/08. For 2008/09, both methods happen to give the same result.

(c) Note that a loan is exempt from the cheap loan provisions for a tax year if it and other employment-related loans (excluding qualifying loans) do not exceed £10,000 in aggregate at any time in the year (£5,000 for 2013/14 and earlier years). [*ITEPA 2003, s 180; FA 2014, s 22*]. See EIM26137 and *Simon's Taxes* E4.632.

(d) There is no taxable benefit in respect of a loan where, if interest were paid on it, the whole of the interest would qualify for tax relief. [*ITEPA 2003, s 178*]. Where such interest only partly qualifies, a benefit continues to arise, with relief being given for the qualifying part of the interest. See EIM26135, EIM26136 and *Simon's Taxes* E4.632.

(e) In order for interest paid by the employee to be taken into account, it need not be paid *in* the tax year, only *for* the tax year. See HMRC Employment Income Manual, EIM26250–26258 for a useful discussion on this.

9.3 IT   Employment Income

(f) This example illustrates the year 2008/09 as that was the latest year in which the official rate was changed in-year. The principles continue to apply for subsequent years.

9.4   BENEFITS — LIVING ACCOMMODATION

[*ITEPA 2003, ss 97–113, 313–315; FA 2016, s 7(2)(3)(9)*]

(A) Expenses

N is employed by the G Property Co Ltd, earning £13,850 p.a. He occupies, rent-free, the basement flat of a block of flats for which he is employed as caretaker/security officer. The annual value of the flat is determined at £250. In 2020/21, G Ltd incurred the following expenditure on the flat

	£
Heat and light	700
Decoration	330
Repairs	210
Cleaning	160
	£1,400
Conversion of large bedroom into two smaller bedrooms	£3,000

In addition, the company pays N's council tax which amounts to £500.

N pays a personal pension premium of £160 net of tax (equivalent to £200 gross) into a registered scheme on 31 October 2020, but, apart from his personal allowance, he has no other reliefs.

N's taxable income for 2020/21 is

Salary	13,850
Annual value of flat	—
Heat and light, decoration, repairs, cleaning	
£1,400 restricted to (note (c))	1,365
	15,215
Deduct Personal allowance	(12,500)
Taxable	£2,715

Notes

(a) N is not chargeable to income tax on the annual value of the flat if he can show that it is necessary for the proper performance of his duties for him to reside in the accommodation. [*ITEPA 2003, s 99(1)*]. He might equally well be able to claim under *ITEPA 2003, s 99(2)*. See EIM11342, EIM11346 and *Simon's Taxes* E4.607.

(b) The structural alterations costing £3,000 will not be regarded as a benefit. [*ITEPA 2003, s 313*]. See EIM21620 and *Simon's Taxes* E4.608A.

Employment Income   IT 9.4

(c) The earnings treated as having arisen in respect of the heat and light, decoration, repairs and cleaning costs will be restricted by *ITEPA 2003, s 315* to the lesser of

(i)	the expenses incurred	£1,400
(ii)	10% × £13,650 (net earnings)	£1,365

The contribution to a registered pension scheme is deductible in arriving at net earnings for this purpose. [*ITEPA 2003, s 315(5)*]. (The contribution is not shown above as a deduction from taxable income as basic rate relief has been given at source and higher/additional rate relief is not applicable.) See EIM21720, EIM21721 and *Simon's Taxes* E4.608A.

(d) Where the benefit of living accommodation is exempt under *ITEPA 2003, s 99(1), s 99(2) or s 100* (accommodation provided as result of security threat), the payment by the employer of the employee's council tax (and/or water rates) is also exempt. [*ITEPA 2003, s 314*]. See EIM15023 and *Simon's Taxes* E4.608A.

(B) **Normal and additional charge**

S, the founder and managing director of S Ltd, a successful transport company, has since April 2015 occupied a house owned by S Ltd. The house was acquired by S Ltd in August 2009 for £150,000 and, since acquisition, but before 6 April 2019, £80,000 has been spent by S Ltd on alterations and improvements to the house. The gross annual value of the house for rating purposes before 1 April 1990 (when the community charge replaced general rates) was £1,663. S pays annual rental of £2,000 to the company for 2020/21 only. He pays all expenses relating to the property.

S's taxable benefits in respect of his occupation of the house for 2019/20 and 2020/21 are as follows

		£	£
2019/20			
Gross annual value			1,663
Additional charge			
Acquisition cost of house		150,000	
Cost of improvements		80,000	
		230,000	
Deduct		(75,000)	
Additional value		£155,000	
Additional value at 2.5%%	note (b)		3,875,
			£5,538
2020/21			
Gross annual value	note (a)		Nil
Additional charge			
Acquisition cost of house		150,000	
Cost of improvements		80,000	
		230,000	

9.4 IT   Employment Income

Deduct		(75,000)	
Additional value		£155,000	
Additional value at 2.25%	note (b)		3,488
			3,488
Rental payable by S		2,000	
Deduct Gross annual value		(1,663)	
			(337)
			£3,151

Notes

(a) No taxable gross annual value arises in 2020/21 because the rental of £2,000 payable by S exceeds the gross annual value of £1,663. The excess is deductible from the amount of the benefit arising under the additional charge.

(b) The percentage to be used in determining the amount of the benefit is that in force for the purposes of taxing cheap loan arrangements (see 9.3(D) above) at the beginning of the tax year.

(c) If S had moved into the house on, say, 6 April 2016 (more than six years after its acquisition by S Ltd), market value at that date would be substituted for cost plus improvements to date. If, however, original cost plus cost of improvements had not exceeded £75,000, the additional charge would not apply (regardless of market value at the date of first occupation by S). [ITEPA 2003, s 107]. See EIM11473 and Simon's Taxes E4.608.

9.5   REMOVAL BENEFITS AND EXPENSES, INCLUDING CHEAP LOAN ARRANGEMENTS

[ITEPA 2003, ss 271–289]

Mr R E Locate lives in Chelsea and is employed as a store manager by T Ltd, a department store chain, at one of their London branches. In June 2020, he is asked by T Ltd to take up a similar position at their main Birmingham store with effect from 1 August 2020. The company agrees to pay Mr Locate's expenses, up to a ceiling of £7,500, in connection with his moving house to the Birmingham area. In the event, the expenses paid or reimbursed by the company amount to £7,000, all paid in 2020, all eligible expenses within ITEPA 2003, ss 272, 277–285 and all reasonably incurred by the employee in connection with his change of residence. As he is unable to move into his new home until 15 August 2020, T Ltd provides Mr Locate with temporary living accommodation near his new place of employment. The accommodation is rented by the company and would give rise to a taxable benefit on the employee of £300 under ITEPA 2003, s 105, but no charge under ITEPA 2003, s 106 (see 9.4 above).

T Ltd also provides Mr Locate with an interest-free bridging loan of £50,000 in connection with the change of residence. The loan is made on 1 August 2020 and is repaid on 10 April 2021 when the sale of the employee's former residence is completed. The official rate of interest under ITEPA 2003, s 181 is assumed to remain at 2.25% throughout. Mr Locate's salary for 2020/21 amounts to £44,000.

9.5 IT   Employment Income

Notes

(a) Eligible expenses and benefits which are reasonably incurred or provided in connection with the change in the employee's residence are qualifying expenses or benefits only if they are incurred or provided on or before the end of the tax year following that in which the employment, new duties or duties at the new location commence, i.e. by 5 April 2022 in this example.

(b) 'Subsistence' provided for the employee is an eligible benefit by virtue of *ITEPA 2003, s 281(4)*. For this purpose, 'subsistence' includes temporary living accommodation as well as food and drink. [*ITEPA 2003, s 281(6)*]. See EIM03113 and *Simon's Taxes* E4.725.

(c) See also 9.3(D) above as regards cheap loans.

9.6   BENEFITS — MISCELLANEOUS

T earns £6,000 p.a. and during the year ended 5 April 2021 his employer provided him with, or paid on his behalf, or reimbursed, the following

	£
BUPA contributions (self and family) of which 25% reimbursed by T	600
Special medical insurance for overseas business visit lasting four nights	250
Voucher exchangeable for rail season ticket	500
Gift token exchangeable for goods at local department store	75
Holiday pay scheme voucher, exchangeable for cash	350
Overnight incidental expenses (telephone, laundry etc.) relating to above-mentioned overseas trip	36

The rail ticket voucher was purchased in March 2020 but was not handed to T until after 6 April 2020. The holiday pay voucher was received by T in June 2020 at which time PAYE was applied. The gift token was received in December 2020.

T's chargeable earnings for 2020/21 are

	£
Salary	6,000
BUPA contributions (£600 less 25% reimbursed) (note (a))	450
Rail ticket voucher (note (c))	500
Gift token (note (d))	75
Holiday pay scheme voucher (note (e))	350
	£7,375

Mr Locate's taxable benefits for 2020/21 in respect of removal expenses and benefits plus cheap loans are calculated as follows

	£
Qualifying removal expenses	7,000
Qualifying removal benefits	300
	£7,300

The total is less than the qualifying limit of £8,000 under *ITEPA 2003, s 287(1)* and is thus exempt from tax by virtue of *ITEPA 2003, s 271(1)*.

Cheap loan arrangements

The interest-free loan is treated by *ITEPA 2003, s 289* as having been made on a date later than that on which it was actually made, as follows.

$$\text{Number of days in the 'exempted discharge period'} = \frac{A}{B \times C} \times 365$$

A = 700 (unused qualifying limit, i.e. £8,000 - £7,300)

B = 50,000 (maximum loan outstanding between the actual date of the loan, 1.8.20, and 5.4.22, the latter being the 'limitation day' — see *ITEPA 2003, s 274* and note (a) below)

C = 2.25% (the official rate of interest as at the actual date of the loan, 1.8.20, disregarding any subsequent changes of rate)

$$\frac{700}{50{,}000 \times 2.25\%} \times 365$$

= 227.11 rounded to 227 days

[*ITEPA 2003, s 288(4)*].

The 'exempted discharge period' of 227 days runs from 1.8.20 to 15.03.21 inclusive. The loan is deemed to have been made on 15.03.21. [*ITEPA 2003, s 289(1)–(3)*].

Calculation of benefit:

(i) Averaging method

$$\frac{£50{,}000 + £50{,}000}{2} \times \frac{1}{12} \times 2.25\% = \qquad £94$$

(ii) Alternative method
15.03.21–5.4.21 = 21 days

$$£50{,}000 \times 2.25\% \times 21/365 \qquad £65$$

Amount chargeable to tax (on the assumption that the alternative method is applied) £65

Notes

(a) All provisions of the benefits code apply in full to all employees (including directors) whatever their level of earnings, subject to special rules for ministers of religion and an exemption for home care workers. [*ITEPA 2003, ss 216–220; FA 2015, s 13(1)(4)*]. The BUPA contributions are now a chargeable benefit, which would not previously have been the case for a 'lower-paid' employee. See EIM60066 and *Simon's Taxes* E4.602.

(b) The special medical insurance for the overseas business trip is exempted from charge by *ITEPA 2003, s 325*. See EIM21766 and *Simon's Taxes* E4.762.

(c) The rail ticket voucher is chargeable in 2020/21 being the later of the year of receipt by the employee and the year of expense incurred by the employer. [*ITEPA 2003, s 88*]. See *Simon's Taxes* E4.605.

(d) The gift token is a non-cash voucher chargeable under *ITEPA 2003, s 87*. See EIM16140 and *Simon's Taxes* E4.1123.

(e) The holiday pay voucher, being a 'cash voucher' within *ITEPA 2003, s 75* is taxable under PAYE by virtue of *ITEPA 2003, s 693*. See EIM16110 and *Simon's Taxes* E4.604.

(f) The reimbursement of incidental overnight expenses is not taxable as the amount does not exceed £10 for each night of absence (£5 for absences within the UK). [*ITEPA 2003, ss 240, 241*]. See EIM02710 and *Simon's Taxes* E4.706.

Enterprise Investment Scheme IT 10.1

10 Enterprise Investment Scheme

[*ITA 2007, ss 156–257; TCGA 1992, ss 150A, 150B; FA 2018, ss 14–16, Sch 4; FA 2020, s 36*]

10.1 CONDITIONS FOR RELIEF AND FORM OF RELIEF

(A)

Marshal Ney is a UK resident with a salary of £185,000 for 2019/20 and no other income. For 2019/20, he is entitled to full income tax relief on an investment of £200,000 in a venture capital trust.

In 2019/20 he subscribes for ordinary shares in two unquoted companies issuing shares under the enterprise investment scheme (EIS).

A Ltd was formed by some people in Ney's neighbourhood to publish a local newspaper. 200,000 ordinary £1 shares were issued at par in August 2019 and the company started trading in September 2019. Ney subscribed for 16,000 of the shares. Ney becomes a director of A Ltd in September 2019, and receives director's fees of £5,000 in 2019/20, a level of remuneration which is considered reasonable for services rendered by him to the company in his capacity as a director.

B Ltd, which is controlled by an old friend of Ney, has acquired the rights to manufacture in the UK a new type of industrial cleaning solvent and requires additional finance. Ney subscribed for 8,000 ordinary £1 shares at a premium of £1.50 per share in October 2019. The issue increases the company's issued share capital to 25,000 ordinary £1 shares.

Ney will obtain tax relief in 2019/20 as follows

Amount eligible for relief

		£
A Ltd	note (a)	16,000
B Ltd	note (b)	Nil
Total (being less than the maximum of £1,000,000)		£16,000

	£
Salary	185,000
Director's remuneration (A Ltd)	5,000
Total income	190,000
Personal allowance (restricted due to level of income)	Nil
Taxable income	£190,000
Tax payable:	
37,500 @ 20%	7,500.00
112,500 @ 40%	45,000.00
40,000 @ 45%	18,000.00
	70,500.00
VCT relief £200,000 @ 30%	(60,000.00)

10.1 IT   Enterprise Investment Scheme

	10,500.00
Deduct EIS relief £16,000 @ 30%	(4,800.00)
Net tax liability 2019/20	£5,700.00

Notes

(a) Marshal Ney is entitled to relief on the full amount of his investment in A Ltd. The fact that he becomes a paid director of A Ltd *after* an issue to him of eligible shares does not prevent his qualifying for relief in respect of those shares providing his remuneration as a director is reasonable and he is not otherwise connected with the company. [*ITA 2007, s 169*]. See VCM11070 and *Simon's Taxes* E3.111.

(b) Ney is not entitled to relief against his income for his investment of £20,000 in B Ltd. As a result of the share issue he owns more than 30% of the issued ordinary share capital (8,000 out of 25,000 shares) and is therefore regarded as connected with the company and denied relief. [*ITA 2007, s 170*]. See VCM11080 and *Simon's Taxes* E3.107.

(c) EIS relief is given at the EIS rate of tax (30%) and by way of an income tax reduction. The relief cannot exceed what would otherwise be the income tax liability (no restriction being necessary in this example). For this purpose, the income tax liability is before taking into account any married couple's allowance, double tax relief and certain other specified items. However, the VCT investment relief must be deducted before the EIS relief. [*ITA 2007, ss 26, 27, 29, 158*]. VCM10530 and *Simon's Taxes* E3.156.

(B)

In 2020/21 Marshal Ney subscribes for shares in three more unquoted UK companies issuing shares under the EIS. None of the companies are knowledge-intensive companies.

C Ltd is a local company engaged in the manufacture of car components. It issues a further 540,000 ordinary £1 shares at £2 per share in June 2020 and Ney subscribes for 14,800 shares costing £29,600, increasing his stake in the company to 10%. He had originally held 24,300 shares, acquired by purchase at arm's length in May 2018 for £32,400.

D Ltd has been trading as a restaurateur for several years and requires an injection of capital to finance a new restaurant. Ney and three other unconnected individuals each subscribe for 75,000 ordinary £1 shares at par in November 2020. The balance of 480,000 shares are held by Ney's sister and niece. D Ltd has the equivalent of 80 full-time employees in November 2020 when the new shares are issued.

E Ltd is an electronics company, with 60 employees, controlled by two cousins of Marshal Ney. The company has not issued any shares in the previous twelve months but is now seeking £5 million extra capital for expansion, and raises it via the EIS. Ney subscribes for 950,000 ordinary £1 shares at par in December 2020.

Ney's salary is increased by bonus to £277,000 for 2020/21. His director's fees from A Ltd amount to £5,320, which again is considered reasonable for services rendered. He makes a claim to treat 9,500 of his C Ltd shares (costing £19,000) to be regarded as issued in 2019/20, thus eliminating his tax liability for that year.

Enterprise Investment Scheme IT 10.1

Ney will obtain tax relief as follows

2019/20

C Ltd note (a) £19,000 @ 30% =	£5,700

2020/21

Amount eligible for relief

	£
C Ltd (£29,600 − £19,000 carried back)	10,600
D Ltd	75,000
E Ltd	950,000
Total amount subscribed	£1,035,600
But amount eligible for relief restricted to subscriptions of	£1,000,000

Relief given

	£
Salary	277,000
Director's remuneration	5,320
Total income	282,320
Personal allowance (restricted due to level of income)	Nil
Taxable income	£282,320
Tax payable:	
37,500 @ 20%	7,500.00
112,500 @ 40%	45,000.00
132,320 @ 45%	59,544.00
	112,044.00
Deduct EIS relief:	
£1,000,000 @ 30% = £300,000, but restricted to	112,044.00
Net tax liability 2020/21	Nil

85

10.1 IT   Enterprise Investment Scheme

Attribution of relief to shares   note (b)

		£
CLtd shares	$\dfrac{10,600}{1,035,600} \times £112,044$	1,147
DLtd shares	$\dfrac{75,000}{1,035,600} \times £112,044$	8,114
ELtd shares	$\dfrac{950,000}{1,035,600} \times £112,044$	102,783
		£112,044

Notes

(a) The investor may claim relief as if any number of the shares had been issued in the preceding tax year. The only restriction (not relevant in this example) is that relief in any one tax year may not be given on subscriptions of more than the annual maximum for that year. The relief will be given in addition to that previously claimed for 2019/20 (see (A) above). [*ITA 2007, s 158(4)*]. See VCM10530 and *Simon's Taxes* E3.156.

(b) Relief is restricted in this example by (i) the £1,000,000 maximum, (ii) the available EIS rate (i.e. 30%) and (iii) an insufficiency in Ney's tax liability. The relief attributable to each issue of shares (which will be relevant in the event of a disposal of the shares or withdrawal of relief — see 10.2 below) is found by apportioning the income tax reduction by reference to the amounts subscribed for each issue. (For this purpose, 9,500 of the C Ltd shares are regarded as having been separately issued in the previous year.) The relief so attributed to each issue is then apportioned equally between all the shares comprised in that issue. [*ITA 2007, ss 201, 210(2)*]. See VCM14020 and *Simon's Taxes* E3.160.

(c) An issuing company under the EIS scheme must have fewer than the equivalent of 250 full-time employees (500 for knowledge-intensive companies) when the EIS shares are issued. [*ITA 2007, s 186A*]. See VCM13120 and *Simon's Taxes* E3.134.

(d) With effect for shares issued on or after 6 April 2018, the upper limit on the amount in respect of which an individual may obtain income tax relief for a tax year operates as follows:

   (i) if the shares do not include any 'KIC shares', the limit is £1 million;

   (ii) if the total amount subscribed for KIC shares is £1 million or more, the limit is £2 million; and

   (iii) in any other case, the limit is £1 million plus total amount subscribed for KIC shares.

Enterprise Investment Scheme   IT 10.2

'*KIC shares*' are shares in any company which is a knowledge-intensive company (as defined) at the time the shares are issued.

Prior to the above taking effect the upper limit is in all cases £1 million.

[*ITA 2007, s 158(2)(2ZA)(2ZB); FA 2018, Sch 4 paras 1(2)–(4), 10*]. See VCM10530 and *Simon's Taxes* E3.156.

10.2 WITHDRAWAL OF RELIEF/GAINS AND LOSSES ON EIS SHARES

(A)

In June 2021, Marshal Ney, the investor in 10.1 above, sells 38,100 ordinary £1 shares in C Ltd (see **10.1(B)** above), in an arm's length transaction, for £90,000, leaving him with 1,000 shares.

The position is as follows
Income Tax

	£
2019/20	
Relief attributable to 9,500 shares treated as issued in 2019/20:	
9,500 shares at £2 per share = £19,000 @ 30%	5,700
Consideration received $\left(\dfrac{9,500}{38,100} \times £90,000\right) = £22,441$ @ 30%	6,732
Excess of tax at the EIS rate on consideration over relief	£1,032
Relief withdrawn by assessment for 2019/20	£5,700

	£
2020/21	
Relief attributable to 4,300 shares	
4,300/5,300 × £1,147	931
Consideration received	
$\left(\dfrac{4,300}{38,100} \times £90,000\right) = £10,157 \times 931 / (8,600$ @ 30%) = £3,665 @ 30%	1,100
Excess of tax at the EIS rate on adjusted consideration over relief	£169
Relief withdrawn by assessment for 2020/21	£931

Capital Gains Tax

	£	£
2021/22		
Disposal proceeds (38,100 shares)		90,000
Cost: 24,300 shares acquired May 2018	32,400	
13,800 shares acquired June 2020	27,600	60,000
Chargeable gain		£30,000

10.2 IT   Enterprise Investment Scheme

Notes

(a) For both income tax and capital gains tax purposes, a disposal is matched with acquisitions on a first in/first out basis. [*ITA 2007, s 246*]. See VCM16020 and *Simon's Taxes* E3.167, C3.1006, E3.708. Thus, the 38,100 shares sold in June 2021 are matched with 24,300 shares purchased in May 2018 and with 13,800 of the 14,800 EIS shares subscribed for in June 2020. For these purposes, 9,500 of the EIS shares are treated as having been issued in 2019/20 (by virtue of Marshal Ney's carry-back claim — see note (a) to **10.1(B)** above). [*ITA 2007, s 201(6)*]. Therefore, those shares are treated as disposed of in priority to those on which relief was given in 2020/21.

(b) Following the disposal, Ney is left with 1,000 shares in C Ltd acquired in June 2020 for £2,000, to which the EIS relief attributable is £216 (1,147 – 931).

(c) EIS relief is withdrawn if shares are disposed of before the end of the requisite three-year period. In this example, relief attributable to the shares sold is fully withdrawn as consideration received, reduced as illustrated, exceeds the relief attributable. See (B) below for where the reverse applies. The consideration is reduced where the relief attributable (A) is less than tax at the 'EIS original rate' on the amount subscribed (B), and is so reduced by applying the fraction A/B. [*ITA 2007, ss 209, 210*]. The '*EIS original rate*' is the EIS rate for the tax year for which the relief was obtained, i.e. currently 30%. See VCM15015 and *Simon's Taxes* E3.167 .

(d) Relief is withdrawn by means of an assessment for the year(s) in which relief was given. [*ITA 2007, s 235*]. See *Simon's Taxes* E3.174.

(e) The capital gain on the disposal is fully chargeable as the EIS shares are not held for the requisite three-year period.

(B)

In December 2021 Ney disposes of his 75,000 ordinary £1 shares in D Ltd (see **10.1(B)** above), in an arm's length transaction, for £60,000.

The position is as follows
Income Tax

	£
2020/21	
Relief attributable to shares sold	8,114

$$£60,000 \times \frac{8,114}{£75,000 \times 30\%} = 21,637 @ 30\% \qquad 6,491$$

Excess of relief over tax at the EIS rate on adjusted consideration	£1,623
Relief withdrawn by assessment for 2020/21	£6,491

Capital Gains Tax

2021/22

	£	£
Disposal proceeds (December 2021)		60,000
Cost (November 2020)	75,000	
Less Relief attributable to shares:		
£8,114 − £6,491	(1,623)	
		73,377
Allowable loss		£(13,377)

Notes

(a) See notes (b) and (c) to (A) above.

(b) The EIS relief withdrawn is limited to tax at the EIS original rate (see note (c) to (A) above) on the consideration received, reduced as illustrated. If the disposal had been made otherwise than by way of a bargain made at arm's length, the full relief would have been withdrawn. [*ITA 2007, s 209*].

(c) An allowable loss may arise for capital gains tax purposes on a disposal of EIS shares, whether or not the disposal occurs within the requisite three-year period. In computing such a loss, the allowable cost is reduced by EIS relief attributable to the shares (and not withdrawn). [*TCGA 1992, s 150A(1)*]. See VCM20050 and *Simon's Taxes* C3.1005–C3.1008.

(d) A loss, as computed for capital gains tax purposes, may be relieved against income on a claim under *ITA 2007, s 132* (share loss relief — see **15.5** LOSSES). [*ITA 2007, s 131*]. See VCM74020 and *Simon's Taxes* C1.501.

(C)

(i) In September 2021, Marshal Ney receives from E Ltd (one of the companies in **10.1(B)** above) an asset with a market value of £38,000 but for which he pays the company only £2,000.

(ii) In March 2024, Ney sells his 950,000 shares in E Ltd for their market value of £1,190,000.

Income Tax

(i) The difference of £36,000 between the market value of the asset and the consideration given for it represents value (which is not insignificant value) received by the investor from the company within the period beginning one year before the issue of the shares and ending three years after the issue (or three years after the commencement of trade, if later). The value received (reduced in like manner as is mentioned in note (b) to (A) above) is compared to the relief attributable to the shares.

10.2 IT Enterprise Investment Scheme

2020/21

	£
Relief attributable to 950,000 E Ltd shares (see **10.1**(B) above)	102,783
Value received	

$$£36{,}000 \times \frac{102{,}783}{£950{,}000 \times 30\%} = 12{,}983 \ @ \ 30\% \qquad \underline{3{,}895}$$

Excess of relief over value received	£98,888
Relief withdrawn by assessment for 2020/21	£3,895

[*ITA 2007*, ss 159(4), 213–217, 220, 234(1), 235].

(ii) As Ney holds the shares for the requisite three-year period, there is no withdrawal of relief on disposal.

Capital Gains Tax

As Ney holds the shares for the requisite three-year period, and EIS relief has not been fully withdrawn, any gain on disposal is generally exempt from capital gains tax (although this does not prevent an allowable loss from arising). [*TCGA 1992, s 150A(2)(2A)*]. A proportion of the gain could become chargeable under *TCGA 1992, s 150A(3)* where the relief given was less than tax at the EIS rate on the amount subscribed but this does not apply where, as in Ney's case, the relief fell to be restricted due to his having insufficient income tax liability to cover it. [*TCGA 1992, s 150A(3)*].

A proportion of the gain does, however, become chargeable where value is received leading to a part-withdrawal of relief. [*TCGA 1992, s 150B*]. See VCM20070 and *Simon's Taxes* C3.1006.

2023/24

	£
Disposal proceeds (March 2024)	1,190,000
Cost (December 2020)	950,000
Gain	240,000

Chargeable gain =

$$\text{gain} \times \frac{\text{Relief withdrawn}}{\text{Relief attributable (before reduction)}}$$

i.e.

$$£240{,}000 \times \frac{£3{,}895}{£102{,}783} \qquad \underline{£9{,}095}$$

Exempt gain £(240,000 − 9,095)	£230,905

11 Herd Basis

[*ITTOIA 2005, ss 111–129*]

11.1 A farmer acquires a dairy herd and elects for the herd basis to apply. The movements in the herd and the tax treatment are as follows

Year 1

	No	Value £
Mature		
Bought @ £150	70	10,500
Bought in calf @ £180		
(Market value of calf £35)	5	900
Immature		
Bought @ £75	15	1,125
Herd Account		
70 Friesians		10,500
5 Friesians in calf (5 × £(180 − 35))		725
75 Closing balance		£11,225
Trading Account		
5 Calves (5 × £35)		175
15 Immature Friesians		1,125
Debit to profit and loss account		£1,300

Year 2

	No	Value £
Mature		
Bought @ £185	15	2,775
Sold @ £200	10	2,000
Died	3	—
Immature		
Born	52	—
Matured @ 60% of market value of £200 note (a)	12	1,440

IT   Herd Basis

Herd Account

75	Opening balance		11,225
	Increase in herd		
15	Purchases	2,775	
12	Transferred from trading stock	1,440	
27		4,215	
(13)	Replacement cost £4,215 × 13/27	(2,029)	
14	Non-replacement animals cost		2,186
89	Closing balance		£13,411

Trading Account

Sale of 10 mature cows replaced		(2,000)
Transfer to herd — 14 animals		(1,440)
Cost of 13 mature cows purchased to replace those sold/deceased ($^{13}/_{15}$ × £2,775)		2,405
Net credit to profit and loss account note (b)		£(1,035)

Year 3

	No	Value £
Mature		
Jerseys bought @ £250	70	17,500
Friesians slaughtered @ £175 (market value £185)	52	9,100
Immature		
Friesians born	20	—
Matured		
Friesians @ 60% of market value of £190 note (*a*)	15	1,710

Herd Account

89	Opening balance		13,411
	Increase in herd		
18	Jerseys		4,500
	52 Improvement Jerseys@	250	
	less Market value of Friesians	185	
	52@	65	3,380
	Transfer from trading stock		
15	Friesians		1,710
122	Closing balance		£23,001

Herd Basis IT 11.1

Trading Account

Compensation	(9,100)
Transfer to herd	(1,710)
Purchase of replacements note (c) (52 × £185)	9,620
Net credit to profit and loss account	£(1,190)

Year 4

The farmer ceases dairy farming and sells his whole herd.

	No	Value £
Mature		
Jersey sold @ £320	70	22,400
Friesians sold @ £200	52	10,400
Immature		
Friesians sold @ £100	65	6,500
Herd Account		
Opening balance		23,001
52 Friesians		
70 Jerseys		
(122) Sales		(32,800)
— Profit on sale note (d)		£(9,799)
Trading Account		
Sale of 65 immature Friesians		(6,500)
Credit to profit and loss account		£(6,500)

Notes

(a) The use of 60% of market value was originally by agreement between the National Farmers' Union and HMRC (see now BIM55410). Alternatively, the actual cost of breeding or purchase and rearing could be used.

(b) As the cost of rearing the 12 cows to maturity will already have been debited to the profit and loss account, no additional entry is required to reflect that cost. Due to the fact that the animals were in opening stock at valuation and will not be in closing stock, the trading account will in effect be debited with that valuation.

(c) The cost of the replacements is restricted to the cost of replacing like with like.

(d) Provided these animals are not replaced by a herd of the same type within five years the proceeds will be tax-free.

(e) The herd basis is not available when profits are calculated using the cash basis for smaller businesses. [*ITTOIA 2005, s 111A; FA 2013, Sch 4 paras 24, 56*]. See BIM55410 and *Simon's Taxes* B5.150.

12 Intellectual Property

Cross-reference. See 3.5 CAPITAL ALLOWANCES for allowances for patent rights.

12.1 PATENT ROYALTIES

[*ITA 2007, s 461*]

An inventor received £24,920 after deduction of tax at source (i.e. £31,150 gross) on 1 June 2020, for the use of his patent over a four-year period ending on that date. His only other income for the four years was a salary as set out below.

In the absence of spreading provisions, the assessments for the four years to 5 April 2021 are

Tax year	2017/18	2018/19	2019/20	2020/21
	£	£	£	£
Salary	21,350	23,200	27,350	28,500
Patent rights				31,150
	21,350	23,200	27,350	59,650
Deduct Personal allowance	(11,500)	(11,850)	(12,500)	(12,500)
Taxable income	9,850	11,350	14,850	47,150
Tax thereon	1,970.00	2,270.00	2,970.00	11,360.00
Less tax deducted at source				(6,230.00)
	1,970.00	2,270.00	2,970.00	5,130.00
Total tax payable				12,340.00

The inventor may however claim under *ITA 2007, s 461* for the liability for 2020/21 to be limited to the tax payable if the royalties had been spread over the period to which they relate, subject to a maximum of six years. The tax payable would then have been

	£	£	£	£
Salary	21,350	23,200	27,350	28,500
Patent rights	7,787	7,787	7,787	7,787
	29,137	30,987	35,137	36,287
Deduct Personal allowance	(11,500)	(11,850)	(12,500)	(12,500)
Taxable income	17,637	19,137	22,637	23,787
Tax thereon	3,527.40	3,827.40	4,527.40	£4,757.40
Total tax thereon				16,639.60
Less tax deducted at source				6,230.00
Total tax payable				10,409.60

A claim is beneficial in this case as spreading would reduce the liability by £1,930.40. Upon a claim being made, the saving will be given effect by means of a tax reduction for the year in which the royalty is received (2020/21 in this example). Tax reductions are given effect at Step 6 of the calculation of income tax liability at *ITA 2007, s 23*. See *Simon's Taxes* E1.910, E1.101B.

13 Late Payment Interest and Penalties

13.1 PAYMENTS UNDER SELF-ASSESSMENT

(A) **Interest and penalties arising on late payment**
[FA 2009, ss 101, 107, Sch 56]

Mrs Worthington is a self-employed cook. Her self-assessment for 2017/18 shows a net income tax liability of £9,000. She makes the following interim payments for 2018/19:

31 January 2019	£4,500
31 July 2019	£4,500

Mrs Worthington's profits increase, and her self-assessment liability for 2018/19 amounts to £12,000. Mrs Worthington does not pay the additional income tax of £3,000 until 26 September 2020.

Mrs Worthington will have a liability to late payment interest computed as follows

31.1.20 – 29.3.20	£3,000 × 3.25% × $^{58}/_{365}$	£15.49
30.3.20 to 6.4.20	£3,000 x 2.75% x 8/365	£1.81
7.4.20 – 25.9.20	£3,000 × 2.60% × $^{172}/_{365}$	36.76
Total		£54.06

In addition as the tax is paid more than 30 days late a late payment penalty will arise on 2 March 2020 of £3,000 × 5% = £150.

As the tax is still unpaid more than five months after the initial penalty is incurred, a further late payment penalty will arise on 2 August 2020 of £3,000 × 5% = £150. See also note (b).

Notes

(a) Interest accrues from the due date until date of payment. [FA 2009, s 101(3)(4)]. See *Simon's Taxes* A4.620.

(b) The interest rate on late paid income tax is 2.60% from 7.4.2020 . It was 3.25% from 21 August 2018 to 30 March 2020 and 2.75% from 30 March 2020 to 6 April 2020.

(c) If the tax had remained unpaid on 2 February 2021 (i.e. eleven months after the initial penalty was incurred), there would have been a third late payment penalty of 5% of the amount unpaid). [FA 2009, Sch 56 para 3]. See *Simon's Taxes* A4.560.

(d) A late payment penalty may arise in respect of unpaid tax due in respect of a final payment of income tax or capital gains tax under TMA 1970, s 59B. See CH142240 and *Simon's Taxes* A4.560. For other circumstances in which a late payment penalty may arise, see the Table in FA 2009, Sch 56 para 1.

(e) Late payment interest will accrue on an unpaid late payment penalty with effect from the expiry of 30 days beginning with the date of the notice imposing the penalty. [FA 2009, s 101, Sch 56 para 11]. See *Simon's Taxes* A4.620.

13.1 IT Late Payment Interest and Penalties

(B) Interest arising on insufficient interim payment

[*FA 2009, s 101, Sch 53 para 1*]

Frank is a self-employed butcher with no other income or capital gains who draws up accounts to 31 October each year. His liability under self-assessment for 2017/18 amounts to £25,000. Frank forecasts that his profits for the accounting period ended 31 October 2018 will result in a liability under self-assessment of £10,000 for 2018/19. He makes a claim to that effect under *TMA 1970, s 59A(4)* and duly pays £5,000 each on 31 January 2019 and 31 July 2019. However, actual profits are in excess of his expectations and result in a self-assessment liability of £16,000. Frank pays an additional £6,000 income tax on 25 January 2020.

For each interim payment Frank's interest will be calculated on the difference between £5,000 and the lesser of:

£8,000 being the sum of £5,000 (actual interim payment) and £3,000 (50% of the final tax payment); and

£12,500 being the interim payment based on the preceding year's tax liability.

Interest will be as follows*

First interim payment

31.1.19 – 24.1.20	£3,000 × 3.25% × $^{359}/_{365}$	£95.90

Second interim payment

31.7.19 – 24.1.20	£3,000 × 3.25% × $^{178}/_{365}$	£47.55

Notes

(a) The Government announced in March 2020 that self-assessment taxpayers can choose to delay making their second payment on account for **2019/20**, otherwise due on **31 July 2020**, if they find it difficult to make the payment on time due to the impact of COVID-19. No claim is required. Those opting to delay will have until 31 January 2021 to make the payment. Whilst introduced principally to assist the self-employed, this measure applies to all self-assessment taxpayers. No late payment interest will be charged for the period 1 August 2020 to 31 January 2021 on the deferred payment. (www.gov.uk/guidance/defer-your-self-assessment-payment-on-account-due-to-coronavirus-covid-19).

(b) See *Simon's Taxes* A4.620.

14 Life Assurance Policies

14.1 LIFE ASSURANCE GAINS AND NON-QUALIFYING POLICIES
[*ITTOIA 2005, ss 461–546; FA 2020, s 37*]

(A) **Top slicing relief — single chargeable event**

A single policyholder realises, in 2020/21, a gain of £2,600 on a non-qualifying policy which has been in existence for $2^1/_2$ years. Her other income for 2020/21 comprises employment income of £45,020, bank interest of £1,900 and dividends amounting to £2,000. She is not a Scottish taxpayer.

The tax chargeable on the gain is calculated as follows

	Normal basis	Top slicing relief claim
	£	£
Policy gain	2,600	1,300
Earnings	45,020	45,020
Savings income	1,900	1,900
Dividends	2,000	2,000
	51,520	50,220
Less Personal allowance	(12,500)	(12,500)
	£39,020	£37,720

	Normal basis		Top slicing relief claim
	£		£
Tax applicable to policy gain			
Higher rate			
£1,520 at 40%	608.00		—
£220 at 40%	—		88.00
	608.00		88.00
Deduct			
Basic rate			
£1,520 at 20%	304.00		—
£220 at 20%	—		44.00
			£44.00
Appropriate multiple 2 × £44.00			£88.00
Tax chargeable lower of	£304.00	and	£88.00
Top slicing relief = (£304.00 − £88.00)	£216.00		

14.1 IT   Life Assurance Policies

Tax payable is therefore as follows

32,520	@ 20%	6,504.00
500	@ 0% (personal savings allowance)	—
1,400	@ 20% (basic rate on savings income)	280.00
2,000	@ 0% (dividend nil rate)	—
1,080	@ 20% (policy gain at basic rate)	216.00
37,500		
1,520	@ 40% (policy gain at higher rate)	608.00
£39,020		
		7,608.00
Deduct:	Top slicing relief (as above)	(216.00)
		7,392.00
Deduct:	Basic rate of tax on policy gain (£2,600 @ 20%)	(520.00)
	Tax liability (subject to PAYE deductions)	£6,872.00

Notes

(a) Tax is calculated by treating the policy gain as the top slice of income. Under the top slicing relief calculation, the total policy gain is divided by the number of complete years the policy has run (two) and the resulting tax multiplied by the same factor.

(b) If a qualifying policy is replaced by a new qualifying policy on a different life or lives then, if certain conditions are met, no chargeable event occurs on the surrender of the earlier policy. [*ITTOIA 2005, s 542*]. See IPTM3520 and *Simon's Taxes* E1.451A.

(c) Gains on certain offshore policies do not carry a notional tax credit, though top slicing relief is computed as if a notional tax credit were available. [*ITTOIA 2005, s 531*]. A similar rule applies to gains on policies issued by friendly societies as part of their tax exempt life or endowment business. See IPTM3810 and *Simon's Taxes* E1.455A.

(B) **Top slicing relief — multiple chargeable events in same tax year**

[*ITTOIA 2005, s 537*]

On 1 May 2020, a policyholder realises a gain of £10,000 on the maturity of a four-year non-qualifying policy. On 1 March 2021, he realises a gain of £12,000 on the surrender of a non-qualifying policy which he took out on 1 October 2014. For 2020/21, his *taxable* income excluding the two policy gains is £36,300. He is not a Scottish taxpayer.

Tax on policy gains without top slicing relief

1,200 @ 20% (basic rate)	240.00
20,800 @ 40%	8,320.00
£22,000	8,560.00
Deduct Basic rate tax (£22,000 × 20%)	4,400.00
Tax payable on policy gains	£4,160.00

Tax on policy gains with top slicing relief

£10,000 divided by 4 years =	2,500	
£12,000 divided by 6 years =	2,000	
	£4,500	

Tax on £4,500 as top slice of income:

1,200 @ 20% (basic rate)	240.00
3,300 @ 40%	1,320.00
£4,500	1,560.00
Deduct Basic rate tax (£4,500 × 20%)	900.00
	£660.00

$$£660.00 \times \frac{2,500}{4,500} = £366.67. \quad £366.67 \times 4 = \qquad 1,466.68$$

$$£660.00 \times \frac{2,000}{4,500} = £293.33. \quad £293.33 \times 6 = \qquad 1,760.00$$

Tax payable on policy gains	£3,226.68

Notes

(a) The basic rate limit for 2020/21 is £37,500, so the amount of policy gains falling within the basic rate band in this case is £1,200 (£37,500 − £36,300).

(b) See IPTM3840 and *Simon's Taxes* E1.455B.

14.2 PARTIAL SURRENDERS OF LIFE POLICIES ETC.

[*ITTOIA 2005, s 507*]

Sheridan took out a policy on 4 February 2013 for a single premium of £15,000. The contract permits periodical withdrawals.

(i) Sheridan draws £750 p.a. on 4 February in each subsequent year.

There is no taxable gain because at the end of each insurance year the total value of rights surrendered (VRS) does not exceed the total allowable payments (TAP).

14.2 IT Life Assurance Policies

	£	
At 3.2.17 withdrawals have been	2,250	(VRS)
Deduct 4 × $^1/_{20}$ of the sums paid in	(3,000)	(TAP)
	No gain	

(ii) On 20.7.17 Sheridan withdraws an additional £3,500.

	£	
At 3.2.18 withdrawals have been	6,500	(VRS)
Deduct 5 × $^1/_{20}$ of the sums paid in	(3,750)	(TAP)
Chargeable 2017/18	£2,750	

(iii) Sheridan makes no annual withdrawal on 4.2.18 but on 4.2.19 makes a withdrawal of £1,000.

In the year 2019/20 the position is

	£	£	
At 3.2.20 withdrawals have been		7,500	
Deduct Withdrawals at last charge		(6,500)	
		1,000	(VRS)
Deduct 7 × $^1/_{20}$ of the sums paid in	5,250		
less amount deducted at last charge	(3,750)		
		1,500	(TAP)
		No gain	

(iv) Sheridan surrenders the policy on 1.7.20 for £13,250, having made a further £1,000 withdrawal on 4.2.20.

In the year 2020/21, the position is

	£	£
Proceeds on surrender		13,250
Previous withdrawals		8,500
		21,750
Deduct Premium paid	15,000	
Gains previously charged	2,750	
		(17,750)
Chargeable 2020/21		£4,000

Notes

(a) VRS is the total of all surrenders, withdrawals etc. for each insurance year since commencement *less* the total of such values which have been brought into account in earlier chargeable events.

Life Assurance Policies   IT 14.3

(b) TAP is the total of annual fractions of one-twentieth (with a maximum of 20 twentieths) of the premiums, lump sums etc. paid for each insurance year since commencement *less* the total of such fractions which have been brought into account in earlier chargeable events.

(c) The chargeable event gain is generally treated as arising at the end of the insurance year and is thus chargeable to income for the tax year in which the insurance year ends. [*ITTOIA 2005, s 509*]. See IPTM3580 and *Simon's Taxes* E1.453D, E1.453F.

(d) An insurance year is a year ending twelve months from the commencement of the policy or from an anniversary thereof. [*ITTOIA 2005, s 499*]. See IPTM3505 and *Simon's Taxes* E1.453.

(e) The gain on final surrender of the policy is calculated under *ITTOIA 2005, s 491*. See *Simon's Taxes* E1.452.

(f) The gains in (ii) and (iv) above are subject to any available top slicing relief (see **14.1** above).

14.3 ADJUSTMENTS FOR PERIODS OF NON-UK RESIDENCE

[*ITTOIA 2005, s 528*]

Churchill took out a life policy on 1 May 2012 paying premiums of £100 per month. On 1 May 2015 he exercised a right under the policy to vary the policy so as to increase the benefits payable under it; the premiums then increase to £120 per month. On 31 March 2021 Churchill assigns all the rights under the policy to an unconnected third party for £16,960. Churchill moves to Germany to live and work for 655 days during 2016/17 and 2017/18, but he returns to UK to live and work thereafter. Under the statutory residence test he is treated as non-UK resident throughout 2016/17. 2017/18 is treated as a split year and he is non-UK resident for the first 290 days of that year. Subject to the chargeable event gain, his income for 2020/21 amounts to £49,900, consisting entirely of employment income. Churchill is not a Scottish taxpayer.

The chargeable event gain is calculated as follows

	£	£
Total benefit value (assignment proceeds)		16,960
Deduct: Total allowable deductions (premiums paid):		
1.5.12–30.4.15 (£100 x 36 months)	3,600	
1.5.15–31.3.21 (£120 x 71 months)	8,520	12,120
Chargeable event gain		4,840
Less: Reduction for periods of non-UK residence (note (b)):		
$£4,840 \times \dfrac{655}{3,255 (1.5.12 - 31.3.21)}$		(974)
Taxable gain		£3,866

14.3 IT   Life Assurance Policies

Top slicing relief is calculated as follows

	Normal basis	Top slicing relief claim
	£	£
Taxable gain (note (c))	3,866	552
Earnings	49,900	49,900
	53,766	50,452
Deduct Personal allowance	(12,500)	(12,500)
	£41,266	£37,952

	Normal basis	Top slicing relief claim
	£	£
Tax applicable to policy gain		
Higher rate		
£3,766 at 40%	1,506.40	—
£452 at 40%	—	180.80
	1,506.40	180.80
Deduct		
Basic rate		
£3,766 at 20%	753.20	—
£452 at 20%	—	90.40
		£90.40
Appropriate multiple 7 × £90.40 (note (c))		£632.80
Tax chargeable lower of	£753.20 and	£632.80
Top slicing relief (£753.2 − 632.80) =	£120.40	

Notes

(a) As regards policies issued in respect of insurances made on or after 6 April 2013, a chargeable event gain is reduced to take account of any periods during which the policyholder was not resident in the UK. The reduction also applies in relation to an insurance made before 6 April 2013 if, on or after that date, the policy is varied so as to increase the benefits (an exercise of rights conferred by the policy being treated for this purpose as a variation), is assigned (in whole or in part) or becomes held as security for a debt.

(b) In the reduction fraction, the numerator is the number of days in the 'material interest period' when the individual was not UK resident. The denominator is the total number of days in the material interest period. The *'material interest period'* is

Life Assurance Policies   IT 14.3

broadly the policy period, i.e. the period for which the policy has run before the chargeable event occurs; see *ITTOIA 2005, s 528(5)(10)* for the full definition. See IPTM3732 and *Simon's Taxes* E1.452D.

(c) In computing top slicing relief, the total policy gain is normally divided by the number of *complete* years the policy has run (eight years in this example) and the resulting tax multiplied by the same factor — see **14.1(A)** above. However, where a reduction has been made for periods of non-UK residence, that number is itself reduced by the result of dividing the number of days of non-UK residence by 365 and then rounding down the result to the nearest whole number (one year in this example). Therefore, a factor of 7 (8 minus 1) applies in this example. [*ITTOIA 2005, s 536(6)–(8)*]. See IPTM3736, IPTM3840 and *Simon's Taxes* E1.455B.

(d) The calculation of tax payable would then proceed as in **14.1(A)** above with the top slicing relief given as a tax reduction.

15 Losses

Cross-references. See also **18.2–18.4** PARTNERSHIPS, and see **26.2** SELF-ASSESSMENT for the method of giving effect under self-assessment to the carry-back of losses to earlier years of assessment.

15.1 SET-OFF OF TRADING LOSSES AGAINST GENERAL INCOME

[*ITA 2007, ss 61(2), 64, 65*]

L, a single woman, commences to trade on 1 July 2016, preparing accounts to 30 June, and has the following results (as adjusted for tax purposes) for the first four years.

	Profit/(loss) £
Year ended 30 June 2017	27,000
Year ended 30 June 2018	9,000
Year ended 30 June 2019	(3,000)
Year ended 30 June 2020	(25,000)

L has other income of £19,500 for 2019/20 and £22,000 for 2020/21, having had no other income in the earlier years. The 2020/21 income includes dividend income of £3,000.

The taxable profits for the first five tax years of the business are as follows

	£
2016/17 (1.7.16–5.4.17) (£27,000 × $^9/_{12}$)	20,250*
2017/18 (y/e 30.6.17)	27,000
2018/19 (y/e 30.6.18)	9,000
2019/20 (y/e 30.6.19)	Nil
2020/21 (y/e 30.6.20)	Nil
* Overlap relief accruing – £20,250.	

L claims relief under *ITA 2007, s 64(2)(a)* (set-off against income of the same year) for the 2019/20 loss (£3,000). She also claims relief under *ITA 2007, s 64(2)(b)* (set-off against income of the preceding year) for the 2020/21 loss (£25,000), with a further claim being made under *ITA 2007, s 64(2)(a)* for the balance of that loss.

The tax position for 2019/20 and 2020/21 is as follows

2019/20	£
Total income before loss relief	19,500
Deduct Claim under *ITA 2007, s 64(2)(a) note (b)*	(3,000)
	16,500
Deduct Claim under *ITA 2007, s 64(2)(b)*	(16,500)
Net income	Nil

15.1 IT Losses

2020/21

Total income before loss relief	22,000
Deduct Claim under *ITA 2007, s 64(2)(a)*	(8,500)
Net income	13,500
Deduct Personal allowance	(12,500)
Taxable income	£1,000
Tax payable £1,000 @ 0% (dividend nil rate) (note (d))	—

Loss utilisation

	£
2019/20	
Loss available under *ITA 2007, s 64(2)(a)*	3,000
Deduct Utilised in 2019/20	(3,000)
Loss available under *ITA 2007, s 64(2)(b)*	25,000
Deduct Utilised in 2019/20	(16,500)
Loss available for relief in 2020/21 under *ITA 2007, s 64(2)(a)*	£8,500
2020/21	
Balance of loss available under *ITA 2007, s 64(2)(a)*	8,500
Deduct Utilised in 2020/21	8,500

Notes

(a) Under *ITA 2007, s 64*, relief is available for the tax year in which the loss arises (*section 64(2)(a)*) or the immediately preceding year (*section 64(2)(b)*). See BIM85015 and *Simon's Taxes* B8.202.

(b) Where losses of two different years are set against the income of one tax year, then, regardless of the order of claims, relief for the current year's loss is given in priority to that for the following year's loss. [*ITA 2007, s 65(2)–(4)*]. This is beneficial to the taxpayer in this example as it leaves £8,500 of the 2020/21 loss to be relieved in that year. See *Simon's Taxes* B8.202.

(c) By making the claim under *ITA 2007, s 64(2)(b)* (set-off against income of the preceding year), L has avoided a tax liability for 2019/20 but has also wasted her personal allowance. This claim might not have been made in practice.

(d) Both the personal allowance and loss relief can be deducted in such way as will result in the greatest reduction in the taxpayer's liability to income tax (see **1.4 ALLOWANCES AND TAX RATES**). It is assumed that for 2020/21 L will deduct these firstly from income other than dividend income. This leaves dividend income in charge which will attract the dividend allowance.

(e) See **15.3** below for losses in the opening years of a business.

15.2 SET-OFF OF TRADING LOSSES ETC. AGAINST CAPITAL GAINS

[*ITA 2007, s 71; TCGA 1992, ss 261B, 261C*]

M has carried on a trade for some years, preparing accounts to 30 June each year. For the year ended 30 June 2020 he makes a trading loss of £17,000. Taxable profit for 2019/20 is £5,000 and other income for 2019/20 and 2020/21 amounts to £2,000. He makes a capital gain of £15,900 and a capital loss of £1,000 for 2020/21 and has capital losses brought forward of £11,000. M makes claims for loss relief, against income of 2019/20 and income and gains of 2020/21, under *ITA 2007, s 64(2)(b), s 64(2)(a)* and *TCGA 1992, s 261B*.

Calculation of 'relevant amount'

	£
Trading loss — year ended 30.6.20	17,000
Relieved against other income for 2020/21	(2,000)
Relieved against income for 2019/20	(7,000)
Relevant amount	£8,000

Calculation of 'maximum amount'

	£
Gains for 2020/21	15,900
Losses for 2020/21	(1,000)
Unrelieved losses brought forward	(11,000)
Maximum amount	£3,900

Relief under *TCGA 1992, s 261B*

	£	£
Gains for the year		15,900
Losses for the year	1,000	
Relief under *TCGA 1992, s 261B*	3,900	
		(4,900)
Gain (covered by annual exempt amount)		£11,000
Capital losses brought forward and carried forward		£11,000

Loss memorandum

	£
Trading loss	17,000
Claimed under *ITA 2007, s 64(2)(a)*	(2,000)
Claimed under *ITA 2007, s 64(2)(b)*	(7,000)
Claimed under *TCGA 1992, s 261B*	(3,900)
Unutilised loss	£4,100

15.2 IT Losses

Notes

(a) Where relief is available under *ITA 2007, s 64* (set-off against general income) for a tax year and either a claim is made under that *section* or the person's total income for the year is nil, a claim may also be made to treat an amount of trading loss (determined as above) as an allowable capital loss for the year.

(b) The amount to be set against gains is restricted to so much of the 'relevant amount' as does not exceed the 'maximum amount'. The *'relevant amount'* is so much of the loss that cannot be set against income for the year and has not been otherwise relieved. The *'maximum amount'* is the amount chargeable to capital gains tax for the year, ignoring the annual exemption and the effect of *TCGA 1992, s 261B* itself. See CG15801 and *Simon's Taxes* B8.202.

(c) Capital losses brought forward are deducted in ascertaining the 'maximum amount', and thus the relief due under *TCGA 1992, s 261B*, but the relief itself is treated as an allowable loss for the year of claim and thus given in priority to capital losses brought forward.

(d) In this example, £1,300 of the capital gains tax annual exempt amount of £12,300 is wasted, but the brought forward capital losses are preserved for carry-forward against gains of future years. If M had *not* made the claim under *TCGA 1992, s 261B*, his net gains for the year of £14,900 would have been reduced to the annual exempt amount by deducting £2,600 of the losses brought forward. Only £8,400 of capital losses would remain available for carry-forward against future gains and a further £3,900 of trading losses would have been available for carry-forward against future trading profits. So the effect of the claim is to preserve capital losses at the expense of trading losses.

15.3 LOSSES IN EARLY YEARS OF A BUSINESS

(A) **Losses carried back three years**

[*ITA 2007, ss 72–74*]

F, a single person, commences to trade on 1 December 2017, preparing accounts to 30 November. The first four years of trading produce losses of £12,000, £9,000, £2,000 and £1,000 respectively, these figures being as adjusted for tax purposes. For each of the four tax years 2014/15 to 2017/18, F had other income of £8,000.

The losses for tax purposes are as follows

			£	£
2017/18	(1.12.17–5.4.18) (£12,000 × $^4/_{12}$)			4,000
2018/19	(y/e 30.11.18)		12,000	
	Less already allocated to 2017/18		(4,000)	8,000
2019/20	(y/e 30.11.19)			9,000
2020/21	(y/e 30.11.20)			2,000
2021/22	(y/e 30.11.21)	note (b)		1,000

Losses IT 15.3

Loss relief under *ITA 2007*, s 72 is available as follows

	Losses available			
	2017/18	2018/19	2019/20	2020/21
	£	£	£	£
Losses available	4,000	8,000	9,000	2,000
Set against total income				
2014/15	4,000	—	—	—
2015/16	—	8,000	—	—
2016/17	—	—	8,000	—
2017/18	—	—	1,000	2,000
	£4,000	£8,000	£9,000	£2,000

Revised total income is thus £4,000 for 2014/15, nil for 2015/16 and 2016/17 and £5,000 for 2017/18.

Notes

(a) Losses are computed by reference to the same basis periods as profits. Where any part of a loss would otherwise fall to be included in the computations for two successive tax years (as is the case for 2017/18 and 2018/19 in this example), that part is excluded from the computation for the second of those years. [*ITA 2007, s 61(2)*]. See *Simon's Taxes* B8.201.

(b) The loss for the year ended 30 November 2021 in this example is not available for relief under *ITA 2007*, s 72 as it does not fall into the first four *tax years* of the business (even though it is incurred in the first four years of trading). See BIM85045 and *Simons Taxes* B8.206. It is of course available for relief under *ITA 2007*, s 64 (depending on the level of other income for 2020/21 and 2021/22) or for carry-forward under *ITA 2007*, s 83. See BIM85060 and *Simon's Taxes* E5.625.

(B) **Computation of losses in early years**

Q commenced trading on 1 February 2020 and prepared accounts to 31 December. He made a trading loss of £20,900 in the eleven months to 31 December 2020 and profits of £18,000 and £16,000 in the years to 31 December 2021 and 2022 respectively. He has substantial other income for 2019/20 and 2020/19 and makes claims under *ITA 2007*, s 64 for both years.

15.3 IT Losses

Taxable profits/(allowable losses) are as follows

		£	£
2019/20	(1.2.20–5.4.20) (£20,900) × $^2/_{11}$		(3,800)
2020/21	(1.2.20–31.1.21):		
	1.2.20–31.12.20	(20,900)	
	Less already allocated to 2019/20	3,800	
		(17,100)	
	1.1.21–31.1.21 £18,000 × $^1/_{12}$	1,500	
			(15,600)
2021/22	(y/e 31.12.21)		18,000
	(Overlap relief accruing — £1,500)		
2022/23	(y/e 31.12.22)		16,000

Notes

(a) Losses are computed by reference to the same basis periods as profits. Where any part of a loss would otherwise fall to be included in the computations for two successive tax years (as is the case for 2019/20 and 2020/21 in this example), that part is excluded from the computation for the second of those years. [*ITA 2007, s 61(2)*]. See *Simon's Taxes* B8.201.

(b) Losses available for relief for 2019/20 and 2020/21 are £3,800 and £15,600 respectively. If both years' losses are carried forward under *ITA 2007, s 83* instead of being set against other income (under either *ITA 2007, s 64* or *s 72*), the aggregate loss of £19,400 will extinguish the 2021/22 profit and reduce the 2022/23 profit by £1,400. Note that although the actual loss was £20,900, there is no further amount available for carry-forward: the difference of £1,500 has been used in aggregation in 2020/21.

(c) The net profit for the first three accounting periods is £13,100 (£18,000 + £16,000 – £20,900). The net taxable profit for the first four tax years is £14,600 (£18,000 + £16,000 – £3,800 – £15,600). The difference of £1,500 represents the overlap relief accrued, which will be given on cessation or on a change of accounting date resulting in a basis period of more than one year. Note that the overlap profit of £1,500 is by reference to an overlap period of *three* months, i.e. 1.2.20 to 5.4.20 (two months — overlap profit nil) and 1.1.21 to 31.1.21 (one month — overlap profit £1,500).

15.4 TERMINAL LOSS RELIEF

[*ITA 2007, ss 63, 89–91*]

B, a trader with a 30 September year end, ceases to trade on 30 June 2020. Tax-adjusted results for his last two periods of account are as follows

Losses IT 15.4

	Trading profit/(loss) £
Year ended 30 September 2019	28,000
Nine months to 30 June 2020	(9,000)

At cessation, there is unused overlap relief of £2,000.

The terminal loss relief available is as follows

	£	£
2020/21 (6.4.20 – 30.6.20)		
£9,000 × ³/₉		3,000
plus unused overlap relief		2,000
Terminal loss		5,000
2019/20 (1.7.19 – 5.4.20)		
1.10.19 – 5.4.20 £9,000 × ⁶/₉	6,000	
1.7.19 – 30.9.19 (£28,000) × ³/₁₂	(7,000)	
Net profit	(1,000)	
Terminal loss		Nil
Terminal loss relief		£5,000

Notes

(a) In determining the terminal loss arising in a part of the final twelve months (a terminal loss period) that falls into any one tax year, a profit made in that period must be netted off against a loss in that period. In this example, no loss has been incurred in the terminal loss period that falls within 2019/20. However, two different tax years are looked at separately, so that the 'net profit' of £1,000 arising in the terminal loss period falling within 2019/20 does not have to be netted off against the 2020/21 loss and is instead disregarded. See BIM85055 and *Simon's Taxes* B8.208, E5.624.

(b) Available overlap relief is given as a deduction in computing the profit or loss of the final *tax year* and is thus included in a terminal loss in full. It does not fall to be apportioned between tax years in the same way as a loss sustained for a *period of account*.

(c) The losses which do not form part of the terminal loss claim may be relieved under *ITA 2007, s 64*, and in practice, where other income is sufficient, the whole of the losses would in many cases be claimed under *section 64*.

15.5 IT Losses

15.5 SHARE LOSS RELIEF

[ITA 2007, ss 131–151; FA 2020, s 38]

X subscribed for 3,500 £1 ordinary shares at par in ABC Ltd in May 2011. She purchased a further 1,750 such shares on the stock market in September 2016, by which time their market price had risen to £2.50 per share. By 2020 the company's stock market value had slumped. X feels that it may recover but nonetheless sells 2,625 shares on the market in October 2020 at 40p per share (total proceeds £1,050) and makes a claim for share loss relief. It is accepted that the shares she subscribed for in May 2011 are qualifying shares for share loss relief purposes. At no time have any shares in ABC Ltd qualified for any tax relief under the enterprise investment scheme or seed enterprise investment scheme.

The capital gains tax (CGT) pool is as follows:

		Shares	Cost £
May 2011	Subscription	3,500	3,500
Sept 2016	Purchase	1,750	4,375
		5,250	7,875
Oct 2020	Sale	(2,625)	(3,938)
C/fwd		2,625	£3,937

Allowable loss for CGT purposes for 2020/21 (proceeds £1,050 – cost £3,938) = £2,888.

For share loss relief purposes, 1,750 of the shares sold are matched on a last in/first out (LIFO) basis with the 1,750 shares purchased in September 2016. See note (b). These are not qualifying shares as they were not subscribed for.

875 of the shares sold are matched with part of the 3,500 qualifying shares subscribed for in May 2011.

So one-third (875/2,625) of the shares sold relate to qualifying shares. Therefore, the proportion of the allowable loss attributable to the qualifying shares sold is one-third of £2,888 = £963.

However, the actual cost of the qualifying shares sold is only £875 (£3,500 × 875/3,500). The loss qualifying for share loss relief is restricted to this amount. See note (c).

Share loss relief available to X for 2020/21 and/or 2019/20 = £875.

Allowable loss remaining available for CGT purposes = £2,013 (£2,888 – £875).

Notes

(a) Share loss relief is the term used to describe the relief contained in *ITA 2007, ss 131–151* which enables an individual to claim relief against income for what would otherwise be a capital loss on the disposal of qualifying shares. Qualifying shares are shares subscribed for in a qualifying trading company or shares on which income tax relief under the Enterprise Investment Scheme has been claimed. See VCM70000 and *Simon's Taxes* Division E3.701A.

(b) This example illustrates a disposal out of a mixed holding, i.e. a holding of shares which includes both qualifying shares and other shares. The matching rules are not a replacement for CGT identification rules in computing the amount of the allowable loss. The purpose of the matching rules is to determine the extent, if any, to which a disposal of shares forming part of a mixed holding is of qualifying shares. See *Simon's Taxes* E3.708.

(c) The amount of share loss relief is limited to the sums that would have been allowable as deductions in computing the loss if the qualifying shares had not formed part of the CGT pool. See *Simon's Taxes* E3.708A.

(d) Under share loss relief, losses can be set against current year's income (*ITA 2007, s 132(1)(a)*) or preceding year's income (*ITA 2007, s 132(1)(b)*). See VCM74020 and *Simon's Taxes* E3.701A

(e) X would consider making the share loss relief claim if she has sufficient taxable income in 2020/21 and/or 2019/20 to set off the loss without wasting allowances and if her net chargeable gains for 2020/21 are within the annual exempt amount such that capital losses for the year are wasted. Even if chargeable gains were in excess of the annual exempt amount it might still be worth making the share loss relief claim so as to obtain relief at income tax rates in preference to CGT rates.

(f) If it turned out that any of the 2020/21 loss could not be relieved under *ITA 2007, s 132* due to an insufficiency of income, that part of the loss would revert to being a capital loss for CGT purposes.

16 Married Persons and Civil Partners

16.1 MAINTENANCE PAYMENTS

[*ITA 2007, ss 453–456, Sch 2 para 101*]

Mr Green, who was born on 7 October 1933, separated from his wife in June 2005 and, under a Court Order dated 15 July 2006, pays maintenance of £300 per month to his ex-wife and £100 per month to his daughter, payments being due on the first of each calendar month commencing 1 August 2006. Mr Green has pension income of £18,470 and dividends of £2,200 for 2020/21. He is not a Scottish taxpayer. He re-marries on 6 October 2020.

	Dividends	Non-Savings income	Total
	£	£	£
2020/21			
Mr Green			
Earned income		18,470	18,470
Dividends	2,200		2,200
Total and net income	2,200	18,470	20,670
Deduct Personal allowance		(12,500)	(12,500)
Taxable income	£2,200	£5,970	£8,170

Tax payable:				
5,970	@ 20% (basic rate)		1,194.00	1,194.00
2,000	@ 0% (dividend nil rate)	—		—
200	@ 7.5% (dividend ordinary rate)	15.00		15.00
		15.00	1,194.00	1,209.00
Deduct	Maintenance relief — wife:			
	£3,600 paid, but restricted to £3,510 @ 10%			(351.00)
				858.00
Deduct	Married couple's allowance			
	£9,075 × ⁶/₁₂ = £4,538 @ 10%			(453.80)
Tax liability (subject to PAYE deductions)				£404.20

Notes

(a) Relief for qualifying maintenance payments is restricted to cases where at least one of the parties was aged 65 or over on 5 April 2000. The relief is restricted to an amount equal to a percentage of the basic married couple's allowance for the year.

16.1 IT   Married Persons and Civil Partners

No relief is due for other maintenance payments. Relief is given by way of income tax reduction and is restricted to 10%. The recipient of the maintenance payment must not have remarried. See *Simon's Taxes* E1.102.

(b) Maintenance payments are exempt from tax in the hands of the recipient.

(c) Tax relief for maintenance payments does not affect entitlement to the married couple's allowance either in the year of re-marriage or in later years. The allowance for the year of re-marriage is restricted in the normal way under *ITA 2007, s 54*. See *Simon's Taxes* E1.920.

17 Non-Residents

17.1 LIMIT ON LIABILITY TO INCOME TAX

[*ITA 2007, ss 56, 460, 810–828, Sch 2 paras 14–17; ITTOIA 2005, s 399*)]

Jean-Claude is resident and domiciled in France. He owns a property in the UK from which he receives taxable rental income of £7,000 per annum. He also has a UK bank account on which the amount of interest is £21,000 per annum and he receives dividends from a UK company of £8,500.

The UK bank interest is paid gross and can therefore be ignored when calculating the maximum UK liability. He will be treated as having paid tax of £637.50 (£8,500 at 7.5%) in respect of the dividends.

His UK income tax liability in 2020/21 will be (under *ITA 2007, s 811*):

Amount A—Tax treated as paid in respect of dividends: £637.50

Plus

Amount B—Tax in respect of other income (ignoring personal allowances)

= Rental income (7,000 @ 20%): £1,400

Maximum tax liability: £2,037.50

There will be no liability in respect of the bank interest. However, Jean-Claude will not be able to deduct the UK personal allowance when calculating the tax due in respect of the rental income.

Under the 'normal' rules, Jean-Claude's tax liability for 2020/21 would be:

	£
UK property income	7,000
UK savings income (bank interest)	21,000
Dividend income from UK companies	8,500
Total UK income	36,500
Deduct: personal allowance	(12,500)
Taxable UK income	24,000

	£
UK income tax liability:	
Non-savings income (£0 @ 20%)	Nil
Savings income (£5,000 @ 0%)	Nil
Savings income (£1,000 @ 0%)	Nil
Savings income (£9,500 @ 20%)	1,900
Dividend income (£2,000 @ 0%)	Nil
Dividend income (6,500 @ 7.5%)	487.50
Total tax liability	2,387.50

17.1 IT   Non-Residents

It is therefore not beneficial for Jean-Claude to claim the personal allowance. *ITA 2007, s 811* will therefore limit Jean-Claude's UK tax liability to £2,037.50. This will be reduced by the £637.50 of tax deemed to have been paid in respect of the dividends, resulting in tax payable of £1,400.

Notes

(a) 'Disregarded income' includes interest and other annual payments, dividends from UK resident companies, purchased life annuity payments, profits from deeply discounted securities, distributions from unit trusts, some social security benefits (including state pensions), retirement annuities, certain UK-sourced employment-related annuities and any other income so designated by the Treasury, but generally excluding income from non-UK sources. [*ITA 2007, s 813*]. See INTM269180 and *Simon's Taxes* E6.127 and E6.129A.

(b) Where UK dividends are paid to non-residents, they are deemed to have suffered income tax at the dividend ordinary rate. This tax that is treated as paid does not affect the amount of dividend income taxed in the UK, ie there is no grossing-up, but it can be deducted from the UK income tax liability. It can only reduce the UK tax liability; it cannot generate a repayment. [*ITTOIA 2005, s 399*].

17.2 NON-RESIDENT ENTERTAINERS AND SPORTSMEN

[*ITA 2007, ss 965–970; ITTOIA 2005, ss 13, 14*]

G, a professional golfer who is not resident in the UK, visits the UK in July 2020 to play in a tournament from which he earns £80,000 in appearance and prize money. He directs that the money be paid to a non-resident company which he controls. During his visit, he receives £8,000 from a UK television company for a series of interviews and £15,000 from a national newspaper for a number of exclusive articles. He arranges for 22.5% of the latter sum to be paid direct to his agent, also non-resident and who pays tax on his income at a rate not exceeding 25%, who arranged the deal. G incurs allowable expenses of £14,000 in connection with the trip. He has no other taxable income in the UK during 2020/21. He does not qualify for UK personal reliefs.

G's UK tax position for 2020/21 is as follows

		Taxable income	Tax withheld at source
		£	£
Prize and appearance money	note (b)	80,000	16,000
Fee from television company	note (c)	8,000	—
Fee for newspaper articles	note (d)	15,000	3,000
		103,000	19,000
Deduct Expenses		(14,000)	
		£89,000	

Non-Residents IT 17.2

Tax payable	£	
37,500 at 20%	7,500	
51,500 at 40%	20,600	
£89,000		28,100
Tax payable		£9,100

Notes

(a) G is considered to have carried on a trade in the UK in respect of the payments received, or deemed to have been received, by him in connection with his UK activities. The trade is distinct from any other trade carried on by him. [*ITTOIA 2005, s 13*]. See BIM50600 and *Simon's Taxes* E5.804, E5.805.

(b) A payment to a company under the entertainer's (or sportsman's) control (defined in accordance with *CTA 2010, ss 450, 451*) is treated as a payment to him and withholding tax at the basic rate must be deducted at source. [*ITTOIA 2005, s 14; SI 1987 No 530, Reg 7*]. See CTM60210 and *Simon's Taxes* I6.102, B3.340CA.

(c) No withholding tax falls to be deducted from the television company fee as it does not exceed the de minimis limit. [*SI 1987 No 530, Reg 4(3)*]. The limit is equal to the amount of the basic personal allowance for the year in question (£12,500 for 2020/21). [*SI 2012 No 1359*].

(d) Although a percentage of the fee for newspaper articles was paid not to G but to his agent, it falls to be treated as G's income and is subject to withholding tax by virtue of his agent's being non-resident in the UK and liable to tax at a rate not exceeding 25% in his country of residence. [*SI 1987 No 530, Reg 7(2)(b)*].

(e) It is assumed in the above example that G would not have been able to agree with HMRC a reduced rate of withholding tax. He could have attempted to do so by making written application, under *SI 1987 No 530, Reg 5*, not later than 30 days before any payment fell to be made. However, the total reduced tax payment must represent, as nearly as can be, the actual liability of the performer.

18 Partnerships

18.1 BASIS OF ASSESSMENT

[*ITTOIA 2005, ss 846–856, 863*].

P and Q commenced trading in partnership on 1 July 2015, making up accounts to 30 June. Under the partnership agreement P is to receive a salary of £10,000 per year and Q a salary of £5,000. Profits are to be shared in the ratio 3:2. On 1 July 2018 R becomes a partner, and profits for the year to 30 June 2019 are shared in the ratio 2:2:1 (P and Q continuing to receive their salaries). On 30 June 2019 P leaves the partnership and profits are thereafter shared between Q and R in the ratio 2:1 (Q continuing to receive his salary).

Results for relevant years up to 30 June 2020 are as follows

Year ended	Partners' salaries			Adjusted Profit
	P	Q	R	
	£	£	£	£
30.6.16	10,000	5,000	—	30,000
30.6.17	10,000	5,000	—	35,000
30.6.18	10,000	5,000	—	38,000
30.6.19	10,000	5,000	—	51,000
30.6.20	—	5,000	—	47,000

The adjusted profit figures above are after adding back partners' salaries, which are not deductible for tax purposes.

The tax position for the years 2015/16 to 2020/21 is as follows

	P	Q	R
	£	£	£
2015/16			
1.7.15–5.4.16			
Profits £(30,000 − 15,000) × $^9/_{12}$	6,750	4,500	
Salaries × $^9/_{12}$	7,500	3,750	
Trading income	£14,250	£8,250	

18.1 IT   Partnerships

2016/17
Y/e 30.6.16

Profits £(30,000 − 15,000)	9,000	6,000
Salaries	10,000	5,000
Trading income	£19,000*	£11,000*
*Overlap relief accrued: (1.7.15–5.4.16)	£14,250	£8,250

2017/18
Y/e 30.6.17

Profits £(35,000 − 15,000)	12,000	8,000
Salaries	10,000	5,000
Trading income	£22,000	£13,000

2018/19
Y/e 30.6.18

Profits £(38,000 − 15,000)	13,800	9,200	
Salaries	10,000	5,000	
1.7.18–5.4.19			
Profits £(51,000 − 15,000) × ($1/5 \times 9/12$)			5,400
Trading income	£23,800	£14,200	£5,400

2019/20
Y/e 30.6.19

Profits £(51,000 − 15,000)	14,400	14,400	7,200
Salaries	10,000	5,000	—
	24,400	19,400	7,200
Less overlap relief (see 2016/17)	(14,250)		
Trading income	£10,150	£19,400	£7,200*
*Overlap relief accrued: (1.7.18–5.4.19)			£5,400

2020/21
Y/e 30.6.20

Profits £(47,000 − 5,000)	28,000	14,000
Salaries	5,000	—
Trading income	£33,000	£14,000

Partnerships IT 18.2

Notes

(a) On a partnership change (e.g. the admission or retirement of a partner), the partnership is automatically regarded as continuing, providing there is at least one continuing partner.

(b) Profits are allocated between partners for tax purposes in accordance with the profit-sharing ratios in force during a period of account. Each partner is taxed on his own share, the partnership not being treated as a separate entity. The normal rules used to determine the basis periods for the early years and closing years of a business apply to individuals joining or leaving a partnership. [*ITTOIA 2005, ss 850(1), 852, 853*]. See BIM82280, PM31500 and *Simon's Taxes* B7.401, B8.201, B8.201.

18.2 UNUSUAL ALLOCATIONS OF PROFITS/LOSSES BETWEEN PARTNERS

[*ITTOIA 2005, s 850(2)–(5)*].

J, K and L are full equity partners, sharing profits and losses equally and preparing accounts to 30 April. The partnership agreement also makes provision for partners' salaries, and for the year to 30 April 2020, J and K are entitled to salaries of £12,000 and £5,000 respectively. However, the firm has an unexpectedly bad year and makes a loss of £13,000, this being the tax-adjusted figure after adding back non-deductible partners' salaries.

The initial allocation between partners is as follows

	Total	J	K	L
	£	£	£	£
Partnership loss	(13,000)			
Allocate salaries	17,000	12,000	5,000	—
Loss after salaries	(£30,000)	(10,000)	(10,000)	(10,000)
Allocation of loss	(£13,000)	£2,000	(£5,000)	(£10,000)

A reallocation must be made as follows

For tax purposes, a profit cannot be allocated to one partner (in this case J) if the partnership as a whole has made a tax loss. (Similarly, if the partnership had made a tax profit, no partner could have a tax loss.) J's allocation must be reduced to nil and the profit initially allocated to K and L must be proportionately reduced as follows.

$$K\text{'s loss} = £13,000 \times \frac{5,000}{5,000 + 10,000} = £\underline{4,333}$$

$$L\text{'s loss} = £13,000 \times \frac{10,000}{5,000 + 10,000} = £\underline{8,667}$$

	Total	J	K	L
Final allocation	(£13,000)	Nil	(£4,333)	(£8,667)

18.2 IT Partnerships

Note

(a) The losses allocated to K and L are losses of the basis period for 2020/21 and are therefore tax losses of that year. [*ITA 2007, s 62*]. It is up to each of K and L individually to decide what to do with his allocated loss, e.g. carry it forward, set it off against other income etc. See BIM82255 and *Simon's Taxes* E1.1004.

18.3 LIMITED PARTNERSHIPS — LOSSES

[*ITA 2007, ss 103–106, 113A, 114*]

R and S, who have been trading in partnership for several years preparing accounts to 30 June, share profits and losses equally. S is a limited partner. For the year ended 30 June 2020, the partnership made a loss of £12,000. Other relevant details are as follows

	R £	S £
Other income 2020/21	10,000	8,000
Capital and accumulated profits At 30.6.20	4,000	5,000

R and S may claim loss relief under ITA 2007, s 64 for 2020/21 as follows

	R £	S £
Other income	10,000	8,000
Share of partnership loss (restricted for S)	(6,000)	(5,000)
	£4,000	£3,000
Loss carried forward against future partnership trading profits	—	£1,000

Notes

(a) The amount of partnership loss which a limited partner may set against general income and gains is restricted to the amount of his 'contribution to the firm' (broadly his capital contribution and accumulated profits) at the end of the basis period for the tax year in which the loss is sustained.

(b) Certain amounts must be excluded from a limited partner's contribution for these purposes, where the cost of providing those amounts is or could be borne by another person.

(c) The relief a limited partner can claim (against general income and gains) for what remains of the loss after applying the above restrictions is capped at £25,000. [*ITA 2007, ss 103, 103C, 103D; ITTOIA 2005, s 863(2)*]. See *Simon's Taxes* B7.107, B7.513, B7.514.

18.4 LIMITED LIABILITY PARTNERSHIPS — LOSSES

[*ITA 2007, ss 107–109, 113A(2)–(4), 114; LLPA 2000, s 10(1)*]

Mr Wainwright becomes a member of a limited liability trading partnership on 6 April 2018. The partnership prepares accounts to 5 April each year. He introduces capital of £20,000 into the partnership on 6 April 2018, and on 1 April 2021 he makes a further capital contribution of £12,000.

His share of the partnership's trading losses are as follows

Y/e 5 April 2019	£12,000
Y/e 5 April 2020	£12,000
Y/e 5 April 2021	£6,000

Mr Wainwright claims relief under *ITA 2007, s 64* for these losses against his general income. The amounts available are as follows:

	£	£
2018/19		
Share of loss y/e 5.4.19		12,000
Capital contribution 6.4.18		20,000
Unrelieved capital contribution c/fwd		£8,000
ITA 2007, s 64 relief available		£12,000
2019/20		
Share of loss y/e 5.4.20		12,000
Unrelieved capital contribution b/fwd		8,000
Total unrelieved loss c/fwd		£4,000
ITA 2007, s 64 relief available		£8,000
2020/21		
Share of loss y/e 5.4.21	6,000	
Total unrelieved loss b/fwd	4,000	10,000
Capital contribution 1.4.21		12,000
Unrelieved capital contribution c/fwd		£2,000
ITA 2007, s 64 relief available		£10,000

Notes

(a) The amounts of partnership trading loss which a member of a limited liability partnership may set against general income and gains are restricted to the amount of his 'contribution to the LLP' (as defined) at the end of the basis period for the tax year in which the loss is sustained.

(b) Amounts relating to a trade carried on by a member of a limited liability partnership which are prevented from being given or allowed by (a) above are referred to as the member's 'total unrelieved loss'. In each subsequent tax year in which the member continues to carry on the trade and any of the total unrelieved loss remains

18.4 IT Partnerships

outstanding, the balance of the total unrelieved loss is treated for the purposes of *ITA 2007, s 64*, *ITA 2007, s 72* and *TCGA 1992, s 261B*, and for the purposes of (a) above, as having been made in that subsequent tax year. See CG15801, BIM85045, INTM165210 and *Simon's Taxes* B8.202, B8.206.

(c) 'Contribution to the LLP' falls to be restricted as in note (b) to **18.3** above.

19 Pension Provision

19.1 RELIEF FOR CONTRIBUTIONS BY INDIVIDUAL MEMBERS

[*FA 2004, ss 188–195, 195A, Sch 36 paras 39, 40; ITA 2007, s 58; FA 2014, Sch 7 paras 13, 16*]

(A) **Henry**

Henry carries on a trade in the UK in which he makes an allowable loss of £1,000 for 2018/19 (for which he claims relief against 2017/18 income), a taxable profit of £17,500 for 2019/20 and a taxable profit of £44,000 for 2020/21. His only other income consists of building society interest and UK dividends. Building society interest received amounted to £11,050 for 2018/19 and £12,000 for 2019/20 and 2020/21. UK dividends received amounted to £900 for each year. He makes net contributions to a registered pension scheme of £2,400 during the tax year 2018/19 and £4,000 during each of the tax years 2019/20 and 2020/21. He is not a Scottish taxpayer.

Henry's tax liabilities are as follows.

2018/19	Savings income £	Dividends £	Total £
Trading income			Nil
Building society interest	11,050		11,050
UK dividends		900	900
Total and net income	11,050	900	11,950
Less Personal Allowance	(11,050)	(800)	(11,850)
Taxable Income		£100	£100
Tax Liability			
100 @ 0% (dividend allowance)		—	—

Henry has made gross pension contributions of £3,000 (£2,400 × 100/80). As his gross contributions do not exceed £3,600, he is entitled to tax relief even though he has no relevant UK earnings for the year. He is not required to repay the basic rate tax of £600 withheld at source from the contributions.

19.1 IT Pension Provision

2019/20	Savings income	Dividends	Non-savings income	Total
	£	£	£	£
Trading income			17,500	17,500
Building society interest	12,000			12,000
UK dividends		900		900
Total and net income	12,000	900	17,500	30,400
Less Personal Allowance			(12,500)	(12,500)
Taxable Income	£12,000	£900	£5,000	£17,900

Tax Liability				
5,000 @ 20% (basic rate)			1,000.00	1,000.00
1,000 @ 0% (personal savings allowance)	—			—
11,000 @ 20% (basic rate on savings income)	2,200.00			2,200.00
900 @ 0% (dividend allowance)		—		—
£17,900				
	2,200.00	3,200.00	1,000.00	3,200.00

Henry has made gross pension contributions of £5,000 (£4,000 × 100/80). His relevant UK earnings are £17,500, which is more than sufficient to cover the gross contributions. He is entitled to full tax relief, which he has already obtained by deduction at source.

2020/21	Savings income	Dividends	Non-Savings income	Total
				£
Trading income			44,000	44,000
Building society interest	12,000			12,000
UK dividends		900		900
Total and net income	12,000	900	44,000	56,900
Less Personal Allowance			(12,500)	(12,500)
Taxable Income	£12,000	£900	£31,500	£44,400

Tax Liability				
31,500 @ 20% (basic rate on earnings)			6,300.00	6,300.00
500 @ 0% (personal savings allowance)	—			—
10,500 @ 20% (basic rate on savings income)	2,100.00			2,100.00
1,000 @ 40% (higher rate on savings income)	400.00			400.00
900 @ 0% (dividend allowance)		—		—
£44,400				
	£2,500.00	—	£6,300.00	£8,800.00

Henry has made gross pension contributions of £5,000 (£4,000 × 100/80). His relevant UK earnings are £44,000, which is more than sufficient to cover the gross contributions. He has obtained basic rate tax relief at 20% by deduction at source. He obtains higher rate relief by extension of the basic rate band; the normal basic rate limit of £37,500 is increased by £5,000 to £42,500. Without that increase, an additional £5,000 of savings income would have fallen into the 40% rate band. (Above the normal basic rate limit, the rate at which the pension contributions save tax will depend on the mix of taxable income, i.e. the extent to which it is dividend income, savings income or other income.)

Notes

(a) A 'relevant UK individual' (see *FA 2004, s 189(1)*) is entitled to relief on contributions to a registered pension scheme up to the total amount of his 'relevant UK earnings' (see *FA 2004, s 189(2)(3)*) within the charge to income tax for the year. Provided, however, the scheme operates tax relief at source, contributions of up to £3,600 (gross) attract relief even if total relevant UK earnings are less than that amount or if there are no such earnings. See PTM044100 and *Simon's Taxes* E7.221, E7.222, E7.223.

(b) Provided the individual has sufficient relevant UK earnings to cover them there is no upper limit on the contributions that can be relieved in each year. Tax relief may, however, be effectively clawed back by the application of the lifetime allowance charge and/or the annual allowance charge.

(B) **Celia**

Celia is a self-employed professional with taxable profits of £280,000 for the year to 30 April 2020. She has bank deposit interest of £4,000 for 2020/21. She makes net contributions to a registered pension scheme of £16,000 during the tax year ending on 5 April 2021. She is not a Scottish taxpayer.

Celia's 2020/21 income tax liability is computed as follows.

	£
Professional income	280,000
Bank interest	4,000
Total and net income	284,000
Less Personal Allowance (note (b))	—
Taxable Income	£284,000
Tax Liability	
57,500 @ 20% (basic rate)	11,500.00
112,500 @ 40% (higher rate)	45,000.00
114,000 @ 45% (additional rate)	51,300.00
£284,000	
	£107,800.00

19.1 IT Pension Provision

Notes

(a) Celia has made gross pension contributions of £20,000 (£16,000 × 100/80) and has obtained basic rate relief at source. She obtains additional rate relief by extension of the basic rate band; the normal basic rate limit of £37,500 is increased by £20,000 to £57,500. The higher rate limit of £150,000 is increased by the same amount, so that the higher rate band remains at £112,500. Without these adjustments, an additional £20,000 of income would have been taxable at 45% instead of 20% (a 25% saving).

(b) No personal allowance is due as income is too far in excess of the £100,000 limit. [*ITA 2007, s 35(2)–(4)*]. See *Simon's Taxes* E1.910.

(c) No personal savings allowance is due as Celia is an additional rate taxpayer.

(d) As a high income individual, Celia may face an annual allowance charge for 2020/21. See the continuation of this example at **19.3(B)** below.

19.2 LIFETIME ALLOWANCE

[*FA 2004, ss 214–226; FA 2013, s 48, Sch 22; TPA 2014, Sch 1 paras 26, 27, 76, Sch 2 paras 19(2), 20–24; FA 2015, Sch 4 paras 4–7; F(No 2)A 2015, s 21(7)(10); FA 2016, s 19, Sch 4*]

(A) With no enhancement factor

Aisleyne starts to receive a pension from a registered pension scheme (a benefit crystallisation event) on 1 November 2006. The amount of benefit crystallised is £600,000. Aisleyne is entitled to the standard lifetime allowance of £1.5 million (for 2006/07). Thus, the crystallisation event does not give rise to a lifetime allowance charge, but Aisleyne has used up two-fifths of her lifetime allowance.

Aisleyne is also a member of another registered pension scheme, from which she receives a lump sum on 1 August 2020 and starts to draw a pension; these are benefit crystallisation events. The total amount of benefit crystallised is £536,550. The standard lifetime allowance for 2020/21 is £1,073,100. Aisleyne's unused lifetime allowance is three-fifths of this, i.e. £643,860. Thus, the crystallisation event does not give rise to a lifetime allowance charge, and Aisleyne has used up 90% of her lifetime allowance (40% + 50% (0.53655/1.0731 × 100)).

(B) With an enhancement factor

(i) Shabnam notified HMRC of her intention to benefit from **primary protection** by reference to relevant pre-2006/07 accrued pension rights of £2.5 million, and HMRC duly certified that she is entitled to a lifetime allowance enhancement factor of 0.667 ((£2.5 million – 1.5 million)/£1.5 million). This means that Shabnam can have benefits of 1.667 times the standard lifetime allowance before incurring any liability to the lifetime allowance charge.

In 2020/21 Shabnam receives a lump sum from the registered scheme and starts to draw a pension; these are benefit crystallisation events. The total amount of benefit crystallised is £2.95 million. Shabnam's enhanced lifetime allowance in 2020/21 is £3 million (£1.8 million × 1.667) (see note (d)). Therefore, she will not become liable to the lifetime allowance charge.

(ii) Winston has primary protection by reference to relevant pre-2006/07 accrued pension rights of £2.25 million and has a lifetime allowance enhancement factor of 0.5 ((£2.25 million − 1.5 million)/£1.5 million). In 2011/12, he took benefits valued at £0.9 million. At this time his enhanced lifetime allowance was £2.7 million (£1.8 million × 1.5), so the benefit crystallisation did not give rise to a lifetime allowance charge.

In 2020/21 Winston takes the remainder of his benefits then worth £1.9 million. The standard lifetime allowance is then £1,073,100. Winston's enhanced lifetime allowance remains at £2.7 million (£1.8 million × 1.5) (see note (d)).

The amount of lifetime allowance used up by Winston's 2011/12 benefit crystallisation is found by multiplying the then crystalised amount of £0.9 million by:

$$\frac{\text{SLA at time of current }(2020/21)\text{ event (but see note (e))}}{\text{SLA at time of previous }(2011/12)\text{ event}}$$

So the used amount is:

$$£900{,}000 \times \frac{1.5}{1.8} = £750{,}000$$

Winston has used up £0.75 million and has £1.95 million (£2.7 million − £0.75 million) still available. As Winston's 2020/21 benefit crystallisation is worth £1.9 million, he does not become liable to the lifetime allowance charge.

Notes

(a) Any excess of crystallised benefits over the unused lifetime allowance is chargeable to income tax at 55% if paid as a lump sum or at 25% otherwise. The charge is not dependent upon any person's being resident or domiciled in the UK. Although chargeable to income tax, the chargeable amount is not treated for any tax purposes as income, which means that, for example, losses, reliefs and allowances cannot be set against it and it does not count as income for the purposes of any double tax treaty.

(b) The tax will normally be paid by the scheme administrator. It will usually be recovered by deduction from the benefits paid by the scheme to the individual. If instead it is paid out of scheme funds, the tax itself is added to the chargeable amount. See, for example, HMRC Pensions Tax Manual PTM085000.

(c) See *FA 2004, Sch 36 paras 7–11D* as regards primary protection under the transitional rules for pension rights accrued at 5 April 2006.

(d) Despite the fall in the standard lifetime allowance from £1.8 million to £1.5 million, then to £1.25 million and to £1 million and with an inflation adjustment in 2019/20 to £1,055,000 and in 2020/21 to £1,073,100, where an individual's lifetime allowance falls to be enhanced under primary protection for 2012/13 or any subsequent year, the amount of the enhancement is computed by applying the primary protection factor to a lifetime allowance of £1.8 million (as long as this remains greater than the actual lifetime allowance). [*FA 2004, s 218(5B)*]. See PTM095100 and *Simon's Taxes* E7.216, E7.218.

(e) When calculating the availability of the lifetime allowance for an individual with primary protection, where a benefit crystallisation event has occurred before 6 April 2014 and a further benefit crystallisation event occurs on or after that date, then in calculating the adjustment of the used amount, the current standard lifetime allowance (£1,073,100 for 2020/21) is replaced by £1.5 million if greater. This ensures that those with primary protection do not benefit from an increase in their

19.2 IT   Pension Provision

available lifetime allowance if the current standard lifetime allowance is less than £1.5 million when the adjustment is made. [*FA 2004, s 219(5A); FA 2013, Sch 22 para 7; FA 2014, Sch 6 para 10*]. See PTM088200 and *Simon's Taxes* E7.217.

19.3 ANNUAL ALLOWANCE

[*FA 2004, ss 227–238A; FA 2011, Sch 17 paras 29–31; FA 2013, s 49; TPA 2014, Sch 1 paras 63–68, 88–91; F(No 2)A 2015, Sch 4*]

(A) Carry-forward of annual allowance

Lily is self-employed and joins a registered pension scheme for the first time on 1 July 2016. The scheme's annual pension input period coincides with the fiscal year. Lily has fluctuating business profits and makes contributions to the scheme under deduction of basic rate tax at source as follows:

2016/17	£6,400 net (£8,000 gross)
2017/18	£40,000 net (£50,000 gross)
2018/19	£16,000 net (£20,000 gross)
2019/20	£44,000 net (£55,000 gross)
2020/21	£68,800 net (£86,000 gross)

No-one else makes contributions to Lily's pension arrangement under the scheme. Lily's total pension input amount for each year will be equal to the gross amount of her contributions. For each year, she will receive higher and additional rate tax relief, where appropriate, on the gross amount of her contributions provided she has sufficient relevant UK earnings to cover that amount, which it is assumed she does.

For 2016/17, Lily has unused annual allowance of £32,000 (£40,000 – £8,000). Note that if her total pension input had exceeded the annual allowance, there would have been no question of her bringing forward any unused annual allowance from earlier years as she was not a member of a registered pension scheme in those years.

For 2017/18, she has excess pension input amounts of £10,000 (£40,000 – £50,000). In the absence of a carry-forward facility, she would have been liable to an annual allowance charge on £10,000 at her marginal rate of tax for the year. However, £10,000 of her unused allowance for 2016/17 is brought forward to extinguish her liability. She still has £22,000 unused allowance remaining from 2016/17.

For 2018/19, she has unused annual allowance of £20,000 (£40,000 – £20,000).

For 2019/20, she has excess pension input amounts of £15,000 (£40,000 – £55,000). £15,000 of her unused allowance for 2016/17 is brought forward to extinguish her liability.

For 2020/21, Lily has excess pension input amounts of £46,000 (£40,000 – £86,000). Although £7,000 of her 2016/17 annual allowance remains unused, it cannot be carried forward more than three years. However, her unused allowance of £20,000 for 2018/19 is available in full. She is liable to an annual allowance charge on £26,000 at her marginal rate of tax for the year and has no more unused allowance to carry forward.

Pension Provision   IT 19.3

The position can be summarised as follows

	Annual allowance	Pension input amounts	Unused allowance b/fwd	Chargeable amount	Unused allowance c/fwd	Cumulative unused allowance c/fwd
	£	£	£	£	£	£
2016/17	(40,000)	8,000		Nil	32,000	32,000
2017/18	(40,000)	50,000	(10,000)	Nil		22,000
2018/19	(40,000)	20,000		Nil	20,000	42,000
2019/20	(40,000)	55,000	(15,000)	Nil		27,000
					3 year dropout	(7,000)
						20,000
2020/21	(40,000)	86,000	(20,000)	26,000		Nil

Notes

(a) A carry-forward facility was introduced by *FA 2011* whereby any unused part of the annual allowance for a tax year can be carried forward for up to three tax years. The first year for which unused allowance could be carried forward was 2008/09, but see (B) below as regards carry-forward from 2008/09, 2009/10 and/or 2010/11. Unused annual allowance is available for carry-forward only if it arises during a tax year in which the individual is a member of a registered pension scheme. If the amount of the annual allowance exceeds the total pension input amount (broadly the pension savings) for that year, the excess is unused allowance. See PTM113310 and *Simon's Taxes* E7.215.

(b) The current year's annual allowance is deemed to be used first. If this is insufficient to avoid an annual allowance charge, any unused annual allowance from the three previous years can then be used; the earliest year's unused allowance is used first and so on. The carry-forward is automatic and does not have to be claimed.

(B) **Annual allowance taper**

Celia, the additional rate taxpayer in **19.1(B)** above, has 'threshold income' of £264,000 (net income £284,000 less gross pension contributions of £20,000) for 2020/21. As her threshold income is over £200,000, she will be a high-income individual and subject to the annual allowance taper if her adjusted income is over £240,000. In fact, Celia's adjusted income is equal to net income in this case and is £284,000.

Her annual allowance of £40,000 is reduced by £22,000 (one-half of (284,000 − 240,000)) and is thus £18,000 (being above the £4,000 minimum). She has a £2,000 excess of pension input amount (£20,000) over annual allowance (£18,000) and is thus subject to an annual allowance charge for 2020/21 at her marginal tax rate (45%) on £2,000.

In practice Celia may well have some unused annual allowance brought forward (see (A) above) from 2017/18 and/or 2018/19, 2019/20 which would operate to reduce or eliminate the charge for 2020/21.

19.3 IT Pension Provision

Notes

(a) For 2020/21, if an individual is a 'high-income individual' for a tax year, the annual allowance is reduced by £1 for every £2 by which 'adjusted income' exceeds £240,000 (previously £150,000), but cannot be reduced below £4,000 (previously £10,000). The £4,000 minimum thus takes effect where adjusted income is £312,000 (previously £210,000) or more. A 'high-income individual' is one whose 'threshold income' is over £200,000 (previously £110,000) and whose 'adjusted income' is over £240,000 (previously £150,000). [*FA 2004, ss 228ZA, 228ZB; F(No 2)A 2015, Sch 4, para 10*]. See PTM057100 and *Simon's Taxes* E7.213.

(b) 'Threshold income' is broadly net income (taxable income before deducting any personal allowance) less the gross equivalent of pension contributions for the year on which basic rate tax relief has been given at source. Certain amounts which would have been included in employment income were it not for salary sacrifice arrangements must be added, and any lump sum death benefits taxable on the individual as pension income for the year are excluded.

(c) 'Adjusted income' is broadly net income after adding back any deductions made for pension contributions and any employer contributions. Lump sum death benefits are excluded as in (b) above.

(C) **Money purchase annual allowance**

Kerensky had a money purchase pension plan at 6 April 2020. He makes contributions of £16,000 net (equivalent to £20,000 gross) during 2020/21. At the beginning of the tax year he made a withdrawal. The withdrawal triggers the money purchase annual allowance test for 2020/21.

Kerensky has taxable income of £125,000 for 2020/21, including all his income withdrawals from the pension plan but excluding any annual allowance chargeable amount.

The calculation of the annual allowance charge is as follows.

Compare the 'alternative chargeable amount' with the 'default chargeable amount'. If the former exceeds the latter, Kerensky's annual allowance charge for 2020/21 will be based on the alternative chargeable amount.

Terms	Definition	Workings
Alternative annual allowance	This is the normal annual allowance of £40,000 minus £4,000 (£10,000 before 6 April 2017).	It is £36,000 for 2020/21
Alternative chargeable amount	This is the total of the amount by which 'defined benefit pension input amounts' (see *FA 2004, s 227B(3)–(5)*) exceed the 'alternative annual allowance' PLUS the amount by which money purchase input amounts (see *FA 2004, s 227C–227F*) exceed £4,000 (£10,000 before 6 April 2017).	There are no defined benefit pension input amounts. Excess of money purchase plan contributions over £4,000 (i.e. £20,000 – £4,000) = £16,000 The alternative chargeable amount is £16,000

| Default chargeable amount | This is the excess (if any) of pension input amounts over the normal annual allowance of £40,000. | Excess of contributions (£20,000) over £40,000 i.e. NIL |

So in this example, the alternative chargeable amount exceeds the default chargeable amount.

Annual allowance charge

As the alternative chargeable amount is greater than the default chargeable amount, Kerensky's annual allowance charge for 2020/21 will be based on the alternative chargeable amount.

£16,000 @ 40% = £6,400

The chargeable amount falls within Kerensky's higher rate band for the year.

Notes

(a) A reduced annual allowance applies where an individual has flexibly accessed his money purchase savings. [FA 2004, ss 227, 227ZA, 227B–227G].

(b) Only the pension input amounts arising after the trigger date are tested against the money purchase annual allowance. Any pension input amounts that do not fall to be thus tested are tested instead against the alternative annual allowance. [FA 2004, ss 227B(3)(c), 227F].

(c) Unused money purchase annual allowance cannot be carried forward to subsequent tax years. Where the alternative chargeable amount applies to an individual for a tax year (instead of the default chargeable amount), the only amount capable of carry-forward from that year is the excess (if any) of the alternative annual allowance over 'defined benefit pension input amounts'. [FA 2004, s 228A(8)].

(d) As regards an individual's option to have his annual allowance charge paid from his pension benefits by the scheme administrator, the amount of the liability is computed *for this purpose only* as if the default chargeable amount applied to him instead of the alternative chargeable amount (i.e. in a case where the alternative chargeable amount does, in fact, apply). [FA 2004, s 237B(2A)].

(e) For further examples on the operation of the money purchase annual allowance, see PTM056510, and where the trigger event occurs part way through the tax year, PTM056540.

20 Personal Service Companies etc.

[*ITEPA 2003, ss 48–61; ITTOIA 2005, ss 163, 164*]

20.1 CALCULATION OF DEEMED EMPLOYMENT PAYMENT

Harry is a systems analyst trading through his own personal service company, ABC Ltd, in which he owns 99% of the ordinary shares. During 2020/21, he is engaged at different times by two independent companies, DEF Ltd and GHJ Ltd (the client companies), in each case under a contract between the client company and ABC Ltd. It is accepted that each engagement is in the nature of employment and is within the special tax and NIC rules for personal service companies and other intermediaries. ABC Ltd is paid £40,000 by DEF Ltd and £20,000 by GHJ Ltd for the services provided by Harry.

For 2020/21, Harry draws a salary of £28,000 from ABC Ltd which is taxed under PAYE and on which employer's NICs of, say, £2,800 are due. He is also provided with a company car on which the taxable benefit is £4,000 and on which Class 1A NICs of, say, £550 are due. ABC Ltd makes pension contributions of £3,100 into a registered pension scheme on Harry's behalf and reimburses expenses of £1,500 which, if Harry had been employed directly by the client companies, would have been qualifying travelling expenses within *ITEPA 2003, ss 337–340* and which do not cover any home-to-work travel (see note (c)). ABC Ltd pays a salary of £8,000 to Harry's wife who acts as company secretary and administrator.

ABC Ltd is deemed to make a payment to Harry on 5 April 2021, chargeable to tax as employment income and computed as follows

			£	£	£
Step (1)	Total amount from relevant engagements				60,000
	Deduct 5%				(3,000)
					57,000
Step (2)	*Add* payments and other benefits received other than from ABC Ltd				—
Step (3)	*Deduct*	(a) Expenses	1,500		
		(b) Capital allowances	—		
		(c) Pension contributions	3,100	4,600	
Step (4)	*Deduct*	Salary	28,000		
		Benefits	4,000		
		Employer's Class 1 NICs	2,800		
		Employer's Class 1A NICs	550	35,350	(39,950)
					£17,050
	Deemed employment payment $£17{,}050 \times \dfrac{100}{113.8}$				14,982
	Employer's NICs due on deemed payment £14,982 @ 13.8%				2,068
	Total as above				£17,050

20.1 IT   Personal Service Companies etc.

Notes

(a) The salary paid by ABC Ltd to Harry's wife is not deductible in arriving at the deemed employment payment, except to the extent that it, and other expenses of the company, are covered by the 5% deduction at Step (1) above. (The salary may of course be deductible in computing ABC Ltd's taxable business profits.) The 5% deduction is a standard allowance intended to cover the company's running costs and is given automatically, regardless of the actual occurrence or amount of such costs. It is computed purely for the purpose of determining the deemed employment payment and is not deductible in computing ABC Ltd's taxable business profits.

(b) The deemed employment payment is generally treated in the same way as an actual payment of remuneration, so that the normal PAYE provisions apply. Subject to special rules where the intermediary is a partnership, the payment (and the related employer's NICs) is an allowable expense in computing the taxable business profits of the intermediary for the period of account in which it is deemed to be made (and for no other period). [*ITEPA 2003, s 56; ITTOIA 2005, ss 163, 164*]. See ESM8000 series and *Simon's Taxes* E4.1006A, E4.1010, E4.1011.

(c) Subject to conditions being met, relief is denied for home-to-work travel expenditure for engagements via personal service companies and other employment intermediaries. [*ITEPA 2003, s 339A*].

(d) For 2020/21 onwards, *FA 2020, Sch 1* shifts responsibility for operating the rules, and deducting any tax and NICs due, from the individual to the organisation, agency or other third party paying the individual's personal service company. Thus, private sector engagements are brought into line with public sector engagements. Where the client (i.e. the person for whom the services are performed) is qualifies as small or does not have a UK connection, the new rules do *not* apply. The individual's personal service company or other intermediary will continue to be subject to the pre-existing IR35 rules.

21 Post-Cessation Receipts and Expenditure

21.1 POST-CESSATION RECEIPTS

[*ITTOIA 2005, ss 241–257; FA 2013, Sch 4 paras 39(2), 56, Sch 5 paras 4, 6, Sch 45 paras 77, 153(2)*]

A trader retired and closed down his trade on 31 March 2020 and, in the year 2020/21, the following subsequent events occurred.

(i) He paid a former customer £100 as compensation for defective work.

(ii) In the accounts at the date of closure a specific provision was made against a debt for £722. All debts were recovered in full.

(iii) Stock in trade incorrectly taken to be valueless at the date of cessation was sold for £215.

(iv) He eventually sold a piece of machinery six months after cessation for £136. This had been valued at nil at cessation.

(v) At 31 March 2020, after obtaining maximum loss relief, there was a trading loss of £333 unrelieved.

The above will be subject to income tax for 2020/21 as follows

		£	£
Sales			215
Bad debts recovered			722
			937
Deduct	Compensation payment	100	
	Balance of losses (£333–£136, note a)	197	
			297
Taxable post-cessation receipts			£640

Notes

(a) The proceeds of sale of the plant are taken into the final capital allowances computation, i.e. for 2019/20 [*CAA 2001, s 61(2)*] and the loss carried forward of £333 has been reduced by the balancing charge to £197. See CA23240, CA23250 and *Simon's Taxes* B3.334, B3.359.

(b) An election could be made under *ITTOIA 2005, s 257* for the post-cessation receipts to be treated as having been received on the date of cessation and thus chargeable at 2019/20 rates. See also *TMA 1970, Sch 1B para 5*.. See BIM90075 and *Simon's Taxes* A4.202, B2.808.

21.2 IT Post-Cessation Receipts and Expenditure

21.2 POST-CESSATION EXPENDITURE

[*ITA 2007, ss 96–101, 125, 126; TCGA 1992, ss 261D, 261E; ITTOIA 2005, ss 248(3)(4), 250, 255(4); FA 2012, s 9*]

Simcock ceased trading in February 2020. In 2020/21, the following events occur in connection with his former trade.

(i) Simcock pays a former customer £9,250 by way of damages for defective work carried out by him in the course of the trade.

(ii) He incurs legal fees of £800 in connection with the above claim.

(iii) He incurs debt collection fees of £200 in connection with trade debts outstanding at cessation and which were taken into account as receipts in computing profits.

(iv) He writes off a trade debt of £500, giving HMRC notice of his having done so.

(v) He incurs legal fees of £175 in relation to a debt of £1,000 owing by him to a supplier which, although disputed, was taken into account as an expense in computing his trading profits.

(vi) He eventually agrees to pay £500 in full settlement of his liability in respect of the debt in (v) above, paying £250 in March 2021 and the remaining £250 in May 2021.

In 2021/22, Simcock receives £3,000 from his insurers in full settlement of their liability with regard to the expense incurred in (i) above.

For 2020/21, Simcock's total income before taking account of the above events is £9,000 and he also has capital gains of £13,400 (with £900 capital losses brought forward from 2019/20).

Simcock makes a claim under *ITA 2007, s 96* (relief for post-cessation expenditure) for 2020/21 and a simultaneous claim under *TCGA 1992, s 261D* to have any excess relief set against capital gains.

Simcock's tax position for 2020/21 is as follows

		£	£
Income			
Total income before claim under *ITA 2007, s 96*			9,000
Deduct Post-cessation expenditure			
(i)		9,250	
(ii)		800	
(iii)		200	
(iv)		500	
(v)	not allowable under these rules	—	
(vi)	*less* unpaid expenses at 5.4.21	(750)	
		10,000	
Restricted to total income		(9,000)	(9,000)
Excess relief			£1,000

Post-Cessation Receipts and Expenditure IT 21.2

Capital gains

Gains before losses brought forward and annual exemption		13,400
Deduct Post-cessation expenditure (excess as above)		(1,000)
Net gains for the year		12,400
Losses brought forward	900	
Used in 2019/20	(100)	(100)
Carried forward	£800	
Net gains (covered by annual exempt amount)		£12,300

For **2021/22**, Simcock will have taxable post-cessation receipts of £3,000 arising from the insurance recovery. He will be able to offset expenses of £175 under (v) above, which, whilst not within these rules, should qualify as a deduction against post-cessation receipts. He will also have post-cessation expenditure of £250 in respect of the further payment in 2021/22 under (vi) above, the 2020/21 post-cessation expenditure having been restricted by at least that amount (see note (b)).

Notes

(a) Under *ITA 2007, s 96* relief is available against total income for specified types of expenditure and for bad debts where the expenditure is incurred or the debt proves to be bad within seven years after the date of cessation of the trade, profession or vocation. Any excess can be claimed against chargeable gains for the year. Any remaining excess relief cannot be carried forward against total income or gains of a subsequent year but is available as a deduction against any future post-cessation receipts. See BIM90100 and *Simon's Taxes* B2.810, B2.805, B2.809.

(b) Allowable post-cessation expenditure is restricted to the extent that any expenses were taken into account in computing profits but remained unpaid at the end of the year to which the claim relates. Any subsequent payment is itself treated as a post-cessation expense to the extent that the unpaid expense previously caused post-cessation expenditure to be restricted.

22 Property Income

[ITTOIA 2005, Pt 3]

22.1 FURNISHED LETTINGS

[ITTOIA 2005, ss 263–272ZA, 273, 274, 275, 276A, 307B–307F, 311A, 334B–334E; F(No 2)A 2017, Sch 2 paras 13–15, 17, 22, 23, 64; FA 2018, s 36]

(A) **Cash basis**

Mrs C has a furnished cottage in a picturesque coastal village. She makes the cottage available for letting. Several lettings are for periods of more than 31 days, and the cottage does not qualify as 'furnished holiday accommodation' under 22.2 below. The letting does not constitute a trade. The rent charged is £800 per month from June to September inclusive and £550 per month for the rest of the year. Mrs C has no other letting income.

During 2020/21 the house was occupied from April until October, lay vacant during November, December and January and was let again for February and March. In March 2021, the tenant defaulted on two weeks' rent, which proved impossible to collect. All of the remaining rent was paid during 2020/21

Expenses paid in 2020/21 were as follows:

Business rates £680, Water rates £184, Electricity £520 (£500 received from tenants through coin operated meters), Advertising £300, Cleaning between lettings £280, House contents insurance £272, Repairs £220.

During the year Mrs C purchased for the cottage a fridge freezer for £400 and a microwave for £85. Both were like-for-like replacements for existing items. No value was received for the items replaced.

The property income computation for 2020/21 is as follows

	£	£
Rent received (4 × £800 + 4 × £550 + £275)		5,675
Business rates	680	
Water rates	184	
Electricity (520 − 500)	20	
Advertising	300	
Cleaning	280	
Insurance	272	
Repairs	220	
Replacement domestic items relief (note (d))	485	(2,441)
Taxable profit		£3,234

Notes

(a) For 2017/18 onwards, the profits of a property business for a tax year must be calculated on the cash basis unless one of the following conditions is met:

22.1 IT Property Income

- an election to disapply the cash basis is made by the person carrying on the property business;
- the business is carried on at any time in the tax year by a company, a limited liability partnership, a partnership in which one or more partners is not an individual, or the trustees of a trust;
- the cash basis receipts, i.e. the amount that would be brought into account as receipts if the cash basis applied, exceed £150,000 (proportionately reduced if the property business is carried on for only part of the tax year);
  - the property business is carried on by an individual and includes a share of 'joint property income' (i,e, income to which spouses or civil partners are treated for income tax purposes as beneficially entitled in equal shares); and
  - a share of that joint property income is included in a property business carried on by that individual's spouse or civil partner for the same tax year, the profits of which are *not* calculated on the cash basis; or
- business premises renovation allowances have been made to the property business at any time and, if profits were to be calculated in accordance with generally accepted accounting practice (GAAP), a balancing event would give rise to a balancing allowance or balancing charge for the tax year.

Where a person has a UK property business and an overseas property business, the conditions apply separately to each.

(b) In calculating profits of a property business on the cash basis, receipts are brought into account at the time they are received, and expenses are brought into account at the time they are paid. This is subject to any adjustment required or authorised by law, and certain special rules apply to the cash basis. Otherwise, the general rule applies that the profits of a property business are calculated in the same way as the profits of a trade. All letting income from UK property, whether furnished or unfurnished, is taxed as income from a single UK property business carried on by the landlord.

(c) Although property income is computed similarly to trading income, it retains its nature as investment income as opposed to earnings and does not count as relevant earnings for pension contribution purposes (subject to the rules for furnished holiday lettings — see **22.2** below).

(d) Subject to conditions being met, replacement domestic items relief enables landlords of residential property to deduct capital expenditure on domestic items, e.g. furniture, furnishings, appliances (including white goods) and kitchenware, where the expenditure is on a replacement item provided for use in the property. The relief applies to both furnished and unfurnished lettings, but not to furnished holiday lettings within **22.2** below. The deduction is made in computing the profits of the property business, and does not require the making of a claim. The amount of the deduction is the cost of the replacement item, but is limited to the cost of an equivalent item if the new item is not the same, or substantially the same, as the old. [*ITTOIA 2005, s 311A*]. See PIM3205 and *Simon's Taxes* B6.401, C2.217.

(e) See (B) below for profits calculated on the GAAP basis, i.e. on the accruals basis in accordance with generally accepted accounting practice.

Property Income   IT 22.1

(B) **GAAP basis**

Mrs A has a furnished cottage in a picturesque coastal village. She makes the cottage available for letting. Several lettings are for periods of more than 31 days, and the cottage does not qualify as 'furnished holiday accommodation' under **22.2** below. The letting does not constitute a trade. The rent charged is £800 per month from June to September inclusive and £550 per month for the rest of the year. Mrs A has no other letting income.

During 2020/21 the house was occupied from April until October, lay vacant during November, December and January and was let again for February and March. In March 2021, the tenant defaulted on two weeks' rent, which proved impossible to collect.

Expenses payable in respect of 2020/21 were as follows:

Business rates £680, Water rates £184, Electricity £520 (£500 received from tenants through coin operated meters), Advertising £300, Cleaning between lettings £280, House contents insurance £272, Repairs £220.

During the year Mrs A purchased for the cottage a fridge freezer for £400 and a microwave for £85. Both were like-for-like replacements for existing items. No value was received for the items replaced.

The property income computation for 2020/21 is as follows

Mrs A has elected under *ITTOIA 2005, s 271A(10)* to use the accruals basis to calculate the taxable profits of her property business. She must do so by 31 January 2023. As such, her profits are calculated in accordance with GAAP.

	£	£
Rent receivable (4 × £800 + 5 × £550)		5,950
Business rates	680	
Water rates	184	
Electricity (520 − 500)	20	
Advertising	300	
Cleaning	280	
Insurance	272	
Repairs	220	
Bad debt written off (550 ÷ 2)	275	
Replacement domestic items relief (note (c))	485	(2,716)
Taxable profit		£3,234

Notes

(a) All letting income from UK property, whether furnished or unfurnished, is taxed as income from a single UK property business carried on by the landlord. The profits of that business are computed according to trading income principles as if the business were a trade.

(b) Although property income is computed similarly to trading income, it retains its nature as investment income as opposed to earnings and does not count as relevant earnings for pension contribution purposes (subject to the rules for furnished holiday lettings — see **22.2** below).

22.1 IT   Property Income

(c) Subject to conditions being met, replacement domestic items relief enables landlords of residential property to deduct capital expenditure on domestic items, e.g. furniture, furnishings, appliances (including white goods) and kitchenware, where the expenditure is on a replacement item provided for use in the property. The relief applies to both furnished and unfurnished lettings, but not to furnished holiday lettings within **22.2** below. The deduction is made in computing the profits of the property business, and does not require the making of a claim. The amount of the deduction is the cost of the replacement item, but is limited to the cost of an equivalent item if the new item is not the same, or substantially the same, as the old. [*ITTOIA 2005, s 311A*].

(d) See (A) above for profits calculated on the cash basis.

22.2 FURNISHED HOLIDAY LETTINGS

[*ITA 2007, ss 127, 127ZA; ITTOIA 2005, ss 322–326, 326A, 327, 328, 328A, 328B*]

Mr B owns and lets out furnished holiday cottages. None is ever let to the same person for more than 31 consecutive days. Three cottages have been owned for many years but Rose Cottage was acquired on 1 June 2020 (and first let on that day) while Ivy Cottage was sold on 30 June 2020 (and last let on that day).

In 2020/21 days available for letting and days let are as follows

	Days available	Days let
Honeysuckle Cottage	270	240
Primrose Cottage	195	150
Bluebell Cottage	225	90
Rose Cottage	225	90
Ivy Cottage	30	5

Additional information

Rose Cottage was let for 45 days between 6 April and 31 May 2021.

Ivy Cottage was let for 103 days in the period 1 July 2019 to 5 April 2020 and was available for letting for 180 days in that period.

Qualification as 'furnished holiday accommodation'

Honeysuckle Cottage qualifies as it meets both the 210-day availability test and the 105-day letting test.

Primrose Cottage does *not* qualify although it is let for more than 105 days as it fails to satisfy the 210-day test. Averaging (see below) is only possible where it is the 105-day test which is not satisfied.

Bluebell Cottage does not qualify by itself as it fails the 105-day test. However, it may be included in an averaging election.

Rose Cottage qualifies as furnished holiday accommodation. It was acquired on 1 June 2020 so qualification in 2020/21 is determined by reference to the period of twelve months beginning on the day it was first let, in which it was let for a total of 135 days.

Property Income IT 22.3

Ivy Cottage was sold on 30 June 2020 so qualification is determined by reference to the period from 1 July 2019 to 30 June 2020 (the last day of letting). It qualifies as it was available for letting for 210 days and let for 108 in this period.

Averaging election for 2020/21

	Days let
Honeysuckle Cottage	240
Bluebell Cottage	90
Rose Cottage	135
Ivy Cottage	108

$$\frac{240 + 90 + 135 + 108}{4} = 143.25 \text{ days}$$

note (c)

Notes

(a) Income from the commercial letting of furnished holiday accommodation is treated as trading income for certain limited purposes; in particular it counts as relevant UK earnings for the purpose of obtaining relief for contributions to a registered pension scheme.

(b) In addition, the commercial letting of furnished holiday accommodation is treated as a trade for the purpose of various capital gains tax reliefs including BUSINESS ASSET DISPOSAL RELIEF (FORMERLY ENTREPRENEURS' RELIEF) (CGT 206) and business assets gifts hold-over relief (see CGT 213 HOLD-OVER RELIEFS). [*TCGA 1992, ss 241, 241A*]. See CG73500 and *Simon's Taxes* C3.1301, D1.1057.

(c) All four cottages included in the averaging election now qualify as furnished holiday accommodation as each is deemed to have been let for 143.25 days in the year 2020/21.

(d) If Bluebell cottage had still not qualified as a result of averaging but qualified in 2019/20, it would have been possible to make a 'period of grace' election, provided there had been a genuine intention to meet the 105-day letting condition for 2020/21. The same applies if the cottage had qualified for 2018/19 and a period of grace election had been made in respect of it for 2019/20. [*ITTOIA 2005, s 326A*]. See *Simon's Taxes* B6.404.

22.3 'RENT-A-ROOM' RELIEF

[*ITTOIA 2005, ss 784–802; FA 2013, Sch 4 paras 40, 56*]

Frankie and Johnny are single persons sharing a house as their main residence. They have for some years taken in lodgers to supplement their income. As Frankie contributed the greater part of the purchase price of the house, she and Johnny have an agreement to share the rental income in the ratio 2:1, although expenses are shared equally. The house was acquired without a mortgage.

Gross rents and allowable expenses are as set out below In the year ended 5 April 2016, the pair faced a heavy repair bill after uninsured damage to one of the rooms

22.3 IT Property Income

	Gross rents	Allowable expenses
	£	£
Year ended 5 April 2015	5,700	1,100
Year ended 5 April 2016	3,600	4,400
Year ended 5 April 2017	11,475	5,450
Year ended 5 April 2018	10,500	4,400
Year ended 5 April 2019	10,500	4,400
Year ended 5 April 2020	13,500	8,000
Year ended 5 April 2021	12,000	1,000

For 2014/15, the position is as follows

Normal computation of property income

	Frankie	Johnny
	£	£
Gross rents (y/e 5.4.15)	3,800	1,900
Allowable expenses	(550)	(550)
Net rents	£3,250	£1,350

Johnny's share of *gross* rents is less than his one half share (£2,125) of the £4,250 basic amount then in place. It is assumed that he would not make the election for full rent-a-room relief not to apply. His share of net rents is thus treated as nil.

Frankie's share of gross rents exceeds £2,125, so full rent-a-room relief cannot apply. She can, however, elect to apply the alternative method of calculation. Under that method, she is taxed on the excess of *gross* rents over £2,125. It is assumed that she will make the election as she will then be taxed on £1,675 rather than £3,250.

For 2015/16, the position is as follows

Normal computation of property income

	Frankie	Johnny
	£	£
Gross rents (y/e 5.4.16)	2,400	1,200
Allowable expenses	(2,200)	(2,200)
Net rents / (loss)	£200	£(1,000)

Johnny's share of gross rents continues to be less than £2,125. Under full rent-a-room relief, his share of net rents will be treated as nil. However, he will obtain no relief, by carry-forward or otherwise, for his loss. In order to preserve his loss, he could elect for full rent-a-room relief not to apply, the election having effect for 2015/16 only.

Frankie's share of gross rents exceeds £2,125. Therefore, her previous election for the alternative method will not be treated as automatically withdrawn. She will be taxed under the alternative method on £275 (£2,400 – £2,125). However, this is greater than the amount taxable on the normal property income computation (£200), so it is assumed she would withdraw the election with effect for 2015/16 and subsequent years. The notice of withdrawal does not prejudice the making of a fresh election for 2016/17 or any subsequent year.

For 2016/17, the position is as follows

Normal computation of property income

	Frankie	Johnny
	£	£
Gross rents (y/e 5.4.17)	7,650	3,825
Allowable expenses	(2,725)	(2,725)
Net rents	£4,925	£1,100

Johnny's share of gross rents now exceeds £3,750, i.e. half of the new £7,500 limit, so full rent-a-room relief will not apply. He could elect for the alternative method to apply, and his chargeable income will then be reduced to £75 (£3,825 − £3,750). This is further reduced to nil by the bringing forward of his £1,000 loss for 2015/16. Johnny then carries forward £925 of losses to 2017/18. If Johnny did not make the election, his chargeable income would be £100 with the whole of his 2015/16 loss having been utilised.

Frankie can make a fresh election for the alternative method, with effect from 2016/17, and she will then be taxed on £3,900 (£7,650 − £3,750).

For 2017/18, the position is as follows

Normal computation of property income

	Frankie	Johnny
	£	£
Gross rents (y/e 5.4.18)	7,000	3,500
Allowable expenses	(2,200)	(2,200)
Net rents	£4,800	£1,300

Johnny's share of gross rents is below £3,750, i.e. half of the £7,500 limit, so that the election to apply the alternative method is treated as having been withdrawn, and full rent-a-room relief applies instead (assuming he makes no election to disapply it). His share of net rents is thus nil. The balance of £925 of his 2015/16 loss is carried forward to 2018/19.

Frankie's election to apply the alternative method will continue to have effect (unless withdrawn), so that her chargeable property income will be £3,250 (£7,000 − £3,750).

22.3 IT   Property Income

For 2018/19, the position is as follows

The normal computation of property income is as for 2017/18. Frankie's election to apply the alternative method continues to have effect, so that her chargeable property income is again £3,250. Full rent-a-room relief continues to apply for Johnny, and the 2015/16 loss of £925 is carried forward to 2019/20.

For 2019/20, the position is as follows

Normal computation of property income

	Frankie £	Johnny £
Gross rents (y/e 5.4.20)	9,000	4,500
Allowable expenses	(4,000)	(4,000)
Net rents	£5,000	£500

For both Frankie and Johnny their shares of gross rents now exceed £3,750, i.e. half of the £7,500 limit, so that full rent-a-room relief will not apply, and since their share of the expenses also exceeds £3,750, the election to apply the alternative method will be unfavourable. It is therefore assumed that Frankie withdraws her election (by 31 January 2022). They are accordingly both charged to tax on the basis of the normal property income computation, with Johnny's £925 loss brought forward being set against his share, the balance of £425 being carried forward to 2020/21.

For 2020/21, the position is as follows

Normal computation of property income

	Frankie £	Johnny £
Gross rents (y/e 5.4.21)	8,000	4,000
Allowable expenses	(500)	(500)
Net rents	£7,500	£3,500

For both Frankie and Johnny, their share of gross rents exceeds £3,750, so that full rent-a-room relief will not apply. Both could now elect to apply the alternative method of calculation (the election to be made by 31 January 2023). Frankie's chargeable property income will be reduced to £4,250 (£8,000 − £3,750). Johnny's chargeable property income will be reduced to £250 (£4,000 − £3,750) and further reduced to nil by offsetting £250 of his remaining 2015/16 loss (of which the balance of £175 is carried forward to 2021/22).

Notes

(a) Rent-a-room relief covers receipts for meals, cleaning, laundry etc. as well as sums (i.e. rents) received for the use of the furnished accommodation. It applies equally where the provision of accommodation and services is chargeable as trading income or as miscellaneous income. [*ITTOIA 2005, s 786*]. See PIM4001 and *Simon's Taxes* B6.601, B6.602.

(b) Where receipts accrue to more than one person in respect of the same residence in one income period, each of those persons who is a qualifying individual is entitled to a limit of one half of the 'basic amount' for the relevant tax year. The basic amount is £4,250 for years up to and including 2015/16 and £7,500 for 2016/17 onwards. [*ITTOIA 2005, ss 789, 790; SI 2015 No 1539*]. See PIM4010 and *Simon's Taxes* B6.603.

(c) The property allowance (see **22.6** below), which became available from 2017/18 onwards, cannot be used in conjunction with rent-a-room relief. [*ITTOIA 2005, s 783BM*]. See *Simon's Taxes* B6.202A.

22.4 MORTGAGE INTEREST AND OTHER FINANCE COSTS

[*ITTOIA 2005, ss 272A, 272B, 274A, 274AA, 274B, 274C*]

Jacob owns a property in Coventry which he acquired with the aid of a mortgage. Part of the building is rented out as office premises and part as residential accommodation. The latter is not furnished holiday accommodation. A comparison of the floor areas of the commercial and residential parts of the building shows that the latter comprise 64% of the total floor area of the building.

For 2020/21, the interest paid on the mortgage amounts to £5,600. The profits of Jacob's UK property business, before deducting any mortgage interest but otherwise as adjusted for tax purposes, amount to £31,104. There is an allowable loss of £3,200 brought forward from 2019/20 under *ITA 2007, s 118*. Jacob has no overseas property business. He is a lecturer with taxable profits of £26,612 for the year to 30 June 2020 but has no other source of taxable income. He has no children and will therefore be unaffected by the high income child benefit charge.

Jacob's property income for 2020/21 is calculated as follows

		£	£
Profits before deducting mortgage interest			31,104
Deduct: Mortgage interest:			
	commercial accommodation £5,600 @ 36%	2,016	
	residential accommodation (£5,600 @ 64%) x 0% (notes (a) and (b))	—	
			(2,016)
			29,088
Deduct:	Loss brought forward		(3,200)
Taxable property income			£25,888

22.4 IT Property Income

Jacob's income tax liability for 2020/21 is calculated as follows

		£	£
Professional income			26,612
Property income as above			25,888
Total and net income			52,500
Deduct: Personal allowance			(12,500)
Taxable income			£40,000
Tax payable:			
	37,500 @ 20%		7,500.00
	2,500 @ 40%		1,000.00
	£40,000		—
			8,500.00
	Less: Basic rate reduction (see below): £3,584 @ 20%		(716.80)
Tax payable			£7,783.20

The basic rate reduction is calculated as follows

The basic rate reduction is based on the lowest of the following:

		£
(i)	interest otherwise unrelieved (£5,600 – £2,016)	3,584
(ii)	the taxable profits of the property business for the year, net of losses brought forward	25,888
(iii)	the individual's 'adjusted total income' for the year, i.e. net income, exclusive of any savings income or dividend income, minus the personal allowance (and any blind person's allowance)	40,000

Notes

(a) Deductions for finance costs, including mortgage interest, incurred on or after 6 April 2017 are restricted in computing residential property income (other than from furnished holiday lettings). Only a percentage of finance costs were deductible in computing property income, with the balance attracting basic rate relief only. For 2020/21 onwards, all finance costs are relieved at basic rate only. The percentage of finance costs deductible was 25% for 2019/20, 50% for 2018/19 and it was 75% for 2017/18. See *Simon's Taxes* B6.202F.

(b) Where a property business consists of the letting of both residential and other property, the restriction to basic rate applies only to the proportion of finance costs that relates to the residential letting. Any apportionment should be made on a just and reasonable basis. In this example, the mortgage interest has been apportioned by reference to floor space. One alternative would have been to apportion it by reference to the respective values of the different parts of the building. See HMRC Property Income Manual PIM2056.

(c) If the amount on which the basic rate deduction is based had been less than the figure given by option (i) (i.e. because option (ii) or (iii) gave a lower figure), the deficit would have been carried forward and added to the option (i) figure for the following tax year.

22.5 PREMIUMS ETC. ON LEASES OF UP TO 50 YEARS

[*ITTOIA 2005, ss 276–307*]

Cross-reference. See also CGT 216.3(C)(H)(I) LAND.

(A)

Mr Green grants a 30-year lease of premises to a trader, Mr Indigo, on 1 March 2021 for a premium of £35,000.

The amount to be included in the profits of Mr Green's property business for 2020/21 is as follows

$$P \times \frac{50 - Y}{50}$$

where

P = the amount of the premium, and

Y = the number of complete periods of 12 months (other than the first) comprised in the effective duration of the lease.

[*ITTOIA 2005, s 277*].

Thus

$$£35,000 \times \frac{50 - 29}{50} = £\underline{14,700}$$

(B) Allowance to lessee carrying on trade etc.

[*ITTOIA 2005, ss 60–67*]

Assuming the same figures as in (A) above and that Mr Indigo prepares accounts to 31 March

Chargeable premium	£14,700
Number of days comprised in the lease period	10,958

The lessee will obtain relief as follows

$$\frac{£14,700}{10,958} = £1.34 \text{ per day treated as a deductible expense.}$$

22.5 IT Property Income

i.e. £42 for period of account to 31.3.21 and £489 for period of account to 31.3.22 and so on.

(C) **Grant of sub-lease**

[*ITTOIA 2005, ss 64, 287, 288*]

On 1 May 2022, Mr Indigo in (A) and (B) above finds that the leased premises are now surplus to his trading requirements, and he grants a 10-year sub-lease at a premium of £12,500.

The amount to be included in the profits of Mr Indigo's property business for 2022/23 is computed as follows

	£
Chargeable premium before reduction	
$£12,500 \times \dfrac{50-9}{50} =$	10,250
Reduced by £14,700 × $^{10}/_{30}$	(4,900)
Reduced chargeable premium	£5,350

The chargeable sub-lease premium is reduced by reference to the premium chargeable on the landlord.

The number of days in the 10-year receipt period of the sub-lease is 3,653. The daily amount of the relief given is therefore £4,900 divided by 3,653 = £1.34. This equals the daily expense computed in (B) above; as there is no deficit, Mr Indigo is not entitled to any deduction under (B) above for any of the 3,653 qualifying days covered by the sublease.

Supposing Mr Indigo had been able to obtain a premium of only £5,000 for the 10-year sub-lease. The amount to be included as a receipt in computing the profits of his property business for 2022/23 would then be as follows.

	£
Chargeable premium before reduction	
$£5,000 \times \dfrac{50-9}{50} =$	4,100
Reduced by	
$£14,700 \times \dfrac{10}{30} = £4,900$ but restricted to	(4,100)
	Nil

The daily amount of the relief given is now £4,100 divided by 3,653 = £1.12. This is less than the daily expense of £1.34 computed in (B) above, the deficit being £0.22. Mr Indigo would be entitled to a deduction of £0.22 under (B) above for each of the 3,653 qualifying days covered by the sub-lease. See PIM1205 and *Simon's Taxes* B6.301.

22.6 PROPERTY ALLOWANCE

[*ITTOIA 2005, ss 783B-783BQ; F(No 2) 2017, Sch 3 paras 1, 8, 13*]

Ariadne is in employment earning £25,000 per annum but earns extra money by renting out a garage to a neighbour. For the year ended 5 April 2021 she receives rent of £1,300. She pays £200 for repairs to the garage roof.

Ariadne's taxable property business profits for the year to 5.4.21 are as follows

		£	£
Rent received (i.e. gross receipts)			1,300
Deduct:	Repairs expenses	500	(200)
Taxable profit			£1,100

Ariadne elects to use the property allowance and is instead taxed as follows

		£
Gross receipts		1,300
Deduct:	Property allowance	(1,000)
Taxable profit for 2020/21		£300

Notes

(a) A £1,000 allowance (the '*property allowance*') was introduced for property income with effect for the tax year 2017/18 onwards. It does not apply to property businesses carried on in partnership or where rent-a-room relief is available (see **22.3** above). See *Simon's Taxes* B6.202A.

(b) Where an individual's gross receipts do not exceed the £1,000 allowance, profits are treated as nil ('*full relief*'). The individual can elect for full relief not to be given. Where, as in this example, gross receipts exceed the £1,000 allowance, the individual can elect to use an alternative method of calculating income ('*partial relief*'). Under this method the charge to tax is on the excess of gross receipts over £1,000.

23 Remittance Basis

23.1 REMITTANCES FROM MIXED FUNDS

[*ITA 2007, ss 809Q, 809R*]

Van Helsing is resident, but not domiciled or deemed domiciled in the UK. He has regular employment in both the UK and Transylvania and some non-UK shareholdings. He maintains a single bank account in Transylvania which he opened in August 2019. Previously all his transactions went through a UK bank account; part of his UK salary after tax continues to be paid into that account. Van Helsing has made a claim to pay UK tax on the remittance basis for 2019/20 and 2020/21.

Van Helsing's Transylvanian bank account statements show the following

		Money Out	Money In	Balance
		£	£	£
30 August 2019	UK salary (part)		4,200	4,200
15 September 2019	overseas salary		12,000	16,200
30 September 2019	UK salary (part)		4,200	20,400
6 October 2019	overseas dividends		11,000	31,400
30 October 2019	UK salary (part)		4,200	35,600
30 November 2019	UK salary (part)		4,200	39,800
15 December 2019	overseas salary		12,000	51,800
30 December 2019	UK salary (part)		4,200	56,000
30 January 2020	UK salary (part)		4,500	60,500
29 February 2020	UK salary (part)		4,500	65,000
15 March 2020	overseas salary		12,000	77,000
30 March 2020	UK salary (part)		4,500	81,500
4 April 2020	overseas dividends		21,500	103,000
30 April 2020	UK salary (part)		4,500	107,500
30 April 2020	bank interest		6,000	113,500
15 May 2020	sale proceeds of overseas shareholding		794,000	907,500
30 May 2020	UK salary (part)		4,500	912,000
15 June 2020	overseas salary		13,000	925,000
21 June 2020	transfer to UK bank account	450,000		475,000

All amounts of overseas income other than the bank interest were subject to deduction of tax at source in their country of origin. The investment sold in May 2020 was originally inherited from Van Helsing's great aunt's estate; the chargeable gain on disposal is £350,000.

23.1 IT Remittance Basis

Applying the rules in ITA 2007, s 809Q(3)

Step 1

For each of the categories of income and capital in paragraphs (a) to (i) below, find the amount of income or capital for the tax year in question in the mixed fund immediately before the transfer to the UK. The tax year in question is the tax year in which the transfer occurs, i.e. 2020/21. The categories are:

(a) employment income (other than income within (b), (c) or (f));

(b) relevant foreign earnings (other than income within (f));

(c) foreign specific employment income (other than income within (f));

(d) relevant foreign income (other than income within (g));

(e) foreign chargeable gains (other than gains within (h));

(f) employment income subject to a foreign tax;

(g) relevant foreign income subject to a foreign tax;

(h) foreign chargeable gains subject to a foreign tax;

(i) income or capital not within any of the above.

		£
employment income not subject to a foreign tax — (a) above	UK salary	9,000
relevant foreign income not subject to a foreign tax — (d) above	bank interest	6,000
foreign chargeable gains not subject to a foreign tax — (e) above	overseas shareholding	350,000
employment income subject to a foreign tax — (f) above	overseas salary	13,000
relevant foreign income subject to a foreign tax — (g) above	overseas dividends	Nil
		£378,000

Step 2

Identify the earliest category which has an amount of income or gain in the mixed fund. This is category (a) which has £9,000.

Step 3

As the amount of the transfer is greater than the amount identified at Step 2 the amount of the transfer is treated as reduced by the amount identified in Step 2.

£450,000 − £9,000 = £441,000

Step 4

Repeat Steps 2 & 3 for each category in turn until the transfer is reduced to nil or all categories are exhausted.

£441,000 − £6,000 − £350,000 − £13,000 = £72,000

Remittance Basis   IT 23.1

Step 5

As the amount of the transfer is not exhausted, repeat steps 1 to 4 but this time in relation to the immediately preceding year, i.e. 2019/20.

		£
employment income not subject to a foreign tax — (a) above	UK salary	34,500
employment income subject to a foreign tax — (f) above	overseas salary	36,000
relevant foreign income subject to a foreign tax — (g) above	overseas dividends	32,500
		£102,500

Applying Steps 1 to 4 for 2019/20, all of the income in categories (a) and (f) and £1,500 of the income in category (g) is matched with the transfer.

£72,000 − £34,500 − £36,000 − £1,500 = Nil

Outcome

The £450,000 transfer is therefore regarded as a remittance of:

	2020/21	2019/20	Total
	£	£	£
UK employment income — category (a)	9,000	34,500	43,500
relevant foreign income not subject to foreign tax — category (d)	6,000		6,000
foreign chargeable gains not subject to foreign tax — category (e)	350,000		350,000
employment income subject to a foreign tax — category (f)	13,000	36,000	49,000
relevant foreign income subject to a foreign tax — category (g)		1,500	1,500
			£450,000

Conclusions

All of Van Helsing's UK employment income for both years to date (£43,500) is included in the transfer. This is not a taxable remittance as it is taxable in the UK on an arising basis.

£56,500 of overseas income is included in the transfer and treated as remitted to the UK. It is chargeable income for 2020/21, the year in which it is remitted, with credit being available under the double tax relief provisions for foreign taxes paid.

The remaining £350,000 of the £450,000 transfer is taxable as a chargeable gain for 2020/21, the year in which it is remitted.

The balance of £475,000 carried forward in the Transylvanian bank account consists of £31,000 of 2019/20 overseas dividends and £444,000 (£794,000 − £350,000) of capital originally represented by the overseas shareholding sold in May 2020. The capital is 'clean capital', having come from an inheritance, and will not be chargeable to tax when remitted to the UK.

23.1 IT   Remittance Basis

Notes

(a) The remittance basis can only apply to an individual for a particular tax year if, for that tax year, the individual is resident but not domiciled in the UK. In most cases it requires the making of a claim; there are certain exceptions where the amounts involved are small. [*ITA 2007, ss 809B–809D*]. See RDRM32010 and *Simon's Taxes* E4.1319, E4.1315.

(b) Where, for any tax year, an individual makes a *claim* for the remittance basis to apply, he loses entitlement to UK personal reliefs for that year and, if he is a 'long-term UK resident' (as defined), he is also liable to an additional tax charge. [*ITA 2007, ss 809G, 809H*]. See RDRM32040 and *Simon's Taxes* E6.324B, E6.324E, E6.324F, E6.324G, E6.328B, E6.125.

(c) All chargeable income and gains are taxable for the year in which they are remitted and not, if different, the year in which they arose. [*ITEPA 2003, s 22; ITTOIA 2005, s 832; TCGA 1992, s 12*]. See CG12600, CG25313 and *Simon's Taxes* C1.102, C1.603.

(d) If Van Helsing had claimed the remittance basis for 2020/21 but not for 2019/20, his 2019/20 foreign income would have been taxed on the arising basis in that year and would not have been taxable when remitted. If, on the other hand, he had claimed the remittance basis for 2019/20 but not for 2018/19, his 2019/20 foreign income would still have been chargeable when remitted in 2020/21 or any later year.

(e) Subject to conditions, individuals performing the duties of a *single* employment both inside and outside the UK may calculate their tax liability by reference to the total amount transferred out of a mixed fund during a tax year, rather than by reference to individual transfers. The rules are then applied to the total amount transferred out of the fund to the UK in the tax year as if it were a single transfer. This has effect only if the mixed fund account is credited with nothing other than earnings from employment, consideration for the disposal of employment-related securities/options or interest on the account. [*ITA 2007, ss 809RA–809RD; FA 2013, Sch 6 paras 6, 8*]. See ERSM162910 and *Simon's Taxes* E4.1318.

24 Savings and Investment Income

24.1 DEEPLY DISCOUNTED SECURITIES

[*ITTOIA 2005, ss 427–460*]

(A) **Profit on disposal.**

On 28 June 2002 Mr Knight subscribed for £10,000 3% loan stock issued by DDS plc at a price of £55 per £100 stock incurring costs of £60. He sold these same securities on 6 July 2020 for £80 per £100 stock and incurred costs of £90. The 3% loan stock in DDS plc is quoted on the Stock Exchange, was issued on 1 July 2000 at £80 and is redeemable on 30 June 2030 at £100.

Mr Knight's tax position for 2020/21 on the disposal is

			£	£
Disposal proceeds				8,000
Less acquisition cost				(5,500)
				2,500
Deduct Costs of acquisition	note (b)		60	
Costs of disposal	notes (b), (c)		—	
				(60)
Taxable income				£2,440

Notes

(a) Subject to certain exceptions, a security is a '*deeply discounted security*' if, at the time it is issued, the amount payable on maturity (or any possible occasion of redemption) exceeds (or may exceed) the issue price by more than $R \times 0.5\% \times Y$, where R is the amount payable on maturity etc. and Y is the period between issue and redemption, expressed in years (and fractions of years) but with a maximum value of 30. In this example, $R = £100$ and $Y = 30$. $£100 \times 0.5\% \times 30 = £15$. The difference between issue price and redemption price is £20. Thus, the loan stock is a deeply discounted security. Exceptions include company shares, gilts (but not strips), excluded indexed securities, life assurance policies, capital redemption policies and securities issued under the same prospectus as other securities issued previously but not themselves deeply discounted securities. [*ITTOIA 2005, ss 430–436*]. See SAIM3020 and *Simon's Taxes* D9.502.

(b) Subject to note (c), relief is available for costs incurred in connection with the acquisition of the security or with its transfer or redemption, but only if incurred before 27 March 2003 or, if incurred on or after that date, the person transferring or redeeming the security had held it continuously since before that date *and* the security was listed on a recognised stock exchange (within *ITA 2007, s 1005*) at some time before that date. [*FA 1996, Sch 13 para 1(2)–(4); ITTOIA 2005, ss 453, 455*]. See SAIM3080 and *Simon's Taxes* D9.513.

24.1 IT   Savings and Investment Income

(c) Such costs as are referred to in note (b) are not deductible where incurred on or after 6 April 2015. [*ITTOIA 2005, s 455; FA 2012, Sch 39 para 48*]. Thus the disposal costs are not deductible in this example.

(B) **Loss on disposal.**

On the assumption that Mr Knight in (A) above sells the loan stock for £40 per £100 stock instead of £80 the following will apply:

Mr Knight's tax position for 2020/21 on the disposal is

		£	£
Disposal proceeds			4,000
Less acquisition cost			(5,500)
			(1,500)
Deduct	Costs of acquisition	60	
	Costs of disposal	—	
			(60)
Allowable loss			(£1,560)

Notes

(a) Mr Knight will be able to claim loss relief of £1,560 as a deduction in computing net income for 2020/21. The relief must be claimed no later than 31 January 2023.

(b) Loss relief is available only if the person sustaining the loss had held the security continuously since before 27 March 2003 *and* the security was listed on a recognised stock exchange (within *ITA 2007, s 1005*) at some time before that date. [*ITTOIA 2005, ss 453, 454*].

25 Seed Enterprise Investment Scheme

25.1 INCOME TAX INVESTMENT RELIEF

[ITA 2007, ss 257A–257EG; FA 2013, s 56(4)(6); FA 2014, s 54; FA 2018, s 14(2)(4)(5); FA 2020, s 110]

For 2020/21 Ben has taxable earnings of £225,000, dividends of £20,000 and bank interest of £15,000. On 20 May Ben invests £20,000 in a venture capital trust on which he is entitled to full income tax relief. He also makes the following qualifying investments by subscription in companies issuing shares via the Seed Enterprise Investment Scheme (SEIS). He is not a Scottish taxpayer.

	Date shares acquired	Shares acquired (all at par)	Acquisition cost £
X Ltd	25 August 2020	10,000 ordinary £1	10,000
Y Ltd	15 December 2020	40,000 ordinary 50p	20,000
Z Ltd	1 February 2021	30,000 ordinary £1	30,000
			£60,000

On 29 April 2020 Ben also made a qualifying investment of £5,000 under the enterprise investment scheme (EIS).

Ben's investment in Z Ltd represents 25% of that company's issued share capital. He becomes a director of the company and receives director's fees of £6,000 in 2020/21. This is in addition to his earnings quoted above.

Ben will obtain tax relief for 2020/21 as follows

Amount eligible for SEIS relief

	£
X Ltd	10,000
Y Ltd	20,000
Z Ltd note (c)	30,000
Total (being less than the maximum of £100,000)	£60,000

	£
Earnings (including director's fees)	231,000
Dividends	20,000
Bank interest	15,000
Total income	266,000
Personal allowance (restricted due to level of income)	Nil
Taxable income	£266,000

25.1 IT Seed Enterprise Investment Scheme

Tax payable:		
37,500	@ 20%	7,500.00
112,500	@ 40%	45,000.00
96,000	@ 45%	43,200.00
2,000	@ 0% (dividend allowance)	—
18,000	@ 38.1% (dividend additional rate)	6,858.00
		102,558
Deduct VCT relief £20,000 @ 30%		(6,000.00)
		96,558
Deduct EIS relief £5,000 @ 30%		(1,500.00)
		95,058
Deduct SEIS relief £60,000 @ 50%		(30,000.00)
Net tax liability 2020/21 (subject to PAYE deductions)		£65,058.00

Notes

(a) The SEIS is a tax-advantaged venture capital scheme. Income tax relief is available for investment in small companies (i.e. those with 25 or fewer employees and assets of up to £200,000) that are carrying on, or preparing to carry on, a new qualifying business. The relief is available on share subscriptions of up to £100,000 per individual per tax year. The shares must be retained for at least three years. See *Simon's Taxes* E3.801.

(b) SEIS relief is given at the SEIS rate of tax (50%) and by way of an income tax reduction. The relief cannot exceed what would otherwise be the income tax liability (no restriction being necessary in this example). For this purpose, the income tax liability is before taking into account any married couple's allowance, double tax relief and certain other specified items. However, the VCT investment relief must be deducted before the EIS investment relief and SEIS relief. [*ITA 2007, ss 26, 27, 29, 257AB*]. See VCM31130 and *Simon's Taxes* E3.802.

(c) The fact that Ben is a director of Z Ltd and in receipt of director's remuneration does not invalidate his claim for relief. If, however, he had been an employee *other than a director* of the company at any time in the requisite three-year holding period, he would not have been eligible for SEIS income tax relief. [*ITA 2007, ss 257AC, 257BA*]. See VCM31140.

(d) Though not illustrated in this example, any amount of SEIS investment relief can be carried back to the preceding tax year, provided the £100,000 maximum is not thereby exceeded for that year.

(e) Ben is not entitled to a personal savings allowance in respect of his bank interest as he is an additional rate taxpayer.

Seed Enterprise Investment Scheme IT 25.2

25.2 WITHDRAWAL OF RELIEF/CAPITAL LOSSES

[ITA 2007, ss 257F–257GI, 257HA]

(A) Withdrawal of income tax relief

[ITA 2007, ss 257F–257GI, 257HA]

On 1 March 2023 Ben, the investor in **25.1** above, needs to raise some funds urgently and sells half his X Ltd shares at arm's length to another shareholder for £4,250.

The position is as follows

SEIS investment relief falls to be reduced or withdrawn as the shares have not been held for the requisite period of three years.

The tax reduction in 2020/21 is attributed to the three share issues subscribed for according to the amounts claimed for each issue.

The relief attributable to the 10,000 X Ltd shares subscribed for is 10,000/60,000 x £30,000 = £5,000.

The relief attributable to the 5,000 shares sold is therefore £2,500.

If the relief attributable is greater than an amount equal to tax at the SEIS rate on the disposal consideration, the relief is reduced by that amount. Otherwise, the relief is withdrawn in full.

Tax at the SEIS rate on the disposal consideration:

50% x £4,250 = £2,125

This is less than £2,500 so the relief given is reduced by £2,125 by the making of an assessment to income tax for 2020/21.

Notes

(a) If the disposal had not been at arm's length, the relief would have been withdrawn in full.

(b) The disposal consideration would fall to be treated as reduced for the purposes of the above calculation where the relief attributable (A) is less than tax at the SEIS rate on the amount subscribed (B). It is so reduced by applying the fraction A/B. [ITA 2007, ss 209, 210]. This works the same way as for withdrawal of relief under the EIS scheme; see **10.2 ENTERPRISE INVESTMENT SCHEME** for an illustration. See *Simon's Taxes* E3.167.

(B) Capital losses

[TCGA 1992, s 150E]

The disposal in (A) above is also a disposal for capital gains tax purposes.

25.2 IT Seed Enterprise Investment Scheme

The capital gains position is as follows

2022/23

	£	£
Disposal proceeds (March 2023)		4,250
Cost (August 2020)	5,000	
Less Relief attributable to shares:		
£2,500 − £2,125	(375)	
		(4,625)
Allowable loss		(£375)

Note

(a) An allowable loss may arise for capital gains tax purposes on a disposal of SEIS shares, whether or not the disposal occurs within the requisite three-year period. In computing such a loss, the allowable cost is reduced by SEIS relief attributable to the shares (and not withdrawn).

26 Self-Assessment

Cross-references. See also **13.1** LATE PAYMENT INTEREST AND PENALTIES.

26.1 CALCULATION OF INTERIM PAYMENTS
[*TMA 1970, s 59A*]

For 2019/20, Kylie's self-assessment shows the following.

	£
Gross income tax liability	8,164
Capital gains tax liability	2,122
Class 4 NIC liability	198
PAYE tax deducted (all relating to 2019/20)	3,740

The payments on account for 2020/21 (unless, on a claim, Kylie chooses to pay different amounts) are based on relevant amounts as follows.

	£
Income tax (£8,164 − £3,740 =)	4,424
Class 4 NIC	198

Half of the relevant amounts is due on each of 31 January 2021 and 31 July 2021. No payment on account is required in respect of capital gains tax liability.

Note

(a) The Government announced in March 2020 that self-assessment taxpayers can choose to delay making their second payment on account for **2019/20**, otherwise due on 31 July 2020, if they find it difficult to make the payment on time due to the impact of COVID-19. No claim is required. Those opting to delay will have until 31 January 2021 to make the payment. Whilst introduced principally to assist the self-employed, this measure applies to all self-assessment taxpayers. No late payment interest will be charged for the period 1 August 2020 to 31 January 2021 on the deferred payment. (www.gov.uk/guidance/defer-your-self-assessment-payment-on-account-due-to-coronavirus-covid-19).

26.2 CLAIMS INVOLVING MORE THAN ONE YEAR
[*TMA 1970, s 42(11A), Sch 1B*]

(A) **Carry-back claim made after 31 January in the later year**

Ant files his 2019/20 tax return at the end of January 2021. His self-assessment shows an income tax liability of £8,640, of which £2,400 represents higher rate tax charged on the top £6,000 of income. Ant subsequently makes a claim to carry back from 2020/21 (the later year) to 2019/20 a trading loss of £5,000 for the year to 31 December 2020, producing a tax saving of £2,000 (£5,000 @ 40%). All tax due has been paid on the due dates.

26.2 IT Self-Assessment

If the claim is made on, say, 1 April 2021, a repayment of £2,000 will be made.

If the claim is made on, say, 1 July 2021, the relief of £2,000 will be set against the second 2020/21 interim payment on account (POA) of £4,320 (half of £8,640) due on 31 July 2021 (see note (a)).

If the claim is made on, say, 1 September 2021, and the 31 July 2021 POA has been duly made, a repayment of £2,000 will be made. If the claim is made on 1 September 2021, and the 31 July 2021 POA has *not* been made, the relief of £2,000 will be set against the POA (see note (a)), which is then regarded to that extent as having been paid on 1 September 2021 (see note (b)).

In no case will repayment interest be due, as the relief is given before 31 January 2022 (see note (c)).

As he has made no trading profit for 2020/21, Ant might make a separate claim to reduce or dispense with his POAs for that year (see *TMA 1970, s 59A(3)(4)*).

Notes

(a) Once a valid claim involving more than one year, e.g. a carry-back claim, has been made, HMRC will give effect to it as soon as possible, subject to the following policies:

- no repayment of tax will be made for the earlier year unless tax for the earlier year has been paid in full; and
- where liability for any year is outstanding (or will become due within 35 days after HMRC process the claim), relief will be given by set-off rather than by repayment.

(Revenue Tax Bulletins December 1996 361–365, June 1997 p 443; HMRC Self Assessment Claims Manual SACM11020).

(b) Where the tax saving arising from a loss carry-back claim is set against an outstanding tax liability, the effective date of settlement of that liability, for the purpose of calculating any charge to late payment interest or penalties, is the date on which the valid carry-back claim is made (Revenue Tax Bulletins December 1996 p 364, August 2001 p 879).

(c) On a repayment or set-off arising from a loss carry-back claim, repayment interest accrues only from 31 January following the later year (i.e. the year of loss). It follows that if in this example the repayment or set-off is made before 31 January 2022, no repayment interest will be due. [*FA 2009, s 102, Sch 54, para 7*]. See *Simon's Taxes* A4.629.

(d) For loss relief carry-backs generally, see **15.1, 15.3, 15.4** losses.

(B) **Carry-back claim made after 31 July but before 31 January in the later year**

Dec files his 2019/20 tax return in October 2020. On 1 November 2020, he makes a claim to carry back from 2020/21 (the later year) to 2019/20 a trading loss of £5,000 for the year to 30 April 2020. Dec's POAs for 2019/20 (based on his 2018/19 liability) were £3,000 each. All tax due has been paid on the due dates.

What if Dec's self-assessment for 2019/20 shows an income tax liability of £8,640, of which £2,400 represents higher rate tax charged on the top £6,000 of income? The loss produces a tax saving of £2,000 (£5,000 @ 40%). This will be available to set off against the 2019/20 balancing payment (due on 31 January 2021), reducing it from £2,640 to £640. The 2020/21 POAs will be £4,320 each.

What if Dec's self-assessment for 2019/20 shows an income tax liability of £5,500, which represents tax charged at 20%? The 2019/20 POAs will have been adjusted to £2,750 each, and repayments made of £250 in respect of each POA. The loss produces a tax saving of £1,000 (£5,000 @ 20%). As all the tax for 2019/20 has been paid and there are no outstanding liabilities for any year, the £1,000 will be repaid. No repayment interest is due. The 2020/21 POAs will be £2,750 each.

Say the carry-back claim had instead been made on 3 January 2021 (assuming all other facts are as immediately above), the £1,000 tax saving would have been set against the first 2020/21 POA of £2,750 due on 31 January 2021, reducing it to £1,750.

As he has made no trading profit for 2020/21, Dec might make a separate claim to reduce or dispense with his POAs for that year (see *TMA 1970, s 59A(3)(4)*). See EM4660 and *Simon's Taxes* A4.605.

(C) **Carry-back claim made before 31 July in the later year**

The facts are as in (B) above except that Dec files his 2019/20 return on 25 April 2020 and makes his carry-back claim on 31 May 2020. As accounts for the year to 30 April 2020 are not finalised at this stage, the trading loss of £5,000 is a 'best estimate' but does turn out to be an accurate figure. Dec could not have made the claim in the return as the period of account in which the loss is sustained had not yet come to an end when he filed the return.

What if Dec's self-assessment for 2019/20 shows an income tax liability of £8,640, of which £2,400 represents higher rate tax charged on the top £6,000 of income? The loss produces a tax saving of £2,000 (£5,000 @ 40%). This will be available to set off against the 2019/20 balancing payment (due on 31 January 2021), reducing it from £2,640 to £640. The 2020/21 POAs will be £4,320 each.

What if Dec's self-assessment for 2019/20 shows an income tax liability of £5,500, which represents tax charged at 20%? The 2019/20 POAs will be adjusted to £2,750 each and there will be no balancing payment due on 31 January 2021. A repayment of £250 will be made from the first POA paid on 31 January 2020. The tax saving of £1,000 (£5,000 @ 20%) will be set against the second POA due on 31 July 2020, reducing it from £2,750 to £1,750. The 2020/21 POAs will be £2,750 each.

What if the facts were as immediately above but Dec has failed to pay the first POA for 2020/21 due on 31 January 2021? The tax saving of £1,000 (£5,000 @ 20%) will be set against this outstanding liability, reducing the payment required from £2,750 (originally £3,000) to £1,750. The effective date of payment for interest purposes is 31 May 2020, the date of the valid claim (see note (b) to (A) above). The balance of £1,750 is already overdue, and a further POA of £2,750 is due on 31 July 2020. No balancing payment for 2019/20 is due on 31 January 2021. The 2020/21 POAs will be £2,750 each.

As he has made no trading profit for 2020/21, Dec might make a separate claim to reduce or dispense with his POAs for that year (see *TMA 1970, s 59A(3)(4)*).

27 Settlements

27.1 TAX PAYABLE BY TRUSTEES

A is sole life-tenant of a settlement which has income and expenses in the year 2020/21 as follows

	£
Property income	500
Bank interest	1,500
Dividends	1,000
	£3,000
Expenses chargeable to income	£400

The tax payable by the trustees under self-assessment is as follows:

	£
Property income — £500 @ 20% (basic rate)	100.00
Bank interest — £1,500 @ 20% (basic rate)	300.00
Dividends — £1,000 @ 7.5% (dividend ordinary rate)	75.00
	£475.00

The expenses are not deductible in arriving at the tax payable by the trustees. The starting rate for savings, personal savings allowance and dividend allowance are not available to trustees.

Notes

(a) By prior arrangement, where there is a sole life-tenant in a trust, HMRC may allow the interest to be assessed directly on that beneficiary.

(b) For treatment of the trust income in the hands of the beneficiary, see **27.3(A)** below.

27.2 SPECIAL TRUST RATES OF TAX

[*ITA 2007, ss 9, 479–487, 491–498; FA 2016, s 5(4)(10), Sch 1 paras 63(5)–(7), 73*]

(A) **Standard rate band**

For 2020/21, a small discretionary trust has property income of £500, building society interest of £300 and UK dividends of £600. It has no other income or expenses. The settlor has made no other settlements.

27.2 IT Settlements

The tax liability of the trust for 2020/21 is as follows

	£
Standard rate band	
Property income — £500 @ 20% (basic rate)	100.00
Interest — £300 @ 20% (basic rate)	60.00
Dividends — £200 @ 7.5% (dividend ordinary rate)	15.00
	£175.00
Income exceeding standard rate band	
Dividends — £400 @ 38.1% (dividend trust rate)	152.40
	£327.40

Notes

(a) The property income and building society interest form the lowest slice of the total income; thus, it all falls within the standard rate band and is charged at basic rate. £800 of the £1,000 standard rate band is now used up; thus, £200 of the dividend income falls within the standard rate band and is charged at the dividend ordinary rate. The remainder of the dividend income is charged at the dividend trust rate.

(b) Note that if the trustees were to distribute the whole of the net income of £1,072.60 (£500 + £300 + £600 − £327.40) to beneficiaries, they will have further tax to pay (assuming no balance, or insufficient balance, brought forward from earlier years in the trustees' tax pool). The total tax payable will be £877.58 (£1,072.60 × 45/55), from which can be deducted tax paid of £327.40, leaving a further £550.18 to pay (if no balance is brought forward in the pool). See also note (c) to (B) below and, for an illustration of the pool, (C) below.

(c) The standard rate band of £1,000 is divided between all settlements made by the same settlor, subject to a minimum band of £200 for each settlement. [*ITA 2007*, ss 491, 492]. See TSEM3012 and *Simon's Taxes* C4.210.

(B) **General**

An accumulation and maintenance settlement (the 'XYZ trust') set up by W for his grandchildren in 2002 now comprises quoted investments and an industrial property. The property is let to an engineering company. Charges for rates, electricity etc. are paid by the trust and recharged yearly in arrears to the tenant. As a result of the delay in recovering the service costs, the settlement incurs overdraft interest. There are no other settlements in existence in relation to which W is the settlor.

Settlements   IT 27.2

The relevant figures for the year ended 5 April 2021 are as follows

	£
Property rents	40,500
Dividends	5,000
Bank interest	3,500
	£49,000
Trust administration expenses — proportion chargeable to income	1,350
Overdraft interest	1,050
	£2,400

Tax is payable by the trustees of a discretionary trust (including an accumulation and maintenance trust) at the trust rate (45%) or, in the case of dividend income, at the dividend trust rate (38.1%).

The tax liability of the trust for 2020/21 is as follows

	£	£
Property income £1,000 at 20%	200.00	
£39,500 at 45%	17,775.00	17,975.00
Bank interest £3,500 at 45%		1,575.00
Dividends	5,000	
Deduct Expenses (£2,400 grossed at $^{100}/_{92}$)	(2,595)	
	£2,405	
Tax on £2,595 @ 7.5% (dividend ordinary rate)	194.63	
Tax on £2,405 @ 38.1% (dividend trust rate)	916.31	1,110.94
Tax payable		£20,660.94

Notes

(a) Expenses (including in this example the overdraft interest) are set firstly against UK dividends and similar income, then against dividends from non-UK resident companies (not illustrated in this example), then against other savings income and finally against non-savings income. [*ITA 2007, ss 484–486*]. In this example, all the expenses are set against UK dividends. The effect of the calculation is that the expenses, grossed-up at 7.5%, save tax at 30.6% (the difference between the 7.5% dividend ordinary rate and the 38.1% dividend trust rate). See TSEM8220 and *Simon's Taxes* C4.205.

(b) The net income available for distribution to the beneficiaries, at the trustees' discretion, will be £25,939.06 (see (C) below).

(c) If the whole of the distributable income is in fact distributed, then unless there is sufficient balance brought forward from earlier years in the trustees' tax pool, there will be insufficient tax in the pool to frank the distribution (£25,939.06 × 45/55 =

27.2 IT Settlements

£21,222.87). The tax paid of £20,660.94 will partly cover this, but the trustees will have a further liability which they may not have the funds to settle. See also (C) below.

(d) The property income and savings income form the lowest slice of the total income. Thus, the first £1,000 of such income falls within the standard rate band; as it is basic rate income in nature, that £1,000 is chargeable at the basic rate of 20%.

(e) See note (c) to (A) above as regards the standard rate band.

(f) For treatment of the trust income in the hands of a beneficiary, see **27.3(B)** below.

(C) **Trustees' tax**

[*ITA 2007, ss 496–498; FA 2016, Sch 1, paras 63(7), 73*]

The trustees of the XYZ trust in (B) above have distributed to beneficiaries all available income arising before 6 April 2020, and there is no balance brought forward in the trustees' tax pool created under *ITA 2007, s 497*.

The trustees' additional tax liability for 2020/21 are computed as follows

	£
Total income	49,000
Less expenses	(2,400)
	46,600
Less tax payable by trustees as in (B) above	(20,661)
Distributable income	£25,939
Tax added to trustees' tax pool (Y)	£20,661
Position if all income distributed	
Beneficiaries' income	25,939.00
Add tax at $^{45}/_{55}$ (see **27.3(B)** below) (X)	21,222.81
Beneficiaries' gross income	£47,161.81
Additional tax due from trustees (X) − (Y)	£561.81
Optimum position	
Income distributed (£46,600 (income net of expenses) @ 55%)	25,630.00
Tax credit $^{45}/_{55}$	20,970.00
Beneficiaries' gross income	£46,600.00
Additional tax due from trustees £(20,970 − 20,661)	£309.00
Funds available £(25,939 − 25,630)	£309.00

Note

(a) If the trustees distribute the whole of the distributable income, they will have no funds available from income to pay the additional tax due of £561.81. See TSEM3023 and *Simon's Taxes* C4.212.

Settlements IT 27.3

27.3 INCOME OF BENEFICIARIES

(A) Interests in possession

A, as sole life-tenant of the settlement in **27.1** above, is absolutely entitled to receive the whole settlement income.

A's income from the trust for 2020/21 is computed as follows

	£	£	£
Trust dividend income	1,000		
Trust savings income		1,500	
Other trust income			500
Deduct: dividend ordinary rate tax (7.5%)	(75)		
basic rate tax (20%)		(300)	(100)
	925	1,200	400
Deduct Expenses (note (b))	(400)		
Net income entitlement	£525	£1,200	£400

Beneficiary's entitlement

Grossed-up amounts:	£525 × $^{100}/_{92}$	£567.56		
	£1,200 × $^{100}/_{80}$		£1,500.00	
	£400 × $^{100}/_{80}$			£500.00
Tax deducted at source		£42.56	£300.00	£100.00

Notes

(a) This income falls to be included in A's return even if it is not actually paid to him, as he is absolutely entitled to it. He will receive a tax certificate (form R185 (Trust Income)) from the trust agents, showing three figures each for gross income, tax deducted and net income, as illustrated above.

(b) Trust expenses are deductible firstly from UK dividends and similar income, then from dividends from non-UK resident companies (not illustrated in this example), then from savings income and finally from non-savings income. [*ITA 2007, s 503*]. See *Simon's Taxes* C4.508.

(c) That part of A's trust income which is represented by dividend income (£567) is treated in A's hands as if it were dividend income received directly by A. A is entitled to a credit against his tax liability for the £42 dividend ordinary rate tax deducted by the trustees, and this is repayable to him if he has insufficient liability to cover it.

(d) Similarly, that part of A's trust income which is represented by savings income (£1,500) is treated in A's hands as if it were such income received directly by A. It will thus qualify wholly or partly for the 0% starting rate for savings to the extent (if any) that A's other taxable income is less than the starting rate limit of £5,000, and for the personal savings allowance if A is not an additional rate taxpayer.

27.3 IT Settlements

(B) Accumulation or discretionary trusts

M, the 17-year old grandson of W, is one of the five beneficiaries to whom the trustees can pay the settlement income in **27.2(B)** above. The trustees make a payment of £7,095 to M on 31 January 2021. He has no other income in the year 2020/21.

M's income from the trust is

	£
Net income	7,095.00
Tax at $^{45}/_{55}$	5,805.00
Gross income	£12,900.00

He can claim a tax repayment for 2020/21 of

	£
Total income	12,900
Deduct Personal allowance	(12,500)
	£400

Tax payable:	
£400 × 20% (basic rate)	80.00
Tax accounted for by trustees	(5,805.00)
Repayment due	£(5,725.00)

Notes

(a) If no income was actually paid to M from the settlement, nothing would fall to be included in his return.

(b) Unlike the position with interest in possession trusts (see (A) above), no distinction is made between dividend income, savings income and other income in the beneficiary's hands, the full amount of the payment to him being treated as having suffered tax at a single rate of 45% in the hands of the trustees. The beneficiary is not entitled to the dividend allowance, the starting rate for savings or the personal savings allowance as a payment from a discretionary trust is neither dividend income nor savings income in his hands.

(c) For treatment of trust income where the beneficiary is an infant under a parent's settlement, see **27.4** below.

27.4 SETTLEMENT BY PARENT IN FAVOUR OF OWN CHILD

[*ITTOIA 2005, ss 629, 631, 632, Sch 2 para 133*]

L set up an accumulation and maintenance trust for his two children, aged 5 and 3, in 2005. On 31 December 2006 and 31 December 2007, school fees of £990 were paid on behalf of each child. In January 2021 the trust was wound up and the assets transferred to the two beneficiaries, then aged 21 and 19, in equal shares. At that time there was £6,000 of undistributed income.

Settlements   IT 27.5

The income to be treated as the settlor's income will be as follows

2006/07	$£1,980 \times \dfrac{100}{60}$	£3,300
2007/08	$£1,980 \times \dfrac{100}{60}$	£3,300
2020/21	note (b)	Nil

Notes

(a) The payments for 2006/07 and 2007/08 are grossed up in accordance with the 'rate applicable to trusts' for each of those years, i.e. 40% for both the years.

(b) Income is not treated as that of the parent settlor if, at the time of payment, the children have either married or reached the age of eighteen.

27.5 LOANS BY SETTLEMENT TO SETTLOR

[*ITTOIA 2005, ss 633–638*]

The trustees of a settlement with undistributed income of £1,340 at 5 April 2016 made a loan of £30,000 to B, the settlor, on 30 September 2016.

B repays the loan on 31 December 2020. Undistributed income of £3,500 arose in 2016/17, £6,490 in 2017/18, £4,510 in 2018/19, £10,450 in 2019/20 and £9,200 in 2020/21. The trustees duly settle all their liabilities to tax on trust income.

The following income amounts will be treated as part of B's total income

		£
2016/17	$£4,840 \times {}^{100}/_{55}$	8,800
2017/18	$£6,490 \times {}^{100}/_{55}$	11,800
2018/19	$£4,510 \times {}^{100}/_{55}$	8,200
2019/20	$£10,450 \times {}^{100}/_{55}$	19,000
2020/21	$£3,710 \times {}^{100}/_{55}$ note (b)	6,745

The notional tax credit available to B is

		£
2016/17	£8,800 @ 45%	3,960.00
2017/18	£11,800 @ 45%	5,310.00
2018/19	£8,200 @ 45%	3,690.00
2019/20	£19,000 @ 45%	8,550.00
2020/21	£6,745 @ 45%	3,035.25

27.5 IT   Settlements

Notes

(a) Where in any tax year the trustees of a settlement pay any capital sum (including by way of loan) to the settlor, a corresponding amount (grossed up at the trust rate) is treated as income of the settlor to the extent that it falls within the amount of available income in the settlement up to the end of that tax year or, to the extent that it does not fall within that amount, to the end of the next and subsequent tax years (up to a maximum of ten years).

(b) The amount treated as income in 2020/21 is limited to the amount of the loan less amounts previously treated as income (£30,000 − (£4,840 + £6,490 + £4,510 + £10,450)).

28 Share-Related Employment Income and Exemptions

28.1 SHARE OPTIONS — CHARGE TO TAX

[*ITEPA 2003, ss 471–484*]

An employee is granted an option exercisable within 5 years to buy 1,000 shares at £5 each. The option costs 50p per share. He exercises the option on 15 June 2020 when the shares are worth £7.50. The option is not granted under a tax-advantaged scheme. The employee does not incur any expenses in connection with the acquisition of the shares.

The amount taxable as employment income in 2020/21 is as follows

	£	£
Open market value of shares 1,000 × £7.50		7,500
Price paid 1,000 × £5 − shares	5,000	
1,000 × 50p − option	500	
		5,500
Amount taxable as employment income		£2,000

Notes

(a) The result would be the same if, instead of exercising the option, the employee transferred his option to a third party for £2,500.

(b) The capital gains tax base cost of the shares will be £7,500 being the aggregate of the price paid for the shares, the price paid for the option and the amount chargeable to income tax. [*TCGA 1992, ss 119A, 144(3)*]. See CG25395 and *Simon's Taxes* C2.1014.

(c) A share option is taken outside these rules (and into the convertible shares regime at **28.3** below) if it is a right to acquire securities that is itself acquired pursuant to a right or opportunity made available under arrangements having as one of their main purposes the avoidance of tax or national insurance contributions. [*ITEPA 2003, s 420(8)*]. See ERSM20110 and *Simon's Taxes* E4.507A, E4.508H.

28.2 RESTRICTED SHARES

[*ITEPA 2003, ss 422–432*]

Edward and Andrew are employees of Perks Ltd.

Edward is given 2,000 shares in the company on 1 October 2016 on the understanding that he cannot sell them for at least three years. This has the practical effect of restricting the market value by 30 pence per share.

Andrew is given 3,000 shares in the company on the same date on the understanding that they will be forfeited if he leaves the company before 1 January 2021. This has the practical effect of restricting the market value by 50 pence per share. Andrew does not leave the company and thus holds the shares with full rights as from 1 January 2021.

28.2 IT Share-Related Employment Income and Exemptions

The above awards are not made under a tax-advantaged scheme.

The market value per share, disregarding the above restrictions, is as follows.

At 1.10.16	£2.00
At 1.10.19	£4.00
At 1.1.21	£5.00

The following amounts are chargeable to tax as employment income

2016/17

Edward — 2,000 × £1.70 (restricted market value at 1.10.16) = £3,400

Andrew — no charge, as provision for forfeiture persists for no more than five years (see *ITEPA 2003, s 425*) — Nil

2019/20

Edward — chargeable event occurs on 1.10.19 when the shares cease to be restricted shares.

Taxable amount = UMV × (IUP − PCP − OP) − CE (see *ITEPA 2003, s 428*)

UMV (Unrestricted Market Value) = (2,000 × £4) = £8,000

$$\text{IUP (Initial Uncharged Proportion)} = \frac{4{,}000\,(2{,}000 \times £2) - 3{,}400}{4{,}000}$$

PCP (Previously Charged Proportion) = Nil (as there has been no previous chargeable event)

OP (Outstanding Proportion) = Nil (as unrestricted market value and actual market value are the same after the event)

CE (employee's expenses) = Nil

Taxable amount = £8,000 × 15% (600/4,000) = £1,200

2020/21

Andrew — chargeable event occurs on 1.1.21 when the shares cease to be restricted shares.

Taxable amount = UMV × (IUP − PCP − OP) − CE

UMV = (3,000 × £5) = £15,000

$$\text{IUP (Initial Uncharged Proportion)} = \frac{6{,}000\,(3{,}000 \times £2) - \text{Nil}}{6{,}000}$$

Other values = Nil

Taxable amount = £15,000 × 100% (6,000/6,000) = £15,000

Share-Related Employment Income and Exemptions IT 28.3

Available elections and their effect

Andrew could have elected, jointly with his employer, to disapply the exemption on acquisition. The election would have had to be made by 15 October 2016. [*ITEPA 2003, s 425*]. The chargeable amount for 2016/17 would have been 3,000 × £1.50 = £4,500. The chargeable amount in 2020/21 would then have been £15,000 × 25% (1,500/6,000) = £3,750.

Edward and/or Andrew could also (or alternatively) have elected, jointly with the employer, to ignore the restrictions in computing the chargeable amount on acquisition. The election(s) would have had to be made by 15 October 2016. [*ITEPA 2003, s 431*]. The chargeable amounts for 2016/17 would have been £4,000 for Edward (2,000 × £2) and £6,000 for Andrew (3,000 × £2) but there would have been no further charge in subsequent years.

Note

(a) The elections mentioned above are implemented by way of an agreement (between employer and employee), in a form approved by HMRC; there is no requirement for them to be submitted to HMRC. Once made, the elections are irrevocable.

(b) With effect on and after 6 April 2015, irrespective of when the shares in question are acquired, the above election is available only if, at the time of acquisition, the earnings from the employment are (or would be if there were any) general earnings to which any of the charging provisions for employment income apply.

28.3 CONVERTIBLE SHARES

[*ITEPA 2003, ss 435–444*]

Missy is an employee of XYZ Ltd. Under a non-tax-advantaged employee share scheme, she is awarded 1,000 'B' shares in the company on 1 December 2018 which are convertible in exactly two years' time into 1,200 'A' shares. Under the terms of the scheme, Missy is required to pay the company £150 for the conversion. She duly converts the shares on 1 December 2020. Relevant market values (MV) per share are as follows.

MV per 'B' share at 1.12.18 with right to convert after 2 years	£2.00
MV per 'B' share at 1.12.18 ignoring right to convert	£1.80
MV per 'A' share at 1.12.20	£3.75
MV per 'B' share at 1.12.20 ignoring right to convert	£3.00

Chargeable amount on acquisition of 'B' shares (2018/19)

1,000 × £1.80 (conversion right ignored — *ITEPA 2003, s 437*)	£1,800

28.3 IT Share-Related Employment Income and Exemptions

Chargeable amount on conversion into 'A' shares (2020/21) *(ITEPA 2003, ss 440, 441)*

	£	£
1,200 × £3.75 (MV of 'A' shares)		4,500
Less 1,000 × £3.00 (MV of 'B' shares)	3,000	
Consideration given for the conversion	150	(3,150)
Chargeable amount		£1,350

Note

(a) Immediately after the conversion, Missy has shares worth £4,500 for which she has paid £150, a benefit of £4,350 of which only £3,150 has been taxed. The capital growth in the 'B' shares between acquisition and conversion is not charged to income tax.

28.4 TAX-ADVANTAGED SHARE INCENTIVE PLANS

[ITEPA 2003, ss 488–515, Sch 2]

GB plc operates a share incentive plan self-certified as a tax-advantaged plan in August 2020. The plan provides for free shares, partnership shares, matching shares and dividend shares. The following table illustrates the permissible benefits and the tax position of participating employees as regards each of these kinds of share.

	Free shares	Partnership shares	Matching shares	Dividend shares
Brief description	Shares appropriated (without payment) to employees	Shares acquired on employees' behalf from sums deducted from their salary	Shares appropriated (without payment) to employees in proportion to their partnership shares	Shares acquired on employees' behalf out of dividends received on their plan shares
Maximum limits per participant	Shares worth £3,600 (per tax year) at time of award	Salary deductions must be lower of £1,800 per tax year and 10% of salary (plan may specify lower limits)	Two matching shares for each partnership share acquired (plan may specify lower ratio)	No statutory limit but the amount of cash dividends to be reinvested (or how such an amount is to be determined) is at the direction of the company.
Minimum limits — note (a)	N/A	£10 on any occasion or such lesser amount as is specified in the plan	N/A	N/A

Share-Related Employment Income and Exemptions IT 28.4

	Free shares	Partnership shares	Matching shares	Dividend shares
Holding period (i.e. period during which shares must remain in plan) — note (b)	As specified by company — must be at least three years but not more than five, from time of award	None — employee may withdraw shares from plan at any time (see below for tax position)	As specified by company — must be at least three years but not more than five, from time of award	Three years from acquisition
Tax on award of shares	None	None — deductions from salary allowable for income tax	None	None — dividends applied in acquiring shares are not taxable
Income tax on shares leaving the plan (note (c)) within less than three years of award (subject to note (d))	On market value of shares when they leave the plan	On market value of shares when they leave the plan	On market value of shares when they leave the plan	Original dividend becomes taxable, but in tax year in which shares leave plan
Income tax on shares leaving the plan (note (c)) after three years or more, but less than five years, after award (subject to note (d))	On lower of market value at time of award and market value on leaving the plan	On lower of salary used to acquire the shares and market value on leaving the plan	On lower of market value at time of award and market value on leaving the plan	None
Income tax on shares leaving the plan (note (c)) five or more years after award	None	None	None	None
Capital gains tax on shares leaving the plan (note (c)) at any time— note (f)	None	None	None	None

Notes

(a) It is at the option of the company whether or not to include in the plan a minimum limit for partnership shares. [*ITEPA 2003, Sch 2 para 47*].

28.4 IT Share-Related Employment Income and Exemptions

(b) Shares appropriated to employees, or acquired on their behalf, are held within the plan by trustees until leaving the plan as in (d)) below. In all cases, the stipulated holding period automatically ends if the participating employee ceases to be in relevant employment. [*ITEPA 2003, Sch 2 paras 36, 61, 67*].

(c) References to shares leaving the plan are to their ceasing to be subject to the plan. Shares cease to be subject to the plan if they are withdrawn by the participant (i.e. transferred by the plan trustees on his instructions or sold by them on his instructions and his account) or the participant leaves the relevant employment. [*ITEPA 2003, Sch 2 paras 95–97*].

(d) There is no income tax charge on shares ceasing to be subject to the plan *at any time* by reason of the participant's ceasing to be in relevant employment due to death, injury, disability, redundancy, retirement and other specified reasons beyond his control. [*ITEPA 2003, s 498, Sch 2 paras 98, 99*]. See ETASSUM25120 and *Simon's Taxes* E4.538.

(e) The income tax exemptions do not apply if the shares are awarded or acquired under arrangements one of the main purposes of which is the avoidance of tax or national insurance contributions. [*ITEPA 2003, s 489(4)*]. See *Simon's Taxes* E4.538, E1.574.

(f) For capital gains tax purposes, shares ceasing to be subject to the plan at any time are deemed to have been disposed of and immediately reacquired by the participant at that time at their then market value, but no chargeable gain or allowable loss arises on that deemed disposal. [*TCGA 1992, Sch 7D para 5*].

(g) The above table is for illustrative purposes only to summarise key features. For a more detailed explanation see *Simon's Taxes* E4.528 onwards

28.5 ENTERPRISE MANAGEMENT INCENTIVES

[*ITEPA 2003, ss 527–541, Sch 5; FA 2020, s 107*]

Keyman, an executive director of HIP Company Ltd, is granted on 1 September 2018, by reason of his employment, an option, exercisable within ten years, to acquire 8,000 ordinary shares in the company at £2.50 per share. No price is payable for the option itself. The market value of the company's ordinary shares at the date the option is granted is £3.50 per share. Keyman exercises the option on 11 October 2019 when the market value is £4.50 per share. On 19 September 2020, he sells half his holding (i.e. 4,000 shares) for net proceeds of £24,900. No other options have been granted to Keyman by reason of his employment with the company.

HIP Company Ltd is a qualifying company for the purposes of the Enterprise Management Incentives provisions, and gives HMRC notice of the grant of the option by 1 December 2018 (i.e. within 92 days). It obtained a Stock Market quotation in March 2020. Keyman is an eligible employee and, at the time of grant, the total value of shares in the company in respect of which options existed was well below £3 million.

Income tax

2018/19

No charge arises on receipt of the option. [*ITEPA 2003, ss 475, 528*].

2019/20

Charge on exercise of option (note (c))

Lower of

	£	£
Market value of 8,000 shares at time option granted (8,000 × £3.50)	£28,000	
Market value of 8,000 shares at time option exercised (8,000 × £4.50)	£36,000	28,000
Deduct Option Price (8,000 × £2.50)		(20,000)
Amount chargeable to income tax as employment income		£8,000

Capital gains tax

2020/21

	£	£
Net disposal proceeds (4,000 shares)		24,900
Deduct Cost of shares (4,000 × £2.50)	10,000	
Amount charged to income tax: (note (c))		
£8,000 × 4,000/8,000	4,000	(14,000)
Chargeable gain (within £12,300 annual exempt amount)		£10,900

Notes

(a) Under the Enterprise Management Incentives provisions, the company may be quoted or unquoted but must be an independent company carrying on (or preparing to carry on) a qualifying trade, whose gross assets do not exceed £30 million and which has less than 250 full-time employees and a permanent establishment in the UK. Broadly, an employee is eligible if he is employed by the company for at least 25 hours per week or, if less, at least 75% of his total working time, and he controls no more than 30% of the company's ordinary share capital. Any time in the period 19 March 2020 to 5 April 2021 inclusive during which, for reasons connected with COVID-19, the employee is not required to work is treated as a permissible period of absence and so will not result in an employee failing to the meet the working time requirement.

(b) Companies are able to grant options over shares worth (at time of grant) up to £250,000 to eligible employees.

(c) The discount (i.e. the excess of market value at date of grant over the aggregate of any amount paid for the option itself and the option price) is chargeable to income tax under *ITEPA 2003, s 476*. If market value had fallen by the time of exercise, the amount so chargeable is reduced (or extinguished) accordingly. [*ITEPA 2003, s 531*]. The amount chargeable to income tax is deductible for capital gains tax purposes by virtue of *TCGA 1992, s 119A*. It is allocated pro rata to the shares sold, under the normal part disposal rules for shares. See CG25395 and *Simon's Taxes* **C2.1014**.

(d) If the option had been a non-tax-advantaged share option, the income tax charge would have been on £16,000 (£36,000 – £20,000) (see computation at **28.1** above).

(e) Chargeable gains realised on shares acquired by the exercise of qualifying options may be eligible for capital gains tax business asset disposal relief (formerly entrepreneurs' relief). The twenty-four months minimum holding period (twelve-months prior to

28.5 IT   Share-Related Employment Income and Exemptions

6 April 2019) required for business asset disposal relief begins when the option is granted rather than when the shares are acquired. The normal requirement for business asset disposal relief that the individual must hold at least 5% of the company's ordinary share capital does not apply. [*TCGA 1992, s 169I(7A)–(7R); FA 2013, Sch 24 paras 1, 5, 6*]. See CG63975 and *Simon's Taxes* C3.1302A.

(f)   EU State aid approval for the Enterprise Management Incentive scheme expired on 6 April 2018 but has subsequently been renewed. HMRC will treat share options granted during the hiatus between 7 April and 15 May 2018 as qualifying under the scheme. HMRC will also waive the three-year limit under the maximum entitlement rules if a company cancelled options granted during the hiatus and wishes to grant them again Employment Related Securities Bulletin No. 30, October 2018. See *Simon's Taxes* E4.543 – E4.553B.

29 Social Security Income

29.1 HIGH INCOME CHILD BENEFIT CHARGE

[*ITEPA 2003, ss 681B–681H; Social Security Administration Act 1992, s 13A; Social Security Administration (Northern Ireland) Act 1992, s 11A*]

Jill is a single parent of one child and is entitled to child benefit of £20.70 per week throughout 2019/20 and £21.05 per week throughout 2020/21. Her adjusted net income is less than £50,000 for both those tax years. On 14 May 2020 she moves in with her boyfriend Jack, who has an adjusted net income of £56,344 for 2020/21. They continue to live together beyond 5 April 2021.

The income tax consequences for 2019/20 and 2020/21 are as follows

Jill has no liability to the high income child benefit charge for either year as her adjusted net income does not exceed £50,000. Jack is liable to the charge in respect of Jill's child benefit entitlement for the week beginning Monday 18 May 2020 and all subsequent weeks throughout the tax year 2020/21.

The charge is 1% of the amount of child benefit entitlement for every £100 of the chargeable person's adjusted net income above £50,000.

The amount of the charge on Jack is computed as follows. Child benefit entitlement for the 47 weeks beginning Monday 18 May 2020 is £21.05 x 47 = £989.35 which is rounded down to £989. Adjusted net income is rounded down to £56,300. The tax charge is:

£989 x 1% x 6,300/100 = £623.07

This is rounded down to £623, which is added to Jack's income tax liability for the year.

Jill has no liability to the high income child benefit charge for either year as her adjusted net income does not exceed £50,000. Jack is liable to the charge in respect of Jill's child benefit entitlement for the week beginning Monday 18 May 2020 and the subsequent 46 weeks falling in the tax year 2020/21.

Notes

(a) An income tax charge (the '*high income child benefit charge*') is imposed on an individual whose adjusted net income exceeds £50,000 in a tax year and who is, or whose partner is, in receipt of child benefit. In the event that both partners have an adjusted net income that exceeds £50,000, the charge applies only to the partner with the highest income.

(b) The maximum charge is an amount equal to the full amount of child benefit entitlement and applies where the chargeable person's adjusted net income is £60,000 or more.

(c) Child benefit itself is non-taxable but the high income child benefit charge effectively claws back the benefit from high income taxpayers.

(d) Adjusted net income is broadly taxable income before deducting personal reliefs but adjusted by deducting the gross equivalent of any Gift Aid donations or any pension contributions paid net of basic rate tax. [*ITA 2007, s 58*]. See PAYE10010 and *Simon's Taxes* E1.920, E1.911.

30 Trading Income

Cross-reference. See also 31 TRADING INCOME — CASH BASIS FOR SMALLER BUSINESSES.

30.1 OPENING YEARS OF ASSESSMENT

[*ITTOIA 2005, ss 199, 200, 204*]

Simon commences trade on 1 September 2018 and prepares accounts to 30 April, starting with an eight-month period of account to 30 April 2019. His profits (as adjusted for tax purposes) for the first three periods of account are as follows

	£
Eight months to 30 April 2019	24,000
Year to 30 April 2020	39,000
Year to 30 April 2021	40,000

His taxable profits for the first four tax years are as follows

	Basis period		£	£
2018/19	1.9.18 – 5.4.19	£24,000 × $^7/_8$		21,000
2019/20	1.9.18 – 31.8.19:			
	1.9.18 – 30.4.19		24,000	
	1.5.19 – 31.8.19	£39,000 × $^4/_{12}$	13,000	
				37,000
2020/21	Y/e 30.4.20			39,000
2021/22	Y/e 30.4.21			40,000

Overlap relief accrued:	
1.9.18 – 5.4.19 – 7 months	21,000
1.5.19 – 31.8.19 – 4 months	13,000
Total overlap relief accrued note (b)	£34,000

Notes

(a) The taxable profits for the first tax year are those from the commencement date to 5 April. [*ITTOIA 2005, s 199(1)*]. In the second tax year, the period from commencement to the accounting date in that year is less than 12 months, so the basis period is the 12 months from commencement. [*ITTOIA 2005, s 200(2)*]. In the third tax year, there is a period of account of 12 months to the normal accounting date, so the basis period is that period of account. [*ITTOIA 2005, s 198*]. Assessments then continue on that basis. See BIM81010 and *Simon's Taxes* B8.101.

30.1 IT Trading Income

(b) The overlap relief accrued (by reference to an aggregate overlap period of 11 months) will be given on cessation (see **30.3** below) or on a change of accounting date resulting in a basis period exceeding 12 months (the relief given depending on the extent of the excess) (see **30.2**(B) below).

30.2 CHANGE OF ACCOUNTING DATE

[*ITTOIA 2005, ss 214–220*]

(A) Change to a date earlier in the tax year

Miranda commenced trade on 1 September 2016, preparing accounts to 31 August. In 2019, she changes her accounting date to 31 May, preparing accounts for the nine months to 31 May 2019. The conditions of *ITTOIA 2005, s 217* are satisfied in relation to the change. Her profits (as adjusted for tax purposes) are as follows

	£
Year ended 31 August 2017	18,000
Year ended 31 August 2018	21,500
Nine months to 31 May 2019	17,000
Year ended 31 May 2020	23,000

Taxable profits for the first five tax years are as follows

	Basis period		£	£
2016/17	1.9.16 – 5.4.17	£18,000 × $^7/_{12}$		10,500
2017/18	Y/e 31.8.17			18,000
2018/19	Y/e 31.8.18			21,500
2019/20	1.6.18 – 31.5.19:			
	1.6.18 – 31.8.18	£21,500 × $^3/_{12}$	5,375	
	1.9.18 – 31.5.19		17,000	
				22,375
2020/21	Y/e 31.5.20			23,000

Overlap relief accrued:

	£
1.9.16 – 5.4.17 — 7 months	10,500
1.6.18 – 31.8.18 — 3 months	5,375
Total overlap relief accrued note (c)	£15,875

Notes

(a) For a change of accounting date to result in a change of basis period, the conditions in *ITTOIA 2005, s 217* must normally be satisfied. [*ITTOIA 2005, s 216*]. See *Simon's Taxes* B4.110.

(b) In this example, the 'relevant period' is that from 1 September 2018 (the day following the end of the basis period for 2018/19) to 31 May 2019 (the new accounting date in the year 2019/20 — the year of change). As the relevant period is less than 12 months, the basis period for 2019/20 is the 12 months ending on the new accounting date. [*ITTOIA 2005, s 216(2)*].

(c) The overlap relief accrued (by reference to an aggregate overlap period of 10 months) will be given on cessation (see **30.3** below) or on a change of accounting date resulting in a basis period exceeding 12 months (the relief given depending on the extent of the excess) (see (B) below).

(B) **Change to a date later in the tax year**

Dennis starts a business on 1 July 2016, preparing accounts to 30 June. In 2019, he changes his accounting date to 31 December, preparing accounts for the six months to 31 December 2019. The conditions of *ITTOIA 2005, s 217* are satisfied in relation to the change. His profits (as adjusted for tax purposes) are as follows

	£
Year ended 30 June 2017	18,000
Year ended 30 June 2018	21,500
Year ended 30 June 2019	23,000
Six months to 31 December 2019	12,000
Year ended 31 December 2020	27,000

Taxable profits for the first five years are as follows

	Basis period		£	£
2016/17	1.7.16 – 5.4.17	£18,000 × ⁹/₁₂		13,500
2017/18	Y/e 30.6.17			18,000
2018/19	Y/e 30.6.18			21,500
2019/20	1.7.18 – 31.12.19:			
	1.7.18 – 30.6.19		23,000	
	1.7.19 – 31.12.19		12,000	
			35,000	
	Deduct Overlap relief		(9,000)	
				26,000
2020/21	Y/e 31.12.20			27,000

Overlap relief accrued:	
1.7.16 – 5.4.17 — 9 months	13,500
Less utilised in 2019/20 — 6 months	(9,000)
Carried forward — 3 months	£4,500

30.2 IT Trading Income

Utilisation of overlap relief in 2019/20

$$\text{Apply the formula: } A \times \frac{B-C}{D}$$

where

A = aggregate overlap relief accrued (£13,500);

B = length of basis period for 2019/20 (18 months);

C = 12 months; and

D = the length of the overlap period(s) by reference to which the aggregate overlap profits accrued (9 months).

Thus, the deduction to be given in computing profits for 2019/20 is

$$£13,500 \times \frac{18-12}{9} = £9,000$$

Notes

(a) For a change of accounting date to result in a change of basis period, the conditions in *ITTOIA 2005, s 217* must normally be satisfied. [*ITTOIA 2005, s 216*]. See *Simon's Taxes* B4.110.

(b) In this example, the 'relevant period' is that from 1 July 2018 (the day following the end of the basis period for 2018/19) to 31 December 2019 (the new accounting date in the year 2019/20 — the year of change). As the relevant period is more than 12 months, the basis period for 2019/20 is equal to the relevant period. [*ITTOIA 2005, s 216(3)*]. Note that a basis period of 18 months results in this case, even though accounts were prepared for a period of only 6 months to the new date.

(c) The overlap relief accrued (by reference to an overlap period of 9 months) is given on cessation (see **30.3** below) or, as in this example, on a change of accounting date resulting in a basis period exceeding 12 months (the relief given depending on the extent of the excess). The balance of overlap relief (£4,500) is carried forward for future relief on the happening of such an event. [*ITTOIA 2005, s 220*]. If Dennis had changed his accounting date to 31 March or 5 April (instead of 31 December), the overlap relief of £13,500 would have been given in full in 2019/20.

(C) **Change of accounting date carried forward**

[*ITTOIA 2005, s 219*]

Sharon has been trading since 1 September 1992, preparing accounts to 31 August. She has transitional overlap relief of £21,000 brought forward by reference to an overlap period of seven months. She decides to change her accounting date to 30 April, preparing accounts for a period of 20 months from 1 September 2016 to 30 April 2019. Results for relevant periods of account are as follows.

Trading Income IT 30.2

	£
Year ended 31 August 2016	60,000
1 September 2016 to 30 April 2018 (20 months)	90,000
Year ended 30 April 2019	67,500
Year ended 30 April 2020	73,500

The first year of change is 2017/18 being the first year in which accounts are not made up to the old date of 31 August. [*ITTOIA 2005, s 214(1)*]. However, a period of account exceeding 18 months cannot result in a change of basis period. [*ITTOIA 2005, s 217(1)(3)*]. The position is then looked at with regard to 2018/19, but again the period of account ending with the new date in that year, 30 April 2018, is a period exceeding 18 months, so the basis period cannot change. Moving on to 2019/20, however, there is a period of account of less than 18 months to the new date in that year, i.e. the year to 30 April 2019, so there *can* be a change of basis period provided the other conditions of *ITTOIA 2005, s 217* are satisfied.

The assessments are as follows

	Basis period			£	£
2016/17	Y/e 31.8.16				60,000
2017/18	1.9.16 – 31.8.17	(90,000 × $^{12}/_{20}$)			54,000
2018/19	1.9.17 – 31.8.18:				
	1.9.17 – 30.4.18	(£90,000 × $^{8}/_{20}$)	36,000		
	1.5.18 – 31.8.18	(£67,500 × $^{4}/_{12}$)	22,500		58,500
2019/20	1.5.18 – 30.4.19*				67,500
2020/21	Y/e 30.4.20				73,500

*The relevant period is the 8 months from 1.9.18 – 30.4.19. As this is less than 12 months, the basis period for 2019/20 is the 12 months ending on 30.4.19, the new date in the year.

Notes

(a) The period 1.5.18 – 31.8.18 is an overlap period of 4 months for which there is an overlap profit of £22,500 (as computed for the 2018/19 assessment). Thus, the aggregate overlap profit carried forward is increased to £43,500 by reference to an overlap period of 11 months.

(b) The fact that the original overlap relief is transitional relief (applicable only to businesses commenced before 6 April 1994) is of no relevance. Such relief is carried forward, and eventually relieved, in the same way as any other overlap relief.

(c) For the calculation of capital allowances for a period of account exceeding 18 months, see **4.1(B)** CAPITAL ALLOWANCES ON PLANT AND MACHINERY.

30.3 IT Trading Income

30.3 CLOSING YEAR OF ASSESSMENT

[*ITTOIA 2005, s 202*]

Robin commenced to trade on 1 May 2016, preparing accounts to 30 April. He permanently ceases to trade on 30 June 2020, preparing accounts for the two months to that date. His profits (as adjusted for tax purposes) are as follows

	£
Year ended 30 April 2017	24,000
Year ended 30 April 2018	48,000
Year ended 30 April 2019	96,000
Year ended 30 April 2020	36,000
Two months ended 30 June 2020	5,000
	£209,000

Taxable profits for the five tax years of trading are as follows

	Basis period		£	£
2016/17	1.5.16 – 5.4.17	(£24,000 × $^{11}/_{12}$)		22,000
2017/18	Y/e 30.4.17			24,000
2018/19	Y/e 30.4.18			48,000
2019/20	Y/e 30.4.19			96,000
2020/21	1.5.19 – 30.6.20			
	1.5.19 – 30.4.20		36,000	
	1.5.20 – 30.6.20		5,000	
			41,000	
	Deduct Overlap relief		(22,000)	19,000
				£209,000

Overlap relief accrued:	
1.5.16 – 5.4.17 — 11 months	22,000
Utilised in 2020/21	(22,000)

Notes

(a) The basis period for the tax year of cessation is the period beginning immediately after the end of the basis period for the penultimate tax year and ending on the date of cessation. Note that profits taxed over the lifetime of the business equate to profits earned (as adjusted for tax purposes).

(b) The overlap relief accrued as a result of the application of the opening years rules is given in full on cessation (in the absence of an earlier change of accounting date resulting in a basis period exceeding 12 months — see **30.2**(B) above). [*ITTOIA 2005, s 205*]. See BIM81095 and *Simon's Taxes* B8.107.

30.4 PROFIT COMPUTATIONS

A UK trader commences trading on 1 October 2019. His profit and loss account for the year to 30 September 2020 is

	£	£
Sales		110,000
Deduct Purchases	75,000	
Less Stock and work in progress at 30.9.20	15,000	
		(60,000)
Gross profit		50,000
Deduct		
Salaries (all paid by 30.6.21)	15,600	
Rent and rates	2,400	
Telephone	500	
Heat and light	650	
Depreciation	1,000	
Motor expenses	2,700	
Entertainment	600	
Bank interest	900	
Hire-purchase interest	250	
Repairs and renewals	1,000	
Accountant's fee	500	
Bad debts	200	
Sundries	700	
		(27,000)
Net profit		23,000
Gain on sale of fixed asset		300
Rent received		500
Bank interest received		150
Profit		£23,950

Further Information

(i) Rent and rates. £200 of the rates bill relates to the period from 1.6.19 to 30.9.19.

(ii) Telephone. Telephone bills for the trader's private telephone (included in the accounts) amount to £150. It is estimated that 40% of these calls are for business purposes.

30.4 IT Trading Income

(iii) Motor expenses. All the motor expenses are in respect of the proprietor's car. 40% of the annual mileage relates to private use and home to business use.

			£
(iv)	Entertainment	Staff	100
		UK customers	450
		Overseas customers	50
			£600

(v) Hire-purchase interest. This is in respect of the owner's car.
(vi) Repairs and renewals. There is an improvement element of 20% included.
(vii) Bad debts. This is a specific write-off.
(viii) Sundries. Included is £250 being the cost of obtaining a bank loan to finance business expenditure, £200 for agent's fees in obtaining a patent for trading purposes and a £50 inducement to a local official.
(ix) Other. The proprietor obtained goods for his own use from the business costing £400 (resale value £500) without payment.
(x) Capital allowances for the year to 30 September 2020 amount to £1,520.

Computation of taxable trading income — Year to 30.9.20

		£	£
Profit per the accounts			23,950
Add			
Repairs — improvement element			200
Hire-purchase interest (40% private)			100
Entertainment	note (e)		500
Motor expenses (40% private)			1,080
Depreciation			1,000
Telephone (60% × £150)			90
Goods for own use			500
Illegal payment	note (g)		50
			27,470
Deduct			
Bank interest received (savings income)		150	
Rent received (property income)		500	
Gain on sale of fixed asset		300	
			(950)
			26,520
Less Capital allowances			(1,520)
Chargeable trading income			£25,000

Notes

(a) Costs of obtaining loan finance are specifically allowable. [*ITTOIA 2005, s 58*]. See BIM45800 and *Simon's Taxes* B2.437.

(b) Capital allowances are deductible as a trading expense.

(c) The adjusted profit of £25,000 would be subject to the commencement provisions for assessment purposes. See **30.1** above.

(d) Pre-trading expenses are treated as incurred on the day on which trade is commenced if they are incurred within seven years of the commencement and would have been allowable if incurred after commencement. [*ITTOIA 2005, s 57*]. See BIM46351, BIM46355 and *Simon's Taxes* B2.460.

(e) All entertainment expenses, other than staff entertaining, are non-deductible. [*ITTOIA 2005, ss 45–47*]. See BIM45000 onwards and *Simon's Taxes* B2.432.

(f) If wages and salaries remain unpaid nine months after the end of the period of account, they are disallowed. A deduction is then allowable for the period of account in which they are paid. [*ITTOIA 2005, ss 36, 37*]. See BIM47130 and *Simon's Taxes* B2.422.

(g) Trading stock appropriated for personal use must be accounted for at market value. [*ITTOIA 2005, s 172B*]. See BIM51625 and *Simon's Taxes* B2.205.

(h) Expenditure in making a payment which itself constitutes the commission of a criminal offence (or would do if made in the UK) is specifically disallowed. This includes payments which are contrary to the Prevention of Corruption Acts. [*ITTOIA 2005, s 55*]. See BIM43101 and *Simon's Taxes* B2.420.

30.5 TRADING ALLOWANCE

[*ITTOIA 2005, ss 783A–783AR; F(No 2)A 2017, Sch 3 para 1*]

Jennifer is in employment earning £25,000 per annum but for the last few years has been earning extra money by buying and selling rare DVDs online. After taking advice she accepts that her online activities amount to the carrying on of a trade, and she calculates profits to 5 April each year on the cash basis. For the year ended 5 April 2021 she has online sales of £2,100. Her purchases amount to £500 and she has allowable expenses of £100.

Jennifer's taxable profits for the year to 5.4.21 are as follows

			£	£
Sales (i.e. gross receipts)				2,100
Deduct:	Purchases		500	
	Expenses		100	
				(600)
Taxable profit				£1,500

30.5 IT — Trading Income

Jennifer elects to use the trading allowance and is instead taxed as follows

		£
Gross receipts		2,100
Deduct:	Trading allowance	(1,000)
Taxable profit for 2020/21		£1,100

Notes

(a) A £1,000 allowance (the '*trading allowance*') was introduced for trading income with effect for the tax year 2017/18 onwards. It applies to trades, professions and vocations, but not to businesses carried on in partnership. The allowance also covers certain miscellaneous income. A similar, but entirely separate, £1,000 allowance was introduced simultaneously for property income — see **22.3** PROPERTY INCOME.

(b) Where an individual's gross receipts do not exceed the £1,000 allowance, profits will be treated as nil ('*full relief*'). The individual will be able to elect for full relief not to be given. Where, as in this example, gross receipts exceed the £1,000 allowance, the individual can elect to use an alternative method of calculating income ('*partial relief*'). Under this method the charge to tax is on the excess of gross receipts over £1,000.

(c) Although the taxpayer in this example uses the cash basis to calculate profits, the trading allowance is not restricted to such cases.

30.6 CREATIVE ARTISTS — AVERAGING

[*ITTOIA 2005, ss 221, 222, 223–225; FA 2016, s 25(2)(4)–(7)(12)*]

Richard is an established author by profession and has the following profits/losses as adjusted for income tax purposes (including a deduction for capital allowances) for the six years mentioned.

Year ended	Profit/loss £
31.12.15	35,000
31.12.16	30,000
31.12.17	6,000
31.12.18	25,000
31.12.19	13,000
31.12.20	(2,000)

Averaged profits for all years would be

		No averaging claims £	Averaging claims for all possible years £
2015/16	note (a)	35,000	35,000
2016/17	note (b)	30,000	18,000
2017/18	note (c)	6,000	21,500
2018/19	note (d)	25,000	17,250
2019/20	note (e)	13,000	8,625
2020/21	note (e)	Nil	8,625
		£109,000	£109,000

Notes

(a) 2015/16   35,000
    2016/17   30,000
                 £65,000

As £30,000 is not less than 75% of £35,000, no averaging claim is possible.

(b) 2016/17   30,000
    2017/18   6,000
              £36,000 ÷ 2 = £18,000

As £6,000 does not exceed 75% of £30,000, straight averaging applies. Still no claim can be made to average 2016/17 (as adjusted) with 2015/16, even though this would now be possible purely on the figures.

(c) 2017/18   18,000
    2018/19   25,000
              £43,000 ÷ 2 = £21,500

As £18,000 is less than 75% of £25,000, straight averaging applies.

(d) 2018/19   21,500
    2019/20   13,000
              £34,500 ÷ 2 = £17,250

As £13,000 is less than 75% of £21,500, straight averaging applies.

(e) 2019/20   17,250
    2020/21   Nil
              £17,250 ÷ 2 = £8,625

The loss of £2,000 for 2020/21 does not enter into the averaging claim, but is available to reduce either the 2019/20 or the 2020/21 averaged profits of £8,625 on a claim under *ITA 2007, s 64* (see **15.1** losses). See BIM85015.

30.6 IT Trading Income

The 2020/21 averaged profits of £8,625 may themselves be averaged with 2021/22 profits if the 75% rule is satisfied. Any loss claim against income of 2020/21 is disregarded for this purpose.

(f) Averaging does not apply in calculating profits using the cash basis for smaller businesses. [*ITTOIA 2005, ss 221–221A; FA 2013, Sch 4 paras 32, 56*]. See BIM84050 and *Simon's Taxes* B5.326.

30.7 FARMING AND MARKET GARDENING — AVERAGING

[*ITTOIA 2005, ss 221, 222, 222A, 223–225; FA 2016, s 25(2)–(7)(12)*]

(A) **Five-year averaging**

Boycie has been carrying on a farming trade for ten years. In December 2019 the farm suffered heavy flooding. The farm initially had taxable profits as follows for the six years to 30 June 2020.

Year ended	£
30.6.15	34,000
30.6.16	52,000
30.6.17	44,000
30.6.18	50,000
30.6.19	47,000
30.6.20	26,000

Boycie made an averaging claim for the two years 2015/16 and 2016/17. The profits for the first of those years did not exceed 75% of the profits of the other, meaning that a claim was possible. The taxable profit of each of those two years was adjusted to £43,000.

For 2019/20 and 2020/21 a two-year averaging claim is possible, the profits of one year being clearly less than 75% of the profits of the other. If such a claim were made, the taxable profit of each of those two years would be adjusted to £36,500.

As an alternative, after taking into account his other income and his tax rates and allowances for each year, Boycie decides to make a five-year averaging claim for the years 2016/17 to 2020/21 inclusive. The average of the profits of the first four years is £(43,000 + 44,000 + 50,000 + 47,000) divided by 4 = £46,000. (The 2016/17 profit is taken to be £43,000, i.e. the averaged profit resulting from the earlier claim.) The profits of the fifth year are clearly less than 75% of £46,000, so five-year averaging is possible. Following the claim, the taxable profit of each of the five years is now £(43,000 + 44,000 + 50,000 + 47,000 + 26,000) divided by 5 = £42,000.

Notes

(a) As an alternative to two-year averaging, where in relation to five consecutive tax years:

- either A or B is less than 75% of the other (where A is the average of the profits of the first four years and B is the profits of the fifth year); or
- the profits for one or more years, but not all five years, are nil,

Trading Income   IT 30.7

a five-year averaging claim may be made under *ITTOIA 2005, s 222A* by a UK farmer or market gardener. This has effect where the last of the five years is 2016/17 or a subsequent year; for example, a five-year averaging claim could be made with 2016/17 as the final year, which would involve averaging the profits of the years 2012/13 to 2016/17 inclusive. See BIM84115 and *Simon's Taxes* B5.170.

(B)   **Two-year averaging**

Giles, who has been farming for several years, has the following profits as adjusted for income tax purposes.

Year ended	Profit/(loss) £
30.9.12	8,500
30.9.13	12,000
30.9.14	15,000
30.9.15	10,000
30.9.16	4,000
30.9.17	(1,000)
30.9.18	(10,000)
30.9.19	1,600
30.9.20	2,400

Two-year averaged profits for all years would be

		No averaging claims £	Averaging claims for all years £
2012/13	note (a)	8,500	10,000
2013/14	notes (a)(b)	12,000	12,750
2014/15	notes (b)(c)	15,000	12,750
2015/16	notes (c)(d)	10,000	7,000
2016/17	notes (d)(e)	4,000	3,500
2017/18	notes (e)(f)	Nil	1,750
2018/19	notes (g)(h)	Nil	1,750
2019/20	note (j)	1,600	2,000
2020/21	note (k)	2,400	2,000
		£53,500	£53,500

Notes

(a)   2012/13   8,500
      2013/14   _12,000_
                 £20,500

30.7 IT Trading Income

As £8,500 exceeds 70% of £12,000 but does not exceed 75%, the adjustment is computed as follows

Difference £3,500 × 3	10,500	
Deduct ³/₄ × £12,000	(9,000)	
Adjustment	1,500	(1,500)
Existing 2012/13	8,500	
Existing 2013/14		12,000
Revised averaged profits 2012/13 & 2013/14	£10,000	£10,500

Note that this methodology is no longer valid where the second of the two years in question is 2016/17 or a later year. Straightforward averaging applies instead. [*ITTOIA 2005, s 223(4); FA 2016, s 25(5)(12)*]. See BIM84135 and *Simon's Taxes* B5.172, B5.328.

(b) 2013/14   10,500
     2014/15   15,000
              £25,500 ÷ 2 = £12,750

As £10,500 does not exceed 70% of £15,000, the straight average applies.

(c) 2014/15   12,750
     2015/16   10,000
              £22,750

As £10,000 is not less than 75% of £12,750, no averaging is permitted.

(d) 2015/16   10,000
     2016/17   4,000
              £14,000 ÷ 2 = £7,000

As £4,000 does not exceed 75% of £10,000, the straight average applies.

(e) 2016/17   7,000
     2017/18   Nil
              £7,000 ÷ 2 = £3,500

(f) The loss for the year to 30 September 2017 is not taken into account for averaging, but would be available to eliminate the averaged profits for 2017/18 on a claim under *ITA 2007, s 64*. See BIM85015.

(g) 2017/18   3,500
     2018/19   Nil
              £3,500 ÷ 2 = £1,750

(h) The loss for the year to 30 September 2018 is not taken into account for averaging, but would be available to set off against the balance of the averaged profits for 2017/18 and against the averaged profits for 2018/19 on a claim under *ITA 2007, s 64*, with the balance being carried forward.

(j) 2018/19   1,750
     2019/20   1,600
                £3,350

As £1,600 is not less than 75% of £1,750, a two-year averaging claim is not possible. See (A) above as regards five-year averaging.

(k) 2019/20   1,600
     2020/21   2,400 ÷ 2 = £2,000
                £4,000

As £1,600 is less than 75% of £2,400, a two-year averaging claim is possible.

(l) Averaging does not apply in calculating profits using the cash basis for smaller businesses. [*ITTOIA 2005, ss 221–221A; FA 2013, Sch 4, paras 32, 56*]. See BIM84050 and *Simon's Taxes* B5.326.

30.8 FOSTER CARE RELIEF

[*ITTOIA 2005, ss 803–828*]

Dave and Holly, a couple living together, provide foster care by way of trade. Each prepares accounts to 31 December. Foster children are placed with them by their local authority. During the calendar year 2020, they provide care to a twelve-year old (child 1) for the full 52 weeks and to a nine-year old (child 2) for 15 weeks. Their total foster care receipts for the year (before deduction of expenses) are £25,000 each. Their allowable expenses are £14,000 each.

Each of Dave and Holly's individual limits for 2020/21 is computed as follows

		£
Fixed amount for 2020/21: £10,000 ÷ 2		5,000
Amounts per child (y/e 31.12.20):	child 1 (52 × £250)	13,000
	child 2 (15 × £200)	3,000
		£21,000

30.8 IT Trading Income

For 2020/21, their income tax position is as follows

Normal trading income computation

	Dave £	Holly £
Total foster care receipts (y/e 31.12.20)	25,000	25,000
Allowable expenses	(14,000)	(14,000)
Net taxable profit (subject to below)	£11,000	£11,000

Alternative calculation under ITTOIA 2005, ss 815–819

Each could now elect, under *ITTOIA 2005, s 818*, for his or her taxable profits from foster care to be taken as the excess of total foster care receipts over his or her individual limit computed as above. Such an election for any tax year must be made on or before the first anniversary of 31 January following that year and has effect for that tax year only. Under the election, Dave and Holly's taxable profits for 2020/21 will each be reduced to £4,000 (£25,000 - £21,000).

Notes

(a) Foster care receipts are exempt if they do not exceed a limit computed by reference to the individual recipient. If, as in this example, they do exceed that limit, and the recipient so elects, they are subject to the alternative computation above. It is up to each individual recipient whether to make the election.

(b) Some HMRC offices are believed to have taken the view that, in a case such as that illustrated in this example, the amounts per child must be divided between the couple instead of being available separately to each individual. In this example, this would have the effect of reducing each individual's limit by £8,000. In the author's opinion, the legislation does not support such a view. If, however, a couple were trading in partnership (clearly not the case here) it does then become arguable that the partnership takes the place of the individual for the purpose of computing the limits, in which case only one amount per child would be available to the partnership.

30.9 CEMETERIES AND CREMATORIA

[*ITTOIA 2005, ss 169–172*]

GR, who operates a funeral service, owns a cemetery for which accounts to 31 December are prepared. The accounts to 31.12.20 reveal the following

(i) Cost of land representing 110 grave spaces sold in period £3,400
(ii) Number of grave spaces remaining 275
(iii) Residual capital expenditure on buildings and other land unsuitable for £18,250 interments

The allowances available are

			£
(A)	Item (i)		3,400
(B)		$\dfrac{110}{110 + 275} \times £18{,}250$	5,214
			£8,614

Note

(a) £8,614 will be allowed as a deduction in computing GR's trading profits for the period of account ending on 31 December 2020.

31 Trading Income — Cash Basis for Smaller Businesses

Cross-reference. See also **30 TRADING INCOME**.

31.1 CASH BASIS

[*ITTOIA 2005, ss 25A, 31A–31F; SI 2017 No 293*]

Keith has been running a one-man business for a number of years, preparing accounts to 30 September. For the year ended 30 September 2020, his turnover is £95,000 and he elects for his trading profits to be calculated on the cash basis for 2020/21 onwards as provided for by *ITTOIA 2005, s 25A*. His accounts for the year ended 30 September 2019 showed closing stock of £6,300, trade and other creditors of £2,400 and trade debtors of £300.

Keith uses a motor vehicle in the business. On 15 October 2019 he sold his car (Vehicle 1) for £1,400 to an unconnected individual and purchased instead a van (Vehicle 2) for £3,500. Expenditure in connection with Vehicle 1 for the period from 1 October to date of sale amounted to £300, and it had always been accepted that the car was used as to 20% for private purposes. Keith chooses to use the fixed rate deduction scheme (under *ITTOIA 2005, ss 94D–94G*) to calculate allowable expenditure on Vehicle 2. Business mileage was 6,200 miles for the period from date of purchase to 30 September 2020.

Keith also uses a room in his home as an office, working there for 60 hours each month. He chooses to use the fixed rate deduction scheme (under *ITTOIA 2005, s 94H*) to calculate allowable expenditure for use of home for business purposes.

Keith pays out £27,000 on purchases and £4,400 on business overheads in the year to 30 September 2020. The business overheads are all allowable revenue expenses but the figure excludes bank overdraft interest and all expenses connected with the car and van. In addition, Keith spends £2,094 on office furniture and equipment; it is accepted that this is capital expenditure. In the year to 30 September 2020, he is charged interest of £700 on a bank overdraft; the bank account in question includes some personal as well as business transactions.

At 30 September 2019, there were written-down values of £1,560 on the plant and machinery main pool and £2,200 on the pool for Vehicle 1 (which is a single asset pool due to the private use). The main pool includes a computer used only for business purposes which Keith sells for £150 in June 2020 to an acquaintance.

An adjustment expense required to be brought into account under ITTOIA 2005, s 233 as follows

Without an adjustment, the value of £6,300 placed on the previous year's closing stock would be taxed twice, once in the previous year and again when the stock is sold. The £300 brought forward as trade debts would also be taxed twice, once in the previous year and again when the debts are settled. Similarly, the £2,400 brought forward as trade and other creditors would be relieved twice. See note (d).

The adjustment expense is: £(6,300 + 300) – £2,400 = £4,200.

31.1 IT Trading Income — Cash Basis for Smaller Businesses

This is treated as an expense of the trade arising on the last day of the year ending 30.9.20, i.e. the first period of account for which the new basis is adopted.

The capital allowances computation for 2020/21 is as follows

	Main pool	Vehicle 1	Allowances
	£	£	£
Year ended 30.9.20			
WDV at 30.9.19	1,560	2,200	
Expenditure removed from pool (note (e))	(1,560)		
WDV brought forward at 1.10.19	Nil	2,200	
Disposal proceeds		(1,400)	
		800	
Private use adjustment 20%		(160)	
Balancing allowance		£640	640
Total allowances			£640
WDV carried forward	Nil		

The allowable expenditure for Vehicle 2 is

$$M \times R$$

where M is the number of miles of business journeys made by a person (other than as a passenger) using the vehicle in the period; and

R is the rate applicable for that kind of vehicle. The rate applicable to a goods vehicle is 45p per mile up to 10,000 miles and 25p thereafter. See note (f).

6,200 x 45p = £2,790.

The allowable expenditure for use of home as business is as follows

The amount of the fixed rate deduction for the period is the sum of the applicable amounts for each month (or part of a month) falling within the period. The applicable amounts is based on the number of hours worked; it is £18 where the number of hours worked is 51 hours or more but less than 101 hours. See note (f).

£18 x 12 months = £216.

Trading Income — Cash Basis for Smaller Businesses   IT 31.1

Taxable profits for the year to 30.9.20 are computed as follows

	£	£
Turnover		95,000
Deduct Purchases		(27,000)
Gross profit		68,000
Deduct		
Business overheads	4,400	
Expenses relating to Vehicle 1 (£300 x 80% business use)	240	
Fixed rate deduction for Vehicle 2 (see above)	2,790	
Fixed rate deduction for use of home as business (see above)	216	
Capital expenditure (note (g))	3,654	
Interest (note (h))	500	
Adjustment expense (see above)	4,200	
		(16,000)
		52,000
Add Capital receipt (note (i))		150
Net profit		52,150
Deduct Capital allowances on Vehicle 1 (see above)		(640)
Taxable profit		£51,510

Notes

(a) The cash basis is optional, and is available to unincorporated trades, professions and vocations (including those carried on in partnership) with an annual turnover not exceeding the turnover limit. For 2017/18 onwards, the turnover limit is £150,000; previously it was equal to the VAT registration threshold (e.g. £83,000 for 2016/17). Certain types of business are excluded from using the cash basis (see *ITTOIA 2005, s 31C*). Businesses must leave the cash basis the year after their receipts exceed £300,000 (previously twice the VAT registration threshold) unless they once again meet the turnover limit. See *Simon's Taxes* B2.112.

(b) The cash basis is an alternative to preparing accounts for tax purposes on an earnings basis and in accordance with generally accepted accounting practice (GAAP).

(c) In practice, elections to adopt the cash basis are made via the self-assessment tax return by ticking a box.

(d) An adjustment must be made upon entering or leaving the cash basis in the same way as for any other change of accounting basis. [*ITTOIA 2005, s 227A*]. This is to ensure that no receipt is taxed twice and no allowable payment is deducted twice, and similarly that neither receipts nor payments fall out of tax.

(e) No capital allowances are available to a person carrying on a trade in relation to which a cash basis election is in force, other than an allowance for capital expenditure on a car.

31.1 IT   Trading Income — Cash Basis for Smaller Businesses

When a person enters the cash basis for a tax year (Year Z), any qualifying expenditure on plant or machinery which is unrelieved at the end of the basis period for the preceding tax year (Year Y) is allowable as a deduction under the cash basis in Year Z, provided that it would be an allowable deduction were it incurred in Year Z. The rule does not apply where the asset had not been fully paid for as at the end of the basis period for Year Y. [*ITTOIA 2005, ss 240A–240D*]. See also note (g) below. See *Simon's Taxes* B2.304.

(f) The fixed rate deduction schemes are entirely optional and are not restricted to those using the cash basis. If a fixed rate deduction is made for a period of account in respect of qualifying expenditure incurred in relation to a particular vehicle, no other deduction is allowed for such qualifying expenditure. As regards subsequent periods of account, the fixed rate deduction scheme is then compulsory for that vehicle for every period for which it is used for the purposes of the trade. 'Qualifying expenditure', in relation to a vehicle, means expenditure incurred in respect of the acquisition, ownership, hire, leasing or use of the vehicle (other than incidental expenses incurred in connection with a particular journey). [*ITTOIA 2005, ss 94B–94I; CAA 2001, s 38ZA; FA 2016, s 24*].

For cars and goods vehicles, the 10,000 mile limit for the 45p rate takes into account the business mileage of *all* such vehicles used in the trade for which a fixed rate deduction is made; it is not 10,000 miles per vehicle.

For use of home as business, HMRC regard the number of hours worked as relating to hours worked wholly and exclusively for the purposes of the trade on core business activities, i.e. providing goods and/or services, maintaining business records and marketing/obtaining new business. The fixed rate deduction covers heat, light, power, telephone and internet connection. A separate deduction can still be claimed for fixed costs, such as council tax (or domestic rates in NI), insurance and mortgage interest, if an identifiable proportion can be attributed to business use. See *Simon's Taxes* B2.439A.

(g) Under the cash basis there is no general prohibition on deductions for expenditure of a capital nature. Instead, there is a list of capital expenditure for which no deduction is allowed. This list includes expenditure on acquiring a business, education, training, assets that are not depreciating assets, non-business assets, cars, land, non-qualifying intangible assets and financial assets. Any capital expenditure on the provision of a car is therefore prohibited. [*ITTOIA 2005, s 33A*].

The deduction of £3,654 for capital expenditure comprises both the plant and machinery bought in the year (totalling £2,094) and the brought forward written-down value capital allowances for plant and machinery bought in earlier years (£1,560). This is an allowable deduction provided that it would be allowed were it purchased in the current tax year. It is assumed that all the assets purchased constitute depreciating assets. These are defined in *ITTOIA 2005, s 33A(6)* as an asset which can reasonably be expected to have a useful life of less than 20 years or be worth only 10% of its original value in 20 years' time. No deduction is allowed for the van, as explained in note (f) due to the use of the fixed rate deduction. [*ITTOIA 2005, s2 240B–240C*]. See *Simon's Taxes* B2.304.

(h) Interest paid on cash borrowings is deductible up to a limit of £500. It does not matter whether or not the interest was paid wholly and exclusively for the purposes of the trade. [*ITTOIA 2005, ss 51A, 57B*]. See *Simon's Taxes* B2.436.

(i) Where a person using the cash basis receives amounts that would be capital in nature, these may be taxed under the cash basis. Of relevance to this particular example, capital receipts are brought into account where the person receives disposal

Trading Income — Cash Basis for Smaller Businesses   IT 31.1

proceeds in relation to capital expenditure that has been deducted under the cash basis, or would be were it incurred in the current year. [*ITTOIA 2005*, ss 96A–96B; *F(No 2)A 2017*, s 16, Sch 2, paras 1,4]. See *Simon's Taxes* B2.202.

32 Venture Capital Trusts

[*ITA 2007, ss 258–332; TCGA 1992, ss 151A, 151B, Sch 5C; FA 2016, ss 28–31; FA 2018, ss 14–17, Schs 4, 5*]

32.1 INCOME TAX INVESTMENT RELIEF

(A) **Form of relief**

On 1 May 2020, Miss K, who has annual earnings of £72,000, subscribes for 100,000 eligible £1 shares issued at par to raise money by VCT plc, an approved venture capital trust. On 1 September 2020 she purchases a further 225,000 £1 shares in VCT plc for £175,000 on the open market. The VCT makes no distribution in 2020/21. Miss K's other income for 2020/21 consists of dividends of £18,000. PAYE tax deducted is £16,300. She is not a Scottish taxpayer.

Miss K's tax computation for 2020/21 is as follows

	£
Employment income	72,000
Dividends	18,000
Total and net income	90,000
Deduct Personal allowance	(12,500)
Taxable income	£77,500
Tax payable:	
37,500 @ 20%	7,500.00
34,500 @ 40%	13,800.00
2,000 @ 0% (dividend allowance)	—
16,000 @ 32.5% (dividend upper rate)	5,200.00
£90,000	26,500
Deduct VCT investment relief:	
£100,000 @ 30% = £30,000 but restricted to	(26,500)
Income tax liability	Nil
Deduct: PAYE	(16,300.00)
Income tax repayable	£(16,300.00)

32.1 IT   Venture Capital Trusts

Note

(a)   VCT investment relief is available at the rate of 30% on the amount *subscribed for* up to a maximum subscription of £200,000 per tax year. The relief is restricted to the income tax liability (before taking into account certain reductions etc.). [*ITA 2007, ss 261–263*]. See VCM51030 and *Simon's Taxes* E3.210.

(B)   **Withdrawal of relief**

[*ITA 2007, ss 266–270*]

On 1 May 2022, Miss K in (A) above, who has since 2020/21 neither acquired nor disposed of any shares in VCT plc, gives 62,500 shares to her son. On 1 January 2023, she disposes of the remaining 262,500 shares on the open market for £212,500.

The relief given as in (A) above is withdrawn as follows

Disposal on 1 May 2022

The shares disposed of are identified, on a first in, first out basis, with 62,500 of the 100,000 shares subscribed for in May 2020. Since the disposal was not at arm's length, the relief given on those shares is fully withdrawn.

$$\text{Relief withdrawn } \frac{62,500}{100,000} \times £26,500 = \underline{£16,563}$$

Disposal on 1 January 2023

The balance of £9,937 of the relief originally given was in respect of 37,500 of the 262,500 shares disposed of. The disposal consideration for those 37,500 shares is

$$£212,500 \times \frac{37,500}{262,500} = \underline{£30,357}$$

As the disposal was at arm's length, the relief withdrawn is the lesser of the relief originally given (£9,937) and 30% of the consideration received, i.e. 30% of £30,357 = £9,107. Relief withdrawn is therefore £9,107.

The 2020/21 assessment on relief withdrawn will therefore charge tax of £(16,563 + 9,107)   £25,670

Notes

(a)   VCT investment relief is withdrawn on a disposal (or deemed disposal) within five years following the issue of the shares. Withdrawal of relief is by assessment for the tax year for which the relief was given.

(b)   If the disposal is at arm's length, the relief given by reference to those shares is reduced by the appropriate percentage of the consideration received for the disposal and is withdrawn entirely if thereby reduced to nil. The appropriate percentage is 30%, i.e. the rate at which investment relief was available.

Venture Capital Trusts   IT 32.2

32.2 INCOME TAX DIVIDEND RELIEF

On 1 June 2019, W subscribes for 100,000 eligible £1 shares issued at par to raise money by XYZ plc, an approved venture capital trust. On 1 October 2019, he purchases on the open market a further 200,000 shares in XYZ plc for £120,000. On 30 June 2020 W receives a distribution from XYZ plc of 2p per share. W's other income in 2020/21 is a salary of £87,850 and dividends from other companies of £20,000. Tax paid under PAYE amounts to £22,640.00. W is not a Scottish taxpayer.

W's taxable distribution from XYZ plc is arrived at as follows

The shares in XYZ plc were acquired in 2019/20 for £220,000. Distributions in respect of shares representing the £20,000 excess over the permitted maximum are not exempt. The 100,000 shares first acquired for £100,000 are first identified, so that the shares representing the excess are one-sixth of the 200,000 shares subsequently acquired for £120,000, i.e. 33,333 of those shares. The taxable dividend is therefore 33,333 @ 2p per share = £666.66. The dividend on the balance of 266,667 shares (266,667 @ 2p = £5,333.34) is exempt.

W's tax computation for 2020/21 is as follows

	£	£
Employment income		87,850
Dividends (other than from XYZ plc)		20,000
Taxable dividends from XYZ plc		666
Total and net income		108,516
Deduct Personal allowance	12,500	
Restricted by excess of income over £100,000: (£8,516 x /)	(4,258)	£(8,242)
Taxable income		£100,274
Tax payable.		
37,500 @ 20%		7,500.00
42,108 @ 40%		16,843.20
2,000 @ 0% (dividend allowance)		—
18,666 @ 32.5% (dividend upper rate)		6,066.45
£100,274		30,409.65
Deduct: PAYE		(22,640.00)
Net income tax liability		£7,769.65

Notes

(a) Dividends paid to a qualifying individual from a VCT are exempt from tax to the extent that they are made in respect of shares *acquired* (not necessarily subscribed for) for up to £200,000 in any tax year [*ITTOIA 2005, ss 709–712*]. See VCM51200 and *Simon's Taxes* E1.535.

32.2 IT Venture Capital Trusts

(b) The personal allowance is reduced by one-half of the excess of 'adjusted net income' over £100,000. [*ITA 2007, s 35*]. '*Adjusted net income*' is broadly net income less the grossed up amount of any allowable pension contributions and Gift Aid donations. [*ITA 2007, s 58*]. See PAYE10010 and *Simon's Taxes* E1.910.

32.3 CAPITAL GAINS TAX RELIEF ON DISPOSAL

On the disposals in **32.1(B)** above, a chargeable gain or allowable loss arises only on the disposal of shares acquired in excess of the permitted maximum (£200,000) for 2020/21. The 100,000 shares first acquired for £100,000 are first identified, so that the shares representing the excess are three-sevenths (75,000/175,000) of the 225,000 shares acquired for £175,000 on 1 September 2020, i.e. 96,429 of those shares. The disposal identified with those shares (on a first in, first out basis) is a corresponding proportion of the 262,500 shares disposed of for a consideration of £212,500 on 1 January 2023.

Miss K's capital gains tax computation for 2022/23 is therefore as follows

	£
Disposal consideration for 96,429 shares: $£212,500 \times \dfrac{96,429}{262,500} =$	78,061
Deduct Cost of 96,429 shares: $£175,000 \times \dfrac{96,429}{225,000} =$	(75,000)
Chargeable gain	£3,061

Notes

(a) On disposals by an individual of VCT shares (whether or not they were subscribed for), capital gains are exempt and losses not allowable to the extent that the shares disposed of were not acquired in excess of the £200,000 maximum in any tax year. [*TCGA 1992, s 151A*]. See VCM50010 and *Simon's Taxes* E3.221.

(b) The capital gains tax share identification provisions are disapplied as regards VCT shares within the above exemption. [*TCGA 1992, s 151B(1)*].

Corporation Tax

Contents

101	Accounting Periods
102	Capital Allowances
103	Capital Gains
104	Close Companies
105	Double Tax Relief
106	Group Relief
107	Income Tax in relation to a Company
108	Intangible Assets
109	Interest on Overpaid Tax
110	Interest on Unpaid Tax
111	Investment Companies and Investment Business
112	Liquidation
113	Loan Relationships
114	Losses
115	Payment of Tax
116	Profit Computations
117	Research and Development
118	Returns
119	Transfer Pricing

101 Accounting Periods

101.1 THE START AND END OF AN ACCOUNTING PERIOD

[*CTA 2009, ss 9, 10, 12*]

Plantagenet Ltd is incorporated on 1 January 2020. The company opens a bank account on 1 March 2020 which pays interest at 1%. It begins to trade on 1 June 2020. The company prepares its first set of accounts to 31 August 2021 and adopts 31 August as its annual accounting date.

Plantagenet Ltd's first three accounting periods are:

1 March 2020 – 31 May 2020 (beginning on the day on which the company comes within the charge to corporation tax and ending immediately before the day on which the company begins to trade).

1 June 2020 – 31 May 2021 (beginning immediately after the end of the previous accounting period and ending on the expiration of twelve months).

1 June 2021 – 31 August 2021 (beginning immediately after the end of the previous accounting period and ending on the company's accounting date).

Notes

(a) An accounting period of a company begins:
- when the company comes within the charge to corporation tax; or
- immediately after the end of the previous accounting period, if the company is still within the charge to corporation tax; or
- in the case of a company being wound up, when the winding up starts.

[*CTA 2009, ss 9(1), 12(3)*]. See CTM01410 and *Simon's Taxes* D1.108.

(b) An accounting period of a company comes to an end on the first occurrence of any of the following:
- the expiration of twelve months from the beginning of the accounting period;
- an accounting date of the company;
- if there is a period for which the company does not make up accounts, the end of that period;
- the company's beginning or ceasing to trade;
- if the company carries on a single trade, its coming, or ceasing to be, within the charge to corporation tax in respect of that trade;
- if the company carries on more than one trade, its coming, or ceasing to be, within the charge to corporation tax in respect of all the trades;
- the company's becoming, or ceasing to be, UK resident;
- the company's ceasing to be within the charge to corporation tax;

101.1 CT Accounting Periods

- the company's entering administration (in which case the accounting period is treated as ending immediately before the day on which the company enters into administration); or

- the company's ceasing to be in administration under *Insolvency Act 1986, Sch B1* (or any corresponding event otherwise than under that Act).

[*CTA 2009, s 10*]. See CTM01500 and *Simon's Taxes* D1.108.

101.2 EFFECT OF AN ACCOUNTING PERIOD OVERLAPPING TWO FINANCIAL YEARS HAVING DIFFERENT RATES OF CORPORATION TAX

[*CTA 2009, ss 5, 6, 8*]

For the year ended 30 June 2017, the following information is relevant to A Ltd.

	£
Trading income	1,200,600
UK property income	350,000
Income from non-trading loan relationships	30,000

The main rate of corporation tax for the financial year 2016 is 20% and the rate for the financial year 2017 is 19%.

The corporation tax computation of A Ltd for the 12-month accounting period ended on 30.6.17 is

	£	
Trading income	1,200,600	
UK property income	350,000	
Income from non-trading loan relationships	30,000	
Total taxable profits	£1,580,600	
Total profits apportioned		
1.7.16 – 31.3.17	$^9/_{12}$ × £1,580,600	£1,185,450
1.4.17 – 30.6.17	$^3/_{12}$ × £1,580,600	£395,150
Tax chargeable		
20% × £1,185,450		237,090
19% × £395,150		75,079
Total tax charge		£312,169

Accounting Periods CT 101.3

Notes

(a) Where an accounting period does not coincide with a financial year, apportionment is necessary to calculate the tax payable. Apportionment is on a time basis, between the financial years which overlap the accounting period. Corporation tax is then charged on each proportion so computed at the rate fixed for the financial year concerned. [*CTA 2009, s 8*]. See BIM40685, CTM01405.

(b) In order to illustrate the effect of time apportionment, the example above deals with FY 2016 and FY 2017, as the main rate of corporation tax was different for these two years (20% and 19% respectively). Where two financial years have the same rate (as is the case for FY 2018, FY 2019 and FY 2020), there is no practical necessity to perform the time apportionment calculation – therefore, for a tax year ended 30 June 2020 where the total taxable profits are £1,580,600, the tax charge is £300,314 (19% × £1,580,600).

101.3 PERIODS OF ACCOUNT EXCEEDING 12 MONTHS

[*CTA 2009, ss 10(1), 53, 1307; CTA 2010, s 1172*]

B Ltd prepares accounts for 16 months ending on 31 March 2021. The following information is relevant

	£
Profit for 16 months	1,500,000
Capital gain (after indexation calculated to 31 December 2017) arising on 1.6.20	100,000
Tax written down value of plant and machinery main pool	
At 1.12.19	40,000
Plant purchased 1.4.20	900,000
Plant purchased 10.12.20	500,000
Proceeds of plant sold 31.12.20 (less than cost)	4,000

B Ltd has no related 51% group companies

B Ltd will be chargeable to corporation tax as follows

	Accounting period 12 months to 30.11.20	Accounting period 4 months to 31.3.21
	£	£
Adjusted profits (apportioned 12:4)	1,125,000	375,000
Deduct Capital allowances	(907,200)	(157,062)
Trading income	217,800	217,938
Chargeable gain	100,000	
Chargeable profits	£317,800	£217,938

101.3 CT   Accounting Periods

Notes

(a) Capital allowances
    12 months to 30 November 2020

	AIA £	Main pool £	Allowances £
Main pool		40,000	
Additions	900,000	—	
AIA	(900,000)		900,000
		40,000	
WDA 18%		(7,200)	7,200
Total allowances			£907,200
WDV c/f		£32,800	

4 months to 31 March 2021

	AIA £	Main pool £	Allowances £
WDV b/f		32,800	
Additions	500,000		
AIA (£1,000,000 x ¹/₁₂ + (£200,000 x ³/₁₂	(133,334)		133,334
	366,666		
Transfer to pool	(366,666)	366,666	
Disposals		(4,000)	
		395,466	
WDA 18% x 4/12		(23,728)	23,728
Total allowances			£157,062
WDV c/f		£371,738	

Writing-down allowances, but not first-year allowances, are proportionately reduced percentage of 18% if the accounting period is only part of a year. [*CAA 2001, s 56(3)*].

Annual investment allowance on £1,000,000 is available in a 12-month period from 1 January 2019 until 31 December 2020. The AIA for investments before and after these dates is £200,000. It is proportionately reduced for shorter periods or where there are related companies. Transitional rules apply for accounting periods straddling 1 January 2019 and 31 December 2020. [*CAA 2001, s 51A; FA 2019, s 32, Sch 13*]. See IT 4 CAPITAL ALLOWANCES ON PLANT AND MACHINERY.

(b) The capital gain is not apportioned on a time basis, but is included for the period in which it arises [*TCGA 1992 s 2A(1); FA 2019 Sch 1 paras 2, 120*].

(c) The tax for the two accounting periods ended 30.11.20 and 31.3.21 will be due for payment on 1.9.21 and 1.1.22 respectively. [*TMA 1970, s 59D*]. The CT return(s) for both accounting periods will be due by 31.3.22, i.e. the first anniversary of the last day of the sixteen-month period of account, or, if later, three months after the issue of the notice requiring the return. [*FA 1998, Sch 18 para 14*]. See also 118 RETURNS.

102 Capital Allowances

102.1 TRANSFER OF TRADE WITHIN GROUP: PERIOD OF ACCOUNT EXCEEDING 12 MONTHS

[*CTA 2010, ss 938–953; CAA 2001, ss 55, 56, 310–313*]

A Ltd owns 80% of the ordinary share capital of both B Ltd and C Ltd, the latter companies carrying on similar trades.

A Ltd and C Ltd prepare accounts annually to 31 July. B Ltd which previously prepared accounts to 30 April each year has prepared accounts for 15 months ending on 31 July 2020.

On 31 December 2019, C Ltd transferred the whole of its trade to B Ltd under circumstances covered by *CTA 2010, ss 938–953*.

The following information is relevant to B Ltd

		£
Trading profit for 15 months to 31.7.20 before deduction of capital allowances		200,000
1.5.19	Tax written-down value of plant and machinery main pool	10,800
11.6.19	Plant purchased	3,000
3.9.19	Plant purchased	2,000
4.10.19	Plant sold (original cost £9,000)	6,800
1.3.20	Plant purchased	8,000
10.5.20	Plant sold (original cost £40,000)	9,560
15.6.20	Plant purchased	30,000
1.8.19	Tax written-down value of plant and machinery main pool owned by C Ltd	9,216

B Ltd will have chargeable profits as follows

	Accounting period 12 months to 30.4.20 £	Accounting period 3 months to 31.7.20 £
Trading profits	160,000	40,000
Capital allowances on plant and machinery	(14,231)	(30,078)
Chargeable profits	£145,769	£9,922

102.1 CT   Capital Allowances

Capital allowances

Plant and machinery
12 months to 30.4.20

	AIA	Main Pool	Total allow-ances
	£	£	£
WDV b/f		10,800	
Additions	13,000		
Transfer from C Ltd (note (a))		8,525	
		19,325	
Disposals		(6,800)	
		12,525	
AIA £13,000 × 100% (note (e))	(13,000)		13,000
WDA on assets transferred from C Ltd £8,525 × 18% × $^4/_{12}$ (note (a))		(511)	511
WDA on balance of expenditure £(12,525 − 8,525) × 18%		(720)	720
WDV c/f		£11,294	
Total allowances			£14,231

3 months to 31.7.20

	AIA	Main Pool	Total allow-ances
	£	£	£
WDV b/f		11,294	
Additions	30,000		
Disposals		(9,560)	
		1,734	
AIA (note (e))	(30,000)		30,000
WDA (18% × $^3/_{12}$)		(78)	78
WDV c/f		£1,656	
Total allowances			£30,078

Capital Allowances   CT 102.1

Notes

(a) Where a trade is transferred part-way through an accounting period, HMRC take the view that writing-down allowances are calculated for the predecessor for a notional accounting period ending on the date of the transfer. The successor is then treated, in relation to the assets transferred, as having a chargeable period starting on that date and running to the end of its accounting period. (See CA15400.)

	£
The transfer value of machinery and plant obtained from C Ltd is	
Tax written-down value at 1.8.19	9,216
WDA due to C Ltd (£9,216 × 18% × $^5/_{12}$)	(691)
	£8,525

(b) The 'successor' company (B Ltd) is entitled to the capital allowances which the 'predecessor' company (C Ltd) would have been able to claim if it had continued to trade. [*CTA 2010, s 948(2)*]. See CTM06110 and *Simon's Taxes* D6.316, B3.390.

(c) No annual investment allowance, first-year or initial allowance is available to the successor on assets transferred to it by the predecessor. [*CTA 2010, s 948(3)*]. See CTM06110 and *Simon's Taxes* D6.316, B3.390.

(d) Writing-down allowances are reduced proportionately where the accounting period is less than one year. [*CAA 2001, ss 56(3), 310(2)*]. See CA23220.

(e) A Ltd's group is entitled to only one annual investment allowance between all the companies, which can be allocated as the companies think fit. [*CAA 2001, s 51C*]. For the year ended 30 April 2020 it is assumed that B Ltd is allocated £13,000 to allow all of its expenditure in the period to qualify. For the three months to 31 July 2020 it is assumed that B Ltd is allocated £30,000 to allow all of its expenditure in the period to qualify.

103 Capital Gains

103.1 CAPITAL LOSSES

[*TCGA 1992, s 2A(1)(3)(4); FA 2019, Sch 1 paras 2, 120; FA 2020, Sch 4 paras 39, 42*]

P Ltd has the following capital gains/(losses)

Year ended		£
31.7.17	Gains	27,000
	Losses	(7,000)
31.7.18	Losses	(12,000)
31.7.19	Gains	5,000
	Losses	(13,000)
31.7.20	Gains	40,000
	Losses	(30,000)

The gains and losses would be dealt with as follows in the CT computations of P Ltd

	£	£
31.7.17		
Gains chargeable to CT		£20,000
31.7.18		
Unrelieved losses carried forward	£(12,000)	Nil
31.7.19		
Losses (net)	(8,000)	Nil
Add Unrelieved losses brought forward	(12,000)	
Unrelieved losses carried forward	£(20,000)	
31.7.20		
Chargeable gains (net)	10,000	
Deduct Unrelieved losses brought forward	(20,000)	
Unrelieved losses carried forward	£(10,000)	Nil

Notes

(a) Unrelieved losses cannot be set off against trading profits, but are available to relieve future gains.

(b) Gains otherwise chargeable to CT may be covered by trading losses for the same or previous accounting periods or trading losses carried back from a succeeding period under *CTA 2010, s 37(3)*—see **114 LOSSES**. See CTM04510, CTM045904.

103.1 CT   Capital Gains

(c) For accounting periods beginning on or after 1 April 2020 (subject to transitional rules for periods straddling that date), there is a restriction on the amount of chargeable gains that can be relieved by brought-forward capital losses. Subject to a group wide £5m deductions allowance (encompassing the offset of all carried forward losses), companies can only offset up to 50% of chargeable gains using carried forward capital losses. See CGT **207.3** LOSSES.

(d) A special rule applies for financial year 2020 and subsequent years where a company has two or more accounting periods falling wholly within the same financial year, is chargeable to corporation tax for each period only because of a chargeable gain (or allowable loss) arising on the disposal of an asset, and during any gaps between those periods is not chargeable to corporation tax. So far as not otherwise deducted, losses arising in one of the periods can be deducted from gains arising in any of the other periods. The effect is that a loss arising in a later period can be carried back to an earlier period and a loss in an earlier period can be carried forward. To the extent that the loss is carried forward to an accounting period falling wholly within the same financial year, it can be deducted without the application of the restriction on deduction of losses rules (see (c) above). The restriction will apply to its deduction in any later accounting period. This provision will be relevant in particular to non-UK resident companies making direct or indirect disposals of UK land.

(e) See also **103.3(A)** below.

103.2 CLOSE COMPANY TRANSFERRING ASSET AT UNDERVALUE

[*TCGA 1992, s 125*]

(A)

G Ltd (a close company) sold a building in 2019 to an associated company Q Ltd, which is not a member of the same group as G Ltd, at a price below market value at the time. Relevant values relating to the asset were

	£
Cost 1999	45,000
Market value at date of disposal	95,000
Sale proceeds received	75,000

The issued share capital of G Ltd was held at the time of disposal as follows

	£1 ordinary shares	Value prior to sale of asset £
C	25,000	50,000
D	30,000	60,000
E	20,000	40,000
F	25,000	50,000
	100,000	£200,000

Sale proceeds on subsequent sale (at market value) in July 2020 of C's total shareholding (originally purchased at £0.80 per share in 1993) in G Ltd were £55,000.

Capital Gains   CT 103.2

G Ltd's chargeable gain on the sale of the building in 2019 is

	£
Market value (note (b))	95,000
Cost	(45,000)
Unindexed gain	50,000
Indexation allowance at, say, 40% on £45,000 (note (c))	(18,000)
Chargeable gain	£32,000

C's gain on the disposal of the shares in July 2020 is

		£	£
Sale proceeds			55,000
Deduct	Allowable cost:		
	Purchase price (25,000 × £0.80)	20,000	
	Less Apportioned undervalue (note (a))	(5,000)	(15,000)
Chargeable gain			£40,000

Notes

(a) The apportionment of undervalue on disposal is

	£
Market value at time of sale	95,000
Sale proceeds	(75,000)
	£20,000

Proportion of shareholding		Value apportioned
		£
C	$^{25}/_{100}$ × £20,000	5,000
D	$^{30}/_{100}$ × £20,000	6,000
E	$^{20}/_{100}$ × £20,000	4,000
F	$^{25}/_{100}$ × £20,000	5,000
		£20,000

(b) In the computation of the company's gain, market value is substituted for proceeds under *TCGA 1992, s 17*. See CG14530, CG14540 *Simon's Taxes* C2.109, C2.204.

(c) Indexation allowance is frozen at its December 2017 level. No indexation allowance is available in respect of expenditure incurred after 31 December 2017, and for expenditure incurred on or before that date and falling to be deducted on a disposal

103.2 CT Capital Gains

after that date, indexation allowance is computed up to and including December 2017 only. [*TCGA 1992, ss 53(1)(1B), 54(1B); FA 2018, s 26(2)(3)(6)*].See CG17232, CG17270 and *Simon's Taxes* D2.326. See **CGT 214.1** INDEXATION.

(B)

Assume the same facts as in (A) above except that the building had a market value of £155,000 at the date of disposal and the market value of C's shares on the subsequent disposal was £40,000. Assume now also that C purchased his shares at £0.70 per share before 31 March 1982 and that their value on that date was £21,000.

G Ltd's chargeable gain will be computed under the same principles as in (A) above. C's gain on the disposal of the shares will be as follows

		£	£
Sale proceeds			40,000
Deduct Allowable cost:			
31 March 1982 value		21,000	
Less Apportioned undervalue	(note (a))	(20,000)	
			(1,000)
Chargeable gain			£39,000

Notes

(a) The apportionment of undervalue on disposal is

	£
Market value at time of sale	155,000
Deduct Sale proceeds	(75,000)
	£80,000

Proportion of shareholding		Value apportioned
		£
C	$^{25}/_{100} \times £80,000$	20,000
D	$^{30}/_{100} \times £80,000$	24,000
E	$^{20}/_{100} \times £80,000$	16,000
F	$^{25}/_{100} \times £80,000$	20,000
		£80,000

(b) Transfers of assets on or before 31 March 1982 are disregarded in respect of disposals after 5 April 1988 to which re-basing applies (not illustrated in this example). [*TCGA 1992, s 125(1)(5)*]. See *Simon's Taxes* D1.919.

(c) Indexation allowance is frozen at its December 2017 level. No indexation allowance is available in respect of expenditure incurred after 31 December 2017, and for expenditure incurred on or before that date and falling to be deducted on a disposal after that date, indexation allowance is computed up to and including December 2017 only. [*TCGA 1992, ss 53(1)(1B), 54(1B); FA 2018, s 26(2)(3)(6)*]. See CG17232, CG17270 and *Simon's Taxes* D2.326. See **CGT 214.1** INDEXATION.

103.3 GROUPS OF COMPANIES

(A) Re-allocation of gains and losses within a group

[*TCGA 1992, ss 171A–171C; FA 2019, Sch 1 paras 62, 63*]

A Ltd and B Ltd are members of the same group of companies, preparing accounts each year to 31 March. On 30 September 2020, A Ltd sold an asset (asset 1) to an unconnected third party for £100,000. The asset had been acquired in June 2015 for £40,000. On 29 January 2021 B Ltd sold an asset (asset 2), which had cost £70,000 in January 2013, for £50,000 to C Ltd, an unconnected third party. B Ltd incurred costs on the disposal of £2,000. Neither company disposes of any other assets in the year ended 31 March 2021.

A Ltd and B Ltd jointly elect before 31 March 2023 under *TCGA 1992, s 171A* for the chargeable gain or loss on asset 2 to be treated as accruing to company A at the time it would otherwise have accrued to B.

The chargeable gains computations for the year ended 31 March 2021 for A Ltd and B Ltd are as follows.

B Ltd

Deemed disposal of asset 2 in April 2020: consideration deemed to be such that neither gain nor loss arises.

	£
Deemed consideration	84,000
Cost of asset to B Ltd	(70,000)
Indexation allowance £70,000 × say 20%	(14,000)
Gain	Nil

A Ltd

Disposal of asset 1 in September 2020

	£
Consideration	100,000
Cost	(40,000)
Indexation allowance £40,000 × say 10%	(4,000)
Chargeable gain	£56,000

103.3 CT Capital Gains

Disposal of asset 2 in January 2021

	£
Consideration	50,000
Cost to A Ltd	(70,000)
Cost of disposal incurred by B Ltd	(2,000)
Allowable loss	£(22,000)

Net chargeable gains £56,000 − £22,000 = £34,000

Notes

(a) The election under *TCGA 1992, s 171A* must be made in writing to HMRC within two years after the end of the accounting period of A Ltd in which the gain accrued. The election can only be made if a disposal of asset 2 by B Ltd to A Ltd would have been a no gain, no loss disposal within *TCGA 1992, s 171*. See CG45320 and *Simon's Taxes* D2.310, D2.314 and D2.311

(b) Indexation allowance is frozen at its December 2017 level. No indexation allowance is available in respect of expenditure incurred after 31 December 2017, and for expenditure incurred on or before that date and falling to be deducted on a disposal after that date, indexation allowance is computed up to and including December 2017 only. [*TCGA 1992, ss 53(1)(1B), 54(1B); FA 2018, s 26(2)(3)(6)*]. See CG17232, CG17270 and *Simon's Taxes* D2.326. See **CGT 214.1** INDEXATION.

(B) **Intra-group transfers of assets which are trading stock of one company but not of the other — transfer from a 'capital asset' company to a 'trading stock' company**

[*TCGA 1992, ss 161, 173(1); FA 2019, Sch 1 para 54*]

In June 2020, X Ltd transfers an item classed as a fixed asset to another group company Y Ltd, which treats it as trading stock.

The following information is relevant

	Case (i) £	Case (ii) £
Original cost (after 31.3.1982)	100,000	100,000
Market value at date of transfer	120,000	40,000
Eventual sale proceeds	140,000	140,000
Indexation allowance due on original cost at date of transfer	17,000	17,000

Capital Gains CT 103.3

The position of Y Ltd will be as follows if there is no election under *TCGA 1992, s 161(3)*

Chargeable gain/(allowable loss) on appropriation		
Market value	120,000	40,000
Deemed cost of asset (note (a))	(117,000)	(117,000)
Gain/(loss)	3,000	(77,000)
Deduct Indexation allowance included in cost (note (b))	—	17,000
Chargeable gain/(allowable loss)	£3,000	£(60,000)
Trading profit at date of sale		
Sale proceeds	140,000	140,000
Deemed cost of asset	(120,000)	(40,000)
Trading profit	£20,000	£100,000

With an election under *TCGA 1992, s 161(3)*

No chargeable gain arises on appropriation

	£	£
Trading profit at date of sale		
Sale proceeds		140,000
Market value at appropriation	120,000	
Adjustment for (gain)/loss otherwise (chargeable)/allowable	(3,000)	117,000
Trading profit		£23,000

Notes

(a) The intra-group transfer by X Ltd to Y Ltd is treated as a disposal on which neither a gain nor a loss accrues after taking account of any indexation allowance due. X Ltd has no liability on the transfer and Y Ltd has a deemed acquisition cost of £117,000 on the appropriation to stock. [*TCGA 1992, ss 56(2), 171(1)*]. See CG17740, CG45320 and *Simon's Taxes* C2.304 and C2.404.

(b) The indexation allowance on a no gain/no loss transfer must be excluded on a subsequent disposal to the extent that it would otherwise contribute to an allowable loss. [*TCGA 1992, s 56(3)*].

(c) With effect for appropriations on or after 8 March 2017 an election under *TCGA 1992, s 161(3)* can only be made where the appropriation would, in the absence of the election, result in a chargeable gain. Previously an election could be made where either a chargeable gain or an allowable loss would otherwise arise. See CG45900, CG69200 and *Simon's Taxes* C3.801, C3.802, C1.317, D2.415.

(d) Indexation allowance is frozen at its December 2017 level. No indexation allowance is available in respect of expenditure incurred after 31 December 2017, and for expenditure incurred on or before that date and falling to be deducted on a disposal

103.3 CT   Capital Gains

after that date, indexation allowance is computed up to and including December 2017 only. [*TCGA 1992, ss 53(1)(1B), 54(1B); FA 2018, s 26(2)(3)(6)*]. See CG17232, CG17270 and *Simon's Taxes* D2.326. See **CGT 214.1** INDEXATION.

(C) **Intra-group transfers of assets which are trading stock of one company but not of the other — transfer from a 'trading stock' company to a 'capital asset' company**

[*TCGA 1992, ss 161, 173(2); FA 2019, Sch 1 para 54*]

P Ltd acquires from another group company Q Ltd as a fixed asset an item previously treated as trading stock.

	£
Cost to Q Ltd (after 31.3.1982)	100,000
Market value at date of transfer	150,000
Eventual sale proceeds	200,000
Indexation allowance due on transfer value from date of transfer to date of sale	10,000

The group will have the following trading profits and chargeable gains

	£	£
Q Ltd trading profit [*TCGA 1992, s 161(2)*]		
Deemed sale proceeds		150,000
Cost to Q Ltd		(100,000)
Trading profit		£50,000
P Ltd chargeable gain [*TCGA 1992, s 171(1)*]		
Sale proceeds		200,000
Cost of asset	150,000	
Indexation allowance	10,000	
		(160,000)
Chargeable gain		£40,000

Notes

(a) Indexation allowance is frozen at its December 2017 level. No indexation allowance is available in respect of expenditure incurred after 31 December 2017, and for expenditure incurred on or before that date and falling to be deducted on a disposal after that date, indexation allowance is computed up to and including December 2017 only. [*TCGA 1992, ss 53(1)(1B), 54(1B); FA 2018, s 26(2)(3)(6)*]. See CG17232, CG17270 and *Simon's Taxes* D2.326. See **CGT 214.1** INDEXATION.

(D) **Rollover relief on the replacement of business assets**

[*TCGA 1992, ss 152, 153, 155, 175*]

M Ltd and N Ltd are 75% subsidiaries of H Ltd. On 1 February 2019 M Ltd sold a showroom for £200,000, realising a chargeable gain of £110,000. N Ltd purchased a factory for £150,000 in March 2021, within three years after the date of sale of the showroom.

Rollover relief could be claimed as follows

	£	£
Gain otherwise chargeable to corporation tax		110,000
Deduct Unrelieved gain:		
Sale proceeds	200,000	
Less Amount reinvested	(150,000)	
Chargeable gain	£50,000	50,000
Rollover relief		£60,000
New base cost of factory		
Purchase price		150,000
Deduct Rollover relief		(60,000)
		£90,000

Notes

(a) To qualify for relief, the two companies concerned need not be members of the same group throughout the period between the transactions but each must be a member at the time of its own particular transaction.

(b) No indexation will be available to N Ltd as the asset was acquired after 31 December 2017.

(c) See CGT **205.2** ASSETS HELD ON 31 MARCH 1982 and **226** ROLLOVER RELIEF.

(E) **Degrouping charge**

A Ltd had the following transactions

1.3.80 Purchased a freehold property £10,000.

31.3.82 Market value £24,000.

1.3.86 Purchased the entire share capital of B Ltd for £120,000.

1.12.14 Sold the freehold to B Ltd for £20,000 (market value £80,000).

31.9.20 Sold its shares in B Ltd (at which time B Ltd continued to own the freehold property) for £1 million.

Both companies prepare accounts to 30 April.

Relevant values of the RPI are: March 1982: 79.44, March 1986: 96.73, December 2014: 257.5, December 2017: 278.1.

103.3 CT Capital Gains

The taxation consequences are

(i) There will be no chargeable gain on A Ltd's disposal of the property to B Ltd as the disposal is one on which, after taking account of indexation allowance, neither gain nor loss arises. [*TCGA 1992, ss 56(2), 171(1)*].

Indexation factor $(257.5 - 79.44)/79.44 = 2.241$

	£
Cost to A Ltd	10,000
Indexation allowance £24,000 × 2.241 (note (a))	53,784
Deemed cost to B Ltd	£63,784

(ii) On the sale of A Ltd's shares in B Ltd on 31.9.20 (i.e. within six years after the transaction in (i) above), *A Ltd* will have a deemed disposal as follows.

Deemed disposal on 1.12.14

	£	£	£
Market value at 1.12.14		80,000	80,000
Cost (as above)	63,784		
Less indexation to date	(53,784)		
		(10,000)	
Market value at 31.3.82			(24,000)
Unindexed gain		70,000	56,000
Indexation allowance			
£24,000 ×2.241		(53,784)	(53,784)
Indexed gain		£16,216	£2,216
Deemed gain			£2,216

The deemed gain is not charged to corporation tax directly, but is treated as follows.

A Ltd's chargeable gain on disposal of B Ltd shares on 31.9.20

	£
Consideration	1,000,000
Add degrouping gain	2,216
	1,002,216
Less acquisition cost	(120,000)
Unindexed gain	882,216
Indexation allowance $(278.1 - 96.73/96.73) \times £120,000$	(225,001)
Chargeable gain subject to note (c)	£657,215

Notes

(a) Indexation allowance is frozen at its December 2017 level. No indexation allowance is available in respect of expenditure incurred after 31 December 2017, and for expenditure incurred on or before that date and falling to be deducted on a disposal

Capital Gains CT 103.3

after that date, indexation allowance is computed up to and including December 2017 only. [*TCGA 1992, ss 53(1)(1B), 54(1B); FA 2018, s 26(2)(3)(6)*]. See **CGT 214.1** INDEXATION. See also CG17232, CG17270 and *Simon's Taxes* D2.326.

(b) Where the conditions listed below are satisfied, a degrouping gain or loss is not treated as a separate gain or loss accruing to the transferee company, but instead the gain or loss accruing on a 'group disposal' (see below) is adjusted to take account of the degrouping gain or loss. The conditions are as follows:

(A) the transferee company ceases to be a member of the group as a result of one or more disposals ('*group disposals*') by a group member of the transferee's shares or those of another group member;

(B) either:

(i) the company making the group disposal (or, if there is more than one such disposal, at least one of them) is UK resident at the time of disposal, the shares are within the charge to corporation tax (or would be but for the substantial shareholdings exemption — see **103.4**), or any part of the gains or loss on the disposal (or at least one of them) is treated as accruing to a person under *TCGA 1992, s 3(2)* (attribution of gains to members of non-resident companies), or

(ii) had (i) above applied to the group disposal or to each of them, any gain arising would not have been a chargeable gain as a result of the substantial shareholdings exemption; and

(C) *CTA 2010, s 535* (UK real estate investment trusts: exemption of gains) would not apply to the degrouping gain or loss.

See GREIT05005, GREIT05010 and *Simon's Taxes* D7.1135, D7.1125, D7.1120, D7.1152, D7.1156.

Where the conditions are satisfied, a chargeable gain or allowable loss on a single group disposal is calculated by adding any degrouping gain which would otherwise have arisen but for these provisions to the consideration for the group disposal (and a degrouping loss is treated as an allowable deduction).

[*TCGA 1992, s 179(3A)–(3H)*].

(c) Where a company is treated as making a gain under the degrouping charge provisions or such a gain is taken into account in calculating a gain on a disposal of shares as illustrated in this example, a claim can be made to defer part of the gain. Where the degrouping gain is taken into account in calculating a gain on a disposal of shares, the claim can be made by the company making the share disposal or, if there is more than one such disposal, the companies making those disposals acting jointly. In any other case the claim is to be made by the company to whom the degrouping gain is deemed to accrue. The effect is to reduce the amount of the gain by the amount specified in the claim. The reduction must be just and reasonable with regard to any transaction as a direct or indirect result of which the asset to which the gain relates was acquired. Where a gain is reduced in this way, the consideration for the deemed reacquisition of the asset by the transferee company is taken to be its market value less the amount of the adjustment to the gain. In effect the part of the gain excluded is deferred until final disposal of the asset by the transferee company (to whom the liability will then fall). [*TCGA 1992, s 179ZA*].

103.3 CT   Capital Gains

(F) **Restriction on set-off of pre-entry losses**

[*TCGA 1992, s 177A, Sch 7A*]

Wooster Ltd, the holding company of a group, acquires the entire share capital of House Ltd on 1 January 2012. At that date, House Ltd is trading as a gun seller and has an unrelieved allowable pre-entry loss of £150,000. House Ltd makes no further disposals of assets until, in accounting period ended 31 March 2021, it disposes of four assets as follows.

	Date of acquisition	Chargeable gain/ (allowable loss)
Asset A	31/3/10	£50,000
Asset B	1/5/13	£30,000
Asset C	1/11/12	£100,000
Asset D	8/6/08	£(25,000)

Asset B was acquired from an unconnected company and has been used throughout the period of House Ltd's ownership for the purposes of the company's gun selling trade. Asset C is a building which has been leased to an unconnected company throughout. House Ltd had not carried on a property business before acquiring the asset.

House Ltd's total taxable gains for the year ended 31 March 2021 are as follows.

	£	£
Asset A (note (b))		
Chargeable gain	50,000	
Less pre-entry loss (part)	(50,000)	—
Asset B (note (b))		
Chargeable gain	30,000	
Less pre-entry loss (part)	(30,000)	—
Asset C (note (b))		
Chargeable gain	100,000	
Less loss on Asset D (note (b))	(25,000)	75,000
Total taxable gains		£75,000

The pre-entry loss has been utilised as follows.

Loss brought forward	150,000
Set against gain on Asset A	50,000
Set against gain on Asset B	30,000
Unrelieved loss carried forward	£70,000

Capital Gains CT 103.4

Notes

(a) Broadly, the provisions of *TCGA 1992, Sch 7A* restrict the use of losses realised by a company before it joins a group and remaining unrelieved at that time. Such pre-entry losses can be set only against gains on assets held by the company at the time it joined the group or subsequently acquired by the company from outside the group and used by it in a continuing trade.

(b) Further restrictions on the deduction of pre-entry losses may apply for accounting periods beginning on or after 1 April 2020 (subject to transitional rules for accounting periods straddling that date) under the corporate capital loss restriction. See note (c) at **103.1** above and CGT **207.3** LOSSES.

(c) The pre-entry loss in this example can be set off against the gain on Asset A as Asset A was owned by House Ltd before it joined Wooster Ltd's group. The loss can also be set off against the gain on Asset B as, although Asset B was acquired by House Ltd after it joined the group, it was acquired by the company from outside the group and has been used by it in a continuing trade throughout its period of ownership. Asset C fails to meet either of these conditions and so the loss cannot be set against the gain arising on its disposal.

(d) Although Asset D was acquired before House Ltd joined the group, the loss is not a pre-entry loss because it accrues on or after 19 July 2011. Had Asset D been disposed of before that date, the pre-entry proportion of the loss would have been subject to the pre-entry loss restrictions until that date. The loss would have been treated on and after that date as if it had accrued immediately before the company became a member of the group (and therefore as a pre-entry loss).

(e) The provisions do not apply where *TCGA 1992, s 184A* (restrictions on buying losses: avoidance schemes) applies. [*TCGA 1992, Sch 7A para 1(1)*]. See CG47020, CG47021, CG47035, CG47322 and *Simon's Taxes* D2.402–D2.404.

103.4 SUBSTANTIAL SHAREHOLDING EXEMPTION

[*TCGA 1992, Sch 7AC; F(No 2)A 2017, ss 27, 28*]

Swallow Ltd acquired 1,500 shares in Summer Ltd in April 1994. Swallow Ltd holds no other investments in any company, has been a trading company throughout its existence, and is not a member of a group. Summer Ltd has 10,000 issued shares and has been a trading company since its formation. Swallow Ltd makes the following disposals of Summer Ltd shares. All disposals are to persons who are not connected with Swallow Ltd.

31 May 2015	600 shares
30 April 2020	400 shares
30 June 2020	500 shares

The effect of the disposals for the purposes of corporation tax on chargeable gains is as follows
31 May 2015 disposal

Swallow Ltd has held at least 10% of the ordinary share capital of Summer Ltd throughout the two years prior to the disposal. The disposal is therefore of part of a substantial shareholding and no chargeable gain or allowable loss arises on the disposal.

103.4 CT   Capital Gains

30 April 2020 disposal

Although Swallow Ltd did not hold at least 10% of the shares in Summer Ltd immediately before the disposal (the remaining holding being only 900 of 10,000 shares), there is a twelve month period beginning within six years prior to the disposal throughout which it did hold at least 10%. That period is 1 June 2014 to 31 May 2015. Accordingly, the substantial shareholding exemption applies and no chargeable gain or allowable loss arises on the disposal.

30 June 2020 disposal

Swallow Ltd holds only 5% of the share capital of Summer Ltd immediately before the disposal. In the period from 1 July 2014 to 30 June 2020, the company held at least 10% of Summer Ltd's shares only from 1 July 2014 to 31 May 2015. This is not a continuous twelve month period beginning within six years prior to the disposal, and therefore the substantial shareholding exemption will not apply. A gain on the disposal of 500 shares will be a chargeable gain, and a loss an allowable loss.

Note

(a) For disposals on or after 1 April 2017, a gain on a disposal by a company of shares in another company is not a chargeable gain (and a loss is not an allowable loss) if, broadly, the company held at least 10% of the other company's ordinary share capital throughout a twelve month period beginning within six years prior to the disposal. For disposals before 1 April 2017, the company must have held at least 10% of the other company's ordinary share capital throughout a twelve month period beginning within two years prior to the disposal, and both companies had to be trading companies.

104 Close Companies

104.1 CLOSE COMPANY — DEFINITION

[*CTA 2010, ss 439–453*]

(A)

A plc is a quoted company whose ordinary share capital is owned as follows

		%
B	a director	10
C	wife of B	5
D	father of B	4
E		17
F	business partner of E	2
G	a director	10
H		8
I Ltd	a non-close company	30
J		7
100	other shareholders	7
		100

It can be shown that A plc is a close company by considering the following three steps

(i) Is A plc controlled by five or fewer participators or by its directors?

		%	%
I Ltd			30
B	own shares	10	
	C's shares	5	
	D's shares	4	
			19
E	own shares	17	
	F's shares	2	
			19
			68

As A plc is controlled by three participators, the initial conclusion is that the company is close. [*CTA 2010, s 439(2)*].

104.1 CT Close Companies

(ii) Is A plc a quoted company, with at least 35% of the voting power owned by the public?

		%
I Ltd		30
J		7
100	other shareholders	7
		44

As at least 35% of the voting power is owned by the public it appears that A plc is exempt from close company status, subject to step (iii). [CTA 2010, s 446(1)].

(iii) Is more than 85% of the voting power in A plc owned by its principal members?

	%
I Ltd	30
B	19
E	19
G	10
H	8
	86

Because the principal members own more than 85% of the voting power A plc is a close company. [CTA 2010, s 446(2)-(4)].

Note

(a) Although J owns more than 5% of the share capital, he is not a principal member because five other persons each hold more than J's 7% and so themselves constitute the principal members. [CTA 2010, s 446(4)].

(B)

The ordinary share capital of A Ltd (an unquoted company) is owned as follows

		%
B	a director	9
C	son of B	9
D	works manager	5
E	wife of D	15
F	a director	9
G	a director	1
H	a director	1
J	a director	1
K	a director	1
49	other shareholders with 1% each	49
		100

Close Companies   CT 104.1

A Ltd is a close company because it is controlled by its directors, thus

			%	%
B	own shares		9	
	C's shares		9	
				18
D	own shares		5	
	E's shares		15	
				20
F				9
G				1
H				1
J				1
K				1
				51

Note

(a) A manager is deemed to be a director if he and his associates own 20% or more of the ordinary share capital. [*CTA 2010, s 452(2)*]. See CTM60180 and *Simon's Taxes* D3.106.

(C)

The ordinary share capital of A Ltd is owned as follows

		%
B	a director	9
C	a director	9
D	a director	9
E		9
F		9
G Ltd	a close company	8
47	other shareholders with 1% each	47
		100

The ordinary share capital of G Ltd is owned as follows

		%
B	a director	50
C	a director	50
		100

A Ltd is not a close company under the control test because it is not under the control of five or fewer participators. The five largest shareholdings comprise only 45% of the share capital. [*CTA 2010, ss 439(2), 450(3)*].

245

104.1 CT   Close Companies

A Ltd is a close company under the distribution of assets test because B and C would each become entitled to one-half of G Ltd's share of the assets of A Ltd. [*CTA 2010, s 439(3)*]. The shares of assets attributable to the five largest shareholdings become

		%	%
B	own share	9	
	50% of G Ltd's share	4	
			13
C	own share	9	
	50% of G Ltd's share	4	
			13
D			9
E			9
F			9
			53

Note

(a) See CTM60060, CTM60210 and *Simon's Taxes* D3.110, D7.203, D3.102.

(D)

A Ltd is an unquoted company with the following capital structure, owned as shown

	£1 ordinary shares	£1 non-participating preference shares (no votes attached)
B	6,000	—
C	15,000	25,000
D	6,000	19,000
E	5,000	10,000
F	1,600	13,000
G	2,000	—
Other shareholders owning less than 1,000 shares each	64,400	33,000
	100,000	100,000

The company is close by reference to share capital as follows

	Control by votes	Control of issued capital
B	6,000	6,000
C	15,000	40,000
D	6,000	25,000
E	5,000	15,000

	Control by votes	Control of issued capital
F	—	14,600
G	2,000	—
	34,000	100,600

Note

(a) Control of the company includes control of more than one-half of:

　(i)　voting power; or

　(ii)　issued share capital.

[*CTA 2010, s 450(3)*]. See CTM60210.

104.2 LOANS TO PARTICIPATORS

[*CTA 2010, ss 455–464D*]

(A)

P is a participator in Q Ltd, a close company which makes up accounts to 30 September. Q Ltd loaned P £80,000 on 29 August 2018. On 24 May 2020 P repays the loan.

The effect of these transactions on Q Ltd is as follows

1 July 2019	The company is liable to pay corporation tax of £80,000 × 32.5%	£26,000
30 June 2021	On a claim, Q Ltd is entitled to a repayment of	£26,000

Notes

(a) An amount equal to 32.5% of the loan must be self-assessed by the company as if it were corporation tax chargeable for the accounting period in which the loan was made.

(b) If the company is not liable to pay its corporation tax by instalments, the tax is due on the day following the expiry of nine months after the end of the accounting period in which the loan or advance was made.

(c) Where loans or advances are repaid after the due date on which tax is charged, relief by claim in respect of the repayment is not given at any time before the expiry of nine months from the end of the accounting period in which the repayment takes place.

(d) Where a loan is repaid, the tax, or part of the tax, is not repaid if either:

　• within a period of 30 days, a repayment of £5,000 or more is made by a participator and the company makes further chargeable payments (i.e. loans or benefits chargeable under *CTA 2010, s 464A*) of at least £5,000 to the participator, provided that the further chargeable payments are made in an accounting period after that in which the original loan was made; or

104.2 CT   Close Companies

- the amount outstanding is at least £15,000, arrangements have been made at the time of the repayment for one or more chargeable payments to be made to replace some or all of the loan, and further chargeable payments of at least £5,000 are made by the company to the participator.

In either case, the repayment is treated as a repayment of the further chargeable payments and only any excess amount is treated as a repayment of the original loan.

[*CTA 2010, ss 464C, 464D*].

(B)

T is a participator in (but not an employee of) V Ltd, a close company. V Ltd loaned T £100,000 on 10 May 2019. On 2 March 2020, T repays £73,000 and on 15 February 2021, V Ltd agrees to waive the balance of the loan. V Ltd has a year end of 31 March and is not a large company or very large company for instalment payment purposes. T is a higher rate (but not an additional rate) taxpayer for 2020/21.

The effect of these transactions is as follows

V Ltd

On 1.1.2021	The company becomes liable to pay corporation tax of (£100,000 − £73,000) £27,000 × 32.5%	£8,775
On 31.12.2021	The company is due a repayment of £27,000 × 32.5%	£8,775

T

On 15.2.2021	T's 2020/21 taxable income is increased by	£27,000
	As T pays tax at the higher rate, and assuming that T has used his dividend allowance against other dividends, the deemed income will be	
	subject to tax at the dividend upper rate of 32.5% on £27,000	£8,775

Notes

(a) Where a loan or advance which gave rise to a charge under *CTA 2010, s 455* is released or written off, a claim can be made for repayment of the tax. [*CTA 2010, s 458(2)(b)*].

(b) Companies are required to include *section 455* tax in their self-assessment.

104.3 BENEFITS IN KIND FOR PARTICIPATORS

[*CTA 2010, ss 1064–1069*]

R is a participator in S Ltd, a close company, but he is neither a director nor an employee. For the whole of 2020/21, S Ltd provided R with a new petrol fuelled car of which the 'price' for tax purposes (i.e. under *ITEPA 2003, ss 122–124*) was £21,200, and the carbon dioxide emission figure for which was 180g/km. R was required to, and did, pay S Ltd £500 a year for the use of the car. The cost of providing the car, charged in S Ltd's accounts for its year ended 31 March 2021, was £5,000.

Deemed distribution

If the benefit of the car were assessable to tax as income from employment, the cash equivalent would be

	£
£21,200 @ 37%	7,844
Less contribution	(500)
Income of R for 2020/21	£7,344

S Ltd's taxable profits

In computing S Ltd's profits chargeable to corporation tax, the actual expenditure charged (£5,000) must be added back.

105 Double Tax Relief

105.1 MEASURE OF RELIEF

[*TIOPA 2010, ss 2–6, 18–20, 31–34, 42–56*]

The following facts relate to A Ltd's accounting period for the year ended 31 March 2021.

	£
Trading profits	1,500,000
Overseas chargeable gain (tax 40%)	80,000

A Ltd's tax liability is

		Trading income	Overseas gain	Total
		£	£	£
Profits		1,500,000	80,000	1,580,000
CT at 19%		285,000	15,200	300,200
Relief for foreign tax	(note (a))	—	(15,200)	(15,200)
		£285,000	—	£285,000

Note

(a) The maximum amount of relief for foreign tax is the amount of the gain multiplied by the company's corporation tax rate (£80,000 × 19% = £15,200). [*TIOPA 2010, s 42*]. The unrelieved foreign tax (£32,000 – £15,200 = £16,800) cannot be relieved by way of deduction from the gain under *TIOPA 2010, s 113*. See INTM169090 and *Simon's Taxes* E6.438, E6.416. [*TIOPA 2010, s 31*].

105.2 EXEMPTION FOR PROFITS OF FOREIGN PERMANENT ESTABLISHMENTS

[*CTA 2009, ss 18A–18S; FA 2019, Sch 1 paras 111, 120, Sch 5 paras 12, 35*]

(A) **Exclusion of permanent establishment profits**

Wiggo Ltd is a UK company trading as a bike wholesaler. The company also operates through a permanent establishment in Tourland and has made an election under *CTA 2009, s 18A* which took effect at the start of the accounting period ending 31 December 2020. For the accounting period ending 31 December 2020, Wiggo Ltd's total taxable profits, before applying the foreign permanent establishments exemption, consists of trading profits of £5,000,000 and non-trading loan relationships income of £120,000. The company had no opening negative amount (see (B) below) and its foreign permanent establishments amount for the accounting period is calculated as follows.

105.2 CT Double Tax Relief

Profits amount	£
Trading profits	250,000

Losses amount	
Non-trading loan relationship deficit	(40,000)
Foreign permanent establishments amount	£210,000

Exemption adjustments under *CTA 2009, s 18A* are made to Wiggo Ltd's total taxable profits for the year ended 31 December 2020 as follows.

	£	£
Trading profits	5,000,000	
Less Tourland trading profits	(250,000)	4,750,000
Non-trading loan relationship income	120,000	
Add Tourland non-trading loan relationship deficit	40,000	160,000
Total taxable profits		£4,910,000

Notes

(a) A company can make an election for profits arising from its foreign permanent establishments, including chargeable gains, to be exempt from corporation tax (and for losses from those permanent establishments to be excluded). This election can be made by UK resident companies and non-UK resident companies which expect to become UK resident. An election will apply to all accounting periods of the company beginning on or after the 'relevant day'. The 'relevant day' is the day on which, at the time of the election, the next or first accounting period is expected to begin or, in the case of a non-resident company, the day on which the company becomes UK resident. If, in the event, an accounting period begins before and ends on or after the relevant day, then for corporation tax purposes that period is treated as two accounting periods, the first ending immediately before the relevant day and the second starting on that day. Profits and losses are to be apportioned to the two periods on a just and reasonable basis. An election can only be revoked before the relevant day; otherwise it is irrevocable. Profits and losses are not left out of account if they are:

   (1) (for disposals of land on or after 5 July 2016) profits or losses of a trade of dealing in or developing UK land or would be such profits or losses if the company were non-UK resident;

   (2) (for disposals on or after 6 April 2019) gains or losses which would be, were the company non-UK resident, gains or losses on disposals on or after 6 April 2019 of direct and indirect interests in UK land;

   (3) with effect from 6 April 2020 (subject to transitional provisions) profits or losses of a UK property business;

   (4) with effect from 6 April 2020 (subject to transitional provisions) profits consisting of other UK property income; or

Double Tax Relief   CT 105.2

(5) with effect from 6 April 2020 (subject to transitional provisions) profits or losses arising from loan relationships or derivative contracts to which the company is a party for the purposes of its UK property business or to generate other UK property income.

[*CTA 2009, ss 18A(1)–(3), 18F; FA 2019, Sch 1 paras 111, 120, Sch 5 paras 12, 35.*] See INTM281020.

(b) The '*foreign permanent establishments amount*' is the aggregate of the 'profits amount' for each territory outside the UK in which the company carries on, or has carried on, business through a permanent establishment, less the aggregate of the 'losses amount' for each such territory. Where there is a double tax treaty between the territory and the UK which includes a provision non-discrimination provision, the '*profits amount*' is the profits which would be taken to be attributable to the permanent establishment in ascertaining the amount of any credit relief for foreign tax. The '*losses amount*' is calculated on the same basis. If an amount of credit relief does not depend on the profits taken to be attributable to the permanent establishment because, under the treaty, the foreign tax is not charged by reference to such profits, then only profits which would be taken to be attributable to the permanent establishment if the foreign tax were charged by reference to such profits are included in the profits amount (and only such losses are included in the losses amount). Where there is no such treaty, the profits amount and losses amount are the amounts which would be taken to be so attributable to the permanent establishment if there were such a treaty and it was in the terms of the OECD model tax convention. [*CTA 2009, ss 18A(4)–(10), 18R*]. See INTM281010.

(c) Although profits amounts and losses amounts are aggregated in computing the foreign permanent establishments amount, they nevertheless retain their identity for the purpose of making the necessary adjustments to the company's total taxable profits.

(B) **Pre-entry losses**

A company with three foreign permanent establishments makes an election under *CTA 2009, s 18A* which takes effect for the accounting period ending 31 December 2020. The profits amounts and losses amounts (excluding chargeable gains and allowable losses) for the three territories in the preceding six years are as follows.

Year ended 31 December	Territory 1	Territory 2	Territory 3	Foreign permanent establishments amount
2014	2,000	0	(6,000)	(4,000)
2015	1,000	(2,000)	1,000	0
2016	(5,000)	(2,000)	2,000	(5,000)
2017	2,000	4,000	(3,000)	3,000
2018	(10,000)	1,000	2,000	(7,000)
2019	2,000	2,000	2,000	6,000
Opening negative amount				£7,000

253

105.2 CT Double Tax Relief

The opening negative amount must be extinguished by matching with the aggregate profits amount (see note (b) to (A) above) for each subsequent accounting period, starting with the first period for which the election takes effect (i.e. the year ended 31 December 2020). No adjustments can be made to the company's total taxable profits under *CTA 2009, s 18A* until the opening negative amount has been so extinguished.

Alternatively, the company could have elected for the opening negative amount for territory 1 to be streamed, so that it need be matched only with profits amounts for that territory. The opening negative amount is calculated as follows.

Year ended 31 December	Territory 1
2014	2,000
2015	1,000
2016	(5,000)
2017	2,000
2018	(10,000)
2019	2,000
Total	(£8,000)

The streamed negative amount for that territory is the lower of £8,000 and the aggregate total opening negative amount, i.e. £7,000. The company streams no other territory, so the residual negative amount is the difference between the aggregate negative amount £7,000 and the streamed negative amount £7,000, i.e. nil. The profits amounts for Territory 1 must therefore be matched with the negative amount £7,000 before exemption can apply (i.e. the first £7,000 of such amounts are not exempt), but there is no restriction on exemption for profits amounts of Territories 2 and 3.

Notes

(a) Where losses have arisen in any of the company's foreign permanent establishments in the six-year period ending at the end of the accounting period in which the election is made, and those losses have not been eliminated by profits from those establishments before the end of that period, then the company will have an 'opening negative amount' and no adjustments can be made to the company's total taxable profits until that amount has been eliminated. The '*opening negative amount*' is ascertained by calculating the foreign permanent establishments amount (excluding chargeable gains and allowable losses) for each accounting period ending less than six years before the end of the accounting period in which the election is made and for that accounting period. The earliest negative amount is carried forward to the next period where it is either increased by another negative amount or reduced or eliminated by a positive amount, but not so as to cause the result to be positive. This process continues through each accounting period and if there is a negative amount remaining after applying it to the last period, that amount is the opening negative amount. The period for which this process must be carried out is extended if there is a losses amount of more than £50 million in an accounting period beginning within the six-year period ending on 18 July 2011, if that period would not otherwise fall within the normal six-year period. Where the period is extended in this way, the process must be carried out for the period of the losses amount and each subsequent accounting period up to and including that in which the election is made. [*CTA 2009, ss 18J, 18K*].

(b) Alternatively, the company can elect for the opening negative amount to be streamed. If such an election is made then, in effect, the above provisions are applied separately to losses in a particular territory so that they do not delay the application of the exemption to other permanent establishments which would otherwise have no, or a shorter, transitional period. The election must be made at the same time as the exemption election and can only be revoked before the first accounting period to which the exemption election applies. It must specify the territories which are to be streamed. Where not all of the negative opening amount is streamed in this way, the residual amount must be eliminated against the residual profits amounts (i.e. for each accounting period, the total profits amount less the streamed profits amounts) in the same way. [*CTA 2009, ss 18L–18N*]. See INTM284040.

106 Group Relief

106.1 CALCULATION OF GROUP RELIEF

[*CTA 2010, ss 97–156*]

A Ltd has a subsidiary company, B Ltd, in which it owns 75% of the ordinary share capital. Relevant information for the year ended 31 March 2021 is as follows

		£
A Ltd	Trading profit	30,000
	Property income	10,000
	Chargeable gain	15,000
	Qualifying charitable donations	2,000
B Ltd	Trading loss	48,000
	Qualifying charitable donations	2,000

There are no losses brought forward from previous accounting periods.

Group relief is available as follows

	£
A Ltd	
Trading profit	30,000
Property income	10,000
Chargeable gain	15,000
	55,000
Deduct Charitable donation	(2,000)
Profits	53,000
Deduct Loss surrendered by B Ltd	(50,000)
Chargeable profits	£3,000
B Ltd	
Trading loss for the year	48,000
Charitable donation	2,000
	50,000
Deduct Loss surrendered to A Ltd	(50,000)
Losses carried forward	—

106.2 CT   Group Relief

106.2 KINDS OF GROUP RELIEF

[*CTA 2010, s 99(1)(2), 100–104*]

A Ltd is an investment company which has one trading subsidiary, D Ltd in which it owns 100% of the share capital. A Ltd acquires 100% of the share capital of two further trading subsidiaries B Ltd and C Ltd on 1 April 2020. The companies have the following relevant results for the two years ending 31 March 2020 and 31 March 2021.

		Year ended 31.3.20 £	Year ended 31.3.21 £
A Ltd	Profits	10,000	20,000
	Management expenses	(20,000)	(50,000)
B Ltd	Trading loss		(10,000)
	Property income (after capital allowances)		30,000
	Non-trading loan relationship deficit		(10,000)
C Ltd	Trading profit/(loss)		30,000
	Property income (before capital allowances)		1,000
	Capital allowances — trading assets		(5,000)
	— property assets		(2,000)
	Management expenses		(40,000)
D Ltd	Profits		100,000

In addition, C Ltd has trading losses brought forward of £10,000 which arose in the year ended 31 March 2017.

Group relief may be claimed for trading losses, management expenses and property business losses as follows

		Year ended 31.3.20 £	Year ended 31.3.21 £
A Ltd			
Profits		10,000	20,000
Management expenses	(note (a))	(20,000)	(60,000)
Excess management expenses		(10,000)	(40,000)
Deduct Surrendered to D Ltd		—	40,000
Management expenses carried forward to year ended 31.3.21	(note (a))	£(10,000)	—
B Ltd			
Trading loss			(10,000)
Deduct Surrendered to D Ltd	(note (b))		10,000
Non-trading loan relationship deficit			(10,000)

Group Relief CT 106.2

		Year ended 31.3.20 £	Year ended 31.3.21 £
Deduct Surrendered to D Ltd	(note (b))		10,000
Property income			30,000
Profits chargeable to corporation tax			£30,000

C Ltd

Trading profit (£30,000) *less* trade capital allowances (£5,000)			25,000
Less trading loss brought forward			(10,000)
			15,000
UK property income (£1,000) less UK property capital allowances (£2,000) less surrendered to D Ltd (£1,000)	(note (c))		—
			15,000
Management expenses (£40,000) less surrendered to D Ltd (£15,000)	(note (c))		(25,000)
Management expenses carried forward			£10,000

D Ltd

Profits			100,000
Deduct	Surrendered by A Ltd		(40,000)
	Surrendered by B Ltd:		
	– trading loss		(10,000)
	– loan relationship deficit		(10,000)
	Surrendered by C Ltd		
	– UK property losses and management expenses		(16,000)
Profits chargeable to corporation tax			£24,000

Notes

(a) It is not possible in the year ended 31 March 2021 to deduct the excess management expenses brought forward from the year ended 31 March 2020 before deducting the current year management expenses to arrive at the amount available for group relief. However, the excess management expenses of £10,000 arising in the year ended 31 March 2020 carried forward to the year ended 31 March 2021 may be surrendered as group relief for carried-forward losses (see further **106.6** below). [*CTA 2009, s 1223; CTA 2010, ss 103, 188BB*]. See CTM80450 and *Simon's Taxes* D2.220.

(b) Although a company might normally relieve a trading loss and a non-trading loan relationship deficit against other income of the year before surrendering the loss or deficit, it is not obliged to do so. Thus, B Ltd could have reduced its chargeable profits in the year ended 31 March 2021 by £20,000 instead of surrendering that amount to D Ltd. [*CTA 2010, s 99(3)*]. See CTM80110 and *Simon's Taxes* D2.215.

106.2 CT   Group Relief

(c) Qualifying charitable donations, qualifying expenditure on grassroots sport, UK property losses, management expenses and non-trading losses on intangible assets can be surrendered as group relief only to the extent that in aggregate they exceed the surrendering company's 'gross profits' (plus any CFC profits apportioned to it) for the accounting period. The 'gross profits' of the accounting period are, broadly, the profits of the period without any deduction for any amounts qualifying for group relief relating to that period or any amounts of any other period. [*CTA 2010, ss 99(4), 105*]. Therefore, the amount which C Ltd can surrender as group relief is restricted as follows

Management expenses	40,000
UK property loss	1,000
	41,000
Deduct gross profits (before *CTA 2010, s 45* relief)	25,000
Group relief	£16,000

The amount surrendered is taken to consist first of qualifying charitable donations, then of grassroots sport expenditure, then of UK property losses, then of management expenses, and finally of losses on intangible assets. The amount surrendered by C Ltd is therefore identified as the UK property loss of £1,000 and management expenses of £15,000.

C Ltd's management expenses have been relieved as follows

Management expenses	40,000
Deduct Management expenses relieved against income	(15,000)
Surrendered to D Ltd	(15,000)
Excess management expenses carried forward	£10,000

106.3 'OVERLAPPING PERIODS'

[*CTA 2010, ss 138–142*]

D Ltd has several wholly owned subsidiaries, including E Ltd and F Ltd. D Ltd prepares accounts to 30 September, the other two companies to 31 December. Their results were

			£
D Ltd	year ended 30.9.20	loss	(240,000)
E Ltd	year ended 31.12.20	profit	120,000
F Ltd	year ended 31.12.20	profit	150,000

D Ltd makes a profit for the year ended 30.9.21. None of the companies have any brought-forward losses or other unrelieved amounts.

The overlapping period is the nine months to 30.9.20. The surrenderable amount of D Ltd's loss for the overlapping period is $^9/_{12} \times £240,000 = £180,000$. D Ltd surrenders the loss as follows

(i) Surrender to E Ltd — see note (a)

		£
Surrender the smaller of:		
Unused part of the surrenderable amount for the overlapping period		180,000
Unrelieved part of E Ltd's total profits for the overlapping period	$^9/_{12} \times £120,000$	90,000
Surrender		£90,000

(ii) Surrender to F Ltd — see note (b)

		£	£
Surrender the smaller of:			
Unused part of the surrenderable amount for the overlapping period			
surrenderable amount		180,000	
deduct amount surrendered to E Ltd		(90,000)	90,000
Unrelieved part of F Ltd's total profits for the overlapping period	$^9/_{12} \times £150,000$		112,500
Surrender			£90,000

Notes

(a) The effect of the rules is to restrict the overall surrender by D Ltd to $^9/_{12}$ of its loss for the year ended 30 September 2020.

(b) Where more than one claim relates to the whole or part of the same overlapping period, the claims must be considered in the order in which they are made (determined by the date on which the claim ceases to be capable of being withdrawn). Where, as in this case, two or more claims are deemed to be made at the same time, they are treated as made in such order as the companies involved may elect. In the absence of such an election, HMRC may direct. [*CTA 2010, ss 139–141*]. See CTM80230 and *Simon's Taxes* D2.216.

106.4 COMPANIES JOINING OR LEAVING THE GROUP

[*CTA 2010, ss 138–142*]

On 1 April 2020 B Ltd was held as to 90% by A Ltd and 10% by a non-resident.

On 1 September 2020 C Ltd became a 75% subsidiary of A Ltd.

106.4 CT   Group Relief

On 31 December 2020 A Ltd sells 30% of the shares in B Ltd (retaining 60%). A Ltd, B Ltd and C Ltd all prepare accounts to 31 March each year. During the year ended 31 March 2021 the results of the companies are as follows

A Ltd	Profit	£60,000
B Ltd	Loss	£(240,000)
C Ltd	Profit	£30,000

None of the companies have any carried-forward loss or other unrelieved amounts.

Group relief for the loss sustained by B Ltd in the year ended 31.3.21 is available as follows

During the year ended 31 March 2021, B Ltd was a '75% subsidiary' of A Ltd only in the nine-month period 1 April 2020 to 31 December 2020. The period during which both B Ltd and C Ltd were '75% subsidiaries' of A Ltd was the four months 1 September 2020 to 31 December 2020.

Calculation of loss relieved
(i) Against profits of A Ltd

Smaller of:

Unused part of the surrenderable amount for the overlapping period	$9/12 \times £240,000$	£180,000
Unrelieved part of A Ltd's total profits for the overlapping period	$9/12 \times £60,000$	£45,000
Therefore, loss relieved		£45,000

(ii) Against profits of C Ltd

Smaller of:

Unused part of the surrenderable amount for the overlapping period			
surrenderable amount	$4/12 \times £240,000$	80,000	
deduct proportion of amount surrendered to A Ltd relating to overlapping period	$4/9 \times £45,000$	(20,000)	£60,000
Unrelieved part of C Ltd's total profits for the overlapping period	$4/12 \times £30,000$		10,000
Therefore, loss relieved			£10,000

Summary

	A Ltd £	B Ltd £	C Ltd £
Profit/(loss)	60,000	(240,000)	30,000
Group relief (claim)/surrender	(45,000)	55,000	(10,000)
Chargeable profit/(loss carried forward)	£15,000	£(185,000)	£20,000

Notes

(a) When a company joins or leaves a group, the profit or loss is apportioned on a time basis unless this method would work unreasonably or unjustly. In the latter event a just and reasonable method of apportionment must be used. [*CTA 2010, s 141(3)*]. See CTM80260 and *Simon's Taxes* D2.216.

(b) See notes (a) and (b) to **106.3** above.

106.5 RELATIONSHIP TO OTHER RELIEFS

[*CTA 2010, ss 37, 45, 45A, 99, 105*]

B Ltd is a subsidiary of A Ltd and commenced trading on 1 April 2005. Both companies prepare accounts to 31 March each year. The results for the three years ended 31 March 2021 were as follows.

				£
A Ltd	Year ended 31 March	2019	Loss	(4,000)
		2020	Loss	(3,000)
		2021	Loss	(5,000)
B Ltd	Year ended 31 March	2019	Loss	(5,000)
		2020	Profit	10,000
		2021	Loss	(20,000)
		2019	UK property income	1,000
		2020	UK property income	1,000
		2021	UK property income	1,000
		2021	Chargeable gains	5,000

106.5 CT   Group Relief

The losses can be used as follows

	Year ended 31.3.19 £	Year ended 31.3.20 £	Year ended 31.3.21 £
B Ltd			
Trading profit/(loss)	(5,000)	10,000	(20,000)
Trading income	—	10,000	—
UK property income	1,000	1,000	1,000
Income	1,000	11,000	1,000
Chargeable gains	—	—	5,000
CTA 2010, s 37(3)(a) loss relief	(1,000)	—	(6,000)
CTA 2010, s 45A loss relief	—	(4,000)	—
Profits subject to group relief	—	7,000	—
Losses surrendered by A Ltd	—	(3,000)	—
	—	4,000	—
CTA 2010, s 37(3)(b) loss relief	—	(4,000)	—
Chargeable profits	—	—	—
Losses brought forward	—	(4,000)	—
Loss of the period	(5,000)	—	(20,000)
CTA 2010, s 45A relief	—	4,000	—
CTA 2010, s 37(3)(a) relief	1,000	—	6,000
CTA 2010, s 37(3)(b) relief	—	—	4,000
Losses carried forward	£(4,000)	—	£(10,000)
A Ltd			
Trading loss	4,000	3,000	5,000
Deduct Surrendered to B Ltd	—	(3,000)	—
Loss for the period	4,000	—	5,000
Loss brought forward	—	4,000	4,000
Loss carried forward	£4,000	£4,000	£9,000

Note

(a) The trading losses arise on or after 1 April 2017 and so, if not utilised or group relieved in the current period, are to be carried forward and can be utilised against future total profits of the company or group relieved as carried forward losses. [*CTA 2010, s 45A*]. See *Simon's Taxes* D1.1106.

(b) Losses brought forward from previous periods must be used before claiming group relief, as must losses incurred in the current period and available for set-off under *CTA 2010, s 37(3)(a)*. However, group relief takes priority to losses carried back from subsequent periods under *CTA 2010, s 37(3)(b)*.

(c) For illustration purposes, it is assumed that B Ltd claims to carry back trading losses of £4,000 from the year ended 31 March 2021. Alternatively, B Ltd could have claimed group relief for carried-forward losses in respect of the trading loss of £4,000 carried forward by A Ltd from the year ended 31 March 2019. See **106.6** below.

106.6 GROUP RELIEF FOR CARRIED-FORWARD LOSSES

[*CTA 2010, ss 188AA–EK; F(No 2)A 2017, Sch 4 paras 23, 190–192*].

A Ltd has a subsidiary company, B Ltd, in which it owns 75% of the ordinary share capital. The companies commence trading on 1 April 2019 and have the following results for the two years ending 31 March 2020 and 31 March 2021.

	Year ended 31.3.20 £	Year ended 31.3.21 £
A Ltd Trade profits/(loss)	(20,000)	110,000
Property income		30,000
B Ltd Trade profits/(loss)	(150,000)	10,000

Group relief may be claimed for B Ltd's carried-forward trade loss as follows.

	Year ended 31.3.20 £	Year ended 31.3.21 £
A Ltd		
Trade profit/(loss)	(20,000)	110,000
Property income	—	30,000
		140,000
Deduct trade loss carried forward	—	(20,000)
Trade loss surrendered by B Ltd	—	(120,000)
Total taxable profits	£Nil	£Nil
B Ltd		
Trade profit/(loss)	(150,000)	10,000
Unrelieved loss brought forward		(150,000)
Loss surrender to A Ltd	—	120,000
Unrelieved loss carried forward	£(150,000)	£(20,000)

106.6 CT Group Relief

	Year ended 31.3.20 £	Year ended 31.3.21 £
B Ltd loss memoranda		
Trade loss		150,000
Carried forward against total profits of y/e 31.3.21		(10,000)
Surrendered to A Ltd for y/e 31.3.21		(120,000)
Unrelieved loss c/fwd to y/e 31.3.22		£20,000

Notes

(a) The following carried-forward amounts can be surrendered as group relief for carried-forward losses for accounting periods beginning on or after 1 April 2017:

- post-1 April 2017 non-trading deficits from loan relationships;
- non-trading losses on intangible fixed assets;
- expenses of management of investment business;
- post-1 April 2017 trade losses; and
- losses of a UK property business.

Where an accounting period straddles 1 April 2017 it is treated for this purpose as two separate accounting periods, the first ending on 31 March 2017 and the second beginning on 1 April 2017. Apportionments between the two accounting periods are made on a time basis unless that would produce an unjust or unreasonable result, in which case the apportionment must be made on a just and reasonable basis.

(b) A company can only claim group relief for carried-forward losses after it has used its own carried-forward losses to the full extent possible.

(c) Group relief for carry-forward losses is subject to restriction where the total set-off of carried-forward amounts exceeds £5,000,000. See **114.7** LOSSES.

106.7 CONSORTIUM RELIEF

(A) **Loss by company owned by consortium**

[*CTA 2010, ss 130, 132, 133*]

On 1 April 2020 the share capital of E Ltd was owned as follows

	%
A Ltd	40
B Ltd	40
C Ltd	20
	100

Group Relief CT 106.7

All the companies were UK resident for tax purposes.

During the year ended 31 March 2021 the following events took place

| On 1.7.20 | D Ltd bought | 20% from A Ltd |
| On 1.10.20 | C Ltd bought | 10% from B Ltd |

The companies had the following results for the year ended 31 March 2021

		£
A Ltd	Profit	40,000
B Ltd	Profit	33,000
C Ltd	Profit	10,000
D Ltd	Profit	18,000
E Ltd	Loss	(100,000)

None of the companies have any carried-forward losses or other unrelieved amounts.

All the member companies claim consortium relief in respect of the loss sustained by E Ltd. The companies elect that the claims be treated as made first by A Ltd, then by B Ltd, C Ltd and finally by D Ltd. For each company the consortium relief available is the lowest of the following three amounts:

(i) the unused part of the surrenderable amount for the overlapping period;

(ii) the unrelieved part of the claimant company's total profits for the overlapping period; and

(iii) the surrenderable amount for the overlapping period multiplied by the claimant member's share in the consortium in that period.

[*CTA 2010, ss 139, 140, 143*]

A Ltd

The overlapping period is the twelve months to 31.3.21. The amounts are

	£
(i)	100,000
(ii)	40,000
(iii) $100,000 \times 25\%$ ($40\% \times {}^3/_{12} + 20\% \times {}^9/_{12}$)	25,000
Therefore, loss relieved	£25,000

B Ltd

The overlapping period is the twelve months to 31.3.21. The amounts are

106.7 CT   Group Relief

		£	£
(i)	Surrenderable amount	100,000	
	Deduct loss previously surrendered	(25,000)	75,000
(ii)			33,000
(iii)	$100{,}000 \times 35\% \ (40\% \times {}^6/_{12} + 30\% \times {}^6/_{12})$		35,000
	Therefore, loss relieved		£33,000

C Ltd

The overlapping period is the twelve months to 31.3.21. The amounts are

		£	£
(i)	Surrenderable amount	100,000	
	Deduct losses previously surrendered (£25,000 + £33,000)	(58,000)	42,000
(ii)			10,000
(iii)	$100{,}000 \times 25\% \ (20\% \times {}^6/_{12} + 30\% \times {}^6/_{12})$		25,000
	Therefore, loss relieved		£10,000

D Ltd

As D Ltd only became a member of the consortium on 1.7.20, the overlapping period is the nine months to 31.3.21. The amounts are

		£	£
(i)	Surrenderable amount $100{,}000 \times {}^9/_{12}$	75,000	
	Deduct ${}^9/_{12} \times$ losses previously surrendered (£25,000 + £33,000 + £10,000)	(51,000)	24,000
(ii)	$18{,}000 \times {}^9/_{12}$		13,500
(iii)	$100{,}000 \times {}^9/_{12} \times 20\%$		15,000
	Therefore, loss relieved		£13,500

Summary

	A Ltd	B Ltd	C Ltd	D Ltd
	£	£	£	£
Profits for the year ended 31.3.21	40,000	33,000	10,000	18,000
Deduct Loss surrendered by E Ltd	(25,000)	(33,000)	(10,000)	(13,500)
Chargeable profits	£15,000	—	—	£4,500

E Ltd

		£	£
Loss for the year ended 31.3.21			100,000
Deduct Loss surrendered to A Ltd		(25,000)	
B Ltd		(33,000)	
C Ltd		(10,000)	
D Ltd		(13,500)	(81,500)
Not available for consortium relief			£18,500

(B) **Loss by company owned by consortium: claim by member of consortium company's group**

[*CTA 2010, ss 133, 146, 148*]

A Ltd owns 100% of the share capital of B Ltd

B Ltd owns 40% of the share capital of D Ltd

C Ltd owns 60% of the share capital of D Ltd

D Ltd owns 100% of the share capital of E Ltd

D Ltd owns 100% of the share capital of F Ltd

This can be shown as follows

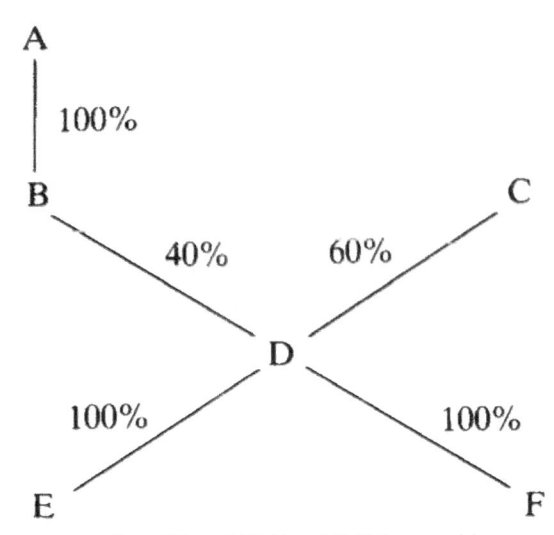

```
        A
        |
        | 100%
        |
        B                    C
          \                /
           40%         60%
             \        /
                D
            /       \
         100%       100%
          /           \
        E             F
```

There are two groups, A and B, and D, E and F. D is owned by a consortium of B and C. This relationship has existed for a number of years with all companies having the same accounting periods. None of the companies has any losses brought forward.

106.7 CT   Group Relief

The companies have the following results for year ended 31 July 2020

A Ltd	£100,000 profit
B Ltd	£(30,000) loss
C Ltd	£Nil
D Ltd	£(20,000) loss
E Ltd	£10,000 profit
F Ltd	£(3,000) loss

E Ltd claims group relief as follows

				£	£
Profit					10,000
Deduct	Group relief: loss surrendered by F Ltd	(note (b))		(3,000)	
	Group relief: loss surrendered by D Ltd	(note (b))		(7,000)	(10,000)
					=

A Ltd can claim group relief and consortium relief as follows

			£	£
Profit				100,000
Deduct	Group relief: loss surrendered by B Ltd	(note (c))	(30,000)	
	Consortium relief: loss surrendered by D Ltd	(note (d))	(5,200)	(35,200)
Chargeable profit				£64,800

Notes

(a) Where a company owned by a consortium is also a member of a group, its losses may be surrendered partly as group relief and partly as consortium relief.

(b) Where a loss of a company owned by a consortium or of a company within its group may be used both as group relief and consortium relief, the consortium relief is restricted. In determining the amount of consortium relief available, it is assumed that the maximum possible group relief is deducted after taking account of any other actual group relief claims within the consortium owned company's group. [*CTA 2010, s 148*]. See CTM80580 and *Simon's Taxes* D2.232. As F Ltd has surrendered losses of £3,000 to E Ltd, D Ltd can only surrender £7,000 to E Ltd as group relief. The surrenderable amount for the period for the purpose of consortium relief is restricted to the balance of D Ltd's loss, i.e. £13,000. If E Ltd had not claimed £3,000 group relief for F Ltd's loss, D Ltd could have surrendered £10,000 to E Ltd by way of group relief and this would have reduced D Ltd's surrenderable amount for consortium relief purposes to £10,000.

(c) Group relief available to A Ltd is the lower of £100,000 and £30,000.

(d) Consortium relief available to A Ltd is the lower of £13,000 (the unused surrenderable amount for the period), £70,000 (its unrelieved profits for the period (£100,000 less £30,000 group relief previously claimed) and £5,200 (40% of £13,000). The relief available to A Ltd is the same as that which B Ltd could have claimed if it had had sufficient profits. A Ltd could also have claimed consortium relief in respect of F Ltd's loss if that had exceeded the £10,000 necessary to cover E Ltd's profit. [*CTA 2010, s 133(1), 146.* See CTM80502 and *Simon's Taxes* D2.232].

(C) **Loss by subsidiary of company owned by consortium**

[*CTA 2010, ss 143, 151(4), 153(3)*]

Throughout 2020 and 2021 the share capital of E Ltd was owned as follows

	%
A Ltd	35
B Ltd	30
C Ltd	25
D Ltd	10
	100

E Ltd owned 90% of the share capital of F Ltd, a trading company. The companies had the following results for the year ended 31 March 2021.

		£
A Ltd	Profit	100,000
B Ltd	Loss	(40,000)
C Ltd	Profit	30,000
D Ltd	Profit	80,000
E Ltd	Profit	40,000
F Ltd	Loss	(240,000)

All the above companies were UK resident for tax purposes. Group relief of £40,000 of the loss sustained by F Ltd is claimed by E Ltd (note (c)).

Consortium relief for the loss sustained by F Ltd would be available as follows

	A Ltd	B Ltd	C Ltd	D Ltd
	£	£	£	£
Profits for the year ended 31.3.21	100,000	—	30,000	80,000
Deduct Loss surrendered by F Ltd (note (a))	(70,000)	—	(30,000)	(20,000)
Chargeable profits	£30,000	—	—	£60,000

106.7 CT   Group Relief

		Losses
F Ltd	£	£
Loss for the year ended 31.3.21		240,000
Deduct Loss surrendered to E Ltd		(40,000)
Available for consortium relief		200,000
Deduct Loss surrendered to A Ltd	(70,000)	
C Ltd	(30,000)	
D Ltd	(20,000)	(120,000)
Losses carried forward		£80,000

Notes

(a) Loss relief for each consortium member is the lower of

  (i) the unused part of the surrenderable amount for the year;

  (ii) the unrelieved part of the claimant company's total profits for the year; and

  (iii) the surrenderable amount for the year multiplied by the claimant member's share in the consortium.

  In this instance, the order in which the claims are deemed to be made does not affect the amounts which can be claimed, as (i) is greater than (ii) and (iii) in all cases.

(b) The surrenderable amount (see note (c)) multiplied by the share in the consortium appropriate to each member is

	%	£
A Ltd	35	70,000
B Ltd	30	60,000
C Ltd	25	50,000
D Ltd	10	20,000
	100	£200,000

(c) The loss available for consortium relief (the surrenderable amount) is reduced by any potentially available group relief. See also notes (a) and (b) to (B) above.

Group Relief   CT 106.7

(D) **Loss by consortium member**

[*CTA 2010, ss 132, 144*]

A Ltd, B Ltd, C Ltd and D Ltd have for many years held 40%, 30%, 20% and 10% respectively of the ordinary share capital of E Ltd. All five companies are UK resident and have always previously had taxable profits. However, for the year ending 30 June 2020 D Ltd has a tax loss of £100,000, followed by taxable profits of £40,000 for the subsequent year. E Ltd's taxable profits are £80,000 and £140,000 for the two years ending 31 December 2019 and 31 December 2020 respectively.

With the consent of A Ltd, B Ltd and C Ltd, D Ltd can (if it wishes) surrender the following part of its loss of £100,000 to E Ltd (assuming no other group/consortium relief claims are made involving either company)

Overlapping period 1.7.19 to 31.12.19

Unused part of the surrenderable amount for the overlapping period	$6/12 \times £100,000$	£50,000
Unrelieved part of E Ltd's total profits for the overlapping period	$6/12 \times £80,000$	£40,000
E Ltd's total profits for the overlapping period multiplied by D Ltd's share in consortium	$6/12 \times £80,000 \times 10\%$	£4,000

Overlapping period 1.1.20 to 30.6.20

Unused part of the surrenderable amount for the overlapping period	$6/12 \times £100,000$	£50,000
Unrelieved part of E Ltd's total profits for the overlapping period	$6/12 \times £140,000$	£70,000
E Ltd's total profits for the overlapping period multiplied by D Ltd's share in consortium	$6/12 \times £140,000 \times 10\%$	£7,000

The lowest figures for the two periods are £4,000 and £7,000.

Therefore, E Ltd can claim £4,000 of D Ltd's loss against its own profits for the year ended 31.12.19 and £7,000 against its profits for the year ending 31.12.20.

107 Income Tax in Relation to a Company

107.1 ACCOUNTING FOR INCOME TAX ON RECEIPTS AND PAYMENTS

[ITA 2007, ss 874–938; CTA 2010, s 967; FA 2017, Sch 5]

S Ltd prepares accounts each year to 31 October. During the two years ending 31 October 2019 and 31 October 2020 it pays and receives several sums (not being interest) from which basic rate income tax is deducted.

The following items are shown net

	Receipts (£)	Payments (£)
21.12.18		8,000
4.1.19	4,000	
9.8.19	8,000	
24.10.19	12,000	
25.3.20		8,000
14.8.20		9,600

The adjusted profits (*before* taking account of the gross equivalents of the above amounts) were

Year ended 31.10.19	£630,000
Year ended 31.10.20	£860,000

S Ltd will use the following figures in connection with the CT61 returns rendered to HMRC and will also be able to set off against its corporation tax liability the income tax suffered as shown

Return period	Payments	Receipts	Cumulative payments less receipts	Income tax paid/(repaid) with return
Year ended 31.10.19	£	£	£	£
1.11.18 to 31.12.18	8,000		8,000	2,000
1.1.19 to 31.3.19		4,000	4,000	(1,000)
1.4.19 to 30.6.19 (No return)			4,000	
1.7.19 to 30.9.19		8,000	(4,000)	(1,000)
1.10.19 to 31.10.19		12,000	(16,000)	—

107.1 CT Income Tax in Relation to a Company

Return period		Payments	Receipts	Cumulative payments less receipts	Income tax paid/ (repaid) with return
Year ended 31.10.20					
1.11.19 to 31.12.19	(No return)				
1.1.20 to 31.3.20		8,000		8,000	2,000
1.4.20 to 30.6.20	(No return)			8,000	
1.7.20 to 30.9.20	(No return)	9,600		17,600	2,400
1.10.20 to 31.10.20	(No return)			17,600	
					£4,400

Taxable profits

	Year ended 31.10.19 £	Year ended 31.10.20 £
Adjusted profits as stated	630,000	860,000
Add Cumulative receipts £16,000 + tax £4,000	20,000	
Deduct Cumulative payments £17,600 + tax of £4,400		(22,000)
Taxable profits	£650,000	£838,000

Tax payable

		Year ended 31.10.19 £	Year ended 31.10.20 £
CT @ 19% on profits		123,500	159,220
Deduct Income tax suffered	(note (a))	(4,000)	
Net liability		£119,500	£159,220

276

Notes

(a) This represents tax suffered on receipts, less that which has been offset against tax deducted from payments.

	£
Tax on receipts	6,000
Tax deducted from payments and recovered from HMRC	2,000
	£4,000

(b) Payments made by companies under the following provisions do not have to be made under deduction of income tax where the company reasonably believes that, at the time of payment, the recipient is a UK company (or a partnership of such companies), a non-UK resident company trading in the UK through a permanent establishment and in computing whose profits the payment falls to be brought into account or one of certain specified bodies or persons. The provisions concerned are:

(i) *ITA 2007, s 874(2)* (payments of yearly interest);

(ii) *ITA 2007, s 889(4)* (payments in respect of building society securities);

(iii) *ITA 2007, s 901(4)* (annual payments by persons other than companies);

(iv) *ITA 2007, s 903(7)* (patent royalties);

(v) *ITA 2007, s 906(5)* (royalty payments etc. where the owner lives abroad);

(vi) *ITA 2007, s 910(2)* (proceeds of sale of patent rights paid to non-UK residents);

(vii) *ITA 2007, s 919(2)* (manufactured interest on UK securities: payments to UK residents etc.); and

(viii) *ITA 2007, s 928(2)* (chargeable payments connected with exempt distributions).

108 Intangible Assets

108.1 DEBITS AND CREDITS

[*CTA 2009, 726–744*]

(A) **Writing-down on accounting basis**

On 1 April 2016, Oval Ltd purchased an intangible asset from an unrelated company, Edgbaston Ltd, for £100,000. The asset is to be used for trading purposes and has a remaining useful economic life of 15 years. The cost of the asset is capitalised in Oval Ltd's accounts and in accordance with generally accepted accounting practice is amortised on a straight-line basis over the remaining 15 year life. On 1 April 2020, the company sells the asset to another unrelated company, Riverside Ltd, for £150,000.

Oval Ltd will bring into account for tax purposes the following debits and credits in respect of the intangible asset.

	£
Y/e 31.3.17	
Cost of asset	100,000
Debit for year (1/15 of cost)	(6,667)
WDV at 31.3.17	93,333
Y/e 31.3.18	
Debit for year (1/15 of cost)	(6,667)
WDV at 31.3.18	86,666
Y/e 31.3.19	
Debit for year (1/15 of cost)	(6,666)
WDV at 31.3.19	£80,000
Y/e 31.3.20	
Debit for year (1/15 of cost)	(6,667)
WDV at 31.3.20	£73,333
Y/e 31.3.21	
Proceeds of realisation	150,000
Less Tax written-down value	(73,333)
Taxable credit	£76,667

As the asset was held for trading purposes, the debits of £6,667 for each of the years ended 31 March 2017, 2018, 2019 and 2020 are allowable trading deductions, and the credit of £76,667 for the year ended 31 March 2021 is a trading receipt.

108.1 CT Intangible Assets

Notes

(a) See **108.3** below for the rollover relief available on reinvestment of disposal proceeds in new intangible assets.

(b) No debits, other than realisation debits, are allowable in respect of goodwill or certain other customer-related intangible assets which were acquired on or after 8 July 2015 and before 1 April 2019. Realisation debits arising on such assets are treated as non-trading debits. [*CTA 2009, s 879C, FA 2019, Sch 9, para 6*]. See *Simon's Taxes* D1.601, D1.602. Similar restrictions also applied, in certain circumstances, where such assets were acquired from a related individual on or after 3 December 2014. [*CTA 2009, ss 849B–849D; FA 2015, s 26; F(No 2)A 2015, s 33(7)*]. For assets acquired on or after 1 April 2019, see **108.1(C)** below.

(B) **Writing-down at fixed rate**

M Ltd is a UK subsidiary of a multi-national group and prepares its accounts under IFRS. On 1 January 2016, M Ltd, which draws up accounts each year to 31 December, purchases the trade of X Ltd, an unrelated company. It is agreed that, of the purchase price, £500,000 is allocated to X Ltd's brand name, which is particularly well established in the UK and the USA. The brand name is considered to have an indefinite economic life and accordingly the expenditure is not amortised in M Ltd's accounts. Before 31 December 2019 M Ltd elects to write down the cost at the fixed rate of 4% per year. On 1 January 2019, M Ltd sells its rights to the brand name in the USA for £400,000 to Z plc, an unrelated company. £250,000 of the book value of the brand name in the accounts is set off against the disposal, giving an accounting profit of £150,000, and leaving the remaining book value as £250,000. On 1 January 2021, M Ltd sells the remaining rights in the brand name to Z plc for £200,000.

M Ltd must bring into account in calculating its trading profits the following debits and credits in respect of the brand name.

	£
Y/e 31.12.17	
Cost of brand name	500,000
Debit for year (4% of cost)	(20,000)
WDV at 31.12.17	480,000
Y/e 31.12.18	
Debit for year (4% of cost)	(20,000)
WDV at 31.12.18	£460,000
Y/e 31.12.19	
Part-realisation proceeds	400,000
Less Adjusted WDV (note (b))	(230,000)
Gain on part realisation (credit)	£170,000

Intangible Assets CT 108.1

Adjusted WDV of asset after part realisation (note (c))	230,000
Debit for year (4% of cost of remaining asset (note (d)))	(10,000)
WDV at 31.12.19	220,000

Y/e 31.12.20

Debit for year (4% of remaining cost)	(10,000)
WDV at 31.12.20	£210,000

Y/e 31.12.21

Realisation proceeds	200,000
Less WDV at 31.12.20	(210,000)
Loss on realisation (debit)	£(10,000)

Notes

(a) A company may elect for the tax cost of an intangible asset to be written down for tax purposes at a fixed rate. The election must be made in writing to HMRC within two years after the end of the accounting period in which the asset is created or acquired by the company and is irrevocable. Where the election is made, a debit of 4% of the cost (or, if less, the balance of the written-down value) is brought into account in each accounting period beginning with that in which the expenditure is incurred. The debit is proportionately reduced for accounting periods of less than twelve months. [*CTA 2009, ss 730, 731*]. See CIRD12905, CIRD12920, CIRD12910 and *Simon's Taxes* D1.628, D1.1445.

(b) On the part realisation of an asset, a proportion of the written-down value of the asset is deducted from the proceeds to arrive at the amount of the credit or debit arising. The proportion is that given by dividing the reduction in accounting value (i.e. the accounting value immediately before the realisation less the accounting value immediately afterwards) by the accounting value immediately before the realisation. [*CTA 2009, s 737*]. See CIRD13260 and *Simon's Taxes* D1.631. In this case, the reduction in accounting value is (£500,000 − £250,000) = £250,000, and the accounting value immediately before the realisation is £500,000. The amount to be deducted from the proceeds in this case is therefore £460,000 × (£250,000/£500,000) = £230,000.

(c) Following a part realisation, the written-down value of the remaining part of the asset is reduced to that proportion of it that is equal to the accounting value immediately after the realisation divided by the accounting value immediately before the realisation. [*CTA 2009, s 744*]. See CIRD12795, CIRD12920 and *Simon's Taxes* D1.632. In this case, therefore, the adjusted written-down value is £460,000 × (£250,000/£500,000) = £230,000.

(d) Following a part realisation, the fixed rate debit is calculated by reference to 4% of the value of the asset recognised for accounting purposes immediately after the realisation (plus the cost of any subsequent capitalised expenditure on the asset). [*CTA 2009, s 731(6)*].

108.1 CT   Intangible Assets

(C)   **Debits on goodwill and certain customer-related intangibles**

[*CTA 2009, ss 879A-879P; FA 2019, Sch 9 paras 6, 7*]

On 1 April 2020, N Ltd, a trading company, acquires goodwill of £400,000 as part of a business acquisition which also includes a patent with a cost of £50,000. N Ltd makes up accounts to 31 March using UK GAAP. Both the goodwill and the patent are used for the trade, are deemed to have useful lives of 10 years and are written off in the profit and loss account on a straight line basis. In the year to 31 March 2022, N Ltd sells the goodwill for £300,000 and the patent for £40,000. The allowable deductions for goodwill and the patent for the years to 31 March 2021 and 31 March 2022 are as follows.

Year to 31.3.21 – goodwill

The debit under the fixed rate relief is 6.5% x £400,000 = £26,000 (note (a)).

This is restricted by the amount of qualifying intellectual property acquired (the patent) through the following formula (note (a)):

(£50,000 x 6) / £400,000 = £300,000 / £400,000 = 0.75

The restricted debit is 0.75 x £26,000 = £19,500.

The accounts charge for amortisation of goodwill is £400,000 / 10 years = £40,000. Therefore £40,000 is added back to profits and the restricted debit of £19,500 is allowed as a trading deduction.

The tax written down value is £374,000 (ignoring the restriction on debits due to the level of the qualifying IP amount).

Year to 31.3.21 – patent

The accounts charge for amortisation of the patent is £50,000 / 10 years = £5,000. This is an allowable charge to profit and loss and no adjustment is required.

The tax written down value is £45,000.

Year to 31.3.22 – goodwill

On the sale of the goodwill the trading debit on realisation would be £374,000 – £300,000 = £74,000. This is multiplied by the restriction fraction which gives £74,000 x 0.75 = £55,500 (note (c)).

The non-trading debit on the restricted part of the goodwill is then calculated as follows (note (c)).

If the restriction on the debits arising from the level of the qualifying IP amounts was not ignored the tax written down value would be £400,000 – £19,500 = £380,500.

Therefore the debit on realisation for the restricted goodwill would be £380,500 – £300,000 = £80,500. The non-trading debit is £80,500 – £55,500 = £25,000.

The overall loss on goodwill for the company of £100,000 has been allowed as follows:

	£
Year to 31.3.21: trading deduction	19,500
Year to 31.3.22: trading deduction	55,500
Year to 31.3.22: non-trading debit	25,000

Intangible Assets   CT 108.1

	£
Year to 31.3.21: trading deduction	19,500
Total	£100,000

Year to 31.3.22 – patent

The accounting loss on the patent would be £45,000 – £40,000 = £5,000. This is an allowable charge to profit and loss and no adjustment is required.

Notes

(a) For goodwill and certain other customer-related assets acquired on or after 1 April 2019, relief is available for the debits brought into account by the company, including debits which arise from a change of accounting policy. Relief is only available when the relevant assets are acquired as part of a business acquisition that includes the acquisition of qualifying intellectual property (IP) which will be used on a continuing basis in the company's business. The rate of relief is fixed at 6.5% and this is only available on goodwill and certain other customer-related assets expenditure which is up to six times the qualifying IP bought with it. [*CTA 2009, ss 879B, 879I, 879M; FA 2019, Sch 9 para 6*]. See *Simon's Taxes* D1.627A.

(b) If the goodwill and other customer-related assets expenditure is transferred, on or after 1 April 2019, from a related individual or from a partnership which includes a related partner, then relief is only available if the goodwill or customer-related asset was acquired in a third party acquisition by the transferor and is transferred to the company along with the business. The relief is also at a fixed rate of 6.5% and again is only available when the relevant asset is acquired as part of a business acquisition that includes the acquisition of qualifying IP which will be used on a continuing basis in the company's business. The relief is limited to the notional accounting value of the relevant asset. [*CTA 2009, ss 879K, 879L, 879N; FA 2019, Sch 9 para 6*].

(c) On realisation of goodwill and customer-related assets, any debits brought into account are treated as non-trading debits where the relief has been restricted in relation to previous debits. Any debits which arise on the realisation of goodwill and customer-related assets, which have had partial restrictions on the relief of debits, is divided between two parts. The first part is the debit that would have been brought into account on the realisation of the asset, without any restriction, multiplied by any relevant restriction ratio. In order to calculate the amount of the debit arising on realisation, the calculation of the tax written down value of the goodwill and customer-related assets disregards any restriction on the debits previously brought into account. The second part is then the debit that would have arisen on realisation of the relevant asset less the amount in the first part. In this second part, in order to calculate the amount of debit on realisation of the asset, the calculation of the tax written down value does **not** disregard any previous restrictions of the debits. [*CTA 2009, s 879O; FA 2019, Sch 9 para 6*].

(d) No debits, other than realisation debits, are allowable in respect of goodwill or other customer-related intangible assets which were acquired on or after 8 July 2015 and before 1 April 2019. Realisation debits arising on such assets are treated as non-trading debits. [*CTA 2009, s 879C; FA 2019, Sch 9 para 6*]. See *Simon's Taxes* D1.601, D1.602.

(e) These provisions apply to:

    (i) goodwill in a business or part of a business;

108.1 CT   Intangible Assets

    (ii)   intangible fixed assets that consist of information which relates to customers or potential customers of a business or part of a business;

    (iii)   intangible fixed assets that consist of a relationship (whether contractual or not) between a person carrying on a business and one or more customers of that business or part of that business;

    (iv)   unregistered trademarks or other signs used in the course of a business or part of a business; and

    (v)   licences or other rights in respect of an asset within (i)–(iv) above.

[*CTA 2009, s 879A; FA 2019, Sch 9 para 6*].

108.2 NON-TRADING LOSS ON INTANGIBLE ASSETS

[*CTA 2009, ss 751–753; F(No 2)A 2017, Sch 4 paras 5, 190*]

A Ltd is an investment company drawing up accounts each year to 31 March. The following figures are relevant for the two years ended 31 March 2020 and 2021.

	Y/e 31.3.20 £	Y/e 31.3.21 £
UK property income	15,000	16,000
Income from non-trading loan relationships	5,000	20,000
Overseas income (foreign tax paid £3,600)	20,000	—
Management expenses	(5,000)	(5,000)
Non-trading profit/(loss) on intangible fixed assets	(55,000)	11,000

A Ltd wishes to make the most tax-efficient use of the non-trading loss, and so makes a claim to set off £15,000 against profits of the year ended 31 March 2020 under *CTA 2009, s 753(1)*. The corporation tax computations for the two years ended 31 March 2021 are as follows.

	£
Y/e 31.3.20	
UK property income	15,000
Income from non-trading loan relationships	5,000
Overseas income	20,000
	40,000
Deduct Management expenses	(5,000)
Non-trading loss	(15,000)
Profits chargeable to CT	£20,000
Corporation tax: £20,000 @ 19%	3,800
Deduct Double tax relief	(3,600)
Corporation tax payable	200

Intangible Assets CT 108.2

	£
Y/e 31.3.21	
UK property income	16,000
Income from non-trading loan relationships	20,000
Income from non-trading intangible assets (see below)	11,000
	47,000
Deduct Management expenses	(5,000)
Non-trading loss	(40,000)
Profits chargeable to CT	£2,000
Corporation tax: £2,000 @ 19%	£380

Use of non-trading loss

	£
Loss y/e 31.3.20	55,000
Set-off against profits for y/e 31.3.20	(15,000)
Set-off against profits for y/e 31.3.21	(40,000)
Carry-forward as non-trading loss	Nil

Notes

(a) A non-trading loss on intangible fixed assets for an accounting period may be set off against the company's total profits for the period. The company must make a claim for relief within two years after the end of the accounting period, or within such further period as HMRC may allow. Relief for the whole or part of the loss may be claimed in this way. [*CTA 2009, s 753(1)(2)*]. See CIRD13540.

(b) A non-trading loss may alternatively be surrendered as group relief. See **106.2 GROUP RELIEF**.

(c) To the extent that a non-trading loss is not set off against profits of the current accounting period or surrendered as group relief, it is carried forward to the next accounting period and treated as a non-trading loss of that period. [*CTA 2009, s 753(3)*]. The carried-forward loss is available for set-off against profits of that accounting period or alternatively may be surrendered as group relief for carried-forward losses (see **106.6 GROUP RELIEF**). A loss cannot be carried forward to the accounting period in which the company ceases to be a company with investment business (or to any subsequent accounting period).

(d) The rules for the carry forward of losses illustrated in this example apply to accounting periods beginning on or after 1 April 2017. For this purpose, where an accounting period straddles that date it is treated as two separate accounting periods, the first ending on 31 March 2017 and the second beginning on 1 April 2017. Apportionments between the two accounting periods are made on a time basis unless that would produce an unjust or unreasonable result, in which case the apportionment must be made on a just and reasonable basis [*F(No.2)A 2017, Sch 4 para 190*].

108.2 CT   Intangible Assets

Previously, to the extent that a non-trading loss was not set off against profits of the current accounting period or surrendered as group relief, it was carried forward to the next accounting period and treated as a non-trading debit of that period. The carried-forward loss was therefore included in the computation of any non-trading profit or loss on intangible fixed assets for that period. Where a loss resulted, the whole loss was available for set-off against total profits of the period. However, the debit carried forward had to be excluded from the loss for the period in calculating any amount available for surrender as group relief. [*CTA 2010, s 104(2)*].

(e) The carry-forward of non-trading losses is subject to restriction where the total set-off of carried-forward amounts exceeds £5,000,000. See **114.7** LOSSES.

108.3 ROLLOVER RELIEF ON REINVESTMENT

[*CTA 2009, ss 754–763*]

Oval Ltd, the company in **108.1(A)** above, purchases a new intangible fixed asset (asset 2) on 1 April 2021 for £165,000 and claims rollover relief in respect of the asset disposed of in that example (referred to below as asset 1).

The effect of the claim for tax purposes is as follows.

	£
Disposal proceeds of asset 1	150,000
Tax cost of asset 1	(100,000)
Rollover relief available	£50,000

The taxable credit on disposal of asset 1 for the year ended 31.3.21 is therefore recalculated as follows

	£
Proceeds of realisation	150,000
Less Tax written-down value	(73,333)
Amount rolled over	(50,000)
Taxable credit	£26,667

The cost for tax purposes of asset 2 is adjusted as follows

	£
Cost of asset 2	165,000
Less amount rolled over on asset 1	(50,000)
Adjusted cost for tax purposes	£115,000

Notes

(a) A company which realises a chargeable intangible asset and incurs expenditure on other chargeable intangible assets within the period beginning one year before the date of realisation and ending three years after that date, may, subject to meeting detailed conditions, claim rollover relief under *CTA 2009, Pt 8 Ch 7*. The claim must specify the old assets to which the claim relates, the expenditure on other assets by reference to which relief is claimed, and the amount of relief claimed. [*CTA 2009, s 757*]. See CIRD20150 and *Simon's Taxes* D1.639.

(b) On making the claim, the proceeds of realisation of the old asset and the cost recognised for tax purposes of the other assets are both reduced by the amount available for relief. Where the expenditure on the other assets is equal to or exceeds the realisation proceeds the amount available for relief is the excess of the proceeds over the tax cost of the original asset. Where the expenditure on other assets is less than the realisation proceeds, the amount available for relief is the excess of the expenditure over the tax cost of the original asset. The relief does not affect the tax treatment of the other parties to the transactions. [*CTA 2009, s 758*]. See CIRD20205, CIRD20210, CIRD20220, CIRD20230 and *Simon's Taxes* D1.638.

(c) In this case, the relief available is £50,000, leaving £26,667 of the gain on realisation chargeable. This effectively recovers the debits previously given in respect of the asset (£6,667 × 4 = £26,667, see **108.1(A)** above). Only the profit element is rolled over.

109 Interest on Overpaid Tax

[*ICTA 1988, ss 825, 826; FA 1989, s 178; FA 1991, Sch 15 para 22, 23; FA 2019, s 88; SI 1989 No 1297; SI 1993 No 2212*]

109.1 (A) REPAYMENT OF TAX: GENERAL

[*SI 1998 No 3175; SI 1998 No 3176*]

X Ltd prepares accounts to 31 December. On 15 June 2020 it submits its tax return for the year ended 31 December 2019 showing a corporation tax liability for the period of £14,000, and accompanied by a payment of £7,000. On 1 October 2020 it makes a further payment of £7,000. It subsequently submits an amended return showing a reduced liability of £12,500, and £1,500 is repaid to the company on 1 December 2020.

It is assumed that interest rates for corporation tax repayments other than by instalment, and for tax paid before the due date, remain unchanged after 29 September 2009 and 21 September 2009 respectively.

X Ltd will be entitled to interest on overpaid tax, calculated as follows

		£
15.6.20 to 30.9.20	£7,000 × 0.5% × $^{108}/_{365}$ =	10.36
1.10.20 to 30.11.20	£1,500 × 0.5% × $^{61}/_{365}$ =	1.26
Total interest		£11.62

Notes

(a) The rate of interest on corporation tax paid early is the special (usually) higher rate applying to overpaid instalment payments (see (B) below). The special rate does not apply to overpaid tax after nine months after the end of the accounting period, from which date the (usually) lower normal rate applies. At the time of writing the two rates were the same: 0.5%. This is the minimum possible rate.

(b) The unified repayment interest provisions of *FA 2009, s 102, Sch 54* do not yet apply to corporation tax.

(B) REPAYMENT OF TAX: INSTALMENT PAYMENTS

[*SI 1998 No 3175; SI 1998 No 3176; SI 2017 No 1072*]

Z Ltd has no related 51% group companies and had taxable profits in excess of £1,500,000 for the year ended 31 March 2018. For the year ending 31 March 2019, Z Ltd pays £143,000 for the first instalment on 30 September 2018, this being equivalent to a quarter of its estimated corporation tax liability of £572,000. The same amount is paid on the due dates for the second and third instalments and on 5 July 2019 for the fourth instalment. On 3 September 2020, the tax liability is agreed at £506,800 and £65,200 is repaid to the company on 22 September 2020.

It is assumed that interest rates for corporation tax repayments remain unchanged after September 2009.

109.1 CT   Interest on Overpaid Tax

The interest on overpaid tax is calculated as follows

Instalments due on quarter dates £506,800 × $^1/_4$ = £126,700

Interest on overpaid tax

	£
14 October 2018 to 13 January 2019	
143,000 − 126,700 = £16,300 @ 0.5% × $^{92}/_{365}$	20.54
14 January 2019 to 13 April 2019	
286,000 − 253,400 = £32,600 @ 0.5% × $^{90}/_{365}$	40.19
14 April 2019 to 5 July 2019	
429,000 − 380,100 = £48,900 @ 0.5% × $^{83}/_{365}$	55.60
6 July 2019 to 13 July 2019	
572,000 − 380,100 = £191,900 @ 0.5% × $^{8}/_{365}$	21.03
14 July 2019 to 31 December 2019	
572,000 − 506,800 = £65,200 @ 0.5% × $^{171}/_{365}$	152.73
1 January 2020 to 21 September 2020	
572,000 − 506,800 = £65,200 @ 0.5% × $^{264}/_{365}$	235.79
	£525.88

Notes

(a) Interest will not be payable before the due date of the first instalment.

(b) A special (sometimes) higher rate of interest for instalment payments applies from the date the excess arises to the earlier of nine months after the end of the accounting period and the date the tax is repaid. Interest is calculated using the usually lower normal rate from the date of nine months after the end of the accounting period to the date of issue of the repayment order. At the time of writing the two rates were the same: 0.5%. This is the minimum possible rate.

(c) Debit interest works in the same way as the credit interest illustrated in this example (see **110.1(C)**). For example, had Z Ltd paid less than the amount of tax due at any one of the above dates, the interest payable would be worked out on the same basis but using the relevant interest rates for unpaid tax.

(d) The instalment payment dates for very large UK companies (those with profits over £20 million) are in the third, sixth, ninth and twelfth months of each accounting period. These rules apply for accounting periods beginning on or after 1 April 2019.

(e) HMRC use a denominator of 365 in calculations of repayment interest regardless of whether or not a leap year is involved.

Interest on Overpaid Tax   CT 109.2

109.2 REPAYMENT ARISING FROM CARRY-BACK OF LOSSES UNDER *CTA 2010*, *SS 37, 39*: TERMINAL LOSSES

Y Ltd prepares accounts to 31 December. It has chargeable profits of £100,000 and £60,000 for the years to 31 December 2018 and 2019 respectively and pays corporation tax of £19,246 and £11,400 on the due dates (i.e. 1 October 2019 and 1 October 2020 respectively). The company ceases trading on 31 July 2020 and incurs a loss in its last period of £80,000. It claims loss relief under *CTA 2010, ss 37, 39* against profits of previous accounting periods. As a result of the claim, it receives a corporation tax repayment of £15,249 on 25 July 2021 comprising £3,849 for the year to 31 December 2018 and £11,400 for the year to 31 December 2019.

Interest on overpaid tax is calculated as follows

On tax of £11,400 for year ended 31.12.19:

Date of payment	1 October 2020
Material date	1 October 2020
Interest runs from	1 October 2020

Interest runs to 25 July 2021, a total of 297 days.

On tax of £3,849 for year ended 31.12.18:

Date of payment		1 October 2019
Material date	(note (a))	1 May 2021
Interest runs from		1 May 2021

Interest runs to 25 July 2021, a total of 85 days.

Notes

(a) Where, under a *section 37* claim, a loss is carried back to an accounting period not falling wholly within the twelve months preceding the period of loss, the resulting corporation tax repayment is effectively treated as a repayment of tax paid for the period *in* which the loss is incurred, rather than for the period *to* which the loss is carried back. [*ICTA 1988, s 826(7A)*].

(b) HMRC use a denominator of 365 in calculations of repayment interest regardless of whether or not a leap year is involved.

Interest on Unpaid Tax   CT 110.1

110   Interest on Unpaid Tax

110.1 SELF-ASSESSMENT

[*TMA 1970, s 87A; SI 1998, No 3175; SI 1998 No 3176; SI 1999 No 1928; SI 1999 No 1929; SI 2017 No 1072*]

(A)   **General**

S Ltd (which has no related 51% group companies) prepares accounts to 31 July. On 31 May 2020, it makes a payment of £80,000 in respect of its corporation tax liability for the year to 31 July 2019, the due date being 1 May 2020. On completing its corporation tax return, the company ascertains its total tax liability for the year to be £105,000 and makes a further payment of £25,000 on 16 July 2020. The final CT liability is agreed at £107,500 on 27 November 2020 and the company pays a further £2,500 on 5 January 2021.

It is assumed that the interest rates remain unchanged after 7 April 2020.

Interest on unpaid tax will be payable as follows

1.5.20 to 31.5.20	£80,000 × 2.60% × $^{30}/_{366}$	=	170.49
1.5.20 to 16.7.20	£25,000 × 2.60% × $^{76}/_{366}$	=	134.97
1.5.20 to 5.1.21	£2,500 × 2.60% × $^{249}/_{366}$	=	44.22
Total interest charge			£349.68

Notes

(a)   HMRC use a denominator of 366 in calculations of interest on unpaid tax regardless of whether or not a leap year is involved.

(b)   The unified late payment interest provisions of *FA 2009, s 101, Sch 53* (see IT 13 LATE PAYMENT INTEREST AND PENALTIES) do not yet apply to corporation tax.

(B)   **Refund of interest charged**

On 1 November 2020, T Ltd pays corporation tax of £100,000 for its year ended 31 December 2019. The due date for payment was 1 October 2020. The liability is finally agreed at £80,000 and a repayment of £20,000 is made to T Ltd on 1 May 2021.

The rates of interest are assumed for the purposes of this example to remain unchanged after 7 April 2020.

The interest position will be as follows

(i) T Ltd will be charged interest on £100,000 for the period 1.10.20 to 1.11.20 (31 days). The charge will be raised following payment of the £100,000 on 1.11.20.

£100,000 × 2.60% × $^{31}/_{366}$ = £220.22

110.1 CT   Interest on Unpaid Tax

(ii) The company will be entitled to interest on overpaid tax of £20,000 for the period 1.11.20 (date of payment) to 1.5.21 (date of repayment) (181 days ignoring leap year).

$£20,000 \times 0.5\% \times {}^{181}/_{365} = £49.59$

(iii) T Ltd will also receive a refund of interest charged on £20,000 for the period 1.10.20 to 1.11.20.

$£20,000 \times 2.60\% \times {}^{31}/_{366} = £44.04$

(C) **Instalment payments**

R Ltd has no related 51% group companies and had taxable profits in excess of £1,500,000 for the year ended 31 March 2018. For the year ending 31 March 2019, R Ltd makes instalment payments of £110,000 (this being equivalent to a quarter of its estimated corporation tax liability of £440,000) on the first three due dates. The last instalment is not paid until 24 July 2019. On 3 September 2020, the tax liability is finally agreed at £524,800. R Ltd pays the balance due of £84,800 on 10 September 2020.

The rates of interest are assumed for the purposes of this example to remain unchanged after 30 March 2020 for quarterly payments and after 7 April 2020 otherwise.

The interest on unpaid tax is calculated as follows

Instalments due on quarter dates £524,800 × 1/4 = £131,200

	£
1st instalment	
14 October 2018 to 13 January 2019	
131,200 – 110,000 = £21,200 @ 1.75% × ${}^{92}/_{366}$ =	93.25
1st and 2nd instalment	
14 January 2019 to 13 April 2019	
262,400 – 220,000 = £42,400 @ 1.75% × ${}^{90}/_{366}$ =	182.45
1st, 2nd and 3rd instalments	
14 April 2019 to 13 July 2019	
393,600 – 330,000 = £63,600 @ 1.75% × ${}^{91}/_{366}$ =	276.72
1st, 2nd, 3rd and 4th instalments	
14 July 2019 to 23 July 2019	
524,800 – 330,000 = £194,800 @ 1.75% × ${}^{10}/_{366}$ =	93.14
24 July 2019 to 31 December 2019	
524,800 – 440,000 = 84,800 @ 1.75% × ${}^{161}/_{366}$ =	652.79
Normal due date for payment — 1 January 2020	
1 January 2020 to 29 March 2020	
524,800 – 440,000 = 84,800 @ 3.25% × ${}^{89}/_{366}$ =	670.17

Interest on Unpaid Tax   CT 110.1

30 March 2020 to 6 April 2020
524,800 − 440,000 = 84,800 @ 2.75% × $^{8}/_{366}$ =   50.97

7 April 2020 to 10 September 2020
524,800 − 440,000 = 84,800 @ 2.60% × $^{156}/_{366}$ =   939.75

Interest on unpaid tax   2,959.24

Notes

(a) A special lower rate of interest for instalment payments applies from the due date of payment to the earlier of nine months after the end of the accounting period and the date the tax is paid. Interest is calculated using the higher normal rate from the date of nine months after the end of the accounting period to the date the tax is paid.

(b) Credit interest works in the same way as the debit interest illustrated in this example (see 109.1(B)). For example, had R Ltd paid more than the amount of tax due at any one of the above dates, the interest payable by HMRC would be worked out on the same basis but using the relevant interest rates for overpaid tax.

(c) Instalment payment dates for very large UK companies (those with profits over £20 million) are in the third, sixth, ninth and twelfth months of each accounting period. These rules apply for accounting periods beginning on or after 1 April 2019.

(D) **Surrenders of tax refunds within a group of companies**

[*CTA 2010, ss 963–966; FA 1989, s 102*]

V Ltd has had, for some years, a 75% subsidiary, W Ltd, and both prepare accounts to 30 November. On 1 September 2019 (the due date), both companies make payments on account of their CT liabilities for the year ended 30 November 2018. V Ltd pays £250,000 and W Ltd pays £150,000. In August 2020, the liabilities are eventually agreed at £200,000 and £180,000 respectively. Before any tax repayment is made to V Ltd, the two companies jointly give notice under *CTA 2010, s 963(2)* that £30,000 of the £50,000 tax repayment due to V Ltd is to be surrendered to W Ltd. W Ltd makes a payment of £20,000 to V Ltd in consideration for the tax refund surrendered.

The rates of interest are assumed for the purposes of this example to remain unchanged after 7 April 2020.

If no surrender had been made, and all outstanding tax payments/repayments made on, say, 1 September 2020, the interest position would have been as follows

£

V Ltd
Interest on CT repayment of £50,000
for the period 1.9.19 to 1.9.20   £50,000 × 0.5% =   250

110.1 CT Interest on Unpaid Tax

W Ltd
Interest on late paid CT of £30,000

for the period 1.9.19 to 29.3.20	£30,000 × 3.25% × $^{211}/_{365}$ =	564
for the period 30.3.20 to 6.4.20	£30,000 × 2.75% × $^{8}/_{365}$ =	18
for the period 7.4.20 to 1.9.20	£30,000 × 2.60% × $^{146}/_{365}$ =	312
Net interest payable by the group		£644

The surrender has the following consequences

(i) Only £20,000 of the repayment (the unsurrendered amount) is actually made, and is made to V Ltd together with interest of £100 (at 0.5% for 365 days).

(ii) V Ltd, the surrendering company, is treated as having received a CT repayment of £30,000 (the surrendered amount) on the 'relevant date' which in this case is the normal due date of 1.9.19 V Ltd having made its CT payment on time. V Ltd is thus not entitled to any interest on this amount.

(iii) W Ltd, the recipient company, is deemed to have paid CT of £30,000 on the 'relevant date', 1.9.19 as above. It thus incurs no interest charge.

(iv) The group has turned a net interest charge of £644 into a net interest receipt of £100, a saving of £744. This arises from the differential in the rates of interest charged on unpaid and overpaid tax.

(v) The payment of £20,000 by W Ltd to V Ltd, not being a payment in excess of the surrendered refund, has no tax effect on either company.

Note

(a) V Ltd could have given notice to surrender its full refund of £50,000 to W Ltd, instead of just £30,000. There would, in fact, have been no point in doing so, but if W Ltd had made its original CT payment later than the due date, so as to incur an interest charge on the £150,000 originally paid, a full surrender would have produced a saving as the amount surrendered would be treated as having been paid on the due date.

111 Investment Companies and Investment Business

111.1 MANAGEMENT EXPENSES

[*CTA 2009 ss 1218–1220, 1223, 1248; CAA 2001, ss 18, 253*]

XYZ Ltd, an investment company, rents out rooms, halls and equipment to conference providers. It makes up accounts to 31 March. The following details are relevant

	31.3.19 £	31.3.20 £
Rents receivable	38,000	107,000
Interest receivable accrued gross	10,000	5,000
Chargeable gains	18,000	48,000
Management expenses		
attributable to property	20,000	25,000
attributable to management	50,000	40,000
Capital allowances		
attributable to property	1,000	500
attributable to management	2,000	1,000

The corporation tax computations are as follows
Year ended 31.3.19

		£	£
Property income			
Rents			38,000
Deduct	Capital allowances	1,000	
	Expenses	20,000	(21,000)
			17,000
Non-trading loan relationships			10,000
Chargeable gains			18,000
			45,000
Deduct	Management expenses	50,000	
	Capital allowances	2,000	(52,000)
Unrelieved balance carried forward			£(7,000)

111.1 CT Investment Companies and Investment Business

Year ended 31.3.20

		£	£
Property income			
Rents			107,000
Deduct	Capital allowances	500	
	Expenses	25,000	(25,500)
			81,500
Non-trading loan relationships			5,000
Chargeable gains			48,000
			£134,500
Deduct	Management expenses	40,000	
	Capital allowances	1,000	
	Unrelieved balance from previous accounting period	7,000	(48,000)
Profit chargeable to CT			£86,500

On 1 April 2020, XYZ Ltd diversified and began to provide conference services itself. The following details are relevant for the year ending 31 March 2021.

	31.3.21
	£
Income from conferences	65,000
Rents receivable	40,000
Interest receivable accrued (gross)	5,000
Conference costs	22,000
Management expenses	
attributable to property	20,000
attributable to management	73,000
Capital allowances	
attributable to conferences	2,000
attributable to property	400
attributable to management	800

Investment Companies and Investment Business   CT 111.1

The corporation tax computations are as follows.
Year ended 31.3.21

	£	£	£
Trading income			65,000
Deduct Conference costs		22,000	
Capital allowances		2,000	
			(24,000)
			41,000
Property income			
Rents		40,000	
Deduct Capital allowances	400		
Expenses	20,000	(20,400)	
			19,600
Income from non-trading loan relationships			5,000
Deduct Management expenses	73,000		
Capital allowances	800		
			(73,800)
Unrelieved balance carried forward			£(8,200)

Notes

(a) Relief for management expenses is available to companies with investment business whether or not they are investment companies. Such expenses are deductible for corporation tax purposes for the accounting period in which they are charged to the accounts. [*CTA 2009, ss 1218–1231, 1248, 1255*]. A company with investment business is defined as 'any company whose business consists wholly or partly in the making of investments'. [*CTA 2009, s 1218*]. (It will include, for example, a trading company with shares in subsidiary companies.)

(b) The excess management expenses (including capital allowances) in the accounting period ended 31.3.19 are carried forward to the accounting period ended 31.3.20 and are set against total profits of that period. If profits in the year ended 31.3.20 had been insufficient, the excess management expenses could have been carried forward to subsequent periods until fully used. Similarly, the excess management expenses in the accounting period ended 31.3.21 can be carried forward to subsequent accounting periods. For accounting periods beginning on or after 1 April 2017, a claim is required for carried-forward management expenses to be set off against total profits of the next accounting period. A claim can be made for the whole or part of the excess carried forward. For this purpose, where an accounting period straddles 1 April 2017 it is treated as two separate accounting periods, the first ending on 31 March 2017 and the second beginning on 1 April 2017. Apportionments between the two accounting periods are made on a time basis unless that would produce an unjust or unreasonable result, in which case the apportionment must be made on a just and reasonable basis [*CTA 2009, s 1223; F (No 2) A 2017, Sch 4 paras 6, 190*]. See also note (d) below. See CTM08620 and *Simon's Taxes* D7.311, D7.313, D8.122, D1.1114, D1.122, D1.1109.

111.1 CT Investment Companies and Investment Business

(c) Management expenses brought forward from earlier accounting periods beginning on or after 1 April 2017 (see note (b) above) can be included in a group relief for carried-forward losses claim. See **106.6** GROUP RELIEF.

(d) Surplus management expenses may not be carried forward if there is a change of ownership of a company with investment business and one of the following occurs:

   (i)   a significant increase (as defined) in the company's capital after the change of ownership,

   (ii) a major change in the nature or conduct of the business of the company in the period beginning three years before the change and ending five years after (three years where either the change in ownership or the change in the nature or conduct of the business occurs before 1 April 2017),

   (iii) a considerable revival of the company's business which before the change was small or negligible.

   [*CTA 2010*, ss 677–703].

(e) The carry-forward of excess management expenses is subject to restriction where the total set-off of carried-forward amounts exceeds £5,000,000. See **114.7** LOSSES.

112 Liquidation

112.1 ACCOUNTING PERIODS IN A LIQUIDATION

[*CTA 2009, ss 9, 12; CTA 2010, ss 626–629*]

On 31 August 2018 a resolution was passed to wind up X Ltd. The company's normal accounting date was 31 December.

It was later agreed between the liquidator and HMRC that 31 January 2020 would be the assumed date of completion of winding-up. The actual date of completion is 30 April 2021.

The last accounting period of the company before liquidation is

1.1.18 to 31.8.18	—	8 months

The accounting periods during the liquidation are as follows

1.9.18 to 31.8.19	—	12 months
1.9.19 to 31.1.20	—	5 months
1.2.20 to 31.1.21	—	12 months
1.2.21 to 30.4.21	—	3 months

Note

(a) If the rate for the financial year in which the winding-up is completed (the 'final year') has not been fixed or proposed by Budget resolution before completion of the winding-up, the rate for the penultimate financial year will apply to the income of that year. In this case, the final and penultimate financial years for the above accounting periods are 2021 and 2020 respectively.

113 Loan Relationships

113.1 TRADING PURPOSE

[*CTA 2009 ss 295–301, 304, 306A–310, 328*]

A Ltd requires additional trade finance and on 1 January 2019 enters into an agreement with XY Bank plc to borrow £100,000 for 3 years. Interest is payable every 6 months commencing 1 July 2019 at 6% per annum. Legal fees and negotiation expenses of £2,800 which were directly incurred in bringing this loan into existence were paid in December 2018. The company's accounting reference date is 31 March and it adopts an amortised cost basis for all loan relationships.

A Ltd's accounts for the year ended 31 March 2019 show the following

	£	£
Turnover		1,400,000
Purchases and expenses		
(all allowable for corporation tax purposes)	900,000	
Finance Charges		
XY Bank plc – interest to 31 March 2019	1,500	
Legal fees and negotiation expenses	2,800	
Depreciation*	120,000	
		1,024,300
Net profit per accounts		£375,700

*Capital allowances for the same year are £95,000.

The company's corporation tax computation for the same period is as follows

	£
Net profit per accounts	375,700
Add: Depreciation	120,000
Less: Capital allowances	(95,000)
Adjusted profit for corporation tax purposes	£400,700

For corporation tax purposes the accrued interest on the loan with XY Bank plc taken out for trading purposes is treated as a trading expense.

113.1 CT   Loan Relationships

The profit and loss charge for each of the following accounting periods will be

	Year ended 31.3.19 £	Year ended 31.3.20 £	Year ended 31.3.21 £	Year ended 31.3.22 £
'Debits'				
Expenses	2,800	—	—	—
Interest payable	1,500	6,000	6,000	4,500

This conforms to the amortised cost basis of accounting as interest will be allocated to the period to which it relates. Where the directly-incurred expenses are material then under GAAP they should be deducted from the proceeds of the loan and spread over the life of the loan within the overall finance charge.

Notes

(a) A company has a loan relationship whenever it stands in the position of debtor or creditor in respect of a money debt. (A money debt being any debt not arising in the normal course of purchase and sale of goods and services for resale.) [*CTA 2009 ss 302, 303*]. See CFM31010, CTM47535, CFM92060, CFM31030, CFM31050.

(b) The taxation of the loan relationship follows accounts drawn up in accordance with generally accepted accounting practice. [*CTA 2009, ss 306A–310; F(No 2)A 2015, Sch 7 paras 4, 5, 103*].

(c) Interest payments on current loans for trading purposes are treated as a trading expense. [*CTA 2009, ss 296, 297, 301*].

(d) Only expenses directly incurred in relation to the origination of a loan would be allowable under the loan relationships' code. [*CTA 2009, s 306A(2)(a)*].

113.2 NON-TRADING PURPOSES

Tradissimo Ltd, a non-financial trading company, bought £10,000 nominal of corporate bonds at £94 per £100 nominal stock as an investment on 1 January 2018. The bonds will be redeemed on 1 January 2021 at par. Interest at 5% is payable annually on 31 December each year. The company uses an amortised cost accounting method for all its loan relationships. The accounting reference date is 31 March.

As the purchase of the bonds does not relate to the company's trade, its income and expenditure is chargeable as income from a non-trading loan relationship. In addition to the interest, the company will also be taxable on the discount which will be spread over three years on an effective interest rate method. For illustration purposes, a straight-line method has been used below.

Loan Relationships CT 113.3

	Year ended 31.3.18 £	Year ended 31.3.19 £	Year ended 31.3.20 £	Year ended 31.3.21 £
'Credits'				
Interest received	125	500	500	375
Discount	50	200	200	150
Income from non-trading loan relationships	£175	£700	£700	£525

Note

(a) Profits and losses from non-trading loan relationships are taxable as income from non-trading loan relationships. [*CTA 2009, s 299*]. See CFM32030, CFM51020, CFM32010, BIM64295 and *Simon's Taxes* A4.423, A4.424.

113.3 NON-TRADING DEFICIT ON A LOAN RELATIONSHIP

(A) Deficit arising before 1 April 2017

[*CTA 2009, ss 456–463*]

The Beta Trading Co Ltd, which is a single company and not part of a group, has a non-trading loan relationship deficit of £8,400 for the year ended 31 March 2017.

The Beta Trading Co Ltd's computations for relevant years are as follows

	Year ended 31.3.15 £	Year ended 31.3.16 £	Year ended 31.3.17 £	Year ended 31.3.18 £
Trading income	10,000	11,000	800	12,000
Non-trading loan relationship income/(deficit)	2,000	2,000	(8,400)	400

113.3 CT Loan Relationships

The deficit of £8,400 may be relieved in whole or in part in three different ways (group relief not being available).

		£
Non-trading deficit		8,400
1.	Set off against total profits of the year ended 31 March 2017	(800)
2.	Carry back against profits from non-trading loan relationships of the preceding accounting period	(2,000)
3.	Carry forward against non-trading profits of the company for year ended 31 March 2018	(400)
Net deficit to carry forward against subsequent non-trading profits		£5,200

Notes

(a) Relief for a non-trading deficit may be claimed (to the extent not already surrendered as group relief) either:

   (i) by set-off against profits of the company of whatever description for the deficit period; or

   (ii) by carry back and set-off against profits of the preceding accounting period arising from non-trading loan relationships.

(b) Where relief is not claimed as in (a) above, the non-trading deficit is automatically carried forward for set-off against non-trading profits of the subsequent accounting period, subject to a claim for it to be not so carried forward, in which case it is treated as a non-trading deficit of that period to be carried forward for offset against non-trading profits of succeeding accounting periods.

(c) The £5,200 deficit balance (which income from non trading loan relationships for the year ended 31 March 2017 is insufficient to relieve) will be carried forward for relief against non-trading profits of the next and subsequent accounting periods subject to a claim as in (b) above. [*CTA 2009, s 457(1)(2)*]. See CFM32030, CFM32100 and *Simon's Taxes* D1.740, D4.807, D1.1109, D7.705.

(d) The rules illustrated in this example apply to non-trading deficits arising in accounting periods beginning before 1 April 2017. For this purpose, where an accounting period straddles that date it is treated as two separate accounting periods, the first ending on 31 March 2017 and the second beginning on 1 April 2017. Apportionments between the two accounting periods are made on a time basis unless that would produce an unjust or unreasonable result, in which case the apportionment must be made on a just and reasonable basis. See (B) below for the new rules. The rules illustrated here continue to apply, however, where the company is a charity. [*F (No 2) A 2017, Sch 4 para 190*].

(e) See note (e) to (B) below.

Loan Relationships CT 113.3

(B) **Deficit arising after 31 March 2017**

[*CTA 2009, ss 463A–463I; F(No 2)A 2017, Sch 4 paras 4, 190*]

Sigma Ltd, which is a single company and not part of a group, has a non-trading loan relationship deficit of £8,500 for the year ended 31 March 2020.

Sigma Ltd's computations for relevant years are as follows

	Year ended 31.3.18 £	Year ended 31.3.19 £	Year ended 31.3.20 £	Year ended 31.3.21 £
Trading income	10,000	11,000	800	2,500
Non-trading loan relationship income/(deficit)	2,000	2,000	(8,500)	2,000

The non-trading loan relationship deficit of £8,500 may be relieved in whole or in part in three different ways (group relief not being available).

		£
Non-trading deficit		8,500
1.	Set off against total profits of the year ended 31 March 2020	(800)
2.	Carry back against profits from non-trading loan relationships of the preceding accounting period	(2,000)
3.	Carry forward against total profits of the company for year ended 31 March 2021	(4,500)
Net deficit to carry forward against subsequent total profits		£1,200

Notes

(a) The rules illustrated in this example apply to non-trading deficits arising in accounting periods beginning on or after 1 April 2017. For this purpose, where an accounting period straddles that date it is treated as two separate accounting periods, the first ending on 31 March 2017 and the second beginning on 1 April 2017. Apportionments between the two accounting periods are made on a time basis unless that would produce an unjust or unreasonable result, in which case the apportionment must be made on a just and reasonable basis. [*F (No 2) A 2017, Sch 4 para 190*].

(b) Relief for a non-trading deficit may be claimed (to the extent not already surrendered as group relief) either:

(i) by set-off against profits of the company of whatever description for the deficit period; or

(ii) by carry back and set-off against profits of the preceding accounting period arising from non-trading loan relationships.

113.3 CT   Loan Relationships

(c) Where relief is not claimed as in (a) above or the deficit is not fully relieved, the company may make a claim for the whole or part of the remaining non-trading deficit to be carried forward for set-off against total profits of the subsequent accounting period. In relevant cases, the deficit may instead be surrendered as group relief for carried-forward losses. A claim cannot be made if either the company ceased to be a company with investment business in the period in which the deficit arose or (if it were such a company immediately before the deficit period) its investment business became small or negligible in the deficit period. In the latter case, the unrelieved deficit is automatically carried forward for relief against non-trading profits of the subsequent accounting period, subject to a claim for it to be not so carried forward, in which case it is carried forward for offset against non-trading profits of succeeding accounting periods. This treatment also applies where the company's investment business became small or negligible in an accounting period after the deficit period (but only in respect of that later period and subsequent accounting periods).

(d) The £1,200 deficit balance (which profits for the year ended 31 March 2021 are insufficient to relieve) can, on a claim, be carried forward for relief against total profits of the next accounting period subject to the provisions in (c) above.

(e) From 1 April 2017, the carry-forward of non-trading loan relationship deficits (whether arising pre- or post- April 2017) against total profits or non-trading profits is subject to restriction where the total set-off of carried-forward amounts exceeds £5,000,000. See **114.7** LOSSES.

114 Losses

114.1 CURRENT YEAR SET-OFF OF TRADING LOSSES

[*CTA 2010, s 37(3)(a)*]

A Ltd is a trading company with investment business (see **111.1** INVESTMENT COMPANIES AND INVESTMENT BUSINESS). Its results for the year ended 31 March 2021 show

	£
Trading loss	(100,000)
Property income	30,000
Income from non-trading loan relationships	40,000
Chargeable gains	72,000
Management expenses	(20,000)
Qualifying charitable donations	(10,000)

The loss may be relieved as follows

	£
Property income	30,000
Income from non-trading loan relationships	40,000
Chargeable gains	72,000
	142,000
Deduct Management expenses	(20,000)
	122,000
Deduct Trading loss	(100,000)
	22,000
Deduct Qualifying charitable donations	(10,000)
Taxable total profits	£12,000

Note

(a) Loss relief (other than group relief) against profits for the current year is given in priority to qualifying charitable donations. [*CTA 2010, s 189(1)(3)*]. See CTM09005 and *Simon's Taxes* D7.907, D7.822, D7.201.

114.2 CARRY-FORWARD OF TRADING LOSSES

[*CTA 2010, ss 45A–45E; F(No 2)A 2017, Sch 4 paras 10, 11, 190*]

(A)

Z Ltd has been trading for many years and draws up accounts to 31 March each year. For the year ended 31 March 2021 it has trading profits of £75,000 and property income of £130,000. It has trading losses brought forward as follows:

114.2 CT   Losses

	£
Pre-1 April 2017 losses	100,000
Post-1 April 2017 losses	100,000

The losses can be set off as follows

Y/e 31.3.21

	£	£
Trading income	75,000	
Deduct pre-1 April 2017 losses brought forward	(75,000)	—
Property income		130,000
		130,000
Deduct post-1 April 2017 losses brought forward		(100,000)
Carried forward trading losses		£30,000

Loss memorandum	
Pre-1 April 2007 loss brought forward	100,000
Relieved in y/e 31.3.21	(75,000)
Pre-1 April 2017 loss carried forward	£25,000

Notes

(a) Trading losses arising in accounting periods beginning on or after 1 April 2017 can be carried forward for set-off against total profits of the subsequent accounting period. In relevant cases, the loss may instead be surrendered as group relief for carried-forward losses. For this purpose, where an accounting period straddles that date it is treated as two separate accounting periods, the first ending on 31 March 2017 and the second beginning on 1 April 2017. Apportionments between the two accounting periods are made on a time basis unless that would produce an unjust or unreasonable result, in which case the apportionment must be made on a just and reasonable basis. A claim cannot be made if a claim for set-off against current year profits could not have been made in respect of the loss or if the trade became small or negligible in the loss-making period. In such cases, the loss is automatically carried forward for relief against trading profits of the subsequent accounting period, subject to a claim for it to be not so carried forward, in which case it is carried forward for offset against trading profits of succeeding accounting periods. This treatment also applies to pre-April 2017 losses carried forward to accounting periods beginning on or after 1 April 2017 and where the company's trade became small or negligible or the conditions for current-year set-off are not met in an accounting period after the loss-making period. (In the latter case, the restriction applies only in respect of that later period and subsequent accounting periods). [CTA 2010, ss 45A–45E and Part 5A; F(No 2)A 2017, Sch 4 paras 11, 190].

(b) The carry-forward of trading losses (whether pre- or post- April 2017) against total profits or trading profits is subject to restriction where the total set-off of carried-forward amounts exceeds £5,000,000. See **114.7** below.

(B)

B Ltd has carried on the same trade for many years. The results for the years ended 31 March 2017 to 31 March 2021, are shown below

	2017	2018	2019	2020	2021
	£	£	£	£	£
Trading profit/(loss)	(25,000)	10,000	5,000	(52,000)	45,000
Property income	3,000	1,000	2,000	—	—
Income from non-trading loan relationships	2,000	2,000	3,000	2,000	4,000
Chargeable gains	5,600	4,700	4,000	—	—

B Ltd may claim under *CTA 2010, s 37* to set off the trading losses for the years ended 31 March 2017 and 31 March 2020 against other profits of the same accounting period. Assuming the claims are made (and that no claims are made to carry back the balance of the losses), the losses will be set off as follows

Year ended 31 March 2017		Loss memorandum
	£	£
Trading loss		(25,000)
Property income	3,000	
Income from non-trading loan relationships	2,000	
Chargeable gains	5,600	
	10,600	
Deduct Trading loss	(10,600)	10,600
Taxable total profits	—	
		(14,400)
Year ended 31 March 2018		
Trading income	10,000	
Deduct Loss brought forward	(10,000)	10,000
	—	(4,400)
Property income	1,000	
Income from non-trading loan relationships	2,000	
Chargeable gains	4,700	
Taxable total profits	7,700	
Year ended 31 March 2019		
Trading income	5,000	
Deduct Loss brought forward	(4,400)	4,400
	600	
Property income	2,000	
Income from non-trading loan relationships	3,000	

114.2 CT Losses

Chargeable gains	4,000
Taxable total profits	9,600

Year ended 31 March 2020
Trading loss
Income from non-trading loan relationships
Loss carried forward

Year ended 31 March 2021
Trading income
Income from non-trading loan relationships

Deduct Loss brought forward
Loss carried forward

114.3 CARRY-BACK OF TRADING LOSSES

[*CTA 2010, ss 37–44, 45F–45G*]

(A) **Terminal losses**

X Ltd has the following results for the two years ending 31 December 2018 and 2019 and its final period to 30 September 2020 when it ceases trading.

	31.12.18	31.12.19	30.9.20
	£	£	£
Trading profit/(loss)	30,000	4,500	(30,000)
Property income	1,000	1,000	3,000
Income from non-trading loan relationships	500	500	4,000
Chargeable gains	—	1,500	2,250
Management expenses	—	(4,000)	(4,000)

	£	Loss memorandum £
The loss can be relieved as follows		
Period ended 30 September 2020		
Trading loss		(30,000)
Property income	3,000	
Income from non-trading loan relationships	4,000	
Chargeable gains	2,250	
	9,250	

Deduct Management expenses	(4,000)	
Trading loss (*CTA 2010, s 37(3)(a)*)	(5,250)	5,250
Taxable total profits	—	
		(24,750)

Year ended 31 December 2019

Trading income	4,500	
Property income	1,000	
Income from non-trading loan relationships	500	
Chargeable gains	1,500	
	7,500	
Deduct Management expenses	(4,000)	
	3,500	
Deduct Loss carried back	(3,500)	3,500
(*CTA 2010, ss 37(3)(b), 39*)		
Taxable total profits	—	
		£(21,250)

Year ended 31 December 2018

Trading income	30,000	
Property income	1,000	
Income from non-trading loan relationships	500	
	31,500	
Deduct Loss carried back	(21,250)	21,250
(*CTA 2010, ss 37(3)(b), 39*)		
Taxable total profits	£10,250	
Losses remaining (note (a))		—

Notes

(a) Where a loss is incurred in the accounting period in which the trade is discontinued, it may be carried back for three years prior to the period in which the loss occurred. In this example, the losses are fully utilised in the year ended 31 December 2018 but if this were not the case, they could have been carried back to the year ended 31 December 2017. Similar relief is available where the loss is incurred in an accounting period ending within the 12 months immediately before the cessation but in this case the three year carry-back is limited to an apportioned part of the loss for that penultimate period. This apportionment is on a time basis, by reference to the proportion of the accounting period falling within the final 12-month period. The balance attributable to the earlier part of the accounting period can be carried back one year in the normal way. [*CTA 2010, s 39*]. See CTM04510, CTM04520, CTM04530, CTM04570 and *Simon's Taxes* D1.1101, D1.1105, D6.710.

114.3 CT   Losses

(b) Losses must be set against current year profits before being carried back. If carried back, they must be carried back to the full extent possible, i.e. if losses are not fully relieved in the immediately preceding period, any balance must then be carried back to the period before that, and so on. [*CTA 2010, s 37(3)(4)*]. See CTM04510 and *Simon's Taxes* D1.1104.

(c) Where a loss is incurred on or after 1 April 2017, an additional form of terminal loss relief is available. New-style terminal loss relief includes trading losses brought forward to the period of cessation under *CTA 2010, ss 45, 45A–45B* which can then be carried back three years from the end of the 'terminal period' on an unrestricted basis. [*CTA 2010, s 45F; F(No 2)A 2017, Sch 4 paras 11, 190*]. See *Simon's Taxes* D1.1110. The effect of this might be to negate the original 50% restriction that applied to losses carried forward into one or more of those periods. Losses carried back under a terminal loss relief claim can only be set off against the 'relevant profits' (i.e. trading profits or total profits) that would have been allowable when those losses were carried forward. The carry back period cannot include any of the following:

- the period in which the loss originated;
- any period before the period in which the loss originated;
- any period before 1 April 2017.

[*CTA 2010, s 45F; F(No 2)A 2017, Sch 4 paras 11, 190*].

(B) **Accounting periods of different lengths**

Y Ltd, which previously made up accounts to 31 March, changed its accounting date to 31 December. Its results for the three accounting periods up to 31 December 2020 were as follows

	12 months 31.3.19 £	9 months 31.12.19 £	12 months 31.12.20 £
Trading profit/(loss)	5,500	9,000	(66,000)
Income from non-trading loan relationships	2,500	3,000	—
Chargeable gains	—	—	2,000

Y Ltd makes all available loss relief claims so as to obtain relief against the earliest possible profits. The computations are summarised as follows—

Losses CT 114.4

	12 months 31.3.19 £	9 months 31.12.19 £	12 months 31.12.20 £
Trading income	5,500	9,000	—
Income from non-trading loan relationships	2,500	3,000	—
Chargeable gains	—	—	2,000
	8,000	12,000	2,000
Loss relief			
CTA 2010, s 37(3)(a)			(2,000)
CTA 2010, s 37(3)(b)	(2,000)	(12,000)	
Taxable total profits	£6,000	—	—

Loss memoranda

	12 months 31.12.20 £
Trading loss	66,000
Relieved against current year profits	(2,000)
Relieved by carry-back:	
To p/e 31.12.19	(12,000)
To y/e 31.3.19	(2,000)
Carried forward under CTA 2010, s 45	£50,000

Note

(a) Relief under CTA 2010, s 37(3)(b) (carry-back of losses) is not restricted by reference to the length of the accounting period of loss. However, where a loss is carried back to an accounting period falling partly outside the carry-back period, relief is restricted to an appropriate proportion of profits. [CTA 2010, s 38]. In this example, the one-year period, as regards the loss for the year to 31 December 2020, begins on 1 January 2019 and, therefore, only three-twelfths of the profit for the year to 31 March 2019 can be relieved. See CTM04510 and *Simon's Taxes* D1.1105.

114.4 LOSSES ON UNLISTED SHARES

[*CTA 2010, ss 68–90; FA 2020, s 38*]

Z Ltd has been an investment company since its incorporation in 1973. It is not part of a trading group and has no associated companies. It makes up accounts to 31 December. On 6 February 2020, Z Ltd disposed of part of its holding of shares in T Ltd for full market value. Z Ltd makes no global re-basing election under *TCGA 1992, s 35(5)*.

114.4 CT Losses

Details of disposal
- Contract date — 6.2.20
- Shares sold — 2,000 Ord
- Proceeds (after expenses) — £4,500

Z acquired its shares in T Ltd as follows

				£
6.4.81 subscribed for	1,000 shares	cost (with expenses)		5,000
6.4.91 acquired	1,500 shares	cost (with expenses)		4,000
	2,500			£9,000

T Ltd shares were valued at £3 per share at 31 March 1982. T Ltd has been a UK resident trading company since 1980. Its shares are not quoted on a recognised stock exchange.

Z Ltd may claim that part of the loss incurred be set off against its income as follows

Identification on last in, first out basis

(i) Shares acquired 6.4.91 (not subscribed for)

	£
Proceeds of 1,500 shares $\dfrac{1,500}{2,000} \times £4,500$	3,375
Cost of 1,500 shares	(4,000)
Capital loss *not* available for set-off against income	£(625)

(ii) Shares acquired 6.4.81 (subscribed for)

	Cost basis £	31.3.82 value basis £
Proceeds of 500 shares $\dfrac{500}{2,000} \times £4,500$	1,125	1,125
Cost of 500 shares	(2,500)	
31.3.82 value		(1,500)
	£(1,375)	£(375)
Capital loss available for set-off against income		£(375)

316

Notes

(a) A claim under *CTA 2010, s 70* is restricted to the loss in respect of the shares *subscribed* for. See VCM77040 and *Simon's Taxes* D1.1120, D1.1445.

(b) The claim must be submitted within two years of the end of the accounting period in which the loss was incurred.

(c) The loss of £(375) is available primarily against income of the year ended 31 December 2020, with any balance being available against, broadly speaking, income of the 12 months ended 31 December 2019.

(d) See IT **14.5** losses and CGT **216.3** losses for further examples on this topic.

114.5 RESTRICTION OF TRADING LOSSES ON RECONSTRUCTION WITHOUT CHANGE OF OWNERSHIP

[*CTA 2010, ss 940A–953; F(No 2)A 2017, Sch 4 paras 62–68*]

(A) **Transfer of trade**

A Ltd and B Ltd are two wholly-owned subsidiaries of X Ltd. All are within the charge to corporation tax, although A Ltd has accumulated trading losses brought forward and unrelieved of £200,000 and has not paid tax for several years. As part of a group reorganisation, A Ltd's trade is transferred to B Ltd on 31 October 2020.

A Ltd's balance sheet immediately before the transfer is as follows

	£		£
Share capital	100,000	Property	90,000
Debenture secured		Plant	20,000
on property	50,000	Stock	130,000
Group loan	10,000	Trade debtors	120,000
Trade creditors	300,000		
Bank overdraft	60,000		
	520,000		
Deficit on			
reserves	(160,000)		
	£360,000		£360,000

Book values represent the approximate open market values of assets. B Ltd takes over the stock and plant to continue the trade, paying £150,000 to A Ltd and taking over £15,000 of trade creditors relating to stock. A Ltd is to collect outstanding debts and pay remaining creditors.

114.5 CT Losses

B Ltd becomes entitled to A Ltd's trading losses as follows.

	£
Amount 'A' (i.e. broadly A Ltd's assets not transferred to B Ltd plus any consideration given for the transfer (in this case nil))	
Freehold property (£90,000 − £50,000)	40,000
Trade debtors	120,000
Consideration from B Ltd	150,000
	£310,000

	£
Amount 'L' (i.e. A Ltd's liabilities not transferred to B Ltd)	
Bank overdraft	60,000
Group loan	10,000
Trade creditors (£300,000 − £15,000)	285,000
	£355,000

Trading losses transferable with trade

£200,000 − £(355,000 − 310,000) = £155,000

Notes

(a) Where amount L exceeds amount A the amount of relief given to the successor for losses of the predecessor carried forward is reduced by the excess of L over A. [*CTA 2010, ss 945–947*].

(b) Assets taken over by the successor to the trade are not included in amount A. Loan stock is not included in amount L, but where the loan is secured on an asset which is not transferred, the value of the asset is reduced by the amount secured.

(c) The assumption by B Ltd of liability for £15,000 of trade creditors does not constitute the giving of consideration and is not, therefore, included in amount A. Amount L is, however, reduced by the amount taken over.

(B) **Transfer of part of a trade**

D Ltd and E Ltd are wholly-owned subsidiaries of X Ltd. On 1 November 2020 D Ltd transfers the manufacturing part of what has been an integrated trade to E Ltd. D Ltd has accumulated trading losses brought forward and unrelieved of £150,000, of which £50,000 are attributable to the manufacturing operations.

Immediately before the transfer D Ltd's balance sheet is as follows

Losses CT 114.5

	£			£
Share capital	100,000	Property	— shops	110,000
Share premium	18,000		— factory	70,000
Loan stock	50,000		Plant	45,000
Trade creditors	290,000		Vehicles	20,000
Bank overdraft	42,000		Stock	30,000
			Trade debtors	65,000
	500,000			
Deficit on reserves	(160,000)			
	£340,000			£340,000

Book values represent the approximate open market value of assets. E Ltd takes over the manufacturing business together with the factory, plant and £18,000 of stock for a total consideration of £134,000.

Approximately 60% of D Ltd's turnover relates to manufacturing, and it is agreed that trade debtors and creditors are proportional to turnover.

Amount A (see A above) apportioned to the trade transferred is

	£
Trade debtors (60%)	39,000
Consideration received from E Ltd	134,000
	£173,000

Amount L apportioned to the trade is

	£
Trade creditors (60%)	174,000
Overdraft (33%) note (a)	14,000
	£188,000

Tax losses transferable are restricted to

£50,000 − £(188,000 − 173,000) = £35,000

Notes

(a) On the transfer of part of a trade, such apportionments of receipts, expenses, assets or liabilities are made as may be just and reasonable. [*CTA 2010, s 952(1)*]. It is assumed that it is reasonable to apportion trade debtors and creditors in proportion to turnover and the overdraft in proportion to losses. See CTM06130 and *Simon's Taxes* D6.317.

114.5 CT   Losses

(b) Loan stock, share premium and share capital are not relevant liabilities unless they have arisen in replacing relevant liabilities within the preceding year.

(c) If the trade were transferred as a whole for market value of the assets, no restriction would apply to the losses transferable.

114.6 PROPERTY BUSINESS LOSSES

[CTA 2010, ss 62–67; F(No 2)A 2017, Sch 4 paras 13, 14, 190]

JW Ltd, an investment company which is not a member of a group, has the following results for the three years ended 31 March 2020:

	y/e 31.3.18 £	y/e 31.3.19 £	y/e 31.3.20 £
Income from non-trading loan relationships	6,000	6,000	6,000
Property profit/(loss)	(7,500)	2,000	(8,500)
Management expenses	300	300	500

In view of the continuing losses, JW Ltd closes down its UK property business on 31 March 2020. It sells its properties in the year ended 31 March 2021, realising chargeable gains of £155,000. The company has income from non-trading loan relationships for that year of £6,000 and incurs management expenses of £3,600.

The company's profits chargeable to corporation tax for the four years are as follows.

	£	£
y/e 31.3.18		
Income from non-trading loan relationships		6,000
Deduct management expenses	300	
Property loss (restricted)	5,700	(6,000)
Taxable total profits		Nil
y/e 31.3.19		
Income from non-trading loan relationships		6,000
Property income		2,000
		8,000
Deduct management expenses	300	
Property loss (y/e 31.3.18)	1,800	(2,100)
Taxable total profits		£5,900

320

y/e 31.3.20

Income from non-trading loan relationships		6,000
Deduct management expenses	500	
Property loss (restricted)	5,500	(6,000)
Taxable total profits		Nil

y/e 31.3.21

Income from non-trading loan relationships	6,000
Chargeable gains	155,000
	161,000
Deduct management expenses	(3,600)
Taxable total profits	£157,400

Loss memorandum	£
Loss for y/e 31.3.18	7,500
Used y/e 31.3.18	(5,700)
Used y/e 31.3.19	(1,800)
	Nil

	£
Loss for y/e 31.3.20	8,500
Used y/e 31.3.20	(5,500)
Carried forward as management expenses (relieved y/e 31.3.21)	£3,000

Notes

(a) Relief for UK property business losses is only available where the UK property business is carried on as a commercial business or in the exercise of a statutory function.

(b) UK property business losses arising in accounting periods beginning on or after 1 April 2017 can be carried forward only on the making of a claim. The company can claim some or all of the amount available.

(c) As A Ltd is a company with investment business, on ceasing the UK property business, the unrelieved losses of £3,000 are treated as excess management expenses. [*CTA 2010, s 63*]. For losses arising in accounting periods beginning on or after 1 April 2017, a claim must be made for this treatment to apply. The company can claim some or all of the amount available. See PIM4230 and *Simon's Taxes* B6.203, D1.1109, D1.1114, D1.1116.

(d) The carry-forward of UK property business losses (whether pre- or post- April 2017) against total profits is subject to restriction where the total set-off of carried-forward amounts exceeds £5,000,000. See **114.7** below. See also **106.6** GROUP RELIEF for group relief for carried-forward losses

(e) For the purposes of the changes mentioned in notes (b) to (d) above, where an accounting period straddles 1 April 2017, it is treated as two separate accounting periods, the first ending on 31 March 2017 and the second beginning on 1 April 2017.

114.6 CT   Losses

Apportionments between the two accounting periods are made on a time basis unless that would produce an unjust or unreasonable result, in which case the apportionment must be made on a just and reasonable basis. [*F(No 2)A 2017, Sch 4, paras 190–192*].

[*F (No 2) A 2017, Sch 4*].

114.7 RESTRICTION ON DEDUCTIONS FOR CARRIED-FORWARD LOSSES

[*CTA 2010, ss 269ZA–269ZZB; F(No 2)A 2017, Sch 4 paras 16, 190; FA 2019, Sch 10 para 12; FA 2020, Sch 4*]

(A) Single company

Stephenson Ltd, which is not a member of a group, begins to trade on 1 April 2019. It has the following results for the two years ending 31 March 2020 and 2021.

	y/e 31.3.20 £	y/e 31.3.21 £
Trading profit/(loss)	(9,000,000)	8,000,000
Property income	—	2,000,000

Taxable profits for the two years are computed as follows

	y/e 31.3.20 £	y/e 31.3.21 £
Trading profit	—	8,000,000
Property income	—	2,000,000
	—	10,000,000
Less loss brought forward from y/e 31.3.20 (restricted)		(7,500,000)
Taxable profits	—	£2,500,000

The restriction on the set-off of the carried-forward loss against profits for the year ending 31 March 2021 is calculated as follows.

	£
Qualifying profits	10,000,000
Less deductions allowance	(5,000,000)
Relevant profits	5,000,000
Relevant profits × 50%	2,500,000
Add deductions allowance	5,000,000
Maximum set-off	£7,500,000

Loss memorandum

	£
Loss y/e 31.3.20	9,000,000
Less relieved y/e 31.3.21	(7,500,000)
Carried forward to y/e 31.3.22	£1,500,000

Notes

(a) For accounting periods beginning on or after 1 April 2017, the set-off of losses carried forward from previous accounting periods is restricted for companies with profits in excess of the 'deductions allowance'. Broadly, a company's profits after deduction of any current year reliefs and the deductions allowance can only be reduced by up to 50% by carried-forward losses. For this purpose, where an accounting period straddles 1 April 2017, it is treated as two separate accounting periods, the first ending on 31 March 2017 and the second beginning on 1 April 2017. Apportionments between the two accounting periods are made on a time basis unless that would produce an unjust or unreasonable result, in which case the apportionment must be made on a just and reasonable basis. [*CTA 2010, ss 269ZA–269ZZB; F(No 2)A 2017, Sch 4 paras 16, 190*].

(b) The restriction applies to the following carried-forward amounts: trade losses, losses of a UK property business, non-trading deficits from loan relationships, non-trading losses on intangible fixed assets and expenses of management of investment business. For accounting periods beginning on or after 1 April 2020, the provisions extend to carried-forward capital losses (see CGT **207.3** COMPANIES). For this purpose, an accounting period which straddles 1 April 2020 is treated as if it were two separate accounting periods, the first ending on 31 March 2020 and the second beginning on 1 April 2020. Special rules apply to the calculation of the restriction for such straddling periods.

The restriction applies to both pre-April 2017 and post-April 2017 amounts and to amounts which can be set off against total profits or only against a profits of a particular type. Where the carried-forward amounts include losses which can only be set against particular types of profits, the maximum set-off must be computed separately for trading profits and non-trading profits. The company may decide how its deductions allowance should be allocated between trading and non-trading profits.

(c) If a company is not a member of a group, the deductions allowance is £5 million. If the accounting period is less than twelve months, the amount is reduced proportionally. If a company has profits for an accounting period that do not exceed the amount of the deductions allowance, carried-forward losses may be set against those profits without restriction.

(d) See also **106.6** GROUP RELIEF for group relief for carried-forward losses.

(B) **Groups of companies**

A Ltd is the ultimate parent company of B Ltd and C Ltd. All companies make up accounts to 31 March each year. The companies' results for the year ended 31 March 2021 are as follows.

114.7 CT   Losses

		£
A Ltd	Trading profit	800,000
	Property income	185,000
	Chargeable gain	15,000
B Ltd	Trading profit	5,000,000
C Ltd	Trading profit	400,000
	Non-trading loan relationships	100,000

In addition, each company has the following trading losses brought forward from the year ended 31 March 2020: A Ltd £1,000,000, B Ltd £5,000,000 and C Ltd £500,000. All of the carried-forward losses arose in the year ended 31 March 2020. A Ltd is the group's nominated company for the purpose of allocating the group deductions allowance.

If A Ltd allocates £1,000,000 of the group deductions allowance to itself and the remainder to B Ltd, the companies' taxable profits for the year ended 31 March 2021 are as follows.

	£
A Ltd	
Trading profit	800,000
Property income	185,000
Chargeable gain	15,000
	1,000,000
Deduct Loss brought forward from y/e 31.3.20	(1,000,000)
Chargeable profits	£Nil
B Ltd	
Trading profit	5,000,000
Deduct Loss brought forward from y/e 31.3.20	(4,500,000)
Chargeable profits	£500,000
C Ltd	
Trading profit	400,000
Non-trading loan relationships	100,000
	500,000
Deduct Loss brought forward from y/e 31.3.20	(250,000)
Chargeable profits	£250,000

The restriction on the set-off of the carried-forward losses against profits for the year ending 31 March 2021 is calculated as follows.

	£
A Ltd	
Qualifying profits	1,000,000

Less allocated group deductions allowance	(1,000,000)
Relevant profits	—
Relevant profits × 50%	—
Add allocated group deductions allowance	1,000,000
Maximum set-off	£1,000,000

B Ltd

Qualifying profits	5,000,000
Less allocated group deductions allowance	(4,000,000)
Relevant profits	1,000,000
Relevant profits × 50%	500,000
Add allocated group deductions allowance	4,000,000
Maximum set-off	£4,500,000

C Ltd

Qualifying profits	500,000
Less allocated group deductions allowance	—
Relevant profits	500,000
Relevant profits × 50%	250,000
Add allocated group deductions allowance	—
Maximum set-off	£250,000

Loss memoranda

£

A Ltd

Loss brought forward from y/e 31.3.20	1,000,000
Less relieved y/e 31.3.21	(1,000,000)
	—

B Ltd

Loss brought forward from y/e 31.3.20	5,000,000
Less relieved y/e 31.3.21	(4,500,000)
Carried forward to y/e 31.3.22	£500,000

C Ltd

Loss brought forward from y/e 31.3.20	500,000
Less relieved y/e 31.3.21	(250,000)
Carried forward to y/e 31.3.22	£250,000

114.7 CT Losses

Notes

(a) A group of companies has a single deductions allowance known as the group deductions allowance and can allocate this to any company or companies in the group as it chooses. This is done through a nominated company. The maximum amount of the allowance that is available to be shared amongst all group companies is £5 million (reduced proportionately for accounting periods of less than twelve months). The nomination must be made by all the companies in the group that are within the charge to corporation tax and must state the date the nomination takes effect, which may be before the date the nomination is made. [*CTA 2010, s 269ZR; F(No 2)A 2017, Sch 4 para 16*].

(b) A group for this purpose is two or more companies where one company is the ultimate parent of each of the other companies and is not the ultimate parent of any other company. A company (A) is the ultimate parent of another company (B) if A is the parent of B and no company is the parent of both A and B. A is the parent of B if B is a 75% subsidiary of A, A is beneficially entitled to at least 75% of any profits available for distribution to equity holders of B or A would be beneficially entitled to at least 75% of the assets of B distributed to equity holders on a winding-up. [*CTA 2010, s 269ZZB; F(No 2)A 2017, Sch 4 para 16*].

(c) See also **106.6 GROUP RELIEF** for group relief for carried-forward losses.

115 Payment of Tax

Cross-reference. See **109.1** and **110.1** for interest on overpaid and unpaid tax, and **118.1** and **118.2** for returns and filing dates.

115.1 PAYMENTS BY LARGE COMPANIES

[*TMA 1970, ss 59D, 59E; SI 1998 No 3175; SI 2014 No 2409; SI 2017 No 1072*]

(A) Large companies

BG Ltd, which has five related 51% group companies, draws up accounts to 31 December each year. Its taxable profits and tax liabilities are as follows. Note that the tax liabilities are assumed for the purposes of the example only.

Accounting period ended	Profits	Tax
	£	£
31.12.14	240,000	22,500
31.12.15	260,000	20,000
31.12.16	275,000	25,000
31.12.17	255,000	9,500
31.12.18	270,000	68,000
31.12.19	260,000	60,000
31.12.20	200,000	40,000

The upper limit is as follows

£1,500,000 ÷ 6 = £250,000

Year ended 31.12.14

The company is not large as its profits do not exceed the upper limit.

Year ended 31.12.15

Although the company's profits exceed the upper limit, it will not have to make quarterly instalments payments because it was not large during the previous twelve months.

Year ended 31.12.16

The company is a large company in this period as it would have been a large company in the previous year but for the exclusion in *SI 1998 No 3175, reg 3*.

Year ended 31.12.17

Although the company's profits exceed the upper limit, its tax liability does not exceed £10,000 so it is not a large company.

Year ended 31.12.18

Although the company's profits exceed the upper limit, it will not have to make quarterly instalment payments because it was not large during the previous twelve months.

115.1 CT   Payment of Tax

Year ended 31.12.19

The company is a large company in this period as it would have been a large company in the previous year but for the exclusion in *SI 1998 No 3175, reg 3*.

Year ended 31.12.20

The company is not large as its profits do not exceed the upper limit.

Notes

(a) A company is 'large' for the purpose of quarterly instalment payments (see B below) if its augmented profits for an accounting period exceed the *CTA 2010, s 24* 'upper limit' which is in force at the end of that period. This is £1,500,000 divided by one plus the number of 'related 51% group companies' (as defined at *CTA 2010, s 279F*). 'Augmented profits' mean total profits chargeable to corporation tax plus 'exempt ABGH distributions' (as defined) of the period other than any such distributions or FII received from fellow group members. See *Simon's Taxes* D1.1202, D1.1204, D1.1204A.

(b) A company is not large in an accounting period for which its total corporation tax liability (reduced by any deductions from payments in the period under the construction industry tax scheme) does not exceed £10,000, proportionately reduced if the accounting period is less than twelve months, or if its profits do not exceed £10,000,000 provided it was not a large company (disregarding this exclusion) in the previous 12-month period. The £10,000,000 threshold is reduced by dividing it by one plus the number of related 51% group companies and is reduced proportionately where the accounting period is less than 12 months.

(B) **Instalment payments**

HP Ltd, a large company, draws up accounts to 30 September each year. The company's return for the year ended 30 September 2020 shows total taxable profits of £4,000,000 and corporation tax payable £760,000.

Tax is due and payable by the company for the year ended 30 September 2020 as follows.

Instalments due:	£
14.4.20	190,000
14.7.20	190,000
14.10.20	190,000
14.1.21	190,000
	£760,000

Payment of Tax   CT 115.1

Notes

(a) Large companies (see (A) above) are required to pay corporation tax by instalments. Instalments are due at intervals of three months commencing six months and thirteen days from the start of the accounting period and culminating three months and fourteen days from its end. Therefore, for a twelve-month accounting period there will be four instalments.

(b) Instalment payments are calculated by reference to the total liability of the accounting period to which they relate. Where four instalments are due, each will be one quarter of the liability. Each instalment is calculated by reference to the formula $3 \times CTI/n$ where CTI is the total liability and n is the number of whole months in the accounting period plus the 'relevant decimal' (which adjusts for any odd days in the period). Clearly, an estimate of the liability will be required for making instalments before the final liability is known. Where those estimates turn out to be incorrect, interest will be charged to the extent that the instalment payments were insufficient (and interest will be paid on overpayments). Top-up payments may be made at any time. Where the company has grounds for believing that its instalment payments were excessive it may claim a repayment. For interest on instalment payments see **109.1(B)** INTEREST ON OVERPAID TAX and **110.1(C)** INTEREST ON UNPAID TAX.

(c) For accounting periods beginning on or after 1 April 2019, companies with profits exceeding £20 million have to pay instalments in the third, sixth, ninth and twelfth months of the accounting period. The £20 million threshold is divided between members of a group. See (C) below.

(d) If a company is chargeable to corporation tax for an accounting period beginning on or after 11 March 2020 only because of a chargeable gain and would otherwise be very large for that period it is instead treated as only large. [*SI 1998 No 3175, Reg 3(11); FA 2020, s 26*].

Such companies are likely to have short accounting periods, in some cases of only one day. For a one day accounting period this rule may apply to relatively small gains, owing to the requirement to reduce the relevant thresholds on a time basis. The effect for such a period is that the tax is due three months and 14 days after the one day accounting period instead of on the day itself. This rule affects, in particular, non-resident companies which dispose of direct or indirect interests in UK land. It replaces a previous HMRC concessionary treatment for one day accounting periods with the same effect which has applied since April 2019.

(C) **Instalment payments by very large companies**

KW plc, a very large company, draws up accounts to 31 March each year. The company's return for the year ended 31 March 2021 shows total taxable profits of £24,000,000 and corporation tax payable £4,560,000.

Tax is due and payable by the company for the year ended 31 March 2021 as follows.

115.1 CT   Payment of Tax

Instalments due:	£
14.6.20	1,140,000
14.9.20	1,140,000
14.12.20	1,140,000
14.3.21	1,140,000
	£4,560,000

Notes

(a) For accounting periods beginning on or after 1 April 2019, the timing of instalment payments by a company depends on whether or not it is a 'very large' company. Where the company is very large, the first instalment is due two months and 13 days after the first day of the accounting period. The second, third and final instalments are then due at three-monthly intervals. If the accounting period is less than 12 months, the final instalment is generally due 14 days after the date falling one month before the end of the period. Earlier instalments are required only if they fall due before the final instalment date. If the accounting period does not end on the last day of the month and there is no day in the previous month with the same date, the final instalment is due 14 days after the last day of the previous month. Therefore, for a twelve-month accounting period there will be four instalments.

(b) Instalment payments are calculated by reference to the total liability of the accounting period to which they relate. Where four instalments are due, each will be one quarter of the liability. Each instalment is calculated by reference to the formula $3 \times CTI/(wm + wmd)$ where CTI is the total liability and wm is the number of whole months in the accounting period and wmd is a decimal which adjusts for any odd days in the period. Clearly, an estimate of the liability will be required for making instalments before the final liability is known. Where those estimates turn out to be incorrect, interest will be charged to the extent that the instalment payments were insufficient (and interest will be paid on overpayments). Top-up payments may be made at any time. Where the company has grounds for believing that its instalment payments were excessive it may claim a repayment. For interest on instalment payments see **109.1(B)** INTEREST ON OVERPAID TAX and **110.1(C)** INTEREST ON UNPAID TAX.

(c) A '*very large*' company is one whose profits (including UK dividend income, other than intra-group dividends) exceed £20,000,000 in an accounting period, divided by one plus the number of related 51% group companies (as defined at *CTA 2010, s 279F*). The threshold is proportionately reduced where the accounting period is less than 12 months. If a company is not a large company for an accounting period as a result of the rules described in note (b) to (A) above, it is not a very large company for that period. See also note (d) to (B) above.

116 Profit Computations

116.1 COMPUTATIONS

Y Ltd's accounts for the 12 months to 31 December 2020 show the following.

	£		£
Wages and salaries	77,500	Gross trading profit	209,160
Rent, rates and insurance	5,000	Net rents	1,510
Motor expenses	8,000	Government securities	340
Car hire	6,000	Dividend from UK company (received 30.9.20)	4,500
Legal expenses	2,000		
Directors' remuneration	22,875	Profit on sale of investment	5,500
Audit and accountancy	2,500		
Miscellaneous expenses	2,600		
Debenture finance charges	2,450		
Ordinary dividend paid	15,000		
Depreciation	6,125		
Premium on lease written off	14,000		
Net profit	56,960		
	£221,010		£221,010

Analysis of various items gave the following additional information

(i) Legal expenses:

	£
Re staff service agreements	250
Re debt collecting	600
Re new issue of debentures (see (vii) below)	1,150
	£2,000
Miscellaneous expenses:	
Staff outing	400
Subscriptions: Chamber of Commerce	250
Political party	100
Interest on overdue tax	250
Contribution to training and enterprise council	350
Charitable donation to trade benevolent fund	150
Qualifying charitable donations	1,100
	£2,600

116.1 CT   Profit Computations

(ii) On 1 July 2020, Y Ltd was granted a lease on office accommodation for a period of seven years from that date for which it paid a premium of £14,000.

(iii) Car hire of £6,000 represents the hire, under a contract dated 1 July 2020, of a car with emissions 180g/km.

(iv) All wages and salaries were paid during the period of account apart from directors' bonuses of £20,000, accrued in the accounts, voted at the AGM on 1 November 2021 and not previously paid or credited to directors' accounts with the company.

(v) Profit on sale of investment is the unindexed gain arising from the sale of quoted securities on 28 February 2020. The chargeable gain after indexation is £2,070.

(vi) Capital allowances for the year to 31 December 2020 are £10,000.

(vii) Debenture finance charges relate to £50,000 nominal stock issued on 1 January 2020 for trade finance at £96 per £100, carrying interest at 4.5% payable annually in arrears, for redemption 31 December 2027. The charge to profit and loss comprises interest of £2,250 and redemption reserve costs of £200 on a straight line basis. As these are arrived at under an amortised cost basis, the charges are allowable for tax purposes. The issue costs included in legal expenses (see (i) above) are also allowable.

(viii) The £340 Government securities credit relates to £4,000 nominal stock acquired in May 2019 at £4,040 with two years to redemption. It represents gross interest £360 less £20 premium amortisation charge on a straight line basis. It is thus properly chargeable as income from a non-trading loan relationship. The interest was received gross on 31 March and 30 September.

The corporation tax computation is as follows

		£	£
Net profit			56,960
Add			
Depreciation		6,125	
Directors' remuneration	(note (a))	20,000	
Subscription to political party		100	
Charitable donations	(notes (c) and (d))	1,100	
Car hire	(note (e))	900	
Dividend paid		15,000	
Premium on lease written off	(note (f))	14,000	
Interest on overdue tax (note (g))		250	57,475
			114,435
Deduct			
Net rents		1,510	
Government securities		340	
Dividend received		4,500	
Profit on sale of investment		5,500	(11,850)
			102,585

Deduct
Capital allowances   10,000
Allowance for lease premium (note (f))

$$\frac{1}{7} \times \left(\frac{£14{,}000}{50} \times (50 - (7-1)) \right) \times \frac{6}{12} \qquad \underline{880}$$

	(10,880)
CT trading profit	91,705
Income from non-trading loan relationships (note (g))	90
Property Income	1,510
Chargeable gains	2,070
	95,375
Deduct Qualifying charitable donations	(1,100)
(note (d))	
Profits chargeable to corporation tax	£94,275

Notes

(a) Director's remuneration of £20,000 is disallowed as it remained unpaid nine months after the end of the period of account. It will, however, be allowable in the tax computation for the year to 31 December 2021, i.e. the period of account in which it is paid. See also *CTA 2009, s 1289; ITEPA 2003, s 18*. See BIM47140, BIM47135, BIM47140, CIRD12650, EIM42260 and *Simon's Taxes* B2.422, E4.736A, E4.1180.

(b) The contribution to a training and enterprise council is allowable under *CTA 2009, ss 82–86*.

(c) The charitable donation to trade benevolent fund is allowable under *CTA 2009, s 1300*. See BIM45070, BIM45072 and *Simon's Taxes* B2.441, B2.432.

(d) The qualifying charitable donations are deducted from the company's total profits under the Gift Aid provisions. [*CTA 2010, ss 189, 190*]. See CTM09005, CTM0901 and *Simon's Taxes* D7.907, D7.201, D1.315.

(e) The allowable proportion of the car hire expenditure is £6,000@85%

[*CTA 2009, s 56*]. See BIM47725, BIM47740, BIM47730, BIM47745 and *Simon's Taxes* B2.413.

(f) The proportion of the lease premium allowable is calculated under *CTA 2009 ss 217–220*.

(g) Interest on the overdue tax is treated as a non-trading loan relationship debit. The income from non-trading loan relationships for the year ended 31 December 2020 is therefore (£340 − £250 =) £90.

117 Research and Development

117.1 SMALL OR MEDIUM-SIZED ENTERPRISE

[*CTA 2009, ss 104B, 1044–1062*]

D Ltd is a small or medium-sized enterprise established on 1 January 2019. The company incurs qualifying research and development expenditure of £80,000 in the year ended 31 December 2019, in addition to other revenue expenditure of £50,000 (all of which would have been allowable expenditure had the company been trading). On 1 January 2020 D Ltd commences a trade derived from the research and development expenditure, making a taxable profit (before adjustment for research and development relief or pre-trading expenditure) of £160,000 for the year ended 31 December 2020. Further qualifying research and development expenditure is incurred in that year of £41,000. If the company does not make a claim under *CTA 2009, s 104A* (see **117.2** below) the corporation tax position is as follows.

Y/e 31.12.19

D Ltd may elect, under *CTA 2009, s 1045*, by 31 December 2021, to be treated as having incurred a trading loss in the period of an amount equal to 230% of the qualifying research and development expenditure, i.e. £184,000 (£80,000 × 230%). There are then a number of possible alternatives open to D Ltd to make use of the loss. It may:

(1) set the loss against other profits for the accounting period under *CTA 2010, s 37(3)(a)*;

(2) surrender the loss as group relief under *CTA 2010, s 99*;

(3) claim a research and development tax credit equal to 14.5% of the loss (as reduced by any part of it relieved under (1) or (2)) under *CTA 2010, s 1060*; or

(4) carry the losses forward for set-off against future total profits or surrender as group relief under *CTA 2010, s 45B*.

D Ltd claims a tax credit as in (3) above in respect of the deemed loss for the year ended 31 December 2019. Assuming that all of the loss qualifies for the 14.5% tax credit rate, the credit is £184,000 × 14.5% = £26,680.

Y/e 31.12.20

D Ltd claims for the qualifying research and development expenditure to be treated as if it were 230% of the actual amount, i.e. £94,300 (£41,000 × 230%). The company's taxable trading profits for the year are therefore as follows.

117.1 CT Research and Development

	£
Adjusted profit as above	160,000
Less Research and development relief	(94,300)
Other pre-trading expenditure	(50,000)
Trading profits chargeable to CT	£15,700

Notes

(a) Relief for expenditure on research and development is available for expenditure of a revenue nature incurred by a 'small or medium-sized' company on qualifying 'research and development'. A 'small or medium-sized' enterprise is one that has less than 500 employees and either or both annual turnover not exceeding 100 million euros and annual balance sheet total not exceeding 86 million euros. A company is generally excluded if any company in which it holds, or which holds in it, more than 25% of the capital or voting rights, is not a small or medium-sized enterprise.

Where a claim is made, qualifying research and development expenditure is to be treated as if it were 230% of the actual amount. [*CTA 2009, s 1044*]. See CIRD81450, CIRD81700, CIRD81800 and *Simon's Taxes* D1.420, B3.708, D1.401.

(b) The Government has announced that, with effect from April 2021, the amount of payable R&D tax credit (see (3) above) which an SME can receive in any one year will be capped at three times the company's total PAYE and NICs liability for the year.

117.2 ABOVE THE LINE R&D EXPENDITURE CREDITS ('RDEC')

[*CTA 2009, ss 104A–104Y; FA 2020, s 28*].

R Ltd, a large company has trade profits of £6,000,000 before deducting research and development expenditure of £2,000,000 for the year ended 31 March 2021. The research and development expenditure is qualifying expenditure for the purposes of the RDEC. If R Ltd's claims relief, its corporation tax liability will be as follows.

	£'000
Trade profits before R&D expenditure	6,000
Qualifying R&D expenditure	(2,000)
	4,000
R&D expenditure credit	260
Trade profits	4,260

	£
Corporation tax at 19%	809,400
Deduct R&D expenditure credit	(260,000)
Corporation tax payable	549,400

Note

(a) Where a company claims RDEC, the amount of the credit is included as a receipt in the company's tax computation. The amount of the credit is 13% of the qualifying expenditure (12% for expenditure incurred before 1 April 2020, 11% for expenditure incurred before 1 January 2018; 49% in the case of a ring fence trade). [*CTA 2009, ss 104A, 104M; FA 2020, s 28*]. The tax credit is set off against the company's corporation tax liability for the period. If the credit exceeds the corporation tax liability then a specified order of set off applies, which allows for it to be surrendered as group relief, as well as carried forward, or back, against the company's tax liability for other accounting periods. See *CTA 2009, s 104N*. See CIRD89705, CIRD89710, CIRD89780 and *Simon's Taxes* D1.414, D1.420, D1.401, D1.409, D1.436.

118 Returns

118.1 RETURN PERIODS

[*FA 1998, Sch 18 paras 3–7*]

(A)

Aquarius Ltd has always prepared its accounts to 31 October. In 2020, it changes its accounting date, preparing accounts for the nine months to 31 July 2020. On 31 January 2020, HMRC issues a notice specifying a return period of 1 November 2018 to 31 October 2019. On 31 January 2021, they issue a notice specifying a return period of 1 November 2019 to 31 October 2020.

In respect of the first-mentioned notice, Aquarius Ltd is required to make a return for the period 1.11.18 to 31.10.19 accompanied by accounts and tax computations for that period.

In respect of the second of the above-mentioned notices, the company is required to make a return for the period 1.11.19 to 31.7.20 accompanied by accounts and tax computations for that period. [*FA 1998, Sch 18 para 5(1)(2)*].

(B)

Pisces Ltd has always prepared its accounts to 31 December. In 2020, it changes its accounting date, preparing accounts for the nine months to 30 September 2020. On 15 December 2020, HMRC issue a notice specifying a return period of 1 October 2019 to 30 September 2020.

Pisces Ltd is required to make returns both for the period 1.1.19 to 31.12.19 and for the period 1.1.20 to 30.9.20, each return being accompanied by accounts and tax computations for the period covered by it. [*FA 1998, Sch 18 para 5(1)(2)*].

(C)

Aries Ltd has always prepared accounts to 31 October. After 2019, it changes its accounting date, preparing accounts for the fifteen months to 31 January 2021. On 21 August 2020, HMRC issue a notice specifying a return period of 1 November 2018 to 31 October 2019. On 31 January 2020, they issue a notice specifying a return period of 1 November 2019 to 31 October 2020.

In respect of the first-mentioned notice, Aries Ltd is required to make a return for the period 1.11.18 to 31.10.19 accompanied by accounts and tax computations for that period.

In respect of the second of the above-mentioned notices, the company is required to make a return for the accounting period 1.11.19 to 31.10.20, accompanied by accounts and tax computations for the period of account 1.11.19 to 31.1.21. [*FA 1998, Sch 18 para 5(1)(3)*].

(D)

Taurus Ltd has always prepared accounts to 31 October. After 2019, it changes its accounting date, preparing accounts for the fifteen months to 31 January 2021. On 31 January 2020, HMRC issue a notice specifying a return period of 1 November 2018 to 31 October 2019. On 1 April 2020, HMRC issue a notice specifying a return period of 1 November 2019 to 31 January 2020.

118.1 CT Returns

In respect of the first-mentioned notice, the position is as in (C) above.

In respect of the second of the above-mentioned notices, Taurus Ltd is not required to make a return, but should notify HMRC of the correct accounting dates and periods. [*FA 1998, Sch 18 para 5(3)(5)*].

(E)

Gemini Ltd was incorporated on 1 July 2017 but remains dormant until 1 April 2019 when it begins to trade. The first trading accounts are prepared for the year to 31 March 2020 and the company retains that accounting date. On 1 May 2021, HMRC issue notices specifying return periods of 1 July 2017 to 30 June 2018, 1 July 2018 to 30 June 2019, 1 July 2019 to 30 June 2020 and 1 July 2020 to 31 March 2021.

In respect of the notice for the period 1.7.17 to 30.6.18, Gemini Ltd is required to make a return for that period.

In respect of the notice for the period 1.7.18 to 30.6.19, the company is required to make a return for the period 1.7.18 to 31.3.19.

In respect of the notice for the period 1.7.19 to 30.6.20, the company is required to make a return for the period 1.4.19 to 31.3.20 accompanied by accounts and tax computations for that period.

In respect of the notice for the period 1.7.20 to 31.3.21, the company is required to make a return for the period 1.4.20 to 31.3.21 accompanied by accounts and tax computations for that period. [*FA 1998, Sch 18 para 5(1)(2)*].

118.2 FILING DATES

[*FA 1998, Sch 18 para 14*]

The final dates for the filing with HMRC of the returns in **118.1** above, and for the payment of corporation tax (assuming none of the companies concerned falls within the definition of a 'large company' or a 'very large company' to which the instalment payment provisions apply—see **115.1** PAYMENT OF TAX), are as follows

Return period	Filing date		Payment date (note (f))
118.1(A) above			
1.11.18 – 31.10.19	31.10.20	(note (a))	1.8.20
1.11.19 – 31.7.20	31.7.21		1.5.21
118.1(B) above			
1.1.19 – 31.12.19	15.3.21	(note (b))	1.10.20
1.1.20 – 30.9.20	30.9.21		1.7.21
118.1(C) above			
1.11.18 – 31.10.19	21.11.20	(note (b))	1.8.20
1.11.19 – 31.10.20	31.1.22	(note (c))	1.8.21

Returns   CT 118.2

Return period	Filing date	Payment date
118.1(D) above		
1.11.18 – 31.10.19	31.10.20	1.8.20
118.1(E) above		
1.7.17 – 30.6.18	1.8.21	—
1.7.18 – 31.3.19	1.8.21	—
1.4.19 – 31.3.20	1.8.21	1.1.21
1.4.20 – 31.3.21	31.3.22	1.1.22

Notes

(a) The normal filing date is the first anniversary of the last day of the return period.

(b) If later than the date in (a) above (or, where relevant, (c) below), the filing date is three months after the date on which the notice is issued by the Inspector.

(c) Where a company's period of account extends beyond the end of the return period, the filing date is extended to the first anniversary of the last day of that period of account. This is subject to a limit of 30 months from the beginning of the period of account, although this would come into play only in the exceptional case where accounts are prepared for a period exceeding 18 months.

(d) The time allowed for filing returns is effectively extended to the time allowed under the *Companies Act 2006* if this would give a later filing date than under (a)–(c) above. [*FA 1998, Sch 18 para 19*]. This will not be so in the majority of cases.

(e) HMRC may grant an extension, on an application by the company, if they are satisfied that the company has a 'reasonable excuse' for not being able to meet the filing date under (a)–(c) above. [*TMA 1970, s 118(2)*].

(f) Nothing in (a)–(e) above affects a company's liability to pay corporation tax within nine months and one day following the end of an accounting period. [*TMA 1970, s 59D(1)*]. See **115** PAYMENT OF TAX for the instalment payment provisions applicable to large companies. See CTM95010 and *Simon's Taxes* D1.1320, C1.108, D1.115.

119 Transfer Pricing

119.1 ADJUSTMENTS FOR TRANSFER PRICING

[*TIOPA 2010, ss 146–230*]

(A) **Transfer pricing adjustment**

A Ltd provides management and administrative services to a number of its wholly-owned subsidiaries. All companies in the group have accounting periods ending on 31 March and do not qualify as small or medium-sized enterprises for transfer pricing purposes. For the accounting period ending 31 March 2021, A Ltd makes a charge for its management and administrative services to B Ltd of £450,000. Following an enquiry into A Ltd's return for that period, it is agreed that the arm's length value of the services to A Ltd was £600,000. An adjustment is accordingly made of £150,000 to increase A Ltd's taxable profits by that amount.

B Ltd can claim to apply a corresponding adjustment (see note (c) below) to reduce its taxable profits for the same period by £150,000 (increasing its deductible expenses to £600,000). B Ltd may also make a balancing payment to A Ltd of up to £150,000 without it being treated as a distribution or otherwise taken into account for tax purposes.

Notes

(a) The transfer pricing rules apply broadly where transactions between connected parties take place at other than arm's length prices conferring an advantage to the parties in terms of a reduction in the liability to UK tax. A transfer pricing adjustment may then be made to restore the tax position to what it would have been had the transaction been at arm's length. The regime applies to both UK and cross-border transactions. Dormant companies and small and medium-sized enterprises will, in most circumstances, be exempt from applying the transfer pricing and thin capitalisation rules. Where an adjustment is required by the provisions to increase the profits of one party, the corresponding adjustment provisions apply so that the connected UK party can make a compensating reduction in their taxable profits.

(b) A 'dormant' company is one which is dormant (under the *Companies Act 2006, s 1169*) throughout the accounting period ending on 31 March 2004 (or if there is no such accounting period, the three-month period ending on that date); and has continued to be dormant at all times since the end of that period apart from any transfer pricing adjustments. Very broadly, a small enterprise is defined as a business with less than 50 employees and either turnover or assets of less than €10 million and a small or medium-sized enterprise as a business with less than 250 employees and either turnover of less than €50 million or assets of less than €43 million. A medium-sized enterprise can still be subject to a transfer pricing notice.

(c) Where a transfer pricing adjustment has been made by the advantaged party (either in the return or following a determination) the disadvantaged party may claim a corresponding adjustment in applying the arm's length rule rather than the actual provision. Claims must be made within two years of the making of the return or the giving of the notice taking account of the determination, and a claim based on a return which is subsequently the subject of such a notice may be amended within

119.1 CT   Transfer Pricing

two years of the giving of the notice. (These time limits may be extended in certain cases where HMRC fails to give proper notice to disadvantaged persons under *TIOPA 2010, s 185*.) A corresponding adjustment may not be claimed by a disadvantaged person which is not a company and which is within the charge to income tax if the advantaged person is a company. See *Simon's Taxes* D2.619.

(d) Where a transfer pricing adjustment is made, the disadvantaged company may make a corresponding balancing payment to the advantaged company. Provided the balancing payment does not exceed the amount of the 'available compensating adjustment', it is not taken into account when computing profits or losses for tax purposes or regarded as a distribution or charge on income. The *'available compensating adjustment'* is the difference between the profits and losses of the disadvantaged company computed on the basis of the actual provision and computed for the purposes of making a compensating adjustment (see note (c) above).

(B) **Transfer pricing and thin capitalisation**

On 1 July 2019, B Ltd is granted a loan of £5,000,000 at 6% interest p.a. from an unassociated bank. The loan is guaranteed by B Ltd's parent company, G plc. Both companies draw up accounts for the year ended 30 June and neither company qualifies as a small or medium-sized enterprise for transfer pricing purposes. Following an enquiry into B Ltd's return for the accounting period ending 30 June 2020, HMRC successfully maintain that, in the absence of the guarantee from G plc, the bank would not have advanced more than £1,000,000 to B Ltd. Accordingly, an adjustment is made to increase B Ltd's profits for the period by £240,000 in disallowing the interest on £4,000,000 of the loan.

G plc could make a claim (or B Ltd could claim on its behalf) for a corresponding adjustment before or after the transfer pricing adjustment is made in B Ltd's return, or following the determination so that it is treated as having paid the interest subject to the disallowance. Accordingly, provided the interest in G plc's case would not be subject to a transfer pricing adjustment, G plc could claim a deduction for £240,000 in respect of the interest paid by B Ltd. G plc can make a balancing payment of up to £240,000 to B Ltd without it being treated as a distribution or charge on income or otherwise taken into account for tax purposes.

Notes

(a) A compensating adjustment may be claimed by the disadvantaged party or by the advantaged person on his behalf before or after the arm's length provision has been applied in the case of the advantaged party (in his return or following a determination). Where a transfer pricing adjustment to disallow interest follows from the provision of a guarantee, the guarantor can claim a compensating adjustment as if it was the borrower and had paid the interest subject to the disallowance, and adjust its accounts accordingly. A claim can also be made by the lender on behalf of the guarantor. Claims must be made or amended before the expiry of the time limits in note (c) to (A) above.

(b) Where a transfer pricing adjustment applies to disallow interest and the lender claims a compensating adjustment under either *TIOPA 2010, ss 174–178* or *ss 181–184*, the interest disallowed as a deduction for the borrower is correspondingly not treated as from non-trading loan relationships income for the lending company. See INTM440030, INTM413140, INTM413140 and *Simon's Taxes* D4.321.

(c) Where a transfer pricing adjustment applies in the case of the advantaged company, the guarantor company may make a corresponding balancing payment to the borrower. Provided such a balancing payment does not in aggregate exceed the amount of the compensating adjustment, it is not taken into account for corporation tax purposes when computing profits or losses of the guarantor or the borrower, or regarded as a distribution or charge on income. The compensating adjustment in this case is the total reduction in interest or other amounts payable under the loan subject to the guarantee (and thus treated as paid by the guarantor).

(d) For accounting periods commencing on or after 1 April 2017 (subject to transitional rules), the group would also be subject to the corporate interest restriction (CIR) rules in *TIOPA 2010, ss 372–498* and *Sch 7A*. Broadly, the CIR restricts interest and similar finance amounts to 30% of 'tax-EBITDA' ('the fixed ratio method') subject to a modified debt cap. There is also an election for an alternative group ratio method with its own modified debt cap. Groups with finance costs below £2m per annum are unaffected by CIR. The CIR applies *after* transfer pricing and anti-hybrid rules, etc. but *before* the loss restriction rules. See CHAPTER 114 for details on loss restriction.

(e) See also the notes to (A) above.

Capital Gains Tax

201	Annual Rates and Exemptions
202	Anti-Avoidance
203	Assets
204	Assets held on 6 April 1965
205	Assets held on 31 March 1982
206	Business Asset Disposal Relief (formerly Entrepreneurs' Relief)
207	Capital Sums Derived from Assets
208	Companies
209	Computation of Gains and Losses
210	Double Tax Relief
211	Enterprise Investment Scheme
212	Exemptions and Reliefs
213	Hold-Over Reliefs
214	Indexation
215	Investors' Relief
216	Land
217	Losses
218	Married Persons and Civil Partners
219	Offshore Settlements
220	Overseas Matters
221	Partnerships
222	Payment of Tax
223	Private Residences
224	Qualifying Corporate Bonds
225	Remittance Basis
226	Rollover Relief — Replacement of Business Assets
227	Seed Enterprise Investment Scheme
228	Settlements
229	Shares and Securities
230	Shares and Securities — Identification Rules
231	Social Investment Relief
232	Wasting Assets

201 Annual Rates and Exemptions

201.1 RATES OF TAX
[*TCGA 1992, ss 1H–1J; FA 2019, Sch 1 paras 2, 120*]

(A)

Erica owns an established business and has taxable profits of £40,000 for her accounting year ended 5 April 2021. She has no other income for 2020/21 but she makes a chargeable gain (before deduction of the annual exempt amount) of £30,300. The gain is not an upper rate gain and does not qualify for business asset disposal relief (formerly entrepreneurs' relief). Her capital gains tax liability for 2020/21 is computed as follows.

	£
Trade profits	40,000
Deduct Personal allowance	(12,500)
Step 3 income	£27,500
Unused part of the basic rate band (£37,500 – £27,500)	£10,000
Chargeable gain	30,300
Deduct Annual exempt amount	(12,300)
Taxable gain	£18,000

£		
10,000	@ 10%	1,000
8,000	@ 20%	1,600
£18,000		£2,600

Notes

(a) Except for upper rate gains (see (C) below), an individual's gains are chargeable at a rate of 10%. However, to any extent that gains, if treated as the top slice of income, exceed the basic rate limit (£37,500 for 2020/21), they are chargeable at 20%. Note that, for Scottish and Welsh taxpayers, the basic rate limit remains at £37,500 for the purpose of determining the applicable rate of capital gains tax. [*TCGA 1992, s 1J(6); FA 2019, Sch 1 paras 2, 120*]. See CG10246 and *Simon's Taxes* C1.107.

(b) See (B) below for the 10% rate applicable to gains in respect of which a claim to business asset disposal relief (formerly entrepreneurs' relief) is made.

(B)

Felix owns an established business and has taxable profits of £44,000 for his accounting year ended 31 March 2021. He has no other income for 2020/21 but he makes two chargeable gains (before deducting the annual exempt amount) of £17,000 each. Neither gain is an upper rate gain but one of them qualifies for business asset disposal relief (formerly entrepreneurs' relief). His capital gains tax liability for 2020/21 is computed as follows.

CGT Annual Rates and Exemptions

Disposal qualifying for business asset disposal relief

	£
Capital gains tax £17,000 × 10%	£1,700

Disposal not qualifying for business asset disposal relief

Chargeable gain	17,000
Deduct Annual exempt amount	(12,300)
Taxable gain	£4,700
Capital gains tax £4,700 × 20%	£940
Total capital gains tax for 2020/21 (£1,700 + £940)	£2,640

Notes

(a) Gains qualifying for business asset disposal relief (formerly entrepreneurs' relief) are treated as the lowest part of the gains for the year. The unused part of the basic rate band, i.e. £6,000 (£37,500 − (£44,000 − £12,500)), is set against the gain qualifying for business asset disposal relief even though it does not affect the rate of tax for that gain. The whole of the gain not qualifying for business asset disposal relief is therefore chargeable to tax at 20%.

(b) It is assumed that Felix sets his annual exempt amount against the gain chargeable at 20% as this achieves the greater tax saving.

(C)

Marley owns an established business and has taxable profits of £44,000 for her accounting year ended 31 March 2021. She has no other income for 2020/21 but she makes two chargeable gains (before deducting the annual exempt amount) of £17,000 each. Neither gain qualifies for business asset disposal relief (formerly entrepreneurs' relief) but one of them is an upper rate gain. Her capital gains tax liability for 2020/21 is computed as follows.

	£
Trade profits	44,000
Deduct Personal allowance	(12,500)
Step 3 income	£31,500
Unused part of the basic rate band (£37,500 − £31,500)	£6,000

Standard rate gain

£		£
6,000 @ 10%		600
11,000 @ 20%		2,200
£17,000		£2,800

Annual Rates and Exemptions   CGT 201.1

Upper rate gain

Chargeable gain	17,000
Deduct Annual exempt amount	(12,300)
Taxable gain	£4,700
Capital gains tax £4,700 × 28%	£1,316
Total capital gains tax for 2020/21 (£2,800 + £1,316)	£4,116

Notes

(a) 'Upper rate gains' are:

- residential property gains (including gains by non-residents on disposals of interests in UK residential property); and

- carried interest gains (i.e. gains accruing under *TCGA 1992, s 103KA(2)(3)* (carried interest) or gains resulting from carried interest (other than a co-investment repayment or return) arising under arrangements not involving a partnership and under which the individual performs investment management services in respect of an investment scheme).

(b) An individual's upper rate gains are chargeable at a rate of 18%. However, to any extent that gains, if treated as the top slice of income, exceed the basic rate limit (£37,500 for 2020/21), they are chargeable at 28%. Note that, for Scottish and Welsh taxpayers, the basic rate limit remains at £37,500 for the purpose of determining the applicable rate of capital gains tax. [*TCGA 1992, s 1J(6); FA 2019, Sch 1 paras 2, 120*]. See CG10246 and *Simon's Taxes* C1.107.

(c) The taxpayer can choose to set the unused part of the basic rate band (£6,000) against either the upper rate gain or the other gain. In practice the effect is the same as there is a 10% reduction in the rate of CGT applicable to the gain falling within the unused part of the band. In this example the unused part is set against the standard rate gain for illustration purposes.

(d) It is assumed that Marley sets her annual exempt amount against the gain chargeable at 28% as this achieves the greater tax saving.

(e) A person who makes a disposal of UK land on which a residential property gain arises must make a special return to HMRC in respect of the disposal on or before the 30th day following the day of the 'completion' of the disposal (and, where appropriate, make a payment on account of CGT no later than the filing date for that return). For UK-resident taxpayers, this applies only for disposals on or after 6 April 2020. For non-UK residents, a return is required for any disposal of UK land and whether or not a gain is made. The '*completion*' of a disposal occurs at the time of the disposal or, where the disposal is under a contract completed by conveyance, transfer or other instrument, at the time the instrument takes effect. [*FA 2019, Sch 2*].

201.2 CGT   Annual Rates and Exemptions

201.2 ANNUAL EXEMPT AMOUNT

[*TCGA 1992, s 1K; FA 2019, Sch 1 paras 2, 120; SI 2020 No 333*]

(A) **Interaction with losses**

For 2020/21, R, who is UK-resident throughout the year, has chargeable gains of £17,300 and allowable losses of £4,000. He also has allowable losses of £14,000 brought forward.

	£
Net gains (£17,300 − £4,000)	13,300
Deduct Annual exempt amount	(12,300)
	1,000
Deduct Losses brought forward (part)	(1,000)
Taxable gains	Nil
Losses brought forward	14,000
Less utilised in 2020/21	(1,000)
Losses carried forward	£13,000

(B) **Interaction with losses and settlement gains attributed under TCGA 1992, s 87**

For 2020/21, P, who is resident in the UK, has the same gains and losses (including brought-forward losses) as R above, but is also a beneficiary of an offshore trust. Trust gains of £12,600 are attributed to her for 2020/21 under *TCGA 1992, s 87*.

	£
Gains (£17,000 + £12,600)	29,600
Deduct current year loss	4,000
	25,600
Deduct Annual exempt amount	(12,300)
	13,300
Deduct Losses brought forward (part)	(13,000)
Taxable gains	£300
Losses brought forward	14,000
Less utilised in 2020/21	(13,000)
Losses carried forward	£1,000

Annual Rates and Exemptions   CGT 201.2

Notes

(a) Attributed gains (as in (b) below) cannot be covered by personal losses. The exempt amount is therefore allocated to attributed gains in priority to personal gains as this results in the greatest reduction in taxable gains. £300 (£12,600 − £12,300) of the attributed gains remain taxable.

(b) For the purposes of (a) above, 'attributed gains' are non-resident settlement gains attributed to a beneficiary under *TCGA 1992, s 87* (as in this example) and those similarly attributed to a beneficiary or onward recipient under *TCGA 1992, ss 87K, 87L, 89(2)*. See CG38575 and *Simon's Taxes* C4.440.

202 Anti-Avoidance

202.1 VALUE SHIFTING

[*TCGA 1992, s 29*]

Jak owns all the 1,000 £1 ordinary shares of K Ltd. The shares were acquired on subscription in 1979 for £1,000 and had a value of £65,250 on 31 March 1982. In December 2020, the trustees of Jak's family settlement subscribed at par for 250 £1 ordinary shares in K Ltd, thereby acquiring 20% of the voting power in the company.

It is agreed that the value per share of Jak's holding immediately before the December 2020 share issue was £175 and immediately afterwards was £150. The value per share of the trust's holding, on issue, was £97 per share.

The proceeds of the deemed disposal are computed as follows

Value passing out of Jak's 1,000 shares is £25,000 (1,000 × £25 per share (£175 − £150)).

Value passing into the trust's 250 shares is £24,250 (250 × £97 per share) *less* the subscription price paid of £250 (250 × £1 per share) = £24,000.

The proceeds of the deemed disposal are equal to the value passing into the new shares, i.e. £24,000. (The trust's acquisition cost is £24,250, i.e. actual plus deemed consideration given.)

The disposal is a part disposal (see **209.2** COMPUTATION OF GAINS AND LOSSES), the value of the part retained being £150,000 (1,000 × £150 per share).

Jak will have a capital gain for 2020/21 as follows

	£
Proceeds of deemed disposal	24,000
Allowable cost $\dfrac{24,000}{24,000 + 150,000} \times £65,250$	(9,000)
Chargeable gain	£15,000

Note

(a) The legislation taxes the amount of value passing *into* the transferee holdings, not (if different) the amount passing from the transferor. The deemed proceeds are thus equal to the value received by the transferee(s). See CG58855 and *Simon's Taxes* C1.335, C2.115.

202.2 CGT   Anti-Avoidance

202.2 VALUE-SHIFTING TO GIVE TAX-FREE BENEFIT

[*TCGA 1992, s 30*]

M owns the whole of the issued share capital in C Ltd, an unquoted company. He is also a director of the company. M receives an offer from a public company for his shares. Prior to sale, C Ltd pays M £30,000 for loss of his office as director. M then sells the shares for £100,000.

On the sale of M's shares, HMRC may seek to adjust the consideration in computing M's chargeable gain on the grounds that M has received a tax-free benefit and the value of his shares has thereby been materially reduced.

202.3 ASSETS DISPOSED OF IN A SERIES OF TRANSACTIONS

[*TCGA 1992, ss 19, 20*]

L purchased a set of 6 antique chairs in June 1992 at a cost of £12,000. He gave 2 chairs to his daughter in February 2015, another pair to his son in November 2017, and sold the final pair to his brother for their market value in August 2020.

The market value of the chairs at the relevant dates were

	2 chairs £	4 chairs £	6 chairs £
February 2015	6,000	14,000	26,000
November 2017	7,800	18,000	34,200
August 2020	10,400	24,000	46,200

The capital gains tax computations are as follows
February 2015

Disposal to daughter

Deemed consideration	£6,000

As the consideration does not exceed £6,000, the disposal is covered by the chattel exemption (see note (a)).

November 2017

(i) 2014/15 disposal to daughter recomputed

Original market value (deemed disposal consideration at February 2015)	£6,000
Reasonable proportion of aggregate market value as at February 2015 of all assets disposed of to date	
£14,000 × 2/4	£7,000

	£
Deemed consideration (greater of £6,000 and £7,000)	7,000
Cost $\dfrac{7,000}{7,000 + 14,000} \times £12,000$	(4,000)
Chargeable gain 2014/15	£3,000

(ii) 2017/18 disposal to son

Original market value (deemed disposal consideration)	£7,800
Reasonable proportion of aggregate market value as at November 2017 of all assets disposed of to date	
£18,000 × 2/4	£9,000

	£
Deemed consideration (greater of £7,800 and £9,000)	9,000
Cost $\dfrac{9,000}{9,000 + 7,800} \times (£12,000 - £4,000)$	(4,286)
Chargeable gain 2017/18	£4,714

202.3 CGT Anti-Avoidance

August 2020

(i) Gain on 2014/15 disposal to daughter recomputed

Original market value (deemed consideration in recomputation at November 2017)	£7,000
Reasonable proportion of aggregate market value as at February 2015 of all assets disposed of to date	
£26,000 × 2/6	£8,667
Deemed consideration (greater of £7,000 and £8,667)	£8,667
Cost $\dfrac{8,667}{8,667 + 14,000} \times £12,000$	(£4,588)
Revised chargeable gain 2014/15	£4,079

(ii) Gain on 2017/18 disposal to son recomputed

Original market value (deemed consideration in computation at November 2017)	£9,000
Reasonable proportion of aggregate market value as at November 2017 of all assets disposed of to date	
£34,200 × 2/6	£11,400
Deemed consideration (greater of £9,000 and £11,400)	11,400
Cost $\dfrac{11,400}{11,400 + 7,800} \times (£12,000 - £4,588)$	(4,401)
Revised chargeable gain 2017/18	£6,999

(iii) Gain on 2020/21 disposal to brother

Original market value (actual consideration)	£10,400
Reasonable proportion of aggregate market value as at August 2020 of all assets disposed of to date	
£46,200 × 2/6	£15,400
Deemed consideration (greater of £10,400 and £15,400)	£15,400
Cost (£12,000 − £4,588 − £4,401)	(£3,011)
Chargeable gain 2020/21	£12,389

Anti-Avoidance CGT 202.4

Notes

(a) The disposal in February 2015 is at first covered by the chattel exemption of £6,000. As the second disposal in November 2017 is to a person connected with the recipient of the first disposal, the two must then be looked at together for the purposes of the chattel exemption, and, as the combined proceeds exceed the chattel exemption limit, the exemption is not available. [*TCGA 1992, s 262*]. See **212.1(C)** EXEMPTIONS AND RELIEFS. See also CG76573 and *Simon's Taxes* C3.1811.

(b) The three disposals are linked transactions within *TCGA 1992, s 19* as they are made by the same transferor to persons with whom he is connected, and take place within a six-year period. See CG14650–14795 and *Simon's Taxes* C2.114.

(c) It is assumed in the above example that it is 'reasonable' to apportion the aggregate market value in proportion to the number of items. In other instances a different basis may be needed to give the 'reasonable' apportionment required by *TCGA 1992, s 20(4)*. See CG14653 and *Simon's Taxes* C2.114.

202.4 DEPRECIATORY TRANSACTIONS: GROUPS OF COMPANIES

[*TCGA 1992, s 176; FA 2018, s 28*]

G Ltd owns 100% of the share capital of Q Ltd, which it acquired in June 1990 for £75,000. Q Ltd owns land which it purchased in 1986 for £50,000. In 2016, the land, then with a market value of £120,000, was transferred to G Ltd for £50,000. In April 2020, Q Ltd was put into liquidation, and G Ltd received liquidation distributions totalling £30,000.

The loss on the Q Ltd shares is £45,000 (£75,000 – £30,000). The whole or part of the loss is likely to be disallowed on the grounds that it resulted from the depreciatory transaction involving the transfer of land at less than market value.

Note

(a) Where the ultimate disposal of the shares or securities takes place on or after 22 November 2017 (or is treated as taking place before 22 November 2017 as a result of a negligible value claim (see **217.1(B)** LOSSES)) made on or after that date), any depreciatory transactions occurring on or after 31 March 1982 are taken into account. Previously, only depreciatory transactions occurring in the six-years ending with that disposal were taken into account. See CG46500 and *Simon's Taxes* D2.350.

203 Assets

203.1 OPTIONS

[*TCGA 1992, ss 44, 46, 144, 144ZA–144ZD, 145*]

Cross-reference. See also **232.2** WASTING ASSETS.

On 1 February 2017 F granted an option to G for £10,000 to acquire freehold land bought by F for £50,000 in September 1997. The option is for a period of 5 years, and the option price is £100,000 plus 1% thereof for each month since the option was granted. On 1 February 2018, G sold the option to H for £20,000. On 30 June 2020, H exercises the option and pays F £141,000 for the land. Neither G nor H intended to use the land for the purposes of a trade.

2017 Grant of option by F

		£
Disposal proceeds		10,000
Allowable cost		—
Chargeable gain 2016/17		£10,000

2018 Disposal of option by G

	£	
Disposal proceeds		20,000
Allowable cost	10,000	
Less: Wasted — £10,000 × $^2/_5$	(4,000)	(6,000)
Chargeable gain 2017/18		£14,000

2020 Exercise of option

(i) Earlier assessment on F vacated
(ii) Aggregate disposal proceeds

(£10,000 + £141,000)	151,000
Allowable cost of land	(50,000)
Chargeable gain (on F) 2020/21	£101,000

H's allowable expenditure is

Cost of option	20,000
Cost of land	141,000
	£161,000

203.1 CGT   Assets

Note

(a) The wasting asset rules (see **232** WASTING ASSETS) apply on the disposal of the option by G (though certain options are exempted from these rules — see *TCGA 1992, s 144*). As these rules can only apply on a disposal, they cannot apply on the exercise of the option by H (as the exercise of an option is not treated as a disposal), so his acquisition cost remains intact. See *Simon's Taxes* C2.1009.

204 Assets held on 6 April 1965

Note

The general re-basing rule for ASSETS HELD ON 31 MARCH 1982 (205) applies automatically and without exception for capital gains tax purposes, so that special rules for assets held on 6 April 1965 are not required. Accordingly, the provisions in this chapter apply only for the purposes of corporation tax on chargeable gains. [*TCGA 1992, s 35(9)*].

204.1 QUOTED SHARES AND SECURITIES

[*TCGA 1992, s 109(4)(5), Sch 2 paras 1–8*]

(A) **Basic computation of gain**

H Ltd acquired 3,000 U plc ordinary shares in 1963 for £15,000. Their market value was £10 per share on 6 April 1965 and £12 per share on 31 March 1982. In September 2020, H Ltd sells 2,000 of the shares for £45 per share. The indexation factor for the period March 1982 to December 2017 is 2.501.

	£	£	£
Sale proceeds	90,000	90,000	90,000
Cost	(10,000)		
6 April 1965 value		(20,000)	
31 March 1982 value			(24,000)
Unindexed gain	80,000	70,000	66,000
Indexation allowance:			
£24,000 × 2.501	(60,024)	(60,024)	(60,024)
Indexed gain	£19,976	£9,976	£5,976
Chargeable gain			£5,976

Notes

(a) The comparison is firstly between the gain arrived at by deducting cost and that arrived at by deducting 6 April 1965 value. The smaller of the two gains is taken. If, however, an election had been made under either *TCGA 1992, Sch 2 para 4* or *TCGA 1992, s 109(4)* for 6 April 1965 value to be used in computing all gains and losses on quoted shares held at that date, this comparison need not be made and the taxable gain, subject to (c) below, would be £10,000. See CG51633 and *Simon's Taxes* C2.719.

(b) The second comparison is between the figure arrived at in (a) above and the gain using 31 March 1982 value. As the latter is smaller, it is substituted for the figure in (b) above by virtue of *TCGA 1992, s 35(2)*. If, however, an election had been made under *TCGA 1992, s 35(5)* for 31 March 1982 value to be used in computing all gains and losses on assets held at that date, neither this comparison nor that in (a) above need be made and the taxable gain would still be £6,000. See CG15500 and *Simon's Taxes* C2.601.

204.1 CGT   Assets held on 6 April 1965

    (c)   Indexation is based on 31 March 1982 value in all three calculations as this gives the greater allowance. [*TCGA 1992, s 55(1)(2)*]. See CG17405 and *Simon's Taxes* C2.608.

    (d)   Indexation allowance is frozen at its December 2017 level. No indexation allowance is available in respect of expenditure incurred after 31 December 2017, and for expenditure incurred on or before that date and falling to be deducted on a disposal after that date, indexation allowance is computed up to and including December 2017 only. [*TCGA 1992, ss 53(1)(1B), 54(1B); FA 2018, s 26(2)(3)(6)*]. See **214.1** INDEXATION. See CG17230 and *Simon's Taxes* C2.301.

    (e)   All comparisons are between gains *after* indexation.

(B)   **Basic computation—no gain/no loss disposals**

J Ltd acquired a holding of quoted shares in 1957 for £1,000. The market value of the holding at 6 April 1965 and 31 March 1982 respectively was £19,000 and £20,000. J Ltd sells the holding in September 2020 for £18,000. The indexation factor for the period March 1982 to December 2017 is 2.501.

(i) Assuming no elections made to use 1965 value or 1982 value

	£	£
Sale proceeds	18,000	18,000
Cost	(1,000)	
6 April 1965 value		(19,000)
Unindexed gain/(loss)	17,000	(1,000)
Indexation allowance:		
£20,000 × 2.501 (see below) = £50,020 but restricted to	(17,000)	—
Indexed gain/(loss)	Nil	£(1,000)
Chargeable gain/allowable loss		Nil

As one computation shows no gain/no loss and the other a loss, the disposal is a no gain/no loss disposal. [*TCGA 1992, Sch 2 para 2(1)*]. There is no need to compute the gain or loss using 31 March 1982 value as re-basing cannot disturb a no gain/no loss position. [*TCGA 1992, s 35(3)(c)*].

(ii) Election made to use 6 April 1965 value

	£	£
Sale proceeds	18,000	18,000
6 April 1965 value	(19,000)	
31 March 1982 value		(20,000)
(Loss)	(1,000)	(2,000)
Allowable loss	£1,000	

The allowable loss is £1,000 as re-basing cannot increase a loss. [*TCGA 1992, s 35(3)(b)*].

Assets held on 6 April 1965   CGT 204.1

(iii) Election made to use 31 March 1982 value

There is an allowable loss of £2,000.

(C) **Parts of holding acquired at different times**

L Ltd has the following transactions in shares of A plc, a quoted company

Date	Number of shares bought/(sold)	Cost/(proceeds)
9.1.57	1,500	1,050
10.11.62	750	600
15.7.69	1,200	3,000
12.10.80	1,400	5,000
16.12.83	850	5,950
17.9.95	1,150	5,200
19.12.20	(6,000)	(120,000)
	850	

Market value of A shares at 6 April 1965 was £1.60

Market value of A shares at 31 March 1982 was £4.00

Indexation factors	March 1982 to December 2017	2.501
	December 1983 to April 1985	0.091
	April 1985 to September 1995	0.589
	September 1995 to December 2017	0.847

(i) No election made to substitute 1965 market value

Identify 6,000 shares sold as follows

Section 104 holding	Shares	Qualifying Expenditure £	Indexed Pool £
16.12.83 acquisition	850	5,950	5,950
£5,950 × 0.091			541
6.4.85 pool	850	5,950	6,491
Indexed rise: April 1985 to September 1995			
£6,491 × 0.589			3,823
17.9.95 acquisition	1,150	5,200	5,200
	2,000	11,150	15,514
Indexed rise: September 1995 to December 2017			
£15,514 × 0.847			13,140
			28,654

365

204.1 CGT Assets held on 6 April 1965

Section 104 holding	Shares	Qualifying Expenditure £	Indexed Pool £
19.12.20 disposal	(2,000)	(11,150)	(28,654)
Balance of pool	—	—	—

	£
Sale proceeds (2,000 × £20)	40,000
Cost (as above)	(11,150)
Unindexed gain	28,850
Indexation allowance (£28,654 − £11,150)	(17,504)
Chargeable gain	£11,346

1982 holding		£	£
Sale proceeds (1,200 + 1,400) × £20		52,000	52,000
Cost (£3,000 + £5,000)		(8,000)	
Market value 31.3.82 (2,600 × £4)			(10,400)
Unindexed gain		44,000	41,600
Indexation allowance £10,400 × 2.501		(26,010)	(26,010)
Gain after indexation		£17,990	£15,590
Chargeable gain			£15,590

10.11.62 acquisition	£	£	£
Sale proceeds (750 × £20)	15,000	15,000	15,000
Cost	(600)		
Market value 6.4.65 (750 × £1.60)		(1,200)	
Market value 31.3.82 (750 × £4)			(3,000)
Unindexed gain	14,400	13,800	12,000
Indexation allowance £3,000 × 2.501	(7,503)	(7,503)	(7,503)
Gain after indexation	£6,897	£6,297	£4,497
Chargeable gain			£4,497

Assets held on 6 April 1965

9.1.57 acquisition (part)

	£	£	£
Sale proceeds (650 × £20)	13,000	13,000	13,000
Cost (650 × £0.70)	(455)		
Market value 6.4.65 (650 × £1.60)		(1,040)	
Market value 31.3.82 (650 × £4)			(2,600)
Unindexed gain	12,545	11,960	10,400
Indexation allowance £2,600 × 2.501	(6,503)	(6,503)	(6,503)
Gain after indexation	£6,042	£5,457	£3,897

Chargeable gain   £3,897

Summary of chargeable gains

	Number of shares	Chargeable gain £
Section 104 holding	2,000	11,346
1982 holding	2,600	15,590
10.11.62 acquisition	750	4,497
9.1.57 acquisition (part)	650	3,897
	6,000	£35,330

Remaining shares
850 acquired on 9.1.57 for £595

(ii) Election made to substitute 1965 market value

Identify 6,000 shares as follows

Section 104 holding

Disposal of 2,000 shares as in (i) above			£11,346

1982 holding

	Shares		Pool cost £
9.1.57	1,500	× £1.60	2,400
10.11.62	750	× £1.60	1,200
15.7.69	1,200		3,000
12.10.80	1,400		5,000
	4,850		11,600
19.12.20 disposal	(4,000)	4,000/4,850 × £11,600	(9,567)
Remaining shares	850		£2,033

204.1 CGT   Assets held on 6 April 1965

	£	£
Sale proceeds (4,000 × £20)	80,000	80,000
Cost (as above)	(9,567)	
Market value 31.3.82 (4,000 × £4)		(16,000)
Unindexed gain	70,433	64,000
Indexation allowance £16,000 × 2.501	(40,016)	(40,016)
Gain after indexation	£30,417	£23,984
Chargeable gain		£23,984

Summary of chargeable gains/allowable losses	Number of shares	Chargeable gain/ (loss) £
Section 104 holding	2,000	11,346
1982 holding	4,000	23,984
	6,000	£35,330

Notes

(a) Because re-basing to 31 March 1982 applies in this case, the result is the same whether or not the election to substitute 6 April 1965 value has been made, but with a lower 31 March 1982 value the computations could produce differing overall gains/losses.

(b) Note that indexation is based on 31 March 1982 value whenever this gives the greater allowance.

(c) Indexation allowance is frozen at its December 2017 level. No indexation allowance is available in respect of expenditure incurred after 31 December 2017, and for expenditure incurred on or before that date and falling to be deducted on a disposal after that date, indexation allowance is computed up to and including December 2017 only. [*TCGA 1992, ss 53(1)(1B), 54(1B); FA 2018, s 26(2)(3)(6)*]. See **214.1** INDEXATION. See also CG17230 and *Simon's Taxes* C2.301.

204.2 LAND REFLECTING DEVELOPMENT VALUE

[*TCGA 1992, Sch 2 paras 9–15*]

K Ltd sells a building plot, on which planning permission has just been obtained, in November 2020 for £200,000. The company acquired the plot in 1958 when its value was £2,000. The market value was £5,000 at 6 April 1965 and £10,000 at 31 March 1982, and the current use value in November 2020 is £15,000. The indexation factor for the period March 1982 to December 2017 is 2.501.

Assets held on 6 April 1965   CGT 204.3

	£	£	£
Sale proceeds	200,000	200,000	200,000
Cost	(2,000)		
Market value 6.4.65		(5,000)	
Market value 31.3.82			(10,000)
Unindexed gain	198,000	195,000	190,000
Indexation allowance			
£10,000 × 2.501	(25,010)	(25,010)	(25,010)
Gain after indexation	£172,990	£169,990	£164,990
Chargeable gain			£164,990

Notes

(a) Time apportionment would have substantially reduced the gain of £172,990, using cost, such that re-basing to 31 March 1982 would have given a greater gain than that based on cost and would not therefore have applied. However, as the plot has been sold for a price in excess of its current use value, no time apportionment can be claimed.

(b) Gains must be compared after applying the indexation allowance, which is based on 31 March 1982 value, this being greater than either cost or 6 April 1965 value.

(c) In this case, the gain is computed in accordance with the rules in 205 ASSETS HELD ON 31 MARCH 1982 as the gain by reference to 31 March 1982 value is lower than the gain by reference to 6 April 1965 value which in turn is lower than the gain by reference to cost.

(d) Indexation allowance is frozen at its December 2017 level. No indexation allowance is available in respect of expenditure incurred after 31 December 2017, and for expenditure incurred on or before that date and falling to be deducted on a disposal after that date, indexation allowance is computed up to and including December 2017 only. [*TCGA 1992*, ss 53(1)(1B), 54(1B); *FA 2018*, s 26(2)(3)(6)]. See **214.1** INDEXATION. See also CG17230 and *Simon's Taxes* C2.301.

204.3 OTHER ASSETS

[*TCGA 1992, Sch 2 paras 16–19*]

(A) **Chattels**

M Ltd purchased a painting in 1942 for £5,000 to hang on the boardroom wall. On 5 October 2020 the company sold the painting for £470,000 net. The painting's value was £129,000 at 6 April 1965, but only £125,000 at 31 March 1982. The indexation factor for the period March 1982 to December 2017 is 2.501.

204.3 CGT   Assets held on 6 April 1965

(i) Time apportionment

Period of ownership since 6 April 1945	(note (a))	75 years 6 months
Period of ownership since 6 April 1965		55 years 6 months

		£
Unindexed gain (£470,000 − £5,000)		465,000
Indexation allowance £125,000 × 2.501	(note (b))	(312,625)
		£152,375
Gain after indexation £152,375 × (55y 6m/75y 6m) (note (c))		£112,011

(ii) Election for 6.4.65 value

		£
Sale proceeds		470,000
Market value 6.4.65		(129,000)
Unindexed gain		341,000
Indexation allowance £129,000 × 2.501	(note (b))	(322,629)
Gain after indexation		£18,371

Election for 6.4.65 value is beneficial, subject to re-basing.

(iii) Re-basing to 1982

		£
Sale proceeds		470,000
Market value 31.3.82		(125,000)
Unindexed gain		345,000
Indexation allowance £129,000 × 2.501	(note (b))	(322,629)
Gain after indexation		£22,371

Re-basing cannot increase a gain. [*TCGA 1992, s 35(3)(a)*]. Therefore, the gain of £18,371 stands and the election for 6.4.65 value is beneficial.

Notes

(a)   Under time apportionment, the period of ownership is limited to that after 5 April 1945.

(b)   In (i) above, indexation is based on 31.3.82 value, being greater than cost — it cannot be based on 6 April 1965 value as this does not enter into the calculation. In (ii), indexation is on the higher of 31.3.82 value and 6.4.65 value. This is also the case in (iii) as one is comparing the position using 6.4.65 value and 31.3.82 value. See *TCGA 1992, s 55(1)(2)*. See CG17405 and *Simon's Taxes* C2.607.

(c) Indexation allowance is frozen at its December 2017 level. No indexation allowance is available in respect of expenditure incurred after 31 December 2017, and for expenditure incurred on or before that date and falling to be deducted on a disposal after that date, indexation allowance is computed up to and including December 2017 only. [*TCGA 1992, ss 53(1)(1B), 54(1B); FA 2018, s 26(2)(3)(6)*]. See **214.1** INDEXATION. See also CG17230 and *Simon's Taxes* C2.301.

(d) The time apportionment calculation is applied to the gain *after* indexation (*Smith v Schofield* HL 1993, 65 TC 669, [1993] STC 268).

(B) **Land and buildings**

X Ltd acquired land on 5 June 1960 for £7,250. The company acquired access land adjoining the property for £2,750 on 1 January 1961 and, having obtained planning consent, on 30 July 1963 incurred expenditure of £15,000 in building houses on the land, which were let. On 6 September 2020, X Ltd sells the houses with vacant possession for £400,000, net of expenses. The value of the houses and land is £20,000 at 6 April 1965 and £100,000 at 31 March 1982. The indexation factor for the period March 1982 to December 2017 is 2.501.

The gain using time apportionment is

	£	£
Net proceeds of sale		400,000
Deduct Cost of land	7,250	
Cost of addition	2,750	
Cost of building	15,000	(25,000)
Unindexed gain		375,000
Indexation allowance £100,000 × 2.501		(250,100)
Gain after indexation		£124,900
Apportion to allowable expenditure (note (c))		

	£	£
(i) Land 7,250/25,000 × £124,900	36,221	
Time apportion £36,221 × (55y 5m/60y 3m)		33,315
(ii) Addition 2,750/25,000 × £124,900	13,739	
Time apportion £13,739 × (55y 5m/59y 8m)		12,760
(iii) Building 15,000/25,000 × £124,900	74,940	
Time apportion £74,940 × (55y 5m/57y 1m)		72,752
Gain after indexation and time apportionment		£118,827

204.3 CGT   Assets held on 6 April 1965

The gain using re-basing to 1982 is

	£
Net proceeds of sale	400,000
Market value at 31.3.82	(100,000)
Unindexed gain	300,000
Indexation allowance	
£100,000 × 2.501	(250,100)
Gain	£49,900
Chargeable gain	£49,900

Notes

(a) An election for 6 April 1965 valuation could not be favourable, even were it not for the effect of re-basing, as the value is less than historic costs.

(b) It is the gain/loss *after* time apportionment that is compared with the gain/loss produced by re-basing. [*TCGA 1992, Sch 3 para 6*]. See *Simon's Taxes* C2.611.

(c) The time apportionment calculation is applied to the gain *after* indexation (*Smith v Schofield* HL 1993, 65 TC 669, [1993] STC 268).

(d) Indexation allowance is frozen at its December 2017 level. No indexation allowance is available in respect of expenditure incurred after 31 December 2017, and for expenditure incurred on or before that date and falling to be deducted on a disposal after that date, indexation allowance is computed up to and including December 2017 only. [*TCGA 1992, ss 53(1)(1B), 54(1B); FA 2018, s 26(2)(3)(6)*]. See **214.1** INDEXATION. See also CG17230 and *Simon's Taxes* C2.301.

(C) **Unquoted shares**

On 6 April 1954, A Ltd acquired 5,000 shares in C Ltd, an unquoted company, for £15,201. At 6 April 1965, the value of the holding was £15,000. A Ltd sells the shares (its entire holding in the company) on 6 April 2020 for £95,000.

The indexation factor for the period March 1982 to December 2017 is 2.501. No election for universal 31 March 1982 re-basing is made but the market value of the holding at that date is agreed at £17,000.

Assets held on 6 April 1965

The gain using time apportionment is as follows

Total period of ownership:	66 years
Period after 6 April 1965:	55 years

	£
Proceeds	95,000
Cost	(15,201)
Unindexed gain	79,799
Indexation allowance:	
31.3.82 value £17,000 × 2.501	(42,517)
Gain after indexation	£37,282
Gain after time apportionment: £37,282 × 55/66	£31,068

The gain with an election to use 6.4.65 value is as follows

	£
Proceeds	95,000
6.4.65 value	(15,000)
Unindexed gain	80,000
Indexation allowance:	
31.3.82 value £17,000 × 2.501	(42,517)
Gain after indexation	£37,483

The gain with re-basing to 1982 is as follows

	£
Proceeds	95,000
31.3.82 value	(17,000)
Unindexed gain	78,000
Indexation allowance:	
31.3.82 value £17,000 × 2.501	(42,517)
Gain after indexation	£35,483

Time apportionment is more beneficial than an election for 6 April 1965 value. Re-basing does not apply as it cannot increase a gain. The chargeable gain is therefore £31,068.

(D) Unquoted shares — share exchange before 6 April 1965

[*TCGA 1992, Sch 2 para 19(1)(3)*]

204.3 CGT Assets held on 6 April 1965

N Ltd purchased 5,000 £1 ordinary shares in R Ltd, an unquoted company, on 1 January 1961. The purchase price was £3 per share, a total of £15,000. On 1 December 1964, R Ltd was acquired by D Ltd, an unquoted company, as a result of which N Ltd received 10,000 8% convertible preference shares in D Ltd in exchange for its holding of R shares. In November 2020, N Ltd sold the D Ltd shares for £8.45 per share.

The market value of the D Ltd shares was £2.03 per share at 6 April 1965 but only £1.50 per share at 31 March 1982. The indexation factor for the period March 1982 to December 2017 is 2.501.

The gain, disregarding re-basing, is

		£
Disposal consideration	10,000 at £8.45	84,500
Allowable cost	10,000 at £2.03	(20,300)
Unindexed gain		64,200
Indexation allowance £20,300 × 2.501		(50,770)
Gain after indexation		£13,430

The gain using re-basing to 1982 is

	£
Disposal consideration (as above)	84,500
Market value 31.3.82 10,000 at £1.50	(15,000)
Unindexed gain	69,500
Indexation allowance £20,300 × 2.501	(50,770)
Gain after indexation	£18,730
The overall result is	
Chargeable gain	£13,430

Notes

(a) Subject to re-basing, allowable cost *must* be taken as 6.4.65 value.

(b) Indexation is based on the greater of 31.3.82 value and 6.4.65 value. [*TCGA 1992, s 55(1)(2)*].

(c) Where the effect of re-basing would be to increase a gain, re-basing does not apply (but see note (e) below). [*TCGA 1992, s 35(3)(a)*]. See CG16760 onwards and *Simon's Taxes* C2.601.

(d) By concession (ESC D10), tax is not charged on a disposal of the *entire* new shareholding on more than the actual gain realised, i.e. by reference to original cost but without time apportionment.

(e) Indexation allowance is frozen at its December 2017 level. No indexation allowance is available in respect of expenditure incurred after 31 December 2017, and for expenditure incurred on or before that date and falling to be deducted on a disposal after that date, indexation allowance is computed up to and including December 2017 only. [*TCGA 1992, ss 53(1)(1B), 54(1B); FA 2018, s 26(2)(3)(6)*]. See **214.1** INDEXATION. See also CG17230 and *Simon's Taxes* C2.301.

Assets held on 6 April 1965 CGT 204.3

(E) **Unquoted shares — share exchange after 5 April 1965**

[*TCGA 1992, Sch 2 para 19(2)(3)*]

S Ltd acquired 10,000 £1 ordinary shares in L Ltd for £5,000 on 31 May 1959. The shares are not quoted, and their value at 6 April 1965 was £6,000. On 1 September 1989, the shares were acquired by R plc, in exchange for its own ordinary shares on the basis of 1 for 2. The offer valued L ordinary shares at £2.23 per share. In February 2021, S Ltd sells its 5,000 R shares for £14.60 per share. The agreed value of the L Ltd shares at 31 March 1982 was £2.05 per share.

Indexation factors	March 1982 to September 1989	0.468
	September 1989 to December 2017	1.385
	March 1982 to December 2017	2.501

The gain without re-basing to 1982 is computed as follows

(i) Using time apportionment

Deemed disposal at 1.9.89:

	£
Proceeds (market value £2.23 × 10,000)	22,300
Cost	(5,000)
Unindexed gain	17,300
Indexation allowance	
MV 31.3.82 10,000 × £2.05 × 0.468	(9,594)
Gain after indexation	£7,706
Gain after time apportionment:	
£7,706 × (24y 5m/30y 3m)	£6,219

Actual disposal in February 2021:

	£
Proceeds 5,000 × £14.60	73,000
Deemed acquisition cost at 1.9.89	(22,300)
Unindexed gain	50,700
Indexation allowance £22,300 × 1.385	(30,886)
Gain after indexation	£19,814
Total gain £(6,219 + 19,814)	£26,033

(ii) With election for 6.4.65 value

	£
Disposal consideration	73,000
Allowable cost	(6,000)

204.3 CGT   Assets held on 6 April 1965

Unindexed gain	67,000
Indexation allowance 10,000 × £2.05 × 2.501	(51,271)
Gain	£15,729

Subject to re-basing, the election is beneficial.

The gain using re-basing to 1982 is

	£
Disposal consideration	73,000
Market value 31.3.82 10,000 × £2.05	(20,500)
Unindexed gain	52,500
Indexation allowance £20,500 × 2.501	(51,271)
Gain after indexation	£1,229
The overall result is	
Chargeable gain	£1,229

Re-basing applies as it produces a smaller gain than that using 6 April 1965 value.

Notes

(a) The deemed disposal on 1 September 1989 is *only* for the purposes of *TCGA 1992, Sch 2 para 16* (time apportionment). See CG15500P and *Simon's Taxes* C2.611.

(b) If an election is made for 6 April 1965 value, no valuation is required at 1 September 1989.

(c) Indexation allowance is frozen at its December 2017 level. No indexation allowance is available in respect of expenditure incurred after 31 December 2017, and for expenditure incurred on or before that date and falling to be deducted on a disposal after that date, indexation allowance is computed up to and including December 2017 only. [*TCGA 1992, ss 53(1)(1B), 54(1B); FA 2018, s 26(2)(3)(6)*]. See **214.1** INDEXATION. See also CG17230 and *Simon's Taxes* C2.301.

(F) **Part disposals after 5 April 1965**

[*TCGA 1992, s 42, Sch 2 para 16(8)*]

H Ltd bought land for £15,000 on 31 October 1960. Its value at 6 April 1965 was £17,200. On 1 February 1988, H Ltd sold part of the land for £50,000, the balance being then worth £200,000. On 9 April 2020, H Ltd sells the remaining land for £450,000. The agreed value of the total estate at 31 March 1982 was £150,000 and H Ltd made a claim on the February 1988 disposal for that value to be used for indexation purposes under the law then in force.

Indexation factors	March 1982 to February 1988	0.305
	March 1982 to December 2017	2.501

1988 disposal

	£
Proceeds of part disposal	50,000
Deduct allowable cost $\dfrac{50,000}{50,000 + 200,000} \times £15,000$	(3,000)
Unindexed gain	47,000

Indexation allowance $£150,000 \times \dfrac{50,000}{50,000 + 200,000} = £30,000$

	£
$£30,000 \times 0.305$	(9,150)
Gain after indexation	£37,850

Time apportionment

$$\text{Chargeable gain } \dfrac{22\text{y } 10\text{m}}{27\text{y } 3\text{m}} \times £37,850 \qquad £31,715$$

If an election were made to substitute 6 April 1965 valuation, the computation would be

	£
Proceeds of part disposal	50,000
Deduct allowable cost $\dfrac{50,000}{50,000 + 200,000} \times £17,200$	(3,440)
Unindexed gain	46,560

Indexation allowance $£150,000 \times \dfrac{50,000}{50,000 + 200,000} = £30,000$

	£
$£30,000 \times 0.305$	(9,150)
Chargeable gain	£37,410

An election would not be beneficial.

204.3 CGT   Assets held on 6 April 1965

2020 disposal
The gain without re-basing to 1982 is as follows

Computation of entire gain over period of ownership:

	£
Proceeds	450,000
Cost £(15,000 – 3,000)	(12,000)
Unindexed gain	438,000
Indexation allowance	
MV 31.3.82 £(150,000 – 30,000) × 2.501	(300,120)
Gain after indexation	£137,880 (A)

Computation of gain for period 31.10.60 - 1.2.88:

	£
Market value at date of part disposal	200,000
Cost £(15,000 – 3,000)	(12,000)
Unindexed gain	188,000
Indexation allowance £(150,000 – 30,000) × 0.305	(36,600)
Gain after indexation	£151,400 (B)

$$\text{Time apportionment } £151,400 \times \frac{22y\ 10m}{27y\ 3m} \qquad £126,861 \text{ (C)}$$

	£
Balance of gain (1.2.88 to 9.4.20) ((A) – (B))	£(13,520) (D)
Chargeable gain (subject to re-basing) ((C) + (D))	£113,341

The gain using re-basing to 1982 is as follows

		£
Disposal proceeds		450,000
Market value 31.3.82 £150,000 × $\frac{12,000}{15,000}$	(note (b))	(120,000)
Unindexed gain		330,000
Indexation allowance £120,000 × 2.501		(300,120)
Gain after indexation		£29,880

The overall result is
Chargeable gain £29,880

Assets held on 6 April 1965 CGT 204.3

Re-basing applies as it produces neither a larger gain nor a loss.

Notes

(a) The deemed disposal on 1 February 1988 is only for the purposes of *TCGA 1992, Sch 2 para 16(3)–(5)* (time apportionment). For re-basing purposes, the asset is still regarded as having been held at 31 March 1982.

(b) Where there has been a part disposal after 31 March 1982 and before 6 April 1988 of an asset held at 31 March 1982, the proportion of 31 March 1982 value to be brought into account in the re-basing calculation is that which the cost previously unallowed bears to the total cost, giving the same effect as if re-basing had applied to the part disposal. [*TCGA 1992, Sch 3 para 4(1)*]. See CG16940 and *Simon's Taxes* C2.606.

(c) HMRC will also accept an alternative basis of calculation on the part disposal of land. Under this method, the part disposed of is treated as a separate asset and any fair and reasonable method of apportioning part of the total cost to it will be accepted e.g. a reasonable valuation of that part at the acquisition date. (HMRC Statement of Practice SP D1.)

(d) Indexation allowance is frozen at its December 2017 level. No indexation allowance is available in respect of expenditure incurred after 31 December 2017, and for expenditure incurred on or before that date and falling to be deducted on a disposal after that date, indexation allowance is computed up to and including December 2017 only. [*TCGA 1992, ss 53(1)(1B), 54(1B); FA 2018, s 26(2)(3)(6)*]. See **214.1** INDEXATION. See also CG17230 and *Simon's Taxes* C2.301.

(e) The time apportionment calculation is applied to the gain *after* indexation (*Smith v Schofield HL 1993*, 65 TC 669, [1993] STC 268).

205 Assets held on 31 March 1982

205.1 CAPITAL GAINS TAX

[*TCGA 1992, s 35(1)(2)*]

Robbie sells an asset (which is neither tangible movable property nor otherwise exempt) on 25 April 2020 for £200,000. He had purchased the asset in 1979 for £50,000, and its value at 31 March 1982 was £42,000. The chargeable gain on the asset is computed as follows.

	£
Sale proceeds	200,000
31.3.1982 value	(42,000)
Chargeable gain 2020/21	£158,000

Notes

(a) The asset is deemed to have been sold and immediately re-acquired at its market value at 31 March 1982. For capital gains tax purposes (i.e. in relation to disposals by individuals, trustees and personal representatives), this rule (known as 're-basing') applies to all disposals. [*TCGA 1992, s 35(1)(2)*]. See CG15500 and *Simon's Taxes* C2.601.

(b) Exceptions to re-basing apply for the purposes of corporation tax on chargeable gains. See 205.2 below.

205.2 CORPORATION TAX

[*TCGA 1992, s 35, Sch 3*]

(A)

R Ltd purchased a painting on 1 October 1979 for £50,000 (including costs of acquisition) and sold it at auction for £260,000 (net of selling expenses) on 15 August 2020. Its value at 31 March 1982 was £70,000 and the indexation factor for the period March 1982 to December 2017 is 2.501.

205.2 CGT   Assets held on 31 March 1982

	£	£
Net sale proceeds	260,000	260,000
Cost	(50,000)	
Market value 31.3.82		(70,000)
Unindexed gain	210,000	190,000
Indexation allowance £70,000 × 2.501	(175,070)	(175,070)
Gain after indexation	£34,930	£14,930
Chargeable gain		£14,930

Notes

(a) The asset is deemed to have been sold and immediately re-acquired at its market value at 31 March 1982. [*TCGA 1992, s 35(1)(2)*]. See CG15500 and *Simon's Taxes* C2.602.

(b) Re-basing does not apply if it would produce a larger gain or larger loss than would otherwise be the case, nor if it would turn a gain into a loss or vice versa, nor if the disposal would otherwise be a no gain/no loss disposal. [*TCGA 1992, s 35(3)(4)*].

(c) An *irrevocable* election may be made to treat, broadly speaking, *all* assets held on 31 March 1982 as having been sold and re-acquired at their market value on that date, in which case the restrictions in (b) above will not apply. [*TCGA 1992, s 35(5)*]. If the election had been made in this example, the gain would still be £14,930, but there would have been no need to compute the gain by reference to cost and make a comparison with that using re-basing.

There are some minor exclusions from the rule that the election must extend to all assets. [*TCGA 1992, Sch 3 para 7*]. There are also special rules for groups of companies. [*TCGA 1992, Sch 3 paras 8, 9*].

(d) Indexation is automatically based on 31 March 1982 value, without the need to claim such treatment, unless a greater allowance would be produced by reference to cost. [*TCGA 1992, s 55(1)(2)*]. See also **214.1(C)** INDEXATION.

(e) See also **204** ASSETS HELD ON **6** APRIL **1965** for the general application of the re-basing provisions to such assets. See **214.2(A)(C)** INDEXATION for the position as regards an asset acquired by means of a no gain/no loss transfer from a person who held it at 31 March 1982.

(f) For capital gains tax purposes (i.e. in relation to disposals by individuals, trustees and personal representatives), re-basing applies to all disposals with no exceptions. See **205.1** above.

(g) Indexation allowance is frozen at its December 2017 level. No indexation allowance is available in respect of expenditure incurred after 31 December 2017, and for expenditure incurred on or before that date and falling to be deducted on a disposal after that date, indexation allowance is computed up to and including December 2017 only. [*TCGA 1992, ss 53(1)(1B), 54(1B); FA 2018, s 26(2)(3)(6)*]. See **214.1** INDEXATION. See also CG17230 and *Simon's Taxes* C2.301.

Assets held on 31 March 1982   CGT 205.2

(B)

The facts are as in (A) above, except that net sale proceeds amount to £60,000.

	£	£
Net sale proceeds	60,000	60,000
Cost	(50,000)	
Market value 31.3.82		(70,000)
Unindexed gain/(loss)	10,000	(10,000)
Indexation allowance (as in (A)) but restricted to	(10,000)	—
Gain/(loss)	Nil	£(10,000)
Chargeable gain/(allowable loss)	Nil	

Notes

(a) Re-basing does not apply as it cannot disturb a no gain/no loss position. [*TCGA 1992, s 35(3)(c)*].

(b) A universal re-basing election under *TCGA 1992, s 35(5)* would produce an allowable loss of £10,000 (but must extend to all assets). See CG16760 and *Simon's Taxes* C2.604.

(c) See **205.1** above for the application of re-basing for capital gains tax purposes.

(C)

The facts are as in (A) above, except that net sale proceeds amount to £230,000.

	£	£
Net sale proceeds	230,000	230,000
Cost	(50,000)	
Market value 31.3.82		(70,000)
Unindexed gain	180,000	160,000
Indexation allowance (as in (A))	(175,070)	
Indexation allowance (as in (A)) but restricted to		(160,000)
Gain	£4,930	Nil
Chargeable gain/(allowable loss)		Nil

205.2 CGT   Assets held on 31 March 1982

Note

(a) Re-basing applies as it produces a no gain/no loss position compared to a gain otherwise.

(b) Indexation allowance is frozen at its December 2017 level. No indexation allowance is available in respect of expenditure incurred after 31 December 2017, and for expenditure incurred on or before that date and falling to be deducted on a disposal after that date, indexation allowance is computed up to and including December 2017 only. [*TCGA 1992, ss 53(1)(1B), 54(1B); FA 2018, s 26(2)(3)(6)*]. See **214.1** INDEXATION. See also CG17230 and *Simon's Taxes* C2.301.

(D)

A Ltd acquired a holding of D plc quoted shares for £11,000 net in January 1980. At 31 March 1982, their value had fallen to £8,000. On 29 April 2020, A Ltd sold the entire holding for £50,000 net. The indexation factor for the period March 1982 to December 2017 is 2.501.

	£	£
Proceeds	50,000	50,000
Cost	(11,000)	
Market value 31.3.82		(8,000)
Unindexed gain	39,000	42,000
Indexation allowance £11,000 × 2.501	(27,511)	(27,511)
Gain after indexation	£11,489	£14,489
Chargeable gain		£11,489

Notes

(a) Re-basing does not apply as its effect would be to increase a gain.

(b) Indexation is based on cost as that is greater than 31 March 1982 value.

(c) If a universal re-basing election had been made (under *TCGA 1992, s 35(5)*), the chargeable gain would have been £14,489.

(d) Indexation allowance is frozen at its December 2017 level. No indexation allowance is available in respect of expenditure incurred after 31 December 2017, and for expenditure incurred on or before that date and falling to be deducted on a disposal after that date, indexation allowance is computed up to and including December 2017 only. [*TCGA 1992, ss 53(1)(1B), 54(1B); FA 2018, s 26(2)(3)(6)*]. See **214.1** INDEXATION. See also CG17230 and *Simon's Taxes* C2.301.

(E)

C Ltd acquired a holding of E Ltd shares for £14,000 net in January 1980. At 31 March 1982, their value stood at £17,000. C Ltd sold the shares in April 2020 for £10,000 net.

Assets held on 31 March 1982   CGT 205.3

	£	£
Proceeds	10,000	10,000
Cost	(14,000)	
Market value 31.3.82		(17,000)
Unindexed loss (no indexation due)	£(4,000)	£(7,000)
Allowable loss	£(4,000)	

Notes

(a) Re-basing does not apply as its effect would be to increase a loss.

(b) Indexation is not available in either calculation as it cannot increase a loss.

(c) If a universal re-basing election had been made (under *TCGA 1992, s 35(5)*), the allowable loss would have been £7,000, but the election must extend to all assets. See CG16760 and *Simon's Taxes* C2.604.

205.3 DEFERRED CHARGES ON GAINS BEFORE 31 MARCH 1982

[*TCGA 1992, s 36, Sch 4*]

K Ltd, a farming company, purchased farmland for £25,000 in 1975. The company sold the land in August 1984 for £45,000 but purchased further farmland in September 1984 for £50,000 and claimed rollover relief in respect of the disposal of the original farmland. K Ltd sells the replacement farmland in April 2020 for £250,000 and claims relief under *TCGA 1992, Sch 4*. The relevant indexation factors are

March 1982 to August 1984	0.133
September 1984 to December 2017	2.086

The gain on the original farmland is rolled over as follows

	£
Allowable cost	25,000
Indexation allowance £25,000 × 0.133	3,325
	28,325
Actual consideration	45,000
Chargeable gain rolled over	£16,675
Cost of replacement farmland	50,000
Deduct amount rolled over	(16,675)
Deemed allowable cost	£33,325

205.3 CGT Assets held on 31 March 1982

K Ltd's chargeable gain on disposal of the replacement farmland in April 2020 is as follows

	£	£
Proceeds		250,000
Deemed allowable cost	33,325	
Add one-half of rolled-over gain	8,338	
	41,663	
Indexation allowance £41,663 × 2.086	86,909	(128,572)
Chargeable gain		£121,428

Notes

(a) K Ltd cannot benefit from re-basing to 1982 as it did not hold the replacement farmland on 31 March 1982. Instead, the company claims relief under *TCGA 1992, s 36, Sch 4* so that the reduction in the cost of the replacement farmland resulting from the rollover relief on the original farmland is itself reduced by one half. [*TCGA 1992, Sch 4 para 1*]. See *Simon's Taxes* C2.605.

(b) Relief under *TCGA 1992, Sch 4* must be claimed within two years of the end of the accounting period in which the ultimate disposal takes place. [*TCGA 1992, Sch 4 para 9*].

(c) The relief applies only for the purposes of corporation tax on chargeable gains. [*TCGA 1992, s 36, Sch 4 para A1*].

(d) Indexation allowance is frozen at its December 2017 level. No indexation allowance is available in respect of expenditure incurred after 31 December 2017, and for expenditure incurred on or before that date and falling to be deducted on a disposal after that date, indexation allowance is computed up to and including December 2017 only. [*TCGA 1992, ss 53(1)(1B), 54(1B); FA 2018, s 26(2)(3)(6)*]. See **214.1** INDEXATION. See also CG17230 and *Simon's Taxes* C2.301.

(e) For further rollover relief examples, see **226** ROLLOVER RELIEF — REPLACEMENT OF BUSINESS ASSETS.

206 Business Asset Disposal Relief (formerly Entrepreneurs' Relief)

206.1 COMPUTATION OF RELIEF

[*TCGA 1992, ss 169L–169M; FA 2019, s 39, Sch 16 para 2; FA 2020, s 23, Sch 3*]

(A) **Basic computation**

In May 2020, Mr Henry sells his business, Joe's Toys, which he has owned since 1998, to an unrelated party, realising the following chargeable gains and allowable loss.

	Gain/(loss)
	£
Goodwill	700,000
Freehold shop 1	200,000
Freehold shop 2	200,000
Freehold shop 3	(150,000)

Mr Henry claims business asset disposal relief in respect of the sale of the business. He makes no other disposals in 2020/21 and has made no previous claim to business asset disposal relief.

Mr Henry's capital gains tax liability for 2020/21 is calculated as follows.

	£
Gains qualifying for business asset disposal relief	
Goodwill	700,000
Freehold shop 1	200,000
Freehold shop 2	200,000
	1,100,000
Less Loss on freehold shop 3	(150,000)
Deemed chargeable gain qualifying for business asset disposal relief	950,000
Annual exempt amount	(12,300)
Gain chargeable to tax	£937,700
Capital gains tax payable (£937,700 × 10%)	£93,770

Notes

(a) Prior to 2020/21 business asset disposal relief was called entrepreneurs' relief.

(b) Business asset disposal relief can be claimed in respect of 'qualifying business disposals' (as defined in *TCGA 1992, ss 169H–169K*) made on or after 6 April 2008. Relief can also apply to certain chargeable gains deferred before that date which are

206.1 CGT   Business Asset Disposal Relief

deemed to accrue on or after that date — see *FA 2008, Sch 3 paras 7, 8*. The relief applies for capital gains tax purposes only and is not available to companies. Relief is given by deducting the aggregate losses arising on the disposal from the aggregate gains and, where the resulting amount is positive, charging it to tax at 10%. See CG63955 and *Simon's Taxes* C3.1301.

(c) Business asset disposal relief must be claimed on or before the first anniversary of the 31 January following the tax year in which the qualifying business disposal is made. In the case of a disposal of trust business assets, the claim must be made jointly by the trustees and the qualifying beneficiary. [*TCGA 1992, s 169M(1)–(3)*]. Mr Henry must therefore make a claim on or before 31 January 2023. See CG63970 and *Simon's Taxes* C3.1307.

(d) Where a disposal qualifies for both business asset disposal relief and EIS deferral relief or social investment deferral relief, deferral relief can be claimed and business asset disposal relief can then be claimed when the deferred gain comes back into charge on the happening of a chargeable event. [*TCGA 1992, ss 169T–169V*]. See **211.5** below. See *Simon's Taxes* C3.1310.

(e) A disposal of goodwill to a close company (or a non-UK resident company which would be a close company if it were UK-resident) does not qualify for business asset disposal relief if, immediately after the disposal:

- the person making the disposal (P) and any 'relevant connected person' together own 5% or more of the ordinary share capital of the company or of any company in the same group; or

- P and any relevant connected person together hold 5% of the voting rights in the company or in any company in the same group; or

- for disposals on or after 29 October 2018, either:

    (i) P and any relevant connected person together are beneficially entitled to at least 5% of the profits available for distribution to the 'equity holders' of the company and would be beneficially entitled, on a winding up, to at least 5% of the assets of the company available for distribution to the equity holders; or

    (ii) (for disposals on or after 21 December 2018) in the event of a disposal of the whole of the company's ordinary share capital, P and any relevant connected person together would be beneficially entitled to at least 5% of the proceeds.

In determining whether (ii) above applies, it must be assumed that the disposal takes place at the market value of the shares immediately after the disposal, and that the taxpayer is entitled to the proceeds which it would be reasonable to expect him to be entitled to, with regard to all the circumstances at that time. The effect of any avoidance arrangements (i.e. arrangements with a main purpose to secure that any business asset disposal relief provision does or does not apply) is ignored for this purpose.

The exclusion does not, however, apply if P and any relevant connected person dispose of the close company's share capital to another company (company A) so that neither P nor any relevant connected person own any of the ordinary share capital immediately before the end of the period of 28 days beginning with the date of the qualifying business disposal (or such longer period as HMRC allow). If company A is itself a close company (or a non-UK resident company which would be a close company if it were UK-resident), P and any relevant connected person must, immediately before the end of that period, together own less than 5% of the ordinary share capital or voting rights of company A or of any company in the same group. A *'relevant connected person'* means a company connected with P or trustees connected with P.

A disposal of goodwill is also excluded from relief if the person making the disposal is a party to arrangements one of the main purposes of which is to secure that the above exclusion does not apply to the goodwill.

[*TCGA 1992, s 169LA; FA 2016, s 85; FA 2019, Sch 16 paras 2(3), 4*]. See CG64006 and *Simon' Taxes* C3.1302B.

(f) The relief is available where the relevant conditions are met throughout a period of two years (one year for disposals before 6 April 2019 and for later disposals where the business in question ceased before 29 October 2018).

(B) **Lifetime limit**

In August 2020 Mr Robertson sells his entire shareholding in Robbie Ltd, realising a gain of £1,050,000, which qualifies for business asset disposal relief. Mr Robertson makes no other disposals in 2020/21 and has made no previous disposals qualifying for business asset disposal relief. He is an additional rate income tax payer for 2020/21.

Mr Robertson's capital gains tax liability for 2020/21 is calculated as follows.

	£
Deemed chargeable gain qualifying for business asset disposal relief (subject to lifetime limit £1,000,000)	1,050,000
Annual exempt amount	(12,300)
Gain chargeable to tax	£1,037,700
Capital gains tax payable	
£1,000,000 × 10%	100,000
£37,700 × 20%	7,540
	£107,540

Notes

(a) Business asset disposal relief is subject to a lifetime limit which is currently £1 million. For disposals prior to 11 March 2020 the limit was £10 million. The amount to which relief would otherwise apply in respect of a qualifying business disposal is added to any amounts to which relief applied in respect of earlier qualifying business disposals. Where the total exceeds the limit, only so much (if any) of the amount to which relief would otherwise apply in respect of the current disposal as, together with the earlier amounts, does not exceed the limit qualifies for the 10% rate. Any part of the deemed gain excluded by the application of this rule is chargeable at the normal rates of CGT. Where one of the previous lower lifetime limits was exceeded on disposals made before the increases, no further relief can be obtained for those disposals following the increases. Relief can, however, be obtained for qualifying business disposals on or after the dates of increase up to the appropriate new limit. See (D) below.

[*TCGA 1992, s 169N*]. See CG64125 and *Simon's Taxes* C3.1307.

206.1 CGT   Business Asset Disposal Relief

(b)   Three anti-forestalling rules apply to disposals where arrangements were made before 11 March 2020 to circumvent the reduction in the lifetime limit for disposals on or after that date. The effect in each case is to treat a disposal that would otherwise be treated as occurring before 11 March 2020 as occurring on or after that date, so that a lifetime limit of only £1 million is available. [See *FA 2020, Sch 3 paras 2–6*].

(c)   Disposals before 6 April 2008 do not affect the lifetime limit except in the case of deferred gains on which business asset disposal relief is claimed under the transitional rules of *FA 2008, Sch 3 paras 7, 8*.

(d)   The annual exempt amount of £12,300 is allocated against the part of the gain chargeable to tax at 20% as this gives the greater tax saving. [*TCGA 1992, s 1K(5); FA 2019, Sch 1 para 2*]. See CG21610 and *Simon's Taxes* C1.401.

(C)   **Lifetime limit — further example**

In May 2020, Mr Helm sells his entire shareholding in Levon Ltd for £400,000. He had acquired the shares in March 2001 for £150,000 and has been a director of the company since that time. Levon Ltd is a trading company and qualifies as Mr Helm's personal company. He makes no other disposals in 2020/21 and claims business asset disposal relief in respect of the gain on the shares. He has made no previous business asset disposal relief claims.

Mr Helm's capital gains tax liability for 2020/21 is calculated as follows.

	£
Sale proceeds	400,000
Cost	(150,000)
Chargeable gain qualifying for business asset disposal relief	250,000
Annual exempt amount	(12,300)
Gain chargeable to tax 2020/21	£237,700
Capital gains tax payable (£237,700 × 10%)	£23,770

Following the disposal of his shares in Levon Ltd, Mr Helm buys a 25% shareholding in Amy Ltd, another trading company, for £200,000, and starts work as a director of the company. He continues as a director of the company until May 2024 when he sells his entire shareholding for £1,010,000. He claims business asset disposal relief in respect of the disposal. He makes no other disposals in 2024/25, but pays income tax at the additional rate. It is assumed for the purpose of this example only that the annual exempt amount for 2024/25 is £13,000 and the rates of tax remain as for 2020/21.

Mr Helm's capital gains tax liability for 2024/25 is calculated as follows.

	£
Sale proceeds	1,010,000
Cost	(200,000)
Chargeable gain qualifying for business asset disposal relief (subject to lifetime limit £1,000,000)	810,000

Annual exempt amount	(13,000)
Taxable gain 2024/25	£797,000
Capital gains tax payable (note (a))	
£750,000 × 10%	75,000
£47,000 × 20%	9,400
	£84,400

Notes

(a) The lifetime limit applies to restrict the amount of the gain in 2024/25 which qualifies for business asset disposal relief as follows. Of the limit of £1,000,000, £250,000 was used in 2020/21 leaving (£1,000,000 - £250,000 =) £750,000 unused. As the otherwise qualifying gain for 2024/25 is greater than the unused part of the limit, business asset disposal relief is restricted to £750,000.

(b) For a disposal of shares or securities (other than EMI shares — see (c) below) in a company to qualify for business asset disposal relief, the company must be the taxpayer's 'personal company' and must be either a 'trading company' or the 'holding company of a trading group' (both as defined). The taxpayer must be an officer or employee of the company or, where the company is a member of a trading group, of one or more companies which are members of the group. .

An individual's *'personal company'* is a company in which he holds at least 5% of the ordinary share capital (within *ITA 2007, s 989*) and in which, by virtue of that holding:

- he is able to exercise at least 5% of the voting rights by virtue of that holding; and

- for disposals on or after 29 October 2018, either:

    (i) by virtue of that holding, he is beneficially entitled to at least 5% of the profits available for distribution to the 'equity holders' (as defined) of the company and would be beneficially entitled, on a winding up, to at least 5% of the assets of the company available for distribution to the equity holders; or

    (ii) in the event of a disposal of the whole of the company's ordinary share capital, he would be beneficially entitled to at least 5% of the proceeds.

In determining whether (B) above applies at any time in a particular period, it must be assumed that the disposal takes place at that time at the market value of the shares on the final day of the period, and that the taxpayer is entitled to the proceeds which it would be reasonable to expect him to be entitled to, with regard to all the circumstances at that time. The effect of any avoidance arrangements (i.e. arrangements with a main purpose to secure that any business asset disposal relief provision does or does not apply) is ignored for this purpose.

These conditions must be met throughout the two-year period ending with the date of disposal or the two-year period ending with the date on which the company ceases to be a trading company without continuing to be or becoming a member of a trading group or ceases to be a member of a trading group without continuing to be or becoming a trading company. For disposals before 6 April 2019 and for later disposals where the cessation occurs before 29 October 2018, the period throughout which the conditions must be satisfied is only one year.

206.1 CGT   Business Asset Disposal Relief

[*TCGA 1992, ss 169I, 169S(2)–(5); FA 2019, Sch 16 paras 2(4), 4*]. See CG63975 and *Simon's Taxes* C3.1302A, C3.1302B.

See also **206.6** below for the relief available where an individual's interest in a company falls below the 5% threshold as a result of an issue of shares.

(c) A disposal of shares in a company also qualifies for business asset disposal relief if the shares were acquired on or after 6 April 2012 as a result of the exercise of an option under the enterprise management incentives (EMI) scheme and the company is either a 'trading company' or the 'holding company of a trading group' (both as defined). The taxpayer must be an officer or employee of the company or, where the company is a member of a trading group, of one or more companies which are members of the group. These conditions must be met throughout the one-year period ending with the date of disposal (or the one-year period ending with the date, within three years before the disposal, on which the company ceases to be a trading company without continuing to be or becoming a member of a trading group or ceases to be a member of a trading group without continuing to be or becoming a trading company). The taxpayer does not have to have held the shares throughout the one year period, but the EMI option must have been granted on or before the first day of that period. [*TCGA 1992, s 169I*].

(d) The annual exempt amount of £13,000 is allocated against the part of the gain chargeable to tax at 20% as this gives the greater tax saving. [*TCGA 1992, s 1K(5); FA 2019, Sch 1 para 2*]. See CG21610 and *Simon's Taxes* C1.401.

(D) **Change in lifetime limit**

If, in (C) above, Mr Helm's initial gain had been in May 2010 and had been, say, £2,500,000, his entrepreneurs' relief would have been restricted to the then lifetime limit of £2 million. On the disposal in 2024/25 the cumulative total of gains which have obtained relief **exceeds** the lifetime limit (£1 million) at the date of disposal and no further relief can be claimed. Relief in excess of the reduced lifetime limit in respect of the May 2010 disposal is not withdrawn.

206.2 PARTNERSHIPS

[*TCGA 1992, s 169I(8)*]

Martha has been a member of a trading partnership for ten years. In November 2020 she retires from the partnership and sells her interest in the partnership assets to the other partners, realising the following chargeable gains.

	£
Goodwill	100,000
Property	150,000
	£250,000

Martha claims business asset disposal relief in respect of the sale. She makes no other disposals in 2020/21 and has made no previous business asset disposal relief claims.

Business Asset Disposal Relief   CGT 206.3

Martha's capital gains tax liability for 2020/21 is calculated as follows.

	£
Gains qualifying for business asset disposal relief	
Goodwill	100,000
Property	150,000
Deemed chargeable gain qualifying for business asset disposal relief	250,000
Annual exempt amount	(12,300)
Gain chargeable to tax	£237,700
Capital gains tax payable (£237,700 × 10%)	£23,770

Note

(a) A disposal by an individual of the whole or part of his interest in the assets of a partnership is treated for business asset disposal relief purposes as a disposal by him of the whole or part of the partnership business and may therefore be a qualifying business disposal where the necessary conditions are satisfied. [*TCGA 1992, s 169I(8)(b)*]. See CG64040 and *Simon's Taxes* C3.1302C.

206.3 ASSOCIATED DISPOSALS

[*TCGA 1992, ss 169K, 169P; FA 2016, s 84; FA 2019, Sch 16 paras 1(4), 2(2), 4*]

The facts are as in 211.2 above, except that Martha also sells an office which she owns personally and has let to the partnership rent-free since she first purchased it in 2006. The office has been used by the partnership for trade purposes throughout. The chargeable gain on the sale of the office is £56,000 and Martha claims business asset disposal relief.

Martha's capital gains tax liability for 2020/21 is calculated as follows.

	£
Gains qualifying for business asset disposal relief	
Goodwill	100,000
Property	150,000
Office	56,000
Deemed chargeable gain qualifying for business asset disposal relief	306,000
Annual exempt amount	(12,300)
Gain chargeable to tax	£293,700
Capital gains tax payable (£293,700 × 10%)	£29,370

Notes

(a) Where an individual makes a disposal of either all or part of his interest in the assets of a partnership or shares in or securities of a company (or an interest in such shares or securities) which qualifies for business asset disposal relief, an associated disposal of assets owned personally also qualifies for relief. The assets which are disposed of must have been in use for the purposes of the business of the partnership or company (or, where the company is a member of a trading group, the business of a member of the trading group) throughout the two year period (one year for disposals before 6 April 2019 and for later disposals where the business ceases before

206.3 CGT   Business Asset Disposal Relief

29 October 2018) ending with the earlier of the date of the disposal of the partnership assets or shares etc. and the cessation of the business of the partnership or company. The disposal must be made as part of the individual's withdrawal from participation in the business. For disposals of assets acquired on or after 13 June 2016, the disposal must be of an asset or assets which the individual has owned throughout the three years ending with the date of disposal.

Where the disposal of business assets consists of the disposal of all or part of the individual's interest in the assets of a partnership, either:

- the disposed of interest must be at least a 5% interest in the partnership's assets and there must be no 'partnership purchase arrangements' at the date of the disposal; or
- if the disposed of interest is an interest of less than 5%, the individual must have held at least a 5% interest in the partnership's assets for a continuous period of at least three years in the eight years ending on the date of the disposal and there must be no partnership purchase arrangements at the date of the disposal.

For this purpose, *'partnership purchase arrangements'* are arrangements (other than the material disposal) under which the individual or a connected person is entitled to acquire an interest in, or an increased interest in, the partnership (including a share of its profits or assets or an interest in such a share). Arrangements are not, however, partnership purchase arrangements if they were made before both the material disposal and the associated disposal and without regard to either of them.

Where the material disposal of business assets consists of the disposal of shares in a company (or an interest in such shares), all or some of which are ordinary shares, the ordinary shares disposed of must constitute at least 5% of the company's ordinary share capital and be shares in the individual's 'personal company'.

For the meaning of *'personal company'* see note (b) to **206.1(C)** above.

In addition, there must be no 'share purchase arrangements' at the date of the disposal. For this purpose, *'share purchase arrangements'* are arrangements (other than the material disposal) under which the individual or a connected person is entitled to acquire shares or securities in the company or a company which is a member of the same trading group. Arrangements are not, however, share purchase arrangements if they were made before both the material disposal and the associated disposal and without regard to either of them. Two companies are treated as members of the same trading group if, at the date of the disposal, arrangements exist which it is reasonable to assume will result in them becoming such members. This requirement is not met if the disposal of shares is a deemed disposal in consideration of a capital distribution within *TCGA 1992, s 122* other than one made in the course of dissolving or winding up the company.

[*TCGA 1992, s 169K; FA 2016, s 84; FA 2019, Sch 16 paras 1(4), 2(2), 4*]. See CG63995, CG63996 and *Simon's Taxes* C3.1305.

(b) Business asset disposal relief in respect of an associated disposal is restricted where the assets were in use for the purposes of the business only for part of the period of ownership; where only part of the assets are in use for business purposes for that period; where the individual is concerned in carrying on the business (personally, in partnership or as an officer or employee of his personal company) for only part of the period in which the assets are in use for the purposes of the business; and where, for any part of the period for which the assets are in use for the purposes of the business (but ignoring any part of the period which falls before 6 April 2008), their

206.4 REORGANISATIONS ETC.

[*TCGA 1992, s 169Q*]

Mr Prosser is a shareholder in Oyster Ltd, a trading company which qualifies as his personal company for the purposes of business asset disposal relief. He acquired the shares in March 2002 for £150,000 and has been a director of the company since that time. In January 2021, the shareholders of Oyster Ltd accept an offer by a public company, Lobster plc, and Mr Prosser receives shares in Lobster plc in exchange for his entire shareholding in Oyster Ltd. His Lobster plc shares are valued at £550,000 at the time of the exchange, and the company does not qualify as his personal company. Mr Prosser makes no other disposals in 2020/21 and has made no previous claims to business asset disposal relief.

If Mr Prosser elects under *TCGA 1992, s 169Q* to disapply *TCGA 1992, s 127* in respect of the share exchange and claims business asset disposal relief in respect of the gain on the Oyster Ltd shares, his capital gains tax liability for 2020/21 is calculated as follows.

	£
Sale proceeds	550,000
Cost	(150,000)
Chargeable gain qualifying for business asset disposal relief	400,000
Annual exempt amount	(12,300)
Gain chargeable to tax	£387,700
Capital gains tax payable (£387,700 × 10%)	38,770

Notes

(a) Where an exchange of securities (within *TCGA 1992, s 135*) takes place and *TCGA 1992, s 127* would otherwise apply to treat the 'original shares' and the 'new holding' (as defined for the purposes of that section) as the same asset, an election can be made to disapply that section so that business asset disposal relief can be claimed in respect of the disposal of the original shares. See CG52523 and *Simon's Taxes* C3.1308.

(b) The election must be made on or before the first anniversary of the 31 January following the tax year in which the reorganisation takes place. In this case, therefore, the claim must be made by 31 January 2023 (which is the same date by which the claim to business asset disposal relief must be made). An election takes effect only where a claim to business asset disposal relief is also made; without such a claim, the election has no effect.

(c) Mr Prosser cannot claim business asset disposal relief on an eventual disposal of his shares in Lobster plc. If he had not made an election under *TCGA 1992, s 169Q* the opportunity to claim relief would have been lost. See CG64155 and *Simon's Taxes* C3.1308.

(d) The above provisions apply also to reorganisations within *TCGA 1992, s 126* and to schemes of reconstruction within *TCGA 1992, s 136* to which *TCGA 1992, s 127* applies. See CG51745 and *Simon's Taxes* D6.102, D6.202.

206.4 CGT Business Asset Disposal Relief

(e) An anti-forestalling rules applies where there is a reorganisation on or after 6 April 2019 and before 11 March 2020. If an election under the above provisions is made on or after 11 March 2020 in respect of such a reorganisation, the disposal is treated as taking place when the election is made rather than at the time of the reorganisation. The effect is to treat a disposal that would otherwise be treated as occurring before 11 March 2020 as occurring on or after that date, so that a lifetime limit of only £1 million is available. [*FA 2020, Sch 3 para 4*].

206.5 DEFERRED GAINS

[*TCGA 1992, ss 169T–169V*]

In May 2002, Charlotte sells her entire shareholding in Gochenauer Ltd, realising a gain of £137,000. The gain qualifies for business asset disposal relief. In August 2020, Charlotte acquires by subscription 51% of the issued ordinary share capital of Thorn Ltd for £137,000. This is a qualifying investment for the purposes of EIS deferral relief and Charlotte makes a claim to defer the whole of the May 2020 gain.

On 1 May 2024, Charlotte sells her shares in Thorn Ltd, realising a chargeable gain of £80,000, which qualifies for business asset disposal relief. She makes no other disposals in 2024/25 and has made no previous business asset disposal relief claims.

If Charlotte claims business asset disposal relief in respect of both the deferred May 2020 gain and the May 2024 gain, her CGT position for 2024/25 as follows. It is assumed that the annual exempt amount for 2024/25 is £13,000.

	£
Deferred May 2020 gain brought into charge	137,000
May 2024 gain	80,000
Chargeable gains qualifying for business asset disposal relief	217,000
Annual exempt amount	(13,000)
Gain chargeable to tax	£204,000
Capital gains tax payable (£204,000 × 10%)	£20,400

Notes

(a) Where a disposal qualifies for both business asset disposal relief and EIS deferral relief or social investment deferral relief, deferral relief can be claimed and business asset disposal relief can then be claimed when the deferred gain comes back into charge on the happening of a chargeable event. A claim for relief must be made on or before the first anniversary of 31 January following the tax year in which the deferred gain comes back into charge. [*TCGA 1992, ss 169T–169V*]. See *Simon's Taxes* C3.1310.

(b) See **211.3 ENTERPRISE INVESTMENT SCHEME** for a further example of EIS deferral relief.

206.6 RELIEF WHERE SHAREHOLDING IN PERSONAL COMPANY DILUTED BY SHARE ISSUE

[*TCGA 1992, ss 169SB–169SH; FA 2019, Sch 16 paras 3, 4*]

Business Asset Disposal Relief   CGT 206.6

Issey owns 100 shares in Westall Ltd, representing 5% of the issued share capital, which she subscribed for in January 2011 for £100. Throughout the period from January 2011 to 1 February 2021, the company is Issey's personal company but, on the latter date, the company issues 1,000 new shares to an outside investor; as a result Issey's shareholding falls below the 5% threshold and Westall Ltd ceases to be her personal company. The 'relevant value' of Issey's shares on 1 February 2021 is £1,000,000. Issey sells her entire shareholding on 30 November 2023 for £1,500,000. Issey makes no other disposals.

Following the issue of shares to the outside investor on 1 February 2021, Westall Ltd is no longer Issey's personal company and so the gain on the disposal of the shares on 30 November 2023 will not qualify for business asset disposal relief.

If Issey makes an election under *TCGA 1992, s 169SC* by 31 January 2023 she is deemed to have disposed and immediately reacquired her shares on 1 February 2021 and to have realised a chargeable gain as follows.

	£
Relevant value of shares	1,000,000
Cost	(100)
Chargeable gain qualifying for business asset disposal relief	999,000
Annual exempt amount	(12,300)
Gain chargeable to tax 2020/21	£986,700
Capital gains tax payable (£986,700 × 10%)	£98,670

If Issey then makes an election under *TCGA 1992, s 169SD* by 5 April 2025 the deemed gain is deferred until she disposes of the shares on 30 November 2023. The deemed gain is brought back into charge and, if Issey makes a claim by 31 January 2026, qualifies for business asset disposal relief. Issey's capital gains tax liability for 2023/24 is then as follows.

Gain on disposal of shares

	£
Relevant value of shares	1,500,000
Cost (relevant value on 1 February 2021)	(1,000,000)
Chargeable gain	500,000
Deferred February 2021 gain brought into charge	999,000
	1,499,000
Annual exempt amount (say)	(12,300)
Gains chargeable to tax 2023/24	£1,486,700
Capital gains tax payable:	
£999,000 × 10%	99,900
487,700 × 20%	97,540
	£197,440

206.6 CGT Business Asset Disposal Relief

Notes

(a) An individual can make an election under *TCGA 1992, s 169SC* where, as a result of an issue on or after 6 April 2019 of shares by a company for consideration wholly in cash, the company ceases to be his personal company. The shares must be subscribed and issued for genuine commercial reasons and not as part of arrangements to secure a tax advantage (as defined) for any person. An election can only be made if a disposal of all the individual's shares and/or securities in the company immediately before the share issue at their 'relevant value' would have been a material disposal of business assets resulting in a single chargeable gain qualifying for business asset disposal relief (the '*notional gain*').

Where such an election is made, the individual is treated for CGT purposes as having disposed of all of his shares or securities in the company immediately before the share issue and having reacquired them immediately afterwards at their relevant value. The effect of the election is therefore to trigger a chargeable gain, equal to the notional gain, which qualifies for business asset disposal relief.

For a deemed disposal of shares, the '*relevant value*' is the amount that would be apportioned to the shares on a sale of the entire issued share capital at market value immediately before the share issue. Otherwise, the relevant value is the market value of the asset at the time of the share issue.

[*TCGA 1992, s 169SC; FA 2019, Sch 16 paras 3, 4*]. See *Simon's Taxes* C3.1302A.

(b) Where an individual makes an election under *TCGA 1992, s 169SC*, an additional election may be made so that no chargeable gain or allowable loss is treated as arising on the deemed disposal but instead all or part of the notional gain is deferred and treated as arising when the individual subsequently disposes of the shares or securities. The gain is in addition to any actual gain or loss arising on the disposal. If only some of the shares or securities are disposed of there are rules to determine how much of the notional gain is brought back into charge. [*TCGA 1992, s 169SD; FA 2019, Sch 16 paras 3, 4*]. See *Simon's Taxes* C3.1302A.

(c) An election for a deemed disposal of shares or securities must be made on or before the first anniversary of 31 January following the tax year in which the deemed disposal is made. An election to defer the gain until the shares or securities are disposed of must be made within four years of the end of that tax year. Both elections are irrevocable. Where an election to defer the deemed gain has been made, the taxpayer must make a claim for entrepreneurs' relief on or before the first anniversary of 31 January following the first tax year in which the gain is brought into charge. Relief is then given as if the gain arises from a qualifying business disposal made when the gain is brought into charge. Where only a part of the gain is brought back into charge, relief for subsequent gains is similarly given as if they arose from a qualifying business disposal made when they are brought back into charge. In either case, the company is deemed to be the taxpayer's personal company throughout the two years ending with the time the gain is brought into charge. [*TCGA 1992, ss 169SG, 169SH; FA 2019, Sch 16 paras 3, 4*]. See *Simon's Taxes* C3.1302A.

(d) For the meaning of 'personal company' see note (b) to **206.1(C)** above.

207 Capital Sums Derived from Assets

207.1 GENERAL

[*TCGA 1992, s 22(1)*]

A Ltd holds the remainder of a 99-year lease of land, under which it has mineral rights. The lease, which commenced in 2002, was acquired in April 2011 by assignment for £80,000. Following a proposal to extract minerals, the freeholder pays A Ltd £100,000 in June 2020 in consideration of relinquishing the mineral rights, in order to prevent such development. The value of the lease after the alteration is £150,000.

	£
Disposal proceeds	100,000
Allowable cost $\dfrac{100,000}{100,000 + 150,000} \times £80,000$	(32,000)
Gain subject to indexation from April 2011 to December 2017	£68,000

207.2 DEFERRED CONSIDERATION

Z owns 2,000 £1 ordinary shares in B Ltd, for which he subscribed at par in August 2005. On 31 March 2016, he and the other shareholders in B Ltd sold their shares to another company for £10 per share plus a further unquantified cash amount calculated by means of a formula relating to the future profits of B Ltd. The value in March 2016 of the deferred consideration was estimated at £2 per share. On 30 April 2020, Z receives a further £4.20 per share under the sale agreement.

2015/16

		£	£
Disposal proceeds	2,000 at £10	20,000	
Value of rights	2,000 at £2	4,000	24,000
Cost of acquisition			(2,000)
Chargeable gain			£22,000

2020/21

	£
Disposal of rights to deferred consideration	
Proceeds 2,000 × £4.20	8,400
Deemed cost of acquiring rights	(4,000)
Chargeable gain	£4,400

207.2 CGT   Capital Sums Derived from Assets

Notes

(a) A right to unquantified and contingent future consideration on the disposal of an asset is itself an asset, and the future consideration when received is a capital sum derived from that asset (*Marren v Ingles* HL 1980, 54 TC 76 and *Marson v Marriage* Ch D 1979, 54 TC 59).

(b) See **229.4 SHARES AND SECURITIES** for the position where deferred consideration is to be satisfied in shares and/or debentures in the acquiring company.

(c) See also **217.4 LOSSES** for the election to treat a loss on disposal of a right to deferred unascertainable consideration as accruing in an earlier year.

207.3 RECEIPT OF COMPENSATION

[*TCGA 1992, ss 22, 23*]

(A)

C owns a freehold warehouse which is badly damaged by fire as a result of inflammable goods having been inadequately packaged. The value of the warehouse after the fire is £90,000, and it cost £120,000 in 1998. The owner of the goods is held liable for the damage and pays C £60,000 compensation in October 2020.

		£
Disposal proceeds		60,000
Allowable cost $\dfrac{60,000}{60,000 + 90,000} \times £120,000$		(48,000)
Chargeable gain 2020/21		£12,000

(B) Restoration using insurance moneys

A diamond necklace owned by D cost £100,000 in 2009. D is involved in a motor accident in which the necklace is damaged. Its value is reduced to £80,000. D receives £40,000 under an insurance policy in May 2020 and spends £45,000 on having the necklace restored.

(i) *No claim under TCGA 1992, s 23*

		£
Disposal proceeds		40,000
Allowable cost $\dfrac{40,000}{40,000 + 80,000} \times £100,000$		(33,333)
Chargeable gain 2020/21		£6,667
Allowable cost in relation to subsequent disposal		
£100,000 − £33,333 + £45,000		£111,667

(ii) *Claim under TCGA 1992, s 23*

No chargeable gain arises in 2020/21	
Allowable cost originally	100,000
Deduct Amount received on claim	(40,000)
	60,000
Add Expenditure on restoration	45,000
Allowable cost in relation to subsequent disposal	£105,000

(C) **Part application of capital sum received**

E Ltd is the owner of a large estate consisting mainly of parkland which it acquired for £150,000 in August 1997. It grants a one-year licence in August 2020 to an exploration company to prospect for minerals, in consideration for a capital sum of £50,000. The exploration proves unsuccessful and on expiry of the licence E Ltd spends £20,000 on restoration of the drilling sites to their former state. The market value of the estate after granting the licence is £350,000, and it is £400,000 after restoration.

(i) *No claim under TCGA 1992, s 23(3)*

	£
Disposal proceeds	50,000
Deduct Allowable cost $\dfrac{50,000}{50,000 + 350,000} \times £150,000$	(18,750)
Gain subject to indexation from August 1997 to December 2017	£31,250
Allowable expenditure remaining	
£150,000 − £18,750 + £20,000	£151,250

(ii) *Claim made under TCGA 1992, s 23(3)*

	£
Deemed disposal proceeds (£50,000 − £20,000)	30,000
Deduct	
Allowable cost $\dfrac{30,000}{30,000 + 400,000} \times £(150,000 + 20,000)$	(11,860)
Gain subject to indexation to December 2017	£18,140
Allowable expenditure remaining	
£150,000 − £20,000 − £11,860 + £20,000	£138,140

207.3 CGT   Capital Sums Derived from Assets

Notes

(a) Indexation allowance is frozen at its December 2017 level. No indexation allowance is available in respect of expenditure incurred after 31 December 2017, and for expenditure incurred on or before that date and falling to be deducted on a disposal after that date, indexation allowance must be computed up to and including December 2017 only. [*TCGA 1992, ss 53(1)(1B), 54(1B); FA 2018, s 26(2)(3)(6)*]. See **214.1** INDEXATION.

(b) See also CG17230 and *Simon's Taxes* C2.301.

(D) **Capital sum exceeding allowable expenditure**

F inherited a painting in 1980 when it was valued at £2,000. Its value at 31 March 1982 was £3,000. In March 1988, by which time its value had increased considerably, the painting suffered damage whilst on loan to an art gallery and F received £10,000 compensation. The value of the painting was then £30,000. It then cost F £9,800 to have the painting restored. In June 2020, he sells the painting for £50,000.

(i) *No election under TCGA 1992, s 23(2)*

	£
Disposal proceeds March 1988	10,000
Allowable cost $\dfrac{10,000}{10,000 + 30,000} \times £2,000$	(500)
Gain subject to indexation 1987/88	£9,500
Allowable cost in relation to subsequent disposal	
£2,000 − £500 + £9,800	£11,300

	£
Disposal proceeds June 2020	50,000
Allowable cost with re-basing	
$£3,000 \times \dfrac{30,000}{10,000 + 30,000} = £2,250 + £9,800$	(12,050)
Chargeable gain 2020/21	£37,950

(ii) *Election under TCGA 1992, s 23(2)*

	£
Disposal proceeds March 1988	10,000
Less allowable expenditure	(2,000)
Gain subject to indexation 1987/88	£8,000
Allowable cost in relation to subsequent disposal	
£2,000 − £2,000 + £9,800	£9,800

Capital Sums Derived from Assets   CGT 207.3

	£
Disposal proceeds June 2020	50,000
Allowable cost with re-basing (note (b))	
£3,000 − £2,000 + £9,800	(10,800)
Chargeable gain 2020/21	£39,200

Notes

(a) For capital gains tax purposes (i.e. in relation to disposals by individuals, trustees and personal representatives), re-basing applies to all disposals with no exceptions. See **205.1 ASSETS HELD ON 31 MARCH 1982**.

(b) Where there is a disposal after 5 April 1989 to which re-basing applies and, if re-basing had not applied, the allowable expenditure would have fallen to be reduced under *TCGA 1992, s 23(2)* by reference to a capital sum received after 31 March 1982 but before 6 April 1988, the 31 March 1982 value is reduced by the amount previously allowed against the capital sum. [*TCGA 1992, Sch 3 para 4(2)*]. See *Simon's Taxes* C2.606.

208 Companies

Cross-references. See also **CT 103** CAPITAL GAINS.

208.1 BASIC COMPUTATION

A company, Crow Ltd, has an accounting date of 30 June. Crow Ltd acquired an asset in November 1988 for £28,000 and sells the asset on 11 June 2020 for £99,000. The company incurs allowable sale costs of £5,000. It makes no other disposals in the year ended 30 June 2020. The indexation factor for the period November 1988 to December 2017 is 1.528. The company's taxable gain for the accounting period ended 30 June 2020 is as follows.

	£
Sale consideration	99,000
Less costs of sale	(5,000)
Cost of asset	(28,000)
Unindexed gain	66,000
Less indexation allowance £28,000 × 1.528	(42,784)
Chargeable (and taxable) gain	£23,216

Notes

(a) Companies do not pay capital gains tax. Instead they pay corporation tax on their chargeable gains. Gains are included in a company's profits liable to corporation tax and taxed at the applicable rate. [*TCGA 1992, s 2A; CTA 2009, s 2; FA 2019, Sch 1 para 2*]. For disposals before 6 April 2019, there were two exceptions to the rule that companies do not pay capital gains tax; the capital gains tax charge on high value disposals of dwellings subject to the annual tax on enveloped dwellings under *TCGA 1992, ss 2B–2F* and the non-resident capital gains tax charge on disposals of UK residential property interests under *TCGA 1992, ss 14B–14H*. For later disposals the charge on high value disposals of dwellings is abolished and the charge on UK residential property interests is replaced by the corporation tax charge on disposals by non-resident companies of direct and indirect interests in UK land under *TCGA 1992, s 2B(4)*. See *Simon's Taxes* B6.701, C2.1131.

(b) Chargeable gains and allowable losses are nevertheless computed according to capital gains tax principles, although there are now many important differences in the computational rules. The main differences are as follows.

    (i) Computations are made by reference to accounting periods instead of tax years. [*TCGA 1992, s 2A(1); FA 2019, Sch 1 para 2*].

    (ii) Re-basing to market value at 31 March 1982 applies to individuals etc. automatically and without any exceptions for disposals on or after 6 April 2008, but the exceptions continue to apply to companies (see **205** ASSETS HELD ON **31 MARCH 1982**). The rules for ASSETS HELD ON **6 APRIL 1965 (204)** therefore apply only to companies.

    (iii) Special provisions apply to tax as income gains and losses in respect of loan relationships, derivative contracts and intangible assets (see **CT 108** INTANGIBLE ASSETS and **CT 113** LOAN RELATIONSHIPS).

208.1 CGT Companies

    (iv)   BUSINESS ASSET DISPOSAL RELIEF (**206**) (formerly entrepreneurs' relief) applies to qualifying business disposals by individuals, etc., but not by companies.

    (v)   INVESTORS' RELIEF (**215**) applies to qualifying disposals of shares by individuals, etc., but not by companies.

    (vi)   Indexation allowance is available to companies (see **214** INDEXATION) but is frozen at its December 2017 level. No indexation allowance is available in respect of expenditure incurred after 31 December 2017, and for expenditure incurred on or before that date and falling to be deducted on a disposal after that date, indexation allowance is computed up to and including December 2017 only. [*TCGA 1992, ss 53(1)(1B), 54(1B); FA 2018, s 26(2)(3)(6)*]. See CG17230 and *Simon's Taxes* C2.301.

    (vii)   The rules for matching shares and securities sold with those acquired are not the same for corporation tax as for capital gains tax (see **230.2** SHARES AND SECURITIES — IDENTIFICATION RULES).

208.2 CAPITAL LOSSES

P Ltd, which makes up accounts to 30 June annually, changes its accounting date to 31 December. It makes up 18-month accounts to 31 December 2020, and its chargeable gains and allowable losses are as follows

	Gains/(losses) £
31.7.19	4,600
19.10.19	11,500
1.12.19	3,500
28.3.20	(8,300)
21.7.20	8,500
1.9.20	(25,000)
20.12.20	7,000

The period of account is split into two accounting periods

1.7.19 – 30.6.20	
Net chargeable gain	£11,300
1.7.20 – 31.12.20	
Net allowable loss	£9,500

Notes

(a)   The loss cannot be set off against the £11,300 net gain in the earlier accounting period (but *can* be carried forward against subsequent gains).

(b)   A loss accruing to a company is not an allowable loss if it arises directly or indirectly in consequence of, or otherwise in connection with, any arrangements one of the main purposes of which is to secure a tax advantage. [*TCGA 1992, s 16A*]. See CG15835 and *Simon's Taxes* C4.227.

(c)   For a further example, see CT **103.1** CAPITAL GAINS.

(d) See 208.3 below for the restriction on deduction of carried-forward capital losses.

208.3 CORPORATE CAPITAL LOSS RESTRICTION

ABC Ltd, which is not a member of a group, has a 31 March year end. At 1 April 2020, it has an allowable capital loss brought forward of £8 million. Its profits for the year ended 31 March 2021 are as follows:

	£'000
Trading profits	3,000
Chargeable gains	6,000
Total	£9,000

ABC Ltd taxable total profits for the year ended 31 March 2021 will be as follows:

	£'000
Trading profits	3,000
Capital gains	6,000
Less loss brought forward from y/e 31.3.20 (restricted)	(5,500)
TTP	3,500

The restriction on the set-off of the carried-forward loss against profits for the year ending 31 March 2021 is calculated as follows.

	£'000
Qualifying chargeable gains	6,000
Less deductions allowance	(5,000)
Relevant chargeable gains	£1,000
Relevant chargeable gains × 50%	500
Add deductions allowance	5,000
Maximum set-off	£5,500

Losses Summary:

	£'000
Capital losses b/fwd	8,000
Current year setoff	(5,500)
Capital losses c/fwd	£2,500

Notes

(a) *FA 2020* introduced provisions extending the existing restriction on the deduction of carried-forward losses (*CTA 2010, ss 269ZA–269ZZB*) to allowable capital losses for accounting periods beginning on or after 1 April 2020 (subject to transitional rules for accounting periods straddling that date). Broadly, the restriction limits the

208.3 CGT Companies

amount of profits against which any carried-forward losses can be relieved to 50% of profits over an annual 'deductions allowance' of £5 million. A single £5 million limit is shared between all of the members of a group, but can be allocated to each company as the group sees fit.

(b) This example illustrates a simple case where the only losses carried forward are allowable capital losses. Where a company or group has carried forward losses of different types, the provisions operate by separating the losses between those which can be set off against total profits, profits of the same trade, non-trading income profits or chargeable gains and applying a maximum deduction in each case. A company can choose how to allocate its deductions allowance to each category by dividing it up and specifying the amount of a trading profits deductions allowance, a chargeable gains deductions allowance and so on. ABC Ltd allocates its entire deductions allowance of £5 million to chargeable gains. For the application of the corporate loss restriction generally see CT **114.7**.

(c) The basic rule is that the maximum offset of brought forward allowable capital losses is the chargeable gains deductions allowance (£5 million) plus 50% of the relevant chargeable gains of £1 million. Therefore, the maximum offset is capped at £5 million plus 50% of £1 million = £500,000. This gives a maximum offset of brought forward losses of £5.5 million. [*CTA 2010, s 269ZBA; FA 2020, Sch 4 para 2*].

209 Computation of Gains and Losses

209.1 ALLOWABLE AND NON-ALLOWABLE EXPENDITURE

(A) **Allowable expenditure**

[*TCGA 1992, s 38*]

In 2020/21 T sold a house which he had owned since 1994 and which was let throughout the period of ownership (other than as furnished holiday accommodation). The house cost £34,000, with legal costs of £900, in June 1994. T spent £2,000 on initial dilapidations in July 1994. In November 2001, he added an extension at a cost of £5,500 for which he received a local authority grant of £2,500 on completion. Legal costs of £500 were incurred on obtaining vacant possession at the end of the final tenancy in May 2020. The sale proceeds were £170,000 before deducting incidental costs (including valuation fees) of £1,200.

		£	£	£
Sale proceeds			170,000	
Deduct Costs of sale			(1,200)	168,800
Cost of house			34,000	
Add Incidental costs of purchase			900	
			34,900	
Improvement costs:				
Initial dilapidations	(note (a))	2,000		
Extension, less grant		3,000	5,000	
Cost of obtaining vacant possession				
(enhancement cost)			500	(40,400)
Chargeable gain 2020/21				£128,400

Note

(a) It is assumed that the cost of the initial dilapidations were disallowed for income tax purposes under the rule in *Law Shipping Co Ltd v CIR, CS 1923, 12 TC 621*. If any of the expenditure had been so allowed, a deduction would to that extent be precluded as an allowable deduction for CGT purposes by *TCGA 1992, s 39*. See CG14305 and *Simon's Taxes* C2.215.

(B) **Non-allowable expenditure — capital allowances**

[*TCGA 1992, s 41*]

209.1 CGT Computation of Gains and Losses

S Ltd purchased an item of plant and machinery in March 2016 for £90,000. In April 2021, the company sold the asset for £10,000. Annual investment allowance of £90,000 had been given in respect of the asset and a disposal value of £10,000 was added to the main pool in April 2021. S Ltd's capital gains computation is as follows.

	£	£
Disposal consideration		10,000
Allowable cost	90,000	
Deduct net allowances given (£90,000 – £10,000)	80,000	(10,000)
Chargeable gain		£Nil

Note

(a) Where a loss would otherwise be shown, expenditure otherwise allowable as a deduction is reduced to the extent that capital allowances have been made in respect of it. The capital allowances taken into account are those granted (less any balancing charge) to the disposer. Structures and buildings allowances are, however, excluded from the definition of capital allowances for this purpose. Where the loss-making disposal is of plant or machinery in relation to expenditure on which allowances or charges have been made for capital allowance purposes and which has been used solely for trade purposes and has not attracted partial depreciation subsidies which would deny capital allowances, the capital allowances (if any) are deemed to be the difference between the qualifying expenditure incurred (or treated as incurred) by the disposer, and the disposal value. See also CG15400 onwards and *Simon's Taxes* C2.217.

(C) **Enhancement expenditure**

[*TCGA 1992, s 38*]

Mr Hopkins bought a second home in August 1978 for £15,000. Mr Hopkins' neighbour, Mr Douglas, claimed that part of the garden of the house belonged to him. Mr Hopkins won the court case resulting, but incurred legal fees of £5,000 in September 1985.

In 2000 Mr Hopkins had a tennis court built for £5,000, but this was demolished in 2007.

Mr Hopkins sold the house in November 2020 for £126,000. It was agreed that the value of the house at 31 March 1982 was £25,000. The house has never been treated as Mr Hopkins' main residence.

The chargeable gain is as follows.

	£
Sale consideration	126,000
Less 31 March 1982 value	(25,000)
Legal fees re boundary dispute	(5,000)
Chargeable gain	£96,000

Notes

(a) The expenditure on the tennis court in 2000 is not allowable as it is not reflected in the state or nature of the asset at the time of disposal in November 2020 as required by *TCGA 1992, s 38(1)(b)*. HMRC consider that the demolition of the tennis court is not a deemed disposal within *TCGA 1992, s 24(1)* as it is not the 'entire loss, destruction, dissipation or extinction' of an asset because it is not an 'asset': it is only part of an asset, the land. See CG15190 and *Simon's Taxes* C1.320.

(b) Expenditure wholly and exclusively incurred in establishing, preserving or defending title to, or to a right over, an asset is allowable expenditure. [*TCGA 1992, s 38(1)(b)*]. See CG15180–CG15230 and *Simon's Taxes* C2.206, C2.207.

(c) Where a person makes a disposal of UK residential property on which a chargeable gain arises on or after 6 April 2020, that person must make a return to HMRC in respect of the disposal on or before the 30th day following the day of the completion of the disposal (and, where appropriate, make a payment on account of CGT). The requirements also apply to any direct or indirect disposal of UK land on or after 6 April 2019 by a non-resident or in the overseas part of a split tax year, whether or not a gain is made. See *FA 2019, Sch 2*.

209.2 PART DISPOSALS

[*TCGA 1992, s 42*]

Note

See also **216.1 LAND** for small part disposals of land.

(A)

T purchased a 300-acre estate in March 1988 for £1m plus legal and other costs of £50,000. In January 1991 he spent £47,000 on improvements to the main house on the estate (not his main residence), which he sells in September 2020 for £660,000. The costs of sale are £40,000. The value of the remaining land is £2.34m.

	£	£
Sale proceeds		660,000
Deduct incidental costs		(40,000)
		620,000
Cost £1,050,000 × $\frac{660,000}{660,000 + 2,340,000}$	231,000	
Improvement costs	47,000	(278,000)
Chargeable gain		£342,000

Notes

(a) The improvements expenditure is not apportioned as it relates entirely to the part of the estate being sold. [*TCGA 1992, s 42(4)*]. See CG15430 and *Simon's Taxes* C2.402, C2.403.

209.2 CGT   Computation of Gains and Losses

(b) Where a person makes a disposal which includes UK residential property on which a chargeable gain arises on or after 6 April 2020, that person must make a return to HMRC in respect of the disposal on or before the 30th day following the day of the completion of the disposal (and, where appropriate, make a payment on account of CGT). The requirements also apply to any direct or indirect disposal of UK land on or after 6 April 2019 by a non-resident or in the overseas part of a split tax year, whether or not a gain is made. See *FA 2019, Sch 2*.

(B)

U inherited some land at a probate value of £500,000 in November 1981. Its market value at 31 March 1982 was £540,000. In November 1987, he sold part of the land for £240,000, the remaining land then being worth £480,000. He sells the remaining land in April 2020 for £600,000.

The gain, subject to indexation, on the part disposal in November 1987 is

	£
Proceeds	240,000
Cost £500,000 × $\dfrac{240,000}{240,000 + 480,000}$	(166,667)
Gain subject to indexation	£73,333

The gain on the disposal in April 2020 is

	£
Proceeds	600,000
Market value 31.3.82	
£540,000 × $\dfrac{480,000}{240,000 + 480,000}$	(360,000)
Chargeable gain	£240,000

Notes

(a) Where re-basing applies and there has been a part disposal after 31 March 1982 and before 6 April 1988, the proportion of 31 March 1982 value to be brought into account on the ultimate disposal is the same as the proportion of cost not allowed on the part disposal, as if the re-basing provisions had applied to the part disposal. [*TCGA 1992, Sch 3 para 4(1)*]. See CG16940 and *Simon's Taxes* C2.606.

(b) For capital gains tax purposes (i.e. in relation to disposals by individuals, trustees and personal representatives), re-basing applies to all disposals with no exceptions. See **205.1 ASSETS HELD ON 31 MARCH 1982**.

Computation of Gains and Losses CGT 209.2

(C)

V bought the film rights of a novel for £50,000 in May 2014. A one-third share of the rights was sold to W Ltd in March 2015 for £20,000, when the rights retained had a value of £45,000. In December 2020, V's rights were sold to a film company for £100,000 plus a right to royalties, such right being estimated to be worth £150,000.

	£
March 2015	
Sale proceeds	20,000
Cost £50,000 × $\dfrac{20,000}{20,000 + 45,000}$	(15,385)
Chargeable gain 2014/15	4,615

	£
December 2020	
Sale proceeds (£100,000 + £150,000)	250,000
Cost (£50,000 − £15,385)	(34,615)
Chargeable gain 2020/21	£215,385

Note

(a) The right to royalties is itself an asset and could be the subject of a future disposal by V. See **207.2** CAPITAL SUMS DERIVED FROM ASSETS and, where applicable, **232** WASTING ASSETS.

(D)

C inherited land valued at £72,000 in May 1989. He granted rights of way over the land to a neighbouring landowner in March 1994, in consideration for a parcel of land adjacent to his, valued at £21,000. The value of the original land, subject to the right of way, was then £147,000. In March 2021, C sold the whole of the land for £170,000.

Indexation factor May 1989 to March 1994	0.239

	£
Part disposal in March 1994	
Disposal consideration	21,000
Allowable expenditure	
$\dfrac{21,000}{21,000 + 147,000} \times £72,000$	(9,000)
Unindexed gain	12,000
Indexation allowance £9,000 × 0.239	(2,151)
Chargeable gain 1993/94	£9,849

413

209.2 CGT Computation of Gains and Losses

Disposal in March 2021		£
Disposal consideration		170,000
Deduct Original land £(72,000 − 9,000)	63,000	
Addition	21,000	(84,000)
Chargeable gain 2020/21		£86,000

Notes

(a) It is assumed that the additional land is merged with the existing land to give a single asset.

(b) A claim under *TCGA 1992, s 242* (small part disposals of land — see **216.1** LAND) could not be made in respect of the March 1994 part disposal as the consideration exceeded £20,000. See CG71870 and *Simon's Taxes* C2.1103.

210 Double Tax Relief

210.1 RELIEF BY CREDIT

[*TIOPA 2010, ss 18–41*]

Lyra, a higher rate income tax payer, has the following chargeable gains for 2020/21.

UK gain	£30,800	
Foreign gain	£16,000	(Foreign tax £6,400)

Neither gain is an upper rate gain. Lyra claims credit relief for the foreign tax paid. Her capital gains tax liability for 2020/21 is as follows.

	UK gain £	Foreign gain £
Chargeable gain	30,800	16,000
Less annual exempt amount	(12,300)	
Gain chargeable to tax	18,500	16,000
Capital gains tax: £18,500/£16,000 × 20%	3,700	3,200
Less credit for foreign tax	—	3,200
Tax payable	£3,700	Nil

Notes

(a) No relief is available for the excess of the foreign tax over the CGT liability in respect of the foreign gain (£6,400 − £3,200 = £3,200).

(b) Strictly, the double tax relief is limited to the difference between the total CGT liability for the year before relief (i.e. £6,900) and what the CGT liability would be if the foreign gain were excluded (i.e. £3,700) [*TIOPA 2010, s 40*]. In practice, the effect of this provision is that the annual exempt amount is allocated against the UK gain. If Lyra had been a basic rate income tax payer, any unused part of the basic rate band would likewise have been allocated against the UK gain in priority to the foreign gain (gains within that unused part being chargeable to CGT at 10%). See *Simon's Taxes* E6.433B.

(c) A claim for credit relief must normally be made not more than four years after the end of the tax year for which the gain is chargeable. The claim deadline is extended to 31 January following the tax year in which the foreign tax is paid, where this is later than the above deadline. [*TIOPA 2010, s 19*]. See INTM162560 and *Simon's Taxes* E6.429A.

211 Enterprise Investment Scheme

Cross-reference. See also **IT 10.2** ENTERPRISE INVESTMENT SCHEME.

211.1 DISPOSAL OF EIS SHARES MORE THAN THREE YEARS AFTER ISSUE

[*TCGA 1992, s 150A(2)(3); ITA 2007, s 159(2)*]

On 8 November 2020 P subscribes £1,350,000 for 900,000 shares in the EIS company, S Ltd. S Ltd is not a knowledge-intensive company and P obtains the maximum EIS income tax relief of £300,000 (£1,000,000 × 30%) for 2020. On 3 April 2025 he sells the entire holding for £2,790,000.

The chargeable gain arising is calculated as follows

	£
Disposal proceeds	2,790,000
Cost	(1,350,000)
Gain	1,440,000
Less *TCGA 1992, s 150A(2)(3)* exemption	
£1,440,000 × (£300,000/£405,000) (note (b))	(1,066,667)
Chargeable gain 2024/25	£373,333

Notes

(a) Gains arising on the sale more than three years after issue of shares qualifying for EIS income tax relief are not chargeable gains unless the EIS relief is fully withdrawn before disposal. The exemption begins three years after the date of commencement of the qualifying trade if this is later than three years after issue.

(b) Where the income tax relief is not given on the full EIS subscription (otherwise than because of insufficient income), capital gains tax relief is given on a proportion of the gain on the disposal or part disposal.

The gain is reduced by the multiple A/B where

A = the actual income tax reduction and

B = the tax at the EIS rate for the year of relief on the amount subscribed for the issue.

A = £1,000,000 × 30% = £300,000

B = £1,350,000 × 30% = £405,000

(c) With effect for shares issued on or after 6 April 2018, the upper limit on the amount in respect of which an individual may obtain income tax relief for a tax year operates as follows:

(i) if the shares do not include any 'KIC shares', the limit is £1 million;

(ii) if the total amount subscribed for KIC shares is £1 million or more, the limit is £2 million; and

211.1 CGT   Enterprise Investment Scheme

   (iii) in any other case, the limit is £1 million plus total amount subscribed for KIC shares.

   'KIC shares' are shares in any company which is a knowledge-intensive company (as defined) at the time the shares are issued.

   Prior to the above taking effect the upper limit is in all cases £1 million.

   [ITA 2007, s 158(2)(2ZA)(2ZB); FA 2018, Sch 4 paras 1(2)–(4), 10; SI 2018 No 931, Reg 3]. See VCM10530 and *Simon's Taxes* E3.156.

211.2 LOSS ON DISPOSAL OF EIS SHARES

[TCGA 1992, s 150A(1)(2A)]

(A) **Disposal more than three years after issue**

Assuming the facts otherwise remain the same as in 211.1 above but that the shares are sold for £1,010,000 on 3 April 2025.

The allowable loss arising is calculated as follows

	£	£
Disposal proceeds		1,010,000
Less Cost	1,350,000	
Less Income tax relief given (and not withdrawn)	300,000	(1,050,000)
Allowable loss 2024/25		£40,000

Note

(a) Any loss arising is reduced by deducting the amount of the EIS relief (given and not withdrawn) from the acquisition cost. On the question of income tax withdrawal, see note (b) to (B) below.

(B) **Disposal within three years of issue**

The facts are otherwise as in (A) above except that the shares are sold in an arm's length bargain on 6 April 2022, i.e. within three years after their issue.

Income tax relief given for 2020/21 is withdrawn as follows

   Relief attributable (£1,000,000 @ 30%)   £300,000 (1)

   Consideration

   $£1,010,000 \times \dfrac{300,000\ (£1,000,000\ @\ 30\%)}{405,000\ (£1,350,000\ @\ 30\%)}$ @ 30%   (£224,444) (2)

Enterprise Investment Scheme   CGT 211.3

The amount at (1) is greater than that at (2), so income tax relief of £224,444 is withdrawn. [*ITA 2007, ss 209, 210*].

The relief not withdrawn is therefore £(300,000 − 224,444) =   £75,556

The allowable loss arising is calculated as follows

	£	£
Disposal proceeds		1,010,000
Less Cost	1,350,000	
Less Income tax relief not withdrawn	75,556	(1,274,444)
Allowable loss 2022/23		£264,444

Notes

(a) For the purposes of computing an allowable loss, the consideration is reduced by the relief attributable to the shares. [*TCGA 1992, s 150A(1)*]. The relief attributable is that remaining following any withdrawal of relief.

(b) A withdrawal of income tax relief arises on a disposal of EIS shares within 'period A' under *ITA 2007, s 159(2)*, i.e. within three years after their issue or, if later, within the period ending immediately before the third anniversary of the date of commencement of the qualifying trade. [*ITA 2007, s 209*]. See VCM10540 and *Simon's Taxes* C3.1005.

211.3 EIS DEFERRAL RELIEF

[*TCGA 1992, Sch 5B*]

On 1 June 2020, X realises a gain of £300,000 on the disposal of an asset he had owned since September 2006. X makes no other disposals in 2020/21. On 1 February 2022, X acquires by subscription 65% of the issued ordinary share capital of ABC Ltd at a total subscription price of £248,000. This is a qualifying investment for the purposes of EIS deferral relief. X makes a claim to defer the maximum £248,000 of the June 2020 gain against the qualifying investment.

On 1 July 2026, X sells 40% of his holding in ABC Ltd for £199,200. He makes no other disposals in 2026/27.

X's CGT position for 2020/21 is as follows

	£
Gain	300,000
Less EIS deferral relief	(248,000)
	52,000
Less annual exempt amount	(12,300)
Taxable gain 2020/21	£39,700

211.3 CGT   Enterprise Investment Scheme

X's CGT position for 2026/27 is as follows

	£
Gain on ABC Ltd shares	
Disposal proceeds	199,200
Less cost (£248,000 @ 40%)	(99,200)
Chargeable gain	£100,000
Deferred gain brought into charge	
Total gain deferred	£248,000
Clawback restricted to expenditure to which disposal relates	£99,200
Taxable gains 2026/27 (subject to annual exempt amount) (£100,000 + £99,200)	£199,200
Gain remaining deferred until any future chargeable event (£248,000 − £99,200)	£148,800

Notes

(a) No part of X's subscription for ABC Ltd shares can qualify for EIS income tax relief. X is connected with the company by virtue of his shareholding being greater than 30%. (In practice, the holdings of his associates, e.g. wife and children, must also be taken into account in applying the 30% limit.) [*ITA 2007, ss 163, 166–171*]. See VCM11050 and *Simon's Taxes* E3.109.

(b) As the ABC Ltd shares do not qualify for income tax relief, there is no CGT exemption for the gain arising on disposal even though the shares were held for the requisite three-year period.

(c) Where a disposal qualifies for both BUSINESS ASSET DISPOSAL RELIEF (**206**) (formerly entrepreneurs' relief) and EIS deferral relief, deferral relief can be claimed and business asset disposal relief can then be claimed when the deferred gain comes back into charge on the happening of a chargeable event. [*TCGA 1992, ss 169T–169V*]. See **206.5** BUSINESS ASSET DISPOSAL RELIEF. See *Simon's Taxes* C3.1310.

212 Exemptions and Reliefs

Cross-references. See also **223** PRIVATE RESIDENCES, **224** QUALIFYING CORPORATE BONDS and **232** WASTING ASSETS.

212.1 CHATTELS

(A) **Marginal relief**

[*TCGA 1992, s 262(2)*]

On 1 April 1989, Y acquired by inheritance a painting valued for probate at £900. He sold it for £7,200 on 30 October 2020, incurring costs of £150.

	£	£
Disposal proceeds	7,200	
Incidental costs	(150)	7,050
Acquisition cost		(900)
Chargeable gain		£6,150
Marginal relief		
Chargeable gain limited to $^5/_3 \times$ (£7,200 − £6,000)		£2,000

Note

(a) See CG76577 and *Simon's Taxes* C1.409

(B) **Loss relief**

[*TCGA 1992, s 262(3)*]

Z bought a piece of antique jewellery for £7,000 in February 1992. In January 2021 he is forced to sell it, but at auction it realises only £1,500 and Z incurs costs of £100.

	£	£
Deemed disposal consideration		6,000
Cost of disposal	100	
Cost of acquisition	7,000	(7,100)
Allowable loss		£1,100

Note

(a) Where the disposal consideration for tangible movable property is less than £6,000 and there would otherwise be a loss, the consideration is deemed to be £6,000.

(b) See CG76590 and *Simon's Taxes* C1.409

212.1 CGT   Exemptions and Reliefs

(C) **Partial disposal of assets forming sets**

[*TCGA 1992, s 262(4)*]

AB purchased a set of six 18th century dining chairs in 1986 for £1,200. After incurring restoration costs of £300 in 1992, he sold two of them in March 2016 to an unconnected person for £2,900. In August 2020, he sold the other four to the same buyer for £4,900.

The two disposals are treated as one for the purposes of the chattel exemption and marginal relief, the consideration for which is £7,800. Marginal relief on this basis would give a total chargeable gain of £3,000 ([£7,800 − £6,000] × $^5/_3$) which is to be compared with the following:

March 2016	£	£
Disposal proceeds		2,900
Acquisition cost	1,200	
Enhancement cost	300	
	1,500	
Cost of two chairs sold £1,500 × $^2/_6$		(500)
Chargeable gain		£2,400
2020		£
Disposal proceeds		4,900
Cost £1,500 × $^4/_6$		(1,000)
Chargeable gain		£3,900
Total chargeable gains (£2,400 + £3,900)		£6,300

The total gain of £6,300 compares with a gain of £3,000 using marginal relief. Marginal relief is therefore effective and the total chargeable gain is £3,000.

The gain is apportioned to tax years as follows (note (b))

2015/16	£3,000 × $\dfrac{2,900}{7,800}$ =	£1,115
2020/21	£3,000 × $\dfrac{4,900}{7,800}$ =	£1,885

Notes

(a) Prior to the second disposal, the first disposal would have been exempt, the proceeds being within the £6,000 chattel exemption.

(b) The gain as reduced by marginal relief is apportioned between tax years in the same ratio as the proportion of total sale proceeds applicable to each year. See CG76637 and *Simon's Taxes* C1.409.

(c) See also **202.3** ANTI-AVOIDANCE.

213 Hold-Over Reliefs

213.1 RELIEF FOR GIFTS

[*TCGA 1992, s 260*]

(A) **Chargeable lifetime transfers**

B owns a house which he has not occupied as a private residence. He purchased the house for £15,200 inclusive of costs in 1979 and in January 2021 he gives it to a discretionary trust of which he is the settlor. The settlement is not a settlor-interested settlement for the purposes of *TCGA 1992, ss 169B–169G*. The market value of the house is agreed to be £200,000 at the date of transfer, and B incurs transfer costs of £1,000. The house had a value of £21,000 at 31 March 1982.

	£
Disposal consideration	200,000
Deduct Costs of disposal	(1,000)
	199,000
Market value 31.3.82	(21,000)
Chargeable gain	£178,000

If B elects under *TCGA 1992, s 260*, his chargeable gain is reduced to nil, and the trustees' acquisition cost of the house is treated as £22,000 (£200,000 - £178,000).

Notes

(a) Relief under *TCGA 1992, s 260* is restricted, generally, to transfers which are, or would but for annual exemptions be, chargeable lifetime transfers for inheritance tax purposes. See CG67040 and *Simon's Taxes* C1.425.

(b) Separate rules apply to transfers of assets between MARRIED PERSONS AND CIVIL PARTNERS **(218)**.

(c) Relief under *TCGA 1992, s 260* is not available on a disposal to the trustees of a settlor-interested settlement (as defined). [*TCGA 1992, ss 169B–169G*]. See CG67064 and *Simon's Taxes* C3.512.

(d) Where a UK-resident person makes a disposal of UK residential property on which a chargeable gain arises on or after 6 April 2020, that person must normally make a return to HMRC in respect of the disposal on or before the 30th day following the day of the completion of the disposal (and, where appropriate, make a payment on account of CGT). It must, however, be assumed that any election which can, at the date of completion, reasonably be expected to be made, will be made. In this case, if it were reasonable to make the assumption that an election under *TCGA 1992, s 260* would be made, no payment on account need be made and no return filed. See *FA 2019, Sch 2 paras 4, 14(2)*.

The requirement to make a return also applies to any direct or indirect disposal of UK land on or after 6 April 2019 by a non-resident or in the overseas part of a split tax year, whether or not a gain is made. See *FA 2019, Sch 2*.

213.1 CGT   Hold-Over Reliefs

(B) **Disposal consideration**

[TCGA 1992, s 260(5)]

The facts are as in (A) above except that B sells the house to the trustees for £30,000.

	£	£
Chargeable gain (as above) (note (a))		178,000
Deduct		
Actual consideration passing	30,000	
B's allowable costs	(22,000)	
		(8,000)
Held-over gain		£170,000
(i) B's chargeable gain is reduced to £178,000 − £170,000		£8,000
(ii) The trustees' allowable cost is reduced to £200,000 − £170,000		£30,000

Note

(a) The disposal consideration is taken as the open market value of the house at the date of disposal because B and the trustees are connected persons. Thus, the computation of the gain is as in (A) above. See CG67090.

(C) **Relief for IHT**

[TCGA 1992, s 260(7)]

The facts are as in (A) above. Before transferring the house, B had made substantial chargeable transfers. Inheritance tax of £20,000 is payable on the transfer. The trustees sell the house in December 2021 for £195,000.

	£	£
Disposal proceeds		195,000
Acquisition cost	200,000	
Deduct held-over gain	178,000	
		(22,000)
Gain		173,000
IHT attributable to earlier transfer		(20,000)
Chargeable gain		£153,000

Notes

(a) Where the IHT attributable to the earlier transfer is greater than the gain, the IHT deduction is limited to the amount of the gain and cannot create or increase a loss. [TCGA 1992, s 260(7)]. See CG67050 and *Simon's Taxes* C1.425, I5.915.

(b) A similar inheritance tax relief operates where the original gain was held over under TCGA 1992, s 165 or FA 1980, s 79. [TCGA 1992, ss 67, 165(10)].

Hold-Over Reliefs   CGT 213.3

213.2 RELIEF FOR GIFTS OF BUSINESS ASSETS

[*TCGA 1992, s 165, Sch 7*]

Zoë owns a freehold property which she lets to the family trading company, Sphere Ltd, in which she and her father each own half the shares and voting rights. Zoë inherited the property in April 1990 at a probate value of £50,000, and since then the whole of the property has been used for the purposes of the company's trade. In November 2020, Zoë transfers the property to her boyfriend. Its market value at that time is £115,000. The intention is that he should give sufficient consideration to leave Zoë with a chargeable gain exactly equal to the annual exempt amount (there being no other disposals in 2020/21).

Actual consideration should be £62,300 as shown by the following computation

		£
Deemed consideration		115,000
Deduct: Cost		(50,000)
Unrelieved gain		65,000
Held-over gain (see below)		(52,700)
Chargeable gain covered by annual exempt amount		£12,300
Computation of held-over gain		
	£	£
Unrelieved gain		65,000
Actual consideration	62,300	
Less allowable expenditure	50,000	(12,300)
Held-over gain		£52,700

Note

(a) On a subsequent disposal of the property, the allowable expenditure would be £62,300 (deemed proceeds of £115,000 less held-over gain of £52,700). See CG66980 and *Simon's Taxes* C3.501–C3.503, I3.612.

213.3 TRANSFER OF BUSINESS TO A COMPANY — INCORPORATION RELIEF

[*TCGA 1992, s 162*]

W has carried on an antiquarian bookselling business for many years. He decides to form an unquoted company, P Ltd, to carry on the business. He transfers, in May 2020, the whole of the business undertaking, assets and liabilities to P Ltd, in consideration for the issue of shares, plus an amount left outstanding on interest-free loan. W becomes a director of P Ltd. The business assets and liabilities transferred are valued as follows

213.3 CGT   Hold-Over Reliefs

	£	Value £	Chargeable gain £
Freehold shop premises (acquired in 2000)		80,000	42,000
Goodwill		36,000	16,000
Fixtures and fittings		4,000	—
Trading stock		52,000	—
Debtors		18,000	—
		190,000	
Mortgage on shop	50,000		
Trade creditors	20,000	70,000	—
		£120,000	£58,000

The company issues 100,000 £1 ordinary shares, valued at par, to W in May 2020, and the amount left outstanding is £20,000. If W does not elect to disapply *TCGA 1992, s 162* treatment, the amount of the chargeable gain rolled over on transfer of the business is as follows.

$$\frac{100,000}{120,000} \times £58,000 \qquad £48,333$$

Of the chargeable gain, £9,667 (£58,000 − £48,333) remains taxable and is covered by the annual exempt amount.

The allowable cost of W's shares is £51,667 (£100,000 − £48,333).

Note

(a)   See CG65710 and *Simon's Taxes* C3.401–C3.403.

214 Indexation

Note

Indexation allowance is available only for the purposes of corporation tax on chargeable gains.

214.1 INDEXATION ALLOWANCE — GENERAL RULES

[*TCGA 1992, ss 53–56*]

(A) **Calculation of indexation factor — companies — disposal before 1 January 2018**

M Ltd bought a freehold factory in December 1984 for £500,000. Further buildings are erected at a cost of £200,000 in May 1992. In May 2017 the factory is sold for £2m. The relevant values of the retail price index (RPI) are as follows:

December 1984	90.87
May 1992	139.3
May 2017	271.1

	£	£
Disposal consideration		2,000,000
Deduct Cost of factory and site	500,000	
Cost of additions	200,000	(700,000)
Unindexed gain		1,300,000
Indexation allowance		
(i) Factory and site		
Indexation factor		

$$\frac{271.7 - 90.87}{90.87} = 1.990$$

Indexed rise
£500,000 × 1.990   995,000

(ii) Additions
Indexation factor

$$\frac{271.7 - 139.3}{139.3} = 0.950$$

Indexed rise		
£200,000 × 0.950	190,000	1,185,000
Gain chargeable to corporation tax		£115,000

214.1 CGT   Indexation

Note

(a) See CG12740, CG46101 and *Simon's Taxes* C2.304, C2.404.

(B) **Calculation of indexation factor — companies — disposal on or after 1 January 2018**

The facts are as in (A) above, except that the factory is sold in May 2020. The relevant values of the retail price index (RPI) are as follows

December 1984	90.87
May 1992	139.3
December 2017)	278.1

	£	£
Disposal consideration		2,000,000
Deduct Cost of factory and site	500,000	
Cost of additions	200,000	(700,000)
Unindexed gain		1,300,000
Indexation allowance		
(i) Factory and site		
Indexation factor		

$$\frac{278.1 - 90.87}{90.87} = 2.060$$

Indexed rise		
£500,000 × 2.060	1,030,000	
(ii) Additions		
Indexation factor		

$$\frac{278.1 - 139.3}{139.3} = 0.996$$

Indexed rise		
£200,000 × 0.996	199,200	1,229,200
Gain chargeable to corporation tax		£70,800

Note

(a) Indexation allowance is frozen at its December 2017 level. No indexation allowance is available in respect of expenditure incurred after 31 December 2017, and for expenditure incurred on or before that date and falling to be deducted on a disposal after that date, indexation allowance is computed up to and including December 2017 only. [*TCGA 1992, ss 53(1)(1B), 54(1B); FA 2018, s 26(2)(3)(6)*]. See *Simon's Taxes* C2.301–C2.303.

Indexation CGT 214.1

(C) Disposal of asset held on 31 March 1982

X Ltd acquired an asset for £6,000 in August 1979. The company sold it for £29,000 in December 2020. The agreed market value of the asset at 31 March 1982 is £7,500. The indexation factor for March 1982 to December 2017 is 2.501.

	£	£
Disposal consideration	29,000	29,000
Deduct Cost	(6,000)	
Market value 31.3.82		(7,500)
Unindexed gain	23,000	21,500
Indexation allowance £7,500 × 2.501	(18,758)	(18,758)
Gain after indexation	£4,242	£2,742
Chargeable gain		£2,742

Notes

(a) In both the calculation using cost and that using 31 March 1982 value, indexation is automatically based on 31 March 1982 value. If, however, a greater allowance would have been produced by basing indexation on cost, that would automatically have applied instead. If, however, an irrevocable election were to be made under *TCGA 1992, s 35(5)* for all assets to be treated as sold and re-acquired at 31 March 1982, indexation must then be based on 31 March 1982 value whether it is beneficial or not. [*TCGA 1992, s 55(1)(2)*]. See CG16760, CG17405 and *Simon's Taxes* C2.607

(b) Indexation allowance is frozen at its December 2017 level. No indexation allowance is available in respect of expenditure incurred after 31 December 2017, and for expenditure incurred on or before that date and falling to be deducted on a disposal after that date, indexation allowance is computed up to and including December 2017 only. [*TCGA 1992, ss 53(1)(1B), 54(1B); FA 2018, s 26(2)(3)(6)*].

(c) See also **205.1 ASSETS HELD ON 31 MARCH 1982**.

(D) Losses — indexation allowance restriction

[*TCGA 1992, s 53(1)(b)(2A); FA 1994, s 93(1)–(3)(11)*]

In June 1993, M Ltd had purchased two assets, each for £25,000. In September 2020, the company sells the assets for £30,000 (A) and £23,000 (B) respectively. Incidental costs of purchase and sale are ignored for the purposes of this example. The indexation factor for the period June 1993 to December 2017 is 0.972.

The gains/losses on the sales are as follows

	(A)	(B)
	£	£
Proceeds	30,000	23,000
Cost	(25,000)	(25,000)
Unindexed gain/(loss)	5,000	(2,000)

214.1 CGT Indexation

Indexation allowance £25,000 × 0.972 = £24,300 but restricted to		(5,000)	Nil
Chargeable gain/(allowable loss)		Nil	£(2,000)

Note

(a) Indexation allowance can reduce an unindexed gain to nil but cannot create or increase a loss.

(b) Indexation allowance is frozen at its December 2017 level. No indexation allowance is available in respect of expenditure incurred after 31 December 2017, and for expenditure incurred on or before that date and falling to be deducted on a disposal after that date, indexation allowance is computed up to and including December 2017 only. [*TCGA 1992, ss 53(1)(1B), 54(1B); FA 2018, s 26(2)(3)(6)*].

214.2 NO GAIN/NO LOSS TRANSFERS

(A) **Transfers between spouses or civil partners before 6 April 2008 — asset acquired by first spouse before 1 April 1982 — gain on ultimate disposal after 5 April 2008**

[*TCGA 1992, s 35A, s 52A, s 55(5)(6), s 56(2), s 58; FA 2008, Sch 2 paras 59, 60, 65(2), 71, 78, 83*]

Mr N inherited a country cottage in 1977 at a probate value of £12,000. Its market value at 31 March 1982 was £30,000. In July 1988, Mr N incurred enhancement expenditure of £5,000 on the cottage. In May 1990, he gave the cottage to his wife. In November 2020, Mrs N sells it for £205,000. At no time was the cottage the main residence of either spouse. The relevant indexation factors are as follows

March 1982 to May 1990	0.589
July 1988 to May 1990	0.183

(i) *Disposal in May 1990*

Consideration deemed to be such that neither gain nor loss arises.

	£	£
Cost of cottage to Mr N		12,000
Enhancement expenditure		5,000
		17,000
Indexation allowance:		
£30,000 × 0.589	17,670	
£5,000 × 0.183	915	18,585
Cost of cottage to Mrs N		£35,585

(ii) *Disposal in November 2020*

Re-computation of Mrs N's acquisition cost

	£
Market value 31.3.82	30,000
Enhancement expenditure	5,000
	35,000
Indexation allowance (as above)	18,585
Cost of cottage to Mrs N	£53,585

Mrs N's chargeable gain

	£
Sale proceeds	205,000
Deduct cost	(53,585)
Chargeable gain 2020/21	£151,415

Notes

(a) The cottage having been acquired by Mrs N by means of a no gain/no loss disposal from her husband to which re-basing did not apply, in computing the gain on her disposal of the cottage after 5 April 2008 re-basing is assumed to have applied to the no gain/no loss disposal. [*TCGA 1992, s 35A; FA 2008, Sch 2 paras 59, 71*]. Therefore, in computing the gain or loss on the post-5 April 2008 disposal, the allowable expenditure includes the value of the cottage at 31 March 1982 and the indexation allowance due for the period from that date to the date on which Mrs N acquired the cottage (May 1990). This rule does not affect the position of Mr N. See CG17402 and *Simon's Taxes* C2.607.

(b) Indexation allowance is abolished for capital gains tax purposes (i.e. for disposals by individuals, trustees and personal representatives) for disposals on or after 6 April 2008. [*TCGA 1992, s 52A; FA 2008, Sch 2 paras 78, 83*]. No indexation allowance is due therefore on the disposal by Mrs N, but as a result of the rule in note (a) above, she effectively obtains indexation allowance up to the date on which she acquired the cottage (or April 1998 if earlier). See CG17209 and *Simon's Taxes* C2.717, C2.717A.

(c) See also (B) below and **218 MARRIED PERSONS AND CIVIL PARTNERS**.

(B) **Transfers between spouses or civil partners before 6 April 2008 — asset acquired by first spouse after 31 March 1982 — gain on ultimate disposal after 5 April 2008**

[*TCGA 1992, s 56(2)*]

The facts are as in (A) above except that Mr N inherited the cottage in April 1982 at a probate value of £30,000. The relevant indexation factors are

214.2 CGT   Indexation

April 1982 to May 1990	0.557
July 1988 to May 1990	0.183

(i) *Disposal in May 1990*

Consideration deemed to be such that neither gain nor loss arises.

	£	£
Cost of cottage to Mr N		30,000
Enhancement expenditure		5,000
		35,000
Indexation allowance:		
£30,000 × 0.557	16,710	
£5,000 × 0.183	915	17,625
Cost of cottage to Mrs N		£52,625

(ii) *Disposal in November 2020*

Sale proceeds	205,000
Cost (as above)	(52,625)
Chargeable gain 2020/21	£152,375

Notes

(a) For further examples on transfers between spouses or civil partners, see (A) above and **218** MARRIED PERSONS AND CIVIL PARTNERS.

(b) See note (b) to (A) above.

(c) See CG46101 and *Simon's Taxes* C2.304.

(C) **Intra-group transfers — asset acquired by group before 1 April 1982**

[*TCGA 1992, s 55(5)–(9), s 56(2), s 171*]

J Ltd and K Ltd are 75% subsidiaries of H Ltd. J Ltd acquired a property in 1980 for £20,000. Its market value at 31 March 1982 was £25,000. In May 1990, J Ltd transferred the property to K Ltd. In May 2020, K Ltd sells the property outside the group. The sale proceeds are (1) £90,000, (2) £18,000 or (3) £29,000. The relevant indexation factors are as follows

March 1982 to May 1990	0.589
March 1982 to December 2017	2.501

Indexation CGT 214.2

(i) *Disposal in May 1990*

Consideration deemed to be such that neither gain nor loss arises.

	£
Cost of asset to J Ltd	20,000
Indexation allowance £25,000 × 0.589	14,725
Cost of asset to K Ltd	£34,725

(ii) *Disposal in May 2020*

(1) Proceeds £90,000

	£	£	£
Proceeds		90,000	90,000
Cost	34,725		
Deduct Indexation allowance previously given	14,725	(20,000)	
Market value 31.3.82			(25,000)
Unindexed gain		70,000	65,000
Indexation allowance £25,000 × 2.501		(62,525)	(62,525)
Gain after indexation		£7,475	£2,475
Chargeable gain			£2,475

(2) Proceeds £18,000

	£	£	£
Proceeds		18,000	18,000
Cost	34,725		
Deduct Indexation allowance previously given	14,725	(20,000)	
Market value 31.3.82			(25,000)
		(2,000)	(7,000)
Add Rolled-up indexation		(14,725)	(14,725)
Loss after rolled-up indexation		£(16,725)	£(21,725)
Allowable loss		£16,725	

214.2 CGT Indexation

(3) Proceeds £29,000

	£	£	£
Proceeds		29,000	29,000
Cost	34,725		
Deduct Indexation allowance previously given	14,725		
		(20,000)	
Market value 31.3.82			(25,000)
Unindexed gain		9,000	4,000
Indexation allowance:			
£25,000 × 2.501 = £62,525 but restricted to		(9,000)	(4,000)
		Nil	Nil
Excess of rolled-up indexation (£14,725) over indexation allowance given above		(5,725)	(10,725)
Loss after rolled-up indexation		£(5,725)	£(10,725)
Allowable loss		£5,725	

Notes

(a) Having acquired the property by means of a no gain/no loss disposal from J Ltd, who held it at 31 March 1982, K Ltd is deemed to have held the asset at 31 March 1982 for the purposes of the re-basing provisions, and also the provisions under which indexation allowance is computed using value at 31 March 1982. [*TCGA 1992, s 55(5)(6), Sch 3 para 1*]. See CG17760 and *Simon's Taxes* C2.607.

(b) In (2) and (3) above, as the ultimate disposal is after 29 November 1993 and indexation allowance is either unavailable in (2) above or restricted in (3) above, special provisions enable the person making the disposal to obtain the benefit of any indexation allowance already accrued on no gain/no loss transfers made *before* 30 November 1993 (called 'rolled-up indexation'). [*TCGA 1992, s 55(7)–(9)*]. See CG17760 and *Simon's Taxes* C2.607.

(c) Indexation allowance is frozen at its December 2017 level. No indexation allowance is available in respect of expenditure incurred after 31 December 2017, and for expenditure incurred on or before that date and falling to be deducted on a disposal after that date, indexation allowance is computed up to and including December 2017 only. [*TCGA 1992, ss 53(1)(1B), 54(1B); FA 2018, s 26(2)(3)(6)*]. See **214.1** INDEXATION.

(D) **Intra-group transfers — asset acquired by group after 31 March 1982 — loss on ultimate disposal**

[*TCGA 1992, s 56(2)–(4), s 171*]

L Ltd, M Ltd and N Ltd are members of a 75% group of companies. L Ltd acquired a property in June 1990 for £50,000 and transferred it to M Ltd in June 1993. M Ltd transferred the property to N Ltd in June 1996, and N Ltd sold it outside the group in June 2020 for £55,000. The relevant indexation factors are as follows

June 1990 to June 1993	0.113
June 1993 to June 1996	0.085

(i) *Disposal in June 1993*

Consideration deemed to be such that neither gain nor loss arises.

	£
Cost of asset to L Ltd	50,000
Indexation allowance £50,000 × 0.113	5,650
Cost of asset to M Ltd	£55,650

(ii) *Disposal in June 1996*

Cost of asset to M Ltd	55,650
Indexation allowance £55,650 × 0.085	4,730
Cost of asset to N Ltd	£60,380

(iii) *Disposal in June 2020*

Proceeds	55,000
Cost (as above)	(60,380)
Loss before adjustment under *TCGA 1992, s 56(3)*	(5,380)
Deduct Indexation on June 1996 disposal	4,730
Allowable loss	£(650)

Note

(a) Where a loss accrues on the ultimate disposal, it is reduced by any indexation allowance included in the cost of the asset by virtue of a no gain/no loss disposal made *after* 29 November 1993. If this adjustment would otherwise convert a loss into a gain, the disposal is treated as giving rise to neither a gain nor a loss [*TCGA 1992, s 56(3)*]. See CG17740 and *Simon's Taxes* C2.304.

215 Investors' Relief

215.1 COMPUTATION OF RELIEF

[*TCGA 1992, ss 169VC, 169VK; FA 2016, Sch 14 para 2*]

(A) Basic computation

In May 2020, Sara sells her entire holding of shares in Watkins Ltd, an unlisted trading company, for £900,000. Sara subscribed for the shares in April 2017 for £200,000. She claims investors' relief in respect of the disposal. She has made no previous claim to the relief and makes no other disposals in 2020/21.

Sara's capital gains tax liability for 2020/21 is calculated as follows.

	£
Sale consideration	900,000
Less cost of shares	(200,000)
Chargeable gain	700,000
Less Annual exempt amount	(12,300)
Gain chargeable to tax	£687,700
Capital gains tax payable (£687,700 × 10%)	£68,770

Notes

(a) Investors' relief can be claimed by individuals or trustees in respect of certain disposals on or after 6 April 2019 of qualifying ordinary shares in unlisted trading companies subscribed for on or after 17 March 2016. The relief applies for capital gains tax purposes only and is not available to companies. The investor must have held the shares continuously throughout the period beginning with the date they were issued and ending with the date of disposal. That period must be at least three years, or, where the share was issued before 6 April 2016, at least three years plus the period beginning with the date of issue and ending on 5 April 2016. With limited exceptions, the investor must not be an officer of employee of the company or a connected company. Relief is given by charging the gain to capital gains tax at 10%.

(b) Investors' relief must be claimed on or before the first anniversary of the 31 January following the tax year in which the qualifying business disposal is made. In the case of a disposal by trustees, the claim must be made jointly by the trustees and the eligible beneficiary or beneficiaries. [*TCGA 1992, s 169VM; FA 2016, Sch 14 para 2*]. Sara must therefore make a claim on or before 31 January 2023. See HMRC Capital Gains Manual CG63560 and *Simon's Taxes* C3.1324.

(c) There are provisions for the disqualification of shares from relief where the investor receives any value, other than insignificant value, from the company at any time in the period beginning one year before, and ending immediately before the third anniversary of, the date on which the shares were issued. See *TCGA 1992, Sch 7ZB*. (See HMRC Capital Gains Manual CG63640 and *Simon's Taxes* C3.1327).

215.1 CGT   Investors' Relief

(B) **Qualifying and non-qualifying shares**

Charlie has the following transactions in ordinary 25p shares in Surf Ltd, an unlisted trading company.

Date		No. of shares acquired/(sold)	Cost/(proceeds) £
1 May 2017	subscribes for	2,000	20,000
1 July 2017	purchases	2,000	25,000
1 August 2018	subscribes for	2,000	30,000
1 August 2020	sells	(3,000)	(120,000)
1 September 2021	sells	(3,000)	(200,000)

Charlie and the company meet all the conditions necessary for the shares issued to Charlie to qualify for investors' relief. Charlie makes no other disposals in 2020/21 or 2021/22. For the purpose only of this example it is assumed that the annual exempt amount for 2021/22 remains same as for 2020/21 (£12,300). Charlie is a higher rate income tax payer for both years. If Charlie makes all of the available investors' relief claims, his capital gains liability is as follows.

2020/21

Section 104 holding	Shares	Qualifying expenditure £
May 2017 acquisition	2,000	20,000
July 2017 acquisition	2,000	25,000
	4,000	45,000
August 2018 acquisition	2,000	30,000
	6,000	75,000
August 2020 disposal	(3,000)	(37,500)
Pool carried forward	3,000	£37,500

Calculation of chargeable gain	£
Disposal consideration	120,000
Allowable cost $\dfrac{3,000}{6,000} \times £75,000$	(37,500)
Chargeable gain	82,500
Less: Annual exempt amount	(12,300)
Gain chargeable to tax	£70,200

Investors' Relief CGT 215.1

Capital gains tax payable (see note (a))
£55,000 × 10%	5,500
£15,200 × 20%	3,040
	£8,540

2021/22

Section 104 holding	Shares	Qualifying expenditure
		£
Pool brought forward	3,000	37,500
September 2021 disposal	(3,000)	(37,500)
Pool carried forward	—	—

Calculation of chargeable gain	£
Disposal consideration	200,000
Allowable cost	(37,500)
Chargeable gain	162,500
Less Annual exempt amount	(12,300)
Gain chargeable to tax	£150,200

Capital gains tax payable (see note (b))
£108,333 × 10%	10,833
£41,867 × 20%	8,373
	£19,206

Notes

(a) Where only some of the shares in a holding are qualifying shares, only a corresponding proportion of the gain (after deduction of any allowable losses) is taxable at the rate of 10%. The proportion is the number of qualifying shares treated as disposed of divided by the total number of shares disposed of. For this purpose, qualifying shares are treated as disposed of in priority to non-qualifying shares. See (b) below where there has been a previous disposal of shares from the holding. [*TCGA 1992, s 169VD; FA 2016, Sch 14 para 2*]. See HMRC Capital Gains Manual CG63570 and *Simon's Taxes* C3.1324.

In the case of the disposal in August 2020, Charlie's holding immediately before the disposal consists of 2,000 qualifying shares (the shares subscribed for in May 2017) and 4,000 non-qualifying shares. The non-qualifying shares consist of 2,000 excluded shares (i.e. shares which can never be qualifying shares) acquired in July 2017 and the 2,000 shares subscribed for in August 2018 which are potentially qualifying shares (i.e. shares which would be qualifying shares if they had been held by Charlie for sufficient time). Therefore 2,000 of the 3,000 shares disposed of are treated as qualifying shares. The part of the chargeable gain qualifying for investors' relief is therefore £82,500 × (2,000/3,000) = £55,000.

215.1 CGT   Investors' Relief

(b) Where, before a disposal in respect of which a claim to investors' relief is made, there have been one or more previous disposals of shares from the same holding, special rules apply, where needed, to determine which shares are treated as having been previously disposed of (and therefore which shares are treated as in the holding immediately before the current disposal). The rules operate to preserve the maximum potential relief for future disposals.

Where a claim to investors' relief was made in respect of the previous disposal:

(i) all of the qualifying shares in the holding immediately before the previous disposal are treated as having been disposed of or, if less, so many of the qualifying shares as equals the total number of shares disposed of;

(ii) if the number of qualifying shares in the holding immediately before the previous disposal was less than the total number of shares disposed of and excluded shares were in the holding at that time, then the excluded shares are also treated as having been disposed of, up to a maximum of the total number of shares in the disposal less those treated as having been disposed of in (i) above; and

(iii) if the total number of shares treated as having been disposed of under (i) and (ii) above is less than the total number of shares disposed of, so many of the potentially qualifying shares in the holding as make up the difference are treated as having been disposed of (on a last in first out basis).

If no claim to investors' relief was made in respect of the previous disposal that disposal is taken to consist of first excluded shares, then potentially qualifying shares and finally qualifying shares. [*TCGA 1992, ss 169VE–169VG; FA 2016, Sch 14 para 2*]. See HMRC Capital Gains Manual CG63580 and *Simon's Taxes* C3.1325.

The August 2020 disposal is therefore taken to consist of 2,000 qualifying shares and 1,000 of the excluded shares acquired in July 2017. The remaining shares are taken to consist of 1,000 excluded shares and 2,000 potentially qualifying shares. By the time of the disposal in September 2021 the potentially qualifying shares have become qualifying shares. Applying the rules in (a) above to the September 2021 disposal, the part of the chargeable gain qualifying for investors' relief is £162,500 × (2,000/3,000) = £108,333

(c) The annual exempt amount of £12,300 is allocated against the part of the gain chargeable to tax at 20% as this gives the greater tax saving. [*TCGA 1992, s 4B*]. See CG21610.

(C) **Lifetime limit**

In August 2020 Ms Moorer sells her entire shareholding in Alison Ltd, realising a gain of £10,050,000, which qualifies for investors' relief. Ms Moorer makes no other disposals in 2020/21 and has made no previous disposals qualifying for investors' relief. She is an additional rate income tax payer for 2020/21. Ms Moorer's capital gains tax liability for 2020/21 is calculated as follows.

	£
Chargeable gain	10,050,000
Less Annual exempt amount	(12,300)
Gain chargeable to tax	£10,037,700

Investors' Relief   CGT 215.2

Capital gains tax payable
£10,000,000 × 10%   1,000,000
£37,700 × 20%   7,540
                                                                                £1,007,540

Notes

(a) Investors' relief is subject to a lifetime limit of £10 million. The amount to which relief would otherwise apply in respect of a disposal is added to any amounts to which relief applied in respect of earlier disposals. Where the total exceeds the limit, only so much (if any) of the amount to which relief would otherwise apply in respect of the current disposal as, together with the earlier amounts, does not exceed the limit qualifies for the 10% rate. Any part of a gain excluded by the application of this rule is chargeable at the normal rates of CGT. [*TCGA 1992, s 169VK; FA 2016, Sch 14 para 2*]. See HMRC Capital Gains Manual CG63600 and *Simon's Taxes* C3.1324.

(b) The annual exempt amount of £12,300 is allocated against the part of the gain chargeable to tax at 20% as this gives the greater tax saving. [*TCGA 1992, s 1K(5); FA 2019, Sch 1 para 2*].

215.2 REORGANISATIONS ETC.

[*TCGA 1992, s 169VT; FA 2016, Sch 14 para 2*]

In May 2017, Mr W subscribed for 5,000 shares in Smith Ltd, an unlisted trading company for £10,000. The shares are potentially qualifying shares for the purposes of investors' relief. In January 2021, the shareholders of Smith Ltd accept an offer by a public company, Capaldi plc, and Mr W receives shares in Capaldi plc in exchange for his entire shareholding in Smith Ltd. His Capaldi plc shares are valued at £150,000 at the time of the exchange, and they are excluded from qualifying for investors' relief. Mr W makes no other disposals in 2020/21 and has made no previous claims to investors' relief.

If Mr W elects under *TCGA 1992, s 169VT* to disapply *TCGA 1992, s 127* in respect of the share exchange and claims investors' relief in respect of the gain on the Smith Ltd shares, his capital gains tax liability for 2020/21 is calculated as follows.

	£
Sale proceeds	150,000
Cost	(10,000)
Chargeable gain qualifying for investors' relief	140,000
Less Annual exempt amount	(12,300)
Gain chargeable to tax	£127,700
Capital gains tax payable (£127,700 × 10%)	£12,770

Notes

(a) Where an exchange of securities (within *TCGA 1992, s 135*) takes place and *TCGA 1992, s 127* would otherwise apply to treat the 'original shares' and the 'new holding' (as defined for the purposes of that section) as the same asset, an election can be

215.2 CGT   Investors' Relief

(b) made to disapply that section so that investors' relief can be claimed in respect of the disposal of the original shares. See HMRC Capital Gains Manual CG45552 and *Simon's Taxes* D6.206.

(b) The election must be made on or before the first anniversary of the 31 January following the tax year in which the reorganisation takes place. In this case, therefore, the claim must be made by 31 January 2023 (which is the same date by which the claim to investors' relief must be made). An election takes effect only where a claim to investors' relief is also made; without such a claim, the election has no effect.

(c) Mr W cannot claim investors' relief on an eventual disposal of his shares in Capaldi plc. If he had not made an election under *TCGA 1992, s 169VT* the opportunity to claim relief would have been lost. See HMRC Capital Gains Manual CG63630 and *Simon's Taxes* C3.1326.

(d) The above provisions apply also to reorganisations within *TCGA 1992, s 126* and to schemes of reconstruction within *TCGA 1992, s 136* to which *TCGA 1992, s 127* applies.

216 Land

216.1 SMALL PART DISPOSALS

[*TCGA 1992, s 242*]

C owns farmland which cost £134,000 in May 1988. In February 1996, a small plot of land is exchanged with an adjoining landowner for another piece of land. The value placed on the transaction is £18,000. The value of the remaining estate excluding the new piece of land is estimated at £250,000. In March 2021, C sells the whole estate for £300,000. He makes no other disposals in 2020/21. The indexation factor for May 1988 to February 1996 is 0.421.

(i) **No claim made under TCGA 1992, s 242(2)**

			£	£
(a)	*Disposal in February 1996*			
	Disposal proceeds			18,000
	Allowable cost $\dfrac{18,000}{18,000 + 250,000} \times £134,000$			(9,000)
	Unindexed gain			9,000
	Indexation allowance £9,000 × 0.421			(3,789)
	Chargeable gain 1995/96			£5,211
(b)	*Disposal in March 2021*			
	Disposal proceeds			300,000
	Allowable cost			
	Original land £(134,000 − 9,000)		125,000	
	Exchanged land		18,000	(143,000)
	Chargeable gain 2020/21			£157,000

(ii) **Claim made under TCGA 1992, s 242(2)**

		£	£
(a)	*No disposal in February 1996*		
	Allowable cost of original land		134,000
	Deduct Disposal proceeds		(18,000)
	Adjusted allowable cost		£116,000
	Allowable cost of additional land		£18,000

216.1 CGT   Land

(b) *Disposal in March 2021*

Disposal proceeds		300,000
Allowable cost		
Original land	116,000	
Additional land	18,000	(134,000)
Chargeable gain 2020/21		£166,000

Notes

(a) A claim under *TCGA 1992, s 242* may be made where the consideration for the part disposal does not exceed one-fifth of the value of the whole, up to a maximum of £20,000. See CG71870 and *Simon's Taxes* C2.1103.

(b) If the second disposal had also been made in 1995/96 no claim under *section 242(2)* could have been made on the part disposal as proceeds of all disposals of land in the year would have exceeded £20,000.

(c) If the original land had been held at 31 March 1982 and the part disposal took place after that date, the disposal proceeds, on a claim under *section 242(2)*, would be deducted from the 31 March 1982 value for the purpose of the re-basing provisions.

216.2 COMPULSORY PURCHASE

[*TCGA 1992, ss 243–248*]

(A) **Rollover where new land acquired**

(i) *Rollover not claimed*

D owns freehold land purchased for £77,000 in 1978. Part of the land is made the subject of a compulsory purchase order. The compensation of £70,000 is agreed on 10 August 2020. The market value of the remaining land is £175,000. The value of the total freehold land at 31 March 1982 was £98,000.

	£
Disposal consideration	70,000
Market value 31.3.82	
$£98,000 \times \dfrac{70,000}{70,000 + 175,000}$	(28,000)
Chargeable gain 2020/21	£42,000

(ii) *Rollover claimed under TCGA 1992, s 247*

If, in (i), D acquires new land costing, say, £80,000 in, say, December 2020, relief may be claimed as follows.

	£
Allowable cost of land compulsorily purchased	28,000
Actual consideration	70,000
Chargeable gain rolled over	£42,000
Allowable cost of new land (£80,000 − £42,000)	£38,000

Note

(a) See CG61900 and *Simon's Taxes* C2.1116

(B) **Small disposals**

(i) *No rollover relief claimed*

T inherited land in June 1988 at a probate value of £290,000. Under a compulsory purchase order, a part of the land is acquired for highway improvements. Compensation of £32,000 and a further £10,000 for severance, neither sum including any amount in respect of loss of profits, is agreed on 14 May 2020. The value of the remaining land is £900,000. Prior to the compulsory purchase, the value of all the land had been £950,000.

	£
Total consideration for disposal (£32,000 + £10,000)	42,000
Deduct Allowable cost $\dfrac{42,000}{42,000 + 900,000} \times £290,000$	(12,930)
Chargeable gain 2020/21	£29,070

(ii) *Rollover relief claimed under TCGA 1992, s 243*

Total consideration for disposal is £42,000, less than 5% of the value of the estate before the disposal (£950,000). T may therefore claim that the consideration be deducted from the allowable cost of the estate.

Revised allowable cost (£290,000 − £42,000)	£248,000

No chargeable gain then arises in 2020/21.

Note

(a) HMRC additionally regard consideration of £3,000 or less as 'small', whether or not it would pass the 5% test illustrated here. (Revenue Tax Bulletin February 1997, p 397). See CG61940, CG72200 and *Simon's Taxes* C2.1117.

216.3 CGT   Land

216.3 LEASES

(A) Short leases which are not initially wasting assets

[*TCGA 1992, Sch 8 para 1*]

On 31 August 2015 N purchased the remaining term of a lease of commercial premises for £55,000. The lease was subject to a 25-year sub-lease granted on 1 July 1993 at a fixed rental of £1,000 a year. The market rental was estimated at £15,000 a year. The term of the lease held by N is 60 years from 1 April 1991. The value of the lease in 2018, when the sub-lease expired, was estimated at 31 August 2015 as being £70,000. Immediately upon expiry of the sub-lease, N has refurbishment work done at a cost of £50,000, of which £40,000 qualifies as enhancement expenditure. On 31 March 2021, N sells the lease for £130,000.

Term of lease at date of expiry of sub-lease	32 years 9 months
Relevant percentage $89.354 + {}^9/_{12} \times (90.280 - 89.354)$	90.049%
Term of lease at date of assignment	30 years
Relevant percentage	87.330%

	£	£
Disposal consideration		130,000
Deduct Allowable cost	55,000	
Enhancement costs	40,000	
	95,000	
Less Wasted		
$\dfrac{90.049 - 87.330}{90.049} \times 95,000$	2,868	
		(92,132)
Chargeable gain 2020/21		£37,868

Note

(a) The head-lease becomes a wasting asset on the expiry of the sub-lease. [*TCGA 1992, Sch 8 para 1(2)*]. See *Simon's Taxes* C2.1201, C2.1204, C2.1210, C2.1211.

(B) Grant of long lease

[*TCGA 1992, s 42, Sch 8 para 2*]

In 1982, K acquired a long lease by assignment for £44,000. At the time he acquired it, the lease had an unexpired term of 95 years. On 10 April 2020, he granted a 55-year sublease for a premium of £110,000 and a peppercorn rent. The value of the reversion plus the capitalised value of the rents is £10,000. The value of the lease at 31 March 1982 was estimated at £54,000.

		£
Disposal consideration		110,000
Market value 31.3.82	$£54{,}000 \times \dfrac{110{,}000}{110{,}000 + 10{,}000}$	(49,500)
Chargeable gain 2020/21		£60,500

(C) Grant of short lease

[*TCGA 1992, Sch 8 paras 2, 5; ITTOIA 2005, ss 277–281; CTA 2009, ss 215–218*]

L is the owner of a freehold factory which he leases for a term of 25 years commencing in December 2020. The cost of the factory was £100,000 in April 2001. The lease is granted for a premium of £30,000 and an annual rent. The reversion to the lease plus the capitalised value of the rents amount to £120,000.

		£	£
Amount chargeable to income tax			
Amount of premium			30,000
Deduct Excluded $\dfrac{25-1}{50} \times £30{,}000$			(14,400)
Amount chargeable to income tax			£15,600
Chargeable gain			
Premium received		30,000	
Deduct Charged to income tax		(15,600)	
			14,400
Allowable cost $\dfrac{14{,}400}{30{,}000 + 120{,}000} \times £100{,}000$			(9,600)
Chargeable gain 2020/21			£4,800

Notes

(a) A short lease is one the duration of which, at the time of grant, does not exceed 50 years.

(b) The amount chargeable to income tax is not deducted from the amount of premium appearing in the denominator of the CGT apportionment fraction.

(c) See PIM1205 and *Simon's Taxes* B6.301.

216.3 CGT   Land

(D) **Disposal by assignment of short lease: without enhancement expenditure**

[TCGA 1992, Sch 8 para 1]

X buys a lease for £200,000 on 1 October 2016. The lease commenced on 1 June 2007 for a term of 60 years. X assigns the lease for £300,000 at the end of March 2021.

Term of lease unexpired at date of acquisition		50 years 8 months
Relevant percentage		100%
Term of lease unexpired at date of assignment		46 years 2 months
Relevant percentage 98.490 + ($^2/_{12}$ × (98.902 − 98.490))		98.559%

		£	£
Disposal consideration			300,000
Allowable cost		200,000	
Deduct Wasted $\dfrac{100 - 98.559}{100} \times £200,000$		2,882	
			(197,118)
Chargeable gain 2020/21			£102,882

(E) **Disposal by assignment of short lease held at 31 March 1982**

[TCGA 1992, s 35, Sch 8 para 1]

A Ltd buys a lease for £100,000 on 1 March 1982. The lease commenced on 31 March 1972 for a term of 60 years. Its value at 31 March 1982 was estimated at £104,000. On 31 March 2021 A Ltd assigns the lease for £270,000. The indexation factor for the period March 1982 to December 2017 is 2.501.

(i) *The computation without re-basing to 1982 is as follows*

Term of lease unexpired at date of acquisition (1.3.82)		50 years 1 month
Relevant percentage		100%
Term of lease unexpired at date of assignment		11 years 0 months
Relevant percentage		50.038%

		£	£
Disposal consideration			270,000
Cost		100,000	
Deduct Wasted $\dfrac{100 - 50.038}{100} \times £100,000$		(49,962)	(50,038)

448

Unindexed gain		219,962
Indexation allowance (see (ii) below)		(130,152)
Gain after indexation		£89,810

(ii) *The computation with re-basing to 1982 is as follows*

Term of lease unexpired at deemed date of acquisition (31.3.82)	50 years
Relevant percentage	100%
Term of lease unexpired at date of assignment	11 years
Relevant percentage	50.038%

	£	£
Disposal consideration		270,000
Market value 31.3.82	104,000	
Deduct Wasted $\dfrac{100 - 50.038}{100} \times £104,000$	(51,960)	(52,040)
Unindexed gain		217,960
Indexation allowance £52,040 × 2.501		(130,152)
Gain after indexation		£87,808
Chargeable gain		£87,808

Notes

(a) A Ltd is deemed, under *TCGA 1992, s 35*, to have disposed of and immediately re-acquired the lease on 31 March 1982 at its market value at that date.

(b) Both calculations produce a gain with the re-basing calculation producing the smaller gain. Therefore, re-basing applies. [*TCGA 1992, s 35(2)(3)(a)*]. See CG17405.

(c) Indexation is based, in both calculations, on the assumption that the asset was sold and re-acquired at market value on 31 March 1982 since this gives a greater allowance than if based on original cost as reduced by the wasting asset provisions. [*TCGA 1992, s 55(1)(2)*].

(d) Indexation allowance is frozen at its December 2017 level. No indexation allowance is available in respect of expenditure incurred after 31 December 2017, and for that incurred on or before that date and falling to be deducted on a disposal after that date, indexation allowance is computed up to and including December 2017 only. [*TCGA 1992, ss 53(1)(1B), 54(1B); FA 2018, s 26(2)(3)(6)*]. **214.1** INDEXATION.

(F) **Disposal by assignment of short lease: with enhancement expenditure**

[*TCGA 1992, Sch 8 para 1*]. D Ltd acquires the lease of office premises for £100,000 on 1 July 2012. On 1 January 2014, the company contracts for complete refurbishment of the premises at a total cost of £180,000, of which £120,000 can be regarded as capital

216.3 CGT Land

enhancement expenditure. Work is done at the beginning of January 2014, and money is payable in equal tranches in March 2014 and May 2014. The lease is for a 50 year term commencing 1 April 2005. On 1 January 2021, the lease is assigned to a new lessee for £450,000.

Indexation factors	July 2012 to December 2017	0.149
	March 2014 to December 2017	0.091
	May 2014 to December 2017	0.087

Term of lease unexpired at date of acquisition — 42 years 9 months
Relevant percentage $96.593 + {}^{9}/_{12} \times (97.107 - 96.593)$ — 96.979%

Term of lease unexpired at date of expenditure
incurred (January 2014 — see note (a)) — 41 years 3 months
Relevant percentage $96.041 + {}^{3}/_{12} \times (96.593 - 96.041)$ — 96.179%

Term of lease unexpired at date of assignment — 34 years 3 months
Relevant percentage $91.156 + {}^{3}/_{12} \times (91.981 - 91.156)$ — 91.362%

	£	£	£
Disposal consideration			450,000
Cost of acquisition	100,000		
Deduct Wasted			
$\dfrac{96.979 - 91.362}{96.979} \times 100,000$	(5,792)	94,208	
Enhancement expenditure	120,000		
Deduct Wasted			
$\dfrac{96.179 - 91.362}{96.179} \times 120,000$	(6,010)	113,990	(208,198)
Unindexed gain			241,802
Indexation allowance			
Cost of lease £94,208 × 0.149		14,037	
Enhancement costs			
March 2014 £56,995 × 0.091		5,187	
May 2014 £56,995 × 0.087		4,959	
			(24,183)
Chargeable gain			£217,619

Land CGT 216.3

Notes

(a) The wasting provisions apply to enhancement expenditure by reference to the time when it is first reflected in the nature of the lease. The indexation provisions apply by reference to the date the expenditure became due and payable. [*TCGA 1992, s 54(4)(b), Sch 8 para 1(4)(b)*]. See CG17251 and *Simon's Taxes* C2.302, C2.303.

(b) Indexation allowance is frozen at its December 2017 level. No indexation allowance is available in respect of expenditure incurred after 31 December 2017, and for expenditure incurred on or before that date and falling to be deducted on a disposal after that date, indexation allowance is computed up to and including December 2017 only. [*TCGA 1992, ss 53(1)(1B), 54(1B); FA 2018, s 26(2)(3)(6)*]. See **214.1** INDEXATION.

(G) **Disposal of short lease where premium partly relieved as trading deduction**

[*ITTOIA 2005, ss 60–67; CTA 2009, ss 62–67*]

Butcher acquired a 36-year lease of shop premises from Baker on 1 July 2013 at a premium of £33,000. Butcher prepares trading accounts to 30 June each year. On 1 July 2020, when the unexpired term of the lease is 29 years and property values have risen sharply in the locality, he assigns the lease for £76,000. He makes no other chargeable disposals in 2020/21.

The annual trading deduction under *ITTOIA 2005, ss 60–67* is computed as follows

	£
Premium on 36-year lease	33,000
Deduct (36 − 1) × 2% × £33,000	(23,100)
Premium chargeable on Baker	£9,900

In addition to actual rent payable under the lease, Butcher is entitled to a deduction in computing trading profits in respect of the part of the premium chargeable on Baker, accruing on a day-to-day basis for up to 36 years, of

$$\frac{£9,900}{36} = £275 \text{ p.a.}$$

In his seven accounting years to 30 June 2020, Butcher has thus received a total deduction of (£275 × 7) = £1,925

The chargeable gain on disposal of the lease in July 2020 is computed as below.

Term of lease unexpired at date of acquisition	36 years
Relevant percentage	92.761%
Term of lease unexpired at date of disposal	29 years
Relevant percentage	86.226%

216.3 CGT   Land

		£	£
Disposal consideration			76,000
Cost of acquisition		33,000	
Deduct Income tax relief given (see above) (note (a))		(1,925)	
		31,075	
Deduct Wasted $\dfrac{92.761 - 86.226}{92.761} \times £31,075$		(2,189)	(28,886)
Chargeable gain			47,114
Deduct Annual exempt amount			(12,300)
Taxable gain 2020/21			£34,814

Notes

(a) The allowable expenditure for CGT is reduced, by virtue of *TCGA 1992, s 39* (exclusion of double relief), by the amount on which income tax relief has been given. This reduction is made *before* the wasting asset reduction required by *TCGA 1992, Sch 8 para 1(4)*. See CG71200.

(b) For further examples on the *income tax* treatment of lease premiums, see (C) above, (H) and (J) below, and **IT 22.5 PROPERTY INCOME**.

(H) **Sub-lease granted out of short lease: premium not less than potential premium**

[*TCGA 1992, Sch 8 paras 4, 5*]

On 1 November 2018, S purchased a lease of shop premises then having 50 years to run for a premium of £100,000 and an annual rental of £40,000. After occupying the premises for the purposes of his own business, S granted a sub-lease to N Ltd. The sub-lease was for a term of 21 years commencing on 1 August 2020, for a premium of £50,000 and an annual rental of £30,000. It is agreed that, had the rent under the sub-lease been £40,000, the premium obtainable would have been £20,000.

Term of lease at date granted	50 years
Relevant percentage	100%
Term of lease at date sub-lease granted	48 years 3 months
Relevant percentage $99.289 + {}^3/_{12} \times (99.657 - 99.289)$	99.381%
Term of lease at date sub-lease expires	27 years 3 months
Relevant percentage $83.816 + {}^3/_{12} \times (85.053 - 83.816)$	84.125%

	£
Premium chargeable to income tax on S	
Amount of premium	50,000
$\text{Deduct } \dfrac{21-1}{50} \times £50{,}000$	(20,000)
Amount chargeable	£30,000
Chargeable gain	
Disposal consideration	50,000
Allowable expenditure	
$£100{,}000 \times \dfrac{99.381 - 84.125}{100}$	(15,256)
Chargeable gain	34,744
Deduct Amount chargeable to income tax	(30,000)
Net chargeable gain 2020/21	£4,744

Note

(a) If the amount chargeable to income tax had exceeded the chargeable gain, the net gain would have been nil. The deduction cannot create or increase a loss. [*TCGA 1992, Sch 8 para 5(2)*]. See *Simon's Taxes* C2.1218.

(I) **Sub-lease granted out of short lease: premium less than potential premium**

[*TCGA 1992, Sch 8 paras 4, 5*]

C bought a lease of a house on 1 May 2016, when the unexpired term was 49 years. The cost of the lease was £20,000, and the ground rent payable is £500 p.a. C then let the house on a monthly tenancy until 30 November 2020 when he granted a 10-year lease for a premium of £5,000 and an annual rent of £8,000. Had the rent under the sub-lease been £500 a year, the premium obtainable would have been £40,000. C does not at any time occupy the house as a private residence.

Term of lease at date of acquisition	49 years
Relevant percentage	99.657%
Term of lease when sub-lease granted	44 years 5 months
Relevant percentage $97.595 + {}^5/_{12} \times (98.059 - 97.595)$	97.788%
Term of lease when sub-lease expires	34 years 5 months
Relevant percentage $91.156 + {}^5/_{12} \times (91.981 - 91.156)$	91.500%

216.3 CGT   Land

	£
Amount chargeable to income tax	
Amount of premium	5,000
Deduct Exclusion $\dfrac{10-1}{50} \times £5,000$	900
Chargeable to income tax	£4,100
Chargeable gain	
Disposal consideration	5,000
Deduct Allowable expenditure	
$£20,000 \times \dfrac{97.788 - 91.500}{99.657} \times \dfrac{5,000}{40,000}$	(158)
Gain	4,842
Deduct Amount chargeable to income tax	(4,100)
Net chargeable gain 2020/21	£742

Note

(a) If the amount chargeable to income tax had exceeded the chargeable gain, the net gain would have been nil. The deduction cannot create or increase a loss. [*TCGA 1992, Sch 8 para 5(2)*]. See *Simon's Taxes* C2.1218

216.4 DIRECT DISPOSALS OF INTERESTS IN UK LAND BY NON-RESIDENTS

[*TCGA 1992, ss 1A(3), 1C, 1G, 2B(4)(5), Sch 4AA; FA 2019, Sch 1*]

(A) Land acquired on or after 6 April 2019

Aanya, a resident in Spain, acquired a commercial property in London on 1 September 2019 for £1m. She rents out the property to a third party. The costs of acquisition in 2019 totalled £350,000. Aanya sells the property on 1 April 2021 for £1.8m. The costs of sale were £100,000. Aanya's taxable gain for 202/21 is calculated as follows.

	£
Sales proceeds	1,800,000
Less: Cost of sale	(100,000)
Net proceeds	1,700,00
Less: Cost	(1,000,000)
Less: Acquisition costs	(350,000)
Less: Annual exempt amount	(12,300)
Taxable gain	337,700

Notes

(a) For 2019/20 onwards, a person who is not UK resident for a tax year is chargeable to capital gains tax on gains arising on the disposal in that year of any interests in UK land. The charge applies also if the tax year is a split year for an individual under the statutory residence test and the disposal is made in the overseas part of the year. [*TCGA 1992, ss 1A(3)(b), 1G; FA 2019, Sch 1 paras 2, 120*]. These provisions replace and extend the provisions for non-resident disposals of UK residential property which applied for disposals in 2015/16 to 2018/19. The provisions are subject to rebasing rules for land acquired before 6 April 2019. See (B)–(D) below.

(b) Similarly, for disposals on or after 6 April 2019, non-UK resident companies are chargeable to corporation tax on gains on interests in UK land. [*TCGA 1992, ss 2B(4)(5); FA 2019, Sch 1 paras 2, 120*].

(c) An '*interest in UK land*' is an estate, interest, right or power in or over land in the UK, or the benefit of an obligation, restriction or condition affecting the value of such, but not including:

- any interest or right (other than a rentcharge or, in Scotland, a feu duty) held to secure payment of money or performance of any other obligation; or
- a licence to use or occupy land;
- in England, Wales or Northern Ireland, a tenancy at will or an advowson, franchise (i.e. a grant from the Crown, such as the right to hold a market or fair, or the right to take tolls) or manor; or
- any other interest or right specified in Treasury regulations.

'*Land*' includes buildings and structures and any land under the sea or otherwise covered by water.

[*TCGA 1992, s 1C; FA 2019, Sch 1 paras 2, 120*].

(d) For 2019/20 onwards, a person who is not UK resident for a tax year is also chargeable to capital gains tax on gains arising on the disposal in that year of assets deriving at least 75% of their value from UK land if he has a 'substantial indirect interest' in that land. The charge applies also if the tax year is a split year for an individual under the statutory residence test and the disposal is made in the overseas part of the year. Non-UK resident companies are likewise chargeable to corporation tax on such gains arising on or after 6 April 2019. [*TCGA 1992, ss 1A(3)(c), 1G, 2B(4)(6); FA 2019, Sch 1 paras 2, 120*].

216.4 CGT   Land

(e) Where a non-UK resident person (other than a company) makes a disposal within (a) or (d) above on or after 6 April 2019, that person must normally make a return to HMRC in respect of the disposal on or before the 30th day following the day of the completion of the disposal (and, where appropriate, make a payment on account of CGT). The requirement applies whether or not a gain arises from the disposal. A payment on account in respect of a disposal in 2019/20 is not required if the taxpayer has been given a notice to deliver a self-assessment return or 2019/20 or 2018/19 (and the notice has not been withdrawn). See *FA 2019, Sch 2*.

The requirement to make a return also applies to any direct disposal of UK land by a UK-resident person (other than a company) on or after 6 April 2019 where a residential property gain arises.

(f) See CG73960 and *Simon's Taxes* C2.1128.

(B) **Direct disposals not chargeable before 6 April 2019**

Mr A, a resident in Spain, acquired a commercial property in London on 1 September 2010 for £5m. The company rents out the property to a third party. The costs of acquisition in 2010 totalled £350,000. The property is valued at £15m on 5 April 2019 with professional valuation costs of £10,000. Mr A sells the property on 1 April 2021 for £18m. The costs of sale were £100,000.

Commercial properties held as an investment by non-residents were not within the scope of the NRCGT provisions prior to 6 April 2019.

Under the post-5 April 2019 rules for non-residents, Mr A can choose one of two different methods of calculation under *TCGA 1992, Sch 4AA, Pt 2*. These are considered in turn.

Default method

Under the default method, which applies unless Mr A elects for an alternative, the property is rebased to its market value on 5 April 2019 and it is only the gain arising after this date that is taxed:

	£
Sales proceeds	18,000,000
Less: Cost of sale	(100,000)
Net proceeds	17,900,000
Less: Value at 5 April 2019 (plus valuation costs)	(15,010,000)
Less: Annual exempt amount	(12,300)
Chargeable gain	2,877,700

As this requires a valuation the default method will incur higher professional expenses than the retrospective method, although the valuer's fees are allowable in the capital gains tax calculation.

Retrospective basis

Under the retrospective basis the entire gain is chargeable, not just the post-5 April 2019 gain. Similarly, if there is a loss, the entire loss is allowable.

Land CGT 216.4

	£
Sales proceeds	18,000,000
Less: Cost of sale	(100,000)
Net proceeds	17,900,000
Less: Cost (£5,000,000 plus £350,000 acquisition costs)	(5,350,000)
Less : annual exempt amount	(12,300)
Chargeable gain	12,537,700

Clearly, it is not beneficial to make the election in this case. This method of calculation is only likely to be used where the original cost is higher than the market value of the property at 5 April 2019.

Therefore, The default method produces the lowest chargeable gain and no election to use the retrospective basis should be made.

Notes

(a) See CG73960 and CG73894 and *Simon Taxes* C2.1128.

(b) An election for the retrospective (or time-apportionment — see (C) below) basis of computation can only be made in a self-assessment tax return for the tax year in which the disposal is made or in the UK land disposal return (see note (e) to (A) above) for the disposal (or in an amendment to either type of return). An election made in a UK land disposal return can be revoked in the self-assessment return (or amendment), provided that the latter return is delivered by the filing date. Otherwise, an election is irrevocable. [*TCGA 1992, Sch 4AA para 21; FA 2019, Sch 1 para 17*].

(C) **Direct disposals of pre-April 2015 assets fully chargeable before 6 April 2019**

Mr B, who is resident in Ireland, purchased a residential property in Belfast for £200,000 on 10 April 2001. The costs of acquisition were £2,000. The property was extended in June 2007 at a cost of £200,000. The property has been let throughout Mr B's period of onwerhsip and has never been his main residence.

The property is valued at £1,000,000 on 5 April 2015, with valuation costs of £7,500.

The property was sold on 6 June 2020 for £1,500,000.

As the property has been a dwelling throughout the period from 6 April 2015 until 5 April 2019, it is fully chargeable under the NRCGT rules. Under the post-5 April 2019 rules for non-residents, Mr B can choose one of three different methods of calculation under *TCGA 1992, Sch 4AA, Pt 3*. These are considered in turn.

Default method

Under the default method, which applies unless B Ltd elects for an alternative, the property is rebased to its market value on 5 April 2015:

216.4 CGT   Land

	£
Sales proceeds	1,500,000
Less: Cost of sale	(10,000)
Net proceeds	1,490,000
Less: value at 5 April 2015 (see note below)	(1,007,500)
Less : Annual Exempt Amount	(12,300)
Chargeable gain	£470,200

Note

(a) As the valuation takes account of the earlier enhancement to the property (the extension), the cost of the enhancement is not taken into account. The costs of the valuation on 5 April 2015 are allowable. [*TCGA 1992, Sch 4AA, para 7; FA 2019, Sch 1, para 17*].

Retrospective method

If B Ltd elects to use the retrospective basis, the entire gain is chargeable, not just the post-5 April 2015 gain. Similarly, if there is a loss, the entire loss is allowable.

	£
Sales proceeds	1,500,000
Less: Cost of sale	(10,000)
Net proceeds	1,490,000
Less: Original cost (£200,000 plus £2,000 costs)	(202,000)
Less: Cost of enhancement	(200,000)
Less : Annual exempt amount	(12,300)
Chargeable gain	£1,075,700

Straight-line time apportionment method

If Mr B elects for the straight-line method of apportioning the gain, the UK chargeable gain is determined on a days basis (to the date of disposal):

	£
Sales proceeds	1,500,000
Less: Cost of sale	(10,000)
Net proceeds	1,490,000
Less: Original cost (£200,000 plus £2,000 costs	(202,000)
Less: Cost of enhancement	(200,000)
Less : Annual exempt amount	(12,300)
Gain	1,075,700
Less: pre-6 April 2015 gain (£1,075,700 x 5,109/6,998) (see note (a))	(785,332)
Chargeable gain	£290,368

Therefore, The time apportionment method produces the lowest chargeable gain. For the chargeable gain to be calculated on this basis, Mr B must make an irrevocable election via his tax return for the accounting period in which the disposal takes place.

Notes

(a) To apportion the gain on a straight-line basis, the pre-6 April 2015 gain must be excluded. The ownership period begins on the date of acquisition, or 31 March 1982 if later (in this example, it is therefore 10 April 2001). The pre-6 April 2015 period ends on 5 April 2015. The total ownership period ends on the day date of disposal, which for capital gains tax purposes is the date the contracts are exchanged. The total ownership period is 6,998 days (10 April 2001 to 6 June 2020) and the period which falls before 6 April 2015 is 5,109 days. See CG73924

(b) For the time limit for making an election see note (b) to (B) above.

(c) For the requirement to make a UK land disposal return see note (e) to (A) above.

(d) See *Simon's Taxes* C2.1148.

(D) **Direct disposals of assets partially chargeable before 6 April 2019**

A building was acquired by a non-resident, Mr C, on 6 April 1990 for £60,000 and comprises of a shop with a flat above it. The building is disposed of in June 2021 for £380,000. The shop represented half of the building throughout.

Market value at 5 April 2015 is £300,000.

Market value at 5 April 2019 is £350,000.

As the property has had mixed usage during the ownership period, it is partially chargeable before 6 April 2019.

Mr C can choose one of two different methods of calculation under TCGA 1992, Sch 4AA, Pt 4. These are considered in turn

Default method

Under the default method, which applies unless Mr B elects for an alternative, the property (because it was acquired before 6 April 2015) is rebased twice — once on 5 April 2015 and again on 5 April 2019. For the assumed sale on 5 April 2019, the gain or loss calculated is treated as accruing on the actual disposal in addition to the gain or loss that accrues on the actual disposal:

	£
Actual disposal	
Sales proceeds	380,000
Less: value at 5 April 2019	350,000
Gain on actual disposal June 2021	£30,000
Assumed disposal in April 2019	
Value at 5 April 2019	350,000

216.4 CGT Land

Less: value at 5 April 2015		(300,000)
		50,000
Less: non-residential element (see note (a))		(25,000)
Gain on assumed sale in April 2019		£25,000
Total gain accruing (£30,000 + £25,000)		£55,000

Note

(a) Only the residential element on the property is chargeable on the assumed sale. As the shop represented half of the building throughout, only 50% of the gain is chargeable. [*TCGA 1992, Sch 4AA, para 13; FA 2019, Sch 1, para 17*].

Retrospective method

	£
Sales proceeds	380,000
Less: Less: original cost	(60,000)
Gain	320,000
Less: Annual exempt amount	(12,300)
Chargeable gain	£307,700

Therefore, the default method produces the lowest chargeable gain and no election to use the retrospective basis should be made.

Notes

(a) See *Simon's Taxes* C2.1149.

(b) For the time limit for making an election see note (b) to (B) above.

(c) For the requirement to make a UK land disposal return see note (e) to (A) above.

217 Losses

Cross-references. See **IT 15.2** LOSSES for the set-off of trading losses against chargeable gains made by individuals. See **201.2** ANNUAL RATES AND EXEMPTIONS for the interaction between losses and the annual exempt amount.

217.1 RELIEF FOR ALLOWABLE LOSSES

[*TCGA 1992, ss 1(3), 1E, 1F, 24, 62(2); FA 2019, Sch 1 paras 2, 120*]

(A) General

On 30 April 2020 Q sells for £40,000 a part of the land which he owns. The market value of the remaining estate is £160,000. Q bought the land for £250,000 in March 1996.

	£
Disposal consideration	40,000
Allowable cost $\dfrac{40,000}{40,000 + 160,000} \times £250,000$	50,000
Allowable loss	£10,000

(B) Asset of negligible value

In June 2020, John sells an asset, realising a chargeable gain of £25,000. In December 2020, John learns that his shareholding in Jones Ltd has become worthless. He acquired the shares in 1995 for their then market value of £15,000. John makes no other disposals in 2020/21.

If John makes a negligible value claim under *TCGA 1992, s 24* no later than 5 April 2023, then his capital gains tax computation for 2020/21 is as follows.

	£
Chargeable gain	25,000
Less allowable loss	(15,000)
	10,000
Less annual exempt amount (£12,300 restricted to)	(10,000)
Gains chargeable to tax 2020/21	Nil

Notes

(a) Where the owner of an asset which has become of 'negligible value' makes a claim to that effect he is treated as if he had sold, and immediately reacquired, the asset for a consideration of an amount equal to the value specified in the claim. Such a claim can also be made if the disposal by which the claimant acquired the asset was a no gain/no loss disposal at the time of which the asset was of negligible value and, between the time at which the asset became of negligible value and that disposal, any other disposal of the asset was a no gain/no loss disposal. The deemed sale is treated

217.1 CGT   Losses

as having occurred at the time of the claim or at an earlier time specified in the claim. An earlier time can be specified only if the claimant owned the asset at that time, the asset had become of negligible value at that time and that time is not more than two years before the beginning of the tax year in which the claim is made or, for corporation tax, is on or after the first day of the earliest accounting period ending not more than two years before the time of the claim. [*TCGA 1992, s 24*].

(b) '*Negligible value*' is not defined but is taken by HMRC to mean 'worth next to nothing'. See CG13125 and *Simon's Taxes* C1.320, C1.321, C1.505, C1.506, C2.1107, C1.307.

(C) Loss carried back from year of death

Rick dies on 30 March 2021. Before his death, he makes one disposal in 2020/21, realising an allowable loss of £19,000. In 2019/20 and 2018/19 he had realised chargeable gains of £16,000 and £27,000 respectively.

Following Rick's death his capital gains position for 2018/19 and 2019/20 is revised as follows.

	£
2019/20	
Chargeable gain	16,000
Less 2020/21 allowable loss carried back (part)	(4,000)
	12,000
Less annual exempt amount	(12,000)
Gains chargeable to tax 2019/20	Nil
2018/19	
Chargeable gain	27,000
Less 2020/21 allowable loss carried back (remainder)	(15,000)
	12,000
Less annual exempt amount	(11,700
Taxable gain 2018/19	£300

Notes

(a) Allowable losses in excess of chargeable gains incurred by the deceased in the tax year in which death occurs can be carried back and set off against chargeable gains in the three preceding tax years. Chargeable gains accruing in a later year must be relieved before those of an earlier year. Losses carried back cannot be set against gains treated under *TCGA 1992, s 87* or *s 89(2)* as accruing to the individual as a beneficiary of a non-UK resident settlement. [*TCGA 1992, s 62(2)(2A); FA 2019, Sch 1 para 29*]. See CG38570 and *Simon's Taxes* C4.440, C4.449A.

(b) Any remaining unused losses *cannot* be carried forward and set off against gains made by the personal representatives or legatees.

(c) Losses carried back to 2019/20 or a later year are deducted *after* the annual exempt amount. [*TCGA 1992, s 1K(4); FA 2019, Sch 1 paras 2, 120*]. Note that the result is in effect the same as for earlier years where the amount carried back is restricted so as to allow gains covered by the annual exempt amount to remain in charge.

217.2 PERSONAL LOSSES SET AGAINST ATTRIBUTED SETTLEMENT GAINS

[*TCGA 1992, ss 1E(4), 86; FA 2019, Sch 1 paras 2, 33, 120*]

In May 2003, R created an offshore settlement in which he retained the reversionary interest. It is accepted that *TCGA 1992, s 86* applies to the settlement such that any chargeable gains accruing to the trustees are chargeable on R as settlor. In July 2020, the trustees realised a gain of £18,418 on a disposal of quoted securities which they had held since creation of the settlement. They made no other disposal in the year. R, meanwhile, made two disposals in 2020/21 on which he realised a chargeable gain of £4,000 and an allowable loss of £9,000. Neither the trustees nor R have any losses brought forward from earlier years. R pays income tax for 2020/21 at the higher rate.

R's CGT position for 2020/21 is as follows.

	£
Personal gains	4,000
Attributed gains	18,418
Deduct Personal losses	(9,000)
	13,418
Deduct Annual exempt amount	(12,300)
Taxable gains 2020/21	£1,118
CGT payable by R at 20% (recoverable from trustees)	£223.60
Personal losses carried forward	Nil

Note

(a) Personal losses can be set against gains attributed to the taxpayer under *TCGA 1992, s 86* (charge on settlor of non-UK resident settlement in which he has an interest). Such losses cannot, however, be set off against gains treated under *TCGA 1992, ss 87, 87K, 87L or 89(2)* as accruing to a beneficiary or the settlor of a non-UK resident settlement or the recipient of an onward gift from such a beneficiary — see **201.2(B)** ANNUAL RATES AND EXEMPTIONS. See CG38435 and *Simon's Taxes* C4.425.

217.3 LOSSES ON SHARES IN UNLISTED TRADING COMPANIES

[*TCGA 1992, s 125A; ITA 2007, ss 131–151; FA 2020, s 38*]

P subscribed for 3,000 £1 ordinary shares at par in W Ltd, a qualifying trading company, in June 1988. In September 1995, P acquired a further 2,200 shares at £3 per share from another shareholder. In December 2020, P sold 3,900 shares at 40p per share.

217.3 CGT Losses

Procedure

Firstly, establish the 'section 104 holding' pool.

	Shares	Qualifying expenditure
		£
June 1988 subscription	3,000	3,000
September 1995 acquisition	2,200	6,600
	5,200	9,600
December 2020 disposal	(3,900)	(7,200)
Pool carried forward	1,300	£2,400

Step 1. Calculate the CGT loss in the normal way, as follows

	£
Disposal consideration 3,900 × £0.40	1,560
Allowable cost	(7,200)
Allowable loss	£(5,640)

Step 2. Applying a LIFO basis, identify the qualifying shares (1,700) and the non-qualifying shares (2,200) comprised in the disposal.

Step 3. Calculate the proportion of the loss attributable to the qualifying shares.

$$\text{Loss referable to 1,700 qualifying shares } \frac{1,700}{3,900} \times £5,640 \qquad £2,458$$

Step 4. Compare the loss in Step 3 with the actual cost of the qualifying shares, *viz.*

$$\text{Cost of 1,700 qualifying shares } \frac{1,700}{3,000} \times £3,000 \qquad £1,700$$

The loss available against income is restricted to £1,700 (being lower than £2,458).

The loss not relieved against income remains an allowable loss for CGT purposes.

£5,640 − £1,700 = £3,940

Note

(a) For further examples on this topic, see **IT 15.5 LOSSES** and **CT 114.4 LOSSES**.

(b) See VCM74050, 75400–75490 and *Simon's Taxes* D1.1120

217.4 DEFERRED UNASCERTAINABLE CONSIDERATION: ELECTION TO TREAT LOSS AS ARISING IN EARLIER YEAR

[*TCGA 1992, ss 279A–279D*]

Tanya owns 2,000 £1 ordinary shares in Be Good Ltd, for which she subscribed at par in January 1997. On 31 March 2014, she and the other shareholders in Be Good Ltd sold their shares to another company for £20 per share plus a further unquantified cash amount calculated by means of a formula relating to the future profits of Be Good Ltd. The value in March 2014 of the deferred consideration was estimated at £5.10 per share. Tanya makes no other disposals of chargeable assets in 2013/14. On 30 April 2020, Tanya receives a further £3.60 per share under the sale agreement.

Without an election under *TCGA 1992, s 279A*, Tanya's capital gains position is as follows.

2013/14

	£	£
Disposal proceeds	40,000	
Value of rights	10,200	50,200
Cost of acquisition		(2,000)
Chargeable gain 2013/14		£48,200

2020/21

	£
Disposal of rights to deferred consideration	
Proceeds 2,000 × £3.60	7,200
Deemed cost of acquiring rights	(10,200)
Allowable loss 2020/21	£(3,000)

If Tanya makes an election under *TCGA 1992, s 279A* by 31 January 2023 the 2020/21 loss is treated as arising in 2013/14 and can be set off against the gain of that year as follows.

2013/14

	£
Gain as above	47,842
Less Allowable loss	(3,000)
Chargeable gain 2013/14	£44,842

Notes

(a) Where a person within the charge to capital gains tax makes a disposal of a right to 'future unascertainable consideration' (as defined) acquired as consideration for the disposal of another asset, and a loss accrues, he may, subject to conditions, make an election for the loss to be treated as arising in the year in which that other asset was disposed of. Where the right was acquired as consideration for two or more disposals in different tax years (referred to as '*eligible years*'), the loss is utilised in the earliest year first. [*TCGA 1992, s 279A*]. See CG15083–15086 and *Simon's Taxes* C2.107A.

217.4 CGT   Losses

(b) To the extent that the loss cannot be utilised in the earliest eligible year it may be carried forward for set-off against gains of later years. In the case of tax years falling between that year and the year of the loss, any remaining part of the loss can only be deducted if the year concerned is an eligible year. [*TCGA 1992, s 279C; FA 2008, Sch 2 paras 43, 56(2)*]. See CG15100, CG15104–15106 and *Simon's Taxes* C2.107A.

(c) The election is irrevocable and must be made by notice in writing to HMRC on or before the first anniversary of 31 January following the year of the loss. The notice must specify the amount of the relevant loss, the right disposed of, the tax year of the right's disposal, and, if different, the year of the loss, the tax year in which the right was acquired, the original asset or assets on disposal of which the right was acquired, the eligible year in which the loss is to be treated as accruing, and the amount to be deducted from gains of that year. [*TCGA 1992, s 279D*]. See CG15121–15122 and *Simon's Taxes* C2.107A.

218 Married Persons and Civil Partners

218.1 TRANSFERS BETWEEN SPOUSES OR CIVIL PARTNERS

[*TCGA 1992, s 58*]

(A) **No transfer between spouses or civil partners**

Paul and Heidi are a married couple. For 2020/21 Heidi's taxable income (after personal allowance) is £50,000 and Paul's is £15,000. On 4 July 2020, Heidi sells two paintings which she had acquired in June 1994 at a cost of £5,000 each. Net sale proceeds amount to £16,000 and £25,000. Neither spouse disposed of any other chargeable assets during 2020/21.

Chargeable gains — Heidi

	£
Net proceeds of painting 1	16,000
Cost	(5,000)
Chargeable gain	£11,000
Net proceeds of painting 2	25,000
Cost	(5,000)
Chargeable gain	£20,000
Total chargeable gains (£11,000 + £20,000)	31,000
Annual exempt amount	(12,300)
Taxable gains 2020/21	£18,700
Tax payable £18,700 × 20%	£3,740.00

Note

(a) See CG22210 and *Simon's Taxes* C1.202, C2.112.

(B) **Transfer between spouses or civil partners**

The facts are as in (A) above except that in April 2020, Heidi gives painting 2 to Paul who then makes the sale on 4 July 2020.

218.1 CGT   Married Persons and Civil Partners

Chargeable gains – Heidi

	£
Deemed consideration for painting 2 (April 2020) (note (a))	5,000
Cost	(5,000)
Chargeable gain	Nil
Net proceeds of painting 1	16,000
Cost	(5,000)
Chargeable gain	£11,000
Total chargeable gains	11,000
Annual exempt amount (restricted)	(11,000)
Taxable gains 2020/21	£Nil

Chargeable gain — Paul

	£
Net proceeds (4.7.20)	25,000
Cost (April 2020)	(5,000)
Chargeable gain	20,000
Annual exempt amount	(12,300)
Taxable gain 2020/21	£7,700
Capital gains tax £7,700 × 10%	£770.00
Tax saving compared with (A) above (£3,740 − £770)	£2,970

Notes

(a) The inter-spouse transfer is deemed to be for such consideration as to ensure that no gain or loss accrues. [*TCGA 1992, s 58*]. See CG22210 and *Simon's Taxes* C1.202, C2.112.

(b) The fact that transfers of assets between husband and wife or between civil partners are no gain/no loss transfers enables savings to be made by ensuring that disposals are made by a spouse or partner who has an unused annual exempt amount and/or pays CGT at a lower rate.

(c) A transfer between spouses or civil partners followed by a sale could be attacked by HMRC as an anti-avoidance device. To minimise the risk, there should be a clear time interval between the two transactions and no arrangements made to effect the ultimate sale until after the transfer. The gift should be outright with no strings attached and with no 'arrangement' for eventual proceeds to be passed to the transferor.

Married Persons and Civil Partners CGT 218.1

(C) **Transfer between spouses or civil partners before 6 April 2008**

The facts are as in (B) above except that Heidi gives painting 2 to Paul in January 2008. The indexation factor for the period June 1994 to April 1998 is 0.124.

Chargeable gains — Heidi

2007/08

	£
Deemed consideration for painting 2 (January 2008) (note (a))	5,620
Cost	(5,000)
Unindexed gain	620
Indexation allowance (to April 1998) £5,000 × 0.124	(620)
Chargeable gain	Nil

2020/21

Net proceeds of painting 1	16,000
Cost	(5,000)
Chargeable gain	11,000
Annual exempt amount (restricted)	(11,000)
Taxable gains 2020/21	£Nil

Chargeable gain — Paul

	£
Net proceeds (4.7.20)	25,000
Cost (January 2008)	(5,620)
Chargeable gain	19,380
Annual exempt amount	(12,300)
Taxable gain	£7,080
Capital gains tax £7,080 × 10%	£708.00
Tax saving compared with (A) above (£3,740 − £708))	£3,032

218.1 CGT   Married Persons and Civil Partners

Notes

(a) The consideration for the inter-spouse transfer is equal to cost plus indexation to April 1998. See **214.2** INDEXATION for further examples.

(b) The abolition of indexation allowance for capital gains tax purposes for disposals after 5 April 2008 does not affect the deemed consideration for which Paul is treated as acquiring painting 2.

(c) See CG56715 and *Simon's Taxes* C1.422.

218.2 EMPLOYEE SHAREHOLDER SHARES

[*TCGA 1992, s 58; FA 2013, Sch 23 para 17; FA 2016, s 88(7)–(10); FA 2017, s 13(2)(6)–(8)*]

In May 2021, Amy transfers shares with a market value of £90,000 to her husband Rory. The shares are exempt employee shareholder shares within *TCGA 1992, s 236B* acquired by Amy in May 2016 for £15,000. The capital gains tax consequences of the transfer are as follows.

(i) No previous disposals of exempt employee shareholder shares

Exempt gain — Amy

	£
Deemed consideration (market value)	90,000
Cost	(15,000)
Exempt gain	£75,000
Lifetime limit remaining unused (£100,000 – £75,000)	£25,000

Rory is deemed to have acquired the shares at market value for £90,000.

(ii) Lifetime limit previously used up

Chargeable gain — Amy

	£
Deemed consideration (no gain/no loss)	15,000
Cost	(15,000)
Exempt gain	£Nil

Rory is deemed to have acquired the shares for £15,000.

(iii) £60,000 of lifetime limit previously used

Balance of lifetime limit (£100,000 − £60,000)   £40,000

Chargeable gain — Amy

	£
Deemed consideration (amount resulting in gain equal to balance of lifetime limit)	55,000
Cost	(15,000)
Gain (exempt as equal to the balance of the lifetime limit)	£40,000

Rory is deemed to have acquired the shares for £55,000.

Notes

(a) The exemption for employee shareholder shares is abolished for such shares acquired under an employee shareholder agreement entered into on or after the 'relevant day'. The *'relevant day'* is in most cases 1 December 2016 but, where the individual received the necessary legal advice on 23 November 2016 before 1.30 pm, it is 2 December 2016. [*FA 2017, s 13(6)–(8)*].

(b) The no gain/no loss rule does not apply to a transfer of exempt employee shareholder shares between spouses or civil partners who are living together where any gain would be wholly exempt. [*TCGA 1992, s 58(2)(3); FA 2016, s 88(8)(9); FA 2017, s 13(2)(6)–(8)*].

(c) A lifetime limit of gains of £100,000 applies to disposals of exempt employee shareholder shares acquired under employee shareholder agreements entered into on or after 17 March 2016 and before the relevant day (see note (a) above). Gains falling partly within the limit are exempt to the extent that they do not exceed the unused balance of the limit. Gains on disposals of shares acquired under agreements entered into before that date do not count in applying the limit. [*TCGA 1992, s 236B(1A)–(1C)(3A); FA 2016, s 88(2)(3); FA 2017, s 13(4)(6)–(8)*].

(d) Where a transfer of employee shareholder shares would only be partly exempt as a result of the lifetime limit, the transfer is treated as made for a consideration equal to the amount (not exceeding market value) which results in a gain of an amount equal to the balance of the lifetime limit. [*TCGA 1992, s 58(4)(5); FA 2016, s 88(9); FA 2017, s 13(2)(6)–(8)*].

(e) See CG22210, CG56715 and Simon's C1.202, C2.112, C1.422.

218.3 JOINTLY OWNED ASSETS

Derek and Raquel are a married couple. Derek had for many years owned an investment property which he purchased for £70,000 in May 1988. On 5 January 1996, he transferred to Raquel a 10% share in the property which was thereafter held in their joint names as tenants in common. At the time of the transfer, a 10% share of the property is worth £10,000 on the open market and a 90% share is worth £90,000. No declaration is made for income tax purposes under what is now *ITA 2007, s 837*, with the result that the rental income from the property is treated, by virtue of *ITA 2007, s 836*, as arising in equal shares. On 29 June 2020, the property is sold for £140,000. The indexation factor for May 1988 to January 1996 is 0.414.

218.3 CGT   Married Persons and Civil Partners

(i) **Inter-spouse transfer**

	£
Deemed consideration (January 1996)	9,898
Cost £70,000 × $\dfrac{10{,}000}{10{,}000 + 90{,}000}$ (see note (c))	(7,000)
Unindexed gain	2,898
Indexation allowance £7,000 × 0.414	(2,898)
Chargeable gain 1995/96	Nil

(ii) **2020/21 disposal**

	Derek	Raquel
	£	£
Disposal proceeds	126,000	14,000
Cost: Derek (£70,000 − £7,000)	(63,000)	
Raquel (see (i) above)		(9,898)
Chargeable gains 2020/21	£63,000	£4,102

Notes

(a) Where a joint declaration of unequal beneficial interests is made under *ITA 2007, s 837* it is presumed that the same split applies for capital gains tax purposes. In the absence of a declaration, and regardless of the income tax treatment of income derived from the asset, a gain on an asset held in the joint names of husband and wife is apportioned in accordance with their respective beneficial interests at the time of disposal. (Revenue Press Release 21 November 1990). See *Simon's Taxes* E5.103A.

(b) See 218.1(C) above as to how the consideration for the inter-spouse transfer is arrived at.

(c) The allowable expenditure on the inter-spouse transfer is apportioned in accordance with the part disposal rules in *TCGA 1992, s 42* (see **209.2** COMPUTATION OF GAINS AND LOSSES).

219 Offshore Settlements

Cross-reference. See also **217.2** LOSSES.

219.1 CHARGE ON BENEFICIARY IN RECEIPT OF CAPITAL PAYMENTS

(A) **Charge under TCGA 1992, s 87**

C, resident and domiciled in the UK, is the sole beneficiary of a discretionary settlement created by his father in 5 and administered in the Cayman Islands. The trustees are all individuals resident in the Cayman Islands. The trustees make no gains or capital payments in 2016/17 or any earlier year, but make the following capital payments to C in 2017/18 onwards.

	£
2017/18	50,000
2018/19	60,000
2019/20	50,000
2020/21	70,000

In 2020/21, the trustees sell two settlement assets (which are not UK residential property interests) realising a gain of £350,000 and a loss of £50,000. They make no other disposals in that year. C makes only one disposal in 2020/21, realising an allowable loss of £25,000. C pays income tax in 2020/21 at the higher rate.

The settlement's 'section 1(3) amount' for 2020/21 is:

	£
Gain	350,000
Less Loss	(50,000)
Section 1(3) amount for 2020/21	£300,000

The section 1(3) amount is matched with the capital payments made to C on a last in first out basis as follows.

	£
Section 1(3) amount	300,000
2020/21 capital payment	70,000
2020/21 capital payment	50,000
2018/19 capital payment	60,000
2017/18 capital payment	50,000
Unmatched amount carried forward	£70,000

219.1 CGT   Offshore Settlements

C's liability to capital gains tax for 2020/21 is as follows.

	£
Matched section 1(3) amount (£70,000 + £50,000 + £60,000+ £50,000)	230,000
Less Annual exempt amount	(12,300)
Amount chargeable to capital gains tax 2020/21	£217,700
Capital gains tax (£217,700 × 20%)	£43,540

Notes

(a) *TCGA 1992, s 87* applies to a settlement for a tax year if there is no time in the year when the trustees are resident in the UK. [*TCGA 1992, s 87(1)(6)*]. See CG38570, CG38575 and *Simon's Taxes* C4.440, C4.449A.

(b) There are detailed rules for matching gains with capital payments. Broadly, capital payments are matched with section 1(3) amounts on a last in first out basis by applying the five step process in *TCGA 1992, s 87A*. See CG38721 and *Simon's Taxes* C4.455.

(c) The '*section 1(3) amount*' for a tax year for which the settlement is within *TCGA 1992, s 87* is the amount which would have been chargeable on the trustees under *TCGA 1992, s 1(3)* (i.e. chargeable gains less current year and brought forward losses) had they been resident in the UK in that year *less*, if *TCGA 1992, s 86* (offshore settlement where settlor has interest) applies to the settlement for the year, any chargeable gains for the year under that section. The section 1(3) amount for a tax year for which *section 87* does not apply is nil. In determining the section 1(3) amount, where an amount on which the trustees would be chargeable accrues on a non-resident disposal of a direct or indirect interest in land (for disposals on or after 6 April 2019) or a non-resident CGT disposal (for disposals before 6 April 2019) any amount on which the trustees are in fact chargeable as such a gain is not chargeable on the beneficiary. [*TCGA 1992, s 87(4)–(5A); FA 2019, Sch 1 paras 35, 120*]. See CG10919 and *Simon's Taxes* C1.102, C1.106, C1.502.

Note that for 2018/19 and earlier years, the section 1(3) amount was known as the 'section 2(2) amount'. The change is a result of the rewriting of part of *TCGA 1992* by *FA 2019*.

(d) C's personal loss of £25,000 for 2020/21 cannot be relieved against gains chargeable under *TCGA 1991, s 87*.

(e) Subject to certain exceptions, capital payments received in 2018/19 or a subsequent year are disregarded for these purposes if received (or treated as received) from the trustee by a beneficiary who is non-UK resident throughout the tax year. This provision also applies for 2018/19 onwards to capital payments received before 2018/19 which have not been matched under the above provisions as they apply for 2017/18 and earlier years. [*TCGA 1992, ss 87D–87F, 87H; FA 2018, Sch 10 paras 1(1)(12)(13), 2*].

(f) Where a capital payment is received in 2018/19 or a later year by a beneficiary who is a close member (as above) of the settlor's family at the time of receipt and the settlor is resident in the UK in the tax year of receipt, the above provisions apply as if the payment were received by the settlor as a beneficiary (whether or not he is in fact a beneficiary) and not by the actual recipient. The settlor can recover any resulting tax from the actual recipient of the payment and can require HMRC to

(g) *FA 2018* introduced provisions to tax capital payments by offshore settlements in circumstances where the beneficiary receiving the payment is not liable to CGT under these provisions (because he is non-UK resident or a remittance basis user) and he makes an onward gift of the proceeds to a UK resident. Broadly, the UK resident is treated as if they had received the payment from the trust as a beneficiary. The provisions apply where the onward gift is made on or after 6 April 2018 (and do so even if the original capital payment is received before that date). [*TCGA 1992, ss 87I–87M; FA 2018, Sch 10 para 1(1)(14)*].

provide a certificate specifying the amount of the gains and the amount of tax for the purpose of recovering the tax. Any such certificate is conclusive evidence of the facts stated in it. [*TCGA 1992, s 87G; FA 2018, Sch 10 para 1(1)(13)*].

(B) **Surcharge on CGT under TCGA 1992, s 87**

[*TCGA 1992, s 91; FA 2019, Sch 1 para 43*]

D, resident and domiciled in the UK, is the sole beneficiary of a discretionary settlement created by his father in May 2010 and administered in the Cayman Islands. The trustees are all individuals resident in the Cayman Islands. In 2016/17, the trustees sell an asset realising a gain of £120,000, but otherwise make no disposals. In 2020/21, the trustees make a capital payment to D of £120,000, having made no previous capital payments. D makes no other disposals in 2020/21 but pays income tax for that year at the higher rate.

D's capital gains tax liability for 2020/21 is calculated as follows.

	£
CGT (subject to surcharge)	
(£120,000 − £12,300 annual exempt amount) × 20%	21,540
Surcharge £21,540 × 10% × 4 years (1.12.17–30.11.21)	8,616
Total tax payable 2020/21	£30,156

Notes

(a) The capital payment of £120,000 in 2020/21 is matched under *TCGA 1992, s 87A* with the section 1(3) amount for 2020/21 of £120,000. See (A) above.

(b) The surcharge is 10% per annum for a period beginning on 1 December following the end of the tax year the section 1(3) amount for which is matched with the capital payment and ending on 30 November in the tax year following that in which the capital payment is made but subject to a maximum period of six years. [*TCGA 1992, s 91(3)–(5)*]. See CG38795 and *Simon's Taxes* C4.449E.

220 Overseas Matters

220.1 COMPANY MIGRATION

[*TCGA 1992, ss 185, 187, 187B; FA 2019, Sch 1 paras 67, 120, Sch 8 para 9*]

Z Ltd is a company incorporated in Ruritania, but regarded as resident in the UK by virtue of its being managed and controlled in the UK. It is the 75% subsidiary of Y plc, a UK resident company. On 1 October 2020, the management and control of Z Ltd is transferred to Ruritania and it thus ceases to be UK resident, although it continues to trade in the UK, on a much reduced basis, via a UK permanent establishment.

Details of the company's chargeable assets immediately before 1 October 2020 were as follows.

	Market value	Capital gain after indexation (where applicable) if all assets sold
	£	£
Factory in UK	480,000	230,000
Warehouse in UK	300,000	180,000
Factory in Ruritania	350,000	200,000
Warehouse in Ruritania	190,000	100,000
UK quoted investments	110,000	80,000
Foreign trade investments	100,000	Loss (60,000)

The UK warehouse continues to be used in the UK trade. The UK factory does not, and is later sold. On 1 June 2021, the Ruritanian warehouse is sold for the equivalent of £210,000. On 1 October 2022, Y plc sells its shareholding in Z Ltd.

Prior to becoming non-UK resident, Z Ltd had unrelieved capital losses brought forward of £40,000.

The corporation tax consequences are as follows

Chargeable gain accruing to Z Ltd on 1.10.20

	£
Factory (Ruritania)	200,000
Warehouse (Ruritania)	100,000
UK quoted investments	80,000
Foreign trade investments	(60,000)
	320,000
Losses brought forward	(40,000)
Net gain chargeable to corporation tax	£280,000

A deemed gain of £230,000 also arises on the UK factory but is deferred until the factory is sold. The deferred gain is in addition to any actual gain arising on the disposal of the factory under *TCGA 1992, s 2B(4)(a)* (disposals of UK land by non-resident companies).

220.1 CGT   Overseas Matters

The sale of the overseas warehouse, and of any other overseas assets, is outside the scope of corporation tax on chargeable gains.

Any subsequent disposal of the UK warehouse *will* be within the charge to corporation tax, having been omitted from the deemed disposal on 1 October 2020, due to its being used in a trade carried on in the UK through a permanent establishment. On disposal, the gain will be computed by reference to original cost, or 31.3.82 value if appropriate, rather than to market value immediately before 1 October 2020 — see also note (f).

Y plc will realise a capital gain (or loss) on the sale of its shareholding in Z Ltd on 1 October 2021.

Notes

(a) The provisions of *TCGA 1992, s 185* apply where a company ceases to be resident in the UK. All companies incorporated in the UK are regarded as UK resident. As such a company cannot therefore cease to be resident, *section 185* can apply only to companies incorporated abroad which are UK resident. See also HMRC Statement of Practice SP 1/90 as regards company residence generally. See CG42370, CG42380 and *Simon's Taxes* D4.131.

(b) Unless a company so elects (within two years after ceasing to be UK-resident), neither a gain nor a loss accrue on the deemed disposal of an interest in UK land. For deemed disposals before 6 April 2019, this rule applies if the gain or loss on the deemed disposal would have been an NRCGT gain or loss on the assumption that the disposal was a non-resident CGT disposal. In either case, the gain or loss that would have accrued on the deemed disposal is treated as accruing at the time of any subsequent disposal of the interest, in addition to any gain or loss which actually accrues. [*TCGA 1992, s 187B; FA 2019, Sch 1 paras 67, 120*]. See CG73834.

(c) Where a company ceased to be UK-resident before 1 January 2020, there was a facility to postpone a charge under *TCGA 1992, s 185* by making an election under *s 187*. The facility is withdrawn for companies ceasing to be UK-resident on or after 1 January 2020. Payment of the charge can, however, be postponed by way of a CT exit charge payment plan if the company becomes resident in an EEA state (see note (g) below).

(d) *TMA 1970, ss 109B–109F* contain management provisions designed to secure payment of all outstanding tax liabilities on a company becoming non-UK resident. See also HMRC Statement of Practice SP 2/90. See CT34160–34190 and *Simon's Taxes* D4.131, D4.132.

(e) If the UK warehouse ceases to be a chargeable asset by virtue of Z Ltd's ceasing to carry on a trade in the UK through a permanent establishment, there will be a deemed disposal at market value at that time, under *TCGA 1992, s 25*. Unless an election is made, any gain will be deferred until the warehouse is disposed of (and will be in addition to the actual gain on disposal under *TCGA 1992, s 2B(4)(a)* (disposals of UK land by non-resident companies)). See CG25530, CG42130 and *Simon's Taxes* C1.602, D4.120. See 220.2 below.

(f) A company which becomes non-UK resident can enter into a CT exit charge payment plan if it becomes resident in an EEA state. Under such a plan, corporation tax arising under various exit charges, including *TCGA 1992, s 185* can be deferred. [*TMA 1970, s 59FA, Sch3ZB; FA 2019, Sch 8 paras 1–9*]. See *Simon's Taxes* D1.1359.

220.2 NON-RESIDENTS CARRYING ON TRADE, ETC. THROUGH UK BRANCH OR AGENCY

[*TCGA 1992, ss 1A(3), 1B, 25, 25ZA; FA 2019, Sch 1 paras 2, 25, 26, 120*]

Overseas Matters CGT 220.2

X, who is not resident in the UK, practises abroad as a tax consultant and also practises in the UK through a London branch, preparing accounts to 5 April. The assets of the UK branch include freehold premises bought in 1988 for £60,000 and a computer system acquired in March 2016 for £20,000. On 31 January 2021, the computer ceases to be used in the UK branch and is immediately shipped abroad, and on 28 February 2021, X closes down the UK branch. He sells the premises in June 2021 for £118,000. Capital allowances claimed on the computer up to and including 2019/20 were £20,000 and short-life asset treatment had been claimed.

Relevant market values of the assets are as follows

		£
Computer,	at 31 January 2021	11,000
Premises,	at 14 March 1989	65,000
	at 28 February 2021	110,000

The UK capital gains tax consequences are as follows

2020/21

		£	£
Computer			
Market value 31.1.21			11,000
Deduct			
Cost		20,000	
Less capital allowances claimed	(note (f))	(9,000)	(11,000)
Chargeable gain 2020/21			Nil

There is also a deemed disposal of the premises (see note (c) below). Unless X elects otherwise, the gain on the premises is deferred until they are disposed of. The gain to be deferred is calculated as follows.

	£
Market value 28.2.21	110,000
Deduct Market value 14.3.89	(65,000)
Deferred chargeable gain	£45,000

2021/22

Premises	£
Sale proceeds	118,000
Deduct Cost (market value 28.2.21)	(110,000)
Chargeable gain	£8,000
Deferred gain brought back into charge	£45,000
Total chargeable gains 2021/22	£53,000

220.2 CGT   Overseas Matters

Notes

(a) X is within the charge to UK capital gains tax for disposals after 13 March 1989 by virtue of his carrying on a profession in the UK through a branch or agency. Previously, the charge applied only to non-residents carrying on a *trade* in this manner. X is deemed to have disposed of (with no capital gains tax consequences) and reacquired immediately before 14 March 1989 all chargeable assets used in the UK branch at market value, so that any subsequent CGT charge will be by reference only to post-13 March 1989 gains. [*FA 1989, s 126(3)–(5); TCGA 1992, s 10(5)*]. See CG25510, CG25500 and *Simon's Taxes* C1.602, C1.604.

(b) There is a deemed disposal, at market value, of the computer on 31 January 2021 as a result of its ceasing to be a chargeable asset by virtue of its becoming situated outside the UK. [*TCGA 1992, s 25(1)*]. See CG25530, CG42130 and *Simon's Taxes* C1.602, D4.120.

(c) There is a deemed disposal, at market value, of the premises on 28 February 2021 as a result of the asset ceasing to be a chargeable asset by virtue of X's ceasing to carry on a trade, profession or vocation in the UK through a branch or agency. The premises continue, however, to be a chargeable asset by virtue of being an interest in UK land. As a result, unless X makes an election, the deemed gain is deferred until a subsequent disposal of all or part of the premises. The gain is then treated as arising on the subsequent disposal in June 2021 (in addition to the actual gain on that disposal). On a disposal of only part of an interest in UK land, only a corresponding part of a deemed gain or loss would be treated as arising. [*TCGA 1992, ss 25(3)(8), 25ZA; FA 2019, Sch 1 paras 25, 26, 120*]. See CG73769, CG73988.

(d) X is entitled to the £12,300 annual exempt amount against UK gains, regardless of his residence status (but taxpayers who make a claim under *ITA 2007, s 809B* for the remittance basis are not entitled to the annual exempt amount).

(e) Where a chargeable asset has qualified for capital allowances and a loss accrues on its disposal, the allowable expenditure is restricted, under *TCGA 1992, s 41*, by the net allowances given, which in this example amount to £9,000 (annual investment allowance £20,000 less balancing charge £11,000 arising on the asset's ceasing to be used in the trade).

220.3 TRANSFER OF ASSETS TO NON-RESIDENT COMPANY

[*TCGA 1992, s 140; FA 2018, s 27*]

Q Ltd, a UK resident company, carries on business in a foreign country through a branch there. In September 2014, it is decreed that all enterprises in that country be carried on by locally resident companies. Q Ltd forms a wholly-owned non-UK resident subsidiary R and transfers all the assets of the branch to R wholly in consideration for the issue of shares. The assets transferred include the following

	Value	Charge-able gains
	£	£
Goodwill	100,000	95,000
Freehold land	200,000	120,000
Plant (items worth more than £6,000)	50,000	20,000

	Value	Chargeable gains
	£	£
Other assets	150,000	—
	£500,000	£235,000

On 1 January 2016, there is a compulsory acquisition of 50% of the share capital of R for £300,000 (market value). The value of the whole shareholding immediately before disposal is £750,000. The value of Q Ltd's remaining 50% holding is £300,000.

In June 2020, R is forced to sell its freehold land to the government.

Q Ltd's capital gains position is as follows

2014

The gain of £235,000 is deferred. The allowable cost of the shares in R is £500,000.

2016

	£
Consideration on disposal	300,000
Deduct	
Cost of shares sold $£500,000 \times \dfrac{300,000}{300,000 + 300,000}$	(250,000)
Gain subject to indexation	£50,000
Proportion of deferred gain becoming chaargeable $£235,000 \times \dfrac{300,000}{750,000}$	£94,000

2020

	£
Proportion of deferred gain chargeable	
Gain arising $\dfrac{120,000}{235,000} \times £235,000$	£120,000
Balance of gain still held over (£235,000 − £94,000 − £120,000)	£21,000

220.3 CGT   Overseas Matters

Notes

(a) The 2020 gain arises under *section 140(5)*. If the sale of freehold land had taken place more than six years after the original transfer of assets, no part of the deferred gain would have become chargeable as a result. See CG45660–45680 and *Simon's Taxes* D6.523.

(b) The 2016 gain arises under *section 140(4)*. In this case, there is no time limit as in (a) above. The appropriate proportion of the deferred gain is treated as a separate chargeable gain.

220.4 INDIVIDUAL TEMPORARILY NON-RESIDENT IN THE UK

[*TCGA 1992, ss 1M, 1N, 3E; FA 2013, Sch 45 paras 109–115; FA 2019, Sch 1 paras 2, 120*]

Mr Stephenson, who has lived in the UK all his life, leaves the UK on 1 May 2015 for a four year employment contract abroad. Under the statutory residence test, Mr Stephenson is resident outside the UK for the whole of 2015/16 to 2019/20 inclusive. On 16 May 2017 he sells his entire shareholding in Snow plc for £30,000. He had purchased the shares for £10,000 in April 2007. Mr Stephenson returns to the UK on 6 April 2020 and, under the statutory residence test, is UK-resident from that date. He makes no other disposals in the period 1 May 2015 to 5 April 2021 inclusive.

No chargeable gain accrues on the disposal of the shares in 2017/18 as Mr Stephenson is not resident in the UK.

A chargeable gain is deemed to accrue in respect of the disposal of the shares in 2020/21, the year of Mr Stephenson's return to the UK, computed as follows.

	£
Proceeds	30,000
Acquisition cost	(10,000)
Chargeable gain	£20,000

Notes

(a) *TCGA 1992, s 1M* applies where an individual leaves the UK for a period of temporary residence outside the UK and four out of the seven tax years immediately preceding the year of departure were years for which the individual had sole UK residence or were split years which included a period for which the individual had sole UK residence, provided that the period of non-residence is five years or less. [*TCGA 1992, s 1M(1); FA 2013, Sch 45 paras 110–115; FA 2019, Sch 1 para 2*]. See CG26500 and *Simon's Taxes* E6.137B–E6.137C.

(b) Where the year of return is a split year under the statutory residence test, the deemed gain is treated as arising in the UK part of the year.

221 Partnerships

221.1 ASSETS

[*TCGA 1992, s 59; FA 2019, Sch 1 para 28*]

G, H and I trade in partnership. They share capital in the ratio 5:4:3. Land occupied by the firm is sold on 15 April 2020 for £240,000, having been acquired for £54,000 in 2001. G has personal gains in 2020/21 of £2,500, H has losses of £1,000 and I made no disposals of personal assets. None of the partners has any capital losses brought forward from earlier years.

The gains of G, H and I in respect of the land are as follows

	G($^5/_{12}$)	H($^4/_{12}$)	I($^3/_{12}$)
	£	£	£
Disposal consideration	100,000	80,000	60,000
Less: Cost	(22,500)	(18,000)	(13,500)
Chargeable gain	£77,500	£62,000	£46,500

Summary

	G	H	I
	£	£	£
Share of partnership gain	77,500	62,000	46,500
Personal gains/(losses)	2,500	(1,000)	—
Chargeable gain	80,000	61,000	46,500
Annual exempt amount	(12,300)	(12,300)	(12,300)
Taxable gain 2020/21	£67,700	£48,700	£34,200

Notes

(a) Each partner is regarded as owning a fractional share of each partnership asset, which is calculated by reference to his capital sharing ratio.

(b) See CG10731, CG27150 and *Simon's Taxes* B7.406.

221.2 CGT   Partnerships

221.2 CHANGES IN SHARING RATIOS

J and K have traded in partnership since 1990, sharing capital and income equally. The acquisition costs of the chargeable assets of the firm are as follows

	Cost £
Premises	60,000
Goodwill	10,000

The assets have not been revalued in the firm's balance sheet. On 1 June 2020, J and K admit L to the partnership, and the sharing ratio is J 35%, K 45% and L 20%.

J and K are regarded as disposing of part of their interest in the firm's assets to L as follows

	£
J	
Premises	
Deemed consideration	
£60,000 × (50% − 35%)	9,000
Allowable cost	(9,000)
Chargeable gain	—
Goodwill	
Deemed consideration	
£10,000 × (50% − 35%)	1,500
Allowable cost	(1,500)
Chargeable gain	—

	£
K	
Premises	
Deemed consideration	
£60,000 × (50% − 45%)	3,000
Allowable cost	(3,000)
Chargeable gain	—
Goodwill	
Deemed consideration	
£10,000 × (50% − 45%)	500
Allowable cost	(500)
Chargeable gain	—

Partnerships CGT 221.4

The allowable costs of the three partners are now

	Freehold land £	Goodwill £
J	21,000	3,500
K	27,000	4,500
L	12,000	2,000

Notes

(a) The treatment illustrated above is taken from HMRC Statement of Practice SP D12, para 4 as extended by SP 1/89. Each partner's disposal consideration is equal to his share of current balance sheet value of the asset concerned and each disposal treated as producing no gain and no loss.

(b) L's allowable costs comprise 20% of original cost.

221.3 ACCOUNTING ADJUSTMENTS

A, B and C trade in partnership. They share income and capital profits equally. The firm's only chargeable asset is its premises which cost £51,000 in 1990. C decides to retire. The remaining partners agree to share profits equally. Before C retires (in May 2020), the premises are written up to market value in the accounts, agreed at £180,000. C does not receive any payment directly from the other partners on his retirement.

The capital gains tax consequences are

On retiring, C is regarded as having disposed of his interest in the firm's premises for a consideration equal to his share of the then book value.

		£
Disposal consideration	$1/3 \times £180,000$	60,000
Acquisition cost	$1/3 \times £51,000$	17,000
Chargeable gain, subject to business asset disposal relief		£43,000

A and B will each be treated as acquiring a $1/6$ ($1/2 \times 1/3$) share in the premises, at a cost equal to one half of C's disposal consideration. Their acquisition costs are then

		A £	B £
Cost of original share	$1/3 \times £51,000$	17,000	17,000
Cost of new share	$1/2 \times £60,000$	30,000	30,000
Total		£47,000	£47,000

221.4 CONSIDERATION OUTSIDE ACCOUNTS

D, E and F are partners in a firm of accountants who share all profits in the ratio 7:7:6. G is admitted as a partner in May 2020 and pays the other partners £10,000 for goodwill. The new partnership shares are D $3/10$, E $3/10$, F $1/4$ and G $3/20$. The book value of goodwill is £18,000, its cost on acquisition of the practice from the predecessor in 1991.

221.4 CGT Partnerships

The partners are treated as having disposed of shares in goodwill as follows

	£	£
D		
$^7/_{20} - {}^3/_{10} = {}^1/_{20}$		
Disposal consideration		
Notional $^1/_{20} \times £18,000$	900	
Actual $^7/_{20} \times £10,000$	3,500	
		4,400
Allowable cost $^1/_{20} \times £18,000$		(900)
Chargeable gain		£3,500
E		
$^7/_{20} - {}^3/_{10} = {}^1/_{20}$		
Disposal consideration (as for D)		4,400
Allowable cost (as for D)		(900)
Chargeable gain		£3,500
F		
$^6/_{20} - {}^1/_{4} = {}^1/_{20}$		
Disposal consideration		
Notional $^1/_{20} \times £18,000$	900	
Actual $^6/_{20} \times £10,000$	3,000	
		3,900
Allowable cost		(900)
Chargeable gain		£3,000
G's allowable cost of his share of goodwill is therefore		
Actual consideration paid		10,000
Notional consideration paid $^3/_{20} \times £18,000$		2,700
		£12,700

221.5 SHARES ACQUIRED IN STAGES

Q is a partner in a legal practice. The partnership's only chargeable asset is a freehold house used as an office. The cost of the house to the partnership was £3,600 in 1999 and it was revalued in the partnership accounts to £50,000 in 2015. Q was admitted to the partnership in June 2001 with a share of $^1/_6$ of all profits. As a result of partnership changes, Q's profit share altered as follows

2005	$^1/_5$
2013	$^1/_4$
2020	$^3/_{10}$

For capital gains tax, Q's allowable cost of his share of the freehold house is calculated as follows

		£
2001	$1/6 \times £3,600$	600
2005	$(1/5 - 1/6) \times £3,600$	120
2013	$(1/4 - 1/5) \times £3,600$	180
2020	$(3/10 - 1/4) \times £50,000$	2,500
		£3,400

Note

(a) On Q's acquisition of an increased share of the property in 2020 (subsequent to the revaluation in 2015), any partner with a reduced share will be treated as having made a disposal and thus a gain or loss.

221.6 PARTNERSHIP ASSETS DISTRIBUTED IN KIND

R, S and T are partners sharing all profits in the ratio 4:3:3. Farmland owned by the firm is transferred in November 2020 to T for future use by him as a market gardening enterprise separate from the partnership business. No payment is made by T to the other partners but a reduction is made in T''s future share of income profits. The book value of the farmland is £50,000, its cost in 1996, but the present market value is £150,000.

		£
R		
Deemed disposal consideration	$4/10 \times £150,000$	60,000
Allowable cost	$4/10 \times £50,000$	(20,000)
Gain		£40,000
S		
Deemed disposal consideration	$3/10 \times £150,000$	45,000
Allowable cost	$3/10 \times £50,000$	(15,000)
Gain		£30,000
T		
Partnership share	$3/10 \times £50,000$	15,000
Market value of R's share		60,000
Market value of S's share		45,000
Allowable cost of land for future disposal		£120,000

222 Payment of Tax

222.1 PAYMENT BY INSTALMENTS

(A) **Consideration payable by instalments**

[*TCGA 1992, ss 280, 281*]

Ian, a higher rate income tax payer, sells an asset on 31 March 2021 for £240,000. The consideration is to be paid by twelve annual instalments of £20,000 beginning on 31 March 2021. Ian originally purchased the asset for £15,000 in 1993 and his allowable costs of sale are £4,000. The gain is not an upper rate gain and does not qualify for business asset disposal relief or investors' relief. Ian has no other chargeable gains in 2020/21.

Ian's liability to capital gains tax for 2020/21 is as follows

	£
Consideration	240,000
Less costs of sale	(4,000)
Acquisition cost	(15,000)
Chargeable gain 2020/21	221,000
Annual exempt amount	(12,300)
Gain chargeable to tax	£208,700
Capital gains tax payable (£208,700 × 20%)	£41,740

If Ian opts under *TCGA 1992, s 280* to pay the tax by instalments, the following payments will be due.

31 January 2022	£10,000
31 March 2022	£10,000
31 March 2023	£10,000
31 March 2024	£10,000
31 March 2025	£1,740

222.1 CGT   Payment of Tax

Notes

(a) Where the whole or part of the consideration for a disposal is receivable by instalments over a period exceeding 18 months, beginning not earlier than the date of the disposal, the tax arising may at the option of the taxpayer by paid by such instalments as HMRC allows. The tax instalment period cannot exceed eight years and must end not later than the time at which the final instalment of the consideration is payable. [*TCGA 1992, s 280*]. See *Simon's Taxes* C2.106, D1.902.

(b) HMRC's practice is to ask for instalments of tax equal to half of each instalment of consideration until the total tax liability has been discharged. To the extent that instalments of consideration under the contract fall due on or before the normal due date for the payment of tax (31 January in the tax year following that in which the disposal occurred), the respective instalments of tax are payable on that normal due date. Where instalments of consideration fall due after that time, then the respective instalments of tax are payable on the dates when the taxpayer is contractually entitled to receive the consideration. See CG14910.

(c) Interest on unpaid tax is charged on each instalment only if it is paid late and will run from the date when the instalment was due until the date of payment. See SAM80072.

(d) The above instalment provisions do not apply to deferred consideration which is unquantified and contingent. See **207.2** CAPITAL SUMS DERIVED FROM ASSETS.

(B) **Gifts of land or shares**

On 1 June 2020, Sean gives a parcel of land to his daughter, Erica. The market value of the land on that date is £316,000. Sean purchased the land in 1993 for £37,700 and makes no other disposals in 2020/21. He is a higher rate income taxpayer. For the purposes of this example only, the rate of interest on unpaid capital gains tax is taken to be 4% throughout.

Sean's liability to capital gains tax for 2020/21 is as follows

	£
Market value	316,000
Less acquisition cost	(37,700)
Chargeable gain 2020/21	278,300
Annual exempt amount	(12,300)
Gain chargeable to tax	£266,000
Capital gains tax payable (£266,000 × 20%)	£53,200

Payment of Tax CGT 222.1

If Sean elects under *TCGA 1992, s 281*, before 31 January 2022 to pay the tax by instalments, the following payments will be due.

	£	£
1st instalment due 31.1.22		5,320
2nd instalment due 31.1.23	5,320	
Interest 4% × £47,880	1,915	7,235
3rd instalment due 31.1.24	5,320	
Interest 4% × £42,560	1,702	7,022
4th instalment due 31.1.25	5,320	
Interest 4% × £37,240	1,489	6,809
5th instalment due 31.1.26	5,320	
Interest 4% × £31,920	1,276	6,596
6th instalment due 31.1.27	5,320	
Interest 4% × £26,600	1,064	6,384
7th instalment due 31.1.28	5,320	
Interest 4% × £21,280	851	6,171
8th instalment due 31.1.29	5,320	
Interest 4% × £15,960	638	5,958
9th instalment due 31.1.30	5,320	
Interest 4% × £10,640	425	5,745
10th instalment due 31.1.31	5,320	
Interest 4% × £5,320	212	5,532
Total tax and interest		£62,772

222.1 CGT Payment of Tax

Notes

(a) Capital gains tax chargeable on a gift of land or certain shares or securities can, on election in writing, be paid by ten yearly instalments. The first instalment is due on the ordinary due date. The outstanding balance together with accrued interest may be paid at any time. Where the gift is to a connected person, the tax (and accrued interest) are payable immediately if any part of the subject-matter of the gift is subsequently disposed of for consideration. [*TCGA 1992, s 281(2)(4)(6)(7)*]. See CG66531, CG66540.

(b) Payment by instalments is also available in respect of a deemed disposal by trustees under *TCGA 1992, s 71(1)* (person becoming absolutely entitled to settled property) or *s 72(1)* (termination of life interest on death) and, in certain cases, to a chargeable gain accruing under *TCGA 1992, s 169C(7)* (clawback of hold-over relief under *TCGA 1992, s 165* or *s 260* if settlement becomes settlor-interested). [*TCGA 1992, s 281(1)(8)*].

(c) The disposal must *either* be one to which neither *TCGA 1992, s 165(4)* nor *s 260(3)* (see **213.2** and **213.1** HOLD-OVER RELIEFS) applies (or would apply if a claim was made) *or* one to which either of those *sections* does apply but on which the held-over gain only partly reduces the gain otherwise arising or is nil. [*TCGA 1992, s 281(1)*].

(d) The assets on a disposal of which an election can be made are: land or any interest or estate in land; any shares or securities of a company which, immediately before the disposal, gave control to the person making or deemed to be making the disposal; and any other shares or securities of a company not listed on a recognised stock exchange. [*TCGA 1992, s 281(3)*].

(e) Interest on unpaid tax is charged as if no election had been made. The interest on the unpaid portion of the tax is added to each instalment and must be paid accordingly. [*TCGA 1992, s 281(5)*].

(f) See CG18601 and *Simon's Taxes* C1.109, C4.223.

223 Private Residences

223.1 PERIODS OF OWNERSHIP QUALIFYING FOR EXEMPTION

[*TCGA 1992, ss 222, 223, 223B; FA 2019, Sch 1 paras 74, 120; FA 2020, s 24*]

(A)

P, who is resident in the UK, sold a house on 1 July 2020 realising an otherwise chargeable gain of £154,000. The house was purchased on 1 February 1981 and was occupied as a residence until 30 June 1990 when P moved to another residence, letting pthe house as residential accommodation. He did not reoccupy the house prior to its sale.

	£
Gain on sale	154,000
Deduct Exempt amount under main residence rules	
$\dfrac{8y\ 3m\ +\ 9m}{38y\ 3m} \times £154,000$	(34,118)
Net chargeable gain	£119,882

Notes

(a) The final nine months of ownership (eighteen months for disposals before 6 April 2020) are always included in the exempt period of ownership. A 36-month period applies where, at the time of the disposal:

- the taxpayer is a disabled person or a long-term resident in a care home and does not have any other right in a private residence; or
- the taxpayer's spouse or civil partner is a disabled person or a long-term resident in a care home and neither the individual nor the spouse or civil partner has any other right in a private residence.

'*Disabled person*' is defined for this purpose at *FA 2005, Sch 1A*. An individual is a '*long-term resident*' in a care home at the time of a disposal if at that time he is resident there and has been resident, or can reasonably be expected to be resident there, for at least three months. A '*care home*' is an establishment providing accommodation together with nursing or personal care *TCGA 1992, ss 223(1), 225E; FA 2020, s 24(3)(11)*].

(b) The period of ownership for the exemption calculation does not include any period before 31 March 1982. [*TCGA 1992, s 223(7)*].

(c) The gain attributable to the period in which the house is let does not qualify for relief. For disposals on or after 6 April 2020, letting relief is available only where part of a dwelling-house is the individual's only or main residence and at the same time another part is let out by the individual as residential accommodation (i.e. where there is shared occupancy). See **223.3** below.

(d) See CG64200, CG64236, CG64236, CG64710, CG65030 and *Simon's Taxes* C2.1301–C2.1305, C2.1307, C2.1308.

223.1 CGT   Private Residences

(e) See also **216.4** LAND.

(B)

Q bought a house on 1 August 1981 for £40,000 and used it as his main residence. On 10 February 1982, he was sent by his employer to manage the Melbourne branch of the firm and continued to work in Australia until 4 August 1987, the whole of his duties being performed outside the UK. The house was let as residential accommodation during that period. Q took up residence in the house once again following his return to the UK, but on 30 September 2000 moved to Switzerland for health reasons. The house was again let as residential accommodation. He returned to the UK in August 2003, but did not reside in the house at any time prior to it being sold on 31 December 2020 for £252,350. The house had a market value of £50,000 at 31 March 1982.

Computation of gain before applying exemptions

	£
Disposal consideration	252,350
Market value 31.3.82	(50,000)
Gain before exemptions	£202,350

The gain is reduced by the main residence exemptions as follows

Period of ownership (excluding period before 31.3.82)		38y 9m
Exempt periods since 31.3.82:		
31.3.82 – 30.9.00	18y 6m	
1.4.2020 – 31.12.20 (last nine months)	9m	19y 3m

	£
Gain as above	202,350
Deduct Exempt amount under main residence rules	
$\dfrac{19\text{y 3m}}{38\text{y 9m}} \times £202{,}350$	(100,522)
Net chargeable gain 2020/21	£101,828

Notes

(a) Periods of ownership before 31 March 1982 are excluded in applying the main residence exemptions. [*TCGA 1992, s 223(7)*].

(b) The period spent in Australia (regardless of its length but excluding that part of it before 31 March 1982) counts as a period of residence, as Q worked in an employment all the duties of which were performed outside the UK and used the house as his main residence at some time before and after this period of absence. [*TCGA 1992, s 223(3)(b)*].

Private Residences   CGT 223.2

(c) The period spent in Switzerland would have been exempt, having not exceeded three years, but the exemption is lost as Q did not occupy the property as a main residence at any time after this period. [*TCGA 1992, s 223(3)(a)*].

(d) The last nine months (eighteen months prior to 6 April 2020) of ownership are always exempt providing the property has been used as the owner's only or main residence at some time during the period of ownership, and for this purpose, 'period of ownership' is not restricted to the period after 30 March 1982. See note (a) to (A) above.

(e) The gain attributable to the period in which the house is let does not qualify for relief. For disposals on or after 6 April 2020, letting relief is available only where part of a dwelling-house is the individual's only or main residence and at the same time another part is let out by the individual as residential accommodation (i.e. where there is shared occupancy). See **223.3** below.

(f) See CG65040–CG65068 and *Simon's Taxes* C3.1709.

223.2 ELECTION FOR MAIN RESIDENCE

[*TCGA 1992, s 222(5)*]

S, who is UK-resident throughout, purchased the long lease of a London flat on 1 June 2012. He occupied the flat as his sole residence until 31 July 2014 when he acquired a property in Shropshire. Both properties were thereafter occupied as residences by S until the lease of the London flat was sold on 28 February 2021, realising an otherwise chargeable gain of £75,000.

The possibilities open to S are

(i) **Election for London flat to be treated as main residence throughout**

Exempt gain £75,000

(ii) **Election for Shropshire property to be treated as main residence from 31 July 2014 onwards**

$$\text{Exempt gain } £75{,}000 \times \frac{2y\ 2m + 9m}{8y\ 9m} \qquad £25{,}000$$

223.2 CGT   Private Residences

(iii) Election for London flat to be treated as main residence up to 31 May 2020, with election for the Shropshire property to be so treated thereafter

$$\text{Exempt gain } £75,000 \times \frac{8y + 9m}{8y\ 9m} \qquad £75,000$$

Note

(a) The elections in (iii) are the most favourable, provided they could have been made by 31 July 2016 in respect of the London flat, and by 31 May 2022 in respect of the Shropshire property. Note that the last nine months ownership of the London flat is an exempt period in any case. The advantage of (iii) over (i) is that the period of ownership 1 June 2020 to 28 February 2021 of the Shropshire property will be treated as a period of residence as regards any future disposal of that property. HMRC practice is that the *initial* election (which can be varied) must be made within two years of acquisition of the second property, and this was upheld in *Griffin v Craig-Harvey* Ch D 1993, 66 TC 396, [1994] STC 54. See *Simon's Taxes* C3.1704.

223.3 LETTING RELIEF FOR DISPOSALS ON OR AFTER 6 APRIL 2020

[*TCGA 1992, s 223B; FA 2020, s 24(5)(11)*]

Soraiya sells a house in October 2020 realising a gain before relief of £250,000. She has lived in the house as her main residence throughout her period of ownership but throughout that period 50% of the floor area of the house has been let as residential accommodation. Her chargeable gain for 2020/21 on the house is:

	£	£
Gain before reliefs		250,000
Less: Main residence relief (50%)		(125,000)
		125,000
Less: letting relief–lowest of:		
Main residence relief	125,000	
Gain attributable to letting	125,000	
£40,000	40,000	(40,000)
Chargeable gain		£85,000

Notes

(a) Where a gain to which fractional exemption under *TCGA 1992, s 222* (see **223.1** above) applies accrues to an individual on or after 6 April 2020, further relief (letting relief) is available where at any time in the period of ownership part of the dwellinghouse is the individual's only or main residence and another part is let out by him as residential accommodation (i.e. there is shared occupancy). The part of the gain which would otherwise be chargeable by reason of the letting is exempt to the extent of the lower of:

Private Residences CGT 223.3

- £40,000; and
- the amount of the gain otherwise exempt under *TCGA 1992, s 223* (see **223.1** above).

(b) For disposals before 6 April 2020, letting relief was available where fractional main residence relief was available and the whole dwelling-house or part of it was let out as residential accommodation at any time in the period of ownership. There was no requirement for shared occupancy. Periods of letting before 6 April 2020 where there was no shared occupancy do not give rise to any relief if the disposal is on or after 6 April 2020.

224 Qualifying Corporate Bonds

[*TCGA 1992, ss 115–117*]

224.1 DEFINITION

[*TCGA 1992, s 117*]

B has the following transactions in 5% unsecured loan stock issued in 1983 by F Ltd.

		£
11.11.83	Purchase £2,000	1,800
10.7.89	Gift from wife £1,000 (original cost £800)	—
30.9.97	Purchase £2,000	2,100
5.6.20	Sale £4,000	(3,300)

Apart from the gift on 10.7.89, all acquisitions were arm's length purchases. B's wife acquired her £1,000 holding on 11.11.83. Indexation allowance of £266 arose on the transfer from wife to husband.

For the purposes of the accrued income scheme, the sale is without accrued interest and the rebate amount is £20. The stock is a corporate bond as defined by *TCGA 1992, s 117(1)* and therefore a 'relevant security' as defined by *TCGA 1992, s 108(1)*.

Under the rules for matching relevant securities in *TCGA 1992, s 106A*, the stock disposed of is identified with acquisitions as follows.

(i)   Identify £2,000 with purchase on 30.9.97 (LIFO)

	£
Disposal consideration $£3,300 \times \dfrac{2,000}{4,000}$	1,650
Add rebate amount $£20 \times \dfrac{2,000}{4,000}$	10
	1,660
Allowable cost	(2,100)
Loss	£(440)

The loss is *not* allowable as the £2,000 stock purchased on 30.9.97 is a qualifying corporate bond (note (a)). [*TCGA 1992, s 115*].

224.1 CGT   Qualifying Corporate Bonds

(ii) Identify £1,000 with acquisition on 10.7.89

	£
Disposal consideration £3,300 × $\dfrac{1{,}000}{4{,}000}$	825
Add rebate amount £20 × $\dfrac{1{,}000}{4{,}000}$	5
	830
Allowable cost (including indexation to 10.7.89)	(1,066)
Allowable loss	£(236)

The loss is allowable as the stock acquired on 10.7.89 is not a qualifying corporate bond (note (b)).

(iii) Identify £1,000 with purchase on 11.11.83

	£
Disposal consideration £3,300 × $\dfrac{1{,}000}{4{,}000}$	825
Add rebate amount £20 × $\dfrac{1{,}000}{4{,}000}$	5
	830
Allowable cost £1,800 × $\dfrac{1{,}000}{2{,}000}$	(900)
Allowable loss	£(70)

The loss is allowable as the stock acquired on 11.11.83 is not a qualifying corporate bond (note (c)).

Notes

(a) The acquisition on 30.9.97 is a qualifying corporate bond as it was acquired after 13 March 1984 otherwise than as a result of an excluded disposal. [*TCGA 1992, s 117(7)(b)*].

(b) The acquisition on 10.7.89 was the result of an excluded disposal, being a no gain/no loss transfer between spouses where the first spouse had acquired the stock before 14 March 1984. It is therefore not a qualifying corporate bond. [*TCGA 1992, s 117(7)(b)(8)*].

(c) Securities acquired before 14 March 1984 cannot be qualifying corporate bonds in the hands of the person who so acquired them.

(d) See **IT 2** ACCRUED INCOME SCHEME for the income tax effects of the accrued income scheme.

(e) See CG12608, CG12210, CG54900, CFM45570, CG53706 and *Simon's Taxes* C2.820, C2.821, C2.825, D7.803.

224.2 REORGANISATION OF SHARE CAPITAL

[*TCGA 1992, s 116*]

D holds 5,000 £1 ordinary shares in H Ltd. He acquired the shares in April 1999 by subscription at par. On 1 August 2013, he accepted an offer for the shares from J plc. The terms of the offer were one 25p ordinary share of J plc and £10 J plc 10% unsecured loan stock (a qualifying corporate bond) for each H Ltd ordinary share. Both the shares and the loan stock are listed on the Stock Exchange. In December 2020, D sells £20,000 loan stock at its quoted price of £105 per cent.

The value of J plc ordinary shares at 1 August 2013 was £3.52 per share and the loan stock was £99.20 per cent.

The cost of the H Ltd shares must be apportioned between the J plc ordinary shares and loan stock.

	£
Value of J plc shares	
5,000 × £3.52	17,600
Value of J plc loan stock	
£50,000 × 99.2%	49,600
	£67,200

Allowable cost of J plc shares

$$\frac{17,600}{67,200} \times £5,000 \qquad £1,310$$

Allowable cost of J plc loan stock

$$\frac{49,600}{67,200} \times £5,000 \qquad £3,690$$

Chargeable gain on H Ltd shares attributable to J plc loan stock to date of exchange

	£
Deemed disposal consideration	49,600
Allowable cost	(3,690)
Deferred chargeable gain	£45,910

224.2 CGT Qualifying Corporate Bonds

Deferred chargeable gain accruing on disposal of loan stock in December 2020

Loan stock sold (nominal)	£20,000
Total holding of loan stock before disposal (nominal)	£50,000 |("
Deferred chargeable gain accruing in 2020/21	
$\dfrac{20{,}000}{50{,}000} \times £45{,}910$	£18,364

Notes

(a) The gain on the sale of J plc loan stock is exempt (as the stock is a qualifying corporate bond) except for that part which relates to the gain on the previous holding of H Ltd shares. [*TCGA 1992, s 115, s 116(10)*]. There will also be income tax consequences under the accrued income scheme (see **IT 2** ACCRUED INCOME SCHEME).

(b) The qualifying corporate bond is treated as acquired at the date of the reorganisation, so even if the original shares had been held at 31 March 1982, re-basing would *not* apply on the subsequent disposal of the loan stock.

(c) The exchange of J plc ordinary shares for H Ltd shares is dealt with under *TCGA 1992, ss 127–130*, and no gain or loss will arise until the J plc shares are disposed of. See **229.4** SHARES AND SECURITIES.

(d) See CITM8020 and *Simon's Taxes* D6.111, D6.112.

225 Remittance Basis

225.1 EFFECT OF ELECTION UNDER TCGA 1992, S 16ZA

[*TCGA 1992, s 16ZA, Sch 1; FA 2019, Sch 1 paras 3, 13*]

Kevin, who is domiciled in South Africa, comes to the UK on 6 April 2019 and is resident in the UK with effect from that date. He has substantial non-UK income and assets and makes claims under *ITA 2007, s 809B* for the remittance basis to apply for 2019/20 and 2020/21. Kevin disposes of two non-UK assets in 2019/20 realising a gain of £60,000 and a loss of £20,000. He also disposes of a UK asset on 1 May 2019, realising a gain of £10,000. He makes no disposals in 2020/21 but is treated as having remitted the £60,000 gain to the UK on 1 May 2020. Kevin is a higher rate income taxpayer for both years.

If Kevin makes an election under *TCGA 1992, s 16ZA* for 2019/20, his capital gains tax liabilities are as follows.

2019/20

	£
Gain on UK asset	10,000
Capital gains tax £10,000 × 20%	£2,000
Gain on non-UK asset	60,000
Deduct loss on non-UK asset	(20,000)
Net gain chargeable when remitted to UK	£40,000

2020/21

Net gain on non-UK asset remitted to UK	40,000
Capital gains tax £40,000 × 20%	£8,000

Notes

(a) Where an election has been made under *TCGA 1992, s 16ZA*, capital losses on non-UK assets arising in a tax year must be matched with gains in the following order:

 (I) foreign chargeable gains arising and remitted to the UK in the year or, if the year is a split year, in the UK part of the year;

 (II) foreign chargeable gains arising in the year but not remitted to the UK in that year or, where the year is a split year, remitted to the UK in the overseas part of the year; and

 (III) all other chargeable gains arising in the year (other than gains treated as accruing on the remittance to the UK of foreign chargeable gains arising in a previous year).

If the losses reduce but do not exhaust gains within (II) above, the losses are matched with those gains in reverse chronological order (starting with the last gain to arise in the year). Where necessary, losses are deducted from gains arising on the same day on a pro rata basis.

225.1 CGT Remittance Basis

Only the amounts matched with gains within (I) and (III) above are deducted as allowable losses in calculating the amount on which the individual is chargeable to capital gains tax for the year.

Any losses matched with gains cannot be carried forward, but where a loss is matched with a foreign chargeable gain within (II) above, the amount of that gain is reduced by the matched amount (so that relief for the loss is effectively obtained if the gain is subsequently remitted to the UK).

[*TCGA 1992, Sch 1 paras 2–4; FA 2019, Sch 1 para 13*]. See CG25330A, CG25330C and *Simon's Taxes* C1.603.

The 2019/20 loss cannot therefore be set against the UK gain arising in that year, as it must be set against the foreign gain within (II) above in priority.

(b) The election must be made within four years after the tax year to which it relates.

(c) If no election is made in respect of the first year for which a claim under *ITA 2007, s 809B* to the remittance basis is made (or, for 2017/18 onwards, the first year for which such a claim is made following a period in which the individual has been domiciled (or deemed domiciled) in the UK), losses accruing in that year and any subsequent year (other than one in which the taxpayer is domiciled in the UK) on the disposal of assets situated outside the UK are not allowable losses. [*TCGA 1992, s 16ZA*]. In this case, therefore, if no election had been made, the whole of the remitted gain of £60,000 would have been chargeable in 2020/21.

(d) No annual exempt amount is available for a tax year in respect of which a claim for the remittance basis under *ITA 2007, s 809B* has been made. [*TCGA 1992, s 1K(6); FA 2019, Sch 1 para 2*]. See CG18020 and *Simon's Taxes* C1.503, E6.324B–E6.324F.

(e) An individual who claims the remittance basis for a tax year incurs an additional tax charge of £30,000 for that year if he is 18 years of age or over in that tax year and he has been UK resident in at least seven of the nine tax years immediately preceding that tax year. For 2012/13 onwards, the charge is increased where the individual has been UK resident in at least twelve of the fourteen tax years immediately preceding the tax year in question. For 2012/13 to 2014/15 the increased charge is £50,000; for 2015/16 onwards it is £60,000. For 2015/16 and 2016/17 a higher charge of £90,000 applies where the individual has been UK resident in at least 17 of the 20 tax years immediately preceding the tax year. [*ITA 2007, ss 809C(3)(4), 809H; F(No 2)A 2017, Sch 8 paras 11, 14*]. See RDRM32210 and Simon's Taxes E6.324B–E6.324F.

(f) For 2017/18 onwards, an individual who is not domiciled in the UK is deemed to be so domiciled if either:

(1) he was born in the UK with a UK domicile of origin and is resident in the UK; or

(2) he has been UK-resident for at least 15 of the 20 preceding tax years. This provision does not apply if the individual is not UK-resident in the tax year in question and has not been UK-resident in any previous tax year beginning with 2017/18.

226 Rollover Relief — Replacement of Business Assets

Cross-reference. See also **205.2** ASSETS HELD ON **31** MARCH **1982** for relief under *TCGA 1992, s 36, Sch 4* for certain gains accruing before 31 March 1982.

[*TCGA 1992, ss 152–158*]

226.1 NATURE OF RELIEF

[*TCGA 1992, s 152*]

(A)

N Ltd carries on a manufacturing business. It makes the following disposals and acquisitions of assets during the company's accounting periods ended 31 December 2018, 31 December 2019 and 31 December 2020.

	Asset	Bought/(sold) £	Chargeable gains £
1.10.18	Freehold depot	18,000	—
12.12.18	Leasehold warehouse	(50,000)	28,000
19.7.18	Business formerly carried on by another (unrelated) company:		
	Goodwill (note (c))	20,000	—
	Freehold factory unit	90,000	—
1.2.20	Land adjacent to main factory, now surplus to requirements	(40,000)	19,000
8.9.20	Industrial mincer (fixed plant)	(30,000)	5,000
1.11.20	Extension to new factory	35,000	—

(i) *The gain on the leasehold warehouse may be rolled over against the following*

	Cost £		Gain £
Freehold depot	18,000	$\dfrac{18,000}{50,000} \times £28,000$	10,080
Freehold factory (part)	32,000	$\dfrac{32,000}{50,000} \times £28,000$	17,920
	£50,000		£28,000

226.1 CGT Rollover Relief — Replacement of Business Assets

(ii) *The gain on the surplus land may then be rolled over as follows*

| Freehold factory (part) | £40,000 | Gain rolled over | £19,000 |

(iii) *The gain on the industrial mincer may be rolled over as follows*

| Extension to new factory (part) | £30,000 | Gain rolled over | £5,000 |

The position at 31 December 2020 is then as follows

	£
Freehold depot	
Cost	18,000
Deduct gains rolled over	(10,080)
Allowable cost	£7,920
Freehold factory	
Cost	90,000
Deduct gains rolled over (£17,920 + £19,000)	(36,920)
Allowable cost	£53,080
Extension to new factory	
Cost	35,000
Deduct gains rolled over	(5,000)
Allowable cost	£30,000

Notes

(a) The expenditure still available to match against disposal proceeds is

| Extension to factory (£35,000 − £30,000) | £5,000 |

The expenditure is available only against disposals up to 31 October 2021.

(b) There is no statutory rule prescribing the way in which the gain on an asset must be rolled over against a number of different assets. The taxpayer's allocation of the rolled over gain against the cost of the new assets should be accepted by HMRC, providing specified amounts of consideration are positively earmarked and set against the cost of specified new assets. In (i) the chargeable gain has been rolled over rateably to the costs of the items, but bringing in only part (i.e. the balance of proceeds) of the cost of the freehold factory. See CG60770

(c) For corporation tax purposes, goodwill is *not* a qualifying asset for chargeable gains rollover relief purposes.

Rollover Relief — Replacement of Business Assets   CGT 226.1

(B)

L Ltd carries on a vehicle repair business. In December 2003 it sells a workshop for £90,000 net of costs. The workshop had cost £45,000 inclusive in April 1995. A new workshop is purchased for £144,000 (including incidental costs of acquisition) on 11 January 2005 and sold for £168,000 on 14 January 2021.

Indexation factors	April 1995 to December 2003	0.232
	January 2005 to December 2017	0.472

L Ltd claims rollover of the chargeable gain on the disposal of the workshop.

	£
Allowable cost of original workshop	45,000
Indexation allowance £45,000 × 0.232	10,440
	55,440
Actual disposal consideration	90,000
Chargeable gain rolled over	£34,560
Cost of new workshop	144,000
Deduct Amount rolled over	(34,560)
Deemed allowable cost	£109,440
Disposal consideration, replacement workshop	168,000
Allowable cost	(109,440)
Unindexed gain	58,560
Indexation allowance £109,440 × 0.472	(51,656)
Chargeable gain (January 2021)	£6,904

(C)

The facts are as in (B) above except that the business is carried on by M, an individual. The indexation factor for the period April 1995 to April 1998 is 0.091.

	£
Allowable cost of original workshop	45,000
Indexation allowance £45,000 × 0.091	4,095
	49,095
Actual disposal consideration	90,000
Chargeable gain rolled over	£40,905
Cost of new workshop	144,000
Deduct Amount rolled over	(40,905)
Deemed allowable cost	£103,095
Disposal consideration, replacement workshop	168,000
Allowable cost	103,095
Chargeable gain 2020/21	£64,905

226.1 CGT Rollover Relief — Replacement of Business Assets

226.2 PARTIAL RELIEF

(A) **Assets only partly replaced**

[TCGA 1992, s 153]

G carries on an accountancy practice. In March 2020, he agrees to acquire the practice of another sole practitioner, who is about to retire. As part of the acquisition, G pays £20,000 for goodwill. In January 2021, G moves to new premises, acquiring the remaining 70 years of a 99-year lease for £50,000. The sale of his former office on 25 February 2021 realises £80,000, and a chargeable gain of £59,000 arises.

	£	£
Amount of proceeds of disposal of old office		80,000
Costs against which gains can be rolled over		
Goodwill	20,000	
Lease	50,000	
		(70,000)
Chargeable gain not rolled over		£10,000
Chargeable gain rolled over (£59,000 − £10,000)		£49,000
Allowable cost of assets (see note (a))		
Goodwill	20,000	
Gain rolled over $\frac{20,000}{70,000} \times £49,000$	(14,000)	
		£6,000
Lease	50,000	
Gain rolled over $\frac{50,000}{70,000} \times £49,000$	(35,000)	
		£15,000

Notes

(a) There is no statutory rule prescribing the way in which a gain is to be rolled over against more than one acquisition. See note (b) to **226.1(A)** above.

(b) It would not have been possible to roll over the gain only against the acquisition of the goodwill. The consideration not reinvested (£60,000) would be more than the gain (£59,000).

(c) See CG60400, CG61550 and *Simon's Taxes* C3.305A, C3.303A.

Rollover Relief — Replacement of Business Assets

(B) **Partial business use**

[*TCGA 1992, s 152(7)*]

N carries on a consultancy business from commercial premises formerly used as a shop. N has owned the property since 1 July 1981, but it was let until 1 March 1996 when N moved in, following the expiry of the lease held by the former tenant. On 1 February 2021, N sells the property for £100,000, moving to a new office with a long lease which he acquires for £70,000 and which is wholly used for his business. The value at 31 March 1982 of the property sold was £40,000.

For rollover relief purposes, N is treated as having disposed of two separate assets, one representing his occupation and professional use of the property, the other his ownership of it as an investment. In practice, the proceeds and chargeable gain may be allocated by a simple time apportionment.

Proceeds attributable to business use

£100,000 × 24y11m/38y10m (note (c))   £64,163

Chargeable gain attributable to business use

[£100,000 − £40,000] = £60,000 × 24y11m/38y10m   £38,498

Notes

(a) The proceeds attributable to business use are less than the cost of the new office, so that the whole of the chargeable gain attributable to business use can be rolled over. The allowable cost of the new office is then £31,502 (£70,000 − £38,498).

(b) The balance of the chargeable gain, £21,502 (£60,000 − £38,498) is not eligible for rollover.

(c) The time apportionment takes into account only the period of ownership after 30 March 1982. [*TCGA 1992, s 152(9)*]. See *Simon's Taxes* C3.302A.

226.3 WASTING ASSETS

[*TCGA 1992, s 154*]

(A) **Crystallisation of held-over gain**

In March 2016, a father and son partnership carrying on a car dealing trade sold a freehold showroom for £400,000 realising a chargeable gain of £190,000. On 30 June 2016, the firm purchased for £450,000 the remaining term of a lease due to expire on 30 June 2046 and used the premises as a new showroom. The whole of the gain on the old asset was held over under *TCGA 1992, s 154* on the acquisition of the new asset. In consequence of the father's decision to retire from the business and the resulting need to downsize the operation, the firm assigns the lease for £490,000 on 1 July 2020.

The chargeable gains to be apportioned between the two partners for 2020/21 are as follows

226.3 CGT   Rollover Relief — Replacement of Business Assets

	£	£
Proceeds of assignment		490,000
Cost (see note (a))	450,000	
Deduct Wasted $\dfrac{87.330 - 82.496}{87.330} \times £450,000$	(24,909)	(425,091)
Chargeable gain 2020/21 (see also note (b))		£64,909
Held-over gain becoming chargeable under *TCGA* 1992, s 154(2)(a)		£190,000

Notes

(a) The gain of £190,000 is deferred as opposed to being rolled over and does not reduce the cost of the new asset.

(b) See also **216.3(D)–(G)** LAND for further examples on the assignment of short leases.

(B) Rollover of held-over gain

C Ltd, a manufacturing company, sells an item of fixed plant for £30,000 in February 2016. A chargeable gain of £7,200 arises. In 2018, the company buys storage facilities on a 20-year lease for £40,000. In 2020, an extension to the company's freehold factory is completed at a cost of £25,000.

The position is as follows

(i) The company may claim holdover of the £7,200 chargeable gain in 2016, against the cost of the lease.

(ii) In 2020, part of the chargeable gain can be rolled over against the cost of the factory extension, as follows

	£
Expenditure available for rollover	25,000
Maximum capable of rollover	
£7,200 − (£30,000 − £25,000)	(2,200)
Adjusted base cost of extension	£22,800

Notes

(a) The balance of the chargeable gain, £5,000 (£7,200 - £2,200) may continue to be held over against the cost of the lease, either until it crystallises or until further rollover is possible.

(b) Had the company not claimed holdover against the cost of the lease, a claim against the cost of the extension in 2020 would not have been possible, as the expenditure was incurred outside the normal three-year time limit.

226.4 FURNISHED HOLIDAY LETTINGS

In May 2016, Isobel sells Heene Cottage for £120,000. The cottage had qualified as furnished holiday accommodation throughout Isobel's period of ownership and had originally cost £55,000. The whole proceeds are invested in the acquisition in June 2016 of Croft Cottage at a cost of £150,000 and Isobel claims rollover relief under *TCGA 1992, s 152*. The new property is used as furnished holiday accommodation until June 2020 when it becomes Isobel's only residence. Croft Cottage is sold in June 2022 for £290,000. The chargeable gain on disposal is computed as follows.

Disposal of Heene Cottage

	£	£
Allowable cost		55,000
Actual disposal consideration		120,000
Chargeable gain rolled over		£65,000
Deemed allowable cost of Croft Cottage (£150,000 – £65,000)		£85,000

Disposal of Croft Cottage

		£
Disposal consideration		290,000
Deduct Allowable cost		(85,000)
Gain before main residence relief		£205,000

Main residence relief

	£	£
Gain before relief	205,000	
Less amount of rolled-over gain	(65,000)	65,000
Gain eligible for relief	140,000	
Less relief (2/6 × £140,000)	(46,667)	93,333
Chargeable gain 2022/23		£158,333

Notes

(a) Commercial letting of furnished holiday accommodation is treated as a trade for the purposes of rollover relief. [*TCGA 1992, s 241(3), s 241A(4)(5)*].

(b) Where main residence relief is available to any extent on the disposal of an asset and the acquisition cost has been reduced by rollover relief, the gain to which the main residence relief is applied is reduced by the amount of the rolled-over gain. [*TCGA 1992, s 241(6), s 241A(8)*]. For main residence relief generally see **223** PRIVATE RESIDENCES.

(c) See also IT **22.2** PROPERTY INCOME for the rules which determine whether letting qualifies as the commercial letting of furnished holiday accommodation.

227 Seed Enterprise Investment Scheme

227.1 DISPOSAL OF SEIS SHARES MORE THAN THREE YEARS AFTER ISSUE

[*TCGA 1992, s 150E(2)(4)(5)*]

On 8 November 2020 P subscribes £130,000 for 65,000 shares in the SEIS company, S Ltd, and obtains the maximum SEIS income tax relief of £50,000 (£100,000 × 50%) for 2020/21. On 3 April 2024 he sells the entire holding for £240,000.

The chargeable gain arising is calculated as follows

	£
Disposal proceeds	240,000
Cost	(130,000)
Gain	110,000
Less TCGA 1992, s 150E(2)(4)(5) exemption	
$£110,000 \times \dfrac{50,000}{65,000}$ (note(b))	(84,615)
Chargeable gain 2023/24	£25,385

Notes

(a) Gains arising on the sale more than three years after issue of shares qualifying for SEIS income tax relief are not chargeable gains unless the SEIS relief is fully withdrawn before disposal.

(b) Where the income tax relief is not given on the full SEIS subscription (otherwise than because of insufficient income), capital gains tax relief is given on a proportion of the gain on the disposal or part disposal.

The gain is reduced by the multiple R/T where

R = the actual income tax reduction and

T = the tax at the SEIS rate (50%) on the amount subscribed for the issue.

R = £100,000 × 50% = £50,000

T = £130,000 × 50% = £65,000

(c) See VCM40020, VCM40040 and *Simon's Taxes* E3.880.

227.2 CGT   Seed Enterprise Investment Scheme

227.2 LOSS ON DISPOSAL OF SEIS SHARES

[*TCGA 1992, s 150E(1)(3)*]

(A) **Disposal more than three years after issue**

Assuming the facts otherwise remain the same as in 227.1 above but that the shares are sold for £50,000 on 3 April 2024.

The allowable loss arising is calculated as follows

	£	£
Disposal proceeds		50,000
Less Cost	130,000	
Less Income tax relief given (and not withdrawn)	(50,000)	(80,000)
Allowable loss 2023/24		£(30,000)

Note

(a) Any loss arising is reduced by deducting the amount of the SEIS relief (given and not withdrawn) from the acquisition cost. On the question of income tax withdrawal, see note (b) to (B) below.

(b) See VCM40090, VCM40100 and Simon's Taxes E3.880 - E3.882.

(B) **Disposal within three years of issue**

The facts are otherwise as in (A) above except that the shares are sold in an arm's length bargain on 3 April 2021, i.e. within three years after their issue.

Income tax relief given for 2020/21 is withdrawn as follows

Relief attributable (£100,000 @ 50%)   £50,000 (1)

Consideration

$£50{,}000 \times \dfrac{50{,}000\ (£100{,}000\ @\ 50\%)}{65{,}000\ (£130{,}000\ @\ 50\%)} @ 50\%$ £19,230 (2)

The amount at (1) is greater than that at (2), so income tax relief of £19,230 is withdrawn. [*ITA 2007, ss 257FA, 257FB*].

The relief not withdrawn is therefore £(50,000 − 19,230) =   £30,770

Seed Enterprise Investment Scheme   CGT 227.3

The allowable loss arising is calculated as follows

	£	£
Disposal proceeds		50,000
Less Cost	130,000	
Less Income tax relief not withdrawn	(30,770)	(99,230)
Allowable loss 2020/21		£(49,230)

Notes

(a) For the purposes of computing an allowable loss, the consideration is reduced by the relief attributable to the shares. [*TCGA 1992, s 150E(1)*]. The relief attributable is that remaining following any withdrawal of relief. See VCM40100 and *Simon's Taxes* E3.881.

(b) A withdrawal of income tax relief arises on a disposal of SEIS shares within three years after their issue. [*ITA 2007, s 257FA*]. See VCM36020 and *Simon's Taxes* E3.850.

227.3 SEIS REINVESTMENT RELIEF

[*TCGA 1992, s 150G, Sch 5BB*]

On 1 June 2020, X sells an asset for £365,000. The asset had cost X £240,000 in 2009. X makes no other disposals in 2020/21. On 1 February 2021, X acquires by subscription 50,000 shares in ABC Ltd at a total price of £100,000. X claims SEIS income tax relief in respect of the acquisition.

If X makes a claim for SEIS reinvestment relief under *TCGA 1992, Sch 5BB* then his CGT position for 2020/21 is as follows

	£
Consideration	365,000
Less Acquisition cost	(240,000)
Gain	125,000
Less Reinvestment relief	(50,000)
Chargeable gain	75,000
Less annual exempt amount	(12,300)
Taxable gain 2020/21	£62,700

Notes

(a) SEIS reinvestment relief can be claimed where:

- an individual realises a chargeable gain on a disposal at any time in in a tax year (the 'relevant year'); and
- he is eligible for, and claims, SEIS income tax relief for the relevant year in respect of an amount subscribed for an 'issue of shares' in a company made to him (or treated as made to him) in that year.

227.3 CGT   Seed Enterprise Investment Scheme

(b) The amount of relief is restricted to 50% of the amount on which SEIS income tax relief is claimed.

Where SEIS shares are treated as issued in the previous tax year as a result of a SEIS income tax relief carry-back claim under *ITA 2007, s 257AB(5)*, they will thereby qualify to be used in a reinvestment relief claim for the earlier year. See VCM45010, VCM31130 and *Simon's Taxes* E3.802.

(c) A claim for SEIS reinvestment relief in respect of shares issued in 2020/21 must be made no later than 31 January 2027. [*TCGA 1992, Sch 5BB para 3; ITA 2007, s 257EA*]. See VCM35150 and *Simon's Taxes* E3.846, B8.202.

(d) If SEIS income tax relief attributable to shares is withdrawn, any SEIS reinvestment relief attributable to those shares is also withdrawn. If SEIS income tax relief attributable to shares is reduced, any SEIS reinvestment relief attributable to those shares is reduced in the same proportion. In either case, a chargeable gain is then deemed to accrue to the individual in the relevant year of an amount equal to the amount of reinvestment relief to be withdrawn or the amount by which reinvestment relief falls to be reduced. [*TCGA 1992, Sch 5BB para 5*].

228 Settlements

Cross-reference. See **219.1** OFFSHORE SETTLEMENTS as regards capital gains of non-resident settlements.

228.1 ANNUAL EXEMPT AMOUNTS AND RATES OF TAX

[*TCGA 1992, s 1K, Sch 1C; FA 2019, Sch 1 paras 2, 16, 120*]

The trustees of the E settlement, created in 1974, realise net chargeable gains and allowable losses as follows:

	Chargeable gain/ (allowable loss) £
2016/17	(2,250)
2017/18	3,100
2018/19	5,700
2019/20	3,200
2020/21	12,700

The trustees' capital gains tax liability is computed as follows

	£
2016/17	
Taxable amount	Nil
Losses carried forward	£2,250
2017/18	
Net chargeable gains	3,100
Losses brought forward	—
Taxable amount (covered by annual exempt amount of £5,650)	£(3,100)
CGT	Nil
Losses carried forward	£2,250
2018/19	
Net chargeable gains	5,700
Losses brought forward	(50)
Taxable amount (covered by annual exempt amount)	£5,650
CGT	Nil
Losses carried forward (£2,250 − £50)	£2,200

228.1 CGT   Settlements

2019/20

Net chargeable gains	3,200
Losses brought forward	—
Taxable amount (covered by annual exempt amount of £6,000)	£3,200
CGT	Nil
Losses carried forward	£2,200

2020/21

Net chargeable gains	12,700
Deduct Annual exempt amount	(6,150)
	6,550
Deduct Losses brought forward	(2,200)
Taxable gains	£4,350
CGT at 20% on £4,350	£870
Losses carried forward	Nil

Notes

(a) The rate of capital gains tax accruing to the trustees of any settlement is 20%, unless either the gains are upper rate gains (in which case the rate is 28%) or business asset disposal relief (formerly entrepreneurs' relief) or investors' relief apply (in which case the rate is 10%). For previous years, the rate is 28%, or 10% where business asset disposal relief applies. [*TCGA 1992, s 1H(7)(8); FA 2019, Sch 1 paras 2, 120*]. For the meaning of 'upper rate gains' see **201.1(C) ANNUAL RATES AND EXEMPTIONS**. See CG10246 and *Simon's Taxes* C1.107.

(b) See *TCGA 1992, Sch 1C para 6* for the annual exempt amount available to two or more settlements made by the same settlor after 6 June 1978.

228.2 TRUSTS WITH VULNERABLE BENEFICIARY

[*FA 2005, ss 23–45, Schs 1, 1A; FA 2019, Sch 1 paras 97, 98*]

Harry was born in 2008. In June 2015 both of his parents are killed in a road accident. Neither parent has made a will, so that a statutory trust is established for Harry under the intestacy rules of *Administration of Estates Act 1925, ss 46, 47(1)*. The trustees and Harry's guardian make a vulnerable person election (by 31 January 2019) to take effect on 6 April 2016. On 16 May 2020, the trustees sell an asset, realising a chargeable gain of £20,000. The trustees (who are resident in the UK throughout) make no other disposals in 2020/21. Harry is resident in the UK throughout the tax year and has no personal chargeable gains. His taxable income for 2020/21 is lower than the amount of the personal allowance.

Settlements CGT 228.2

If the trustees make a claim for special tax treatment under *FA 2005, s 24* for 2020/21, their capital gains tax liability is calculated as follows.

	£
Gain	20,000
Annual exemption	(6,150)
Taxable gain 2020/21	£13,850
CGT £13,850 × 20%	2,770
Less reduction under *FA 2005, s 31*	(2,000.00)
CGT payable by trustees	£770.00

The reduction under *FA 2005, s 31* is equal to:

TQTG – (TLVA – TLVB)

where

TQTG = the amount of capital gains tax to which the trustees would, apart from these provisions, be liable for the tax year in respect of qualifying trust gains;

TLVB = the total amount of capital gains tax to which the vulnerable person is liable for the tax year; and

TLVA = what TLVB would be if the qualifying trust gains accrued to the vulnerable person instead of the trustees, and no allowable losses were deducted from them.

In this case, TQTG = £2,800 (as above), TLVB is nil, and TLVA is calculated as follows.

	£
Gain	20,000
Annual exempt amount	(12,300)
Taxable gain	£7,700
CGT £7,700 × 10% (TLVA)	£770.00
The reduction is therefore £2,770 – (£770 – Nil) =	£2,000.00

Notes

(a) The trustees are effectively able to make use of the beneficiary's annual exempt amount and, where applicable, lower rate of tax.

(b) A claim for special tax treatment applies to both income tax and capital gains tax. No separate claim can be made in respect of each tax.

(c) Where the vulnerable beneficiary is not UK resident, see *FA 2005, ss 32, 33, Sch 1*. See *Simon's Taxes* C4.257.

228.3 CGT Settlements

228.3 CREATION OF A SETTLEMENT

[*TCGA 1992, s 70*]

(A)

In December 2020, C transfers to trustees of a settlement for the benefit of his disabled daughter 10,000 shares in W plc, a quoted company. The value of the gift is £85,000. C bought the shares in 1981 for £20,000 and their value at 31 March 1982 was £35,000.

	£
Deemed disposal consideration	85,000
Market value 31.3.82	(35,000)
Chargeable gain	£50,000
Trustees' allowable cost	£85,000

Note

(a) If the transfer had been a chargeable lifetime transfer for inheritance tax purposes, or would be one but for the annual inheritance tax exemption and the settlement is not settlor-interested within *TCGA 1992, ss 169B–169G*, C could have elected under *TCGA 1992, s 260* to roll the gain over against the trustees' base cost of the shares. The trustees do not join in any such election. See CG67064, CG67040-CG67046 and *Simon's Taxes* C4.225, C3.1906, C3.1602, I7.546, I5.915.

(B)

In late April 2020 H settles farmland on trust for himself for life, with interests in reversion to his children. The land cost £20,000 in 1975 and its agreed values are £60,000 at 31 March 1982 and £125,000 at the date of settlement. H's interest in possession in the settled property is valued at £90,000.

The chargeable gain is computed as follows

	£
Deemed disposal proceeds	125,000
Market value 31.3.82	(60,000)
Chargeable gain 2020/21	£65,000

Notes

(a) The value of H's interest in the settled property is ignored and the transfer is not treated as a part disposal.

(b) As the settlement is settlor-interested, H cannot claim hold-over relief under *TCGA 1992, s 260* even though the transfer of the land into settlement is a chargeable lifetime transfer. See note (a) to (A) above.

Settlements   CGT 228.4

228.4 PERSON BECOMING ABSOLUTELY ENTITLED TO SETTLED PROPERTY

[*TCGA 1992, s 71*]

(A)

M is a beneficiary entitled to an interest in possession in settled property, under a settlement made by her mother. The trustees exercise a power of appointment to advance capital to M, and, in September 2020, transfer to her a house valued at £80,000. The house was acquired by the trustees by gift from the settlor in 2004, when its value was £45,000.

The trustees realise a gain of £35,000 (£80,000 - £45,000) on the advancement of capital to M.

Note

(a)   If, while it was settled property, the house had been occupied by M as her private residence with the permission of the trustees, then all or part of the gain would qualify for the private residence exemption under *TCGA 1992, s 225*. See CG65400, CG65407, CG37000 and *Simon's Taxes* C3.1708, C4.516, C4.219.

(B)   **Transfer of settlement losses**

[*TCGA 1992, s 71(2)–(2D)*]

F is the sole remaining beneficiary of an accumulation and maintenance settlement established under his late uncle's will and in which he became entitled to an interest in possession upon reaching the age of 18 in 1996. On 18 September 2003, his 25th birthday, he becomes absolutely entitled as against the trustees to the capital of the trust. At that date, the trust capital consists of the following

- cash of £12,000,
- 10,000 shares in ABC Ltd (purchased for £6,000 in May 2002 and currently valued at £11,000), and
- 15,000 shares in DEF Ltd (transferred into the trust at a CGT value of £27,000 but now valued at only £13,000).

On 30 June 2003, the trustees had sold shares in GHK Ltd at a gain of £3,000 (after deducting indexation allowance to April 1998). On 7 July 2003, they sold shares in LMN Ltd at a loss of £500. None of the above-mentioned trust investments were business assets for taper relief purposes. At 6 April 2003, the trustees had allowable capital losses of £1,000 brought forward from earlier years.

In December 2003, F sells the ABC Ltd shares for £11,600. He also disposes of other assets in 2003/04 realising chargeable gains of £9,400 (with no taper relief due). In 2020/21, he sells the DEF Ltd shares for £15,700 and also disposes of other assets realising chargeable gains of £19,000 and allowable losses of £1,500.

228.4 CGT   Settlements

F takes over entitlement to trust losses as follows

	£	£
Loss on DEF Ltd shares transferred to F £(27,000 − 13,000)		14,000
Deduct Trustees' 'pre-entitlement gains'*:		
(i) gain on ABC Ltd shares transferred to F	5,000	
(ii) other gains in period 6.4.03–18.9.03	3,000	(8,000)
Loss treated as accruing to F (note (a))		£6,000

* See *TCGA 1992, s 71(2A)*.

F's CGT position for 2003/04 and 2020/21 is as follows

2003/04

	£
Gain on sale of ABC Ltd shares £(11,600 − 11,000)	600
Other gains	9,400
	10,000
Deduct Annual exemption	(7,900)
Gains chargeable to tax 2003/04	£2,100
Ex-trust losses carried forward	£6,000

2020/21

	£	£
Gain on sale of DEF Ltd shares £(15,700 − 13,000)	2,700	
Deduct Ex-trust losses brought forward and treated as a loss for the year	(2,700)	—
Other gains	19,000	
Deduct Losses for the year	(1,500)	17,500
		17,500
Deduct Annual exemption		(12,300)
Gains chargeable to tax		£5,200

	£
Ex-trust losses brought forward	6,000
Utilised in 2020/21	(2,700)
Unused balance (note (b))	£3,300

Notes

(a)   Trust losses of £1,000 brought forward and £500 accruing in 2003/04 cannot be transferred to F and in this case are wasted. The 'pre-entitlement gains' cannot be reduced by those losses before being set against the loss on DEF Ltd shares.

(b) In F's hands, the loss can only be set against a gain on the DEF Ltd shares on which it arose. As all those shares are sold in 2020/21, the loss cannot be carried forward any further and the unused balance of £3,300 is written off.

(c) See CG37207, CG37208 and *Simon's Taxes* C4.516.

228.5 TERMINATION OF INTEREST IN POSSESSION ON DEATH

[*TCGA 1992, s 72*]

(A)

K is entitled to an interest in possession under a settlement. The settled property consists of shares and cash. On K's death, L is entitled to a life interest in succession to K. K dies on 1 December 2020, when the shares are valued at £200,000. The trustees' allowable cost in respect of the shares is £40,000.

On K's death, the trustees are deemed to have disposed of and immediately reacquired the shares for £200,000, thus uplifting the CGT base cost, but no chargeable gain then arises.

Note

(a) Where the deceased became entitled to the interest in possession on or after 22 March 2006, the above treatment applies only if

  (i) the deceased died under the age of 18 and, immediately before his death, *IHTA 1984, s 71D* (age 18 to 25 trusts) applies to the property in which the interest subsists; See IHTM42816 and Simon's Taxes I5.502, I5.551, I5.552 or

  (ii) immediately before his death,

   (a) the interest in possession is an immediate post-death interest within *IHTA 1984, s 49A*; See IHTM16061 and *Simon's Taxes* I5.205.

   (b) the interest is a transitional serial interest within *IHTA 1984, s 49C*; See CG36542 and *Simon's Taxes* I5.206.

   (c) the interest is a disabled person's interest within *IHTA 1984, s 89B(1)(c)(d)*; See IHTM42805 and *Simon's Taxes* I5.207 or

   (d) *IHTA 1984, s 71A* (trusts for bereaved minors) applies to the property in which the interest subsists. See IHTM42815 and *Simon's Taxes* I5.546, I5.547

[*TCGA 1992, s 72(1)–(1C)*].

(B)

In 1976, E created a settlement for the benefit of his children M and N and his grandchildren, transferring an investment property valued at £10,000 to the trustees. The terms of the settlement were that M and N each have a life interest in half of the trust income, with the remainder passing to E's grandchildren. In 1990, N assigned his interest to P, an unrelated party, for £35,000, its then market value. In 2020, N dies. The value of a half share of the trust property is then £65,000.

On N's death, his life interest terminates. There is no effect on the trustees as N was no longer the person entitled to the life interest within the meaning of *TCGA 1992, s 72*.

228.5 CGT Settlements

Notes

(a) No chargeable gain arises on the disposal by N of his interest. [*TCGA 1992, s 76*]. See CG12605, CG38040 and Simon's Taxes C4.515, C4.222,

(b) P may claim an allowable loss on extinction of the interest. For an example of the computation if the interest is a wasting asset, see **232.3** WASTING ASSETS.

229 Shares and Securities

Cross-references. See also 204 ASSETS HELD ON 6 APRIL 1965, 205 ASSETS HELD ON 31 MARCH 1982, 214 INDEXATION, 224 QUALIFYING CORPORATE BONDS and 230 SHARES AND SECURITIES — IDENTIFICATION RULES.

229.1 REORGANISATION OF SHARE CAPITAL — VALUATION OF DIFFERENT CLASSES OF SHARE ON SUBSEQUENT DISPOSAL

[*TCGA 1992, ss 126–131*]

(A) **Unquoted shares**

V acquired 10,000 ordinary shares in X Ltd, an unquoted trading company, in April 2001 at a cost of £15,000. In April 2009, as part of a reorganisation of share capital, V was additionally allotted 3,000 new 9% preference shares in X Ltd for which he paid £3,900. In June 2020, V sold his ordinary shareholding, in an arm's length transaction, for £20,000, but retained his preference shares, then valued at £4,000.

The chargeable gain on the disposal of the ordinary shares is calculated as follows

	£
Disposal consideration	20,000
Cost $(£15,000 + £3,900) \times \dfrac{20,000}{20,000 + 4,000}$	(15,750)
Chargeable gain 2020/21	£4,250
Allowable cost of 3,000 preference shares $(£15,000 + £3,900 - £15,750)$	£3,150

Note

(a) The ordinary shares and preference shares held after the reorganisation (the 'new holding') constitute a single asset. [*TCGA 1992, s 127*]. A disposal of part of the new holding is thus a part disposal. If neither class of shares comprising the new holding is quoted on a recognised stock exchange at any time not later than three months after the reorganisation, acquisition cost on a part disposal is apportioned by reference to market values at the date of disposal. [*TCGA 1992, s 129*]. See CG51702, and *Simon's Taxes* D6.224.

(B) **Quoted shares**

Assume the facts to be as in (A) above except that both the ordinary and preference shares are quoted on a recognised stock exchange. On the first day of dealing after the reorganisation took effect, the ordinary shares were quoted at £1.85 and the preference shares at £1.35. V's holdings were therefore valued at £18,500 and £4,050 respectively.

229.1 CGT Shares and Securities

The chargeable gain on the disposal of the ordinary shares is calculated as follows

	£
Disposal consideration	20,000
Cost (£15,000 + £3,900) × $\dfrac{18,500}{18,500 + 4,050}$	(15,506)
Chargeable gain 2020/21	£4,494
Allowable cost of 3,000 preference shares (£15,000 + £3,900 − £15,506)	£3,394

Note

(a) Where one or more of the classes of shares or debentures comprising the new holding is quoted on a recognised stock exchange at any time not later than three months after the reorganisation, acquisition cost on a part disposal is apportioned by reference to market values on the first day of dealing on which the prices quoted reflect the reorganisation. [*TCGA 1992, s 130*]. See CG52002 and *Simon's Taxes* D6.224.

(C) **Quoted shares — reorganisation after 31 March 1982, original holding acquired on or before that date**

In 1980, W subscribed for 5,000 £1 ordinary shares at par in L plc, a quoted company. The value of his holding at 31 March 1982 was £8,000. In November 1991, L plc offered ordinary shareholders two 7% preference shares at £1 per share in respect of each five ordinary shares held. W took up his entitlement of 2,000 preference shares. On the first day of dealing after the reorganisation, the ordinary shares were quoted at £3.00 (making W's holding worth £15,000) and the preference shares at £1.02 (valuing W's holding at £2,040). In June 2020, W sells his preference shares on the market at £2.40 (total proceeds £2,800). (For simplicity, costs of acquisition and disposal are ignored in this example.)

The gain on the disposal of the preference shares is computed as follows

	£
Disposal consideration	4,800
(31.3.82 value £8,000 + cost £2,000) × $\dfrac{2,040}{2,040 + 15,000}$	(1,197)
Chargeable gain 2020/21	£3,603

Note

(a) On a subsequent disposal of the ordinary shares, their cost would be £8,803 (£8,000 + £2,000 − £1,197).

229.2 BONUS ISSUES

[*TCGA 1992, ss 126–128, 130*]

(A) Bonus of same class

In October 2006, Y plc made a scrip issue of one ordinary share for every 10 held. L held 5,000 ordinary shares, which he acquired in May 1998 for £5,500, and therefore received 500 shares in the bonus issue. In October 2020, L sells 3,000 of his shares for £10,000.

Section 104 holding	Shares	Qualifying expenditure £
May 1998 acquisition	5,000	5,500
October 2006 bonus issue	500	—
	5,500	5,500
October 2020 disposal	(3,000)	(3,000)
Pool carried forward	2,500	£2,500

Calculation of chargeable gain	£
Disposal consideration	10,000
Allowable cost $\dfrac{3,000}{5,500} \times £5,500$	(3,000)
Chargeable gain 2020/21	£7,000

(B) Bonus of different class

On 6 April 1996, R bought 2,000 'A' shares in T plc for £3,800. In June 2001, R bought a further 500 'A' shares for £800. In October 2005 T plc made a bonus issue of 2 'B' shares for each 5 'A' shares held, and R received 1,000 'B' shares, valued at £1.20 each (total value £1,200) on the first dealing day after the issue. On the same day, the 'A' shares were quoted at £2 each (total value £5,000). In December 2020 R sells his 1,000 'B' shares for £4,000.

Section 104 holding — 'A' shares	Shares	Qualifying expenditure £
April 1996 acquisition	2,000	3,800
June 2001 acquisition	500	800
	2,500	4,600
October 2005 bonus issue of 'B' shares: transfer proportion of expenditure to 'B' shares (see note (a))		(890)
Pool of 'A' shares carried forward	2,500	£3,710

229.2 CGT   Shares and Securities

	Shares	Qualifying expenditure
Section 104 holding — 'A' shares		£
Section 104 holding — 'B' shares		
October 2005 bonus issue: proportion of pool transferred from 'A' shares holding	1,000	890
December 2020 disposal	(1,000)	(890)
	=	=

Calculation of chargeable gain on disposal of 'B' shares	£
Disposal consideration	4,000
Allowable cost (as allocated)	(890)
Chargeable gain 2020/21	£3,110

Notes

(a) The cost of the 'A' shares is apportioned between 'A' and 'B' shares by reference to market values on the first day of dealing after the reorganisation.

$$\text{Proportion of qualifying expenditure } £4,600 \times \frac{1,200}{1,200 + 5,000} \qquad £890$$

See CG51965 onwards.

(b) A different basis of apportionment applies to unquoted shares. See CG51919 onwards.

229.3 RIGHTS ISSUES

[*TCGA 1992, s 42, s 123(1), s 128(4)*]

Cross-reference.
See **229.8(B)** below as regards sale of rights.

(A) **Rights issue of same class**

W plc is a quoted company which in June 2009 made a rights issue of one £1 ordinary share for every eight £1 ordinary shares held, at £1.35 payable on allotment. V, who held 16,000 £1 ordinary shares purchased in May 2001 for £15,000, took up his entitlement in full, and was allotted 2,000 shares. In December 2020, he sells 6,000 of his shares for £30,000.

Shares and Securities

'Section 104' holding	Shares	Qualifying expenditure
		£
May 2001 acquisition	16,000	15,000
June 2009 rights issue	2,000	2,700
	18,000	17,700
December 2020 disposal	(6,000)	(5,900)
Pool carried forward	12,000	£11,800

Calculation of chargeable gain	£
Disposal consideration	30,000
Allowable cost $\frac{6,000}{18,000} \times £17,700$	(5,900)
Chargeable gain 2020/21	£24,100

(B) **Rights issue of different class**

On 1 March 1999, A acquired 6,000 quoted £1 ordinary shares in S plc at a cost of £7,800. In October 2002, S plc made a rights issue of one 50p 'B' share for every five £1 ordinary shares held, at 60p payable in full on application. A took up his entitlement in full, acquiring 1,200 'B' shares. On the first dealing day after issue, the 'B' shares were quoted at 65p and the £1 ordinary shares at £1.50. A sells his 'B' shares in December 2020 for £20,000.

'Section 104' holding — ordinary shares	Shares	Qualifying expenditure
		£
March 1999 acquisition	6,000	7,800
October 2002 rights issue of 'B' shares		720
	6,000	8,520
Transfer proportion of expenditure to 'B' shares (note (a))		(680)
Pool carried forward	6,000	7,840

'Section 104' holding — 'B' shares	Shares	Qualifying expenditure
		£
October 2002 rights issue: proportion of pool transferred from ordinary shares holding	1,200	680
December 2020 disposal	(1,200)	(680)
Pool carried forward	—	—

229.3 CGT   Shares and Securities

Calculation of chargeable gain on disposal of 'B' shares	£
Disposal consideration	20,000
Allowable cost (as allocated)	(680)
Chargeable gain 2020/21	£19,320

Notes

(a) The cost of the original shares is apportioned between the original shares and the 'B' shares by reference to market values on the first day of dealing after the reorganisation.

Proportion of qualifying expenditure

$$£8,520 \times \frac{1,200 \times 0.65}{(1,200 \times 0.65) + (6,000 \times 1.50)} \qquad £680$$

See CG51965 onwards.

(b) A different basis of apportionment applies to unquoted shares See CG51919 onwards.

(C) **Rights issue of same class: disposal out of *section 104* holding and 1982 holding**

G Ltd has purchased 100,000 25p ordinary shares in C plc as follows

Date	Number of shares acquired	Cost £
22.5.80	20,000	0.78
5.11.83	15,000	1.10
14.9.84	40,000	1.00
30.4.02	25,000	2.30

In May 1992, C made a rights issue of one ordinary share for every five held, at £1.50 payable in full on application. G took up its rights in full (15,000 ordinary shares). It sells 105,000 shares in August 2020 for £4.50 per share. The shares were quoted at 90p on 31 March 1982. Incidental costs of acquisition and disposal are disregarded for the purposes of this example.

Indexation factors	March 1982 to December 2017	2.501
	November 1983 to April 1985	0.094
	September 1984 to April 1985	0.052
	April 1985 to May 1992	0.470
	May 1992 to April 2002	0.261
	May 1992 to December 2017	0.996
	April 2002 to December 2017	0.583

Section 104 holding	Shares	Qualifying expenditure	Indexed pool
		£	£
5.11.83 acquisition	15,000	16,500	16,500
Indexed rise: November 1983 to April 1985			
£16,500 × 0.094			1,551
14.9.84 acquisition	40,000	40,000	40,000
Indexed rise: September 1984 to April 1985			
£40,000 × 0.052			2,080
Pool at 6.4.85	55,000	56,500	60,131
Indexed rise: April 1985 to May 1992			
£60,131 × 0.470			28,262
May 1992 rights issue	11,000	16,500	16,500
	66,000	73,000	104,893
Indexed rise: May 1992 to April 2002			
£104,893 × 0.261			27,377
30.4.02 acquisition	25,000	57,500	57,500
	91,000	130,500	189,770
Indexed rise: April 2002 to December 2017			
£189,770 × 0.583			110,636
	91,000	130,500	300,406
August 2020 disposal	(91,000)	(130,500)	(300,406)
	—	—	—

1982 holding	Shares	Cost	Market value 31.3.82
		£	£
22.5.80 acquisition	20,000	15,600	18,000
May 1992 rights issue (note (a))	4,000	6,000	6,000
	24,000	21,600	24,000
August 2020 disposal	(14,000)	(12,600)	(14,000)
Pool carried forward	10,000	£9,000	£10,000

229.3 CGT   Shares and Securities

Calculation of chargeable gain

(i) Identify 91,000 shares sold with *section 104* holding

	£
Disposal consideration 91,000 × £4.50	409,500
Allowable cost	(130,500)
Unindexed gain	279,000
Indexation allowance £300,406 − £130,500	(169,906)
Chargeable gain	£109,094

(ii) Identify 14,000 shares with 1982 holding

Without re-basing to 1982

	£
Disposal consideration 14,000 × £4.50	63,000
Cost $\dfrac{14,000}{24,000} \times £21,600$	(12,600)
Unindexed gain	50,400
Indexation allowance (see below)	(29,746)
Gain after indexation	£20,654

With re-basing to 1982

	£
Disposal consideration	63,000
Allowable expenditure $\dfrac{14,000}{24,000} \times £24,000$	(14,000)
Unindexed gain	49,000

Indexation allowance

	£	
$£14,000 \times \dfrac{18,000}{24,000} \times 2.501$	26,260	
$£14,000 \times \dfrac{6,000}{24,000} \times 0.996$	3,486	
		(29,746)
Gain after indexation		££19,254
Chargeable gain		£19,254
Total chargeable gain £109,094 + £19,254		£128,348

Shares and Securities CGT 229.4

Notes

(a) The 1982 holding cannot be increased by an 'acquisition', but can be increased by a rights issue as this is not treated as involving an acquisition. [*TCGA 1992, s 109(2), ss 127, 128*]. See *Simon's Taxes* C2.718.

(b) See **230 SHARES AND SECURITIES — IDENTIFICATION RULES** for further examples of the identification rules and the different rules applicable for capital gains tax purposes.

(c) Indexation allowance is frozen at its December 2017 level. No indexation allowance is available in respect of expenditure incurred after 31 December 2017, and for expenditure incurred on or before that date and falling to be deducted on a disposal after that date, indexation allowance is computed up to and including December 2017 only. [*TCGA 1992, ss 53(1)(1B), 54(1B); FA 2018, s 26(2)(3)(6)*]. See **214.1 INDEXATION**. See also CG17230 and *Simon's Taxes* C2.301.

229.4 EXCHANGE OF SECURITIES FOR THOSE IN ANOTHER COMPANY

[*TCGA 1992, ss 135, 137, 138*]

(A) **Takeover by quoted company**

S was a shareholder in N Ltd, an unquoted company. He subscribed for his 20,000 50p ordinary shares at 60p per share in 1979 and the shares were valued at £3 each at 31 March 1982. In July 1987, the shareholders accepted an offer by a public company, M plc, for their shares. Each ordinary shareholder received one £1 ordinary M plc share plus 45p cash for every two N Ltd shares held. S acquired 10,000 M plc shares and received cash of £4,500. The M plc shares were valued at £7.50 each at the time of the acquisition. On 25 April 2020, S sells 4,000 of his 10,000 M plc shares for £84,000. The indexation factor for March 1982 to July 1987 is 0.281.

(i) *On the merger in 1987/88, S makes a disposal only to the extent that he receives cash*

	£
Disposal consideration	4,500
Allowable cost $\dfrac{4,500}{4,500 + (10,000 \times £7.50 = £75,000)} \times £12,000$	(679)
Unindexed gain	3,821
Indexation allowance £679 × 0.281	(191)
Chargeable gain 1987/88	£3,630

Note

(a) The fraction applied to allowable cost corresponds to 5.66%. If the percentage had not exceeded 5% the cash distribution of £4,500 would have been regarded as 'small' and could have been deducted from allowable cost. [*TCGA 1992, s 122*]. No gain would then have arisen in 1987/88, but the allowable cost would have been reduced by £4,500. See also **229.8(B)** below. (A distribution made after 23 February 1997 can additionally be regarded as 'small' if it does not exceed £3,000. See CG57836 and *Simon's Taxes* D6.233.

229.4 CGT   Shares and Securities

(ii) *The chargeable gain on disposal in 2020/21 is*

	£
Disposal consideration	84,000
Market value 31.3.82	
$£(20,000 \times £3) \times \dfrac{75,000}{75,000 + 4,500} \times \dfrac{4,000}{10,000}$ (note (b))	(22,642)
Chargeable gain 2020/21	£61,358

Notes

(a) The M plc shares are regarded as the same asset as the original N Ltd shares. [*TCGA 1992, ss 127, 135*]. Re-basing to 31 March 1982 thus applies, as the original shares were held on that date. See *Simon's Taxes* D6.206.

(b) Where there has been a part disposal after 31 March 1982 and before 6 April 1988 of an asset held on the earlier of those dates, and this is followed by a disposal after 5 April 1988 to which re-basing applies, the re-basing rules are deemed to have applied to the part disposal. [*TCGA 1992, Sch 3 para 4(1)*].

(B) **Takeover by unquoted company**

Y Ltd, a small unquoted company, is taken over in June 2008 by another unquoted company, C Ltd. The terms of the acquisition are that holders of £1 ordinary shares in Y Ltd receive two £1 ordinary shares and one £1 deferred share in C Ltd in exchange for every two ordinary shares held.

B acquired his holding of 500 Y Ltd shares on the death of his wife in May 1994, at probate value of £10,000. In May 2020, B sells his 250 C Ltd deferred shares for £4,500. The value of his 500 C Ltd ordinary shares is then £25,000.

There is no CGT disposal in 2008/09. The chargeable gain on the 2020/21 disposal is calculated as follows

	£
Disposal consideration	4,500
Allowable cost $\dfrac{4,500}{4,500 + 25,000} \times £10,000$	(1,525)
Chargeable gain 2020/21	£2,975
The allowable cost carried forward of the 500 C Ltd ordinary shares is (£10,000 − £1,525)	£8,475

(C) Earn-outs

K owns 10,000 ordinary shares in M Ltd, which he acquired for £12,000 in December 2009. In July 2019, the whole of the issued share capital of M Ltd was acquired by P plc. Under the terms of the takeover, K receives £2 per share plus the right to further consideration up to a maximum of £1.50 per share depending on future profit performance. The initial consideration is receivable in cash, but the deferred consideration is to be satisfied by the issue of shares in P plc. In December 2020, K duly receives 2,000 ordinary shares valued at £6 per share in full settlement of his entitlement. The right to future consideration is valued at £1.40 per share in July 2019.

If K elects to disapply *TCGA 1992, s 138A* the position would be

2019/20

	£	£
Disposal proceeds 10,000 × £2	20,000	
Value of rights 10,000 × £1.40	14,000	34,000
Cost		(12,000)
Chargeable gain 2019/20		£22,000

2020/21

	£
Disposal of rights to deferred consideration:	
Proceeds — 2,000 P plc shares @ £6	12,000
Deemed cost of acquiring rights	(14,000)
Allowable loss 2020/21	£(2,000)
Cost for CGT purposes of 2,000 P plc shares	£12,000

Without an election, the position would be

2019/20

	£
Proceeds (cash) (as above)	20,000
Cost £12,000 × $\dfrac{20,000}{20,000 + 14,000}$	(7,059)
Chargeable gain 2019/20	£12,941
Cost of earn-out right for CGT purposes (£12,000 − £7,059)	£4,941

229.4 CGT   Shares and Securities

2020/21

The shares in P plc stand in the place of the right to deferred consideration and will be regarded as having been acquired in December 2009 for £4,941. No further gain or loss arises until a disposal of the shares takes place.

Notes

(a) Under *TCGA 1992, s 138A* the right to deferred consideration (the 'earn-out right') is treated as a security within *TCGA 1992, s 132*. The gain on the original shares (to the extent that it does not derive from cash consideration) can then be held over against the value of the new shares. This treatment is automatic where the conditions are satisfied, subject to the right to elect for such treatment not to apply. See CG58065 and *Simon's Taxes* D6.208A and D6.208B.

(b) Various conditions must be satisfied for *section 138A* treatment to apply. In particular, the value or quantity of the securities to be received as deferred consideration must be 'unascertainable' (as defined). Any right to receive cash and/or an ascertainable amount of securities as part of the deferred consideration does not fall within these provisions and must be distinguished from the earn-out right, though this does not prevent these provisions from applying to the earn-out right.

(c) See **207.2** CAPITAL SUMS DERIVED FROM ASSETS above for deferred consideration generally.

229.5 SCHEMES OF RECONSTRUCTION

[*TCGA 1992, s 136*]

N Ltd carried on a manufacturing and wholesaling business. In 2011, it was decided that the wholesaling business should be carried on by a separate company. HMRC clearance under *TCGA 1992, s 138* was obtained, and a company, R Ltd, was formed which, in consideration for the transfer to it by N Ltd of the latter's wholesaling undertaking, issued shares to the shareholders of N Ltd. Each holder of ordinary shares in N Ltd additionally received one ordinary share in R Ltd for each N Ltd share he held. W, who purchased his 2,500 N shares for £10,000 in December 1993, received 2,500 R shares. None of the shares involved is quoted. In August 2020, W sells 1,500 of his N shares for £6 each, a total of £9,000, agreed to be their market value. The value of W's remaining 1,000 N shares is also £6 per share, and the value of his R shares is £4.50 per share.

	£
Disposal consideration	9,000
Allowable cost $£10,000 \times \dfrac{9,000}{9,000 + (1,000 \times £6) + (2,500 \times £4.50)}$	(3,429)
Chargeable gain 2020/21	**£5,571**

229.6 CONVERSION OF SECURITIES

[*TCGA 1992, s 132*]

N bought £10,000 8% convertible loan stock in S plc, a quoted company, in June 2008. The cost was £9,800. In August 2015, N exercised his right to convert the loan stock into 'B' ordinary shares of the company, on the basis of 50 shares for £100 loan stock, and acquired 5,000 shares. In June 2020, N sells 3,000 of the shares for £5.00 each.

		£
Disposal consideration		15,000
Cost $\dfrac{3,000}{5,000} \times £9,800$		(5,880)
Chargeable gain 2020/21		£9,120

Notes

(a) The shares acquired on the conversion in 2015 stand in the shoes of the original loan stock. [*TCGA 1992, s 132*]. See CG55016 and *Simon's Taxes* D6.211.

(b) The loan stock cannot be a corporate bond (and thus cannot be a qualifying corporate bond) as it is convertible into securities other than corporate bonds, i.e. into ordinary shares. [*TCGA 1992, s 117(1)*]. See CG53706 and *Simon's Taxes* C2.820.

229.7 SCRIP DIVIDENDS

[*TCGA 1992, ss 141, 142*]

D holds ordinary 20p shares in PLC, a quoted company. The company operates a scrip dividend (also known as a stock dividend) policy whereby shareholders are given the option to take dividends in cash or in new fully-paid ordinary 20p shares, the option being exercisable separately in relation to each dividend. D purchased 2,000 shares for £1,500 in March 1980 and a further 3,000 shares for £8,100 in May 1992 and up until the end of 1997 he has always taken cash dividends. In July 1998, he opts for a scrip dividend and receives 25 shares instead of a cash dividend of £100. On 20 April 2000, he purchases a further 1,000 shares for £3,950. He opts for cash dividends until, in July 2008, he opts for a scrip dividend of 44 shares instead of a cash dividend of £180. He opts for cash dividends thereafter. In May 2020, he sells 2,069 shares for £8,550 (ex div), leaving himself with a holding of 4,000.

In the case of both scrip dividends taken by D, the market value of the new shares is equivalent to the cash dividend forgone. The 'appropriate amount in cash' (see *TCGA 1992, s 142*) is thus the amount of that dividend. The market value at 31 March 1982 of 20p shares in PLC is 80p.

The gain on the disposal in May 2020 is calculated as follows

The '*section 104*' holding' is as follows.

	Shares	Qualifying expenditure
		£
March 1980 acquisition	2,000	1,600
May 1992 acquisition	3,000	8,100
July 1998 scrip dividend	25	100
April 2000 acquisition	1,000	3,950
July 2008 scrip dividend	44	180
	6,069	13,930

229.7 CGT   Shares and Securities

	Shares	Qualifying expenditure
		£
May 2020 disposal	(2,069)	(4,749)
Pool carried forward	4,000	9,181
Proceeds		8,550
Costs £13,930 × 2,069/6,069		(4,749)
Chargeable gain 2020/21		£3,801

Notes

(a) Scrip dividends after 5 April 1998 are treated as free-standing acquisitions. Previously, a scrip dividend received by an individual was treated as a reorganisation within *TCGA 1992, s 128* so that the new shares equated with those already held. See CG14549 and *Simon's Taxes* D6.232.

(b) See also **230.1** and **230.2** SHARES AND SECURITIES — IDENTIFICATION RULES.

229.8 CAPITAL DISTRIBUTIONS

(A)

[*TCGA 1992, s 122*]

T holds 10,000 ordinary shares in a foreign company M SA. The shares were bought in April 1996 for £80,000. In February 2021, M SA has a capital reconstruction involving the cancellation of one-fifth of the existing ordinary shares in consideration of the repayment of £10 to each shareholder per share cancelled. T's holding is reduced to 8,000 shares, valued at £96,000.

	£
Disposal consideration (2,000 × £10)	20,000
Allowable cost $\dfrac{20,000}{20,000 + 96,000} \times £80,000$	(13,793)
Chargeable gain 2020/21	£6,207
The allowable cost of the remaining shares is £80,000 − £13,793	£66,207

(B) **Sale of rights**

[*TCGA 1992, ss 122, 123*]

X is a shareholder in K Ltd, owning 2,500 £1 ordinary shares which were purchased for £7,000 in October 1996. K Ltd makes a rights issue, but X sells his rights, without taking them up, for £700 in August 2020. The ex-rights value of X's 2,500 shares at the date of sale was £14,500.

'Section 104 holding' of K £1 ordinary shares	Shares	Qualifying expenditure
October 1996 acquisition	2,500	£7,000

HMRC cannot require the capital distribution to be treated as a disposal, as the £700 received for the rights does not exceed 5% of (£700 + £14,500) and in any case does not exceed £3,000 (see HMRC Capital Gains Manual CG57836). [*TCGA 1992, s 122(2)*]. If the transaction is not treated as a disposal, the £700 is deducted from the acquisition cost of the shares, leaving a balance of £6,300. If the transaction is treated as a disposal (possibly because X wishes to utilise part of his annual exemption), the computation is as follows.

	£
Disposal proceeds	700
Allowable cost $\dfrac{700}{700 + 14,500} \times £7,000$	(322)
Chargeable gain 2020/21	£378

The allowable cost of the shares is then reduced to £6,678 (£7,000 − £322).

230 Shares and Securities — Identification Rules

Cross-reference. See **229** SHARES AND SECURITIES.

230.1 CAPITAL GAINS TAX IDENTIFICATION RULES

Z, who is resident and ordinarily resident in the UK throughout, has the following acquisitions/disposals of ordinary 25p shares in MIB plc. MIB ordinary 25p shares were worth 210p per share at 31 March 1982. In 2020/21, Z made no disposals of chargeable assets other than as shown below.

Date	No. of shares bought/(sold)	Cost/ (proceeds) £
1 May 1980	1,000	2,000
1 October 1983	2,000	4,500
1 December 1996	500	1,800
1 May 2020	(1,000)	(3,900)
25 May 2020	2,000	7,600
2 January 2021	(3,000)	(18,000)
Remaining holding	1,500	

The disposal on 1 May 2020 is matched with 1,000 of the shares acquired on 25 May 2020 (under the 30-day rule — see note (a)). The resulting chargeable gain is as follows.

	£
Proceeds 1.5.20	3,900
Cost ($£7,600 \times 1,000/2,000$)	(3,800)
Chargeable gain	£100

The disposal of 3,000 shares on 2 January 2021 is matched with 3,000 of the 4,500 forming the '*section 104*' holding' as follows.

	No. of shares	Qualifying expenditure £
Shares acquired 1 May 1980 (note (b))	1,000	2,100
Additional shares 1 October 1983	2,000	4,500
Additional shares 1 December 1996	500	1,800
Additional shares 25 May 2020	1,000	3,800
	4,500	12,200
Disposal 2 January 2021	(3,000)	(8,133)
Pool carried forward	1,500	£4,067

230.1 CGT   Shares and Securities — Identification Rules

The chargeable gain is as follows.

	£
Proceeds 2.1.21	18,000
Cost (£12,200 × 3,000/4,500)	(8,133)
Chargeable gain	£9,867
Total chargeable gains 2020/21 £100 + £9,867	£9,967

Notes

(a) For capital gains tax purposes, disposals are identified (1) with shares acquired on the same day (with certain limited exceptions by election); (2) with acquisitions in the following 30 days; (3) with the '*section 104* holding'; (4) with shares acquired after the disposal (and after the expiry of the 30-day period in (2)) taken in the order in which such acquisitions occur. [*TCGA 1992, ss 104, 105, 106A, 288(7B)*]. See CG51550 onwards and *Simon's Taxes* C2.717.

(b) Re-basing to market value at 31 March 1982 applies automatically for capital gains tax purposes. Accordingly, the qualifying expenditure included in the *section 104* holding in respect of the shares acquired on 1 May 1980 is the market value of those shares on 31 March 1982.

230.2 SHARE IDENTIFICATION RULES FOR COMPANIES

[*TCGA 1992, ss 104, 105–110*]

B Ltd has the following transactions in 25p ordinary shares of H plc, a quoted company.

		Cost/(proceeds)
		£
6.6.78	Purchased 500 at £0.85	425
3.11.81	Purchased 1,300 at £0.80	1,040
15.5.82	Purchased 1,000 at £1.02	1,020
8.9.82	Purchased 400 at £1.08	432
1.2.86	Purchased 1,200 at £1.14	1,368
29.7.87	Sold 2,000 at £1.30	(2,600)
8.6.90	Purchased 1,500 at £1.26	1,890
21.12.93	Received 1,000 from group company (cost £1,250, indexation to date £250)	1,500
10.4.20	Sold 3,900 at £4.00	(15,600)

The shares stood at £1.00 at 31.3.82.

Indexation factors	March 1982 to December 2017	2.501
	May 1982 to April 1985	0.161
	September 1982 to April 1985	0.158
	April 1985 to February 1986	0.019
	February 1986 to July 1987	0.054

Shares and Securities — Identification Rules

July 1987 to June 1990	0.245
June 1990 to December 1993	0.120
December 1993 to December 2017	0.960

Disposal on 10 April 2020

The 'section 104 holding' pool immediately prior to the disposal should be as follows

	Shares	Qualifying expenditure £	Indexed pool £
15.5.82 acquisition	1,000	1,020	1,020
Indexation to April 1985			
£1,020 × 0.161			164
8.9.82 acquisition	400	432	432
Indexation to April 1985			
£432 × 0.158			68
Pool at 6.4.85	1,400	1,452	1,684
Indexed rise: April 1985 – Feb. 1986			
£1,684 × 0.019			32
1.2.86 acquisition	1,200	1,368	1,368
	2,600	2,820	3,084
Indexed rise: February 1986 – July 1987			
£3,084 × 0.054			167
	2,600	2,820	3,251
29.7.87 disposal	(2,000)	(2,169)	(2,501)
c/f	£600	£651	£750
b/f	600	651	750
Indexed rise: July 1987 – June 1990			
£750 × 0.245			184
8.6.90 acquisition	1,500	1,890	1,890
	2,100	2,541	2,824
Indexed rise: June 1990 – December 1993			
£2,824 × 0.120			339
21.12.93 acquisition	1,000	1,250	1,500
	3,100	3,791	4,663
Indexed rise: December 1993 – December 2017			
£4,663 × 0.960			4,476
	3,100	3,791	9,139

230.2 CGT   Shares and Securities — Identification Rules

The '1982 holding' is as follows

	Shares	Allowable expenditure £
6.6.78 acquisition	500	425
3.11.81 acquisition	1,300	1,040
	1,800	1,465

(i) Identify 3,100 shares sold with '*section 104* holding'

	£
Disposal consideration 3,100 × £4.00	12,400
Allowable cost	(3,791)
Unindexed gain	8,609
Indexation allowance £9,139 − £3,791	5,348
Chargeable gain	£3,261

(ii) Identify 800 shares sold with '1982 holding'

	£	£
Disposal consideration 800 × £4.00	3,200	3,200
Cost $\dfrac{800}{1,800} \times £1,465$	(651)	
Market value 31.3.82 $\dfrac{800}{1,800} \times £1,800$		(800)
Unindexed gain	2,549	2,400
Indexation allowance £800 × 2.501	(2,001)	(2,001)
Gain after indexation	£548	£399
Chargeable gain		£399
Total chargeable gain 10 April 2020 (£3,261+ £399)		£3,660

Shares and Securities — Identification Rules CGT 230.2

Notes

(a) Share disposals by companies are identified firstly with the '*section 104* holding' and secondly with the '1982 holding', both of which are regarded as single assets.

(b) On share disposals identified with shares held at 31.3.82, the re-basing provisions have effect, and indexation is based on the higher of cost and 31.3.82 value. If an irrevocable election is made under *TCGA 1992, s 35(5)* for all assets to be treated as disposed of and re-acquired at their market value on 31.3.82, indexation must be based on the 31.3.82 value even if this is less than cost. [*TCGA 1992, s 55(1)(2)*]. See CG13850, CG17405 and *Simon's Taxes* C2.607.

(c) Indexation allowance is frozen at its December 2017 level. No indexation allowance is available in respect of expenditure incurred after 31 December 2017, and for expenditure incurred on or before that date and falling to be deducted on a disposal after that date, indexation allowance is computed up to and including December 2017 only. [*TCGA 1992, ss 53(1)(1B), 54(1B); FA 2018, s 26(2)(3)(6)*]. See **214.1** INDEXATION. See also CG17230 and *Simon's Taxes* C2.301.

231 Social Investment Relief

231.1 DISPOSAL OF SI ASSETS MORE THAN THREE YEARS AFTER ACQUISITION

[TCGA 1992, ss 255B–255D]

On 8 November 2020 Jon subscribes £1,350,000 for 900,000 shares in the community interest company, Snow Ltd, and obtains the maximum SI income tax relief of £300,000 (£1,000,000 × 30%) for 2020/21. On 3 April 2024 he sells the entire holding for £2,000,000.

The chargeable gain arising is calculated as follows

	£
Disposal proceeds	2,000,000
Cost	(1,350,000)
Gain	650,000
Less TCGA 1992, ss 255B, 255C exemption	
£650,000 × 300,000/405,000	(481,481)
Chargeable gain 2023/24	£168,519

Notes

(a) Gains arising on the sale more than three years after the acquisition of an asset qualifying for SI income tax relief are not chargeable gains unless the SI relief is fully withdrawn before disposal.

(b) Where the income tax relief is not given on the full social investment (otherwise than because of insufficient income), capital gains tax relief is given on a proportion of the gain on the disposal or part disposal.

The gain is reduced by the multiple $D/I \times R$ where

D = the actual income tax reduction;

I = the amount invested; and

R = the SI rate for the year of income tax relief.

In this example:

D = £1,000,000 × 30% = £300,000

$I \times R$ = £1,350,000 × 30% = £405,000

(c) See *Simon's Taxes* C3.1913

231.2 CGT   Social Investment Relief

231.2 LOSS ON DISPOSAL OF SI ASSETS

[*TCGA 1992, s 255B(1)*]

(A) **Disposal more than three years after acquisition**

Assuming the facts otherwise remain the same as in 231.1 above but that the shares are sold for £900,000 on 3 April 2024.

The allowable loss arising is calculated as follows

	£	£
Disposal proceeds		900,000
Less Cost	1,350,000	
Less Income tax relief given (and not withdrawn)	300,000	(1,050,000)
Allowable loss 2023/24		£(150,000)

Note

(a) Any loss arising is reduced by deducting the amount of the SI relief (given and not withdrawn) from the acquisition cost. On the question of income tax withdrawal, see note (b) to (B) below.

(B) **Disposal within three years of acquisition**

The facts are otherwise as in (A) above except that the shares are sold in an arm's length bargain on 6 April 2022, i.e. within three years after their issue.

Income tax relief given for 2020/21 is withdrawn as follows

Relief attributable (£1,000,000 @ 30%)	£300,000 (1)
Consideration £900,000 × (300,000 (i.e. £1,000,000 @30%)/405,000 (i.e. £1,350,000 × 30%) @ 30%	£200,000 (2)

The amount at (1) is greater than that at (2), so income tax relief of £200,000 is withdrawn. [*ITA 2007, ss 257R, 257RA*].

The relief not withdrawn is therefore £(300,000 − 200,000) =   £100,000

The allowable loss arising is calculated as follows

	£	£
Disposal proceeds		900,000
Less Cost	1,350,000	
Less Income tax relief not withdrawn	100,000	(1,250,000)
Allowable loss 2022/23		£350,000

Notes

(a) For the purposes of computing an allowable loss, the consideration is reduced by the relief attributable to the assets. [*TCGA 1992, s 255B(1)*]. The relief attributable is that remaining following any withdrawal of relief. See *Simon's Taxes* C1.429A.

(b) A withdrawal of income tax relief arises on a disposal of SI assets within three years of acquisition. [*ITA 2007, ss 257R, 257RA*]. See *Simon's Taxes* E3.925.

231.3 SI DEFERRAL RELIEF

[*TCGA 1992, Sch 8B*]

On 1 August 2018, Robert realises a gain of £500,000 on the disposal of an asset he had owned since September 2005. Robert makes no other disposals in 2018/19. On 1 February 2020, Robert acquires shares in a community interest company for £400,000. Robert claims social investment income tax relief of £120,000 in respect of the investment. Robert makes a claim to defer the maximum £400,000 of the August 2018 gain against the qualifying investment.

On 1 July 2023, Robert sells 40% of his holding in the company for £199,200. He makes no other disposals in 2023/24.

Robert's CGT position for 2018/19 is as follows

	£
Gain	500,000
Less SI deferral relief	(400,000)
	100,000
Less annual exempt amount	(11,700)
Taxable gain 2018/19	£88,300

231.3 CGT   Social Investment Relief

Robert's CGT position for 2023/24 is as follows

The gain of £199,200 on the shares in the SI company is exempt, the shares having been held for more than three years.

	£
Deferred gain brought into charge	
Total gain deferred	£400,000
Clawback restricted to expenditure to which disposal relates	£160,000
Taxable gain 2023/24 (subject to annual exempt amount)	(£160,000)
Gain remaining deferred until any future chargeable event (£400,000 − £160,000)	£240,000

Notes

(a) Only gains accruing on or after 6 April 2014 and before 6 April 2019 can qualify for SI deferral relief. [*TCGA 1992, Sch 8B paras 1(3), 2(2)*]. See *Simon's Taxes* C1.429.

(b) Where a disposal qualifies for both BUSINESS ASSET DISPOSAL RELIEF (**206**) (formerly entrepreneurs' relief) and SI deferral relief, deferral relief can be claimed and entrepreneurs' relief can then be claimed when the deferred gain comes back into charge on the happening of a chargeable event. [*TCGA 1992, ss 169T–169V*]. See **206.5** BUSINESS ASSET DISPOSAL RELIEF. Previously, the taxpayer had to choose between the reliefs. See *Simon's Taxes* C3.1310.

232 Wasting Assets

Cross-references. See also **216.3** LAND, **226.3** ROLLOVER RELIEF — REPLACEMENT OF BUSINESS ASSETS.

232.1 GENERAL

[*TCGA 1992, ss 44–47*]

V bought an aircraft on 31 May 2015 at a cost of £90,000 for use in his air charter business. It has been agreed that V's non-business use of the aircraft amounts to one-tenth, on a flying hours basis, and capital allowances and running costs have accordingly been restricted for income tax purposes. On 1 February 2021, V sells the aircraft for £185,000. The aircraft is agreed as having a useful life of 20 years at the date it was acquired.

		£
Amount qualifying for capital allowances		
Relevant portion of disposal consideration $^9/_{10} \times £185,000$		166,500
Relevant portion of acquisition cost $^9/_{10} \times £90,000$		(81,000)
Chargeable gain 2020/21		£85,500
Amount not qualifying for capital allowances		
Relevant portion of disposal consideration $^1/_{10} \times £185,000$		18,500
Relevant portion of acquisition cost		
$^1/_{10} \times £90,000$	9,000	
Deduct wasted $£9,000 \times \dfrac{5\text{y } 8\text{m}}{20\text{y}}$	(2,550)	(6,450)
Gain		£12,050
The whole of the £12,050 is exempt.		
The total chargeable gain is therefore		£85,500

Note

(a) Gains on tangible movable property which are wasting assets not qualifying for capital allowances are exempt (and any losses would not be allowable). The exemption does not apply where the asset has become plant as a result of its use for the purposes of a trade, profession or vocation carried on by a person other than the owner and it would not otherwise have been a wasting asset. This does not, however, apply if the asset is plant under a long funding lease and the disposal takes place during the term of the lease or it is a deemed disposal on termination of the lease. [*TCGA 1992, s 45*]. See CG15445 and *Simon's Taxes* C2.901A.

232.2 CGT   Wasting Assets

232.2 OPTIONS

[*TCGA 1992, ss 44, 46, 146*]

Cross-reference.

See also **203.1** ASSETS.

(A) **Unquoted shares**

On 1 July 2018, R grants C an option to purchase unquoted shares held by R. The cost of the option is £600 to purchase 10,000 shares at £5 per share, the option to be exercised by 31 December 2020. On 1 September 2020 C assigns the option to W for £500.

	£	£
Disposal consideration		500
Acquisition cost	600	
Deduct wasted £600 × $^{26}/_{30}$	(520)	(80)
Chargeable gain		£420

(B) **Traded options**

On 1 December 2020, C purchases 6-month options on T plc shares for £1,000. Two weeks later, he sells the options, which are quoted on the Stock Exchange, for £1,200.

	£
Disposal consideration	1,200
Allowable cost	(1,000)
Chargeable gain	£200

Note

(a) The wasting asset rules do not apply to traded options. [*TCGA 1992, s 146*]. See CG76745 and *Simon's Taxes* C2.1003.

232.3 LIFE INTERESTS

[*TCGA 1992, s 44(1)(d)*]

(A)

N is a beneficiary under a settlement. On 30 June 2006, when her actuarially estimated life expectancy was 40 years, she sold her life interest to an unrelated individual, R, for £50,000. N dies on 31 December 2020, and the life interest is extinguished.

Wasting Assets CGT 232.3

R will have an allowable loss for 2020/21 as follows

	£	£
Disposal consideration on death of N		Nil
Allowable cost	50,000	
Deduct wasted $\dfrac{14y\ 6m}{40y} \times £50,000$	(18,125)	
		(31,875)
Allowable loss		£31,875

Note

(a) The amount of the cost wasted is computed by reference to the predictable life, not the actual life, of the wasting asset.

(B)

Assume the facts to be as in (A) above except that the sale of the life interest was on 30 June 1981 and N's life expectancy *at that date* was 40 years. The value of the life interest remained at £50,000 at 31 March 1982.

	£	£
Disposal consideration		Nil
Market value 31.3.82	50,000	
Deduct wasted $£50,000 \times \dfrac{38y\ 9m\ (31.3.82 - 31.12.20)}{39y\ 3m\ \text{(life expectancy at 31.3.82)}}$	(49,363)	
		(637)
Allowable loss 2020/21		£637

Note

(a) Where, by virtue of the re-basing rules, an asset is deemed to have been disposed of and re-acquired at its market value on 31 March 1982, that market value must be reduced in accordance with the period of ownership *after* that date and the predictable life of the wasting asset *at* that date.

Inheritance Tax

301	Accumulation and Maintenance Trusts
302	Agricultural Property
303	Anti-Avoidance
304	Business Property
305	Calculation of Tax
306	Charities
307	Close Companies
308	Deeds of Variation and Disclaimers
309	Double Taxation Relief
310	Exempt Transfers
311	Gifts with Reservation
312	Interest on Tax
313	Liability for Tax
314	Mutual Transfers
315	National Heritage
316	Payment of Tax
317	Protective Trusts
318	Quick Succession Relief
319	Settlements: Interests in Possession
320	Settlements: Relevant Property
321	Transfers on Death
322	Trusts for Bereaved Minors
323	Trusts for Disabled Persons
324	Trusts for Employees
325	Valuation
326	Woodlands

301 Accumulation and Maintenance Trusts

[*IHTA 1984, s 71*]

301.1 CHARGE ON FAILURE TO QUALIFY AS ACCUMULATION AND MAINTENANCE TRUST

On 1 January 1996 G settled £50,000 on trust equally for his great nephews and nieces born before 1 January 2016. The beneficiaries were to take absolute interests at age 18, income being accumulated for minor beneficiaries. By 2016 G had three great nephews and nieces, A (his brother's grandson) born in 1989 and B and C (his sister's grandsons) born in January 2006 and 2009 respectively. The settlement was valued at £150,000 on 1 January 2021.

On 1 January 2021 the settlement fails to qualify as an accumulation and maintenance settlement as more than 25 years have elapsed since the date of settlement and the beneficiaries do not have a common grandparent. There will be a charge to IHT on the value of the settlement on 1 January 2021.

The rate of tax is the aggregate of

0.25% for each of the first	40	quarters	10%
0.20% for each of the next	40	quarters	8%
0.15% for each of the next	20	quarters	3%
	100		21%

The IHT charge is 21% × £150,000 = £31,500

Notes

(a) There was no charge to IHT on A becoming entitled to one-third on his eighteenth birthday in January 2007.

(b) Settlements created on or after 22 March 2006 cannot qualify as accumulation and maintenance trusts. [*IHTA 1984, s 71(1A)*]. Accumulation and maintenance settlements created prior to that date continued to be treated under *IHTA 1984, s 71* until 6 April 2008 (unless they qualified as TRUSTS FOR BEREAVED MINORS (323)). From that date onwards any existing settlement must conform to revised rules to continue to receive *section 71* treatment: the beneficiary or beneficiaries must obtain a right to *capital* on or before the age of eighteen. No charge under *section 71* arose where as a consequence a settlement failed to qualify as an accumulation and maintenance trust on 6 April 2008. [*IHTA 1984, s 71(1)(a)*]. See IHTM42807 and *Simon's Taxes* I5.502.

(c) Settlements which failed to qualify as accumulation and maintenance trusts from 6 April 2008 as a result of the provisions in note (b) above are from that date either treated as 18-to-25 trusts (see 301.2 below) or taxed under the rules in 321 SETTLEMENTS: RELEVANT PROPERTY.

(d) See 323 TRUSTS FOR BEREAVED MINORS for certain settlements (including those created on or after 22 March 2006) which are taxed on a similar basis to accumulation and maintenance trusts.

301.2 IHT   Accumulation and Maintenance Trusts

301.2 PRE-22 MARCH 2006 SETTLEMENTS AFTER 5 APRIL 2008

(A)   **18-to-25 Trusts**

[*IHTA 1984, ss 71D–71G*]

On 30 April 1983 George, who had made no chargeable transfers in the previous seven years, settled £100,000 on trust equally for his grandchildren. The beneficiaries were to take absolute entitlements at age 25, income being accumulated for minor beneficiaries. George has two grandchildren; Alex, who is 25 on 28 February 2008, and Stephanie, born 27 September 1995. On Stephanie's 25th birthday on 26 September 2020 the remaining settlement property is valued at £575,000.

An exit charge arises under *IHTA 1984, s 71F* on Stephanie becoming absolutely entitled to the settlement property on reaching age 25 on 26 September 2020 as follows.

	£
Assumed chargeable transfer	575,000
Assumed cumulative total	—
Deduct Nil rate band	(325,000)
	£250,000
IHT at lifetime rates	£50,000

$$\text{Effective rate } \frac{50,000}{600,000} = 8.33\%$$

Relevant faction

The number of complete quarters that have elapsed between the time of Stephanie's 18th birthday and the day before her 25th birthday is 28. The relevant fraction is therefore 28/40.

The IHT is charged at the relevant fraction of the effective rate on the property to which Stephanie becomes absolutely entitled

28/40 × 8.33% = 5.831%

IHT payable: 3/10 × 5.831% × £600,000   £10,496

Notes

(a)   There is no charge to IHT on Alex becoming absolutely entitled to one half of the settled property on 28 February 2008.

(b)   On 6 April 2008, the settlement ceased to be an accumulation and maintenance trust because the remaining beneficiary does not become entitled absolutely to settled property on or before attaining age 18 as required from that date (see note (b) to **301.1** above). No charge to IHT arises.

(c)   From 6 April 2008 the settlement qualifies as an 18-to-25 trust because it has failed to qualify as an accumulation and maintenance trust by reason only of the change in rules on that date and the settlement secures that the remaining beneficiary

Accumulation and Maintenance Trusts   IHT 301.2

becomes absolutely entitled to the settled property, any income arising from it and any accumulated income on or before attaining the age of 25. [*IHTA 1984, s 71D(4)(6)*]. See IHTM42816 and *Simon's Taxes* I5.551.

(d) No charge to tax would arise on a beneficiary becoming absolutely entitled before the age of 18. [*IHTA 1984, s 71E(2)*].

(B) **Failure of 18-to-25 trust**

On 31 December 2005 Gilbert, who had made no cumulative chargeable transfers within the previous 7 years, settled £150,000 on an accumulation and maintenance settlement for his son Charles born on that date. The trust is contingent on Charles attaining the age of 25 years at which time he will become absolutely entitled to the settled property. If Charles dies before reaching age 25, Gilbert's nephew James, born on 22 March 1995, becomes the beneficiary, becoming absolutely entitled on attaining the age of 26. Charles dies on 6 April 2014. The settlement is valued at £640,000 on 30 December 2015. The property in the settlement is valued at £700,000 at 21 March 2021, the day before James's 26th birthday, when the funds are released to him.

Charges to IHT arise in respect of the settlement as follows.

Ten-year anniversary charge 31 December 2015

	£
Value of relevant property on 31.12.15	640,000
Less nil rate band £325,000	(325,000)
IHT at lifetime rates on £315,000 @ 20%	£63,000

$$\text{Effective rate } \frac{63,000}{640,000} = 9.84375\%$$

Appropriate fraction

The number of complete quarters that have elapsed between the date of Charles's death on 6 April 2014 and the tenth anniversary of the date of the settlement is 6. The appropriate fraction is therefore 6/40.

The IHT is charged at 30% of the appropriate fraction of the effective rate on the relevant property

IHT payable = 30% × 6/40 × 9.84375% × £640,000 = £2,835

301.2 IHT   Accumulation and Maintenance Trusts

Exit charge on James becoming absolutely entitled at 22 March 2021

Effective rate (as above, assuming no increase in nil rate band) = 9.84375%

The number of complete successive quarters between 31 December 2015 and 22 March 2021 is 20.

The proportionate charge is therefore:

9.84375% × 30% × 20/40 × £700,000 = £10,336

Notes

(a) The settlement qualifies as an accumulation and maintenance settlement until 5 April 2008 after which date it failed to qualify because Charles does not become absolutely entitled until age 25 (see note (b) to **301.1** above). No charge to IHT arose at that date.

(b) From 6 April 2008 the settlement is an 18-to-25 trust (see note (c) to A above). It ceases to qualify as an 18-to-25 trust on Charles's death on 6 April 2014 because the requirement for the beneficiary to become absolutely entitled on or before reaching age 25 is no longer met (James becomes absolutely entitled only at age 26). No charge to IHT arises on Charles's death. [*IHTA 1984, s 71E(2)(b)*].

(c) Following Charles's death the settlement comes within the relevant property charging regime (see **321** SETTLEMENTS: RELEVANT PROPERTY) resulting in a 10-year anniversary charge on 31 December 2015 and an exit charge on 22 March 2021 when James reaches age 26.

302 Agricultural Property

[*IHTA 1984, ss 115–124B; FA 2009, s 122*]

302.1 RELIEF FOR TRANSFERS AND OTHER EVENTS

(A) **Relief given at 100%**

[*IHTA 1984, ss 116(1)(2)(7), 124A(1)(3)*]

X has owned since 1984 1,000 acres of land. In June 1993 he began to farm the land, utilising 800 acres for that purpose. The remaining 200 acres are not used for any business purposes. On 1 July 2020 X transfers all the land to his son, Y, at a time when its agricultural value was £1,000 per acre and its open market value £1,500 per acre. He had not used his annual exemptions for 2019/20 and 2020/21. X died on 6 September 2023. Y has continued to run the farm business since the date of the gift.

The value of the gift for inheritance tax purposes before relief is

		£	£
1,000 acres at £1,500 per acre			£1,500,000
The transfer subject to tax is			
(i)	Agricultural value of land		
	800 acres × £1,000	800,000	
	Less agricultural property relief at 100%	(800,000)	—
(ii)	Non-agricultural value of land		
	800 acres × £500		400,000
(iii)	Value of land not used in business		
	200 acres at £1,500 per acre		300,000
			700,000
Deduct Annual exemptions (2019/20 and 2020/21)			(6,000)
Value transferred by PET becoming chargeable on death			£694,000

Notes

(a) Relief is at 100% because

(i) immediately before the transfer, X enjoyed the right to vacant possession;

302.1 IHT Agricultural Property

        (ii)   X had farmed the land for two years before the transfer;

        (iii)   X had acquired the land more than seven years before the transfer and it had been farmed throughout those seven years (by X or any other person); and

        (iv)   the land was farmed by Y between the date of gift and X's death.

        Note that although conditions (ii) and (iii) were both satisfied in this case, it is only necessary to satisfy one of them to qualify for 100% relief.

(b)   Annual exemptions are deducted *after* deducting the agricultural property relief.

(c)   Business property relief may be available in respect of the £400,000 excess of the open market value over the agricultural value.

(d)   IHT will be charged at 80% of full rates as X died more than 3 but not more than 4 years after the gift.

(B)   **Transfer where land is held tenanted under an agricultural lease entered into on or after 1 September 1995**

[IHTA 1984, s 116(1)(2)(7)]

A is the freehold owner of agricultural land which at current vacant possession value is estimated to be valued at £850,000. On 29 September 1992, he enters into an agricultural tenancy (with more than two years to run) with a farming partnership comprising his two sons and his grandson for a full market rental of £25,000 p.a. The tenanted value is estimated at £500,000.

In July 2019 his grandson is killed in a farming accident and a new letting agreement is made between the two sons and A for a full market rent of £35,000 p.a. on 15 September 2019.

A dies on 1 October 2020 when the tenanted value of the land has risen to £600,000.

	£
Transfer at death (tenanted valuation)	600,000
Deduct Agricultural property relief at 100%	(600,000)
IHT payable on	Nil

Notes

(a)   No IHT charge arises on the grant of the lease to the partnership on the basis that it is for full consideration. [*IHTA 1984, s 16*]. See IHTM04230 and *Simon's Taxes* I3.159.

(b)   As A terminated the existing agricultural tenancy and entered into a new tenancy on or after 1 September 1995, agricultural property relief of 100% is available. Only 50% relief would have been available if the existing tenancy had continued. [*FA 1995, s 155; FA 1996, s 185*].

Agricultural Property   IHT 302.2

(C) **Interaction with capital gains tax**

A discretionary settlement has 400 acres of tenanted agricultural land, the tenancy having commenced before 1 September 1995. On 31 October 2018, the trustees appoint the agricultural land to a beneficiary who then becomes absolutely entitled to the land. 50% agricultural property relief is available. The value of the 400 acres as tenanted is £450,000. The trustees fail to pay the capital gains tax due of, say, £60,000 by 31 January 2021 and the beneficiary is assessed and pays the liability.

	£
Value transferred	450,000
Deduct Agricultural property relief at 50%	(225,000)
	225,000
Less Capital gains tax	(60,000)
Chargeable transfer (subject to grossing-up)	£165,000

Notes

(a) An election may be made for the CGT to be held over. [*TCGA 1992, s 260(1)–(5)*].

(b) If the trustees fail to pay all or part of the capital gains tax within twelve months of the due date, an assessment may be made on the beneficiary [*TCGA 1992, s 282*] and the amount of such tax borne by the donee is treated as reducing the value transferred. The beneficiary must become absolutely entitled to the property to obtain the relief. [*IHTA 1984, s 165*]. See IHTM42163 and *Simon's Taxes* I3.611.

(c) If it were possible for the trustees to arrange for a new tenancy to begin after 31 August 1995 but before the transfer, the transfer would have attracted 100% agricultural property relief. [*FA 1995, s 155*]. This could possibly be achieved by terminating the existing lease and entering into a new lease with the same tenants, subject to the terms of the existing lease, the tenants' agreement and general legal requirements.

302.2 SHARES ETC. IN AGRICULTURAL COMPANIES

[*IHTA 1984, ss 122, 123*]

AC Ltd is an unquoted agricultural company of which A owns 60% of the shares.

The company owns	£
4,000 acres of land — agricultural value	4M
Other trading assets (net)	2M
Total value of company	£6M
A's shareholding is valued at	£4.5M

All necessary conditions for relief are satisfied.

302.2 IHT   Agricultural Property

If A were to die in, say, November 2020 the position as regards his shareholding would be as follows

	Total Value £	Land £	Other Assets £
Value of assets of company	6M	4M	2M
Value of shares, split in same proportions	4.5M	£3M	£1.5M
Deduct agricultural property relief (100% of £3M)	(3.0M)		
Deduct business property relief (100% of £1.5M)	(1.5M)		
Chargeable to IHT	Nil		

Notes

(a) Part of the value transferred is attributable to the agricultural value of agricultural property, so agricultural property relief is available. [*IHTA 1984, s 122*]. See IHTM24020 and *Simon's Taxes* I7.331.

(b) The legislation appears to require that both agricultural property relief and business property relief be given, each against its appropriate part of the value. [*IHTA 1984, s 114*]. See also **304 BUSINESS PROPERTY**.

303 Anti-Avoidance

303.1 ASSOCIATED OPERATIONS

[*IHTA 1984, s 268*]

(A)

H owns a set of four Chippendale chairs valued, as a set, at £6,000. Individually they would be valued at only £1,000, although a pair would be worth £2,500 and three £4,000.

He gives one chair to his son each year over four years, during which time all values increase at 10% p.a. (simple). In the fifth year H dies.

	£	£
Year 1		
Value of four chairs	6,000	
Deduct value of three	(4,000)	
Value transferred		2,000
Year 2		
Basic computation ignoring the associated operations rule		
Current value of three chairs	4,400	
Deduct value of two	(2,750)	
Value transferred	£1,650	
Revised to take account of associated operations rule		
Current value of four chairs	6,600	
Deduct value of two	(2,750)	
	3,850	
Deduct value transferred in Year 1	(2,000)	
		1,850
Year 3		
Current value of four chairs	7,200	
Deduct value of one	(1,200)	
	6,000	
Deduct value transferred in Years 1 and 2	(3,850)	
		2,150

303.1 IHT   Anti-Avoidance

Year 4

	£	£
Current value of four chairs	7,800	
Deduct value transferred in Years 1, 2 and 3	(6,000)	
Value transferred		1,800
Total values transferred		£7,800

Note

(a) The normal rule would be that the transfer of value is the loss to the donor's estate, as in Year 1. However, if a series of transfers are treated as associated operations, the transfer is treated as if made at the time of the latest transfer, reduced by the value transferred by the earlier transfers.

(B)

If in (A) above H had wished to give away the chairs over two years instead of four, he might first have given two chairs to his wife, so that each could give the son one chair each year.

Year 1

		£	£
(i)	Value transferred by husband to son		
	Value of two chairs (as half of a set of four linked by the related property rule)	3,000	
	Deduct value of one chair (as half of a pair)	(1,250)	
			1,750
(ii)	Value transferred by wife (similar calculation)		1,750

Year 2

		£	£
(i)	Value transferred by husband, applying the associated operations rule		
	Current value of four chairs	6,600	
	Deduct value transferred in Year 1 by H to son	(3,500)	
	Value transferred		3,100
	Total values transferred		£6,600

Notes

(a) In this case, the total of the values transferred can exceed the value of the assets, although it must be doubtful whether HMRC would seek to apply the full rigours of the section unless the transfer by the wife in Year 1 had fallen within her annual exemptions, or she had survived seven years so that the gift was exempt.

(b) See *IHTA 1984, s 161* for the related property rule, and see also **326.2** VALUATION. See IHTM09731–IHTM09739.

(c) The result above could have been achieved in another way. The first transfer by the husband to his spouse is quantified at £3,000 – the second to the son is quantified at £1,750 as in the example. If through *section 268* one looks at the position as if the transfer of value was made on the last of the operations, the calculation would be:

	£
Value in H's estate before any transfer (i.e. value of 4 chairs at the date of last transfer)	6,600
Value in husband's estate after all transfers	Nil
Value transferred	6,600
Deduct value of earlier operations:	
Transfer to wife disregarded *section 268(3)*	Nil
Transfer to son	(1,750)
Value transferred	£4,850

So the value transferred is £1,750 + £4,850 = £6,600. HMRC would not seek to raise a charge to tax on the actual transfers by the wife to the son.

HMRC may ask the District Valuer Service for the value effectively transferred by one transfer being the last of a series of associated operations. If any of the earlier operations were themselves transfers of value, other than transfers between spouses or civil partners [*IHTA 1984, s 18*], then the adjustment will be dealt with by HMRC. See IHTM11031 and *Simon's Taxes* I3.332.

304 Business Property

[*IHTA 1984, ss 103–114, 269*]

304.1 RELEVANT BUSINESS PROPERTY

(A) **Shares in a holding company with a non-qualifying subsidiary**

[*IHTA 1984, s 111*]

A owns 85% of the share capital of H Ltd, an unquoted company which has two wholly-owned subsidiary companies S Ltd and P Ltd. H Ltd and S Ltd are trading companies and P Ltd is a property investment company. The issued share capital of H Ltd is 100,000 ordinary shares of £1 each valued at £8 per share. The values of the issued shares in S Ltd and P Ltd are £250,000 and £300,000 respectively.

A gives 10,000 shares in H Ltd to his son in August 2018. He has already made chargeable transfers using up his basic exemptions. His son agrees to pay any IHT. A dies in January 2021, at which time his son still owns the shares. It is agreed that the fall in value in A's estate (reduction of a 85% holding to a 75% holding), by which the value of the gift for IHT purposes is measured, is equivalent to the actual value of the shares transferred.

	£	£
Value of gift		80,000
Deduct business property relief 100% × £80,000	80,000	
Less 100% × 80,000 × $\frac{300,000}{800,000}$	(30,000)	
		(50,000)
PET becoming chargeable transfer on death		£30,000

(B) **Land used by a business**

M has for many years owned a factory used in the business of Q Ltd, of which he has control. In September 2018, M gives the factory to his son S when its value is £740,000. He has made no previous chargeable transfer, but made a gift of £3,000 in 2018/19. M dies in October 2020, when the factory is being used for business purposes by S's partnership. S agreed to pay any IHT on the gift.

304.1 IHT Business Property

	£
Value of gift	740,000
Deduct business property relief (50%)	(370,000)
	370,000
Deduct annual exemption (2019/20)	(3,000)
PET becoming chargeable transfer on death	£367,000
IHT payable at full rates ((£367,000–325,000) × 40%)) (death within 3 years)	£16,800

Notes

(a) If M wishes also to dispose of shares in Q Ltd by sale or gift after which he would no longer have control, he should give the factory to his son *before* disposing of the shares, or else the business property relief would not be available on the gift of the factory.

(b) If the factory had been used by Q Ltd at the date of M's death, no business property relief would be available on the gift since the factory would not be relevant business property in S's hands at the date of death.

(C) Land and buildings owned by trustees

X died in 1976 leaving a life interest in factory premises to his son A, with remainder to his grandsons B and C. A occupies the premises for the purposes of his trade, rent-free. In September 2019 A gives up his life interest when the value of the premises is £660,000. B and C agree to pay any IHT. A has already made chargeable transfers using up his annual exemptions. A dies in November 2020, when the factory is still being used in the trade which was then being carried on by B and C in partnership.

	£
Value of gift	660,000
Deduct business property relief (50%)	(330,000)
PET becoming chargeable transfer on death	£330,000
IHT payable at full rates ((£330,000–325,000) × 40%)) (death within 3 years)	£2,000

(D) Further conditions for lifetime transfers

X transfers the share of his 25% interest in Amalgam Ltd (an AIM company) to his son Y and also transfers land and buildings in his partnership to his other son Z on 16 June 2017. X has already used his annual exemptions for 2017/18 and 2016/17. The shares are valued at £640,000 and the land and buildings at £676,000. In February 2019 Amalgam Ltd is quoted on the London Stock Exchange and Y's share value increases to £1 million.

Z sells the land and property to one of the partners in May 2019 and invests the whole proceeds in an unquoted company receiving shares to the value of £800,000. X dies on 6 June 2020.

Business Property IHT 304.1

Theoretical computation on death if shares in Amalgam Ltd had remained unquoted

	£	Gross	Tax
Value of shares to Y	640,000		
Deduct BPR 100%	(640,000)	Nil	Nil
Partnership assets to Z	676,000		
Deduct BPR 50%	(338,000)		
PET becoming chargeable transfer on death ((£338,000–325,000) × 40%))	338,000	£13,000	£5,200

Actual computation on death — tax payable on failed BPR and PETs that have become chargeable because of X's death within 7 years

	£	
Value of shares to Y	640,000	
Value of property to Z after BPR	338,000	
	978,000	
Less nil rate band	(325,000)	
	653,000	× 40% = £261,200

Apportionment of tax

Gift to Y $£261,200 \times \dfrac{£640,000}{£978,000}$ =   £170,928

Gift to Z $£261,200 \times \dfrac{£338,000}{£978,000}$ =   £90,272

Notes

(a) X's death within 3 years of the gift of the shares in Amalgam Ltd results in the loss of business property relief, because on a notional transfer by Y immediately before X's death, the shares, being a non-controlling shareholding in a quoted company, would not have qualified as relevant business property. [*IHTA 1984, s 113A(3)*]. In determining whether on the notional transfer an asset qualifies as relevant business property, the requirement for the asset to be held for two years by the transferor prior to the notional transfer is ignored.

(b) Z has sold the business assets in the partnership and reinvested the proceeds in other relevant business property which attracts 100% BPR (i.e. unquoted shares) as opposed to 50% for the original assets (i.e. land and buildings) in the partnership. Z's replacement of the partnership assets with unquoted shares qualifies for

304.1 IHT Business Property

replacement property relief. [*IHTA 1984, s 113B*]. However, Z's position is affected by Y's loss of 100% BPR in respect of the transfer of shares to Y by X. See IHTM25250 and *Simon's Taxes* I7.194.

(c) Z could have taken the view that his position was vulnerable to Y's decision to accept quoted shares (with no control) and X's death within seven years of the gifts. Insurance on a reducing basis could have been taken out by Z to protect his position and cover the liability of £85,072 (i.e. £90,272 − £5,200).

305 Calculation of Tax

305.1 THE CUMULATION PRINCIPLE: POTENTIALLY EXEMPT TRANSFERS

[*IHTA 1984, ss 3, 3A, 7*]

On 1 May 2013 A gave £50,000 to his daughter, D, and on 1 May 2016 he gave £215,000 to his son, S. Both D and S agreed to pay any IHT due on the gifts.

On 7 March 2021 A died, leaving his estate, valued at £300,000, equally to D and S. The only other transfer made by A was an immediately chargeable transfer of £121,000 during 2011/12. A had sold his home in January 2015 and lived in a nursing home until his death.

Gift on 1 May 2013

The gift is a PET, which becomes exempt since A does not die within seven years of the date of the gift. No IHT is payable.

Gift on 1 May 2016

This PET becomes chargeable since A dies between 4 and 5 years after the gift. IHT is payable by S following the death at 60% of full rates on the basis of the Table of rates in force in 2020/21.

As this PET has become chargeable, it must be cumulated with other chargeable transfers made in the seven years before the date of the gift. The PET made on 1 May 2013 has become exempt and is excluded from the computation but the immediately chargeable transfer of £121,000 made during 2011/12 must be cumulated with the 2016 gift. Note that a transfer made more than seven years before the death of the transferor and which is not itself aggregated with the estate on death is thus brought into the computation of the IHT payable on the 2016 gift.

		£	£
Gift			215,000
Deduct annual exemptions	2016/17	(3,000)	
	2015/16	(3,000)	
			(6,000)
			£209,000

IHT on £209,000 charged in band £121,000 to £330,000

121,001–325,000 at nil%	—	
325,001–330,000 at 40%	2,000	
	£2,000	
IHT payable at 60% of full rates — £2,000 at 60%		£1,200

305.1 IHT Calculation of Tax

Death 7 March 2021

The chargeable transfers in the seven years prior to death comprise only the gift on 1 May 2016 of £209,000.

IHT on death on estate of £300,000 chargeable in band £209,001 to £509,000

	£
209,001–325,000 at nil%	—
325,001–509,000 at 40%	73,600
IHT payable	£73,600

Notes

(a) If A directs in his Will that, despite the earlier agreement, any IHT due on the gift to S is to be borne by his estate, this amounts to a pecuniary legacy to S of the amount of the tax. The reduction in A's estate by the transfer is unchanged at £215,000 as is the tax of £1,200. The legacy is paid out of the death estate of £300,000 with previous chargeable transfers of £209,000. Since the whole of the estate is liable on death, the IHT remains at £73,600.

(b) If S has not by 1 April 2022 paid the IHT of £1,200 due on the gift from A, the personal representatives of A become liable for the tax as it has not been paid by S within 12 months after the end of the month in which A died. The IHT due remains £1,200 since the gross chargeable transfer is £209,000. A had no liability for the tax at the time the transfer was made and the reduction in value to his estate was, therefore, the amount of the gift to S, £215,000. The personal representatives have a right under general law to reimbursement for the tax from S. To the extent that reimbursement is probable, the tax is not a deduction from the estate. Since the personal representatives can claim reimbursement from the half estate due to S, no deduction will be given. Tax on the estate remains, therefore, at £73,600. [*IHTA 1984, ss 199, 204*]. If S had not benefited under A's Will so that no assets were available to reimburse the personal representatives, the tax due of £1,200 might fall to be met from the estate.

(c) A's estate does not qualify for the additional residence nil-rate band because his home was sold before 8 July 2015. For examples on the residence nil-rate band see **310.5 EXEMPT TRANSFERS**.

305.2 THE CUMULATION PRINCIPLE: GROSSING UP A CHARGEABLE TRANSFER

[*IHTA 1984, ss 3, 3A, 5, 7*]

(A)

On 13 July 2013 B gave £337,000 to his nephew N, who agreed to pay any IHT on the gift. On 24 December 2014 B settled £332,000 on discretionary trusts for his great-nephews and nieces, paying the IHT himself.

On 9 July 2020 B died with an estate worth £78,000, having made no other gifts.

Gift 13 July 2013

The gift is a PET but becomes chargeable since B dies between 6 and 7 years after the gift. The annual exemption for 2013/14, and that brought forward from 2012/13 are, however, available, reducing the chargeable transfer to £331,000.

Calculation of Tax IHT 305.2

IHT is charged on the transfer at 20% of full rates, using the Table of rates in force in 2020/21.

	£
IHT on gift	
1–325,000 at nil%	—
325,001–331,000 at 40%	2,400
	£2,400
IHT payable by N at 20% of full rates, i.e. 20% × £2,400	£480

Gift 24 December 2014

Initial liability

The gift to the discretionary trust is an immediately chargeable transfer on which the transferor, B, has agreed to pay the IHT. The annual exemption for 2014/15 is set against the chargeable transfer, reducing it to £329,000.

As B is paying the tax on the transfer, his estate is reduced by two amounts: the gross amount of the transfer itself (i.e. before deducting the annual exemptions) and by the tax due on the net transfer (i.e. after deducting the annual exemptions). The total tax will not merely comprise the tax due on the transfer, but the tax upon that tax, and so on. In order to determine the total tax due, where applicable the excess of the chargeable transfer above the nil rate band (or part thereof) is grossed up, using the following formula:

$$E \times \frac{100}{100 - T} \times T\% = G$$

E = excess over nil rate band

T = applicable rate of tax

G = tax due on gross chargeable transfer

In this example, as chargeable lifetime transfers are charged at 20%, being one half of the full death rates, T will be 20. The computation therefore proceeds as follows.

	£
Value of transfer	332,000
Deduct Annual exemption	(3,000)
	329,000
IHT payable on gift	
£(329,000 – 325,000) × $\frac{100}{100 - 20}$ × 20%	1,000
B's gross chargeable transfer	£330,000

Revision on death

B's death occurs between 5 and 6 years after the gift, so the tax on the chargeable transfer is revised to the IHT payable at 40% of full rates. The PET on 13 July 2013 becomes chargeable, so IHT is charged on the gross chargeable transfer of £330,000 in the bracket £331,000 to £661,000.

305.2 IHT   Calculation of Tax

	£
331,001–661,000 at 40%	132,000
IHT at 40% of £132,000	52,800
Less paid on chargeable lifetime transfer	(1,000)
Additional IHT payable following death	£51,800

Death 9 July 2020

Chargeable transfers in the seven years prior to death amount to £661,000, so IHT is charged on the death estate of £78,000 in the bracket £661,000 to £739,000.

IHT payable
661,001–739,000 at 40%   £31,200

(B)

Facts are as in (A) above except that B died on 9 July 2021. It is assumed that the nil rate band remains unchanged at £325,000.

The PET on 13 July 2013 is exempt and thus not cumulated when reworking the IHT on the chargeable transfer on 24 December 2014 or on death.

Gift 24 December 2014

IHT on gift, as before   £1,000

Following B's death between 6 and 7 years after the gift, IHT is reworked at 20% of full rates. IHT is charged on the gross chargeable transfer of £330,000 in the bracket £Nil to £330,000.

	£
325,001–330,000 at 40%	2,000
IHT payable at 20% of full rates, i.e. 20% × £2,000	£400
Deduct paid originally by B	(1,000)
	—

No further IHT is payable as the tax originally paid exceeds the IHT at the death rates.

Death 9 July 2021

Chargeable transfers in the previous 7 years amount to £330,000 so IHT is charged on the death estate of £78,000 in the bracket £330,000 to £408,000.

IHT payable
330,001–408,000 at 40%   £31,200

Note

(a) No IHT is repayable in respect of the chargeable transfer on 24 December 2014, even though the IHT on death is less than the IHT originally paid on the gift.

305.3 PARTLY EXEMPT TRANSFERS

[IHTA 1984, ss 36–42]

(A) **Where the only chargeable part of a transfer is specific gifts which do not bear their own tax**

A, a widow, dies on 8 June 2020. Her estate is valued at £420,000 and her Will provides for a tax-free legacy to her nephew of £348,000 and the residue of her estate to the National Trust. A had made no chargeable transfers during her lifetime.

Gross-up tax-free legacy at 'death' rates

	£
Tax-free legacy	348,000
Tax thereon	
$(348{,}000 - 325{,}000) \times \dfrac{100}{100-40} \times 40\%$	15,333
Gross chargeable transfer	£363,333
Calculation of net residuary estate	£
Value of estate	420,000
Deduct gross value of legacy	(363,333)
Residue	£56,667
Allocation of estate at death	
Nephew	348,000
National Trust	56,667
Tax	15,333
	£420,000

(B) **Where tax-free specific gifts are not the only chargeable gifts**

A dies on 1 January 2021 leaving a widow, son and nephew. His estate is valued at £560,000 before deduction of business property relief of £50,000 and his Will provides for a tax-free legacy to his son of £360,000, a legacy to the nephew of £13,000 bearing its own tax, a bequest to charity of £26,000, with the residue shared three-quarters by his widow and one-quarter by the son. A had made no previous chargeable transfers.

Allocation of business property relief

[IHTA 1984, s 39A]

305.3 IHT Calculation of Tax

Since the Will made no specific gifts of the business property, the business property relief is apportioned between each of the specific gifts and the residue, i.e. each is multiplied by

$$\frac{\text{Estate less business property relief}}{\text{Estate before business property relief}}$$

Son	£360,000 ×	$\frac{510,000}{560,000}$ =	£327,858
Nephew	£13,000 ×	$\frac{510,000}{560,000}$ =	£11,839
Charity	£26,000 ×	$\frac{510,000}{560,000}$ =	£23,678
Residue	£161,000 ×	$\frac{510,000}{560,000}$ =	£146,625
	£560,000		£510,000

	£	£	£
Hypothetical chargeable estate			
Tax-free legacy to son			327,858
Tax thereon			
$£(327,858 - 325,000) \times \frac{100}{100-40} \times 40\%$			1,905
			329,763
Legacy to nephew			11,839
			341,602
Chargeable residue:			
Gross estate		510,000	
Deduct gross legacies	341,602		
charity	23,678		
		(365,280)	
		£144,720	
Son's one-quarter share			36,180
Hypothetical chargeable estate			£377,782

Calculation of Tax   IHT 305.3

Hypothetical chargeable estate — calculation of assumed tax rate

Tax on £377,782   £21,112

$$£(377{,}782 - 325{,}000) \times 40\%$$

$$\text{Assumed rate } \frac{21{,}112}{377{,}782} \times 100 = 5.5884\%$$

Re-gross tax-free legacy to son using assumed rate

$$£327{,}858 \times \frac{100}{100 - 5.5884} \qquad\qquad £347{,}264$$

Calculate chargeable estate and tax thereon	£	£	£
Grossed-up value of tax-free legacy			347,264
Legacy to nephew			11,839
			359,103
Chargeable residue			
Gross estate		510,000	
Deduct gross legacies	359,103		
charity	23,678		
		(382,781)	
		£127,219	
Son's one-quarter share			31,804
Chargeable estate			£390,907
Tax on estate			
0–325,000 at nil %			—
325,001–390,907 at 40%			26,362
			£26,362

$$\text{Estate rate is } \frac{26{,}362}{390{,}907} \times 100 = 6.7438\%$$

Calculation of residue		£	£
Gross estate			560,000
Specific legacies	— son	360,000	
	— nephew	13,000	
	— charity	26,000	
		399,000	

305.3 IHT Calculation of Tax

Tax on son's legacy		
£347,264 at 6.7438%	23,418	
Legacies plus tax thereon		422,418
Residue		£137,582

Distribution of estate	£	£
Widow — three-quarters of residue		103,187
Son — specific legacy	360,000	
— one quarter share of residue	34,395	
	394,395	
Deduct tax on share of residue		
£34,395 × 6.7438%	2,319	
		392,076
Nephew — specific legacy	13,000	
Deduct tax thereon		
£11,839 × 6.7438%	798	
		12,202
Charity		26,000
Tax payable £(23,418 + 2,319 + 798)		26,535
		£560,000

(C) **As (B) above but with settled property**

The facts are as in (B) above except that in addition to his free estate valued at £560,000, A has a life interest acquired before 22 March 2006, worth £100,000 at 1 January 2021, in his late father's estate, with remainder to his son.

The hypothetical chargeable estate is £377,782 as in (B) above and thus the assumed rate remains at 5.5884%. The settled property is ignored at this stage — see note (a).

Calculate chargeable estate and tax thereon	£
Chargeable free estate as in (B) above	390,907
Settled property	100,000
Chargeable estate	£490,907
Tax on estate	
0–325,000 at nil %	—
325,001–490,907 at 40%	66,362
	£66,362

$$\text{Estate rate is } \frac{66,362}{490,907} \times 100 = 13.51824\%$$

Calculation of Tax   IHT 305.3

Calculation of residue

	£	£
Gross estate		560,000
Specific legacies — son	360,000	
— nephew	13,000	
— charity	26,000	
	399,000	
Tax on son's legacy		
£347,264 at 13.51824%	46,943	
Deduct Legacies plus tax thereon		(445,943)
Residue		£114,057

Distribution of estate

	£	£
Widow — three quarters of residue		85,543
Son — specific legacy	360,000	
— one quarter share of residue	28,514	
— settled property	100,000	
Deduct		
tax on share of residue		
£34,395 × 13.51824%	(4,649)	
tax on settled property		
£100,000 × 13.51824%	(13,518)	
		470,347
Nephew — specific legacy	13,000	
Deduct tax thereon		
£11,839 × 13.51824%	(1,600)	
		11,400
Charity		26,000
Tax payable (46,943 + 4,649 + 13,518 + 1,600)		66,710
		£660,000

Notes

(a) Where gifts take effect separately out of the deceased's free estate and out of a settled fund the provisions of *IHTA 1984, ss 36–39A* (partly exempt transfers) apply separately to each fund. [*IHTA 1984, s 40*]. HMRC take the view that the rate of tax to be used for grossing up, i.e. the 'assumed rate' in this example, should be found by looking at each fund separately and in isolation. Thus, the settled property is not taken into account above in the calculation of the assumed rate for gifts out of the free estate. See IHTM26211, IHTM26212 and *Simon's Taxes* I4.242.

(b) The IHT on the settled property, payable by the trustees, is found by applying the estate rate of 13.51824% to the value of that property.

306 Charities

[*IHTA 1984, s 70*]

306.1 PROPERTY LEAVING TEMPORARY CHARITABLE TRUSTS

(A) **Gross payment to beneficiaries**

On 1 January 1974 A settled £100,000 on temporary charitable trusts. The income and capital were to be applied for charitable purposes only for a period of 25 years from the date of settlement, and thereafter could be applied for charitable purposes or to or for the settlor's grandchildren. On 1 January 2021 the trustees paid £50,000 to charity and the balance of the settlement, valued at £75,000, to the three grandchildren.

The relevant period is the period from settlement of the funds or, if later, 13 March 1975 to 1 January 2021, i.e. 183 complete quarters, and the amount on which tax is charged is £75,000 gross.

The rate of tax is

0.25% for 40 quarters	10.00%
0.20% for 40 quarters	8.00%
0.15% for 40 quarters	6.00%
0.10% for 40 quarters	4.00%
0.05% for 23 quarters	1.15%
	29.15%

IHT payable is 29.15% × £75,000 = £21,863

(B) **Net payment to beneficiaries**

Assume the same facts as in (A) above except that the trustees apply £75,000 net for the settlor's three grandchildren, and the balance to charity.

The rate of tax is, as before, 29.15%.

$$\text{IHT payable is } \frac{29.15}{100 - 29.15} \times £75{,}000 = £30{,}857$$

The gross payment to the beneficiaries is £75,000 + £30,857 = £105,857

Note

(a) See IHTM04103, IHTM12803 and *Simon's Taxes* I5.643.

307 Close Companies

[*IHTA 1984, ss 94–98, 102*]

307.1 VALUE TRANSFERRED

The ordinary shares of companies A and B are held as follows (in January 2021)

		A	B
Individuals	X	80%	
	Y	20%	
	Z		10%
Company	A		90%

Company B is non-resident and Z is domiciled in the UK. Company A sells a property valued at £220,000 to a mutual friend of X and Y for £20,000. The following month, company B sells a foreign property worth £100,000 to X for £90,000.

Company A

	£
The transfer of value is £220,000 − £20,000	200,000
Apportioned to X 80% × £200,000	160,000
Y 20% × £200,000	40,000
	£200,000

Company B

The transfer of value of £10,000 is apportioned

		£
To X	80% × 90% × £10,000	7,200
	Deduct increase in X's estate	(10,000)
		—
To Y	20% × 90% × £10,000	1,800
To Z	10% × £10,000 note (c)	1,000
		£2,800

Notes

(a) If the sale by company A were to X (or Y), there would be no apportionment because the undervalue would be treated as a distribution, thus attracting income tax.

(b) On the sale by company B, X would not be liable to income tax.

(c) If Z were not domiciled in the UK, his share of the transfer of value would not be apportioned to him. [*IHTA 1984, s 94(2)(b)*]. See IHTM14854 and *Simon's Taxes* I6.123.

307.2 IHT   Close Companies

307.2 CHARGE ON PARTICIPATORS

Assume the values transferred by X, Y and Z in **307.1** above and that X and Y have each made previous chargeable transfers in excess of £325,000 since January 2014 and have used up their annual exemptions for 2019/20.

Company A

	X	Y	Z
	£	£	£
Value transferred	160,000	40,000	
Annual exemptions 2020/21	(3,000)	(3,000)	
	157,000	37,000	
Tax (25% of net)	39,250	9,250	
Gross transfer	£196,250	£46,250	
IHT thereon at 20%	£39,250	£9,250	

Company B

	X	Y	Z
Value transferred	7,200	1,800	1,000
Deduct increase in X's estate	(10,000)	—	—
		1,800	1,000
Deduct annual exemption		—	(1,000)
		1,800	—
Tax (25% of net)		450	
Gross transfer		£2,250	
IHT thereon at 20%		£450	

Note

(a) Although it is understood that HMRC would follow this method of calculation, there is an alternative view which follows the exact wording of *IHTA 1984, s 94(1)*. This view is that the grossing-up should take place before the increase in X's estate is deducted. In the above example, it makes no difference as the gross transfer would still be less than the increase in X's estate. But suppose that X held 90% of the ordinary shares in Company A. His value transferred would then be £8,100 (90% × 90% × £10,000) and this alternative method would proceed as follows. See IHTM04068 and *Simon's Taxes* I6.121.

	£
Value transferred	8,100
Tax (25% of net)	2,025
	10,125
Deduct increase in X's estate	(10,000)
	£125
IHT thereon at 20%	£25

307.3 ALTERATION OF SHARE CAPITAL

In January 2021 the share capital of company H, an investment company, is owned by P and Q as follows

P	600
Q	400
	1,000 ordinary £1 shares

The shares are valued at £10 per share for P's majority holding and £4 per share for Q's minority holding.

The company issues 2,000 shares at par to Q and the shares are then worth £3.50 per share for Q's majority holding and £1.50 per share for P's minority holding. P has previously made chargeable transfers in excess of £325,000 since January 2014 and has utilised his 2020/21 and 2019/20 annual exemptions.

The transfer of value for P is

	£
Value of holding previously	6,000
Less Value of holding now	(900)
Decrease in value	5,100
Tax (25% of net)	1,275
Gross transfer	£6,375
IHT thereon at 20%	£1,275

Notes

(a) P's transfer of value is *not* a potentially exempt transfer. [*IHTA 1984, s 98(3)*]. See IHTM04069 and *Simon's Taxes* I3.119.

(b) An alternative charge may arise under *IHTA 1984, s 3(3)* (omission to exercise a right) but the transfer would then be potentially exempt and only chargeable if P died within seven years.

308 Deeds of Variation and Disclaimers

[*IHTA 1984, ss 17, 142, 218A*]

308.1 A died in December 2020 leaving his estate of £354,000 to his wife, B, absolutely. A and B had sold their house in June 2015 and moved in with one of their sons, C. B, having an index-linked widow's pension, agreed with her sons, C and D, that they could benefit from the estate to the extent of £325,000 in equal shares, i.e. £162,500 each. A deed of variation is duly executed, incorporating a statement that the variation is to have effect for inheritance tax purposes.

A had made no chargeable transfers before his death.

	£
Exempt transfer to B	29,000
Transfer to C	162,500
Transfer to D	162,500
	£325,000
IHT payable	Nil

Notes

(a) If B died 5 years later when her estate was valued at, say, £354,000, IHT payable would be £11,600 (assuming that the nil rate band was then £325,000). If no deed of family arrangement had been made, the personal representatives of B's estate would be entitled to claim A's unused nil rate band (increased to the amount of the band at that time) and the total estate would potentially be covered by the two nil rate bands. The instrument has in this case potentially increased the IHT liability by £11,600 but has ensured that the sons received their £162,500 five years earlier than would have been the case if B had retained A's property until her death. [*IHTA 1984, s 8A*].

(b) The persons making an instrument of variation and (if additional tax results) the personal representatives, must include in the instrument a statement that the variation is to have effect for inheritance tax purposes. If additional tax results, the persons making the statement must deliver a copy of the instrument to HMRC and notify them of the additional tax payable. [*IHTA 1984, ss 142(2), 218A*]. Where the variation is to any extent in favour of a charity or charitable trust, it is a requirement that the charity or charitable trustees must be notified of the existence of the variation. [*IHTA 1984, s 142(3A)(3B)*].

(c) A's estate does not qualify for the additional residence nil-rate band because A and B's home was sold before 8 July 2015. For examples on the residence nil-rate band see **310.5 EXEMPT TRANSFERS**.

309 Double Taxation Relief

[*IHTA 1984, s 159*]

309.1 UNILATERAL RELIEF

(A) **Where property is situated in an overseas territory only**

A, domiciled in the UK, owns a holiday home abroad valued at £396,000 which he gives to his brother in July 2020. He is liable to local gifts tax of, say, £8,830. He has made no previous transfers and does not use the home again at any time before his death in February 2025. It is assumed for the purposes of this example that the nil rate band is then £325,000.

	£	£
Market value of holiday home		396,000
Annual exemption 2020/21	(3,000)	
2019/20	(3,000)	
		(6,000)
Chargeable transfer		£390,000
IHT payable at 60% of full rates by brother (death between 4 and 5 years after gift)		
£65,000 × 40% × 60%		15,600
Unilateral relief for foreign tax		(8,830)
IHT borne		£6,770

Note

(a) If the overseas tax suffered exceeded the UK liability before relief, there would be no IHT payable but the excess would not be repayable.

(B) **Where property is situated in both the UK and an overseas territory**

M, domiciled in the UK, owns company shares which are regarded as situated both in the UK and country X under the rules of the respective countries. On M's death in June 2020 the shares pass to M's son S. The UK IHT amounts to £5,000 before unilateral relief. The equivalent tax liability arising in country X amounts to £2,000.

$$\text{Applying the formula } \frac{A}{A+B} \times C$$

where

A = amount of IHT

B = amount of overseas tax

C = smaller of A and B

309.1 IHT Double Taxation Relief

The unilateral relief available is

$$\frac{5,000}{5,000 + 2,000} \times £2,000 = £1,429$$

IHT payable = £5,000 − £1,429 = £3,571

(C) **Where tax is imposed in two or more overseas territories on property situated in the UK and each of those territories**

Assume the facts in (B) above except that a third country imposes a tax liability on the death as the shares are regarded as also situated in that country.

UK IHT before unilateral relief	£5,000
Tax in country X	£2,000
Tax in country Y	£400

$$\text{Applying the formula} \frac{A}{A + B} \times C$$

where

A = amount of IHT

B = aggregate of overseas tax

C = aggregate of all, except the largest, of A and the overseas tax imposed in each overseas territory

The unilateral relief available is

$$\frac{5,000}{5,000 + 2,000 + 400} \times (2,000 + 400) = £1,622$$

IHT payable £5,000 − £1,622 = £3,378

(D) **Where tax in one overseas territory is relieved against another overseas territory's tax**

Assume the same facts as in (C) above except that country X allows a credit for tax paid in country Y.

Unilateral relief for IHT

$$\frac{5,000}{5,000 + (2,000 - 400) + 400} \times £((2,000 - 400) + 400) = £1,429$$

IHT payable £5,000 − £1,429 = £3,571

Note

(a) See IHTM27185–IHTM27189 and *Simon's Taxes* F4.104.

310 Exempt Transfers

310.1 ANNUAL EXEMPTION

[*IHTA 1984, s 19*]

(A)

S, who has made no other transfers of value, made gifts to his sister of £5,000 on 1 June 2018 and £4,000 on 1 May 2019. S dies on 1 September 2020 with an estate valued at £325,000.

Annual exemptions are available as follows

	£	£
2018/19		
1 June 2018 Gift		5,000
Deduct 2018/19 annual exemption	3,000	
2017/18 annual exemption (part)	2,000	
		(5,000)
		Nil
2019/20		£
1 May 2019 Gift		4,000
Deduct 2019/20 annual exemption		(3,000)
PET becoming chargeable on death		£1,000

The PET, having become a chargeable transfer as a result of death within seven years, is covered by the nil rate band but is aggregated with the death estate in computing the IHT payable on death.

Note

(a) Although the annual exemption, to the extent that it is not fully utilised in the year, can be carried forward to the following year, the current year's exemption is treated as utilised before any exemption brought forward. [*IHTA 1984, s 19(1)(2)*, IHTM14141]. If S had gifted £6,000 in 2018/19 and £3,000 in 2019/20, the total gifts would have been the same but they would have been fully covered by annual exemptions.

310.1 IHT   Exempt Transfers

(B)

T made a gift to his son of £2,000 on 1 June 2020. On 9 November 2020, he settled £20,000 on a discretionary trust for his children and grandchildren. T had made no other gifts since 6 April 2020, but had used his annual exemptions in each year up to and including 2019/20. T died on 13 February 2026.

The gift on 1 June 2020 is a potentially exempt transfer which becomes chargeable since T died within seven years of the gift. The gift on 9 November 2020 is a chargeable transfer.

	£
1 June 2020 Gift to son — PET becoming chargeable	2,000
Deduct annual exemption 2020/21 (part)	(2,000)
	Nil
9 November 2020 Gift to trust	20,000
Deduct annual exemption 2020/21 (balance)	(1,000)
Chargeable transfer	£19,000

Note

(a)   The annual exemption is allocated to earlier rather than later transfers within the same tax year regardless of whether they are PETs or chargeable transfers when made. Although this approach seems to render *IHTA 1984, s 19(3A)* otiose, this is HMRC's interpretation. See IHTM14143 and *Simon's Taxes* I3.322A.

310.2 NORMAL EXPENDITURE OUT OF INCOME

[*IHTA 1984, s 21*]

A wife pays annual life assurance premiums on a policy in favour of her son. The income of her husband and herself for 2020/21 is

	£
Husband's salary	50,000
Wife's salary	7,600
	£56,600

Income levels are not expected to fluctuate wildly from year to year.

The wife's disposable income is

	£
Salary	7,600
Tax thereon (personal allowance £12,500)	Nil
Personal income	£7,600

Depending on her lifestyle, the wife is probably able to show that she has sufficient income to justify a 'normal expenditure' gift of, say, a £1,000 premium paid annually (and therefore habitual). In form P11 (Notes) HMRC state that, 'examples of usual expenditure are where the deceased was paying a regular premium on an insurance policy for the benefit of another person, or perhaps they were making a monthly or other regular payment.'

If the wife was also accustomed to pay personally for an annual holiday costing, say, £3,500, it might be difficult to show that the life assurance premium was paid out of income.

310.3 NIL RATE BAND — TRANSFER OF UNUSED AMOUNT TO SPOUSE OR CIVIL PARTNER

[*IHTA 1984, ss 8A–8C*]

(A)

John dies on 25 August 2008 with an estate of £312,000 and he leaves by his will £50,000 to each of his two grandchildren on discretionary trusts and the balance is left to his widow, Jean. He has made no transfers in the seven years prior to his death. Jean dies in October 2020 when the nil rate band is £325,000.

If Jean's personal representatives make a claim under *IHTA 1984, s 8A*, the nil rate band maximum available at the time of her death is as follows.

	£
Unused nil rate band at time of death	312,000
Less non-exempt transfers on John's death	(100,000)
Nil rate band unused by John	£212,000

The percentage increase to be made to Jean's nil rate band is therefore

$$\frac{£212,000}{£312,000} \times 100 = 67.95\%$$

Jean's nil rate band is increased to

£325,000 + (£325,000 × 67.95%) = £545,838

Notes

(a) Where a person dies on or after 9 October 2007, his nil rate band maximum at the time of death is, on a claim, treated as increased by the amount of the unused nil rate band of a predeceased spouse or civil partner. The nil rate band maximum is increased by the percentage given by the formula:

$$\frac{E}{NRBMD} \times 100$$

where

E = M - VT;

M = the maximum amount that could be transferred by a chargeable transfer on the predeceased person's death if it were to be wholly chargeable at the nil rate;

310.3 IHT   Exempt Transfers

VT = value actually transferred by the chargeable transfer on the death of the predeceased person (or nil if applicable);

NRBMD = the nil rate band maximum applying at the time of the predeceased person's death.

[*IHTA 1984, s 8A(2)–(4)*]. See Simon's Taxes I4.161A.

(b) The increase in the surviving partner's nil rate band maximum is subject to a maximum of 100% of that band. This could apply where, for example, the person had more than one predeceased spouse or civil partner each of whom died with unused nil rate band. [*IHTA 1984, s 8A(5)*]. See (B) below for the maximum increase in the nil rate band maximum of the survivor.

(c) A claim under *IHTA 1984, s 8A*, must be made by the personal representatives of the surviving partner within two years from the end of the month of death or, if later, within three months beginning with the date the personal representatives first act as such, or within such longer period as HMRC allow. If no such claim is made, a claim can be made by any other person liable to tax on the surviving partner's death within such period as HMRC allow. [*IHTA 1984, s 8B*]. See IHTM43007 and *Simon's Taxes* I4.161A.

(d) Similar provisions apply to allow unused residence nil-rate band (RNRB) to be transferred to a surviving spouse or civil partner who dies on or after 6 April 2017. Where the first death occurred before 6 April 2017, the survivor's RNRB is increased by 100% of whatever the value of the RNRB is at the time of the second death, provided that the value of the estate of the first to die did not exceed £2 million. See **310.5(C)** below.

(B)

Betty has been married and widowed twice before. Her first husband, David, died in October 1974 when estate duty applied. He left all his assets in his will to Betty having made no previous transfers. His estate was wholly within the £15,000 spouse's exemption applying at that time so that none of his tax free band was utilised in 1974. Betty's second husband Jack died on 18 June 2005 and left his assets to Betty excepting a £165,000 gift he made to his daughter in 2003. Betty died in December 2020. Jack and Betty had sold their house on 6 June 2015 and moved in with one of their sons.

If the personal representatives make a claim under *IHTA 1984, s 8A*, Betty's nil rate band maximum is increased as follows.

Increase in respect of David's nil rate band.

David used none of his nil rate band, and the percentage increase to Betty's maximum is therefore 100%.

Increase in respect of Jack's nil rate band.

	£
Unused nil rate band at time of death	275,000
Less non-exempt transfers on John's death	(165,000)
Nil rate band unused by Jack	£110,000

The percentage increase to Betty's maximum is therefore

$$\frac{£110,000}{£275,000} \times 100 = 40\%$$

The total increase to Betty's nil rate band maximum would therefore be (100% + 40%)= 140%. This is, however, restricted to 100%, making Betty's nil rate band maximum on death £650,000 (£325,000 + £325,000).

Notes

(a) The increase in the surviving partner's nil rate band maximum is subject to a maximum of 100% of that band. This could apply where, as in this example, the person had more than one predeceased spouse or civil partner each of whom died with unused nil rate band. [*IHTA 1984, s 8A(5)*]. See IHTM43030.

(b) It is immaterial when the predeceased spouse or civil partner died. Unused nil rate bands can be transferred even if the death was before 25 July 1986 (i.e. when capital transfer tax or estate duty applied) and the provisions of *IHTA 1984, ss 8A–8C* apply as modified by *FA 2008, Sch 4 para 10* to enable this.

(c) Betty's estate does not qualify for the additional residence nil-rate band because Jack and Betty's home was sold before 8 July 2015.

(C) **Charges subsequent to death of predeceased spouse or civil partner**

[*IHTA 1984, s 8C*]

C died in August 2002 having made a conditionally exempt gift of heritage property to his brother, B. C left a property worth £125,000 to B and left the balance of his estate to his wife, D. In October 2008, the heritage property conditional exemption is breached when the property is valued at £104,000. D dies in February 2021.

If the personal representatives make a claim under *IHTA 1984, s 8A*, D's nil rate band maximum is increased as follows.

	£
Unused nil rate band at time of C's death	250,000
Less non-exempt transfers on C's death	(125,000)
Nil rate band unused by C	£125,000

The percentage increase to be made to D's nil rate band is therefore

$$\left(\frac{£125,000}{£250,000} - \frac{£104,000}{£312,000}\right) \times 100 = 16.67\%$$

D's nil rate band is increased to

£325,000 + (£325,000 × 16.67%) = £379,178

Notes

(a) Where, after the death of the first spouse or partner and before the death of the survivor, tax is charged on an amount under *IHTA 1984, ss 32 or 32A* (see **316** NATIONAL HERITAGE) or *IHTA 1984, s 126* (see **327** WOODLANDS) by reference to the rate that would have been applicable if the amount had been included in the estate of the first spouse or partner, *IHTA 1984, s 8A* applies using the following formula to replace that at (A) above:

310.3 IHT   Exempt Transfers

$$\left(\frac{E}{NRBMD} - \frac{TA}{NRBME}\right) \times 100$$

where

$E = M - VT$;

M = the maximum amount that could be transferred by a chargeable transfer on the predeceased person's death if it were to be wholly chargeable at the nil rate;

VT = value actually transferred by the chargeable transfer on the death of the predeceased person (or nil if applicable);

NRBMD = the nil rate band maximum applying at the time of the predeceased person's death;

TA = the amount on which tax is subsequently charged;

NRBME = the nil rate band maximum at the time of the event giving rise to that charge.

[*IHTA 1984, s 8C(1)(2)*]. See IHTM43045 and *Simon's Taxes* I4.161A

(b)   If the tax is charged after the death of the survivor, it is charged as if the personal nil rate band maximum of the predeceased spouse or partner were reduced by the amount by which the survivor's nil rate band was increased under *IHTA 1984, s 8A*. [*IHTA 1984, s 8C(4)(5)*]. See IHTM43046.

310.2 ELECTION TO BE TREATED AS DOMICILED IN THE UK

[*IHTA 1984, ss 267ZA, 267ZB*]

George is UK domiciled and his only asset is a house in the UK worth £3 million. His wife Monique is not domiciled in the UK for inheritance tax purposes and has only foreign assets worth £2 million. George dies on 1 August 2020 leaving his estate to Monique. The couple have no children.

If no election under *IHTA 1984, s 267ZA* is made, the IHT on the death of George is:

	£
Estate	3,000,000
Less spouse exemption	(325,000)
Nil rate band	(325,000)
	£2,350,000
Inheritance tax £2,350,000 @ 40%	£940,000

On the death of Monique on 1 September 2025 when her domicile status for IHT remains unchanged, IHT will once again be due on the UK house. Assuming that its value has not changed, and that the IHT on George's death was paid from her overseas assets, the IHT on Monique's estate will be:

Exempt Transfers IHT 310.2

Estate	3,000,000
Less nil rate band	(325,000)
	£2,675,000
Inheritance tax £2,675,000 @ 40%	£1,070,000
Total inheritance tax on George and Monique's deaths	
£940,000 + £1,070,000 =	£2,010,000

If Monique had elected, under *IHTA 1984, s 267ZA* and before 1 August 2022, to be treated as domiciled in the UK with effect from 1 August 2020, no IHT would be payable on George's death. On Monique's death, IHT would then be due on both her UK and foreign assets. If they remain unchanged from George's death and have the same values, and the nil rate band remains unchanged, the IHT liability would be:

	£
Estate	5,000,000
Less nil rate band	(650,000)
	£4,350,000
Inheritance tax £4,350,000 @ 40%	£1,740,000
Total inheritance tax on George and Monique's deaths	£1,740,000

Notes

(a) An individual who is not domiciled in the UK (disregarding the IHT deemed domicile provisions of *IHTA 1984, s 267*), but whose spouse or civil partner is so domiciled, may elect to be treated as UK domiciled. The election may be either:

- a 'lifetime election' made at any time when the person making the election is non-UK domiciled, or
- a 'death election' made within two years of the death on or after 6 April 2013 of the person's UK domiciled spouse or civil partner.

A death election may be made by the personal representatives of the non-UK domiciled spouse, in the event of that person's death.

An election has effect on the date specified in it, which must be on or after 6 April 2013. Subject to this, a lifetime election may specify a date which is within the period of seven years ending with the date on which it is made, and a death election may specify a date which is within the seven years ending with the date of the death of the UK domiciled spouse or civil partner. In both cases the parties must have been married or civil partners throughout the period covered by the election.

[*IHTA 1984, ss 267ZA, 267ZB*].

(b) Both elections are irrevocable, and apply only for IHT purposes. They have no application to the remittance basis rules for other tax purposes (see IT 23 and CGT 225 REMITTANCE BASIS)

(c) For transfers of value made on or after 6 April 2013, the exemption for transfers to a non-UK domiciled spouse or civil partner is equal to the nil rate band (currently £325,000). [*IHTA 1984, s 18*]. See IHTM11033 and *Simon's Taxes* I3.332.

310.5 IHT   Exempt Transfers

310.5 RESIDENCE NIL RATE BAND

[*IHTA 1984, ss 8D–8M; F(No 2)A 2015, s 9; FA 2016, Sch 15; FA 2019, s 66*]

(A) Inheritance of house by direct descendant

John dies on 5 August 2020 and leaves his estate worth £550,000 to his children. This includes a house worth £200,000 to his son Rob, and other assets worth £400,000 shared equally between son Rob and daughter Ria. John has made no chargeable transfers in the seven years prior to his death.

		£
Estate		550,000
Less Residence nil rate band		(175,000)
(Lower of £200,000 and £175,000)		
Nil rate band		(325,000)
Taxable estate		£50,000
Inheritance tax £50,000 @ 40%		£20,000

Notes

(a) With effect for deaths on or after 6 April 2017 a residence nil rate band is available for transfers on death where the deceased's interest in a qualifying residential interest, which has been their residence at some point and is included in their estate, is inherited by one or more direct descendants on death, whether by Will or on intestacy.

(b) A direct descendant is a child of the deceased, including a step-child, adopted child, foster child, and an infant subject to guardianship arrangement or a special guardianship order. Also included are the lineal descendants of any of these and a person who was the spouse or civil partner of a lineal descendant at the time of the death of the testator or where the descendant predeceased the testator, at the time of the descendant's death so long as such spouse or civil partner has not since remarried or become the civil partner of another.

(c) The maximum available residential nil rate band for 2020/21 is £175,000 (£150,000 for 2019/20).

(B) Downsizing or disposal of house before death and inheritance by children

[*IHTA 1984, s 8FA; FA 2016, Sch 15 paras 1, 5; FA 2019, s 66*]

Monica lived in a house in London. On 10 April 2019 she sold her house for £120,000 and moved into a flat which she bought for £95,000. Monica dies on 15 July 2020. Her estate includes the flat which is now worth £105,000 and other assets worth £395,000 is shared equally between her children.

		£
Estate		500,000
Less Residence nil rate band	(105,000)	
(Lower of £105,000 and £175,000)		
Downsizing addition		

Step 1: Former allowance as on 10 April 2019
$$\frac{120,000}{150,000} \times 100 = 80\%$$

Step 2: Percentage as on Monica's death on 15 July 2020
$$\frac{105,000}{175,000} \times 100 = 60\%$$

Step 3: Percentage of RNRB lost is 20% (80% - 60%)

Step 4: Lost RNRB amount   (35,000)
175,000 × 20%

	(140,000)
Nil rate band	(325,000)
Taxable estate	£35,000
Inheritance tax £35,000 @ 40%	£14,000

Notes

(a) A claim for the residence nil rate band may be made where a person has sold a home in lifetime which they lived in at some stage. The legislation envisages two different circumstances, first that where the deceased downsized from a more valuable residence and there is a less valuable residence left in the estate on death (as illustrated in this example), and second where a residence was previously sold and no other residence purchased. The personal representatives can nominate which former residence is to be used for this relief. The downsizing must have taken place on or after 8 July 2015; there is no relief for any downsizing before that date.

(b) Monica qualifies for the downsizing addition because she sold her house on 10 April 2019 i.e. on or after 8 July 2015, downsizing to a flat which remained in her estate until death but did not fully utilise the residential nil-rate band of £175,000 (see note (c) to (A) above). Both the flat and at least part of the remaining estate are inherited by Monica's children.

(c) The steps used to calculate the downsizing addition are those in *IHTA 1984, s 8FE(9)*.

(C) Transfer of unused band to spouse

[*IHTA 1984, ss 8G, 8L; F(No 2)A 2015, s 9; FA 2016, Sch 15 paras 1, 6*]

Mrs G died on 31 January 2017 leaving an estate worth £1,000,000 which includes a home worth £800,000. She left her estate to her husband Mr G. Mr G dies on 10 June 2020 leaving an estate of £1,500,000 after liabilities, including the interest in the home now worth £900,000 transferred to his daughter. He leaves legacies to friends, nephews and nieces of £400,000 and the residue to their two children in equal shares.

310.5 IHT   Exempt Transfers

Estate		£1,500,000
Less Residence nil rate band (Lower of £900,000 and £175,000)	(175,000)	
Spouse's residence nil rate band transferred to Mr G	(175,000)	
Nil rate band	(325,000)	
Unused nil rate band brought forward	(325,000)	
Net amount available for claim		(1,000,000)
Taxable estate		£500,000
Inheritance tax £500,000 @ 40%		£200,000

Notes

(a) Unused residence nil rate band can be transferred between spouses and civil partners. This transfer is referred to in the legislation as 'brought-forward allowance'.

(b) The brought-forward allowance can be claimed where a person, who dies after 6 April 2017, has been pre-deceased at any time by one or more spouses or civil partners. It is based on the unused proportion of the RNRB at the time of the first death, calculated as follows:

    (1) identify the actual amount of unused RNRB at the time of the first death;

    (2) express this amount as a percentage of the residential enhancement available at the date of the first death;

    (3) if the deceased has survived more than one partner, calculate the unused percentage for each one;

    (4) add the percentages together but if the result is more than 100%, take 100%; and

    (5) apply the total percentage calculated to the residential enhancement at the date of the later death to give the brought forward allowance.

Where the first death occurred before 6 April 2017 and the second death occurs during 2020/21, the actual amount of unused RNRB ((1) above) is deemed to be £175,000. The residential enhancement at the date of the earlier death ((2) above) is also assumed to be £175,000. The effect of this is that the survivor's RNRB is increased by 100% of whatever the value of the RNRB is at the time of the second death (£175,000 in this example).

(c) A claim under *IHTA 1984, s 8L* for a brought-forward allowance must be made within the two years from the end of the month in which the person dies, or if later the period of three months beginning with the date on which the personal representatives first act as such. See IHTM46042.

(D) Tapering for large estate

Robert dies on 10 October 2020 leaving an estate worth £2,100,000 to his two children, which includes main residence of £1,500,000 and other assets of £600,000. He had made no lifetime transfers.

		£
Estate		2,100,000
Less Residential nil rate band		
Lower of £1,500,000 and £175,000	175,000	
RNRB restricted by $\dfrac{2,100,000 - 2,000,000}{2}$	50,000	(125,000)
Less Nil rate band		(325,000)
Taxable estate		£1,650,000
Inheritance tax £1,650,000 @ 40%		£660,000

Note

(a) The residential nil rate band is tapered away by £1 for every £2 that the value of the estate exceeds £2,000,000. [*IHTA 1984, s 8D; F(No 2)A 2015, s 9(1)(4); FA 2016, Sch 15 paras 1, 2*]. See IHTM46023.

311 Gifts with Reservation

[*FA 1986, ss 102–102C, Sch 20; SI 1987 No 1130*]

311.1 GIFTS WITH RESERVATION

(A) **Reservation released within seven years before death**

On 19 June 2002 D gave his house to his grandson G, but continued to live in it alone paying no rent. The house was valued at £130,000. On 5 May 2015 D remarried, and went to live with his new wife F (in a home owned entirely by F). G immediately moved into the house, which was then valued at £333,000.

On 3 January 2020 D died, leaving his estate of £200,000 equally to his granddaughter H and his wife F.

Gift 19 June 2002

As the gift was made more than seven years before death, it is a PET which has become exempt.

5 May 2015 release of reservation

The release of D's reservation is a PET which becomes chargeable by reason of D's death between 4 and 5 years later. IHT is charged, at 60% of full rates on the basis of the Table of rates in force at the time of death, on the value of the house at the date of release of reservation.

		£	£
Gift			333,000
Deduct annual exemptions	2015/16	—	
	2014/15	—	
Chargeable transfer			£333,000
Tax thereon)			
0–325,000 at nil%		—	
325,001–333,000 at 40%		3,200	
		£3,200	
IHT payable at 60% of full rates, 60% × £3,200			£1,920

Death 3 January 2020

IHT is charged at full rates on the chargeable estate of £100,000 (£100,000 passing to the wife is exempt) in the bracket £333,000 to £433,000.

Tax thereon

333,001–433,000 at 40%	£40,000

IHT   Gifts with Reservation

Notes

(a) HMRC consider that the annual exemption is not available against the deemed PET arising on the release of a reservation. See IHTM14343.

(b) The additional residence nil-rate band is not available against a PET becoming chargeable on death. The band is also not available against the death estate. For the purpose of determining entitlement to the band, the house is deemed to have been disposed of when the reservation was released on 5 May 2015. [*IHTA 1984, s 8H(4D)(b); F(No 2)A 2015, s 9; FA 2016, Sch 15 para 7*]. The house was therefore disposed of before 8 July 2015. For examples on the residence nil-rate band see **310.5 EXEMPT TRANSFERS**.

(B) **Reservation not released before death**

On 19 June 2015 X gave a painting to his grandson Y, but continued to hang it on the wall of his living room until he died on 3 January 2021. The painting was valued at £239,000.

On 3 January 2021 X died, leaving his estate of £200,000 (which did not include any residential property) equally to his granddaughter Z and his wife W. The painting was valued at £251,000 at the date of X's death.

Gift 19 June 2015

This is a potentially exempt transfer which becomes chargeable by reason of X's death within seven years.

Death 3 January 2021

As the reservation had not been released at the date of X's death, X is treated as beneficially entitled to the painting, which thus forms part of his chargeable estate on death.

A double charge would arise by virtue of the painting being the subject of a PET and a part of the chargeable estate on death. *The Inheritance Tax (Double Charges Relief) Regulations 1987* [*SI 1987 No 1130*] provide relief as follows.

First calculation under Reg 5(3)(a)

Charge the painting in the death estate and ignore the PET.

	£
Chargeable estate	
Free estate passing to Z	100,000
Painting	251,000
	£351,000

Gifts with Reservation IHT 311.1

There are no chargeable transfers within the previous seven years.

	£
IHT payable	
0–325,000 at nil %	—
325,001–351,000 at 40%	10,400
	£10,400

Second calculation under Reg 5(3)(b)

Charge the PET and ignore the value of the painting in the death estate.

		£	£
Gift 19 June 2015			239,000
Deduct annual exemptions	2015/16	3,000	
	2014/15	3,000	
			(6,000)
Chargeable transfer			£233,000
Tax thereon			
0–233,000		Nil	
		£	
Chargeable estate on death (excluding house)		100,000	
IHT payable in the bracket £325,001 to £333,000			
325,001–333,000 at 40%		£3,200	
Total IHT payable		£3,200	

The first calculation yields the higher amount of tax (£10,400), so tax is charged by reference to the value of the gift with reservation in the estate, ignoring the PET.

Note

(a) The comparison between the two calculations is made *before* credit is given for tax already paid (should there be any). See IHTM14711, IHTM14712.

312 Interest on Tax

[IHTA 1984, s 233; FA 1989, s 178; SI 1989 No 1297]

312.1 B died on 10 February 2020. The executors made a payment on account of IHT of £70,000 on 30 June 2020 on delivery of the account. The final notice of determination was raised by HMRC Inheritance Tax on 19 June 2021 in the sum of £102,500. The rate of interest is assumed to be 5%.

Date of chargeable event (death)	10 February 2020
Date on which interest starts to accrue	1 September 2020
	£
IHT payable	102,500
Payment made on account 30 June 2020	(70,000)
Balance due	£32,500
Assessment raised by HMRC 19 June 2021	
Interest payable (1.9.20 to 19.6.21)	
£32,500 at 5% for 292 days	£1,300

Note

(a) Further interest may be charged if payment of the balance is not made promptly. See IHTM30341 and *Simon's Taxes* I11.405.

312.2 F gave his holiday home in Cornwall to his granddaughter G on 7 August 2016. On 23 May 2020 F died. He had made no use of the property at any time after 7 August 2016. G made a payment of £15,000, on account of the IHT due, on 1 January 2021. The liability was agreed at £27,000, and the balance paid, on 17 February 2021. The rate of interest is assumed to be 5%.

Date of PET	7 August 2016
Date on which PET becomes chargeable	23 May 2020
Date on which IHT is due	1 December 2020
	£
IHT payable	27,000
Payment made on account 1 January 2021	(15,000)
Balance due	£12,000

IHT   Interest on Tax

Interest payable

On £27,000 from 1.12.20–1.1.21	
£27,000 at 5% for 31 days	115
On £12,000 from 1.1.21–17.2.21	
£12,000 at 5% for 47 days	77
Total interest payable	£192

Note

(a)   See IHTM30373, IHTM36253.

313 Liability for Tax

[*IHTA 1984, ss 199(1), 204(2)(3)(5)(6)*]

313.1 LIFETIME TRANSFERS

(A) **Transferor**

A settled £78,000 on discretionary trusts in December 2020, having previously made chargeable transfers on 31 March 2020 totalling £328,000.

A's liability is as follows	£
Gift	78,000
Deduct 2020/21 annual exemption	(3,000)
	£75,000
Grossed at 25%	£93,750
IHT thereon at 20%	£18,750

Note

(a) See IHTM30041–IHTM30044 and *Simon's Taxes* I10.111.

(B) **Transferee**

In example (A) above A pays only £10,000 of IHT and defaults on the balance of £8,750, so that the trustees become liable as transferee.

The trustees' liability is not however £8,750 but is as follows

	£
Original gross	93,750
Deduct IHT unpaid	(8,750)
Revised gross	£85,000
IHT thereon at 20%	17,000
Deduct Paid by A	(10,000)
Now due from trustees	£7,000

Note

(a) See IHTM30051–30054 and *Simon's Taxes* I10.111.

313.1 IHT   Liability for Tax

(C)   **Person in whom property is vested**

In January 2021 C transferred to trustees of a discretionary trust shares in an unquoted property company worth, as a minority holding, £50,000. However, the transfer deprives C of control of the company with the result that the value of his estate is reduced by £210,000. He has already used his nil rate band and annual exemptions.

C's liability is as follows

Net loss to him	£210,000
Grossed at 20%	£262,500
IHT thereon at 20%	£52,500

C fails to pay so that the trustees become liable, as follows

	£
Original gross	262,500
Deduct unpaid IHT	(52,500)
	£210,000
IHT thereon at 20%	£42,000

Note

(a)   The trustees' liability cannot exceed the value of the assets which they hold, namely the proceeds of sale of the shares, less any CGT and costs incurred since acquisition, plus any undistributed income in their hands.

313.2 TRANSFERS ON DEATH

[*IHTA 1984, ss 200(1)(3), 204(1)–(3)(5), 211*]

Personal representatives of E, who died on 30 September 2020, received the following assets:

	£
Free personal property	155,265
Land bequeathed to F (which, under the terms of the will, bears its own IHT)	29,735
Private residence, bequeathed to spouse	51,000

A trust in which E had a pre-April 2006 life interest was valued at £154,000. Under the Will of E, legacies of £15,000, each free of IHT, were given to F and G and the residue was left to H. E had made no chargeable transfers during his lifetime.

	Persons liable	£	IHT £
IHT is borne as to			
chargeable transfer			
Free personal property	PRs	155,265	2,565
Land bequeathed to F	F	29,735	491
Private residence to spouse	—	Exempt	Nil
Trust fund	Trustees	154,000	2,544
		£339,000	£5,600

The residue left to H is as follows		
Free personal property		155,265
Deduct IHT	2,565	
Legacies to F and G	30,000	(32,565)
		£122,700

Note

(a) If the Will had not directed that the IHT on the land bequeathed to F be borne by F, the IHT would be payable out of residue. [*IHTA 1984, s 211*]. See *Simon's Taxes* I10.203A.

313.3 LIFETIME TRANSFER WITH ADDITIONAL LIABILITY ON DEATH

[*IHTA 1984, ss 131, 199(2), 201(2)*]

(A)

On 31 December 2020, H, who had made no earlier chargeable transfers other than to utilise his annual exemptions for 2020/21 and earlier years, transferred £368,000 into a discretionary trust and, a month later, settled an asset worth £20,000 into the same trust. H paid the appropriate IHT. On 30 June 2023, H died. It is assumed that the nil rate band on 30 June 2023 is £350,000.

The trustees become liable to further IHT as follows

	£	£
Original net gift	£368,000	£20,000
Grossed up at half of full rates	£378,750	£25,000
IHT (paid by H)	£10,750	£5,000

313.3 IHT   Liability for Tax

IHT at 80% of death rates applicable in June 2023 on original gross (death between 3 and 4 years after gifts)	5,760	8,000
Deduct paid originally by H	(10,750)	(5,000)
Now due from trustees	—	£3,000

Note

(a) The additional IHT on death is calculated using the rates in force at the date of death. Where the IHT at the new death rates, as tapered, is less than the IHT paid on the original chargeable transfer, there is no repayment.

(B)

The second gift in (A) above had fallen in value to £18,000 by the time of H's death.

The trustees may claim to reduce the IHT payable as follows

	£
Original gross gift	25,000
Deduct drop in value (£20,000 − £18,000)	(2,000)
Revised gross	£23,000
IHT thereon at 80% of death rate applicable in June 2023	7,360
Deduct paid by H	(5,000)
	£2,360

Note

(a) If the asset had fallen in value to £10,625 or less, so that the revised gross became £15,625 or less and the IHT at 80% of death rates £5,000 or less, the trustees would have no liability because H had already paid IHT of £5,000.

313.4 POTENTIALLY EXEMPT TRANSFER BECOMING CHARGEABLE ON DEATH

[*IHTA 1984, ss 199, 201, 204*]

On 19 May 2017 M gave N £336,000. M died on 3 August 2020 having made no other gifts.

		£
Gift		336,000
Deduct annual exemptions	2017/18	(3,000)
	2016/17	(3,000)
		£330,000

Liability for Tax IHT 313.4

The IHT at 80% of full rates on the gift to N is payable by N on 1 March 2021.

	£
0–325,000 at nil%	—
325,001–330,000 at 40%	2,000
	£2,000

IHT payable by N 80% × £2,000 = £1,600

Notes

(a) If N has not paid the IHT due of £1,600 by 1 March 2022 the personal representatives of M are liable, although their liability cannot exceed the death estate of M. The amount is a deductible liability from the estate only to the extent that reimbursement from N cannot be obtained.

(b) See also **305.1** CALCULATION OF TAX for liability to tax on potentially exempt transfers.

314 Mutual Transfers

[*FA 1986, s 104; SI 1987 No 1130*]

314.1 POTENTIALLY EXEMPT TRANSFERS AND DEATH

A, who has made no previous transfers of value other than to use his annual exemptions for 2016/17 and 2017/18, makes a gift of £330,000 to B on 1 July 2017. On 15 July 2018 and 20 January 2019, he makes gifts of £238,000 and £96,000 respectively into a discretionary trust and the trustees pay the IHT due of £1,200 on the later transfer. On 2 January 2020, B dies and the 2016 gift is returned to A by virtue of B's Will. On 4 April 2021, A dies. His taxable estate on death is valued at £410,000 which includes the 2017 gift returned to him in 2020 which is still valued at £330,000. It is assumed that A's estate does not qualify for the additional residence nil-rate band.

First calculation under Reg 4(4)(a)

The gift in 2017 is a PET and would normally become a chargeable transfer by virtue of A's death within seven years of making the gift. However, for the purpose of this calculation, it is ignored and the returned gift is charged as part of A's death estate.

Additional tax due on chargeable lifetime transfers

	£
Gift on 15 July 2018	238,000
Deduct annual exemption 2018/19	(3,000)
	235,000
Gift on 20 January 2019	96,000
	£331,000
IHT at death rates on £331,000	2,400
IHT previously paid	(1,200)
Additional IHT payable by trustees	£1,200
Tax on death estate of £410,000 charged at 40%	
IHT payable note (a)	£164,000
Total IHT payable as consequence of death (£1,200 + £164,000)	£165,200

314.1 IHT Mutual Transfers

Second calculation under Reg 4(4)(b)

The 2017 gift is charged as a PET but the returned gift is ignored in the death estate.

The tax due on PET of £330,000 at death rates

	£
0–325,000 at nil%	Nil
325,001–330,000 at 40%	2,000
	£2,000
IHT payable at 80% of full rates (death between 3 and 4 years after gift)	£1,600

Tax due on chargeable lifetime transfers of £331,000 (after annual exemption) charged at 40%

	£
IHT payable	132,400
IHT paid	(1,200)
Additional IHT payable	£131,200
Tax on death estate of £80,000 charged at 40%	
IHT payable	£32,000
Total IHT payable as consequence of death (£1,600 + £131,200 + £32,000)	£164,800

The first calculation gives the higher amount of tax, so the PET is ignored and the returned gift included in the death estate, the tax liabilities being as in the first calculation above.

Note

(a) Quick succession relief under *IHTA 1984, s 141* (see **318.1** QUICK SUCCESSION RELIEF below) might be due in respect of the returned PET by reference to any tax charged on that PET in connection with B's death. If, as a result of such relief, the first calculation produces a lower tax charge than the second, then the second calculation will prevail, i.e. the PET will be charged and the returned gift ignored in the death estate. See IHTM22091–IHTM22093 and *Simon's Taxes* I4.266.

314.2 CHARGEABLE TRANSFERS AND DEATH

C, who had made no other transfer of value, gifted £320,000 on 31 May 2013 into discretionary trust, on which IHT of £400 was paid. On 5 October 2013, he gave D a life interest in shares worth £85,000; IHT of £17,000 was paid. On 3 January 2019, C makes a PET of £36,000 to E. On 31 December 2019, D dies and the settled shares return to C, the settlor (no tax charge arises on D's death). On 10 August 2020, C dies; his death estate is valued at £320,000 which includes the shares returned from D, now worth £60,000. It is assumed that C's estate does not qualify for the additional residence nil-rate band.

Mutual Transfers   IHT 314.2

First calculation under Reg 7(4)(a)

The gift in October 2013 is ignored and the returned shares included as part of the taxable estate on death.

No additional tax arises on the May 2013 lifetime transfer of £314,000 (after annual exemptions) as it was made more than seven years before death.

Tax due on PET of £30,000 (after annual exemptions) made in January 2019 charged in band £325,001–344,000.

£19,000 at 40% = £7,600.

Tax on death estate of £320,000 charged in band £30,001 to £350,000 (the gift to the discretionary trust having fallen out of cumulation)

30,001–325,000 at nil%	
325,001–350,000 at 40%	£10,000
Total IHT payable as consequence of death	
(£7,600 + £10,000) (but see note (a) below)	£17,600

Second calculation under Reg 7(4)(b)

The October 2013 gift is charged and the returned shares are excluded from the taxable estate on death.

Additional tax due on October 2013 transfer as a result of death — charged in band £325,001 to £399,000.

325,001–399,000 at 40%	£29,600
IHT payable at 20% of full rates	
(death between 6 and 7 years after gift)	5,920
IHT paid £17,000, but credit restricted to	(5,920)
Additional IHT	Nil

Tax due on PET of £30,000 (after annual exemptions) charged in band £399,001 to £429,000.

£30,000 at 40%	£12,000

Tax on death estate of £260,000 charged in band £115,001 to £375,000.

115,001–325,000 at nil %	
325,001–375,000 at 40%	£20,000
Total IHT payable as consequence of death	
(£12,000 + £20,000)	£32,000

314.2 IHT   Mutual Transfers

The second calculation gives the higher amount of tax so the returned gift is excluded from the death estate, the tax liabilities being as in the second calculation above.

Note

(a) If the first calculation had given the higher amount, a credit for IHT would have been due, restricted to the lower of

  (i) the IHT paid on the lifetime transfer (i.e. £17,000); and

  (ii) the IHT attributable to the returned shares on death, calculated as follows:

$$\text{Estate rate } \frac{10,000}{320,000} = 3.125\%$$

£60,000 × 3.125% = £1,875

The IHT actually payable as a consequence of death would have been £15,725 (£17,600 − £1,875).

315 National Heritage

[*IHTA 1984, ss 30–35, 57A, 77–79, 207, Sch 2 paras 5, 6, Sch 4, Sch 5*]

315.1 CONDITIONS FOR EXEMPTION

Lord A died in 1952 leaving Netherington Hall in Wiltshire to his son B together with all its contents. These contents included a painting by Whistler of Netherington Hall and also a rare painting of Mary Queen of Scots alongside Lord Bothwell her second husband. The pictures and other items in the Hall were all exempted from estate duty which, at the time Lord A died, was applied at a marginal rate of 80%.

Unfortunately the son Lord B dies in a hunting accident on Boxing Day 2019 and the Hall together with contents are left to his son, now Lord C. HMRC consider the painting by Whistler of the Hall to be pre-eminent for its artistic interest. The painting is accepted as pre-eminent and is re-exempted on the death of Lord B, subject to a contingent liability to IHT on any breach of undertaking or subsequent disposal by sale when the rate of IHT would be 40%.

HMRC do not consider the painting of Mary Queen of Scots, now valued at £5 million, to be pre-eminent.

As the Mary Queen of Scots painting fails the pre-eminence test IHT of £2 million (£5 million × 40%) is due and paid by the estate. Lord C sells the painting for £8 million (net of expenses and CGT) six months later in June 2020 thereby breaking the estate duty undertaking.

In view of HMRC's decision, there will be a tax charge calculated as follows:

	£
Estate duty at 80% on £8 million	6,400,000
Less credit for IHT paid on Lord B's death	(2,000,000)
Estate duty payable on sale	4,400,000

Note

(a) For claims made on or after 31 July 1998, any picture, print, book, work of art or scientific object, or any other thing not yielding income, or a collection or group of such objects, only qualifies (apart from by virtue of a historical connection with a building of outstanding historic or architectural interest) for conditional exemption, if it appears to HMRC to be *pre-eminent* for its national, scientific, historic or artistic interest [*IHTA 1984, s 31(1)(5)*]. Previously such objects simply had to appear to the Treasury to be of national, scientific, historic or artistic interest. See IHTM11260 and *Simon's Taxes* I7.504.

315.2 IHT   National Heritage

315.2 CONDITIONALLY EXEMPT TRANSFERS AFTER 6 APRIL 1976

(A) **Chargeable event during lifetime of relevant person**

C, who has made previous chargeable transfers during 2013 of £230,000, makes a conditionally exempt gift of property in February 2015. In October 2020, the property is sold for £500,000 and capital gains tax of £80,000 is payable.

		£
Cumulative total of previous chargeable transfers of relevant person		230,000
Net sale proceeds of conditionally exempt property	500,000	
Deduct Capital gains tax payable	(80,000)	
Chargeable transfer		420,000
Revised cumulative total for relevant person		£650,000
Inheritance tax payable (by reference to lifetime rates in October 2020)		
£325,000 at 20% =	£65,000	

(B) **Chargeable event after relevant person is dead**

D died in April 2001 leaving a taxable estate of £350,000 together with conditionally exempt property valued at £600,000 at the breach in October 2020.

	£
Value of relevant person's estate at death	350,000
Value of conditionally exempt property at date of breach	600,000
	£950,000

Inheritance tax payable (by reference to full rates applicable in October 2020).

$$£600,000 \text{ at } 40\% = £240,000$$

Notes

(a) As the chargeable event occurs after tax is reduced by the substitution of a new Table of rates, the new rates are used.

(b) Where a chargeable event arises in respect of property which was allowed conditional exemption on an earlier death, the lower 36% rate of inheritance tax cannot be claimed on that event even if the remaining estate had satisfied the conditions for that rate. [*IHTA 1984, s 33(2ZA)*]. See **321.2** TRANSFERS ON DEATH.

(C) Multiple conditionally exempt transfers

D died in December 1990 leaving a conditionally exempt property to his son E. D's taxable estate at death was £230,000. In 2014 E gave the property to his daughter F. F gave the necessary undertakings so this transfer was also conditionally exempt. In December 2020 F sold the property for its market value of £500,000 and paid capital gains tax of £50,000. During 2014 E had made chargeable transfers of £20,000 and he has made no other transfers.

	£	£
Value of relevant person's estate at death		230,000
Net sale proceeds of conditionally exempt property	500,000	
Deduct capital gains tax	(50,000)	
Chargeable transfer		450,000
		£680,000
Inheritance tax payable by F		
£355,000 at 40% =		£142,000
Previous cumulative total of E		20,000
Add chargeable transfer		450,000
E's revised cumulative total		£470,000

Notes

(a) There have been two conditionally exempt transfers within the period of 30 years ending with the chargeable event in December 2020. HMRC may select either D or E as the 'relevant person' for the purpose of calculating the tax due. The IHT liability will be higher if D is selected. [*IHTA 1984, ss 33(5), 78(3)*].

(b) As F receives the proceeds of sale, she is the person liable to pay the IHT. [*IHTA 1984, s 207(1)*]. See IHTM30121 and *Simon's Taxes* I10.122.

(c) Although the IHT is calculated by reference to D's cumulative total, it is E whose cumulative total is adjusted as he made the last conditionally exempt transfer of the property. [*IHTA 1984, s 34(1)*].

(d) As the chargeable event occurs after a reduction in the rates of tax, the new rates are used to calculate the tax payable. [*IHTA 1984, Sch 2 para 5*].

315.3 CONDITIONALLY EXEMPT TRANSFERS ON DEATH BEFORE 7 APRIL 1976

(A) Chargeable event more than 3 years after death

B died on 31 December 1975 leaving a taxable estate of £100,000 together with a conditionally exempt painting valued at £50,000. In June 2020 the painting was sold for £110,000.

315.3 IHT   National Heritage

		£
Value of deceased's taxable estate		100,000
Value of exempt property at date of chargeable event	note (a)	110,000
		£210,000
Recalculated IHT liability	note (b)	£90,750

IHT payable on conditionally exempt property

$$£90{,}750 \times \frac{110{,}000}{210{,}000} \qquad \qquad £47{,}536$$

No further liability accrues to the estate of the deceased.

Notes

(a) The value of the exempt property will be reduced by any capital gains tax chargeable in respect of the sale. [*TCGA 1992, s 258(8)*]. See CG73325 and Simon's Taxes C3.1905.

(b) The IHT liability is calculated using rates in force at the date of death.

(B) **Estate Duty**

Lord A dies in 1952 (see example at **315.1** above) leaving Netherington Hall and its contents to his son now Lord B. The paintings were exempted from estate duty which was at an 80% marginal rate at the time.

On Boxing Day 2020 Lord B dies in an accident and the Hall and contents are left to his son Lord C. The Executors omit to make claim within the two years to exempt the chattels even though these would have been considered to be pre-eminent under *IHTA 1984, s 31*. The sum of £2,400,000 is paid as IHT on the death in relation to the paintings' value of £6,000,000.

Lord C sells the paintings in the year 2021 for a total sum of £8,000,000 and estate duty at 80% becomes payable on these proceeds (net of expenses), and a credit for the tax previously paid of £2,400,000 is given.

	£
Estate duty 80% × £8m	6,400,000
Less credit for IHT paid on Lord B's death	(2,400,000)
Estate duty payable on sale	4,000,000

Note

(a) If a new exemption claim in respect of the paintings had been made on B's death then the old estate duty liability would have fallen out of account on the chargeable event as only IHT would have been relevant. [*IHTA 1984, Sch 6 para 4(2)(3)*]. The IHT due would have been £8m × 40% = £3,200,000.

315.4 CHARGE TO TAX

Tax credit

[*IHTA 1984, s 33(7)*]

Property inherited in 1984 from A's estate by B, who gave the necessary undertakings so that the property is conditionally exempt, is given in December 2020 by B to C. C agrees to pay any inheritance tax arising from the transfer but does not wish to give the necessary undertakings, so a chargeable event arises. B dies in March 2021.

	£
A's estate at date of death in 1984	180,000
B's cumulative chargeable transfers at date of chargeable event in December 2020 (all in 2019/20)	86,000
Value of property at date of chargeable event	250,000

Inheritance tax on chargeable event (subject to tax credit)

		£
Value of A's estate at date of death		180,000
Value of property at date of chargeable event		250,000
		£430,000
Inheritance tax payable		
£105,000 at 40%		£42,000
Inheritance tax on B's gift		
Cumulative total of previous transfers		86,000
Value of property gifted	250,000	
Deduct Annual exemption 2020/21	(3,000)	247,000
		£333,000
Inheritance tax arising on gift		£3,200
Tax credit		
IHT on B's gift		3,200
IHT on chargeable event	42,000	
Deduct tax credit	(3,200)	
		38,800
Total inheritance tax borne		£42,000

315.5 IHT National Heritage

315.5 SETTLEMENTS — EVENTS AFTER 8 MARCH 1982

(A) Chargeable events following conditionally exempt occasions

A, who is still alive, settled property and investments on discretionary trusts in September 1988, conditional exemption being granted in respect of designated property. In April 2002, the designated property was appointed absolutely to beneficiary C who gave the necessary undertakings for exemption to continue. However, in October 2020, C sold the property for £135,000 net of costs, suffering a capital gains tax liability of £20,000. At the time of C's sale, A had cumulative chargeable transfers of £40,000.

		£
Cumulative total of previous chargeable transfers of relevant person		40,000
Net sale proceeds of conditionally exempt property		115,000
		£155,000
Inheritance tax payable by C		
£110,000 at nil%	—	
£5,000 at 20%	1,000	
£115,000	£1,000	£1,000

Notes

(a) A is the relevant person in relation to the chargeable event as he is the person to effect the only conditionally exempt transfer *and* the person who is settlor in relation to the settlement in respect of which the only conditionally exempt occasion arose. [*IHTA 1984, ss 33(5), 78(3)*].

(b) HMRC have discretion to select either the conditionally exempt transfer (by A to the trustees) in 1988 or the conditionally exempt occasion (from the trustees to C) in 2002 as the 'last transaction' for the purposes of determining who is the relevant person. A is the relevant person regardless of which is selected but HMRC are more likely to choose the earlier transfer as this will result in a greater amount of tax being collected. [*IHTA 1984, ss 33(5), 78(3)(4)*].

(c) The chargeable amount of £115,000 does not increase either A's cumulative total or that of the trustees for the purpose of calculating the IHT liability on any subsequent transfers. As the last conditionally exempt transaction before the chargeable event was a conditionally exempt occasion rather than a conditionally exempt transfer, the provisions of *IHTA 1984, s 34*, (which allow for an increase in the cumulative total) do not apply. [*IHTA 1984, s 78(6)*]. See IHTM11260.

(B) Exemption from the ten-year anniversary charge

[*IHTA 1984, s 79*]

Trustees own National Heritage property for which the necessary undertakings have been given and the property has been designated by the Treasury. The property was settled in January 1975 and is the sole asset of the trust. No appointments or advances of capital have been made. On 30 October 2020, there is a breach of the undertakings. At this date the property is valued at £150,000.

Ten-year anniversary charge

There is no liability in 1985, 1995, 2005 or 2015.

Breach in October 2020

Value of property at time of event	£150,000

The relevant period is the period from the date of settlement or, if later, 13 March 1975 to 29 October 2020, i.e. 182 complete quarters.

The rate of tax is

0.25% for 40 quarters	10.00%
0.20% for 40 quarters	8.00%
0.15% for 40 quarters	6.00%
0.10% for 40 quarters	4.00%
0.05% for 22 quarters	1.1%
	29.1%

IHT payable is 29.1% × £150,000 = £43,650

315.6 MAINTENANCE FUNDS FOR HISTORIC BUILDINGS

[*IHTA 1984, Sch 2 para 6, Sch 4 paras 8, 12–14*]

On 1 January 2001 P settled £500,000 in an approved maintenance fund for his historic mansion during the lives of himself and his wife, W. P died in February 2004, his taxable estate and lifetime transfers chargeable on death amounting to £175,000. On 1 January 2021, the date of death of W, the fund, which has been depleted by extensive repairs to the mansion, is valued at £300,000. £80,000 is transferred to the National Trust, which also accepts the gift of the mansion, and the balance is paid to P's grandson G.

No IHT is payable on the £80,000 paid to the National Trust, but the balance passing to G is liable to IHT at the higher of a tapered scale rate (the 'first rate') and an effective rate calculated by reference to P's estate (the 'second rate'). [*IHTA 1984, Sch 4 paras 12–14*].

First rate

The property was comprised in the maintenance fund for 20 years, i.e. 80 quarters.

The scale rate is

0.25% for each of the first 40 quarters	10.0%
0.20% for each of the next 40 quarters	8.0%
	18.0%

315.6 IHT National Heritage

Second rate

The effective rate is calculated, using half Table rates applying on 1 January 2021, as if the chargeable amount transferred (£220,000) had been added to the value transferred by P on his death (£175,000) and had formed the highest part of the total. Half Table rates are used because the fund was set up in P's lifetime.

	£
£150,000 at nil	—
£70,000 at 20%	14,000
£220,000	£14,000

The effective rate is $\dfrac{14{,}000}{220{,}000} \times 100\% =$ 6.36%

As the second rate (6.36%) is lower than the first rate (18%) the first rate is used.

IHT payable is £220,000 at 18% =   £39,600

316 Payment of Tax

[*IHTA 1984, ss 227, 228, 234*]

316.1 PAYMENT BY INSTALMENTS ON TRANSFER OR DEATH

(A)

F died on 17 December 2020 leaving a free estate of £395,000, including £75,000 (after business property relief at 50%) in respect of plant and machinery in a partnership. An election is made to pay inheritance tax on the plant and machinery by 10 equal yearly instalments.

Inheritance tax on free estate		£
On first	£325,000	Nil
On next	£70,000 at 40%	28,000
	£395,000	£28,000

IHT applicable to plant and machinery

$$\frac{75,000}{395,000} \times 28,000 \qquad £5,316$$

1st instalment due 1.7.21	£531
2nd instalment due 1.7.22	£531
and so on.	

Notes

(a) Instalments continue to be due at yearly intervals for 10 years or until the business property is sold, at which time all unpaid IHT becomes payable.

See IHTM30201.

(b) Interest is payable on each instalment from the day it falls due. If payments are made on time, no interest is payable.

(B)

On 1 December 2020 G gave his land in a partnership of which G was a partner to his son S who agreed to pay any IHT on the transfer. The land was valued at £600,000. G had made prior chargeable transfers of £140,000, had already used his 2019/20 and 2020/21 annual exemptions, and he died on 31 December 2024.

S elected to pay the IHT by 10 yearly instalments and paid the first on 1 August 2025, and the second on 1 September 2026. On 1 December 2026 he sold the land, and paid the balance of the IHT outstanding on 1 February 2027. It is assumed that the rate of interest on unpaid inheritance tax is 3% throughout.

316.1 IHT Payment of Tax

Inheritance tax on gift

		£
Value of land		600,000
Deduct business property relief at 50%		(300,000)
PET becoming chargeable on death		£300,000
IHT payable in the band £140,001–£440,000		

	£	
140,001–325,000 at nil%	Nil	
325,001–440,000 at 40%	46,000	
	£46,000	

		£
Total IHT payable at 60% of full rates (death between 4 and 5 years after gift)		£27,600
1st instalment due 1.7.25	2,760	
Interest at 3% from 1.7.25 to 1.8.25		
$^{31}/_{366} \times £2,760 \times 3\%$	7	
		2,767
2nd instalment due 1.7.26	2,760	
Interest at 3% from 1.7.26 to 1.9.26		
$^{62}/_{366} \times £2,760 \times 3\%$	14	
		2,774
Balance due on sale on 1.12.26	22,080	
Interest at 3% from 1.12.26 to 1.2.27		
$^{62}/_{366} \times £22,080 \times 3\%$	112	
		22,192
Total IHT and interest		£27,733

Note

(a) Interest on unpaid tax is calculated using 366 days as the denominator rather than 365 days.

317 Protective Trusts

317.1 FORFEITURE BEFORE 12 APRIL 1978

[*IHTA 1984, s 73*]

In 1951 X left his estate on protective trusts for his son Z. On 1 January 1978 Z attempted to assign his interest and the protective trusts were accordingly determined. On 1 May 1983 the trustees advanced £25,000 to Z to enable him to purchase a flat. At the same time, they also advanced £10,000 (net) to his granddaughter D. On 1 May 2020 Z died and the trust fund, valued at £200,000, passed equally to his grandchildren absolutely.

1 May 1983

There is no charge to IHT on the payment to Z, but a charge arises on the payment to D. The relevant period is the period from the determination of the protective trusts (1 January 1978) to 1 May 1983 i.e. 21 complete quarters.

The rate of tax is 0.25% for each of 21 quarters   5.25%

$$\text{IHT payable is } \frac{5.25}{100 - 5.25} \times £10,000 = £554$$

The gross payment is £10,554

1 May 2020

There is a charge to IHT when the trust vests on the death of Z. 169 complete quarters have elapsed since the protective trusts determined.

The rate of tax is

0.25% for each of the first 40 quarters	10.0%
0.20% for each of the next 40 quarters	8.0%
0.15% for the next 40 quarters	6.0%
0.10% for the next 40 quarters	4.0%
0.05% for the next 9 quarters	0.45%
	28.45%

IHT payable is 28.45% × £200,000 = £56,900

Note

(a) See IHTM42804.

317.2 IHT   Protective Trusts

317.2 FORFEITURE AFTER 11 APRIL 1978

[*IHTA 1984, s 88*]

Assume the same facts as in 318.1 above but that Z attempted to assign his interest on 1 January 1980.

1 May 1983

There is no charge to IHT on the payment to Z who is treated as beneficially entitled to an interest in possession under the trust. The payment to D is a chargeable transfer. Tax is charged at Z's personal cumulative rate of tax so that if he had made no previous transfers, the payment would be covered by his nil rate tax band. If the payment had been made after 16 March 1987, it would have been a potentially exempt transfer.

1 May 2020

There is a charge to IHT when the trust vests on the death of Z, calculated by aggregating £200,000 with all other chargeable property passing on his death and applying the normal death rates.

Notes

(a) For settlements created on or after 22 March 2006, *IHTA 1984, s 88* applies only if the interest of the principal beneficiary is an immediate post-death interest within *IHTA 1984, s 49A*, a disabled person's interest within *IHTA 1984, s 89B(1)(c)(d)* or a transitional serial interest within *IHTA 1984, ss 49B–49E*. [*IHTA 1988, s 88(4)–(6); FA 2006, Sch 20 para 24*]. See IHTM42801–IHTM42805 and *Simon's Taxes* I5.207.

(b) For settlements created before 22 March 2006, where the protective trusts fail or are determined on or after that date, for inheritance tax purposes the principal beneficiary is treated as if he became beneficially entitled to an interest in possession in the settled property before that date. [*IHTA 1984, s 88(3); FA 2006, Sch 20 para 24*].Therefore the changes to the SETTLEMENTS: INTERESTS IN POSSESSION **(319)** provisions made by *FA 2006* do not apply and the beneficiary continues to be treated under *IHTA 1984, s 49* as beneficially entitled to the settled property concerned whether or not his interest is an immediate post-death interest, a disabled person's interest or a transitional serial interest. See IHTM42804.

318 Quick Succession Relief

[*IHTA 1984, s 141*]

318.1 TRANSFERS AFTER 9 MARCH 1981

On 1 January 2021 A died with a net estate valued at £400,000. In December 2016 he had received a gift from B of £20,000. B died in November 2018 and A paid the IHT (amounting to £8,000) due as a result of B's potentially exempt transfer becoming chargeable.

A was also entitled to an interest in possession in the whole of his father's estate. His father had died in February 2018 with a net estate of £331,000 on which the IHT paid was £2,400. On A's death, the property passed to A's sister and was valued at £145,000. A had made no previous transfers and left his estate to his brother.

	£
Free estate	400,000
Settled property	145,000
Taxable estate	£545,000

IHT on an estate of £545,000 = £88,000

Quick succession relief

The gift from B was made more than four but not more than five years before A's death so quick succession relief at 20% is available.

$$\text{QSR} = 20\% \times £8,000 \times \frac{12,000}{20,000} \qquad £960$$

Interest in possession in father's Will trust	£
Net estate before tax	331,000
Tax	(2,400)
Net estate after tax	£328,600

A's death was more than two but not more than three years after his father's so relief is given at 60%.

$$\text{QSR} = 60\% \times £2,400 \times \frac{328,600}{331,000} \qquad £1,430$$

318.1 IHT   Quick Succession Relief

		£	£
Tax payable on death of A			
IHT on an estate of £545,000			88,000
Deduct QSR			
On gift from B		960	
On father's estate		1,430	
			(2,390)
IHT payable			£85,610

$$\text{On free estate } \frac{400{,}000}{545{,}000} \times £85{,}610 \qquad £62{,}833$$

$$\text{On settled property } \frac{145{,}000}{545{,}000} \times £85{,}610 \qquad £22{,}777$$

Note

(a) The relief is given only by reference to the tax charged on the part of the value received by the donee. Therefore, the tax paid must be apportioned by applying the fraction 'net transfer received divided by gross transfer made'. See IHTM22051–IHTM22081 and Simon's Taxes I5.283.

319 Settlements: Interests in Possession

[IHTA 1984, ss 49–49E, 51(1)–(1B), 52(1)(2A), 54A, 54B, 57]

319.1 TERMINATION OF AN INTEREST IN POSSESSION

A had an interest in possession in a settlement valued at £222,000 with remainder to his son S for life. A's interest in possession commenced in 2002. On 1 July 2020, A released his life interest to S in consideration of S's marriage on 2 July 2020. A had made no gifts since 5 April 2020 but had used his annual exemptions prior to that date. His cumulative total of chargeable transfers at 5 April 2020 was £126,000, and these had all been made since 1 July 2013.

The release of A's life interest is an immediately chargeable transfer.

	£	£
Value of property		222,000
Exemptions		
Annual 2020/21	3,000	
In consideration of marriage	5,000	
		(8,000)
Chargeable transfer		£214,000

IHT on £214,000 is charged in the band £126,001 to £340,000.

	£
126,001–325,000 at nil%	Nil
325,001–340,000 at 20%	3,000
	£3,000
Tax payable by trustees as a consequence of A's release of his interest in possession	£3,000

Notes

(a) The annual gifts exemption and the exemption of gifts in consideration of marriage apply if notice is given to the trustees by the donor within 6 months of the gift.

(b) The tax payable is computed by reference to the transferor's cumulative total of chargeable transfers within the previous seven years, and the chargeable transfer forms part of his cumulative total carried forward.

(c) The interest in possession provisions apply in respect of interests to which a person becomes beneficially entitled on or after 22 March 2006 only if the interest is an immediate post-death interest within *IHTA 1984, s 49A* (see **319.3** below), a disabled person's interest within *IHTA 1984, s 89B(1)(c)(d)* or a transitional serial interest within *IHTA 1984, ss 49B–49E* (see **319.2** below). The provisions also apply where a UK-domiciled person becomes beneficially entitled to an interest in possession on

319.1 IHT   Settlements: Interests in Possession

or after 9 December 2009 by a disposition which is not a transfer of value as a result of *IHTA 1984, s 10* (dispositions not intended to confer gratuitous benefit). [*IHTA 1984, s 49(1A)*]. Otherwise, an interest in possession to which a person becomes beneficially entitled on or after 22 March 2006 is treated as relevant property subject to the rules in **320 SETTLEMENTS: RELEVANT PROPERTY**. [*IHTA 1984, s 59(1)(2)*]. See IHTM16061, IHTM04165.

(d) As the release of A's life interest to S occurred after 5 October 2008, S's interest in possession is not a transitional serial interest and is subject to the rules in **320 SETTLEMENTS: RELEVANT PROPERTY**. The release is an immediately chargeable transfer. See also 319.2 below.

319.2 TRANSITIONAL SERIAL INTERESTS

[*IHTA 1984, ss 49B–49E*]

Rick had an interest in possession in a settlement to which he became beneficially entitled in 1998. The terms of the settlement are that remainder goes to his son Robbie for life. Rick released his life interest to Robbie. At the date of the release, the settlement was valued at £350,000, Rick's cumulative chargeable transfers in the last seven years amounted to £130,000 and he had not used his annual exemptions for any year.

On the assumption that the release takes place on (i) 31 August 2007 and (ii) 5 November 2020, the IHT consequences for Rick are as follows.

(i) **Release on 31 August 2007**

Robbie's interest in possession is a transitional serial interest within *IHTA 1984, s 49C*. The transfer is therefore a potentially exempt transfer and will become chargeable only in the event of Rick's death within seven years.

(ii) **Release on 5 November 2020**

As the release occurs after 5 October 2008 Robbie's interest cannot be a transitional serial interest within *IHTA 1984, s 49C*. As his interest is not a transitional serial interest within *IHTA 1984, s 49D*, the relevant property regime (see **320 SETTLEMENTS: RELEVANT PROPERTY**) applies to it. Rick's transfer is therefore a chargeable transfer and IHT is due as follows.

		£	£
Value transferred by Rick on 5 November 2020			350,000
Deduct annual exemptions	2020/21	3,000	
	2019/20	3,000	(6,000)
			£344,000

Settlements: Interests in Possession   IHT 319.3

IHT on £344,000 is charged in the band £130,001 to £474,000.

	£
£130,001–325,000	Nil
£325,001–474,000 at 20%	29,800
IHT payable	£29,800

Notes

(a) The interest in possession provisions apply in respect of interests to which a person becomes beneficially entitled on or after 22 March 2006 only if the interest is a disabled person's interest within *IHTA 1984, s 89B(1)(c)(d)*, a transitional serial interest within *IHTA 1984, ss 49B–49E* or an immediate post-death interest within *IHTA 1984, s 49A* (see **319.3** below). The provisions also apply where a UK-domiciled person becomes beneficially entitled to an interest in possession on or after 9 December 2009 by a disposition which is not a transfer of value as a result of *IHTA 1984, s 10* (dispositions not intended to confer gratuitous benefit). [*IHTA 1984, s 49(1A)*]. Otherwise, an interest in possession to which a person becomes beneficially entitled on or after 22 March 2006 is treated as relevant property subject to the rules in **320 SETTLEMENTS: RELEVANT PROPERTY**. [*IHTA 1984, s 59(1)(2)*].

(b) An interest in possession to which a person ('B') becomes beneficially entitled during the period 22 March 2006 to 5 October 2008 is a transitional serial interest if the settlement was created before 22 March 2006, immediately before that date a person was beneficially entitled to an interest in possession (the '*prior interest*'), and B became beneficially entitled to his interest on the prior interest coming to an end. B's interest must not be a disabled person's interest and the settlement must not be within the rules for **TRUSTS FOR BEREAVED MINORS (322)**. [*IHTA 1984, s 49C*].

(c) Where a person ('C') becomes beneficially entitled to an interest in possession after 5 October 2008, that interest qualifies as a transitional serial interest only where the interest arises on coming to an end of a prior interest in possession on the death of C's spouse/civil partner. The prior interest must have been held by the spouse or civil partner immediately before 22 March 2006. C's interest must not be a disabled person's interest and the settlement must not be within the rules for **TRUSTS FOR BEREAVED MINORS (322)**. [*IHTA 1984, s 49D*]. See also *IHTA 1984, s 49E* for treatment of an interest as a transitional serial interest where the settled property consists of rights under a life assurance contract.

(d) See IHTM16061 and I5.206.

319.3 IMMEDIATE POST-DEATH INTERESTS

[*IHTA 1984, s 49A*]

Garth, who is married to Maud, dies on 12 January 2019 having already made potentially exempt gifts on 21 May 2016 of £331,000. By his will he leaves his assets to Maud in trust for life and then on her death on trusts to his adult son Richard for life. His estate is valued at £760,000. Garth had made no gifts prior to 5 April 2015 other than to use his annual exemptions prior to 2015/16. Garth and Maud had sold their home in March 2015 and moved into rented sheltered accommodation.

Maud dies on 8 January 2021 when the trust assets are valued at £800,000. Her free estate is valued at £100,000 and she has made no transfers in the preceding seven years, other than to utilise her annual exemptions.

319.3 IHT   Settlements: Interests in Possession

IHT payable on death of Garth

		£	£
Value transferred on 21 May 2016			331,000
Deduct annual exemptions	2016/17	3,000	
	2015/16	3,000	(6,000)
			£325,000

IHT on chargeable gift of £325,000 is charged in the nil rate band up to £325,000. The balance of the estate left on trust for wife Maud is exempt under *IHTA 1984, s 18*. Garth has no unused nil rate band to transfer to Maud.

IHT payable on death of Maud

	£
Trust assets	800,000
Free estate	100,000
	900,000

	£
£0–325,000	Nil
£325,001–£900,000 at 40%	£230,000
IHT payable	£230,000

Notes

(a) The interest in possession provisions apply in respect of interests to which a person becomes beneficially entitled on or after 22 March 2006 only if the interest is a disabled person's interest within *IHTA 1984, s 89B(1)(c)(d)*, a transitional serial interest within *IHTA 1984, ss 49B–49E* (see **319.2** above) or an immediate post-death interest within *IHTA 1984, s 49A*. The provisions also apply where a UK-domiciled person becomes beneficially entitled to an interest in possession on or after 9 December 2009 by a disposition which is not a transfer of value as a result of *IHTA 1984, s 10* (dispositions not intended to confer gratuitous benefit). [*IHTA 1984, s 49(1A)*]. Otherwise, an interest in possession to which a person becomes beneficially entitled on or after 22 March 2006 is treated as relevant property subject to the rules in **320** SETTLEMENTS: RELEVANT PROPERTY. [*IHTA 1984, s 59(1)(2)*].

(b) An interest in possession in a settlement is an immediate post-death interest only if the settlement is effected by Will or intestacy and the person holding the interest became beneficially entitled to it on the death of the testator or intestate. The interest in possession must not be a disabled person's interest and the settlement must not be within the rules for TRUSTS FOR BEREAVED MINORS (**322**). [*IHTA 1984, s 49A*]. See IHTM16061 and *Simon's Taxes* I5.205.

(c) Richard's interest in possession is not an immediate post-death interest as he did not become entitled to his interest in possession on the death of Garth. It is not a transitional serial interest (see note (c) to **319.3** above) or a disabled person's interest. His interest is therefore relevant property subject to the rules in **320** SETTLEMENTS: RELEVANT PROPERTY.

320 Settlements: Relevant Property

Where the value of trust property is given in an example, it is assumed, where relevant, that this includes any undistributed and unaccumulated income treated as included in trust property under *IHTA 1984, s 64(1A)*. Otherwise, such income is excluded as it is not treated as a taxable trust asset (Revenue Statement of Practice SP 8/86).

320.1 RATE OF TEN-YEAR ANNIVERSARY CHARGE

(A) **Post-26 March 1974 settlements**

[*IHTA 1984, ss 64, 66; FA 2020, s 73(5)*]

On 1 May 2000 S settled £150,000 net, £100,000 to be held on discretionary trusts and £50,000 in trust for his brother B for life. At the date of the transfer S had a cumulative total of chargeable transfers of £67,000. £20,000 (gross) was advanced from the discretionary trusts to C on 1 March 2008.

The property held on discretionary trusts was valued at £207,000 on 1 May 2010.

On 1 January 2020 B died, when the property subject to his interest in possession was valued at £95,000. The whole trust property was valued at £322,000 on 1 May 2020 of which £105,000 derived from B's fund. The trustees had made no advances other than that to C.

It is assumed that rates of tax remain at the level for transfers after 5 April 2020.

1 May 2010 Ten-year anniversary charge

		£
Assumed chargeable transfer		
(i)	value of relevant property immediately before the ten-year anniversary	207,000
(ii)	value, at date of settlement, of property which was not, and has not become, relevant property	50,000
(iii)	value, at date of settlement, of property in related settlement	—
		£257,000
Assumed transferor's cumulative total		
(i)	value of chargeable transfers made by settlor in seven-year period ending on date of settlement	67,000
(ii)	amounts on which proportionate charges have been levied in ten years before the anniversary	20,000
		£87,000

320.1 IHT   Settlements: Relevant Property

	Gross £	Tax £
Assumed cumulative total	87,000	—
Assumed transfer	257,000	3,800
	£344,000	£3,800

$$\text{Effective rate of tax } \frac{3,800}{257,000} \times 100 = \underline{1.47860\%}$$

Ten-year anniversary charge

The IHT payable is at 30% of the effective rate on the relevant property

IHT payable = 30% × 1.47860% × £207,000 = £918

1 May 2020 Ten-year anniversary charge

	£
Assumed chargeable transfer (note (a))	
(i) value of relevant property immediately prior to the ten-year anniversary	322,000
(ii) value at date of settlement of property in related settlement	—
	£322,000
Assumed transferor's cumulative total	
(i) value of chargeable transfers made by settlor in seven-year period ending on date of settlement	67,000
(ii) amounts on which proportionate charges have been levied in ten years before the anniversary	—
	£67,000

	Gross £	Tax £
Assumed cumulative total	67,000	—
Assumed transfer	322,000	12,800
	£389,000	£12,800

$$\text{Effective rate of tax } \frac{12,800}{322,000} \times 100 = \underline{3.97516\%}$$

Ten-year anniversary charge

Of the relevant property, £105,000 had not been relevant property for the period 1 May 2010–1 January 2020, i.e. 38 complete quarters.

Settlements: Relevant Property IHT 320.1

IHT payable

			£
At 30% × 3.97516%	= 1.19%	on £217,000	2,582
At 30% × 3.97516%	= 1.19%		
Less 38/40 × 30% × 3.97516%	= 1.13%		
	0.06%	on £105,000	63
Total IHT payable			£2,645

Notes

(a) For charges arising on or after 18 November 2015, the assumed chargeable transfer is the aggregate of:

    (i) the value of relevant property immediately prior to the ten-year anniversary;

    (ii) the value at the date of settlement of relevant property in any related settlement;

    (iii) the value of any same-day addition (as defined) to another settlement with the same settlor; and

    (iv) where an increase in the value of any property in another settlement is represented by the value of a same-day addition within (iii) above and that other settlement is not a related settlement, the value at the date of settlement of the relevant property in that other settlement.

[*IHTA 1984, s 66(4)*]. See IHTM42084.

(b) There is no same-day addition (see (a)(iii)(iv) above) if either or both of the settlements in question are 'protected settlements' which commenced before 10 December 2014. A settlement is a protected settlement if there have been no transfers of value by the settlor on or after 10 December 2014 as a result of which the value of the property comprised in the settlement was increased or if there has been such a transfer of value but that transfer was on the death of the settlor before 6 April 2017 and was effected by provisions of the settlor's will which were, in substance, the same as they were immediately before 10 December 2014. [*IHTA 1984, ss 62B(1)(c), 62C*].

(B) **Pre-27 March 1974 settlements**

[*IHTA 1984, ss 64, 66; FA 2020, s 73(5)*]

On 1 June 1971 T settled property on discretionary trusts. The trustees made the following advances (gross) to beneficiaries

1.1.74	H	£10,000
1.1.77	B	£20,000
1.1.82	C	£60,000
1.1.88	D	£40,000
1.1.94	E	£80,000

320.1 IHT Settlements: Relevant Property

On 1 June 1991 the settled property was valued at £175,000, on 1 June 2001 £180,000.

1 June 1991 Ten-year anniversary charge

		£
Assumed chargeable transfer		
Value of relevant property		£175,000
Assumed transferor's cumulative total		
(i) Aggregate of distribution payments made between 1 June 1981 and 8 March 1982	60,000	
(ii) Aggregate of amounts on which proportionate charge arises between 9 March 1982 and 1 June 1991	40,000	£100,000

	Gross	Tax
	£	£
Assumed cumulative total	100,000	—
Assumed chargeable transfer	175,000	27,000
	£275,000	£27,000

$$\text{Effective rate of tax} = \frac{27{,}000}{175{,}000} \times 100 = \underline{15.429\%}$$

Ten-year anniversary charge

The IHT payable is at 30% of the effective rate on the relevant property.

IHT payable = 30% × 15.429% × £175,000 = £8,100

1 June 2001 Ten-year anniversary charge

	£
Assumed chargeable transfer	
Value of relevant property	£180,000
Assumed transferor's cumulative total	
Aggregate of amount on which proportionate charge arises between 1 June 1991 and 1 June 2001	£80,000

	Gross	Tax
	£	£
Assumed cumulative total	80,000	—
Assumed chargeable transfer	180,000	3,600
	£260,000	£3,600

$$\text{Effective rate of tax} = \frac{3{,}600}{180{,}000} \times 100 = 2\%$$

Settlements: Relevant Property IHT 320.2

Ten-year anniversary charge

The IHT payable is at 30% of the effective rate on the relevant property.

IHT payable = 30% × 2% × £180,000 = £1,080

1 June 2011 Ten-year anniversary charge

Not illustrated.

320.2 RATE OF PROPORTIONATE CHARGE BEFORE THE FIRST TEN-YEAR ANNIVERSARY

(A) **Post-26 March 1974 settlements**

[IHTA 1984, ss 65, 68; FA 2020, s 73(6)]

On 1 April 2011 M settled £60,000 (net) on discretionary trusts. His cumulative total of chargeable transfers (gross) prior to the settlement was £290,000. On 3 December 2019 he added £20,000 (net), having made no chargeable transfers since 1 April 2011.

On 11 October 2019 the trustees had advanced £40,000 to N, and on 1 March 2020 the trustees distributed the whole of the remaining funds equally to P and Q. The remaining funds were valued at £110,000, of which £88,000 derived from the original settlement, and £22,000 from the addition.

11 October 2019 proportionate charge

Assumed chargeable transfer

(i)	Value of property in the settlement at date of settlement	60,000
(ii)	Value at date of settlement of property in related settlement	—
(iii)	Value at date of addition of property added	—
		£60,000

Assumed transferor's cumulative total

Value of chargeable transfers made by settlor in seven-year period ending on date of settlement £290,000

	Gross (£)	Tax (£)
Assumed cumulative total	290,000	—
Assumed transfer	60,000	5,000
	£350,000	£5,000

$$\text{Effective rate of tax} = \frac{5,000}{60,000} \times 100 = 8.33\%$$

Appropriate fraction

The number of complete quarters that have elapsed between the date of settlement, 1 April 2011, and the advance on 11 October 2019 is 34.

320.2 IHT Settlements: Relevant Property

IHT is charged at the appropriate fraction of the effective rate on the property advanced.

$$\text{IHT payable} = 30\% \times \frac{34}{40} \times 8.33\% \times £40,000$$

$$= 2.12\% \times £40,000$$

$$= £848$$

Had the advance of £40,000 been net, the IHT payable would be

$$\frac{2.12}{100 - 2.12} \times £40,000 = £866$$

and the gross advance would be £40,866

1 March 2020 proportionate charge

As property has been added to the settlement, the effective rate of tax is recalculated.

Assumed chargeable transfer	£
(i) Value of property in settlement at date of settlement	60,000
(ii) Value at date of settlement of property in related settlement	—
(iii) Value at date of addition of relevant property added	20,000
	£80,000

Assumed transferor's cumulative total

Value of chargeable transfers made by settlor in seven-year period ending on date of settlement	£290,000

	Gross	Tax
	£	£
Assumed cumulative total	290,000	—
Assumed transfer	80,000	9,000
	£370,000	£9,000

$$\text{Effective rate of tax} = \frac{9,000}{80,000} \times 100 = 11.25\%$$

Appropriate fraction

The number of complete quarters that have elapsed between the date of settlement, 1 April 2011, and the advance on 1 March 2020 is 35.

The number of complete quarters that elapsed between the date of settlement, 1 April 2011, and 3 December 2019, the date on which property was added, was 34.

The IHT is charged at the appropriate fraction of the effective rate on the property advanced

			£
$30\% \times \frac{35}{40} \times 11.25\%$	on	£88,000 =	2,599

Settlements: Relevant Property IHT 320.2

		£
$30\% \times \dfrac{(35-34)}{40} \times 11.25\%$ on £22,000 =		19
	£110,000	
IHT payable on advance of £110,000		£2,618

Notes

(a) For charges arising on or after 18 November 2015, the assumed chargeable transfer is the aggregate of:

  (i) the value of property in the settlement at the date of settlement;

  (ii) the value at the date of settlement of property in any related settlement;

  (iii) the value at the date of addition of property added to the settlement which was then relevant property (whether or not it has remained relevant property);

  (iv) the value at the date it became relevant property of property either in the settlement at date of settlement or subsequently added which was not initially relevant property (whether or not it has remained relevant property);

  (v) the value of any same-day addition (as defined) to another settlement with the same settlor; and

  (vi) where an increase in the value of any property in another settlement is represented by the value of a same-day addition within (v) above and that other settlement is not a related settlement, the value at the date of settlement of the relevant property in that other settlement.

  [*IHTA 1984, s 68(5)*].

(b) There is no same-day addition (see (a)(v)(vi) above) if either or both of the settlements in question are 'protected settlements' which commenced before 10 December 2014. A settlement is a protected settlement if there have been no transfers of value by the settlor on or after 10 December 2014 as a result of which the value of the property comprised in the settlement was increased or if there has been such a transfer of value but that transfer was on the death of the settlor before 6 April 2017 and was effected by provisions of the settlor's will which were, in substance, the same as they were immediately before 10 December 2014. [*IHTA 1984, ss 62B(1)(c), 62C*]. See *Simon's Taxes* I5.361, I5.362.

(B) **Settlor dies within 7 years of settlement — post-26 March 1974 settlement**

On 1 July 2016 T settled £335,000 net on discretionary trusts. His only other transfer had been a gift of £70,000 to his brother B on 1 June 2015. On 7 March 2018 the trustees advanced £70,000 to R, who agreed to pay any IHT due. On 30 August 2020 T died.

Proportionate charge 7 March 2018

At the time of the advance, T had made no chargeable transfers in the seven years prior to the settlement (the gift to B being a PET).

320.2 IHT   Settlements: Relevant Property

Assumed chargeable transfer
Value of property in the settlement at the date of settlement   £335,000

Assumed transferor's cumulative total   Nil

Tax on an assumed transfer of £335,000 =   £2,000

$$\text{Effective rate of tax} = \frac{2,000}{335,000} \times 100 = 0.60\%$$

Appropriate fraction

The number of complete quarters that have elapsed between the date of the settlement, 1 July 2016, and the advance on 7 March 2018 is 6.

IHT is charged at the appropriate fraction of the effective rate on the property advanced.

$$\text{IHT} = 30\% \times \frac{6}{40} \times 0.60\% \times £70,000$$

$$= 0.00027\% \times £70,000$$

$$= £19$$

On the settlor's death within seven years, the PET on 1 June 2015 becomes a chargeable transfer. There will be additional IHT payable by the trustees on the creation of the settlement, and additional IHT payable by B on the advance to him from the settlement.

The gross gift to the settlement, after deducting the 2016/17 annual exemption, was

Gross	Tax	Net
£	£	£
325,000	—	325,000
8,750	1,750	7,000
£333,750	£1,750	£332,000

Additional IHT is payable to increase the charge to 60% of full rates at the time of death (death between 4 and 5 years after gift), with a previous chargeable transfer to B of £67,000 (after deducting the 2015/16 annual exemption).

	Gross	Tax	Net
	£	£	£
Prior transfer	67,000	—	67,000
	333,750	30,300	303,450
	£400,750	£30,300	£370,450

	£
IHT at 60% of full rates 60% × £30,300	18,180
Deduct paid on lifetime chargeable transfer	(1,750)
Additional IHT payable	£16,430

The additional IHT is payable by the trustees, reducing the value of property settled to £335,000 − £16,430 = £318,570

The IHT on the advance to B is recalculated

Assumed chargeable transfer	£318,570
Assumed transferor's cumulative total	
Chargeable transfers made by the settlor in 7 years prior to the settlement (gift 1 June 2015)	£67,000

	Gross £	Tax £
Assumed cumulative total	67,000	—
Assumed transfer	318,570	12,114
	£385,570	£12,114

$$\text{Effective rate of tax} = \frac{12,114}{385,570} \times 100 = 3.14\%$$

The appropriate fraction is $^6/_{40}$ (unchanged).

$$\text{IHT borne} = 30\% \times \frac{6}{40} \times 3.14\% \times £70,000$$

$$= 0.1413\% \times £70,000$$

$$= £99$$

	£
IHT due	99
Deduct already paid	(19)
IHT payable	£80

320.3 RATE OF PROPORTIONATE CHARGE BETWEEN TEN-YEAR ANNIVERSARIES

[*IHTA 1984, ss 65, 69, Sch 2 para 3; FA 2020, s 73(6)*]

On 1 January 2001 G settled £70,000 (net) on discretionary trusts. His cumulative total of chargeable transfers at that date was £185,000. On 1 January 2011 the funds were valued at £150,000, no advances having been made. On 1 February 2013 the trustees advanced

320.3 IHT   Settlements: Relevant Property

£30,000 (gross) to H. On 1 January 2014 G added £80,000 to the settlement, having made cumulative chargeable transfers in the previous seven years of £30,000. On 1 May 2020 the trustees advanced £40,000 to F from the funds originally settled.

1 February 2013 advance to H

8 complete quarters have elapsed since the ten-year anniversary charge so the appropriate fraction is 8/40ths. The rate of tax is therefore 8/40ths of the rate at which IHT would have been charged on the last ten-year anniversary if the Table of Rates in force at 1 February 2013 had been in force at the date of the ten-year anniversary, 1 January 2011.

Tax would have been charged at the last ten-year anniversary as follows

	£
Assumed chargeable transfer	
(i) value of relevant property immediately before the ten-year anniversary	150,000
(ii) value, at date of settlement, of property which was not, and has not become, relevant property	—
(iii) value at date of settlement of property in related settlement	—
	£150,000

	£
Assumed transferor's cumulative total	
(i) value of chargeable transfers made by settlor in seven-year period ending on date of settlement	185,000
(ii) amounts on which proportionate charges have been levied in ten years before the anniversary	—
	£185,000

	Gross	Tax
	£	£
Assumed cumulative total	185,000	—
Assumed transfer	150,000	2,000
	£335,000	£2,000

$$\text{Effective rate} = \frac{2,000}{150,000} \times 100 = 1.333\%$$

Rate of tax at ten-year anniversary = 30% × 1.333% = <u>0.4%</u>

Therefore rate of tax on advance to H

	= 8/40 × 0.4%
IHT payable	= 8/40 × 0.4% × £30,000 = £24

1 May 2020 advance to F

Since property has been added to the settlement, a hypothetical rate of tax at the previous ten-year anniversary must be recalculated as if the added property had been added prior to the anniversary.

		Gross	Tax
	£	£	£
Assumed cumulative total		185,000	—
Assumed transfer			
property at anniversary	150,000		
added property	80,000	230,000	18,000
		£415,000	£18,000

Effective rate = 18,000/230,000 × 100 = 7.83%

Rate of tax that would have been charged at the ten-year anniversary
 = 30% × 7.83%
 = 2.3%

The advance to F took place 37 complete quarters after the ten-year anniversary. The rate of tax is 37/40 × 2.3% = 2.128%

If the advance to F was £40,000 gross

$$\text{IHT payable} = £40,000 \times 2.128\% = £851$$

If the advance to F was £40,000 net

IHT payable = 2.128/(100 − 2.128) × £40,000 = £870

The gross distribution would then be £40,870.

321 Transfers on Death

321.1 POTENTIALLY EXEMPT TRANSFER FOLLOWED BY LOAN FROM DONEE TO DONOR

[*FA 1986, ss 103, 104; SI 1987 No 1130, Reg 6*]

X gives cash of £330,000 to Y on 1 November 2014. On 20 December 2014, Y makes a loan of £330,000 to X. On 31 May 2015, X makes a gift of £20,000 into a discretionary trust. X dies on 15 April 2020, his death estate is worth £345,000 before deducting the liability of £330,000 to Y which remains outstanding. X has made no lifetime transfers other than those specified, except that he has used his annual exemptions for all relevant years.

First calculation under Reg 6(3)(a)

The transfer of £330,000 in November 2014 is a PET which becomes chargeable by virtue of X's death within seven years. However, for the purpose of this calculation the PET is ignored but no deduction is allowed against the death estate for the outstanding loan.

No IHT is due in respect of the chargeable transfer in May 2015 as it is covered by the Nil rate band.

The estate of £345,000 is charged in the band £20,001 to £365,000.

		£
20,001–325,000	at nil%	Nil
325,001–365,000	at 40%	16,000
IHT due		£16,000

Second calculation under Reg 6(3)(b)

The PET in November 2014 is charged on death in the normal way and the loan is deducted from the death estate.

The PET is charged in the band £0 to £330,000.

		£
0–325,000	at nil%	Nil
325,001–330,000	at 40%	2,000
		£2,000
IHT at 40% of full rates		
(death between 5 and 6 years after transfer)		£800

321.1 IHT   Transfers on Death

Additional tax is due on the chargeable transfer in May 2015, £20,000 is charged in the band £330,001 to £350,000.

20,000 at 40%	£8,000
IHT at 60% of full rates	
(death between 4 and 5 years after transfer)	£4,800

Tax is charged on the death estate of £15,000 (£345,000–330,000) in the band £350,001 to £365,000.

350,001–365,000 at 40%	£6,000
Total IHT due £(800 + 4,800 + 6,000)	£11,600

The first calculation gives the higher amount of tax, so the PET is ignored and no deduction is allowed for the outstanding loan against the death estate.

Notes

(a) If the PET had exceeded the loan, the excess would not be ignored for the purpose of the first calculation above.

(b) If X had made more than one PET to Y and the total PETs exceeded the amount of the loan, only PETs up to the amount of the loan are ignored for the purpose of the first calculation above, later PETs being disregarded in preference to earlier ones.

321.2 REDUCED RATE FOR ESTATES WITH 10% GIFTS TO CHARITIES

[*IHTA 1984, Sch 1A*]

(A)

The estate of Percival who died on 30 April 2020 is valued at £425,000, comprising quoted investments and cash. He leaves a legacy of £10,000 to the National Trust and the residue of £415,000 less inheritance tax passes to his children. Percival had made no chargeable transfers in the seven years before his death.

Percival's estate consists of only one component (see note (b)), the general component, and its baseline amount is calculated as follows.

	£
Step 1. Determine value transferred by chargeable transfer attributable to component	
Estate	425,000
Less gift to charity	(10,000)
	415,000

		£
Step 2. Deduct available nil-rate band		(325,000)
		90,000
Step 3. Add back gift to charity		10,000
Baseline amount		£100,000

As the donated amount (£10,000) is at least 10% of the baseline amount for the general component, that component (and in this case the entire estate) qualifies for the 36% rate of inheritance tax.

The inheritance tax due on the chargeable estate (£425,000 − £10,000) is charged in the band £Nil to £415,000.

		£
Nil–325,000	at nil%	Nil
325,001–415,000	at 36%	32,400
IHT due		£32,400

Notes

(a) Inheritance tax is charged on the net chargeable value of any component (see note (b)) of an estate at a rate of 36% where 10% or more of the 'baseline amount' of that component has been left to charity. [*IHTA 1984, Sch 1A paras 1, 2*].

(b) An estate can consist of up to three components:

- the survivorship component, consisting of any joint or common property liable to pass on death by survivorship;
- the settled property component, consisting of settled property comprised in the estate by virtue of an interest in possession to which the deceased was beneficially entitled; and
- the general component, consisting of all other property comprised in the estate other than gifts with reservation.

[*IHTA 1984, Sch 1A para 3*].

(c) The steps taken in calculating the baseline amount are those set out in *IHTA 1984, Sch 1A para 5*. In this simple example the deduction of the gift to charity in step 1 followed by its adding back in step 3 appears redundant but where there is more than one component, this is necessary in apportioning the nil-rate band between components. See (B) below.

(d) The gift to charity reduces the residue by only £2,400 (£10,000 gift less IHT reduction (£40,000 − £32,400)).

(e) Where the conditions are satisfied, the reduced rate applies automatically. An election can, however, be made to disapply the reduced rate for all or any components of the estate. Such an election must be made within two years after the death by all the appropriate persons (as in note (b) to (B) below). [*IHTA 1984, Sch 1A paras 8, 9*].

321.2 IHT Transfers on Death

(B) **Election to merge parts of the estate**

The facts are as in (A) above, except that Percival's legacy to the National Trust is £25,000 and he has also had an interest in possession since 2000 in a settlement valued at death at £100,000.

If no election is made under *IHTA 1984, Sch 1A para 7*, the inheritance tax position is as follows.

General component

	£
Step 1. Determine value transferred by chargeable transfer attributable to component	
Estate	425,000
Less gift to charity	(25,000)
	400,000
Step 2. Deduct appropriate proportion of available nil-rate band*	(260,000)
	140,000
Step 3. Add back gift to charity	25,000
Baseline amount	£165,000

*£325,000 × (£400,000/£500,000) = £260,000

As the donated amount (£25,000) is at least 10% of the baseline amount for the general component (£16,500), that component qualifies for the 36% rate of inheritance tax. No gift to charity is made out of the settled property component, so that component does not qualify for the lower rate. Inheritance tax is chargeable as follows.

	£
Free estate	425,000
Interest in possession	100,000
	525,000
Less gift to charity	(25,000)
	500,000
Less nil-rate band	(325,000)
	175,000
£140,000 @ 36%	50,400
£35,000 @ 40%	14,000
	£64,400

If an election is made under *IHTA 1984, Sch 1A para 7*, the inheritance tax position is as follows.

Merged components

	£
Step 1. Determine value transferred by chargeable transfer attributable to merged components	
Free estate	425,000
Interest in possession	100,000
	525,000
Less gift to charity	(25,000)
	500,000
Step 2. Deduct available nil-rate band*	(325,000)
	175,000
Step 3. Add back gift to charity	25,000
Baseline amount	£200,000

As the donated amount (£25,000) is at least 10% of the baseline amount for the merged components (£20,000), those components qualify for the 36% rate of inheritance tax. Inheritance tax is chargeable as follows.

	£
Free estate	425,000
Interest in possession	100,000
	525,000
Less gift to charity	(25,000)
	500,000
Less nil-rate band	(325,000)
	175,000
£175,000 @ 36%	£63,000

Notes

(a) Where an estate includes more than one component and one of the components qualifies for the reduced rate, an election may be made to treat that component and one or more other eligible parts as one single component. If the 10% test is met for the merged component, then the reduced rate applies to the whole of the merged component. The parts that are eligible to be merged with the qualifying component are the other two components and all the property forming part of the estate by reason of the gifts with reservation provisions. [*IHTA 1984, Sch 1A para 7(1)–(5)*].

(b) The election must be made within two years after the death by all those who are appropriate persons with respect to the qualifying component and each of the eligible parts to be included. The appropriate persons are:

- in relation to the survivorship component, all those to whom the property in the component passes;
- in relation to the settled property component, the trustees;

321.2 IHT Transfers on Death

- in relation to the general component, all the personal representatives (or, if there are none, all those who are liable to inheritance tax attributable to the property in the component); and

- in relation to property forming part of the estate under the gifts with reservation provisions, all those in whom the property concerned is vested when the election is to be made.

[*IHTA 1984, Sch 1A paras 7(6)(7), 9*].

(c) Where there is more than one component, the available nil-rate band is apportioned between the components for the purposes of step 2, in proportion to the amounts determined at step 1 for each component. [*IHTA 1984, Sch 1A para 5*].

322 Trusts for Bereaved Minors

[*IHTA 1984, ss 71A–71H*]

322.1 TRANSITIONAL PROVISIONS FOR PRE-22 MARCH 2006 TRUSTS

(A)

Jacob dies in 2004. Under the terms of his Will he leaves his estate on accumulation and maintenance trusts for the benefit of his two children, Lisa and Luke, then aged one and two. The children are to become absolutely entitled to their share of the settled property at 18.

From its creation in 2004 until 21 March 2006 the trust is within the regime for ACCUMULATION AND MAINTENANCE TRUSTS (**301**).

On and after 22 March 2006 the trust is a trust for bereaved minors within *IHTA 1984, ss 71A–71C*. No IHT charges will arise on the children becoming absolutely entitled, on the death of either of the children, or on the settled property being paid or applied for their advancement or benefit.

Notes

(a) To qualify as a trust for a bereaved minor, the settlement (whether the settled property is settled before, on or after 22 March 2006), must be for the benefit of a bereaved minor and must be established under the Will of a deceased parent (including a step-parent or other person with parental responsibility) of the minor, on the intestacy of a parent or under the Criminal Injuries Compensation Scheme. The minor must become absolutely entitled to the settled property and any income arising (including accumulated income) on or before attaining the age of 18. [*IHTA 1984, s 71A*]. See IHTM42815 and *Simon's Taxes* I5.546.

(b) Existing accumulation and maintenance trusts which meet the above conditions are treated as trusts for bereaved minors from 22 March 2006. [*IHTA 1984, s 71(1B)*].

(B)

The facts are as in (A) above, except that the children become absolutely entitled only at 25.

From its creation in 2004 until 5 April 2008 the trust is within the regime for ACCUMULATION AND MAINTENANCE TRUSTS (**301**).

On and after 6 April 2008, the trust is an 18-to-25 trust within *IHTA 1984, ss 71D–71G*. See **301.2(A)** ACCUMULATION AND MAINTENANCE TRUSTS.

Notes

(a) The settlement does not qualify as a trust for bereaved minors as the beneficiaries do not become entitled absolutely to settled property on or before attaining age 18.

(b) On its failure as an accumulation and maintenance settlement, the trust qualifies as an 18-to-25 trust under both the transitional provisions of *IHTA 1984, s 71D(3)(4)* and the bereaved minors provisions of *IHTA 1984, s 71D(1)(2)*. See IHTM42815, IHTM42816 and *Simon's Taxes* I5.551, I5.552.

322.1 IHT   Trusts for Bereaved Minors

(c)   On 6 April 2008, the settlement ceases to be an accumulation and maintenance trust because the remaining beneficiaries do not become entitled absolutely to settled property on or before attaining age 18 as required from that date (see note (b) to **301.1** ACCUMULATION AND MAINTENANCE TRUSTS). No charge to IHT arises and the settlement becomes an 18-to-25 trust.

(C)

The facts are as in (A) above, except that the children become entitled only to an interest in possession on attaining the age of 18.

From its creation in 2004 until 5 April 2008 the trust is within the regime for ACCUMULATION AND MAINTENANCE TRUSTS **(301)**.

On and after 6 April 2008, the trust is a relevant property trust, subject to the rules in **320**SETTLEMENTS: RELEVANT PROPERTY.

Note

(a)   After 5 April 2008, the settlement does not qualify as an accumulation and maintenance settlement, a trust for bereaved minors or an 18-to-25 trust as the beneficiaries take only an interest in possession at age 18.

323 Trusts for Disabled Persons

[*IHTA 1984, ss 74, 89, 89A*]

323.1 PROPERTY SETTLED BEFORE 10 MARCH 1981

In 1973 Q settled £50,000 in trust mainly for his disabled son P, but with power to apply property to his daughter S. On 1 January 2021 the trustees advanced £5,000 gross to S on her marriage.

There will be a charge to IHT on the payment to S.

The relevant period is the period from settlement of the funds or, if later, 13 March 1975, to 1 January 2021, i.e. 183 complete quarters.

The rate of IHT is the aggregate of

0.25% for each of the first	40	quarters	10.00%
0.20% for each of the next	40	quarters	8.00%
0.15% for each of the next	40	quarters	6.00%
0.10% for each of the next	40	quarters	4.00%
0.05% for each of the next	23		1.15%
	183		29.15%

IHT payable is £5,000 × 29.15% = £1,458

323.2 PROPERTY SETTLED AFTER 9 MARCH 1981 AND BEFORE 8 APRIL 2013

Assume the facts in 323.1 above except that the settlement was made on 1 July 1982.

If the trust secures that not less than half the settled property which is applied during P's life is applied for his benefit, then P is treated as beneficially entitled to an interest in possession in the settled property. The transfer to S is a potentially exempt transfer which may become chargeable in the event of P's death within seven years of the transfer. The gift in consideration of marriage exemption applies (£1,000 on a gift from brother to sister) subject to the required notice.

Otherwise, the trust is discretionary and the IHT liability, if any, would be calculated under the rules applying to SETTLEMENTS: RELEVANT PROPERTY (320).

323.3 PROPERTY SETTLED AFTER 7 APRIL 2013

Assume the facts in 323.1 above except that the settlement was made on 1 July 2013.

The trustees have the power to apply amounts otherwise than for the benefit of the disabled person in excess of the annual limit. The annual limit is the lower of £3,000 and 3% of the maximum value of the settled property in the period in question (in this case £1,500).

The trust is discretionary and falls within the rules applying to SETTLEMENTS: RELEVANT PROPERTY (320).

323.4 IHT   Trusts for Disabled Persons

323.4 SELF-SETTLEMENT BY PERSON WITH CONDITION EXPECTED TO LEAD TO DISABILITY

[*IHTA 1984, s 89A*]

On 31 July 2020 X, who is in the early stages of Alzheimer's disease and currently resides in a care home, settles £300,000 into discretionary trust for his benefit in the future.

X is treated as beneficially entitled to an interest in possession in the settled property. The transfer into settlement of the property is a potentially exempt transfer which may become chargeable in the event of X's death within seven years of the transfer. See *Simon's Taxes* I5.207

324 Trusts for Employees

[*IHTA 1984, s 72*]

324.1 POSITION OF THE TRUST

A qualifying trust for employees of a close company was created on 1 July 1991. On 4 May 2001, £15,000 is paid to a beneficiary who is a participator in the close company and holds 15% of the issued ordinary shares. On 4 August 2020, the whole of the remaining fund of £200,000 ceases to be held on qualifying trusts.

4 May 2001

There is a charge to IHT. The relevant period is the period from 1 July 1991 to 4 May 2001, i.e. 39 complete quarters.

The rate of tax is

0.25% for 39 quarters = 9.75%

$$\text{IHT payable is } \frac{9.75}{100 - 9.75} \times £15,000 = £1,620$$

1 July 2001 and 1 July 2011

There is no liability at the ten-year anniversaries.

4 August 2020

There is a charge to IHT. The relevant period is the period from 1 July 1991 to 4 August 2020, i.e. 116 complete quarters.

The rate of tax is

0.25% for 40 quarters =	10.00%
0.20% for 40 quarters =	8.00%
0.15% for 36 quarters =	5.40%
	23.40%

IHT payable is £200,000 × 23.4% = £46,800

Note

(a) See IHTM42981–IHTM42988 and *Simon's Taxes* I5.631.

325 Valuation

325.1 LAND SOLD WITHIN FOUR YEARS OF DEATH
[*IHTA 1984, ss 190–198*]

(A)

A (a bachelor) died on 1 May 2017 owning four areas of land, as follows.

(i)   10 acres valued at death £50,000

(ii) 15 acres valued at death £60,000

(iii) 20 acres valued at death £60,000

(iv) 30 acres valued at death £70,000

He also owned a freehold house valued at death at £100,000.

In the four years following A's death, his executors made the following sales.

(A) Freehold house sold 15.11.17, proceeds £103,000, expenses £2,000.

(B) Land area (iii) sold 1.6.19, proceeds £59,500, expenses £1,500.

(C) Land area (ii) sold 8.8.20, proceeds £57,000, expenses £1,000.

(D) Land area (iv) sold 19.9.20, proceeds £82,000, expenses £3,000.

The following revisions must be calculated on a claim under IHTA 1984, Pt VI, Chapter IV

	£	
Gross sale proceeds of house	103,000	
Deduct probate value	(100,000)	£3,000
Gross sale proceeds of land area (ii)	57,000	
Deduct probate value	(60,000)	£(3,000)
Gross sale proceeds of land area (iii)	59,500	
Deduct probate value	(60,000)	£(500)

Notes

(a) The sale of area (iii) is disregarded as the loss on sale (before allowing for expenses) is less than 5% of £60,000 (£3,000) and is also lower than £1,000. [*IHTA 1984, s 191*]. See IHTM33083 and *Simon's Taxes* I4.312.

(b) The overall allowable reduction on all sales is therefore nil even though there is a loss after expenses.

(c) For deaths after 15 March 1990, a sale *for less than the value at death* which is made in the fourth year after death is treated as having been made in the three years after death. [*IHTA 1984, s 197A*]. See IHTM33074 and *Simon's Taxes* I4.312.

325.1 IHT   Valuation

(B)   Further purchases of land

A died on 30 June 2020 owning a house and a seaside flat.

At death the valuations were

	£
House	100,000
Flat	50,000
	£150,000
Sales by the executors realised (gross)	
House proceeds 1.7.21	92,000
Flat proceeds 1.12.21	53,000
	£145,000

On 1 May 2021, the executors bought a town house for the daughter for £90,000 (excluding costs).

Initially relief is due of £(150,000 − 145,000) £5,000

Recomputation of relief

$$\text{Appropriate fraction} = \frac{\text{Purchase price}}{\text{Selling price}} = \frac{90,000}{145,000} = \frac{18}{29}$$

		House		Seaside Flat
	£	£	£	£
Value on death		100,000		50,000
Sale price	92,000			
Add (£100,000 − £92,000) × 18/29	4,966			
Revised value for IHT		(96,966)		
Sale price			53,000	
Deduct (£53,000 − £50,000) × 18/29			(1,862)	
Revised value for IHT				(51,138)
Revised relief		£3,034		£(1,138)
Total			£1,896	

Note

(a)   The purchase is taken into account because it is made within the period 30 June 2020 (date of death) and 1 April 2022 (four months after the last of the sales affected by the claim). [*IHTA 1984, s 192(1)*]. If a sale made in the fourth year after death was affected by the claim (under *IHTA 1984, s 197A*), it would *not* be taken into account in determining the above-mentioned period. [*IHTA 1984, s 197A(3)*]. See IHTM33161, IHTM33074 and *Simon's Taxes* I4.316, I4.317, I4.312.

325.2 RELATED PROPERTY

[*IHTA 1984, s 161*]

On the death of a husband on 31 October 2020, the share capital of a private company was held as follows.

	Shares	
Issued capital	10,000	
Husband	4,000	40%
Wife	4,000	40%
Others (employees)	2,000	20%
	10,000	100%

The value of an 80% holding is £80,000, while the value of a 40% holding is £24,000. In his Will, the husband left his 4,000 shares to his daughter.

The related property rules apply to aggregate the shares of

Husband	4,000	
Wife	4,000	
Related property	8,000	shares

Chargeable transfer on legacy to daughter

IHT value of 8,000 shares (80%)	£80,000
IHT value attributed to legacy of husband's shares (4,000)	£40,000

(Subject to 100% business property relief if conditions satisfied).

325.3 SHARES AND SECURITIES

Quoted shares sold within twelve months after death

[*IHTA 1984, ss 178–189*]

An individual died on 30 June 2020 and included in his estate was a portfolio of quoted investments. The executors sold certain investments within twelve months of death. The realisations were as follows

325.3 IHT Valuation

	Probate Value £	Gross Sales £
Share A	7,700	7,200
Share B	400	600
Share C	2,800	2,900
Share D	13,600	11,600
Share E	2,300	2,300
Share F	5,700	5,100
Share G	19,400	17,450
Share H	8,500	8,600
	£60,400	55,750
Incidental costs of sale		(2,750)
Net proceeds of sale		£53,000

On 1 September 2020, share J, having a probate value of £200 and still held by the executors was cancelled.

On 1 December 2020, share K, having a probate value of £1,000 has its stock exchange quotation suspended. On 30 June 2021, the investment is still held by the executors, its estimated value is £49 and the quotation remains suspended.

On 30 April 2021, the executors purchased a new holding for £1,750.

The executors would initially be able to claim a reduction of
(£60,400 − £55,750) + (£200 − £1) + (£1,000 − £49) = £5,800

After the purchase, the reduction is restricted as follows

$$\text{Relevant proportion} = \frac{\text{Reinvestment}}{\text{Total sales}} = \frac{1{,}750}{£55{,}750 + £1 + £49} = \frac{1{,}750}{55{,}800}$$

Original relief restricted by

$$\frac{1{,}750}{55{,}800} \times £5{,}800 = £182$$

Total relief £5,800 less £182   £5,618

Notes

(a) No costs of selling investments may be deducted from the sale proceeds.

(b) The cancelled shares are treated as sold for £1 immediately before cancellation. The suspended shares are treated as sold on the first anniversary of death at their value at that time (provided that value is less than their value on death). [*IHTA 1984, ss 186A, 186B*]. See IHTM34156, IHTM34157 and *Simon's Taxes* I4.302.

(c) The purchase is taken into account as it is made during the period beginning on date of death and ending two months after the end of the last sale taken into account (including deemed sales as in (b) above).

(d) The probate value of each of the investments sold will be adjusted, both for CGT and IHT purposes, to the gross sale proceeds plus the relevant proportion of the fall in value. Thus the probate value of share A will be revised from £7,700 to

$$£7,200 + \left(\frac{1,750}{55,800} \times (7,700 - 7,200) \right) = £7,216$$

(e) Although excluded from computation of the loss on sale for inheritance tax purposes, incidental costs of sale are deductible from proceeds in calculating CGT.

326 Woodlands

[*IHTA 1984, ss 114(2), 125–130, 208, 226(4), Sch 2 para 4*]

326.1 TAX CHARGE

(A)

A died owning woodlands valued at £275,000 being land valued at £200,000 and trees growing on the land valued at £75,000. The woodlands passed to his son D. The executors elected to exclude the value of the trees from the taxable estate on A's death. D died six years later leaving the woodlands to his daughter E. They were then valued at £400,000 being land at £250,000 and trees at £150,000. The rate of tax which would have applied to the value of trees on D's death was 40%, but once again the executors elected to exclude the value of the trees from his estate.

E sold the woodlands for £500,000, including trees valued at £180,000, four years later.

The IHT on the trees is payable when the trees are sold. The trustees of the settlement pay IHT at what would have been the marginal rate on D's death had the tax scale at the time of the sale applied on D's death, e.g. 40% on £180,000 (the proceeds of sale) = £72,000.

Note

(a) If D had gifted the land (with the trees) just before his death, the IHT would have become payable on the trees at what would have been the marginal rate on A's death had the scale at the time of the gift applied on A's death, on the value of the trees at the date of the gift. IHT would also have been payable on D's lifetime transfer (this being a PET but becoming chargeable by virtue of D's death shortly afterwards) but the value transferred by this transfer would have been reduced by the deferred IHT charge. See (B) below.

(B)

B died in 1985 leaving woodlands, including growing timber valued at £100,000, to his daughter C. The executors elected to exclude the value of the timber from the taxable estate on B's death. B had made prior transfers of £50,000 and his taxable estate (excluding the growing timber) was valued at £310,000.

On 1 February 2015 C gave the woodlands to her nephew N, when the land was valued at £355,000 and the growing timber at £125,000. N agreed to pay any IHT on the gift. C died in January 2021, and had made no prior transfers other than to use her annual exemptions each year.

IHT on B's death

No IHT is payable on the growing timber until C's disposal when tax is charged on the net value at that time. The rates are those which would have applied (using the death scale applying on 1 February 2015) if that value had formed the highest part of B's estate on death. The tax was payable on 1 September 2015.

Deferred IHT payable £125,000 at 40%	£50,000

326.1 IHT   Woodlands

IHT on C's lifetime transfer

IHT is payable on C's gift to N as C died within 7 years of the gift. The deferred IHT is deducted from the value transferred.

	£
Value of land and timber	480,000
Deduct deferred IHT	(50,000)
Chargeable transfer	£430,000
IHT at death rates	
On first £325,000	—
On next £105,000 at 40%	42,000
£430,000	£42,000
IHT payable at 20% of full rates (death between 6 and 7 years after gift)	£8,400
Total IHT payable	
Deferred IHT	50,000
Lifetime transfer	8,400
	£58,400

Note

(a) In the above calculations it has been assumed that the woodlands were not run as a business either at the time of B's death or at the time of C's gift. If B had been running the woodlands as a business, such that business property relief would have been available on his death, the amount chargeable on C's disposal would have been reduced by 50%, i.e. to £62,500, on which IHT payable would have been £25,000. [*IHTA 1984, s 127(2)*]. If C ran the woodlands as a business (whether or not B had done so), business property relief would be available on her gift to N provided N also ran the woodlands as a business, but would be given after the credit for the deferred IHT. (With business property relief now usually at 100%, the order of set-off is not so relevant). See *Simon's Taxes* 17.407.

		£
Value of land and timber		480,000
Deduct deferred IHT	say	(25,000)
		455,000
Deduct business property relief at, say, 100%		(455,000)
Chargeable transfer		Nil

Value Added Tax

401 Bad Debt Relief
402 Capital Goods
403 Catering
404 Hotels and Holiday Accommodation
405 Input Tax
406 Motor Cars
407 Output Tax
408 Partial Exemption
409 Records
410 Reduced Rate Supplies
411 Retail Schemes
412 Second-Hand Goods

401 Bad Debt Relief

[*VATA 1994, s 36; SI 1995 No 2518, Regs 165–172E; VAT Notice 700/18/13*]

401.1 PART PAYMENTS AND MUTUAL SUPPLIES

W Ltd has supplied goods to A Ltd. The sales ledger reveals the following amounts due

Invoice	Gross £	Net £	VAT £
16159 dated 31.7.20	487.39	406.16	81.23
15874 dated 12.7.20	364.19	364.19	—
14218 dated 12.6.20	238.04	238.04	—
14104 dated 10.6.20	256.58	213.82	42.76
	1,346.20	£1,222.21	£123.99
Less paid on account on 14104	(100.00)		
Amount due from A Ltd	£1,246.20		

A Ltd was, however, used by W Ltd for delivery work and there is one unpaid invoice for £143.75.

The bad debt relief claimable is as follows

	£
Amount due from A Ltd	1,246.20
Less amount due to A Ltd	(143.75)
Debt due from A Ltd	£1,102.45

The debt is attributed to

	Gross £	VAT £
Invoice 16159	487.39	81.23
Invoice 15874	364.19	—
Invoice 14218	238.04	—
Invoice 14104 (part) *	12.83	2.14
	£1,102.45	£83.37

The amount of bad debt relief claimable is £83.37.

*12.83 / 256.58 × £42.76 = £2.14

Notes

(a) Relief can be claimed provided the debt has been written off as a bad debt in the supplier's accounts and provided six months have elapsed from the date of supply and from the time when the consideration became due and payable.

401.1 VAT   Bad Debt Relief

(b) Where payments on account are specifically allocated by the customer, this allocation must be followed provided the amount paid covers the full value of the supply. General payments on account must be allocated to earliest supplies first, supplies on the same day being aggregated. Where the claimant owes money to the purchaser which can be set off, the amount of the debt for bad debt relief purposes must be reduced by the amount so owed.

401.2 SECOND-HAND GOODS

B, a second-hand dealer, buys a table for £400 and sells it for £500 under the margin scheme, i.e. his profit margin is £100.

If the customer only pays £450, bad debt relief claimable is

$1/6 \times £50 = £8.33$

If the customer only pays £350, bad debt relief claimable is

$1/6 \times £100 = £16.67$

Note

(a) Where a bad debt arises on goods sold under the margin scheme,
  (i) if the debt is equal to or less than the profit margin, relief may be claimed on the VAT fraction of the debt; and
  (ii) if the debt is greater than the profit margin, relief is limited to the VAT fraction of the profit margin.

401.3 REPAYMENT OF REFUND

In July 2020 a business sells goods for £120 (£100 plus £20 VAT). It receives no payment by the relevant date and claims bad debt relief of £20. It subsequently receives £75.00 from the customer for the goods.

The business must repay to HMRC the VAT element of the £75 received, calculated as follows.

$$\frac{75}{120} \times £20 = £12.50$$

402 Capital Goods

402.1 THE CAPITAL GOODS SCHEME

[*SI 1995 No 2518, Regs 112–116; VAT Notice 706/2/18*]

On 1 July 2013, A Ltd, a partly exempt business, acquired the freehold of a five storey office block, incurring VAT of £112,500. The premises are used as the head office administration block for the whole company. On 1 October 2020 the building is sold at a profit for £1.5 million to a company which only makes exempt supplies. The option to tax is not exercised.

A Ltd's partial exemption year runs to 31 March. Its claimable percentage of non-attributable input tax is as follows.

Year ended			
31 March 2014	80%	31 March 2018	75%
31 March 2015	90%	31 March 2019	85%
31 March 2016	75%	31 March 2020	90%
31 March 2017	60%	31 March 2021	95%

The input tax position is as follows

Year ended 31 March 2014 (Interval 1)
Initial input tax claim £112,500 × 80% =   £90,000

Year ended 31 March 2015 (Interval 2)
Additional input tax claimed

$$\frac{112{,}500}{10} \times (90-80)\% =$$ £1,125

Year ended 31 March 2016 (Interval 3)
Input tax repayable

$$\frac{112{,}500}{10} \times (80-75)\% =$$ (£562.50)

Year ended 31 March 2017 (Interval 4)
Input tax repayable

$$\frac{112{,}500}{10} \times (80-60)\% =$$ (£2,250)

402.1 VAT Capital Goods

Year ended 31 March 2018 (Interval 5)
Input tax repayable

$$\frac{112{,}500}{10} \times (80 - 75)\% =$$ (£562.50)

Year ended 31 March 2019 (Interval 6)
Additional input tax claimed

$$\frac{112{,}500}{10} \times (85 - 80)\% =$$ £562.50

Year ended 31 March 2020 (Interval 7)
Additional input tax claimed

$$\frac{112{,}500}{10} \times (90 - 80)\% =$$ £1,125.00

Year ended 31 March 2021 (Interval 8)
Additional input tax claimed

$$\frac{112{,}500}{10} \times (95 - 80)\% =$$ £1,687.50

Adjustment in respect of Intervals 9 and 10
Input tax repayable

$$2 \times \frac{112{,}500}{10} \times (80 - 0)\% =$$ (£18,000.00)

(£16,312.50)

Notes

(a) The adjustment period for buildings is normally ten years.

(b) For the interval in which the building is sold, the adjustment is calculated in the normal way as if it had been used for the whole of the interval. This applies whether it was sold on the first or last day of the interval. For the remaining intervals, the recovery percentage is nil as the option to tax has not been exercised and the supply of the building is therefore exempt.

(c) If the option to tax is exercised on the sale of the building in Interval 8, instead of input tax of £18,000 being repayable in respect of Intervals 9 and 10, further input tax is claimable of

$$2 \times \frac{112{,}500}{10} \times (100-80)\% = \qquad \underline{£4{,}500}$$

On the other hand, VAT of £300,000 is chargeable on the sale which is not recoverable by the exempt company, increasing the effective price to £1,800,000 which might not be acceptable to the purchaser.

(d) See IT **4.7** CAPITAL ALLOWANCES ON PLANT AND MACHINERY for the interaction between the VAT Capital Goods Scheme and capital allowances on assets within the scheme.

403 Catering

403.1 SPECIAL METHOD FOR CATERERS

[*SI 1995 No 2518, Regs 66–75; VAT Notice 727/12, paras 8.3–8.8*]

A fish bar sells both fried fish and chips and wet fish and seafoods. It also has a small restaurant. It is impractical for the owner to keep a record of each sale as it takes place. The business can, however, note its zero-rated supplies over a representative period which are

	£
Receipts from wet fish rounds	724
Shops sales of wet fish and seafoods	285
Sundries (cold leftovers)	28
	£1,037
Overall gross takings	£7,580

At the end of a given quarterly tax period, gross takings total £24,016.28.

Standard-rated percentage is

$$\frac{(7{,}580 - 1{,}037)}{7{,}580} \times 100 = 86\%$$

Output tax for the VAT period is

£24,016.28 × 86% × $\frac{1}{6}$ £3,442.33

Temporary reduced rate

In response to the impact caused to businesses in the hospitality sector as a result of the coronavirus (COVID-19) pandemic, the Government has temporarily reduced that rate of VAT due on catering and hot takeaway supplies to 5%. The rate has been temporarily reduced for supplies made between 15 July 2020 to 12 January 2021. The restaurant does not sell alcohol and all supplies that were standard rated are liable to the reduced rate during this period. The following calculation needs to be done during this period using the figures in the above example:

Reduced-rated percentage is

$$\frac{(7{,}580 - 1{,}037)}{7{,}580} \times 100 = 86\%$$

Output tax for the VAT period is

£24,016.28 × 86% × $\frac{1}{21}$ £983.52

403.1 VAT Catering

Notes

(a) If each sale can be recorded as it takes place, the normal method of accounting can be used. Otherwise either the Point of Sale scheme or, if the business can satisfy HMRC that it is unable to operate the Point of Sale Scheme, the above catering adaptation can be used.

(b) It is not necessary to include the cost of food used for free meals for family and staff but the full cost of any standard-rated items of food taken out of business stock for own or family use should be included.

(c) The representative period chosen depends on the nature of the business but HMRC must be satisfied that it takes account of hourly, daily and seasonal fluctuations. Details of the sample, including dates and times, must be retained and a new calculation must be carried out in each VAT period.

404 Hotels and Holiday Accommodation

404.1 STAYS OVER FOUR WEEKS.

[*VATA 1994, Sch 6 para 9; VAT Notice 709/3/13*]

For the period 15 July 2020 — 12 January 2021 the reduced rate applies to supplies of hotel and holiday accommodation (see below). This calculation is based on a 20% VAT rate applying to the transaction.

In 2020 weekly terms for accommodation, facilities and meals in a hotel are £720.00 (£600.00 + £120.00 VAT) of which £288.00 (£240.00 + £48.00 VAT) represents the charge for meals.

For the first four weeks, the VAT charge is the full £120.00 but thereafter a reduced VAT value may be calculated in one of the following ways. The proportion for meals has been taken to be 40% but this will not always be so.

(a) **If charges are expressed in VAT-exclusive terms**

	£	£
Total VAT-exclusive weekly charge	600.00	
Less VAT-exclusive charge for meals	(240.00)	48.00
	£360.00	
VAT-exclusive value of facilities (20% minimum)	72.00	14.40
VAT due		£62.40

Weekly terms are therefore £600 + £62.40 VAT.

(b) **If charges are expressed in VAT-inclusive terms and the total amount charged to the guest is reduced to take account of the reduced element of VAT**

VAT is as under (a) above but the calculation is

	£	£
Total VAT-inclusive charge	720.00	
Less VAT-inclusive charge for meals	(288.00)	48.00
VAT-inclusive charge for facilities and accommodation	432.00	
Less VAT included 1/6 × £432	(72.00)	
Balance (exclusive of VAT)	£360.00	
VAT-exclusive value of facilities (20% minimum)	72.00	14.40
VAT due		£62.40

The weekly terms are £600 + £62.40 VAT.

404.1 VAT   Hotels and Holiday Accommodation

(c) If charges are expressed in VAT-inclusive terms but the total amount charged to the guest is not reduced to take account of the reduced element of VAT

	£	£
Total VAT inclusive charge	720.00	
Less VAT-inclusive charge for meals	(288.00)	48.00
VAT-inclusive charge for facilities and accommodation	432.00	
Less VAT included *4/104 × £432	(16.62)	16.62
VAT-exclusive charge for facilities and accommodation	£415.38	
Total VAT		£64.62

The weekly terms are not reduced (i.e. £720.00 including £64.62 VAT).

Notes

(a) *At least 20% of the VAT-exclusive charge, after deducting meals, must be treated as being for standard-rated facilities. In this example, the 20% minimum has been used, hence the fraction

$$\frac{20 \times \text{facilities element}\%}{100 + (20 \times \text{facilities element}\%)} = \frac{20 \times 20\%}{100 + (20 \times 20\%)} = \frac{4}{104}$$

If the true value of facilities is more than 20%, the higher value must be used. At a specialist hotel, such as a health farm, the charge for facilities could be as high as 40% and the VAT charge would then be correspondingly higher.

(b) The taxable turnover of a hotel with many long stay guests is very different from its gross takings. It may not therefore need to apply for registration.

LONG STAY ACCOMMODATION — TEMPORARY REDUCED RATE FOR SUPPLIES OF HOLIDAY ACCOMMODATION

The Government has temporarily reduced the rate of VAT t 5% on supplies of hotel and holiday accommodation for the period 15 July 2020 to 12 January 2021. These calculations are based on the 5% VAT rate applying to the transaction.

Hotels and Holiday Accommodation   VAT 404.1

If charges are expressed in VAT-exclusive terms

	£	£
Total VAT-exclusive weekly charge	600.00	
Less VAT-exclusive charge for meals	(240.00)	12
	£360.00	
VAT-exclusive value of facilities (20% minimum)	72.00	3.60
VAT due		£15.60

Weekly terms are therefore £600 + £62.40 VAT.

If charges are expressed in VAT-inclusive terms and the total amount charged to the guest is reduced to take account of the reduced element of VAT

	£	£
Total VAT-inclusive charge	630	
Less VAT-inclusive charge for meals (VAT rate 5%)	(252)	12
VAT-inclusive charge for facilities and accommodation	378	
Less VAT included 1/21 × £432 (VAT rate 5%)	(18)	
Balance (exclusive of VAT)	£360	
VAT-exclusive value of facilities (20% minimum)	72	3.6
VAT due (5%)		£15.60

The weekly terms are £600 + £15.60 VAT.

Notes

(a) *At least 20% of the VAT-exclusive charge, after deducting meals, must be treated as being for standard-rated facilities. In this example, the 20% minimum has been used, hence the fraction

$$\frac{20 \times \text{facilities element\%}}{100 + (20 \times \text{facilities element\%})} = \frac{20 \times 20\%}{100 + (20 \times 20\%)} = \frac{4}{104}$$

If the true value of facilities is more than 20%, the higher value must be used. At a specialist hotel, such as a health farm, the charge for facilities could be as high as 40% and the VAT charge would then be correspondingly higher.

(b) The taxable turnover of a hotel with many long stay guests is very different from its gross takings. It may not therefore need to apply for registration.

405 Input Tax

405.1 REPAYMENT OF INPUT TAX WHERE CONSIDERATION NOT PAID

[*VATA 1994, s 26A; SI 1995/2518, Regs 172F–172J; VAT Notice 700/18/13*]

(A)

In 2020 B purchases goods for £1,200 (£1,000.00 plus £200.00 VAT) and reclaims the full amount of VAT. By the relevant date (see note (a)), it has only paid £500.00 (leaving £700 unpaid).

It must make a repayment of input tax to HMRC of

$$200 \times \frac{700}{1{,}200} = £116.67$$

(B)

After making the repayment of £116.67 to HMRC, B subsequently makes a further payment of £300 for the goods.

B can now reclaim VAT from HMRC of

$$116.67 \times \frac{300}{700} = £50.00$$

Notes

(a) Where a customer claims VAT on a supply as input tax and all or part of the amount due for that supply is not paid to the supplier within six months of

    (i) the date of the supply, or

    (ii) if later, the date on which the consideration for the supply becomes payable

the customer must make a refund to HMRC for the VAT period in which the end of the relevant six-month period falls. This does not apply where the cash accounting scheme is used (so that the date for the recovery of input tax is the date of payment).

(b) Where a customer is in dispute with the supplier, and the supplier agrees to extend the due date for payment of the amount in dispute, repayment is not required until six months after the agreed extended date for payment.

(c) Where, subsequent to making a refund to HMRC under (a) above, a customer pays the whole or part of the consideration for the supply in relation to which the input tax repayment was made, any entitlement to input tax on the supply is restored in proportion to the amount of consideration paid.

405.2 VAT   Input Tax

405.2 NON-BUSINESS ACTIVITIES

[*VATA 1994, s 24(5); VAT Notice 700, paras 32.1–32.7*]

A church receives income not only by way of donations, but also through the sale of books, cards and light refreshments in its bookcentre and coffee shop. For the first quarter its total income is £34,671.49 of which £15,246.22 is donations. VAT on purchases directly attributable to religious activities is £217.95, VAT on purchases related to the bookcentre and coffee shop is £738.95, VAT on general repairs, maintenance and overheads is £2,185.27.

Input tax is calculated as follows	£
VAT on purchases related to business activities	738.95
Add proportion of VAT on general repairs etc.	
$\dfrac{(34{,}671.49 - 15{,}246.22)}{34{,}671.49} \times £2{,}185.27$	1,224.33
	£1,963.28

Notes

(a) VAT on purchases directly attributable to religious activities (non-business) is not input tax and cannot be recovered.

(b) The calculation continues in the same way, quarter by quarter, until the VAT year end when an annual adjustment is made by applying the same calculation to the total figures for the year.

(c) There is no UK legislation covering the apportionment of VAT to arrive at input tax. If computations based on times, attendance, floor areas, etc. produce a fairer result, they can be used.

(d) If some element of business income arises from exempt supplies, input tax may have to be further apportioned to arrive at deductible input tax. See **408** PARTIAL EXEMPTION.

406 Motor Cars

[*VAT Notice 700/64/14*]

406.1 SCALE CHARGE FOR PRIVATE FUEL

[*VATA 1994, ss 56, 57, Schs 4, 6*]

L Ltd provides its employees with cars and pays all day-to-day running expenses, including the cost of any petrol used for private motoring. Each employee submits a monthly return showing opening and closing mileage, together with fuel and servicing receipts for the period. The company chooses to assess the VAT on petrol used for private motoring using the scale charge.

T, the sales director, has a car with CO_2 emission of 220g/km and puts in a monthly claim for April 2020 which includes petrol used for private motoring. The claim is supported with petrol bills totalling £176.49 and a service invoice for £288.00 (£240.00 plus VAT £48.00). The company prepares monthly VAT returns.

The company should code the expenses claim as follows

Debit		£
Servicing		240.00
Fuel £176.49 × $5/6$	147.08	
Scale charge note (a)	27.33	
		174.41
Input VAT — on service	48.00	
— on petrol £176.49 × $1/6$	29.42	
		77.42
		£491.83
Credit		
Expenses reimbursed to T		
£176.49 + £288.00		464.49
Output VAT		27.33
		£491.82

Note

(a) A fuel benefit scale can be used to assess a VAT charge where any petrol or other motor fuel is provided by registered traders for private journeys made by employees, directors, partners or proprietors. Where a trader opts to use the scale charge, all supplies of private fuel must be accounted for on that basis for the prescribed accounting period. The monthly scale charge for prescribed accounting periods beginning after 1 May 2020 for a car with CO_2 emission of 220g/km is £164. The VAT charge is therefore £164 × $1/6$ = £27.33.

407 Output Tax

[*VAT Notice 700, para 31.2*]

407.1 MIXED SUPPLIES

(A) **Apportionment based on cost of both supplies: VAT-inclusive price**

In July 2020 a VAT-inclusive price of £140 is charged for a supply of zero-rated goods which cost £23 and standard-rated goods which cost £40 (excluding VAT).

$$\text{Proportion of the total cost represented by standard-rated goods} = \frac{(40 + \text{VAT})}{(40 + \text{VAT}) + 23} = \frac{48}{71}$$

VAT-inclusive price of standard-rated goods = $^{48}/_{71}$ × £140 = £94.65

VAT included = £94.65 × 1/6 = £15.78

Tax value of zero-rated supply = £140 − £94.65 = £45.35

The total price is therefore apportioned

Value of standard-rated supply	78.87
VAT on standard-rated supply	15.78
Value of zero-rated supply	45.35
	£140

(B) **Apportionment based on cost of both supplies: VAT-exclusive price**

In July 2020 a VAT-exclusive price of £126 is charged for a supply of zero-rated goods which cost £23 and standard-rated goods which cost £40 (excluding VAT).

Proportion of the total cost represented by standard-rated goods = $^{40}/_{63}$

VAT-exclusive value of standard-rated goods = $^{40}/_{63}$ × £126 = £80

VAT on standard-rated goods = £80 × 20% = £16

Tax value of zero-rated supplies = £126 − £80 = £46

The total price is therefore apportioned

Value of standard-rated supply	80
Value of zero-rated supply	46
	126
VAT on £80 at 20%	16
	£142

407.1 VAT   Output Tax

(C) **Apportionment based on the cost of one supply only**

In July 2020 a VAT-inclusive price of £142 is charged for a supply of zero-rated goods which cost £26 and standard-rated services, the cost of which cannot be identified. A fair and reasonable uplift on the zero-rated goods, consistent with actual profit margins of the business, is 50%.

Value of zero-rated supplies = £26 + 50% = £39

VAT-inclusive price of the standard-rated goods = £142 − £39 = £103

VAT on standard-rated goods = £103 × $^1/_6$ = £17.17

The total price is therefore apportioned

Value of zero-rated supply	39.00
Value of standard-rated supply (103 − 17.17)	85.83
	124.83
VAT on £85.83 at 20%	17.17
	£142.00

(D) **Apportionment based on the cost of one supply only: annual calculation (Method 1)**

Assume that the figures in (C) above are representative of similar transactions and the total VAT-inclusive income from such transactions in the year is £25,000.

Zero-rated percentage = $^{39}/_{142}$ × 100 = 27.465%

Value of zero-rated supplies in year = £25,000 × 27.465% = £6,866

Consideration for standard-rated supplies in year = £25,000 − £6,866 = £18,134

Output tax due = £18,134 × $^1/_6$ = £3,022.33

(E) **Apportionment based on the cost of one supply only: annual calculation (Method 2)**

VAT-inclusive subscription income of £400,000 is received in a year in respect of supplies of zero-rated literature with direct costs of £42,000 and standard-rated services, the direct cost of which cannot be identified. The total costs of the business (excluding depreciation) amount to £250,000 in the year. A fair and reasonable uplift to the direct costs of the zero-rated goods to allow for indirect costs is 100%.

Direct cost of zero-rated supplies	42,000
Uplift of 100%	42,000
Full cost of providing zero-rated supplies	£84,000

Proportion of costs attributable to zero-rated supplies

$$\frac{84,000}{250,000} \times 100 = 33.6\%$$

Proportion of costs attributable to standard-rated supplies = 66.4%

Consideration for standard-rated supplies = £400,000 × 66.4% = £265,600

Output tax = £265,600 × $^1/_6$ = £44,266.66

(F) **Apportionment based on normal selling prices (market values): VAT-inclusive price**

A VAT-inclusive price of £200 is charged for a zero-rated supply (which would separately be charged at £50) and a standard-rated supply (which would separately be charged at £200 including VAT).

Proportion of the total normal price represented by standard-rated goods =

$$\frac{200}{200 + 50} = \frac{4}{5}$$

VAT-inclusive price of standard-rated goods = $^4/_5$ × £200 = £160

VAT included = £160 × $^1/_6$ = £26.67

Tax value of zero-rated supply = £200 − £160 = £40

The total price is therefore apportioned

Value of standard-rated supply (£160 − £26.67)	133.33
VAT on standard-rated supply	26.67
Value of zero-rated supply	40.00
	£200.00

408 Partial Exemption

408.1 STANDARD METHOD

[*SI 1995 No 2518, Regs 99–109; VAT Notice 706*]

In its tax year X Ltd makes the following supplies

	Total supplies (excl VAT)	Standard rated supplies (excl VAT)	Exempt supplies
	£	£	£
First quarter	442,004	392,286	49,718
Second quarter	310,929	266,712	44,217
Third quarter	505,867	493,614	12,253
Fourth quarter	897,135	876,387	20,748
	£2,155,935	£2,028,999	£126,936

Input tax for the year is analysed as follows

	Attributable to taxable supplies	Attributable to exempt supplies	Remaining input tax	Total input tax
	£	£	£	£
First quarter	36,409	4,847	11,751	53,007
Second quarter	20,245	311	5,212	25,768
Third quarter	34,698	1,195	10,963	46,856
Fourth quarter	69,707	5,975	9,357	85,039
	£161,059	£12,328	£37,283	£210,670

The proportion of residual input tax attributable to taxable supplies is calculated using the ratio of

$$\frac{\text{Value of taxable supplies}}{\text{Value of all supplies}}$$

expressed as a percentage and, if not a whole number, rounded *up* to the next whole number.

408.1 VAT Partial Exemption

	£	£
First quarter		
Input tax attributable to taxable supplies	36,409	
Proportion of residual input tax deductible		
$\dfrac{392{,}286}{442{,}004} = 88.75\%$		
£11,751 × 89% =	10,458	
		46,867
Second quarter		
Input tax attributable to taxable supplies	20,245	
Proportion of residual input tax deductible		
$\dfrac{266{,}712}{310{,}929} = 85.78\%$		
£5,212 × 86% =	4,482	
	£24,727	

The value of exempt input tax is £1,041 (311 + [5,212 − 4,482]). As this is not more than £625 per month on average and is less than 50% of all input tax in the quarter, all input tax in the quarter is recoverable.

	£	£
Deductible input tax		25,768
Third quarter		
Input tax attributable to taxable supplies	34,698	
Proportion of residual input tax deductible		
$\dfrac{493{,}614}{505{,}867} = 97.58\%$		
£10,963 × 98% =	10,744	
	£45,442	

Partial Exemption   VAT 408.1

	£	£

The value of exempt input tax is £1,414 (1,195 + [10,963 − 10,744]). As this is not more than £625 per month on average and is less than 50% of all input tax in the quarter, all input tax in the quarter is recoverable.

Deductible input tax		46,856

Fourth quarter

Input tax attributable to taxable supplies	69,707	

Proportion of residual input tax deductible

$$\frac{876{,}387}{897{,}135} = 97.69\%$$

£9,357 × 98% =	9,170	
		78,877
		£198,368

Annual adjustment

At the end of the tax year the company carries out an annual adjustment.

	£
Input tax attributable to taxable supplies	161,059

Proportion of residual input tax deductible

$$\frac{2{,}028{,}999}{2{,}155{,}935} = 94.11\%$$

£37,283 × 95% =	35,419
Deductible input tax for year	196,478
Deducted over the four quarters	(198,368)
Under declaration to be paid to HMRC	£(1,890)

408.2 VAT Partial Exemption

408.2 SPECIAL METHOD

[*SI 1995 No 2518, Regs 99–109; VAT Notice 706*]

The facts are the same as in **408.1** above except that HMRC allow X Ltd to use a special method and calculate the proportion of remaining input tax attributable to taxable supplies by the formula

$$\text{Residual input tax} \times \frac{\text{Input tax attributable to taxable supplies}}{\text{Total input tax}}$$

	£	£
First quarter		
Input tax attributable to taxable supplies	36,409	
Proportion of residual input tax deductible		
$£11,751 \times \dfrac{36,409}{53,007} =$	8,071	
		44,480
Second quarter		
Input tax attributable to taxable supplies	20,245	
Proportion of residual input tax deductible		
$£5,212 \times \dfrac{20,245}{25,768} =$	4,095	
	£24,340	

The value of exempt input tax is £1,428 (311 + [5,212 − 4,095]). As this is not more than £625 per month on average and is less than 50% of all input tax in the quarter, all input tax in the quarter is recoverable.

Deductible input tax	25,768
	70,248

Partial Exemption   VAT 408.2

	£	£

Third quarter
Input tax attributable to taxable supplies   34,698

Proportion of residual input tax deductible

$$£10{,}963 \times \frac{34{,}698}{46{,}856} = \qquad 8{,}118$$

                                                               42,816

Fourth quarter
Input tax attributable to taxable supplies   69,707

Proportion of residual input tax deductible

$$£9{,}357 \times \frac{69{,}707}{85{,}039} = \qquad 7{,}670$$

                                                               77,377
                                                             £190,441

Annual adjustment
At the end of the tax year the company carries out
an annual adjustment.

                                                                  £
Input tax attributable to taxable supplies   161,059

Proportion of residual input tax deductible

$$£37{,}283 \times \frac{161{,}059}{210{,}670} = \qquad 28{,}503$$

Deductible input tax for year   189,562
Deducted over the four quarters   (190,441)
Under declaration to be paid to HMRC   £(879)

Note

(a)   In fact, this special method leaves X Ltd worse off than in **408.1** above, but is included here for illustration purposes.

409 Records

409.1 ADJUSTMENTS OF ERRORS ON INVOICES

[*VAT Notice 700, para 19.10; VAT Notice 700/45, paras 3.1–3.3*]

F sells a vast range of foodstuffs. Due to a programming error some wholesale packs of citric acid are incorrectly invoiced as zero-rated 'lemon flavouring'. The company decides not to raise supplementary invoices.

The following adjustment is required

	£
Citric acid sales	1,725.00
VAT charged	64.70
	£1,789.70
£1,789.70 × $1/6$ =	298.28
Less VAT charged	(64.70)
Additional VAT payable	£233.58

Note

(a) With many computer systems it is difficult to raise invoices or credit notes for VAT only. It is essential to ensure that any VAT amount will appear in the correct position on the documentation and will be posted by the system to the VAT account.

410 Reduced Rate Supplies

410.1 GRANT-FUNDED INSTALLATION OF HEATING EQUIPMENT

[*VATA 1994, s 29A, Sch 7A Group 3; VAT Notice 708/6/19*]

(A) **Full grant received covering all work**

A builder installs reduced rate heating equipment to a value of £300 and carries out other building work to a value of £700 (both excluding VAT) for C's main residence. A grant is received to cover the full cost of the work.

	£	£
Value of reduced rate supplies	300	
VAT thereon (5%)	15	
		315
Value of other supplies	700	
VAT thereon (20%)	140	
		840
Total cost covered by grant		£1,155

(B) **Apportionment where partial grant received which the grant-awarding body allocates to the installation of reduced rate heating equipment**

The facts are as in (A) above except that C receives a grant of £200 towards the installation of the reduced rate supplies and pays for the rest of the work personally.

	£	£
Value of reduced rate supplies which are grant-funded	200	
VAT thereon (5%)	10	
		210
Value of other supplies	800	
VAT thereon (20%)	160	
		960
Total cost including VAT		1,170
Less Grant received		(200)
Contribution from C		£970

410.1 VAT Reduced Rate Supplies

(C) **Apportionment where partial grant received which the grant-awarding body does not allocate**

The facts are as in (A) above except that C receives a grant of £200 towards the total cost and pays for the rest of the work personally.

Proportion of total grant allocated to reduced rate supplies

$$£200 \times \frac{300}{1000} = £60$$

	£	£
Value of reduced rate supplies which are grant-funded	60	
VAT thereon (5%)	3	
		63
Value of other supplies	940	
VAT thereon (20%)	188	
		1,128
Total cost including VAT		1,191
Less Grant received		(200)
Contribution from C		£991

411 Retail Schemes

[*VATA 1994, Sch 11 para 2(6); SI 1995 No 2518, Regs 66–75; VAT Notice 727*]

411.1 POINT OF SALE SCHEME

[*VAT Notice 727/3/20*]

N Ltd is a garden centre selling plants and gardening equipment. It also sells gardening books and magazines and barbecue supplies. Due to the product mix, the company splits takings at the time of sale using multi-button tills. At the end of its VAT period, standard-rated takings totalled £125,639.34, zero-rated sales of books, etc. totalled £1,549.28 and reduced rate sales of barbecue fuels totalled £194.32.

Output tax for the period is

$(£125,639.34 \times 1/6) + (£194.32 \times 1/21) = £20,939.89 + £9.25 = £20,949.14$

Notes

(a)   The method of calculation is the same for all VAT periods.

(b)   Taxable turnover must not exceed £130 million.

411.2 APPORTIONMENT SCHEME 1

[*VAT Notice 727/4/20*]

B Ltd has figures for the four quarterly periods in a VAT year as follows.

	Cost of standard-rated goods for resale (incl VAT)	Cost of reduced rate goods for resale (incl VAT)	Total cost of goods for resale (incl VAT)	Gross takings
	£	£	£	£
First quarter	9,429	78	15,701	21,714.55
Second quarter	10,418	124	17,840	24,316.51
Third quarter	9,972	312	15,919	21,899.29
Fourth quarter	7,076	25	11,293	16,149.61
	£36,895	£539	£60,753	£84,079.96

First quarter

Standard-rated sales are

$$\frac{9,429}{15,701} \times £21,714.55 = £13,040.35$$

411.2 VAT Retail Schemes

Reduced rate sales are

$$\frac{78}{15,701} \times £21,714.55 = £107.87$$

Output tax $=(£13,040.35 \times {}^1/_6) + (£107.87 \times {}^1/_{21}) =$ £2,178.53

By similar calculations output tax in the remaining quarters is

Second quarter	2,374.73
Third quarter	2,306.80
Fourth quarter	1,688.21
	£8,548.27

Annual adjustment

Standard-rated sales for the year are

$$\frac{36,895}{60,753} \times £84,079.96 = £51,061.35$$

Reduced rate sales for the year are

$$\frac{539}{60,753} \times £84,079.96 = £745.96$$

Output tax $= (£51,061.35 \times {}^1/_6) + (£745.96 \times {}^1/_{21}) = £8,545.75$

£2.52 must be added to the amount of VAT deductible for the fourth quarter.

Notes

(a) VAT-exclusive retail sales must be less than £1 million.

(b) Any supplies of services, home-grown or self-made goods, or supplies of catering must be dealt with outside the scheme.

(c) The annual adjustment must be made on 31 March, 30 April or 31 May each year, depending upon the VAT return periods. The first adjustment may therefore cover less than a full year.

411.3 APPORTIONMENT SCHEME 2

[*VAT Notice 727/4/20*]

Z Ltd owns a store and can analyse all purchases of stock for resale. It decides to use Apportionment Scheme 2 and calculates that the expected selling price, including VAT, of stock for retail sale at the commencement of using the scheme is £818,703, of which £331,379 represents standard-rated lines. Trading figures for the first four quarters under the scheme are

Retail Schemes VAT 411.3

	ESP of standard-rated goods received for resale (incl VAT)	Total ESP of goods received for resale (incl VAT)	Gross takings
	£	£	£
First quarter	393,741	1,009,199	835,265
Second quarter	400,829	891,685	829,524
Third quarter	314,227	905,859	1,018,784
Fourth quarter	493,207	1,235,087	1,486,381

Output tax is calculated as follows

First quarter

Opening stock	331,379	818,703
First quarter	393,741	1,009,199
	£725,120	£1,827,902

$$\text{Standard-rated sales} = \frac{725,120}{1,827,902} \times £835,265 = £331,345$$

Output tax = £331,345 × 1/6   £55,224.16

Second quarter

Opening stock	331,379	818,703
First quarter	393,741	1,009,199
Second quarter	400,829	891,685
	£1,125,949	£2,719,587

$$\text{Standard-rated sales} = \frac{1,125,949}{2,719,587} \times £829,524 = £343,435$$

Output tax = £343,435 × 1/6   £57,239.17

Third quarter

Opening stock	331,379	818,703
First quarter	393,741	1,009,199
Second quarter	400,829	891,685
Third quarter	314,227	905,859
	£1,440,176	£3,625,446

$$\text{Standard-rated sales} = \frac{1,440,176}{3,625,446} \times £1,018,784 = £404,702$$

Output tax = £404,702 × 1/6   £67,450.33

411.3 VAT Retail Schemes

	ESP of standard-rated goods received for resale (incl VAT) £	Total ESP of goods received for resale (incl VAT) £	Gross takings £
Fourth quarter			
First quarter	393,741	1,009.199	
Second quarter	400,829	891,685	
Third quarter	314,227	905,859	
Fourth quarter	493,207	1,235,087	
	£1,602,004	£4,041,830	

$$\text{Standard-rated sales} = \frac{1{,}602{,}004}{4{,}041{,}830} \times £1{,}486{,}381 = £589{,}136$$

Output tax = £589,136 × 1/6   **£98,189.33**

Notes

(a) For the fifth quarter, the method of calculation continues as in the fourth quarter above, the first quarter's figures being dropped and the fifth quarter's added to produce a rolling average across the last year.

(b) VAT-exclusive retail sales must be less than £130 million.

(c) Any supplies of services or supplies of catering must be dealt with outside the scheme.

(d) If it is not possible to perform a physical stock-take on the date of starting to use the scheme, the ESP values of goods received for resale in the previous three months may be used.

411.4 DIRECT CALCULATION SCHEME 1

[*VAT Notice 727/5/20*]

K runs a newsagent's shop. In addition to sales of newspapers and magazines (zero-rated), K also sells confectionery and tobacco (standard-rated), a limited range of food items (zero-rated) and barbecue fuels (reduced rate supplies). At the end of a VAT period, gross takings are £18,714.55. The expected selling prices of purchases in the period are £11,236.19 for standard-rated goods, £8,154.27 for zero-rated goods and £157.93 for reduced rate goods.

The minority goods are zero-rated and reduced rate supplies (i.e. the main goods are standard-rated).

Retail Schemes   VAT 411.5

Output tax is calculated as follows.

	£	£
Gross takings		18,714.55
Expected selling prices of zero-rated goods	8,154.27	
Expected selling prices of reduced rate goods	157.93	
		(8,312.20)
Standard-rated element of takings		£10,402.35
Output tax = (£10,402.35 × $^1/_6$) + (£157.93 × $^1/_{21}$) =		£1,741.25

Notes

(a) VAT-exclusive retail sales must be less than £1 million.

(b) Minority goods are those at the rate of VAT which forms the smallest proportion of retail supplies or, where goods are supplied at three rates of VAT, which forms the two smallest proportions.

(c) Supplies of services with the same liability as the minority goods must be dealt with outside the scheme, as must supplies of catering.

(d) If the minority goods are standard-rated and reduced rate supplies (i.e. the main goods are zero-rated) output tax is simply:

(ESP of standard-rated goods × $^1/_6$) + (ESP of reduced rate goods × $^1/_{21}$)

411.5 DIRECT CALCULATION SCHEME 2

[*VAT Notice 727/5/20*]

K decides to use Direct Calculation Scheme 2. When the scheme starts to be used, the opening stock, valued at expected selling prices, is

	£
Standard-rated goods	3,145.91
Zero-rated goods	2,250.34
Reduced rate goods	142.51

For the first four quarters, K's relevant details are

	ESP of standard-rated goods purchased	ESP of zero-rated goods purchased	ESP of reduced rate goods purchased	Gross takings
	£	£	£	£
First quarter	11,236.19	8,154.27	157.93	18,714.55
Second quarter	9,075.02	11,667.67	259.32	20,726.40
Third quarter	9,872.90	10,124.75	137.54	20,855.88
Fourth quarter	11,431.39	11,008.62	21.43	22,649.04
	£41,615.50	£40,955.31	£576.22	£82,945.87

411.5 VAT Retail Schemes

At the end of the fourth quarter, K's closing stock, valued at expected selling prices, is

	£
Standard-rated goods	4,217.22
Zero-rated goods	3,151.44
Reduced rate goods	119.19

First quarter

The minority goods are zero-rated and reduced rate supplies. Output tax is calculated as follows.

	£	£
Gross takings		18,714.55
ESP of zero-rated goods	8,154.27	
ESP of reduced rate goods	157.93	
		(8,312.20)
Standard-rated element of takings		£10,402.35
Output tax = (£10,402.35 × $^1/_6$) + (£157.93 × $^1/_{21}$) =		£1,741.25

Second quarter

The minority goods are standard-rated and reduced rate supplies. Output tax is calculated as follows.

(£9,075.02 × $^1/_6$) + (£259.32 × $^1/_{21}$) =   £1,524.85

Third quarter

The minority goods are standard-rated and reduced rate supplies. Output tax is calculated as follows.

(£9,872.90 × $^1/_6$) + (£137.54 × $^1/_{21}$) =   £1,652.03

Retail Schemes   VAT 411.5

Fourth quarter

The minority goods are zero-rated and reduced rate supplies. Output tax is calculated as follows.

	£	£
Gross takings		22,649.04
ESP of zero-rated goods	11,008.62	
ESP of reduced rate goods	21.43	
		(11,030.05)
Standard-rated element of takings		£11,618.99
Output tax = (£11,618.99 × $^1/_6$) + (£21.43 × $^1/_{21}$) =		£1,937.52

The annual adjustment is as follows

The minority goods are zero-rated and reduced rate supplies. Output tax is calculated as follows.

	£	£
Gross takings		82,945.87
Less zero-rated goods		
opening stock	2,250.34	
ESP of goods purchased	40,955.31	
	43,205.65	
closing stock	3,151.44	
		(40,054.21)
		42,891.66
Less reduced rate goods		
opening stock	142.51	
ESP of goods purchased	576.22	
	718.73	
closing stock	119.19	
		(599.54)
Standard-rated element of takings		£42,292.12
Output tax = (£42,292.12 × $^1/_6$) + (£599.54 × $^1/_{21}$) =		7,077.24
Output tax already calculated		
£1,741.25 + £1,524.85 + £1,652.03 + £1,937.52		6,855.65
Additional VAT payable with return for fourth quarter		£221.59

411.5 VAT Retail Schemes

Notes

(a) VAT-exclusive retail sales must be less than £130 million.

(b) Minority goods are those at the rate of VAT which forms the smallest proportion of retail supplies or, where goods are supplied at three rates of VAT, which forms the two smallest proportions.

(c) Supplies of services with the same liability as the minority goods must be dealt with outside the scheme, as must supplies of catering.

412 Second-Hand Goods

412.1 PART EXCHANGE

[*VAT Notice 718, para 13.6*]

A car dealer sells a car for £2,000 cash plus a car for which £1,000 is allowed in part exchange.

Selling price. A selling price of £3,000 must be entered in the stock book.

Purchase price. As the car taken in exchange is eligible to be resold under the scheme, the amount allowed in part exchange (£1,000) is the purchase price. The purchase must also be recorded in the stock book.

412.2 GLOBAL ACCOUNTING SCHEME — NEGATIVE MARGIN

[*SI 1995/1268, Art 13; SI 1999/3120; VAT Notice 718, para 14.8*]

A dealer starts to use the global accounting scheme and values the opening stock on hand at £10,000. In the first VAT period, the total purchases from the purchase summary are £2,000 and the sales from the sales summary are £8,000. In the second VAT period purchases are £1,000 and sales are £7,000.

The margin for the first VAT period is

£8,000 − (£10,000 + £2,000) = (£4,000)

There is a negative margin and no VAT is due. The negative margin is carried forward to the next period.

The margin for the second VAT period is

£7,000 − (£4,000 + £1,000) = £2,000

VAT due = £2,000 × $^1/_6$ = £333.33

Notes

(a) If there is a negative margin (because total purchases exceed total sales), no VAT is due and the negative margin is carried forward to the following VAT period for inclusion in the calculation of the total purchases of that period.

(b) A negative margin cannot be set off against other VAT due in the same VAT period on transactions outside the global accounting scheme.

412.3 VAT   Second-Hand Goods

412.3 AUCTIONEERS' SCHEME

[*SI 1992/3122, Art 8(7); SI 1995/1268, Art 12(7); VAT Notice 718/2, paras 3.1, 8.3*]

Goods are sold at auction for £1,000 (the hammer price). Commission is charged to the seller at 10% net of VAT and a buyer's premium is charged of 15% net of VAT.

Commission = (£1,000 × 10%) + 20% VAT =	£120
Purchase price = £1,000 − £120 =	£880
Buyer's premium = (£1,000 × 15%) + 20% VAT =	£180
Selling price = £1,000 + £180 =	£1,180
Margin = £1,180 − £880 =	£300
Output tax = £300 × $^1/_6$ =	£50

Note

(a) The purchase price, selling price, margin and VAT due are calculated from the successful bid price (hammer price) and commission and other charges.

'*Purchase price*' is the hammer price less commission payable to the auctioneer under the contract with the seller for the sale of the goods.

'*Selling price*' is the hammer price plus the consideration for any supply of services by the auctioneer to the purchaser (e.g. buyer's premium) in connection with the sale of the goods.

The margin is the difference between the purchase price and the selling price. The margin is regarded as being VAT-inclusive i.e. the VAT included is VAT-inclusive margin × VAT fraction (currently $^1/_6$).

National Insurance Contributions

- 501 Age Exception
- 502 Aggregation of Earnings
- 503 Annual Maximum
- 504 Class 1 Contributions: Employed Earners
- 505 Class 1A Contributions: Benefits in Kind
- 506 Class 1B Contributions: PAYE Settlement Agreements
- 507 Class 4 Contributions: On Profits of a Trade etc.
- 508 Company Directors
- 509 Deferment of Payment
- 510 Earnings from Self-Employment
- 511 Earnings Periods
- 512 Intermediaries
- 513 Partners

501 Age Exception

501.1 PERSONS OVER PENSIONABLE AGE

[*SSCBA 1992, s 6(3); SI 2001 No 1004, Regs 7, 28, 29*]

(A)

Gail is approaching state pensionable age on 6 November 2020. She currently works full time earning £500 per week as a PA to the managing director. Although she will attain state pension age in November 2020 both she and the wages clerk are unsure what the position will be if she goes part time for three days of the week from that date earning £300 per week. The managing director is also keen to know whether he will have to pay more Class 1 secondary contributions by employing Jean for the other two days she is away on a wage of £200.

Gail must present her birth certificate or passport to her employer so that the company has proof that age exception is warranted. If it is found that no proof has been obtained then the employer is entirely liable for any underpayment. If Gail does not want her employer to see her birth certificate or passport, HMRC will send her a letter to show them instead. Gail should write to National Insurance Contributions and Employers Office, HM Revenue and Customs BX9 1AN explaining why she doesn't want her employer to see her birth certificate or passport. Although Class 1 primary contributions will cease, the employer must continue to deduct secondary contributions even though Gail is over pensionable age.

	£	Primary* %	£	Secondary† %	£
		Weekly class 1 liabilities before job sharing arrangement in force			
Gail	500.00	Nil/12	38.04	Nil/13.8	45.67
		Weekly class 1 liabilities when job sharing arrangement in force			
Gail	300.00	Nil	Nil	Nil/13.8	18.07
Jean	200.00	Nil/12	2.04	Nil/13.8	4.28
	£500.00		£2.04		£22.35

(* Nil% × £183, 12% × remainder.) († Nil% × £169, 13.8% × remainder.)

The employer will save £23.32 (i.e. £45.67 – £22.35) each week in secondary contributions under the job sharing arrangement.

501.1 NIC   Age Exception

Notes

(a) An employed earner who attains pensionable age is excepted from liability for Class 1 primary contributions on any earnings paid to him or for his benefit after the date he attains pensionable age. The exception does not apply to earnings which would normally have fallen to be paid to him or for his benefit before that date. Earnings which, though paid before he attains pensionable age, would normally fall to be paid to him in a subsequent tax year are within the exception. [*SSCBA 1992, s 6(3); SI 2001 No 1004, Regs 28, 29*]. See *Simon's Taxes* E8.269.

(b) See (B) below for the age at which a person attains state pensionable age.

(B) **Pensionable age**

Imogen was born on 29 March 1954. Applying the table in *Pensions Act 1995, Sch 4 Part 1*, she attains pensionable age on 6 September 2019. Peter was born on 29 March 1955. He attains pensionable age on reaching the age of 66, i.e. on 29 March 2021.

Note

(a) Pensionable age is, in the case of a man born before 6 December 1953, 65, and in the case of a woman born before 6 April 1950, 60. For women born after 5 April 1950 and before 6 October 1954, and for men born after 5 December 1953 and before 6 October 1954, pensionable age rises on a sliding scale contained in *Pensions Act 1995, Sch 4 Pt 1*. For men and women born after 5 October 1954 and before 6 April 1960 pensionable age is 66. A sliding scale under *Sch 4 Pt 1* again applies to gradually increase the pensionable age for men and women born after 5 April 1960 and before 6 March 1961, so that for men and women born after 5 April 1961 pensionable age is 67. A further phased increase applies to those born on or after 6 April 1977 and before 6 April 1978, so that the pensionable age for those born after 5 April 1978 will be 68. The Government announced in 2017 that it intends to amend the law so that the increase in pensionable age to 68 will apply to those born after 5 April 1970. The necessary legislation has not, however, been enacted. See *Simon's Taxes* E8.269.

502 Aggregation of Earnings

502.1 EMPLOYMENT UNDER THE SAME EMPLOYER

[*SSCBA 1992, Sch 1 para 1(1)(a); SI 2001 No 1004, Reg 14*]

(A) Earnings paid for different periods

Arnold is employed by Bauble Bros as a sales representative. He receives a weekly salary, quarterly commission and an annual bonus. Under the earnings period rules, his earnings period is a week (unless HMRC has directed otherwise). In the week ended 10 July 2020, Arnold receives:

	£
Salary for the week ended 10 July 2020	100
Commission for the quarter ended 30 June 2020	387
Bonus for the year ended 31 December 2019	3,300
	£3,787

By virtue of *SSCBA 1992, Sch 1 para 1(1)(a)*, the contribution liabilities of Arnold and of Bauble Bros for that week will be assessed by reference to a single amount of earnings of £3,787.

Notes

(a) All earnings paid to an earner in a given earnings period in respect of one or more employed earner's employments under the same employer are aggregated and treated as a single payment of earnings in respect of one such employment. [*SSCBA 1992, Sch 1 para 1(1)(a); SI 2001 No 1004, Reg 14*]. See **511.1(A)(B)** EARNINGS PERIODS for the rules which determine the earnings period where there are multiple regular pay patterns.

(b) Aggregation does not take place if it is not reasonably practicable. [*SI 2001 No 1004, Reg 14*].

(c) See **502.5** below where an earner has been, but is no longer, a director of a company.

(B) More than one contract

Throughout 2020/21, Cyril is employed by the Dainty Dish Restaurant under two separate contracts of service. As barman, he is paid earnings of £150 per week and, as wine waiter, he is paid earnings of £200 per week.

502.1 NIC   Aggregation of Earnings

The total weekly Class 1 liability is as follows.

			£
Primary	£183	@ Nil	Nil
	£167	@ 12%	20.04
	£350		20.04
Secondary	£169	@ Nil	Nil
	£181	@ 13.8%	24.97
	£350		£24.97
			£45.01

Notes

(a) Because C's two employments are under the same employer, all his earnings in respect of those employments are aggregated and treated as a single weekly payment of £350 in respect of a single employment. [*SSCBA 1992, Sch 1 para 1(1)(a)*].

(b) See notes (b) and (c) to (A) above.

502.2 DIFFERENT EMPLOYMENTS, SECONDARY CONTRIBUTORS IN ASSOCIATION

[*SSCBA 1992, Sch 1 para 1(b); SI 2001 No 1004, Reg 15(1)(a)*]

Throughout 2020/21, Edward is paid earnings of £186 per week in respect of his employment with Fabrications Ltd; £167 per week in respect of his employment with Gudroofs; £88 per week in respect of his employment with Homemakers Ltd and £103 per week with Interiors Ltd. H is in voluntary liquidation under John, a liquidator, but is continuing to play its part in a joint project with F, G and I involving the development of a residential building site. Edward is employed by G, H and I in connection with that joint project but his employment with F is in connection with unassociated activities in which that company is involved.

There are four secondary contributors who pay earnings to Edward: F, G, J (as liquidator of H) and I, but of these only F, G and I are carrying on business in association (J, as liquidator, is not), and of these only G and I are doing so in respect of Edward's employments. Accordingly, only the earnings Edward receives from G and I fall to be aggregated, with Class 1 contribution liabilities arising as follows.

Aggregation of Earnings   NIC 502.4

	£	Primary* %	£	Secondary† %	£
F	186.00	Nil/12	0.36	Nil/13.8	2.35
G	167.00				
I	103.00				
	270.00	Nil/12	10.44	Nil/13.8	13.93
J	88.00	Nil	Nil	Nil	Nil

(* Nil% × £183, 12% × remainder.)
(† Nil% × £169, 13.8% × remainder.)

Notes

(a) All earnings paid to an earner in a given earnings period in respect of more than one employed earner's employments by different secondary contributors who, in respect of those employments, carry on business in association with each other, are aggregated and treated as a single payment of earnings in respect of one such employment. [*SSCBA 1992, Sch 1 para 1(1)(b); SI 2001 No 1004, Reg 15(1)(a)*]. See NIM10004 and *Simon's Taxes* E8.242.

(b) See notes (b) and (c) to 502.1(A) above.

502.3 DIFFERENT EMPLOYMENTS, DIFFERENT EMPLOYERS ONE OF WHOM IS SECONDARY CONTRIBUTOR

[*SSCBA 1992, Sch 1 para 1(1)(b); SI 2001 No 1004, Reg 15(1)(b)*]

From 6 April 2020, Keith is employed by the Lively Lazarites Central Fund as an accountant at a salary of £193 per week. He is also remunerated by that fund at the rate of £186 per week as minister of the LL Free Church in Lincoln.

Under the provisions of *SSCBA 1992, s 6(4)* (which require the earnings from each employment to be viewed in isolation from the other) Class 1 contribution liabilities of £1.20 primary and £3.31 secondary would arise on the earnings of £193 per week. On the earnings of £186 per week, Class 1 contribution liabilities of £0.36 primary and £2.35 secondary would arise. As the fund is not only Keith's employer, however, but also the secondary contributor as regards the earnings paid to him as a minister of religion, his earnings must, by virtue of *SI 2001/1004, Reg 15(1)(b)*, be aggregated and, in consequence, Class 1 contributions of £23.52 primary and £28.98 secondary will be payable on the combined earnings of £379.

502.4 DIFFERENT EMPLOYMENTS, SECONDARY CONTRIBUTOR OTHER THAN ONE OF THE EMPLOYERS

[*SSCBA 1992, Sch 1 para 1(1)(b); SI 2001 No 1004, Reg 15(1)(c)*]

In 2020/21, Marveltipe Agency obtains temporary employment for Norma, a secretary, with O Ltd, P Ltd and Q Ltd. Through Marveltipe, Norma is paid weekly earnings of £98 from O, £108 from P and £78 from Q. Marveltipe also obtains work for Jean with O, P and Q. Through Marveltipe, Jean is paid monthly earnings of £2,500, £1,900 and £1,100 respectively.

Although the earnings are in respect of different employments and are paid by different persons, Marveltipe (though not itself one of Norma or Jean's employers) is the secondary contributor as regards those earnings (see *SI 1978 No 1689, Sch 3 para 2(a)*). Both

502.4 NIC   Aggregation of Earnings

Norma's and Jean's earnings must therefore be aggregated. Class 1 contributions for Norma will therefore be payable on earnings of £284 per week as if it were a single payment in respect of one employment. Class 1 contributions for Jean will likewise be payable on earnings of £5,500 per month.

Notes

(a) All earnings paid by different persons to an earner in a given earnings period in respect of more than one employed earner's employments where some other person is, by regulation, treated as the secondary contributor in relation to those earnings, are aggregated and treated as a single payment of earnings in respect of one such employment. [*SSCBA 1992, Sch 1 para 1(1)(b); SI 2001 No 1004, Reg 15(1)(c)*]. See NIM10006.

(b) But for the requirement to aggregate Norma's earnings, they would have escaped liability as each amount falls below the 2020/21 weekly earnings thresholds of £183 primary and £169 secondary. In Jean's case, primary Class 1 contributions would have been 12% of the earnings (less £792 threshold) from each source – subject to the annual maximum. Aggregation results in a single calculation on the combined earnings so that only 2% is deducted on earnings of £1,333 (total earnings £5,500 less UEL £4,167).

502.5 EARNINGS RELATING TO PERIODS OF FORMER DIRECTORSHIP

[*SI 2001 No 1004, Reg 8(5)(a)*]

Throughout 2020/21, Richard is employed by Stiffs Ltd as an embalmer at a salary of £2,000 per month. Until 31 December 2019 he had been a director of the company but had, on that date, resigned because of worsening health. In September 2020, the board votes him a bonus of £7,000 in respect of his services as director during the year ended 31 December 2019 and a further £5,000 in respect of his services as embalmer during the same period.

Class 1 contributions are as follows.

		Primary		Secondary	
Salary		%	£	%	£
£792/732		Nil		Nil	
£1,208/1,268		12	144.96	13.8	174.98
£2,000					
	(less than *monthly* UEL for primary contribution purposes £4,167)				
Bonuses					
£9,500/8,788		Nil		Nil	
£2,500/3,212		12	300.00	13.8	443.25
£12,000					
	(less than *annual* UEL for primary contribution purposes £50,000)				
Total			£444.96		£618.23

Aggregation of Earnings   NIC 502.6

Notes

(a) Where an earner who was, but is no longer, a director of a company receives earnings in any tax year after that in which he ceased to be a director, those earnings, insofar as they are paid in respect of any period during which he was a director, are not to be aggregated with any other earnings with which they would otherwise fall to be aggregated. [SI 2001 No 1004, Reg 8(5)(a)].

(b) An annual earnings period applies to the earnings relating to the period when Richard was a director. [SI 2001 No 1004, Reg 8(5)(b)]. See NIM12025 and Simon's Taxes E8.246.

(c) Were it not for Reg 8(5)(a), Richard's earnings in September 2020 would fall to be aggregated as the amounts are derived from different employments under the same employer (see 502.1(B) above).

502.6 AGGREGATION WITH GRATUITIES ETC. PAID SEPARATELY

Anthony runs a small hotel in which he employs Bonnie and Clyde as waiters. For the week ending 21 June 2020, Bonnie's earnings are £165 and Clyde's earnings are £196. On the face of it, no contribution liabilities arise as regards Bonnie's earnings as they fall below the thresholds of £183, and liability for primary and secondary Class 1 contributions as regards Clyde's earnings are at only 12% primary and 13.8% secondary on the earnings over £183 and £169 respectively. In the week concerned, however, guests have asked for tips of £50 to be added to their bills and Anthony has passed those tips to David, the hall porter, instructing him that Bonnie is to receive £25 and Clyde is to receive £25. In those circumstances, contribution liabilities for which Anthony is accountable are as follows:

		£		£
Bonnie	Class 1 primary:	183	@ Nil%	0.00
		7	@ 12%	0.84
		190		0.84
	Class 1 secondary:	169	@ Nil%	0.00
		21	@ 13.8%	2.89
		190		2.89
Clyde	Class 1 primary:	183	@ Nil%	0.00
		38	@ 12%	4.56
		221		4.56
	Class 1 secondary:	169	@ Nil%	0.00
		52	@ 13.8%	7.18
		221		7.18

Note

(a) Where tips, gratuities etc. are earnings for contributions purposes and their allocation is not carried out by the person who is the secondary contributor as regards the ordinary earnings of the employed earner to whom they are allocated, the secondary contributor must nevertheless aggregate the tips etc. with the ordinary earnings and account for Class 1 contributions on the aggregate amount. See HMRC leaflet CWG2 (2020), para 2.8.

502.7 NIC   Aggregation of Earnings

502.7   AGGREGATION FOR CLASS 4 PURPOSES

[*SSCBA 1992, s 15*]

Francis is in business as an interior decorator and as a furniture renovator. He is also an equal partner in a firm that supplies fitted kitchens. His interior decorating business was established several years ago with a 31 October accounting date but the furniture renovating business commenced on 1 May 2015 with a 30 April accounting date. The fitted kitchen partnership is long-established (with a 31 December accounting date) and F's share of profits one-half. Trading results adjusted in accordance with the tax and Class 4 rules are as follows

Year ended	Trade	
31 October 2017	Interior decorator	£10,000
31 October 2018	Interior decorator	£12,500
31 October 2019	Interior decorator	£13,500
31 October 2020	Interior decorator	£14,500
30 April 2017	Furniture renovator	£1,200
30 April 2018	Furniture renovator	£1,350
30 April 2019	Furniture renovator	£1,550
30 April 2020	Furniture renovator	£1,950
31 December 2017	Fitted kitchens	£28,500
31 December 2018	Fitted kitchens	£29,000
31 December 2019	Fitted kitchens	£32,000
31 December 2020	Fitted kitchens	£34,000

The amount of trading income chargeable to income tax, and in respect of which Class 4 contributions are calculated, for 2017/18 is as follows

	£
Interior decorator (current year basis)	10,000
Furniture renovator (current year basis)	1,200
Fitted kitchens (current year basis split according to profit share in 2017/18:1/2 × £28,500)	14,250
	£25,450

The amount of trading income chargeable to income tax, and in respect of which Class 4 contributions are calculated, for 2018/19 is as follows

	£
Interior decorator (current year basis)	12,500
Furniture renovator (current year basis)	1,350
Fitted kitchens (current year basis split according to profit share in 2018/19:1/2 × £29,000)	14,500
	£28,350

The amount of trading income chargeable to income tax, and in respect of which Class 4 contributions are calculated, for 2019/20 is as follows

	£
Interior decorator (current year basis)	13,500
Furniture renovator (current year basis)	1,550
Fitted kitchens (current year basis split according to profit share in 2019/20: 1/2 × £32,000)	16,000
	£31,050

The amount of trading income chargeable to income tax, and in respect of which Class 4 contributions are calculated, for 2020/21 is as follows

	£
Interior decorator (current year basis)	14,500
Furniture renovator (current year basis)	1,950
Fitted kitchens (current year basis split according to profit share in 2020/21: 1/2 × £34,000)	17,000
	£33,450

Note

(a) Class 4 contributions are payable in respect of all profits which are immediately derived from the carrying on or exercise of one or more trades, professions or vocations and are profits chargeable to income tax under *ITTOIA 2005, ss 5–23 (Pt 2, Ch 2)*. [*SSCBA 1992, s 15(1)*]. Profits must therefore be aggregated, but time apportionment to the tax year is not required. See also **513 PARTNERS**. See NIM70650 and *Simon's Taxes* E8.317.

503 Annual Maximum

503.1 CLASS 1 AND CLASS 2 LIMITATION

[SI 2001 No 1004, Reg 21]

For the whole of 2020/21, Finch is employed by Grebe at a salary of £3,100 per month, and was paid an annual bonus in March of £8,000. She was also employed by Heron at a salary of £1,875 per month. The Class 1 primary contributions paid on her earnings from her employed earner's employments are as follows

	£			£	£
Grebe	792.00	(monthly earnings threshold)	@ Nil%	0.00 × 11 =	0.00
(First 11 months)	2,308.00		@ 12%	276.96 × 11 =	3046.56
	3,100.00				3046.56
(March)	792.00	(monthly earnings threshold)	@ Nil%	0.00 × 1 =	0.00
	3,375.00		@ 12%	405.00 × 1 =	405.00
	4,167	(monthly UEL)			
	6,933		@ 2%	138.66 × 1 =	138.66
	11,100.00				543.66
(Total)					3,590.22
Heron	792.00	(monthly ET)	@ Nil%	0.00 × 12 =	0.00
	1083.00		@ 12%	129.96 × 12 =	1,559.52
	1,875.00				1,559.52
Total Class 1 paid:					5,149.74

On the face of it, F has paid excessive contributions since the notional annual maximum for 2020/21 is £4,954.44. It is therefore necessary to consider Finch's personalised maximum using the following numbered steps.

Step		£	£
1.	Calculate 53 × (UEL − primary threshold), i.e. 53 × (£962 − £183)		41,287.00
2.	12% thereof		4,954.44
3.	Earnings from each employment that falls between primary threshold and UEL: £2,308 × 11 = £25,388 £3,375 × 1 = £3,375		

503.1 NIC   Annual Maximum

Step		£	£
	£1,083 × 12 = £12,996	41,759	
4.	Deduct figure in step 1. from 3. (£41,759 − £41,287)	472.00	
5.	As the line above gives a positive figure, multiply by 2%		9.44
6.	Earnings from each employment which exceeds UEL	Nil	
7.	Multiply step 6 result by 2%		Nil
8.	Add steps 2, 5, 7 – this gives the personalised annual maximum		£4,963.88

The contributions paid do exceed this personalised maximum and, provided the necessary conditions are met, the excess, suitably adjusted, will be repayable.

Note

(a) Where an earner is employed in more than one employment (including self-employments), liability in any tax year for primary Class 1 contributions and, where payable, Class 2 contributions, cannot exceed an amount equal to 53 primary Class 1 contributions at the primary percentage payable on earnings at the upper earnings limit together with such other liabilities which arise at the additional 2% rate. [*SI 2001 No 1004, Reg 21*]. *Reg 21* sets out an eight step process for calculating an individual's personal maximum, as illustrated in this example. See NIM01251, NIM01270 and *Simon's Taxes* E8.266.

503.2 CLASS 4 LIMITATION

[*SI 2001 No 1004, Reg 100; SI 2016 No 352, Reg 15*]

(A)   **Case 1**

Kate is a self-employed artist with profits chargeable to income tax for 2020/21 (and requiring no further adjustment) of £15,500. She also pays Class 2 contributions for the year. Throughout 2020/21 she is also a director of Kate's Krafts Ltd. Her earnings from the company during the year were £13,450. Contributions are paid as follows:

		£
Class 1 primary	£9,500 × Nil%	0.00
	£3,950 (£13,450 − £9,500) × 12%	474.00
Class 2	£3.05 × 52 Note: There are 52 Sundays in 2020/21	158.60
		£632.60

Annual Maximum NIC 503.2

Her Class 4 liability is not to exceed the amount determined using the following steps:

Step		£	£
1.	Subtract the Class 4 lower profits limit from upper profits limit i.e. £50,000 − £9,500		40,500.00
2.	9% thereof	3,645.00	
3.	Add 52 times the weekly rate of Class 2 i.e. 53 × £3.05	161.65	3,806.65
4.	Subtract from Step 3 the amount of Class 2 paid and Class 1 paid at the main percentage rate (i.e. other than 2%)		
	Class 1	474.00	
	Class 2 − £3.05 × 52	158.60	(632.60)
			3,174.05

This produces a positive result which must be compared with Class 1 and Class 4 − payable at the main rate − and Class 2:

	£
Class 1	474.00
Class 2	158.60
Class 4 (£15,500 − £9,500) × 9%	540.00
	£1,172.60

As £3,174.05, is more than these potential liabilities, the figure of Class 4 payable at the main rate (i.e., 9%) is the figure calculated above (i.e. £540.00). This is a 'Case 1' situation and no further steps are necessary, because there is no liability at the additional rate of 2%.

Class 4 contributions ('Case 1', so equal to Step 4) £540.00

Note

(a) Where for any year Class 4 contributions are payable in addition to primary Class 1 contributions and/or Class 2 contributions, the liability for Class 4 contributions is not to exceed the amount which, when added to the primary Class 1 and Class 2 contributions (after applying the limitation in 503.1 above) equals the sum of the amount of Class 4 contributions which would be payable on profits equal to the upper annual limit plus 53 times the amount of a Class 2 contribution, plus an amount in respect of the additional 2% rate. [*SI 2001 No 1004, Reg 100*]. Reg 100 sets out a multi-step process for calculating each earner's personal maximum, with different further steps for each of three possible results at step four. See (B) and (C) below for cases 2 and 3. See NIM38506 and *Simon's Taxes* E8.321.

503.2 NIC   Annual Maximum

(B) **Case 2**

Iris is a self-employed dressmaker with profits chargeable to income tax for 2020/21 (and requiring no further adjustment) of £19,250. She pays Class 2 contributions for the year. Intermittently, when business is poor, she supplements her income by taking employment with Jeans Ltd. Her earnings from Jeans Ltd during the year were 32 weeks at £631. Contributions are paid as follows

		£
Class 1 primary	£183 × Nil% × 32	0.00
	£448 × 12% × 32	1,720.32
Class 2 Note: There are 52 Sundays in 2020/21	£3.05 × 52	15860
		£1,878.92

In the absence of a relieving provision, Class 4 contributions of £877.50 (i.e. (£19,250 - £9,500) @ 9%) would also be payable. However, the Class 4 liability is not to exceed the amount determined following the numbered steps in the legislation as follows:

Step		£	£
1.	Subtract the Class 4 lower profits limit from upper profits limit i.e. £50,000 − £9,500		40,500.00
2.	9% thereof		3,645.00
3.	Add 53 times the weekly rate of Class 2 i.e. 52 × £3.05	161.65	3,806.65
4.	Subtract from Step 3 the amount of Class 2 paid and Class 1 paid at the main percentage rate (i.e. other than 2%)		
	Class 1	1,720.32	
	Class 2 − £3.05 × 52	158.60	(1,878.92)
	This produces a positive result which must be compared with Class 1 and Class 4 − payable at the main rate − and Class 2:		1,927.73
	Class 1	1,720.32	
	Class 2	158.60	
	Class 4 (£19,250− £9,500) × 9%	877.50	
	As £1,927.73 is less than these potential liabilities, this is the figure of Class 4 payable at the main rate (i.e. 9%) − a 'Case 2' situation.	2,756.42	

Annual Maximum NIC 503.2

	Step		£	£
	5.	Multiply the result of Step 4 (i.e. £1,927.73) by 100/9	21,419.22	
	6.	Subtract the lower profits limit from the lesser of the upper profits limit and the amount of assessable profits	9,750.00	
	7.	Subtract the answer in 5 from the answer in 6. (If negative, treat as nil.)	Nil	
	8.	Multiply the above by 2%		Nil
	9.	Multiply the profits less the upper profits limit by 2%		Nil
	Class 4 contributions ('Case 2', so add 4, 8 and 9)			£1,927.73

In consequence, Iris's liability is limited to that of someone deriving equivalent total earnings exclusively from self-employment.

(C) **Case 3**

Jan is a self-employed printer with profits chargeable to income tax for 2020/21 (and requiring no further adjustment) of £50,850. Throughout the year she pays Class 2 contributions. Throughout the year she is also a director of Jan's Jeans Ltd. Her earnings from the company during the year were £51,050. Contributions are paid as follows:

		£
Class 1 primary	£9,500 × Nil%	0.00
	£40,500 (£50,000 − £9,500) × 12%	4,860.00
	£850 (£50,850 − £50,000) × 2%	17.00
Class 2	£3.05 × 52 Note: There are 52 Sundays in 2020/21	158.60
		£5,035.60

503.2 NIC   Annual Maximum

Her Class 4 liability is not to exceed the amount determined using the following numbered steps:

Step		£	£
1.	Subtract the Class 4 lower profits limit from upper profits limit i.e. £50,000 − £9,500		40,500.00
2.	9% thereof	3,645.00	
3.	Add 53 times the weekly rate of Class 2 i.e. 52 × £3.05	161.65	3,806.65
4.	Subtract from Step 3 the amount of Class 2 paid and Class 1 paid at the main percentage rate (i.e. other than 2%)		
	Class 1	4,860.00	
	Class 2 − £3.05 × 52	158.60	5,018.60
			(1,211.95)
	This produces a negative result, called 'Case 3' in the legislation − see Step 9 also. No Class 4 contributions are payable at the main (9%) rate.		
	The consequence is that the result of this Step 4 is treated as nil.		Nil
5.	Multiply the result of Step 4 by 100/9	Nil	
6.	Subtract the lower profits limit from the lesser of the upper profits limit and the amount of assessable profits	40,500	
7.	Subtract the answer in 5 from the answer in 6. (If negative, treat as nil.)	40,500	
8.	Multiply the above by 2%		810.00
9.	Multiply the profits less the upper profits limit by 2%		
	i.e. £51,050 − £50,000 × 2%		21.00
	Class 4 contributions ('Case 3', so add 4, 8 and 9)		£831.00

504 Class 1 Contributions: Employed Earners

Cross-reference. See also 502 AGGREGATION OF EARNINGS.

504.1 RATES

[*SSCBA 1992, ss 8, 9*]

Kevin employed Glenn at a rate of £1,100 per week from 30 March to 11 April 2020, making payment on Saturday each week.

Primary contributions due are:

Week ended 4 April 2020	166 ×	Nil%	Nil
	796 ×	12%	95.52
	138 ×	2%	2.76
			£98.28
Week ended 11 April 2020	183 ×	Nil%	Nil
	779 ×	12%	93.48
	138 ×	2%	2.76
			£96.24

Kevin's secondary contributions in respect of Glenn's employment are as follows:

Week ended 4 April 2020	166 ×	Nil%	Nil
	934 ×	13.8%	128.89
			£128.89
Week ended 11 April 2020	169 ×	Nil%	Nil
	931 ×	13.8%	128.47
			£128.47

Notes

(a) Most secondary contributors are entitled to an '*employment allowance*' for a tax year which is deducted from the amount due from secondary Class 1 contributions. The allowance is the lower of £4,000 and the amount of the contributions. From 6 April 2020, the employment allowance only applies to employers with an NIC bill of less than £100,000 in the previous tax year. See *National Insurance Contributions Act 2014, ss 1–8*. The allowance is ignored for the purpose of this example (and all of the examples in this work).

(b) An age-related secondary contribution rate of 0% applies to payments to any earner under the age of 21 on the date of payment, unless the earnings payment exceeds the relevant upper earnings limit for the earnings period, in which case the standard employer rate applies to any earnings above that limit. The 0% rate applies also to payments to relevant apprentices under the age of 25. [*SSCBA 1992, ss 9A, 9B; National Insurance Contributions Act 2014, s 9; National Insurance Contributions Act 2015, s 1*]. The primary contribution rate is unaffected, as are the Class 1A and Class 1B rates. See NIM01296 and *Simon's Taxes* E8.2102.

505 Class 1A Contributions: Benefits in Kind

505.1 THE PERSON LIABLE

[*SSCBA 1992, ss 10–10ZB*]

(A) **Benefits provided by third party**

Avant is a sales representative. Throughout 2020/21, his contract of service is with Ballade and they pay Avant his salary and commission, he is provided with a car and private medical insurance; but the car he uses is owned and made available to him by Cavalier, Ballade's parent company and they also pay the medical insurance premium. Because Avant has been provided with benefits and private use of the car, he is chargeable to income tax on an amount arrived at under *ITEPA 2003, ss 201–203*, and, in consequence, a Class 1A contribution is payable for 2020/21 in respect of Avant and the benefits provided to him. But, because the secondary Class 1 contribution on the last payment of earnings made to Avant in 2020/21 is paid by Ballade, Ballade must pay the Class 1A contribution even though Cavalier, not Ballade, is the person who owns the car and paid for the medical insurance.

Note

(a)   See NIM16350 and *Simon's Taxes* E8.272.

(B) **Two or more employers in tax year**

Herald works for Integra until 5 January 2021 when he changes jobs and takes up employment with Jetta. He is provided with a car (which is available for his private use) in each job. A tax charge will arise in respect of each car for 2020/21 so a Class 1A contribution will be payable in respect of each car for that year. Integra will pay secondary Class 1 contributions in relation to Herald's last earnings in his employment with Integra so Integra will be liable to pay a Class 1A contribution in respect of the car provided in that job, while Jetta will pay secondary Class 1 contributions in relation to Herald's last earnings in the tax year so Jetta will be liable to pay a Class 1A contribution in respect of the car provided in the second job.

(C) **Person succeeding to a business**

Orion works for Panda by whom he is provided with a car which is available for his private use. In October 2020, Panda sells his business to Quinta and Quinta continues to employ Orion and to allow him the private use of the car. As Quinta will pay a secondary Class 1 contribution in relation to Orion's last payment of earnings in 2020/21 in respect of the employment by reason of which the car is made available, he (to the exclusion of Panda) will be liable to pay the entire Class 1A contribution for the year in respect of the car – and any other benefits in kind – provided throughout the year.

If, of course, Orion had left Panda's employment before the change took place, the Class 1A liability in respect of the car provided to Orion from 6 April 2020 to the date of his leaving would rest with Panda.

505.2 NIC   Class 1A Contributions: Benefits in Kind

505.2 CARS PROVIDED FOR THE PRIVATE USE OF THE EMPLOYEE

(A) **Reduction for periods when car not available for use**

[*ITEPA 2003, s 143*]

Kadette takes up employment by Legend on 2 June 2020 and a petrol driven, 1,800 cc car (registered before 6 April 2020), with carbon dioxide emissions of 120 g/km costing £15,000 is made available for his business and private use. Petrol is also provided. On 15 June, Kadette is involved in an accident and the car is off the road until 8 July. On 21 September, Kadette is involved in another accident and this time the car is off the road until 29 October. On 2 November, Kadette is moved into a clerical post within the company where he no longer has the use of a company car.

The cash equivalent of the car and fuel benefits for 2020/21 are £4,350 (£15,000 × 29%) and £7,105 (£24,500 × 29%) respectively, but the car is unavailable for 57 days at the start of the tax year, for 37 days in September/October, and for 154 days at the end of the tax year. The period of repair in June/July does not count as unavailability because it lasted for only 22 consecutive days. The cash equivalents of £4,350 and £7,105 are, therefore, reduced by $^{248}/_{365}$ to £1,390 and £2,277.

Note

(a) See EIM25100 and *Simon's Taxes* E8.275

(B) **Car made available by reason of more than one employment**

[*SI 2001 No 1004, Reg 36*]

Robin works for Senator, Trevi and Uno and, by reason of those three employments, is provided with a petrol driven car costing £22,500 and with carbon dioxide emissions of 90 g/km. This is available for his private use but fuel is not provided. In 2020/21 the car benefit of £5,175 (23% × £22,500) is reduced by deducting from it

$$5,175 \times \frac{3-1}{3} = £3,450$$

In other words, each employer will be liable for a Class 1A contribution on £1,725 and the aggregate of those reduced scale amounts (3 × £1,725) is £5,175, i.e. the scale amount on which a single employer of Robin would have been liable for a Class 1A contribution.

(C) **Shared cars**

[*SI 2001 No 1004, Reg 36*]

Accord, Bacara and Clio work for Dedra and, by reason of their employments, are concurrently provided with one car for private use costing £15,790 and with carbon dioxide emissions of 85 g/km. This is available for private use but fuel is not provided. The scale charge in each case is £3,474 (£15,790 × 22%) but these three amounts are then each reduced by deducting

$$£3,474 \times \frac{3-1}{3} = £2,316$$

Class 1A Contributions: Benefits in Kind NIC 505.2

In other words, Dedra will be liable for three Class 1A contributions on £1,158 and the aggregate of those reduced scale amounts (3 × £1,158) is £3,474, i.e. the car benefit on which he would have been liable for a Class 1A contribution if he had made the car available to just one employee.

506 Class 1B Contributions: PAYE Settlement Agreements

506.1 CALCULATION OF CONTRIBUTIONS

[SSCBA 1992, s 10A]

Benevolent Ltd has 500 employees who are all provided with late night taxis each year prior to Christmas when a large, regular and anticipated order is placed by an overseas customer that is time sensitive. The taxi fares amount to an average of £50 per employee during the year ended 5 April 2021. Of the employees affected, 400 are basic rate taxpayers and the other 100 are higher rate (but not additional rate) taxpayers. Also, 100 employees receive expenses amounting to £2,000 in total relating to home to work travel (all higher rate taxpayers). Benevolent Ltd seeks a PSA for 2020/21. The PSA negotiation might be as follows:

	£	£
Tax due under PSA.		
Value of benefits provided to basic rate taxpayers		
(400 × £50)	20,000.00	
Tax thereon @ 20%	4,000.00	
Gross up tax $£4,000 \times \dfrac{100}{100-20}$		5,000.00
Value of benefits provided to higher rate taxpayers		
(100 × £50)	5,000.00	
Value of expenses provided to higher rate taxpayers	2,000.00	
	7,000.00	
Tax thereon @ 40%	2,800.00	
Gross up tax £2,800 × 100 / 100 − 40		£4,666.67
Total tax		£9,666.67
NICs due under PSA.		
Value of expenses otherwise liable for Class 1 NICs	2,000.00	
Class 1B NICs due @ 13.8% on £2,000		276.00
Value of benefits otherwise liable to Class 1A NICs	25,000.00	
Class 1B NICs due @ 13.8% on £25,000		3,450.00
Tax paid by employer liable to Class 1B charge	9,666.67	
Class 1B NICs due re tax paid by employer @ 13.8%		1,334.00
Total NICs and tax payable by Benevolent Ltd		£14,726.67

The tax and Class 1B is payable to HMRC on or before 19 October 2021 (22 October 2021 if paid electronically).

Note

(a) There is no requirement for employers to agree annually with HMRC which employee expenses and benefits may be included in a PAYE settlement agreement. Employers can submit their PSA request at the year end (before 6 July) and make

506.1 NIC   Class 1B Contributions: PAYE Settlement Agreements

ad hoc requests during the year. Where an employer entered into a PSA for 2018/19 or a later year, it will continue for subsequent tax years until either the employer or HMRC cancel it or the employer needs to change it. See NIM18090 and *Simon's Taxes* E8.281.

507 Class 4 Contributions: On Profits of a Trade etc.

Cross-reference. See also **502** AGGREGATION OF EARNINGS; **510** EARNINGS FROM SELF-EMPLOYMENT.

507.1 EXCEPTION OF CLASS 1 CONTRIBUTORS FOR EARNINGS CHARGEABLE TO TAX AS TRADING INCOME

[*SI 2001 No 1004, Reg 94*]

Ariadne is a practising solicitor and also the company secretary of Web Ltd. Her accounting year ends on 30 June and her 2020/21 assessable profits for Class 4 purposes (based on her accounts to 30 June 2020 under *ITTOIA 2005, ss 198(1), 200(3), 201(1)*) are £33,000. During 2020/21 she is paid secretarial fees (under deduction of standard rate primary Class 1 contributions, as appropriate) on a quarterly basis as follows.

	Gross fees	Class 1	
	£	£	
June 2020	500.00	—	(below earnings threshold)
September 2020	500.00	—	(below earnings threshold)
December 2020	2,400.00	Nil	(Nil% on [£9,500 ÷ 4 = £2,375])
		3.00	(12% on remainder [£2,400 − £2,375 = £25])
March 2021	14,000.00	Nil	(Nil% on [£9,500 ÷ 4 = £2,375])
		1,215.00	(12% on remainder up to the UEL [£50,000 ÷ 4 = £12,500] less £2,375)
		30.00	(2% on the remainder up to £14,000 = £1,500).
	£17,400.00	£1,248.00	

As these fees are included gross in Ariadne's accounts (the Class 1 contributions being correctly debited to drawings), the amount of £17,400 is deducted from the profits on which Class 4 contributions would be payable. The position for 2020/21 will be:

	£
Profits as stated	33,000
Less: Class 4 exception	(17,400)
	15,600
Less: lower annual limit	(9,500)
	£6,100
Total Class 4 liability	
£6,100 × 9% =	£549.00

508 Company Directors

Cross-reference. See also **502** AGGREGATION OF EARNINGS; **511** EARNINGS PERIODS.

508.1 EARNINGS

[*SI 2001 No 1004, Reg 22(2)*]

(A)

Gary Newsmith is a director of Lesstain Ltd, which has an accounting date of 5 July. Gary has no balance standing to his credit with the company at 6 July 2020 and fees already voted and paid have exactly equalled his drawings up to that date. G has substantial earnings from other sources and takes only one payment annually from L in respect of his services. A meeting is held on 2 April 2021 at which Gary's fees for the year ending 5 July 2021 are determined at £50,000, but this amount is neither credited to his current account nor made available to him. Due to cash flow problems and the desire to tie Gary to the company, it is agreed that Gary will only become entitled to his emoluments on 4 October 2022.

Gary is taxable on these earnings in 2021/22, since that is the year in which the end of the accounting period falls, and Lesstain Ltd has to apply PAYE to the general earnings on 5 July 2021, despite the fact that Gary may not draw the general earnings before 4 October 2022. When that date arrives, the company must deduct and account for National Insurance contributions, since it is only then that the money is put unreservedly at Gary's disposal.

Note

(a) Fees voted to a director in advance become earnings for contribution purposes on the date the director has an unreserved right to draw on them. (*Garforth v Newsmith Stainless Ltd* [1979] 2 All ER 73).

(B) Fees voted in advance

Dawn is a director of East Ltd. On 31 March 2020 E votes fees to D of £8,000 payable on the last Friday in each month for the next twelve months. D will have earnings for contribution purposes thus:

24 April 2020	£8,000
29 May 2020	£8,000
26 June 2020	£8,000
Etc.	

508.1 NIC   Company Directors

(C) **Fees credited to overdrawn account**

Sherlock is a director of Homes Ltd. On 16 July 2020, his current account with the company is overdrawn by £2,800, of which £2,000 has been treated as earnings for contribution purposes. On 20 July 2020 fees of £30,000 are voted to him and credited to the account. £28,000 of those fees are earnings for contribution purposes.

Note

(a) To the extent that items creating an overdrawn account have already been treated as earnings for contribution purposes, the fees etc. credited will not be earnings for contribution purposes, but any other part of the amount credited will be. [*SI 2001 No 1004, Sch 3 Part X para 2*].

508.2 CALCULATION OF CONTRIBUTIONS

[*SI 2001 No 1004, Regs 8, 22(2)*]

Frederick is appointed a director of Great Ltd on 1 November 2020. Earnings are paid to Frederick as follows:

Date	Payment £	Cumulative £
30 November	700	700
31 December	800	1,500
31 January	5,000	6,500
28 February	900	7,400
31 March	15,600	23,000

There are 23 whole or part contribution weeks left in 2020/21, not counting for this purpose the two days which constitute week 53 (Booklet CA44, Para 25 and page 28). His earnings period as a director is therefore 23 weeks. As the weekly earnings thresholds and the upper earnings limit for 2020/21 are £183.00 (employee), £169.00 (employer) and £962.00 (for both employee and employer) respectively, Frederick's earnings thresholds and upper earnings limit are £4,209.00 (i.e. £183 × 23), £3,887.00 (i.e. £169 × 23) and £22,126.00 (i.e. £962.00 × 23). (The calculation of these limits and thresholds is necessary only if contributions in respect of earnings are to be calculated by use of the modified exact percentage method.)

Contributions can be calculated by use of either the *modified exact percentage method* or the *modified tables method*.

Company Directors NIC 508.2

The *modified exact percentage procedure* would operate as follows:

Cum. Pay £		Cum. Primary £	Primary payable £	Cum. secondary £	Secondary payable £
700	Nil% × £700				
1,500	Nil% × £1,500				
6,500	Nil% × £4,209				
	12% × £2,291	274.92	274.92		
	Nil% × £3,887				
	13.8% × £2,613			360.59	360.59
7,400	Nil% × £4,209				
	12% × £3,191	382.92	108.00		
	Nil% × £3,887				
	13.8% × £3,513			484.79	124.20
23,000	Nil% × £4,209				
	12% × £17,917				
	2% × £874	2,167.52	1,784.60		
	Nil% × £3,887				
	13.8% × £19,113			2,637.59	2,152.80
			£2,167.52		£2,637.59

Alternatively, the *modified tables procedure* could have operated, thus:

Cum.Pay ÷ 23 £	Weekly table band £	Primary per table × 23 £	Primary payable £	Secondary per table × 23 £	Secondary payable £
30.43					
65.22					
282.61	282.00	274.92	274.92	360.59	360.59
321.74	321.00	382.92	108.00	484.79	124.20
1,000	962+38	2,167.52	1,784.60	2,637.59	2,152.80
			£2,167.52		£2,637.59

Note

(a) The above procedures are set out in HMRC booklet CA44, Paras 41 to 44.

509 Deferment of Payment

509.1 CLASS 1 DEFERMENT

[*SSCBA 1992, s 19(1)(2); SI 2001 No 1004, Regs 68, 84*]

Eel is employed by Flounder Ltd, Grunion Ltd and Hake Ltd. In March 2020, when his earnings from the three companies were £700, £300 and £600 per week respectively, he applied for Class 1 deferment for 2020/21.

As his anticipated earnings from Flounder Ltd and Hake Ltd together (£1,300) exceeded the required amount for 2020/21 (£962, plus £183 per additional employment) deferment was granted in respect of the primary Class 1 contribution liability which would otherwise have arisen on his earnings from Grunion Ltd.

If, when the year ends, it is found that earnings from Flounder Ltd and Hake Ltd, contrary to expectations, have not together reached the upper earnings limit throughout the year, HMRC will issue a demand for the balance of contributions due (relating those contributions to Eel's earnings from Grunion Ltd but calculating the amount by reference to his actual total earnings in the year). If (as is more likely), however, the earnings from Flounder Ltd and Hake Ltd have together exceeded the upper earnings limit throughout the year, any excess contributions paid on those earnings will be refunded and the earnings from Grunion Ltd will be automatically excepted from the liability at the main rate which, until its exception, had been merely deferred.

Note

(a) In making application for deferment, a contributor has to agree to pay any amount by which contributions fall short of the total liability within 28 days of demand (see form CA 72A). See NIM01180 and *Simon's Taxes* A6.952.

510 Earnings from Self-Employment

Cross-reference. See also 507 CLASS 4 CONTRIBUTIONS: ON PROFITS OF A TRADE ETC.

510.1 EARNINGS FOR CLASS 4 PURPOSES — LOSS RELIEF

[SSCBA 1992, Sch 2 para 3(1)(4)]

Kit has a sportswear business. His trading results (adjusted for tax purposes) are

Year to		£
5 July 2017	Profit	12,000
5 July 2018	Loss	(17,200)
5 July 2019	Profit	4,000
5 July 2020	Profit	19,400

K's assessable amounts of profit and other income are

	Trade Profit	Investment Income
	£	£
2017/18	12,000	1,500
2018/19	Nil	1,700
2019/20	4,000	1,800
2020/21	19,400	2,200

If K claims relief for his 2018/19 loss of £17,200 under *ITA 2007, s 64*, it will be apportioned against 2017/18 earned income i.e. £12,000 profits, then against 2017/18 investment income i.e. £1,500 and then against 2018/19 investment income i.e. £1,700. The balance of the loss (£2,000) is then carried forward against profits of the same trade only. This will result in revised assessable amounts of profit and income, thus

	Trade Profit	Investment Income
	£	£
2017/18	Nil	Nil
2018/19	Nil	Nil
2019/20	2,000	1,800
2020/21	19,400	2,200

510.1 NIC   Earnings from Self-Employment

For Class 4 purposes, however, only £14,000 of the loss has been relieved (£12,000 in 2017/18 and £2,000 in 2019/20) and the remaining £3,200 must, therefore, also be carried forward to 2019/20 (and subsequent years, if necessary, as in the example), giving revised Class 4 profits as follows

	Class 4
	£
2017/18	Nil
2018/19	Nil
2019/20	Nil
2020/21	18,200

Notes

(a) Loss relief available for income tax purposes under *ITA 2007, s 83* (carry-forward against subsequent profits) and *ITA 2007, s 89* (carry-back of terminal loss) is also available for Class 4 purposes. Relief under *ITA 2007, ss 64, 72* (set-off against general income) is also so available provided that the loss arises from activities of which any profits would have been earnings for Class 4 purposes (and see note (b) below). [*SSCBA 1992, Sch 2 para 3(1)*]. See **IT 15** LOSSES. See also BIM85015, BIM85060 and *Simon's Taxes* E5.622, E5.630

(b) Where a loss deducted for income tax purposes is deducted from income other than trading profits, the loss is, to that extent, carried forward for Class 4 purposes and set off against the first available trading profit for subsequent years. [*SSCBA 1992, Sch 2 para 3(4)*].

511 Earnings Periods

511.1 PAY PATTERNS

[*SI 2001 No 1004, Regs 2–9*]

(A) **Multiple regular pay pattern**

Clive is a salesman for Dubbleglays Ltd. He is paid a monthly salary, a quarterly commission and an annual bonus and has, therefore, three regular pay intervals: a month, a quarter and a year.

As the shortest of these is a month, Clive's earnings period is a month and all the earnings paid to him in a year will be related to one or other of the twelve such periods it contains. If, therefore, he is paid £830 commission on 8 May for the quarter ended 31 March, £500 salary on 15 May for the month of May and £2,500 bonus on 29 May for the year ended 31 December of the preceding year, his earnings for the earnings period from 6 May to 5 June (PAYE month 2) will be £3,830, irrespective of the fact that only £500 of the total is earned within the month and the remainder relates to previous tax years and was earned over a period of between three and twelve months.

Notes

(a) Where two or more regular pay patterns run concurrently, the earnings period is normally the length of the shorter or shortest interval at which any part of the earnings is paid. [*SI 2001 No 1004, Reg 3(1)(2)*]. See NIM08021 and *Simon's Taxes* E8.249.

(b) See (B) below for the power for HMRC to direct that the longer or longest interval should be the earnings period.

(c) See **502.1(A)** AGGREGATION OF EARNINGS for the aggregation of earnings where two or more regular pay patterns run concurrently. See also **502.6, 502.7** AGGREGATION OF EARNINGS for circumstances in which a common earnings period must be determined for related employments.

(B) **Multiple regular pay pattern — HMRC direction**

For the tax year, Everard (one of Clive's colleagues—see (A) above) had total earnings of £15,200 comprising:

	£	Pay interval
Salary	7,200	month
Commission	4,000	quarter
Bonus	4,000	year

A similar pattern had subsisted during the preceding two tax years.

511.1 NIC   Earnings Periods

If HMRC direct on, say, 5 June that, from the date of the direction onwards, and for all future years, E is to have an annual earnings period, E's earnings periods for the tax year would be:

month to	5 May
1 month to	5 June
44-week period to	5 April

and his earnings period for the next and all future tax years would be the tax year concerned.

Note

(a) Where two or more regular pay patterns run concurrently and it appears to HMRC that the greater part of earnings is normally paid at intervals of greater length than the shorter or shortest, HMRC may, by notifying the earner and secondary contributor, specify the longer or longest pay interval as the earnings period. [*SI 2001 No 1004, Reg 3(2A)–(3)*].

(C) **Irregular payments**

On 13 July, Jack is employed by Kwest Films Ltd as a researcher but, because of his age, is not entitled to the adult minimum wage. He is to be paid £5 per hour and to work in his own time and at his own convenience. He has, however, to meet the following deadlines

'Health Service' material	29 August
'Aids' material	26 October
'Disarmament' material	29 October

Jack works 106 hours on the first project, 151 hours on the second and 12 hours on the third. Earnings periods and earnings will be as follows

	£
48 days from 13 July to 29 August	530
58 days from 30 August to 26 October	755
Week ended 31 October (though only a four-day fixed period)	60

Note

(a) Where earnings are paid at irregular intervals and neither follow nor can be treated as following a regular pay pattern, the earnings period is the length of that part of the employment for which the earnings are paid or a week, whichever is the longer. [*SI 2001 No 1004, Reg 4(a)*]. See *Simon's Taxes* E8.249D

511.2 CHANGE OF REGULAR PAY INTERVAL

[*SI 2001 No 1004, Reg 18*]

(A) **Change to longer interval**

Nuthatch and Osprey are both employed by Partridge Ltd. N is paid £400 per week and O is paid £250 per week. In June 2020, they become salaried employees and begin to be paid monthly at £1,800 and £1,050 per month, respectively. The last weekly wage is paid to each of them on 7 June and their first monthly salaries are paid on 5 July.

The first new earnings period is the month from 6 June to 5 July and their last payments of weekly wage fall within this period. Contributions have already been calculated on that wage as follows.

		Primary*		Secondary**	
		%	£	%	£
N	£400	Nil/12	26.04	Nil/13.8	31.88
O	£250	Nil/12	8.04	Nil/13.8	11.17

If contributions on the payment of salary on 5 July are calculated without regard to that wage payment, those contributions will be

		Primary*		Secondary**	
		%	£	%	£
N	£1,800	Nil/12	120.96	Nil/13.8	147.38
O	£1,050	Nil/12	30.96	Nil/13.8	43.88

If, however, contributions are calculated on the total payments in the earnings period, contributions will be

		Primary*		Secondary**	
		%	£	%	£
N	£2,200	Nil/12	168.96	Nil/13.8	202.58
O	£1,300	Nil/12	60.96	Nil/13.8	78.38

*First £792 (monthly) or £183 (weekly) at Nil%.
**First £732 (monthly) or £169 (weekly) at Nil%.

Under *SI 2001/1004, Reg 18(3)*, the contributions due on the two separate parts of earnings are not to exceed the contributions due on the total and they do not.

However, HMRC guidance requires the recalculation to be performed regardless of any comparison and thus, N's separate contributions (primary, £26.04 + £120.96 = £147.00 and secondary, £31.88 + £147.38 = £179.26) become primary, £168.96 and secondary £202.58, and O's separate contributions (primary £8.04 + £30.96 = £39.00 and secondary, £11.17 + £43.88 = £55.05) are to be uplifted to £60.96 primary and £78.38 secondary. Thus, according to HMRC, primary contributions of £142.92 (£168.96 - £26.04) and secondary contributions of £170.70 (£202.58 - £31.88) are to be paid on the first payment of monthly salary to N, while primary contributions of £52.92 (£60.96 - £8.04) and secondary contributions of £67.21 (£78.38 - £11.17) are to be paid on the first payment of monthly salary to O. The legal validity of HMRC's instruction in these circumstances is questionable.

511.2 NIC   Earnings Periods

Notes

(a) An earner's earnings period may be changed as a result of a change in the regular pay interval. If the new earnings period is longer than the old, then where a payment of earnings at the old interval falls within the first new earnings period, contributions on all payments made during the new earnings period are not to exceed the contributions which would have been payable had all those payments been made at the new interval. [*SI 2001 No 1004, Reg 18(3)*]. See *Simon's Taxes* E8.249C

(b) In such circumstances HMRC instruct employers to calculate contribution liabilities on the total of all payments of earnings made in the new earnings period and then to deduct from those amounts the contribution liabilities already calculated on payments of earnings made at the old interval within the new earnings period. (HMRC Leaflet CWG2 (2020), para 1.10).

(B) **Change to shorter interval**

Snipe is employed by Teal Ltd at a salary of £850 per month. He receives £850 on 6 August 2020 but then, from 1 September 2020, his pay arrangement is changed to one under which he receives a weekly wage of £212.50. His first weekly wage under the new arrangement is paid on 2 September 2020. It follows that, in the contribution month ended 5 September, S has received two payments of earnings.

The payments are not aggregated so that liabilities are as follows:

Primary	(on a monthly earnings period basis)	£850 @ Nil%/12% =	£6.96
	(on a weekly earnings period basis)	£212.50 @ Nil%/12% =	£3.54
			£10.50
Secondary	(on a monthly earnings period basis)	£850 @ Nil%/13.8% =	£16.28
	(on a weekly earnings period basis)	£212.50 @ Nil%/13.8% =	£6.00
			£22.28

Note

(a) Where an employed earner's regular pay interval is changed so that the new interval is shorter than the old interval and, as a result, the first of the new earnings periods is contained within the last of the old earnings periods, the two payments are treated separately. (HMRC Leaflet CWG2 (2020), para 1.9).

Earnings Periods   NIC 511.3

511.3 HOLIDAY PAY

[*SI 2001 No 1004, Reg 19*]

Utrillo and Vermeer are both employed by Whistler Ltd. Each is paid a wage of £260 and holiday pay (for the following two weeks) of £250 each per week on 28 June 2020. U works during his holiday period and earns £200 paid to him on 5 July and £220 paid to him on 12 July. His wage on 19 July is £260. V takes his holiday but £140 in overtime pay becomes due for payment to him on 5 July. This is paid (along with a wage of £260) on 19 July after his return to work.

If W adopts *method A*, final calculations will be as follows.

U	£	*Primary*	£	*Secondary*	£
28 June 2020	260	Nil%/12%	9.24	Nil%/13.8%	12.55
5 July 2020	450	Nil%/12%	32.04	Nil%/13.8%	38.77
12 July 2020	470	Nil%/12%	34.44	Nil%/13.8%	41.54
19 July 2020	260	Nil%/12%	9.24	Nil%/13.8%	12.55
	£1,440		£84.96		£105.41

V	£	*Primary*	£	*Secondary*	£
28 June 2020	260	Nil%/12%	9.24	Nil%/13.8%	12.55
5 July 2020	390	Nil%/12%	24.84	Nil%/13.8%	30.49
12 July 2020	250	Nil%/12%	8.04	Nil%/13.8%	11.17
19 July 2020	260	Nil%/12%	9.24	Nil%/13.8%	12.55
	£1,160		£51.36		£66.76

If W adopts *method B*, final calculations will be as follows.

U	£	*Primary*	£	*Secondary*	£
28 June 2020	760 ÷ 3 = 253	Nil%/12%	8.40 × 3 = 25.20	Nil%/13.8%	11.59 × 3 = 34.77
5 July 2020	200	Nil%/12%	2.04	Nil%/13.8%	4.28
12 July 2020	220	Nil%/12%	4.44	Nil%/13.8%	7.03
19 July 2020	260	Nil%/12%	9.24	Nil%/13.8%	12.56
	£1,440		£40.92		£58.64

V	£	*Primary*	£	*Secondary*	£
28 June 2020	760 ÷ 3 = 253	Nil%/12%	8.40 × 3 = 25.20	Nil%/13.8%	11.59 × 3 = 34.77
5 July 2020	—	—	—	—	—
12 July 2020	—	—	—	—	—
19 July 2020	400	Nil%/12%	26.04	Nil%/13.8%	31.88
	£1,160		£51.24		£66.65

511.3 NIC   Earnings Periods

Note

(a) Where a payment of earnings includes a payment in respect of one or more week's holiday, the earnings period may be the length of the interval in respect of which the payment is made ('*method B*'). Alternatively, the holiday pay may simply be treated for contribution purposes as pay in the weeks in which earnings would normally have been paid ('*method A*'). Method B cannot be used in respect of a payment on termination of employment which includes a payment in respect of such holiday. [*SI 2001/1004, Reg 19*]. If method B is used and the length of the interval in respect of which the payment is made includes a fraction of a week, that fraction is treated as a whole week. See *Simon's Taxes* E8.257.

511.4 PAYMENTS TO DIRECTORS AND EX-DIRECTORS

[*SI 2001 No 1004, Reg 8*]

Anchovy is a director of Barracuda Ltd. His drawings (treated as earnings) are £3,600 per month. On 30 June 2020 he resigns his office and begins to work as an ordinary employee of Carp Ltd (a completely unconnected company) who pay him a weekly wage. In May 2021 Anchovy is paid a bonus of £10,000 by B in respect of the year ended 31 March 2021.

An earnings period of one year is to apply to his earnings for the months April, May and June 2021 of £10,800 from B. A weekly earnings period will then apply in respect of his earnings from C. The £10,000 bonus will attract an annual earnings period.

Notes

(a) Where a person is a company director at the beginning of a tax year, the earnings period in respect of his earnings is that tax year. If a person is appointed as a company director during a tax year, the earnings period is the number of weeks remaining in the tax year. [*SI 2001 No 1004, Reg 8(2)(3)*]. See NIM12022, NIM12024 and *Simon's taxes* E8.250.

(b) Where any payments are made to an ex-director in any year *after* that in which his directorship ceased the earnings period is the tax year in which they are paid if they are in respect of any period during which he was a company director. [*SI 2001 No 1004, Reg 8(5)*].

(c) See also **508** COMPANY DIRECTORS.

512 Intermediaries

Cross-reference. See also **IT 20** PERSONAL SERVICE COMPANIES ETC.

512.1 CALCULATION OF DEEMED PAYMENT

[*SI 2000 No 727*]

Graham is an IT consultant working through his own service company and has secured a job with Benevolent Ltd through an agency to work on the computerised accounts system for seven months from October 2020 to April 2021 inclusive. In accounts, a team leader (another IT contractor) tells Graham what work he is to carry out but he is left to his own experience to determine 'how' the work is carried out. Graham is expected to be in attendance at Benevolent Ltd a regular 40 hours per week. Graham's company is paid an hourly rate for his services at 1.5 times the normal hourly rate. Billed monthly, Benevolent Ltd pays the agency who in turn are invoiced by Graham's company. The total invoices for the seven months will amount to £35,000. Graham draws a salary of £10,000 from his company over the period. Allowable expenses up to 5 April 2021 amount to £750 and there are pension contributions of £2,000. The main indications that self-employment arises here is the minimal financial risk from invoicing, the ability to work for others and the existence of Graham's company. In contrast, the engagement is relatively long and he must carry out the services personally. Also Benevolent Ltd provides the equipment and working accommodation and he works the usual working hours of the client. The engagement with Benevolent Ltd would appears to have been an employment had it been between Graham and the client direct rather than through the service company. The intermediary rules therefore apply for 2020/21 as follows:

Relevant income received (October, November, December, January, February; March not paid as at 5 April 2021; April 2021 not yet invoiced)		£25,000
Deduct		
Pension contributions paid	£2,000	
Expenses paid (allowable)	£750	
Flat rate allowance (5% of £25,000)	£1,250	
Salary paid in year to 5 April 2021	£10,000	
Class 1 secondary NICs paid and due on salary paid in year (on £10,000)	£167	(£14,167)
Net deemed payments before NICs		£10,833
Employer's NICs (£10,833 × 13.8/113.8)		(£1,314)
Deemed payment		£9,519

Notes

(a) The post-expense figure before NICs (i.e. £10,833) is multiplied by 100/113.8 to reach the deemed payment figure since the earnings threshold has already been taken into account on the £10,000 salary. Clearly, an adjustment will be necessary if none or only part of the earnings threshold has not been set against salary payments already made in the tax year in question.

512.1 NIC   Intermediaries

(b) Different rules apply where the engagement via the intermediary is with a public authority. In such cases, the liability to pay employment taxes and NICs moves to the public sector body or agency/third party paying the intermediary. These rules were to be extended to private sector engagers with effect from April 2020 but has now been delayed until April 2021 because of the spread of the coronavirus (COVID-19) pandemic. The delay is to help businesses and individuals deal with the economic impact of coronavirus. There will be an exemption for small organisations.

513 Partners

Cross-reference. See also IT 18 PARTNERSHIPS.

513.1 CLASS 4 CONTRIBUTIONS
[*SSCBA 1992, Sch 2 para 4*]

(A)

Alder, Birch and Cypress are in partnership as arboriculturists. Their profit for the year ended 30 June 2020 is £34,000 and during that year C is a salaried partner while A and B share the remaining profit in equal shares. The taxable profits for 2020/21 are £34,000. Although A and B continue to share profits on the same basis, however, C's salary for the year ended 30 June 2020 is £12,000 and for the year ended 30 June 2021 is £14,000. For Class 4 purposes the 2020/21 profit allocation is to be

			£
C		=	12,000
A	1/2 × (£34,000 − £12,000)	=	11,000
B	1/2 × (£34,000 − £12,000)	=	11,000
			£34,000

Note

(a) Where a trade or profession is carried on in partnership, the liability of any partner in respect of Class 4 contributions arises in respect of his share of the profits of that trade or profession. [*SSCBA 1992, Sch 2 para 4(1)*]. The share of profits is determined on the basis of the profit sharing arrangements in the basis period for the year concerned. See also IT 18 PARTNERSHIPS.

(B)

Diamond and Emerald are in partnership as jewellers sharing profits in the ratio of 1:1 until 30 September 2018 and in the ratio of 1:2 after that date. Diamond also runs a nightclub. The partnership profits for the years to 30 September 2018, 30 September 2019 and 30 September 2020 are £40,000, £38,000 and £34,000. D's profits from his nightclub are £28,000 for 2018/19, £24,000 for 2019/20 and £34,000 for 2020/21.

D and E will each separately self-assess their income tax and Class 4 National Insurance liabilities. In the case of D, this will be based on the total income from both sources of self-employment income.

513.1 NIC Partners

D's Class 4 liability for 2018/19 is

		£
£40,000 × 1/2		20,000
Nightclub		28,000
		48,000
Less: Excess over upper annual limit (£46,350)		1,650
		46,350
Less: Lower annual limit		8,424
		£37,926
Class 4 contributions due:		
£37,926 @ 9% =	£3,413.34	
£1,650 @ 2%	33.00	
	£3,446.34	

E's Class 4 liability for 2018/19 is

		£
£40,000 × 1/2		20,000
Less: Lower annual limit		8,424
Class 4 contributions due:		£11,576
£11,576 @ 9% =	£1,041.84	

D's Class 4 liability for 2019/20 is

		£
£38,000 × 1/3		12,667
Nightclub		24,000
		36,667
Less: Lower annual limit		8,632
Class 4 contributions due:		£28,035
£28,035 @ 9% =	£2,523.15	

E's Class 4 liability for 2019/20 is

		£
£38,000 × 2/3		25,333
Less: Lower annual limit		8,632
Class 4 contributions due:		£16,701
£16,701 @ 9% =	£1,503.09	

D's Class 4 liability for 2020/21 is

		£
£34,000 × 1/3		11,333
Nightclub		34,000
		45,333
Less: Lower annual limit		9,500
Class 4 contributions due:		£35,833
£35,833 @ 9% =	£3,224.97	

E's Class 4 liability for 2020/21 is

		£
£34,000 × 2/3		22,667
Less: Lower annual limit		9,500
Class 4 contributions due:		£13,167
£13,167 @ 9% =	£1,185.03	

D and E's Class 4 liabilities for 2018/19 were payable in two equal interim instalments on 31 January 2019 and 31 July 2019 based on the 2017/18 self-assessments, with the balance payable on 31 January 2020. Similarly, their Class 4 liability for 2019/20 is payable in two equal instalments on 31 January 2020 and 31 July 2020 based on the 2018/19 self-assessment, with the balance payable on 31 January 2021 and so on.

The self-assessment payments will, therefore, include the following amounts in relation to Class 4 contributions.

513.1 NIC   Partners

	D	E
	£	£
31 January 2020 (2019/20 POA)	1,723.17	520.92
31 July 2020 (2019/20 POA)	1,723.17	520.92
31 January 2021 (2019/20 repayment/balance)	(923.19)	461.25
31 January 2021 (2020/21 POA)	1,261.57	751.54
31 July 2021 (2020/21 POA)	1,261.58	751.55
31 January 2022 (2020/21 repayment/balance)	701.82	(318.06)
31 January 2022 (2021/22 POA)	1,612.48	592.51
31 July 2022 (2021/22 POA)	1,612.49	592.52

Notes

(a) See note (a) to (A) above.

(b) Where a trade or profession is carried on in partnership, the liability of any partner in respect of Class 4 contributions is calculated by aggregating his share of the profits with his share of the profits of any other trade or profession. [*SSCBA 1992, Sch 2 para 4(1)*].

(c) The Government announced in March 2020 that self-assessment taxpayers can choose to delay making their second payment on account for **2019/20**, otherwise due on 31 July 2020, if they find it difficult to make the payment on time due to the impact of COVID-19. No claim is required. Those opting to delay will have until 31 January 2021 to make the payment. Whilst introduced principally to assist the self-employed, this measure applies to all self-assessment taxpayers. No late payment interest will be charged for the period 1 August 2020 to 31 January 2021 on the deferred payment. (www.gov.uk/guidance/defer-your-self-assessment-payment-on-account-due-to-coronavirus-covid-19).

Index

This index is referenced to chapter and paragraph number within the six main sections of the book. The entries in bold capitals are chapter headings in the text.

A

Accounting date, change of IT 30.2
ACCOUNTING PERIODS CT 101
 See also Periods of Account
 different lengths, of (loss relief) CT 114.3(B)
 end of CT 101.1
 exceeding twelve months CT 101.3
 liquidation, effect of CT 112.1
 overlapping two financial years CT 101.2
 start of CT 101.1
ACCRUED INCOME SCHEME IT 2
 CGT effect CGT 213.3; 224.1
ACCUMULATION AND MAINTENANCE TRUSTS IHT 301
 18-to-25 trusts IHT 301.2
 —failure of IHT 301.2(B)
 after 5 April 2008 IHT 301.2
 charge on failure to qualify IHT 301.1
 income tax IT 27.2; 27.3(B)
AGE EXCEPTION NIC 501.1
Age-related allowances IT 1.7; IT 16.1
AGGREGATION OF EARNINGS NIC 502
 Class 4 contributions NIC 502.7
 different employers NIC 502.3
 different employments NIC 502.2; 502.3; 502.4
 former directorships NIC 502.5
 gratuities paid separately NIC 502.6
 same employer NIC 502.1
 secondary contributors in association NIC 502.2
AGRICULTURAL PROPERTY IHT 302
 interaction of CGT and IHT IHT 302.1(C)
 land with vacant possession IHT 302.1(A)
 shares etc. in agricultural companies IHT 302.2
 tenanted land, transfers of IHT 302.1(B)(C)
Allowable and non-allowable expenditure CGT 209.1
Allowable deductions IT 30.4; CT 116.1
 employment income IT 9.2
ALLOWANCES AND TAX RATES IT 1
 allowances, use of IT 1.1(B)(C)
 losses, use of IT 1.4
 maintenance payments IT 16.2
 marriage allowance IT 1.6
 married couple's allowance IT 1.7; 15.1
 married persons IT 16
 personal savings allowance IT 1.2; 1.8
 rates of tax

ALLOWANCES AND TAX RATES – *cont.*
 —CGT CGT 201.1
 —IT IT 1.1–1.3
 restriction of personal allowance IT 1.5
 Scottish rates IT 1.8
 starting rate for savings IT 1.3
 trading allowance IT 30.5
 transferable tax allowance IT 1.6
Annual allowance IT 19.3
 carry-forward of IT 19.3(A)
 money purchase IT 19.3(C)
 taper of IT 19.3(B)
Annual exemption (IHT) IHT 310.1; 319.1
ANNUAL MAXIMUM NIC 503
 Class 1 and Class 2 limitation NIC 503.1
 Class 4 limitation NIC 503.2
ANNUAL RATES AND EXEMPTIONS CGT 201
 losses, interaction with CGT 201.2
 —attributed settlement gains CGT 201.2(B)
 married persons CGT 218.1
 rates of tax CGT 201.1
 settlements CGT 228.1
ANTI-AVOIDANCE CGT 202; IHT 303
 associated operations IHT 303.1
 disposal to connected person CGT 202.3
 gains of offshore settlements CGT 219.1
 groups of companies
 —depreciatory transactions CGT 202.4
 value-shifting CGT 202.1; 202.2
Approved share option schemes IT 28.3
Assessable profits IT 30.4; CT 116.1
ASSETS CGT 203
 negligible value CGT 217.2(B)
 options CGT 203.1; 232.2
Assets disposed of in series of transactions CGT 202.3; IHT 303.1
ASSETS HELD ON 6 APRIL 1965 CGT 204
 buildings CGT 204.3(B)
 chattels CGT 204.3(A)
 land and buildings CGT 204.3(B)
 land reflecting development value CGT 204.2
 part disposals after 5 April 1965 CGT 204.3(F)
 quoted shares and securities CGT 204.1
 time apportionment CGT 204.3
 unquoted shares CGT 204.3(C)(D)(E)
ASSETS HELD ON 31 MARCH 1982 CGT 205

Index

ASSETS HELD ON 31 MARCH 1982 – *cont.*
  assets transferred at undervalue CT 103.2(B)
  capital gains tax CGT 205.1
  corporation tax CGT 205.2
  deferred gains, relief for CGT 205.3
  no gain/no loss disposals CGT 214.2(A)(C)
  part disposals before 6 April 1988 CGT 209.2(B)
  partnerships, held by CGT 220.1
  private residences CGT 223.1(A)(B)
  short leases CGT 216.3(E)
  wasting assets CGT 232.3(B)
Associated operations IHT 303.1
Averaging, creative artists IT 30.6
Averaging of farming profits IT 30.7

B

BAD DEBT RELIEF VAT 401
  income tax IT 30.4
  mutual supplies VAT 401.1
  part payments VAT 401.1
  repayment of refund VAT 401.3
  second-hand goods VAT 401.2
Basis periods
  trading profits IT 18.1; 30.1–30.3
Benefits code IT 9.3
  close company participators CT 104.3
  —assets given and leased IT 9.3(C)
  —cars IT 9.3(A)
  —loans IT 9.3(D); 9.5
  —petrol IT 9.3(A)
  —vans IT 9.3(B)
  living accommodation IT 9.4
  medical insurance IT 9.6
  miscellaneous IT 9.6
  overnight incidental expenses IT 9.6
  relocation expenses IT 9.5
  removal expenses IT 9.5
  vouchers IT 9.6
Bereaved minors, trusts for IHT 322
Bondwashing IT 2
  CGT effect CGT 224.1
Business assets
  deferment of chargeable gain on replacement of assets CGT 226
  gift of CGT 213.2
  transfer to a company CGT 213.3
BUSINESS ASSET DISPOSAL (FORMERLY ENTREPRENEURS' RELIEF) CGT 206
  associated disposals CGT 206.3
  computation CGT 206.1
  deferred gains CGT 206.5

BUSINESS ASSET DISPOSAL (FORMERLY ENTREPRENEURS' RELIEF) – *cont.*
  dilution of shareholding CGT 206.6
  lifetime limit CGT 206.1(B)–(D)
  partnerships CGT 206.2
  reorganisations CGT 206.4
  transitional provisions CGT 206.5
BUSINESS PROPERTY IHT 304
  allocation of relief IHT 305.4(B)
  further conditions for lifetime transfer IHT 304.1(D)
  land and buildings used by business IHT 304.1(B)(C)
  —owned by trustees IHT 304.1(C)
  shares or securities IHT 304.1(A)
  —non-qualifying subsidiary IHT 304.1(A)

C

CALCULATION OF TAX (Inheritance tax) IHT 305
  cumulation principle IHT 305.1; 305.2
  lifetime chargeable transfers IHT 305.2
  partly exempt transfers IHT 305.3
  potentially exempt transfers IHT 305.1
CAPITAL ALLOWANCES IT 3; CT 102
  See also Capital Allowances on Plant and Machinery
  accounting periods
  —given by reference to CT 102.1
  annual investment allowance, straddling periods IT 4.6
  capital gains, effect on CGT 209.1(B); 219.2; 232.1
  capital goods scheme IT 4.7
  dredging IT 3.2
  FYAs
  long-life assets IT 4.5
  mineral extraction IT 3.3
  mines IT 3.3
  patent rights IT 3.4
  periods of account
  —given by reference to IT 4.1
  plant and machinery IT 4; CT 102.1
  qualifying expenditure IT 4.3
  research and development IT 3.5
  short-life assets IT 4.4
  structures and buildings IT 3.1
  successions IT 4.2
  transfer of trade CT 102.1
  VAT capital goods scheme IT 4.7
CAPITAL ALLOWANCES ON PLANT AND MACHINERY IT 4

Index

CAPITAL ALLOWANCES ON PLANT AND MACHINERY – *cont.*
See also Capital Allowances
long-life assets IT 4.5
periods of account
—given by reference to IT 4.1
qualifying expenditure IT 4.3
short-life assets IT 4.4
successions IT 4.2
CAPITAL GAINS (Companies) CT 103
capital losses CT 103.1
close company transferring asset at undervalue CT 103.2
groups of companies
—degrouping charge CT 103.3(E)
—intra-group transfers of assets CT 103.3(B)(C)
—notional transfer of assets CT 103.3(A)
—pre-entry losses CT 103.3(F)
—rollover relief on replacement of business assets CT 103.3(D)
migration of companies CGT 220.1
substantial shareholdings exemption CT 103.4
CAPITAL GOODS (VAT) VAT 402
capital allowances, interaction with IT 4.7
Capital losses
See Losses
CAPITAL SUMS DERIVED FROM ASSETS CGT 207
deferred consideration CGT 207.2; 217.4; 229.4(C)
receipt of compensation CGT 207.3; 216.2
—capital sum exceeding allowable expenditure CGT 207.3(D)
compulsory acquisition CGT 216.2
—part application of capital sum received CGT 207.3(C)
—restoration using insurance moneys CGT 207.3(B)
Car hire CT 116.1
Cars
See also Motor cars
assessable benefit IT 9.3(A); NIC 505.2
mileage allowances IT 9.2(A)
Cash basis IT 31
property income IT 22.1(A)
trading income IT 31.1
CATERING VAT 403
special method for caterers VAT 403.1
Cemeteries, allowances for IT 30.9
Charitable donations IT 5.1; CT 106.5; 111.1; 114.1; 116.1; 116.2
CHARITIES IT 5; IHT 306
gift aid IT 5.1; CT 116.1

CHARITIES – *cont.*
property leaving temporary charitable trusts IHT 306.1
reduced rate (IHT) for estates with 10% gifts to charity IHT 321.2
Chattels CGT 212.1
held on 6.4.65 CGT 204.3(A)
Cheap loan arrangements IT 9.3(D); 9.5
Child benefit, high income charge IT 29.1
CIVIL PARTNERS
See also Married Persons and Civil Partners
employee shareholder shares and CGT 218.2
transfers between CGT 214.1(E); 214.2(A); 218.1; 218.2; 218.3
Claims
involving more than one year IT 26.2
CLASS 1 CONTRIBUTIONS: EMPLOYED EARNERS NIC 504
annual maximum NIC 503.1
deferment NIC 509.1
rates NIC 504.1
CLASS 1A CONTRIBUTIONS: BENEFITS IN KIND NIC 505
cars for private use NIC 505.2
person liable NIC 505.1
—person succeeding to business NIC 505.1(C)
—third party benefits NIC 505.1(A)
—two or more employers NIC 505.1(B)
CLASS 1B CONTRIBUTIONS: PAYE SETTLEMENT AGREEMENTS NIC 506
calculation of contributions NIC 506.1
CLASS 4 CONTRIBUTIONS: PROFITS OF A TRADE ETC. NIC 507
aggregation of earnings NIC 502.7
annual maximum NIC 503.1
earnings NIC 510.1
exception of Class 1 contributors for trading income NIC 507.1
loss relief NIC 510.1
partners NIC 513.1
CLOSE COMPANIES CT 104; IHT 307
alteration of share capital to transfer value IHT 307.3
benefits in kind for participators CT 104.3
charge on participators IHT 307.2
definition CT 104.1
loans to participators CT 104.2
transfer of asset at undervalue CT 103.2
value transferred IHT 307.1
COMPANIES (Capital gains of) CGT 208
See also Capital Gains
basic computation CGT 208.1
capital losses CT 103.1; CGT 208.2
exchange of securities CGT 229.4
reconstruction schemes CGT 229.5

Index

COMPANIES (Capital gains of) – *cont.*
  transfer of assets to non-resident company CGT 220.3
Companies (migration of) CGT 220.1
COMPANY DIRECTORS NIC 508
  calculation of contributions NIC 508.2
  earnings NIC 508.1
  —fees credited to overdrawn account NIC 508.1(C)
  —fees voted in advance NIC 508.1(B)
Compensation
  CGT on receipt of CGT 207.3; 216.2
COMPENSATION FOR LOSS OF EMPLOYMENT IT 6
  post-employment notice pay IT 6.1
Compulsory acquisition of land CGT 216.2
COMPUTATION OF GAINS AND LOSSES CGT 209
  allowable expenditure CGT 209.1
  —effect of capital allowances CGT 209.1(B)
  —enhancement expenditure CGT 209.1(C)
  compulsory acquisition of land CGT 216.2
  connected persons CGT 202.3
  part disposal CGT 207.1(A); 207.3(A); 209.2; 216.2; 218.3
  —assets held on 6.4.65 CGT 204.3(E)
  —small part disposals of land CGT 216.1
  premiums payable under leases IT 22.5; CGT 216.3
  sets, assets forming CGT 202.3
  value passing out of shares CGT 202.1; 202.2
Conditional exemption from IHT
  See National Heritage
Consortium relief CT 106.7
Convertible shares IT 28.3
Corporate bonds, qualifying CGT 224; 229.6
Creative artists, averaging of profits IT 30.6
Crematoria, allowances for IT 30.9
Cumulation principle (IHT) IHT 305.1; 305.2
Current year basis of assessment
  capital allowances IT 4.1
  losses IT 15.1; 15.3(B)
  partnerships IT 18.1
  trading income IT 30.1; 29.2(B)

D

Death, capital losses on CGT 217.1(C)
Debenture interest CT 116.1
DECEASED ESTATES IT 7
  absolute interest IT 7.1
  limited interest IT 7.2

DEEDS OF VARIATION AND DISCLAIMERS IHT 308
Deeply discounted securities IT 24.1
Deferment of chargeable gain
  See Hold-over reliefs and Rollover relief
Deferred consideration CGT 207.1(B); 229.4(C)
Depreciatory transactions CGT 202.4
Directors' remuneration (unpaid) CT 116.1
Dilution of shareholding CGT 206.6
Disabled persons, trusts for IHT 323
Discretionary trusts IT 27.2; 27.3(B)
  See also Settlements without interests in possession
Dividend income
  See also Franked Investment Income
  accumulation trusts, received by IT 27.2
  personal allowance set against IT 1.1(B)(C)
  deceased estates, received by IT 7.1; 6.2
  discretionary trusts, received by IT 27.2
  individuals, received by IT 1.1
  overseas companies, from 1.1(C); CT 105
  trusts, received by IT 27.1; 27.3(A)
Domicile
  See Residence and Domicile
Double charges relief IHT 311.1(B); 314; 321.1
DOUBLE TAX RELIEF IT 8; CT 105; CGT 210; IHT 309
  exemption for profits of foreign permanent establishments CT 105.2
  limits on IT 8.1(B)
  measure of relief IT 1.1(C); 8.1; CT 105.1; CGT 210.1
  unilateral relief IT 1.1(C); 8.1; CT 105.1; IHT 309.1
Dredging, allowance for IT 3.2
Dwelling house, gains on CGT 223

E

Earn-outs CGT 217.4; 229.4(C)
EARNINGS FROM SELF-EMPLOYMENT NIC 510
  earnings for Class 4 purposes NIC 510.1
  —loss relief NIC 510.1
EARNINGS PERIODS NIC 511
  change of regular pay interval NIC 511.2
  —longer interval NIC 511.2(A)
  —shorter interval NIC 511.2(B)
  directors NIC 511.4
  holiday pay NIC 511.3
  pay patterns NIC 511.1
  —irregular payments NIC 511.1(C)
  —multiple regular NIC 511.1(A)(B)

Index

EARNINGS PERIODS – *cont.*
—HMRC direction NIC 511.1(B)
Emoluments
  See Employment Income
Employee share schemes IT 28
Employee shareholder shares CGT 218.2
Employees, trusts for IHT 324
EMPLOYMENT INCOME IT 9
  benefits IT 9.3–9.6
  —assets given and leased IT 9.3(C)
  —cars IT 9.3(A)
  —living accommodation IT 9.4
  —loans IT 9.3(D); 9.5
  —medical insurance IT 9.6
  —miscellaneous IT 9.6
  —overnight incidental expenses IT 9.6
  —relocation expenses IT 9.5
  —removal expenses IT 9.5
  —travelling expenses IT 9.2(B)
  —vans IT 9.3(B)
  —vouchers IT 9.6
  cars IT 9.2; 9.3(A)
  compensation for loss of employment IT 6
  mileage allowances IT 9.2(A)
  personal service companies etc. IT 20
  termination payments IT 6
  work done abroad
  —travelling expenses IT 9.1
ENTERPRISE INVESTMENT SCHEME IT 10; CGT 211
  capital gains and losses IT 10.2
  —disposal more than three years after acquisition CGT 211.1; 211.2
  carry-back of relief IT 10.1(B)
  conditions for relief IT 10.1
  deferral relief CGT 211.3
  form of relief IT 10.1
  restrictions on relief IT 10.1
  withdrawal of relief IT 10.2
Enterprise management incentives IT 28.5
Entertainers and sportsmen, non-resident IT 17.2
Errors on invoices VAT 409.1
Estate income IT 7
Exempt supplies (VAT)
  See Partial exemption
EXEMPT TRANSFERS IHT 310
  annual exemption IHT 310.1; 319.1
  election to be treated as UK domiciled IHT 310.4
  —termination of an interest in possession IHT 319.1
  gifts in consideration of marriage IHT 319.1; 323.2

EXEMPT TRANSFERS – *cont.*
  Nil-rate band, transfer of unused amount IHT 308.1; 310.3
  normal expenditure out of income IHT 310.2
  residence nil rate band IHT 310.5
Exemption for profits of foreign permanent establishments CT 105.2
EXEMPTIONS AND RELIEFS CGT 212
  chattels CGT 212.1
  dwelling house CGT 223
  qualifying corporate bonds CGT 224
  tangible movable asset CGT 212.1

F

Farming and market gardening
  averaging profits IT 30.7
  herd basis IT 11
  transfer of agricultural property IHT 302
Foreign income
  See Double Tax Relief
Foreign permanent establishments, exemption for profits of CT 105.2
Foster care IT 30.8
Furnished holiday accommodation IT 22.2; CGT 226.4

G

Gifts CGT 213
  assets held on 31 March 1982 CGT 207.2
  business assets CGT 213.2
  charities IT 5.1; CT 116.1
  deduction from trading income CT 116.1
  deferment of gain CGT 213.1; 213.2; 226.3
  exempt transfers IHT 310; 319.1
  land CGT 222.1(B)
  marriage, in consideration of IHT 319.1; 323.2
  shares CGT 222.1(B)
GIFTS WITH RESERVATION IHT 311
  reservation not released before death IHT 311.1(B)
  reservation released before death IHT 311.1(A)
Goodwill CT 108.1(C)
Grossing up (IHT) IHT 305.2
GROUP RELIEF CT 106
  calculation CT 106.1
  carried-forward losses CT 106.6
  companies joining or leaving group CT 106.4
  consortium relief CT 106.7
  overlapping periods CT 106.3

Index

GROUP RELIEF – *cont.*
  relationship to other reliefs CT 106.5
Groups of companies
  consortium relief CT 106.7
  degrouping charge CT 103.3(E)(F)
  depreciatory transactions CGT 202.4
  distribution followed by disposal of shares CGT 202.3
  group relief CT 106
  —carried-forward losses CT 106.6
  —companies joining or leaving group CT 106.4
  —overlapping periods CT 106.3
  —relationship to other reliefs CT 106.5
  intra-group transfers of assets CT 103.3(A)(B)(C); CGT 214.2(C)(D)
  pre-entry losses CT 103.3(F)
  restriction on carried-forward losses CT 114.7(B)
  rollover relief on replacement of business assets CT 103.3(D)
  surrender of tax refunds CT 110.1(D)

H

HERD BASIS IT 11
Heritage property IHT 315
High income child benefit charge IT 29.1
HOLD-OVER RELIEFS CGT 213
  See also Rollover Relief
  assets held on 31 March 1982 CGT 205.2
  chargeable lifetime transfers CGT 213.1(A)
  disposal consideration CGT 213.1(B)
  gifts
  —business assets CGT 213.2
  —chargeable lifetime transfers CGT 213.1
  IHT relief CGT 213.1(C)
  private residences and CGT 222.4
  transfer of business to company CGT 213.3
  —incorporation relief CGT 213.3
HOTELS AND HOLIDAY ACCOMMODATION VAT 404
  furnished holiday accommodation IT 22.2; CGT 226.4
  stays over four weeks VAT 404.1
Husband and wife
  See Married Persons

I

Immediate post-death interests IHT 319.3

INCOME TAX IN RELATION TO A COMPANY CT 107
  accounting for income tax on receipts and payments CT 107.1
Incorporation relief CGT 213.3
INDEXATION CGT 214
  allowance on receipt of compensation CGT 207.3(E)
  assets held on 31.3.82 CGT 214.1(C)
  disposal before 1.1.18 CGT 214.1(A)
  disposal on or after 1.1.18 CGT 214.1(B)
  general rules CGT 214.1
  indexation factor, calculation of
  no gain/no loss disposals CGT 214.2(A)–(C)
  —intra-group transfers CT 103.3(B); CGT 214.2(C)(D)
  —transfers between spouses or civil partners CGT 214.2(A)(B)
  restriction CGT 214.1(D)
  shares and securities, identification rules CGT 230.2
INPUT TAX VAT 405
  non-business activities VAT 405.2
  repayment where consideration not paid VAT 405.1
Installation of heating equipment VAT 410.1
Instalments, payment by IHT 316.1
  interest
  —on overpaid tax CT 109.1(C)
  —on unpaid tax CT 110.2(B)
  large companies CT 115.1
  very large companies CT 115.1
INTANGIBLE ASSETS CT 108
  customer-related CT 108.1(C)
  debits and credits CT 108.1
  goodwill CT 108.1(C)
  non-trading losses CT 108.2
  rollover relief CT 108.3
INTELLECTUAL PROPERTY IT 12
  patent royalties IT 12.1
Inter-spouse transfers CGT 214.1(D); 214.2(A); 218.1; 218.2; 218.3
Interest in possession
  immediate post-death IHT 319.3
  settlements with IHT 319
  settlements without IHT 320
  termination of CGT 228.4; 228.5; IHT 319.1
  transitional serial IHT 319.2
INTEREST ON OVERPAID TAX CT 109; 110.1
INTEREST ON TAX (IHT) IHT 312
  payment by instalments IHT 316.1(B)
INTEREST ON UNPAID TAX IT 13; CT 110; IHT 312; 316.1(B)
Interest received IT 2.1

Index

INTERMEDIARIES NIC 512
calculation of deemed payment NIC 512.1
INVESTMENT COMPANIES AND INVESTMENT BUSINESS CT 111
management expenses CT 111.1
INVESTORS' RELIEF CGT 215
computation of relief CGT 215.1
—basic computation CGT 215.1(A)
—lifetime limit CGT 215.1(C)
—qualifying and non-qualifying shares CGT 215.1(B)
reorganisations CGT 215.2
Invoices, errors on VAT 409.1

L

LAND CGT 216
compulsory purchase CGT 216.2
development value, reflecting CGT 204.2
gifts of CGT 222.1(B)
held on 6.4.65 CGT 204.2; 204.3(B)
leases CGT 216.3
—assignment of short lease CGT 216.3(D)–(G)
—grant of long lease CGT 216.3(B)
—grant of short lease CGT 216.3(C)
—premiums on short leases IT 22.5; CT 116.1; CGT 216.3(C)(G)(H)(J)
—short leases which are not wasting assets CGT 216.3(A)
—sub-lease granted out of short lease CGT 216.3(H)(J)
small part disposals CGT 216.1
valuation IHT 325.1
LATE PAYMENT INTEREST AND PENALTIES IT 13
Leases
See Land *and* Finance leases
Letting of property IT 22
LIABILITY FOR TAX IHT 313
lifetime transfers IHT 313.1
—with additional liability on death IHT 313.3
potentially exempt transfers becoming chargeable IHT 313.4
transfers on death IHT 313.2
LIFE ASSURANCE POLICIES IT 14
adjustments for non-UK residence IT 14.3
gains and non-qualifying policies IT 14.1
partial surrender of IT 14.2
top-slicing relief IT 14.1
Lifetime allowance IT 19.2
Lifetime transfers IHT 305.1; 305.2
liability for tax IHT 313.1
Limited liability partnerships IT 18.4

Limited partner's losses IT 18.3
LIQUIDATION CT 112
accounting periods CT 112.1
LOAN RELATIONSHIPS CT 113
non-trading CT 113.2
non-trading deficits CT 113.3
trading CT 113.1
Loans, from donee to donor IHT 321.1
Loans to employees IT 9.4(D)(E); 9.6
Loans to participators CT 104.2
Loans to settlor of settlement IT 27.5
LOSSES IT 15; CT 114; CGT 217
accounting periods of different length CT 114.3(B)
asset of negligible value CGT 217.1(B)
capital gains, individual's trading losses set-off against IT 15.2
capital losses CT 103.1; CGT 207.2
—election to treat as arising in earlier year CGT 217.4
—indexation losses CGT 214.1(E)
—pre-entry losses CT 103.3(F)
—set-off against settlement gains CGT 217.2
—tangible movable assets CGT 212.1(B)
carry-back of CT 114.3
—death, from year of CGT 217.1(C)
—early losses IT 15.3(A)
—terminal losses IT 15.4; CT 114.3(A)
carry-forward of CT 103.2; 106.6; 114.2; 114.7
cessation of trade IT 15.4; CT 114.3(A)
chattels CGT 212.1(B)
consortium relief CT 106.7
corporate capital loss restriction CGT 208.3
death, year of CGT 217.1(C)
early losses in new business IT 15.3
groups of companies CT 106
intangible assets CT 108.2
interest on overpaid tax CT 109.1(A); 109.2
partnership IT 18.2; 18.3; 18.4
property business CT 114.6
reconstruction
—restriction of trading losses CT 114.5
restriction on carried-forward losses CT 114.7
rights to unascertainable consideration CGT 217.4
set-off of trading losses
—against capital gains (individuals) IT 15.2
—against other income or profits IT 1.4; 14.1; 14.3(A); CT 114.1
terminal IT 15.4; CT 114.3(A)
unlisted companies CGT 217.3
unquoted shares, capital losses available for set-off against income IT 15.5; CT 114.4; CGT 217.3

Index

M

Maintenance funds for historic buildings IHT 315.6
Maintenance payments IT 16.2
Management expenses CT 106.2; 111.1
Married couple's allowance
  transfer of IT 1.7; 16.1
MARRIED PERSONS AND CIVIL PARTNERS IT 16; CGT 218
  age-related allowances IT 1.7; 16.1
  employee shareholder shares and CGT 218.2
  end of marriage IT 16.2
  jointly owned assets CGT 218.3
  maintenance payments IT 16.2
  marriage allowance IT 1.6
  married couple's allowance
  —transfer of IT 1.7; 16.1
  no gain/no loss transfers CGT 214.2(A)(B); 218.1; 218.2; 218.3
  transferable tax allowance IT 1.6
Medical insurance (benefits) IT 9.6
Migration of companies CGT 220.1
Mileage allowances IT 9.2(A)
Mineral extraction IT 3.3
Mines, allowances for IT 3.3
Mixed supplies VAT 407.1
MOTOR CARS VAT 406
  See also Cars
  scale charge for private fuel VAT 406.1
Mutual supplies, bad debt relief where VAT 401.1
MUTUAL TRANSFERS IHT 314
  Chargeable transfers and death IHT 314.2
  Potentially exempt transfers and death IHT 314.1

N

NATIONAL HERITAGE IHT 315
  charge to tax IHT 315.4
  conditionally exempt occasions IHT 315.5
  conditionally exempt transfers IHT 315.2; 315.3; 315.4
  —after 6.4.76 IHT 315.2(A)(B)
  —multiple IHT 315.2(C)
  —on death before 7.4.76 IHT 315.3
  —tax credit on subsequent transfer IHT 315.4
  conditions for exemption IHT 315.1
  estate duty IHT 315.3(B)
  maintenance funds for historic buildings IHT 315.6
  settlements IHT 315.5

NATIONAL HERITAGE – *cont.*
  —conditionally exempt occasions IHT 315.5(A)
  —ten-year anniversary charge exemption IHT 315.5(B)
Negligible value, asset of CGT 217.1(B)
Non-business activities VAT 405.2
Non-resident, company becoming CGT 220.1
Non-resident company, transfer of assets to CGT 220.3
Non-resident entertainers and sportsmen IT 17.2
NON-RESIDENTS IT 17
  life assurance plicies IT 14.3
  limit on liability to income tax IT 17.1
  non-resident entertainers and sportsmen IT 17.2
Non-residents trading through UK permanent establishment CGT 220.2

O

OFFSHORE SETTLEMENTS CGT 219
  gains attributed to UK beneficiary CGT 219.1
Options CGT 203.1; 232.2
  See also Share Incentives and Options
OUTPUT TAX VAT 407
  mixed supplies VAT 407.1
Overdue tax
  See Interest on Tax *and* Interest on Unpaid Tax
Overnight incidental expenses IT 9.6
OVERSEAS MATTERS CGT 220
  See also Double Tax Relief, Offshore Settlements and Residence and Domicile
  company migration CGT 220.1
  earnings abroad
  —travelling expenses IT 9.1
  individual temporarily non-resident CGT 220.4
  non-resident entertainers and sportsmen IT 17.2
  non-residents trading through UK branch or agency CGT 220.2
  overseas resident settlements CGT 219
  transfer of assets to non-resident company CGT 220.3
  UK beneficiary of an overseas resident settlement CGT 219.1

P

Part disposals
  See Disposal
Part exchange
  second-hand goods VAT 412.1

Index

Part payments, bad debt relief where VAT 401.1
PARTIAL EXEMPTION VAT 408
  capital goods scheme VAT 402.1
  self supply
  —stationery VAT 412.1
  special method VAT 408.2
  standard method VAT 408.1
Participators
  See Close Companies
Partly exempt transfers IHT 305.3
PARTNERS NIC 513
  Class 4 contributions NIC 513.1
PARTNERSHIPS IT 18; CGT 221
  accounting adjustments CGT 221.3
  allocation of profits/losses IT 18.2
  assessments IT 18.1
  assets CGT 221.1
  —distribution in kind CGT 221.6
  capital allowances on successions IT 4.2
  changes in partners IT 18.1; CGT 221.2–221.4
  changes in sharing ratios IT 18.1; CGT 221.2–221.5
  consideration outside accounts CGT 221.4
  current year basis IT 18.1
  disposal of partnership asset to partner CGT 221.6
  indexation CGT 214.2(A)(C); 221.2
  investment income IT 18.1(B)
  losses IT 18.2; 18.3
  —limited liability partnerships IT 18.4
  —limited partner IT 18.3
  revaluation of assets CGT 221.3; 221.5
  savings income IT 18.1(B)
  shares acquired in stages CGT 221.5
Patents IT 12
  allowances for IT 3.4
  royalties, spreading of IT 12.1
PAYMENT OF TAX (CGT) CGT 222
  consideration payable by instalments CGT 222.1(A)
  gifts of land or shares CGT 222.1(B)
PAYMENT OF TAX (CT) CT 115
  instalment payments CT 109.1(B); 110.1(C); 115.1(B)(C)
  interest on overpaid CT CT 109.1(A)(B)
  large companies CT 115.1(A)(B)
  very large companies CT 115.1(C)
PAYMENT OF TAX (IHT) IHT 316
  by instalments IHT 316.1
  —with interest IHT 316.1(B)
PENSION PROVISION IT 19
  annual allowance IT 19.3
  contributions by individuals, relief for IT 19.1
  lifetime allowance IT 19.2

Pension schemes
  See Pension Provision
Pensionable age NIC 501.1
Periods of account
  See also Accounting periods
  capital allowances IT 4.1
  exceeding twelve months (CT) CT 101.3
Permanent establishment CGT 220.2
  foreign, exemption for profits of CT 105.2
Personal reliefs
  See Allowances and Tax Rates
PERSONAL SERVICE COMPANIES ETC. IT 20
  calculation of deemed employment payment IT 20.1
Persons liable to IHT
  See Liability for Tax
Petrol, private
  assessable benefit IT 9.3(A)
  VAT scale charge VAT 407.1
Plant and machinery, allowances for IT 4; CT 102.1
POST-CESSATION EXPENDITURE IT 21; 21.2
POST-CESSATION RECEIPTS IT 21; 21.1
Potentially exempt transfers IHT 305.1
  annual exemption, allocation of IHT 310.1(B)
  followed by loan from donee to donor IHT 321.1
  liability for tax on death IHT 313.4
Pre-entry losses CT 103.3(F)
Premiums on short leases IT 22.5; CT 116.1; CGT 216.3(C)(G)(H)
Private medical insurance
  benefit IT 9.6
PRIVATE RESIDENCES CGT 223
  capital gains tax exemption CGT 223
PROFIT COMPUTATIONS CT 116
  allowable deductions CT 116.1
  assessable profits CT 116.1
PROPERTY INCOME IT 22
  cash basis IT 22.1(A)
  expenses deductible IT 22.1; IT 22.4
  furnished holiday accommodation IT 22.2
  GAAP basis IT 22.1(B)
  general IT 22.1
  lodgers IT 22.3
  losses CT 114.6
  mortgage interest and other finance costs IT 22.4
  premiums on leases IT 22.5
  rent-a-room relief IT 22.3
PROTECTIVE TRUSTS IHT 317
  forfeiture IHT 317.1; 317.2
  —after 11.4.78 IHT 317.2

769

Index

PROTECTIVE TRUSTS – *cont.*
—before 12.4.78 IHT 317.1

Q

QUALIFYING CORPORATE BONDS CGT 224
conversion of securities CGT 229.6
definition CGT 224.1
reorganisation of share capital CGT 224.2
QUICK SUCCESSION RELIEF IHT 318
mutual transfers IHT 314.1

R

RECORDS VAT 409
errors on invoices VAT 409.1
REDUCED RATE SUPPLIES VAT 410
installation of energy-saving materials VAT 410.1
Reinvestment relief, SEIS CGT 227.3
Related property, valuation of IHT 303.1(B); 326.2
Relocation expenses IT 9.5
REMITTANCE BASIS IT 23; CGT 225
effect of election CGT 225.1
mixed funds, remittances from IT 23.1
Removal expenses IT 9.5
Rent-a-room relief IT 22.3
Repayments of tax, interest on CT 109; 109.1(A)(B)
RESEARCH AND DEVELOPMENT CT 117
above the line expenditure credits CT 117.2
allowances for IT 3.5
tax credits CT 117.1
Reservation, gifts with IHT 311
reservation not released before death IHT 311.1(B)
reservation released before death IHT 311.1(A)
Residence
See Private Residences
Residence and domicile
election to be treated as UK domiciledt IHT 310.4
individual temporarily non-resident CGT 220.4
life assurance policies and IT 14.3
non-resident company, transfer of assets to CGT 220.2
non-resident entertainers and sportsmen IT 17.1
offshore settlements CGT 219.1
Residence nil rate band IHT 310.5

Restricted shares IT 28.2
RETAIL SCHEMES VAT 411
RETURNS (CT) CT 118
filing dates CT 118.2
return periods CT 118.1
ROLLOVER RELIEF CGT 226
compulsory acquisition of and CGT 216.2
gifts CGT 205.3; 213.1; 213.2; 228.3
receipt of compensation not treated as disposal CGT 207.3(B)–(D); 216.2
replacement of business assets CGT 226
—groups of companies CT 103.3(D)
—nature of relief CGT 226.1
—partial relief CGT 226.2
—wasting assets CGT 226.3
transfer of business to a company CGT 213.3
Royalties and licences
patent rights IT 3.4; 16

S

Salaries
See also Employment Income
deductible against profits IT 31.4; CT 116.1
SAVINGS AND INVESTMENT INCOME IT 24
deeply discounted securities IT 24.1
partnerships IT 18.1(B)
Scottish rates of income tax IT 1.8
SECOND-HAND GOODS VAT 412
auctioneer's scheme VAT 412.3
bad debt relief on VAT 401.2
global accounting scheme VAT 412.2
part exchange VAT 412.1
Securities
See Shares and Securities
SEED ENTERPRISE INVESTMENT SCHEME IT 25; CGT 227
capital gains and losses IT 25.2(B); CGT 227.1; 227.2
income tax investment relief IT 25.1
reinvestment relief CGT 227.3
withdrawal of income tax relief IT 25.2(A)
SELF-ASSESSMENT IT 26
calculation of interim payments IT 26.1
claims involving more than one year IT 26.2
interest arising on insufficient interim payment IT 13.1(B)
interest on unpaid tax IT 13.1; CT 110.1
SETTLEMENTS IT 27; CGT 228
accumulation and maintenance trusts IT 27.2; 27.3(B); IHT 301
annual exemptions CGT 228.1

Index

SETTLEMENTS – *cont.*
beneficiaries, income of IT 27.3
creation of CGT 228.3
death of life tenant CGT 228.5; 232.3
disabled persons, trusts for IHT 323
discretionary trusts IT 27.2; 27.3(B)
—standard rate band IT 27.2(A)
dividends received by IT 27.1; 27.2; 27.3(A)
employees, trusts for IHT 324
interest in possession CGT 228.5
loan to settlor IT 27.5
National Heritage IHT 315.5; 315.6
offshore CGT 219.1
parent's settlement in favour of child IT 27.4
person becoming absolutely entitled to settled property CGT 228.4
proportionate charge IHT 320.2; 320.3
protective trusts IHT 317
rates of tax (CGT) CGT 228.1
tax payable by trustees IT 27.1
temporary charitable trusts IHT 306.1
ten-year anniversary charge IHT 320.1
termination of an interest in possession CGT 228.4; 228.5; 232.3; IHT 319.1
vulnerable beneficiary, with CGT 228.2
Settlements—Accumulation and Maintenance IHT 301
assessments on trust income IT 27.2
beneficiaries, income of IT 27.2(B)
SETTLEMENTS WITH INTERESTS IN POSSESSION CGT 228.5; IHT 319
assessments on trust income IT 27.1
beneficiaries, income of IT 27.3(A)
immediate post-death interests IHT 319.3
termination of an interest in possession CGT 228.4; 228.5; IHT 319.1
—losses (CGT) CGT 228.5(C)
transitional serial interests IHT 319.2
SETTLEMENTS WITHOUT INTERESTS IN POSSESSION IHT 320
post 26.3.74 settlements IHT 320.1(A); 320.2(A)(B)
pre 27.3.74 settlements IHT 320.1(B)
proportionate charge
—before the first ten-year anniversary IHT 320.2
—between ten-year anniversaries IHT 320.3
ten-year anniversary charge IHT 320.1
SHARES AND SECURITIES CGT 229
agricultural property relief IHT 302.2
bonus issues CGT 229.2
business property relief IHT 304.1(A)
capital distributions CGT 229.8
conversion of securities CGT 229.6
corporate bonds, qualifying CGT 224

SHARES AND SECURITIES – *cont.*
deeply discounted securities IT 24.1
deferred consideration CGT 207.2; 217.4; 229.4(C)
earn-outs CGT 217.4; 229.4(C)
exchange of securities CGT 229.4
gifts CGT 222.1(B)
holdings at 6.4.65
—quoted CGT 207.1
—unquoted CGT 207.3(C)(D)
options and incentives IT 28
qualifying corporate bonds CGT 224
reconstruction schemes CGT 229.5
reorganisation of share capital CGT 224.2; 229.1
rights issues CGT 229.1; 229.3
—sale of rights CGT 229.8(B)
scrip dividends CGT 229.7
sold within 12 months after death IHT 325.3
time apportionment
—unquoted shares CGT 204.3(D)
transfer of business to a company for shares CGT 212.3
unquoted shares
—losses relieved against income IT 15.5; CT 114.4; CGT 217.3
—time apportionment CGT 204.3(D)
valuation IHT 325.3
value passing out of CGT 202.1; 202.2
SHARES AND SECURITIES—IDENTIFICATION RULES CGT 230
after 5 April 2008 CGT 230.1
companies CGT 230.2
qualifying corporate bonds CGT 224.1
SHARE-RELATED EMPLOYMENT INCOME AND EXEMPTIONS IT 28
convertible shares IT 28.3
enterprise management incentives IT 28.5
restricted shares IT 28.3
share incentive plans IT 28.4
share options
—charge to tax IT 28.1
Short-life assets IT 4.4
SOCIAL INVESTMENT RELIEF CGT 231
capital gains and losses
—disposal more than three years after acquisition CGT 231.1; 231.2
deferral relief CGT 231.3
SOCIAL SECURITY INCOME IT 29
high income child benefit charge IT 29.1
Special schemes for retailers
  See Retail Schemes
Sportsmen and entertainers, non-resident IT 17.2
Structures and buildings allowances IT 3.1

Index

Substantial shareholdings exemption CT 103.4
Successions to trade
   capital allowances IT 4.2

T

Tangible movable property CGT 212.1
Tax credits
   research and development CT 117.1
Temporary non-residence CGT 220.4
Termination payments (employment) IT 6
Thin capitalisation CT 119.1(B)
Timber, growing IHT 326
Time apportionment CGT 204.3
Top-slicing relief IT 14.1
Trading allowance IT 30.5
TRADING INCOME IT 30
   See also Current year basis of assessment
   cash basis for smaller businesses IT 31.1
   cemeteries IT 30.9
   change of accounting date IT 30.2
   closing year of assessment IT 30.3
   creative artists IT 30.6
   crematoria IT 30.9
   farming and market gardening IT 30.7
   foster care IT 30.8
   opening years of assessment IT 30.1
   profit computations IT 30.4
   trading allowance IT 30.5
TRADING INCOME — CASH BASIS FOR SMALLER BUSINESSES IT 31
   cash basis IT 31.1
Transferable tax allowance IT 1.6
Transfer of business to a company CGT 213.3
Transfer of unused nil-rate band IHT 308.1; 310.3
TRANSFER PRICING CT 119
   thin capitalisation and CT 119.1(B)
TRANSFERS ON DEATH IHT 321
   liability for tax IHT 313.2
   reduced rate for estates with 10% gifts to charities IHT 321.2
Transitional serial interests IHT 319.2
Trusts
   See Settlements
TRUSTS FOR BEREAVED MINORS IHT 322
   Transitional provisions IHT 322.1
TRUSTS FOR DISABLED PERSONS IHT 323
   property settled
   —after 9.3.1981 and before 8.4.2013 IHT 323.2

TRUSTS FOR DISABLED PERSONS – *cont.*
   —after 7.4.2013 IHT 323.3
   —before 10.3.1981 IHT 323.1
   self-settlement where condition expected to lead to disability IHT 323.4
TRUSTS FOR EMPLOYEES IHT 324

V

VALUATION IHT 325
   land sold within four years after death IHT 325.1
   related property IHT 303.1(B); 325.2
   shares and securities sold within 12 months after death IHT 325.3
   stock and work in progress IT 30.4
Value-shifting
   anti-avoidance CGT 202.1; 202.2
Vans, assessable benefit IT 9.3(B)
Variation, Deeds of IHT 308
VENTURE CAPITAL TRUSTS IT 32
   capital gains tax
   —relief on disposal IT 32.3
   distribution relief IT 32.2
   investment relief IT 32.1
   —withdrawal IT 32.1(B)
Vouchers IT 9.6
Vulnerable beneficiary
   trusts with CGT 228.2

W

WASTING ASSETS CGT 232
   eligible for capital allowances CGT 232.1
   leases IT 22.5; CGT 216.3
   —assignment of short lease CGT 216.3(D)–(G)
   —grant of long lease CGT 216.3(B)
   —grant of short lease CGT 216.3(C)
   —short leases which are not wasting assets CGT 216.3(A)
   —sub-lease granted out of short lease CGT 216.3(H)(J)
   life interests CGT 232.3
   options CGT 203.1; 232.2
   rollover relief CGT 226.3
WOODLANDS IHT 326
   deferred IHT charge IHT 326.1
   —credit for, on subsequent transfer IHT 326.1(B)